Lecture Notes in Computer Science 16336

The series Lecture Notes in Computer Science (LNCS), including its subseries Lecture Notes in Artificial Intelligence (LNAI) and Lecture Notes in Bioinformatics (LNBI), has established itself as a medium for the publication of new developments in computer science and information technology research, teaching, and education.

LNCS enjoys close cooperation with the computer science R & D community, the series counts many renowned academics among its volume editors and paper authors, and collaborates with prestigious societies. Its mission is to serve this international community by providing an invaluable service, mainly focused on the publication of conference and workshop proceedings and postproceedings. LNCS commenced publication in 1973.

Pei-Luen Patrick Rau · Heidi Krömker

Editors

HCI International 2025 – Late Breaking Papers

27th International Conference on
Human-Computer Interaction, HCII 2025
Gothenburg, Sweden, June 22–27, 2025
Proceedings, Part VI

 Springer

Editors
Pei-Luen Patrick Rau
Tsinghua University
Beijing, China

Heidi Krömker
Technische Universitat Ilmenau
Ilmenau, Germany

ISSN 0302-9743 ISSN 1611-3349 (electronic)
Lecture Notes in Computer Science
ISBN 978-3-032-12797-6 ISBN 978-3-032-12798-3 (eBook)
https://doi.org/10.1007/978-3-032-12798-3

This Springer imprint is published by the registered company Springer Nature Switzerland AG
The registered company address is: Gewerbestrasse 11, 6330 Cham, Switzerland

If disposing of this product, please recycle the paper.

Foreword

The HCI International (HCII) conference was founded in 1984 by Gavriel Salvendy (Purdue University, USA, Tsinghua University, P.R. China, and University of Central Florida, USA) and the first event of the series, "1st USA-Japan Conference on Human-Computer Interaction", was held in Honolulu, Hawaii, USA, on 18–20 August. Since then, HCI International has been held jointly with several Thematic Areas and Affiliated Conferences, with each one under the auspices of a distinguished international Program Board and under one management and one registration. Twenty-seven HCI International Conferences have been organized so far (every two years until 2013, and annually thereafter).

Last year, we celebrated 40 years since the establishment of the HCII conference, which has been a hub for presenting groundbreaking research and novel ideas and collaboration for people from all over the world. Over the years, this conference has served as a platform for scholars, researchers, industry experts, and students to exchange ideas, connect, and address challenges in the ever-evolving HCI field. The conference has evolved itself, adapting to new technologies and emerging trends, while staying committed to its core mission of advancing knowledge and driving change.

The 27th International Conference on Human-Computer Interaction, HCI International 2025 (HCII 2025), was held as an 'on-site' conference at the Gothia Towers Hotel and Swedish Exhibition & Congress Centre, in Gothenburg, Sweden, on June 22–27, 2025, with the additional option for 'on-line' participation. It incorporated the 21 thematic areas and affiliated conferences listed below.

A total of 7972 individuals from academia, research institutes, industry, and government agencies from 92 countries submitted contributions. 1430 papers and 355 posters (as short research papers) were included in the volumes of the proceedings published just before the start of the conference. Additionally, 439 papers and 104 posters were included in the volumes of the proceedings published after the conference, as "Late Breaking Work". The contributions thoroughly cover the entire field of human-computer interaction, highlight the evolving role of computers in diverse contexts, and demonstrate how HCI research is shaping and improving user experiences across a wide range of domains, influencing technological progress and its effective integration into various sectors. The volumes constituting the full set of the HCII 2025 conference proceedings are listed on the following pages.

I would like to thank the Program Board Chairs and the members of the Program Boards of all thematic areas and affiliated conferences for their contribution towards the high scientific quality and overall success of the HCI International 2025 conference. Their manifold support including paper reviews (via a single-blind review process, with a minimum of two reviews per submission), session organization, and their willingness to act as goodwill ambassadors for the conference is most highly appreciated.

This conference would not have been possible without the continuous and unwavering support and advice of Gavriel Salvendy, founder, General Chair Emeritus, and Scientific Advisor. For his outstanding efforts, I would like to express my sincere appreciation to Abbas Moallem, Communications Chair and Editor of HCI International News.

September 2025   Constantine Stephanidis

HCI International 2025 Thematic Areas and Affiliated Conferences

- HCI: Human-Computer Interaction Thematic Area
- HIMI: Human Interface and the Management of Information Thematic Area
- EPCE: 22nd International Conference on Engineering Psychology and Cognitive Ergonomics
- AC: 19th International Conference on Augmented Cognition
- UAHCI: 19th International Conference on Universal Access in Human-Computer Interaction
- CCD: 17th International Conference on Cross-Cultural Design
- SCSM: 17th International Conference on Social Computing and Social Media
- VAMR: 17th International Conference on Virtual, Augmented and Mixed Reality
- DHM: 16th International Conference on Digital Human Modeling & Applications in Health, Safety, Ergonomics & Risk Management
- DUXU: 14th International Conference on Design, User Experience and Usability
- C&C: 13th International Conference on Culture and Computing
- DAPI: 13th International Conference on Distributed, Ambient and Pervasive Interactions
- HCIBGO: 12th International Conference on HCI in Business, Government and Organizations
- LCT: 12th International Conference on Learning and Collaboration Technologies
- ITAP: 11th International Conference on Human Aspects of IT for the Aged Population
- AIS: 7th International Conference on Adaptive Instructional Systems
- HCI-CPT: 7th International Conference on HCI for Cybersecurity, Privacy and Trust
- HCI-Games: 7th International Conference on HCI in Games
- MobiTAS: 7th International Conference on HCI in Mobility, Transport and Automotive Systems
- AI-HCI: 6th International Conference on Artificial Intelligence in HCI
- MOBILE: 6th International Conference on Human-Centered Design, Operation and Evaluation of Mobile Communications

Conference Proceedings – Full List of Volumes

1. LNCS 15766, Human-Computer Interaction — Part I, edited by Masaaki Kurosu and Ayako Hashizume
2. LNCS 15767, Human-Computer Interaction — Part II, edited by Masaaki Kurosu and Ayako Hashizume
3. LNCS 15768, Human-Computer Interaction — Part III, edited by Masaaki Kurosu and Ayako Hashizume
4. LNCS 15769, Human-Computer Interaction — Part IV, edited by Masaaki Kurosu and Ayako Hashizume
5. LNCS 15770, Human-Computer Interaction — Part V, edited by Masaaki Kurosu and Ayako Hashizume
6. LNCS 15771, Human-Computer Interaction — Part VI, edited by Masaaki Kurosu and Ayako Hashizume
7. LNCS 15772, Human-Computer Interaction — Part VII, edited by Masaaki Kurosu and Ayako Hashizume
8. LNCS 15773, Human Interface and the Management of Information: Part I, edited by Hirohiko Mori and Yumi Asahi
9. LNCS 15774, Human Interface and the Management of Information: Part II, edited by Hirohiko Mori and Yumi Asahi
10. LNCS 15773, Human Interface and the Management of Information: Part III, edited by Hirohiko Mori and Yumi Asahi
11. LNAI 15776, Engineering Psychology and Cognitive Ergonomics: Part I, edited by Don Harris and Wen-Chin Li
12. LNAI 15777, Engineering Psychology and Cognitive Ergonomics: Part II, edited by Don Harris and Wen-Chin Li
13. LNAI 15778, Augmented Cognition, Part I, edited by Dylan D. Schmorrow and Cali M. Fidopiastis
14. LNAI 15779, Augmented Cognition, Part II, edited by Dylan D. Schmorrow and Cali M. Fidopiastis
15. LNCS 15780, Universal Access in Human-Computer Interaction: Part I, edited by Margherita Antona and Constantine Stephanidis
16. LNCS 15781, Universal Access in Human-Computer Interaction: Part II, edited by Margherita Antona and Constantine Stephanidis
17. LNCS 15782, Cross-Cultural Design: Part I, edited by Pei-Luen Patrick Rau
18. LNCS 15783, Cross-Cultural Design: Part II, edited by Pei-Luen Patrick Rau
19. LNCS 15784, Cross-Cultural Design: Part III, edited by Pei-Luen Patrick Rau
20. LNCS 15785, Cross-Cultural Design: Part IV, edited by Pei-Luen Patrick Rau
21. LNCS 15786, Social Computing and Social Media: Part I, edited by Adela Coman and Simona Vasilache

85. CCIS 2772, HCI International 2025 — Late Breaking Posters: Part II, edited by Constantine Stephanidis, Margherita Antona, Stavroula Ntoa, George Margetis and Gavriel Salvendy
86. CCIS 2773, HCI International 2025 — Late Breaking Posters: Part III, edited by Constantine Stephanidis, Margherita Antona, Stavroula Ntoa, George Margetis and Gavriel Salvendy

https://2025.hci.international/proceedings

27th International Conference on Human-Computer Interaction (HCII 2025)

The full list with the Program Board Chairs and the members of the Program Boards of all thematic areas and affiliated conferences of HCII 2025 is available online at:

http://www.hci.international/board-members-2025.php

HCI International 2026 Conference

The 28th International Conference on Human-Computer Interaction, HCI International 2026, will be held jointly with the affiliated conferences at the Montréal Convention Centre (Palais des congrès de Montréal), in Montreal, Canada, 26–31 July 2026. It will cover a broad spectrum of themes related to Human-Computer Interaction, including theoretical issues, methods, tools, processes, and case studies in HCI design, as well as novel interaction techniques, interfaces, and applications. The proceedings will be published by Springer (part of Springer Nature) in a multi-volume set. More information will become available on the conference website: https://2026.hci.international/.

General Chair
Constantine Stephanidis
University of Crete and ICS-FORTH
Heraklion, Crete, Greece
Email: general_chair@2026.hci.international

https://2026.hci.international/

Contents

Design and Engineering of Mobility Experiences

Human Factors, Safety, and Driver Assistance

Designing for Positive Change: Well-Being, Inclusion, and Social Impact

UX Design for AI Literacy in Arabic: A Case Study of the Day of AI Curriculum's Localization

Rahaf Alqahtani[1], Areej Al-Wabil[1,2]([⊠]), Kerem Demirboga[1], Dalal Aldossary[1], Yousef Awartani[1], Arwa Alabdulkarim[3], and Sharifa Alghowinem[4]

[1] Software Engineering Department, Alfaisal University, Riyadh, Saudi Arabia
{rkalqahtani,awabil,kdemirboga,daldossary,
yawartani}@alfaisal.edu
[2] HCI Lab, Alfaisal University, Riyadh, Saudi Arabia
[3] Artificial Intelligence and Robotics Institute, King Abdulaziz City of Science and Technology (KACST), Riyadh, Saudi Arabia
aalabdulkarim@kacst.gov.sa
[4] Personal Robots Group, Massachusetts Institute of Technology (MIT), Cambridge, MA, USA
sharifah@media.mit.edu

Abstract. This study examines human-centered UI/UX design principles tailored to Arabic-speaking populations. By contributing to the localization efforts of the "Day of AI" curriculum into Arabic, the research investigates the challenges and opportunities of generating linguistically and culturally relevant material and designing effective RTL (right-to-left) interfaces that align with the preferences and needs of Arabic-speaking users. The study leverages a semi-automated multimedia translation pipeline to assess its ability to translate diverse educational documents accurately while preserving context and ensuring alignment with sociocultural design considerations. A systematic analysis of the original Day of AI website design was conducted to identify critical areas for adaptation enhancement and development of a multimedia translation pipeline to aid localization efforts. These findings provide actionable insights for designing digital platforms that accommodate Arabic-speaking users' needs, contributing to broader UI/UX localization discussions.

Keywords: User Interface (UI) Design · User Experience (UX) · AI Literacy

1 Introduction

Recent advances in digital learning platforms have significantly reshaped educational delivery, making it more accessible on a global scale. Digital platforms now play a crucial role in academic initiatives, with their potential for success largely contingent on their ability to accommodate and serve diverse users and audiences. Addressing sociocultural and linguistic diversity is no longer a choice but an imperative for successful and engaging user experiences. Considering the most linguistically and culturally diverse populations,

P.-L.P. Rau and H. Krömker (Eds.): HCII 2025, LNCS 16336, pp. 3–17, 2026.
https://doi.org/10.1007/978-3-032-12798-3_1

designing interfaces for Arabic-speaking individuals poses a unique challenge due to the linguistic complexities of the Arabic language and the broad range of cultures in the regions that speak the Arabic language.

The Arabic-speaking population includes over 25 countries, with more than 400 million people [3]. However, it is still underrepresented in the digital world [1]. Most current platforms lack the specific needs of Arabic speakers, which may contribute to unfavorable user experiences. Research has shown that the culture of target users is a key factor that may impact their satisfaction with website utilization [26]. This may restrict access to educational resources and contribute to the persistence of the digital divide, leaving the needs of Arabic-speaking web users unmet.

The "Day of AI" is an initiative led and developed by MIT's RAISE (Responsible AI For Social Empowerment and Education), which is part of a worldwide response to improve learning through modern digital advances. The curriculum offers a collection of free-to-download AI resources, with the goal of making artificial intelligence (AI) literacy accessible to K-12 students, educators, and parents. It is designed to be taught by many instructors, including those with minimal knowledge of technology and AI concepts. Moreover, teaching institutions can adapt this curriculum to fit their unique learning objectives and geographical considerations [11]. While the program has made significant strides in English-speaking regions, localizing it for Arabic-speaking audiences presents complex challenges.

Localizing digital material involves conducting various processes, including accurate translation of multimedia documents for local adaptation of the curriculum and an extensive reimagining of user experience (UX) encompassing interface design, navigation architecture capabilities, and content presentation. For Arabic-speaking audiences, this involves tailoring platforms to accommodate right-to-left (RTL) writing orientation, adapting content to account for the linguistic complexity of Arabic morphology and phonology, and integrating culturally relevant visual and thematic elements. Moreover, effective localization incorporates sociocultural design considerations, ensuring that users not only understand the content but also feel represented, engaged, and valued within the digital learning platform.

Another essential consideration in UX design is the diversity within cultural groups, particularly regarding age. As noted in [28], the age of target users has been shown to influence perceived usability due to variations in cognitive, psychomotor, and psychosocial behaviors. Evidence suggests that younger users may have different interaction preferences and expectations than older users, even within the same cultural context. For instance, children may prioritize playful and engaging interfaces, while older users may value clarity and simplicity [5]. This diversity is especially persistent in educational platforms, where information and communication are increasingly delivered through technology interfaces. Furthermore, taking these considerations into account is essential to ensure effective engagement and learning outcomes for diverse user demographics. This study highlights the culturally sensitive design process in bridging the digital divide between Arabic and non-Arabic speaking populations (Table 1).

Table 1. Terminology and Definitions for Arabization and Localization.

	Translation	Arabization	Localization
Definition	Converting text from one language to another while preserving meaning.	Adapting non-Arabic content and platforms to Arabic, through linguistic and contextual considerations	Adapting content linguistically and culturally to align it with sociocultural design considerations for Arabic-speakers.
Examples	Converting an English website into Arabic through Google Translate [24].	The Arabization efforts of UI interfaces to support RTL orientation [2].	Arabic E-Commerce websites; adapting content, color, symbolism and terminology to suit local needs of Arabic-speaking users [7].

2 Background and Related Work

2.1 Localization Challenges in Educational Platforms

Localization is a comprehensive process that includes various steps and procedures. In the context of educational platforms, these efforts involve translating multimedia content and re-evaluating the current user experience to accommodate the cultural and linguistic nuances of the target audiences [2]. Arabic RTL interfaces present unique challenges, including the need for dynamic text alignment and spacing to accommodate longer phrases. Many platforms may overlook cultural visual hierarchies, color preferences, and familiar icon utilization and tend to create a generalized platform, neglecting users' specific needs, resulting in a suboptimal user experience for Arabic speakers. Prior research highlights the importance of integrating culturally resonant elements and user testing to improve engagement and satisfaction, which may aid in successfully achieving localization objectives [4]. This study aims to address these challenges directly by implementing a semi-automated pipeline that preserves educational content's linguistic and cultural integrity and an interactive platform design to allow accessibility and user satisfaction.

2.2 Gaps in Accurate Multimedia Translation Tools

Machine translation tools have been subject to continuous evolution to meet the needs and standards of fast and accurate automated translation services. Despite advances in machine translation, these tools may face many challenges when translating phrases into Arabic [8, 16]. In the context of translating multimedia, these translation tools have been found to disrupt the formatting and structure of documents, fail to capture and translate embedded elements, and may not accurately preserve the context of the translated material. For instance, these tools may frequently mishandle right-to-left alignment and interactive elements upon translating various media types, resulting in unusable outputs [14]. These gaps necessitate a specialized pipeline to ensure accurate translations across diverse media types. The semi-automated pipeline developed for this research bridges these gaps by combining advanced and specified machine translation tools with targeted human intervention, providing a scalable solution for multimedia localization in educational contexts.

2.3 Existing User Interface Design Methods

The evolution of user interface (UI) design has been characterized by continuous adaptation of principles and methodologies to enhance user experience (UX). Traditional approaches utilized in UI design, such as task-oriented and human-centered design, emphasize the importance of understanding user needs and aligning interface functionalities to meet those needs. Additionally, agile and iterative methodologies, which integrate continuous user feedback, have further enhanced designers' ability to adapt interfaces dynamically.

Despite these methodological advances, applying these methods often assumes an English-speaking user base, leading to designs that overlook the needs of non-English-speaking audiences. Consequently, adapting these principles for culturally diverse populations may require additional considerations, such as integrating linguistic complexity, cultural norms, and visual preferences. These adaptations are particularly critical for Arabic-speaking users, who may encounter unique challenges in navigating digital interfaces primarily designed for English-speaking audiences. This project applies these methods to a localized context, ensuring that the redesigned "Day of AI" platform aligns with Arabic users' preferences.

2.4 Arabic RTL Interface Design Considerations

The RTL interfaces are considered a critical component of digital platforms designed for Arabic-speaking users. However, implementing RTL interfaces often presents challenges due to the differences between Arabic and other languages [10]. The Arabic language, which features variable word lengths, requires interfaces to support dynamic text alignment and spacing to accommodate the transformed content between the two languages. The linguistic structure of Arabic likely results in much longer phrases, as there is no direct translation between English and Arabic text, which further necessitates adjustments to layout and content presentation [29]. The current RTL interface designs may fail to address these nuances, leading to usability issues such as misaligned text, overlapping content, and inconsistencies in navigation capabilities. Furthermore, many RTL designs adopt a direct mirror image of left-to-right (LTR) interfaces, which neglects the cultural and contextual differences that influence user behavior. For instance, the visual hierarchies, the principle of arranging elements in order of their relative importance to the user, color preferences, and icon utilization, may differ between Arabic-speaking users and other user populations. Yet, these factors may be overlooked in RTL designs [7]. Additionally, recent studies have highlighted successful approaches to RTL interface design, such as incorporating culturally relevant visual elements and prioritizing user testing with Arabic-speaking audiences [18]. This study aims to implement the relevant RTL design considerations to ensure user satisfaction through interacting with the localized content.

3 Methodology

3.1 Semi-Automated Translation Pipeline

Through iterative testing and trial phases on automated Python scripts, various machine translation tools (e.g., Google Translate, Microsoft Azure Translate, Google Cloud Translate, and OpenAI's ChatGPT) were evaluated for their effectiveness in translating diverse multimedia types from English to Arabic. These included PowerPoint slides, Word Documents, PDF documents, images, and videos from the Day of AI curriculum. Each tool demonstrated different strengths and limitations depending on the document type.

For text-based files, Microsoft Azure Translate was preferred for its high accuracy value of approximately 90% in Arabic translation and its preservation of formatting in PowerPoint and Word documents. Using ChatGPT's 4o model for these types of files produced disrupted, misformatted text with embedded prompt artifacts, reducing its readability and comprehensibility and resulting in an accuracy value of 60%. Google Cloud's translation services and Optical Character Recognition (OCR) tools excelled in extracting and translating text from PDFs and images, achieving an estimated accuracy of 85%. However, manual reinsertion of the translated content was required to finalize localized versions of files.

For video translation, a multi-step pipeline was implemented: Python libraries extracted audio, OpenAI's Whisper transcribed the speech to English, ChatGPT 4o translated the English speech to Arabic, and ElevenLabs generated the final audio via API [13]. OpenAI was selected for transcription and translation due to its consistency and linguistic accuracy. The translated audio was then re-synced with the original video to complete the translation process.

Despite automation, human verification remains necessary to ensure translations preserve the AI curriculum modules' context, cultural appropriateness, and comprehensibility for Arabic-speaking learners. This pipeline aims to alter a sample of modules from the curriculum to be more aligned with local and cultural educational standards and expectations for usability, translation accuracy, content integrity, and overall course functionality (Figs. 1 and 2).

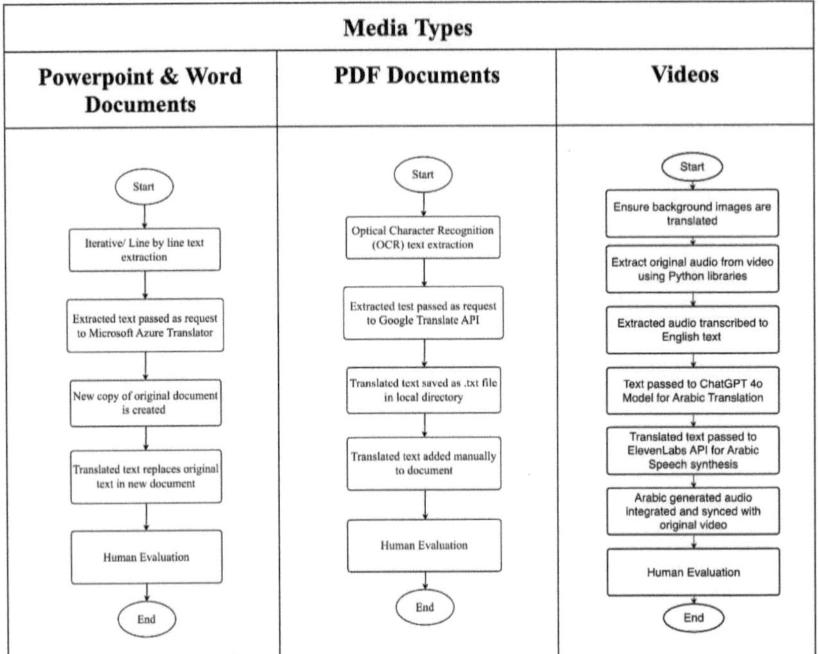

Fig. 1. Flowchart of the Translation Pipeline.

Fig. 2. Example of a Slide from the Day of AI Curriculum after Processing Through the Translation Pipeline.

3.2   Analysis of the Original Day of AI Website

The initial phase of the design aspect involved a detailed review and analysis of the original Day of AI (DOAI) website to identify areas requiring adaptation or improvement for Arabic-speaking audiences. This analysis focused on usability, accessibility, and content presentation. The original website, designed primarily for English-speaking audiences, featured text-heavy layouts and nested links, making navigation challenging for new users. The website provided an auto-translate feature that produced inaccurate translations and disrupted the layouts of pages, reducing readability and usability for non-English speakers. The curriculum page layout, currently structured with vertical drop-down menus, was perceived to be complex when multiple lessons were expanded simultaneously, obscuring the key objectives of creating highly accessible material and content for users. A key issue identified was the emphasis on dense information at the expense of user-friendly navigation. The lack of a clear visual hierarchy and limited use of interactive elements made navigation difficult in the heuristic reviews and was perceived to contribute toward reduced user engagement. These shortcomings highlighted the need for a redesign strategy tailored to the sociocultural design considerations for Arabic UIs and the expectations of Arabic-speaking users for digital content and navigation.

3.3   Co-design Process for Arabic Localization

The co-design process was conducted by engaging stakeholders, including Arabic-speaking users, to implement targeted changes collaboratively. First, the navigation system was simplified to provide a more intuitive experience for the user. The navigation bar was improved in the renewed design for Arabic users, and a separate button was added to allow access to the home page. In contrast, the original website used the Day of AI logo icon as the home button. However, this was not the typical norm of interactions used in Arabic websites and, therefore, was not aligned with what Arabic-speaking users expect in web interfaces. It also neglects the consideration for those who may not be familiar with these interactive shortcuts [9]. The curriculum page was restructured into modular formats, allowing users to identify lesson starting and ending points.

Given the RTL reading orientation of Arabic, all elements were aligned accordingly to ensure a seamless interaction experience. The redesign also incorporated cultural sensitivity by adapting visual and textual content to reflect the preferences of Arabic-speaking audiences. Arabic's linguistic complexity and intricacy required specific adjustments to the website's text and layout. Arabic text typically features longer phrases and sentences than English, posing challenges for maintaining layout consistency [22]. To address this, flexible text containers and additional spacing were introduced, ensuring readability and preventing visual overcrowding. Moreover, carousels were introduced to present non-critical information and reduce the cognitive load from intensive text. These carousels allowed users to navigate content sequentially, using buttons or arrow commands, while avoiding the issue of automated movement, which may cause users to miss key details [19].

To preserve the DOAI initiative's identity in the localized version, the redesigned website retained the original color scheme and visual branding elements. Certain modernized features, such as increased white backgrounds and rounded corners, were added to create a softer and more inviting aesthetic with white space to ensure the accessibility of the Arabic morphology and legibility of RTL flow of textual content [21]. These changes, shown in Figs. 3, 4, 5 and 6, ensured that the Arabic platform-maintained consistency with the original while meeting the unique needs of its target audience.

Fig. 3. Re-Designed Interface for the Arabic version of the DOAI Website.

Fig. 4. Comparison of Re-Designed Arabic Interface and Original Interface (Curriculum Page).

Fig. 5. Comparison of Re-Designed Arabic Interface and Original Interface (Curriculum Page).

Fig. 6. Re-Designed Navigation Bar in Arabic Day of AI Website.

3.4 Usability and UX Reviews

To assess the redesigned platform, the teachability of the localized material, and the educational benefits of the curriculum, a series of Arabic Day of AI workshops were conducted to pilot the content with instructors and participants. These workshops aimed to facilitate user interaction and engagement with the proposed digital platform and initial prototypes of the website design. The workshop sessions consisted of 30 Arabic-speaking individuals to ensure consistency and accurate data collection among the sessions. Moreover, pre- and post-surveys were administered to the workshop participants. These surveys aimed to measure the impact of the localized curriculum on AI literacy among children to ensure that it successfully met the objectives of AI literacy education. The pre-surveys gathered baseline data on participants' familiarity and initial impressions with AI concepts. At the same time, post-surveys assessed changes in AI literacy and user satisfaction from the educational material, such as "What is the most important thing you think you learned about artificial intelligence?" and "What was the most challenging part of the workshop for you?". The results of these surveys have demonstrated that, before the workshop sessions, the children had a limited understanding of AI concepts and faced difficulties with describing the underlying principles. However, the post-surveys indicated that the learning objectives were successfully met, as the children reported understanding how to use LLMs through prompt engineering in the Arabic language and applying advanced generative AI capabilities to design characters. These findings provided critical insights into the benefits of the localized platform and informed further design iterations. Additionally, the System Usability Scale (SUS) surveys were administered to the six instructors of the Arabic Day of AI material to gain insights on the perceived usability of the Arabic digital content for instructors and their reflections on the design considerations in the localized material provided to the instructors for teaching. The SUS survey is a recognized instrument for measuring first impressions with interactive technologies with metrics that can be translated to a quantitative value for further analysis [20]. Moreover, the shared survey included both quantitative and qualitative questions evaluating the accuracy and clarity of the localized digital material, the ease of using this material in teaching students, and the design of the interactive website from which they accessed the Arabic content. Both workshops were conducted in the same space on campus in a university, and consistent layout and setup were considered, as shown in Fig. 7.

Fig. 7. Participants and Instructors in the Arabic DOAI Workshops.

4 Results and Reflections from the UX Reviews

The SUS survey provided insights into users' perceived usability and subjective satisfaction with the localized Arabic interface and curriculum designed for the Arabic Day of AI initiative. This survey gathered responses from a sample of four Arabic-speaking instructors who utilized the website to access the digital content for the sessions. The participants completed the survey after interacting with the localized interface. The SUS survey had a mean score of 64.38 (SD = 10.92). This value reflects a moderate level of perceived usability as compared to the industry benchmark value of 68 [17]. The survey also offered insights into specific areas for improvement and potential weaknesses that may hinder the user experience.

The results indicated that the participants responded positively to the key aspects of the website, with 75% agreeing or strongly agreeing that it was easy to navigate through the web content. Moreover, regarding the inclusion of visuals and interactive elements, all participants strongly agreed these features and additions had enhanced their engagement. Additionally, the design was perceived to support RTL orientation and reflected the cultural norms and expectations, as 87.5% of participants rated this aspect of the website positively. The survey also highlighted specific weaknesses and identified areas for improvement to enhance user satisfaction. Some users found the website unnecessarily complex, and a similar proportion of participants strongly agreed, perceiving interaction as complex. These challenges highlight the need to improve navigation for more straightforward and efficient utilization and reduce cognitive load in navigating and interacting with the website to access digital content. Half of the survey respondents rated the website above the SUS benchmark value of 68; however, a smaller subset of users provided lower usability ratings due to difficulties with navigation and the perception of complexity in the website.

The participants were further asked to answer relevant questions about the accuracy and relevance of the translated curriculum. 50% perceived the curriculum as culturally appropriate and easy to teach to students with minimal knowledge of AI concepts. Furthermore, all instructors provided positive feedback on the importance of localizing this curriculum to strengthen the understanding of children in K-12 levels, as it was demonstrated that many students could not successfully differentiate between which objects and concepts were considered AI and which were not. In addition to localization, instructors emphasized the need for greater contextualization in the translated modules and educators' guides for the curriculum. As noted in [15], contextualization would involve aligning the DOAI modules with students' social, cultural, and environmental contexts.

5   Discussion

5.1   Localization Impact

The UX review highlighted the value of the localization efforts in developing a culturally resonant platform. The utilization and integration of RTL text alignment, culturally relevant visuals, and features were key factors in ensuring user engagement and achieving website localization [4]. Participants provided positive feedback on including culturally relevant interactive elements and unanimously agreed that these features enhanced their engagement with the web platform. This aligns with prior research to indicate that culturally familiar design elements, such as colors, symbols, and images, can improve user satisfaction [7]. An example of the localization efforts in the visual design is depicted in the images used on the UI of the Arabic DOAI interface, shown in Fig. 8.

Fig. 8. Visual Aesthetics in Redesigning Content in the Localization Process.

The platform's use of Arabic terminology further strengthened its accessibility and effectiveness. The website localization efforts aimed to preserve the contextual meanings and linguistic nuances of the original DOAI content. This approach sought to prevent alienation by avoiding direct or literal translations of technical terms and using terminology familiar to local audiences [24]. Moreover, developing a culturally familiar and visually relevant interface aims to help bridge the digital divide experienced by Arabic-speaking audiences. The localization efforts help ensure equitable access to educational digital platforms tailored to local audiences' unique needs. Studies have further highlighted how culturally insensitive designs and considerations may hinder the accessibility for specific user groups, as noted in [12]. Together, these elements play a crucial role in bridging the gap between global educational initiatives and the specific needs of underrepresented audiences, such as Arabic speakers.

5.2 Identified Challenges

While the previously mentioned design considerations for localization are noteworthy, the SUS score also highlighted opportunities for further adjustment and improvement. The results showed that some participants found the website unnecessarily complex to navigate, and this finding suggests that while the platform succeeded in cultural localization, usability may be further optimized. These concerns may be connected to the cognitive load posed by the text layouts or the multiple website pages presenting various information types to users. Moreover, other participants in the survey have shared their experiences with specific curriculum documents, such as PowerPoint presentations and Word documents, that contain translation inconsistencies with modern standard Arabic (MSA) after being processed through the translation pipeline. This concern suggests that the tools and libraries utilized in the automated translation scripts may require upgrades or further testing to ensure correct and complete translation before deployment. These mixed results underscore the significance of human-AI co-design and iterative improvements in automation to tackle identified usability challenges and enhance the overall experience.

5.3 Contributions to Arabic UI Design

This research contributes to the expanding body of knowledge focused on localization efforts and interface design for Arabic-speaking audiences. Similar studies that aim to assess the impact of integrating RTL text alignment and culturally relevant visuals on usability and engagement have shown alignment with the findings of this study. These studies utilized UX reviews, systematic analysis, and direct observational approaches to evaluate Arabic website localization efforts [7]. Moreover, other methods have included the implementation of localization frameworks, such as the proposed five levels of localization, which range from standardized to semi-localized, localized, highly localized, with culturally customized being the highest achievable level [25, 27]. In contrast, this study extracts direct user engagement through subjective satisfaction surveys and gathers feedback from participants interacting with a culturally localized digital learning platform. This aligns more closely with studies following case-study approaches, integrating user response evaluation to assess Arabic localization in commercial and educational platforms like Blackboard Learn [6]. While previous research has primarily focused on evaluating the usability of localized commercial applications, this study aims to expand the body of knowledge by providing insights into the localization of Arabic content in the applied domain of digital learning and educational technology.

Furthermore, previous investigations on Arabic software and website localization have highlighted persistent translation challenges and usability barriers, particularly within the accuracy and reliability of automated translation pipelines [2, 8]. This study examined the effectiveness of a semi-automated multimedia translation pipeline to identify how well current translation and localization efforts align with the linguistic and cultural needs of Arabic-speaking populations in an educational setting.

Additionally, current research on AI literacy in low-resource languages has demonstrated the importance of generative content in native languages to promote digital inclusion [23]. Yet, most of these efforts focus on creating new content from scratch rather than assessing the effectiveness of existing localization efforts. This study differs by measuring the engagement impact of localized parts of AI curricula, ensuring that translation quality and interface design work cohesively to support Arabic-speaking learners. The study also uncovered a positive association between the integration of visual interactive elements that aim to enhance users' engagement and accurate accommodation of RTL orientation throughout the platform. Several studies have treated cultural adaptation and usability as separate concerns; however, this study aims to bridge that gap by integrating usability testing with localization analysis.

6 Conclusion

By integrating cultural and linguistic design elements, this study highlights and addresses the challenges of creating interfaces and educational content that support RTL text orientation, Arabic terminology, and culturally appropriate visuals. The results collected from the SUS survey measured the perceived usability of the digital learning platform by instructors (educators) and the implications of the localization efforts in the design. It also highlighted areas that may require further improvement. These results provided valuable insights into the complexities and considerations of designing localized platforms for Arabic-speaking populations.

6.1 Limitations

While the study's findings shed light on translation and localization for Arabic populations in the context of digital platforms for AI literacy, it also identified several limitations. The SUS score of 64.38 indicated moderate usability levels, and this value also conveys the need for refining the interface to address the issues regarding navigation and the perceived cognitive load in some areas of the platform. These areas reflect the challenges of adapting an English-centric design for Arabic-speaking audiences. The current sample of participants involved in the initiative may not provide a comprehensive view of the preferences of Arabic users. Although the semi-automated translation pipeline was effective in batch processing documents, it occasionally required manual intervention to preserve contextual accuracy, posing scalability challenges.

6.2 Future Work

Future efforts of this initiative would focus on prioritizing and conducting iterative improvements to the platform to address the usability challenges and enhance engagement. The improvements consist of simplifying the website's navigation capabilities while exploring various information layouts to target the key areas from user feedback. Conducting the SUS surveys on an expanded sample size, with participants varying in age, teaching experience, and technical knowledge, would provide a more comprehensive understanding of user preferences. The translation pipeline could also be refined to implement more advanced machine translation technologies tailored to the Arabic language to reduce the current dependency on manual intervention. By addressing the linguistic and cultural needs of Arabic-speaking users, the localization of the Arabic

Day of AI digital content can provide insights for similar initiatives in localization for other regions of world.

Acknowledgments. The authors acknowledge the support of the College of Engineering and Advanced Computing at Alfaisal University and would like to thank the participants and volunteers for the Day of AI workshops at Alfaisal University.

Disclosure of Interests The authors have no competing interests to declare that are relevant to the content of this article.

References

1. Abubaker, H., Salah, K., Al-Muhairi, H., Bentiba, A.: Digital Arabic content: challenges and opportunities. In: Proceedings of the 2015 International Conference on Technology, Research, and Communication, pp. 330–333. IEEE (2015). https://doi.org/10.1109/ICTRC.2015.7156489
2. Abufardeh, S., Magel, K.: Software Localization: The Challenging Aspects of Arabic to the Localization Process (Arabization). In: Proceedings of the IASTED International Conference on Software Engineering, SE 2008, pp. 275–279, North Dakota State University (2008). https://www.scopus.com/pages/publications/62849095997
3. Aldawood, Z., Hand, L., Ballard, E.: Language learning environments for Arabic-speaking children in New Zealand: family demographics and children's Arabic language exposure. Speech Lang. Hear. **26**(4), 266–277 (2023). https://doi.org/10.1080/2050571X.2023.2212537
4. Alexander, R., Thompson, N., McGill, T., Murray, D.: The influence of user culture on website usability. Int. J. Hum. Comput. Stud. **154**, 102688 (2021). https://doi.org/10.1016/j.ijhcs.2021.102688
5. Alrashed, W.A., Alhussayen, A.A.: Examining the user experience (UX) of children's interaction with Arabic interfaces in educational learning contexts. In: Stephanidis, C. (ed.) HCI International 2015 – Posters' Extended Abstracts, vol. 528, pp. 487–492. Springer (2015). https://doi.org/10.1007/978-3-319-21380-4_59
6. Al-Mazrooa, N.: Arabic Localisation: Key Case Studies for Translation Studies. Ph.D. thesis, Cardiff University (2018).
7. Al-Sedrani, A., Al-Khalifa, H.S.: Design considerations for the localization of Arabic e-commerce websites. In: Seventh International Conference on Digital Information Management (ICDIM 2012), pp. 331–335. IEEE (2012). https://doi.org/10.1109/ICDIM.2012.6360094
8. Al-Shaikhli, M.: Problems of machine translation systems in Arabic. J. Lang. Teach. Res. **13**(4), 755–762 (2022). https://doi.org/10.17507/jltr.1304.08
9. Alyahyan, L., Aldabbas, H., Alnafjan, K.: Preferences of Saudi users on Arabic website usability. Int. J. Web Semant. Technol. **7**(4), 1–11 (2016). https://doi.org/10.5121/ijwest.2016.7401
10. Anvari, S., Woods, P.: Localizing graphical user interfaces for right-to-left languages: a practical study. In: Leitner, C., Nägele, R., Bassano, C., Satterfield, D. (eds.) The Human Side of Service Engineering, vol. 143. AHFE International (2024). https://doi.org/10.54941/ahfe1005102
11. Breazeal, C., Du, X., Abelson, H., Klopfer, E., Park, H.W.: Day of AI: Innovating Pedagogical Practices to Bring AI Literacy to Classrooms at Scale. MIT Media Lab (n.d.)
12. Chu, S.: Design factors affect user experience for different cultural populations. J. Educ. Issues. **2**(2), 307 (2016). https://doi.org/10.5296/jei.v2i2.10217

13. Eleven Labs: Text-to-Speech API Documentation. Eleven Labs (2024). https://docs.eleven labs.io/api-reference
14. Goutte, C., Carpuat, M., Foster, G.: The impact of sentence alignment errors on phrase-based machine translation performance. In: Proceedings of the 10th Conference of the Association for Machine Translation in the Americas: Research Papers, San Diego, California, USA. Association for Machine Translation in the Americas (2012)
15. Giamellaro, M.: Dewey's yardstick: contextualization as a crosscutting measure of experience in education and learning. SAGE Open. **7**(1) (2017). https://doi.org/10.1177/215824401770 0463
16. Hadj Ameur, M.S., Meziane, F., Guessoum, A.: Arabic machine translation: a survey of the latest trends and challenges. Comput. Sci. Rev. **38**, 100305 (2020). https://doi.org/10.1016/j. cosrev.2020.100305
17. Hyzy, M., et al.: System usability scale benchmarking for digital health apps: meta-analysis. JMIR Mhealth Uhealth. **10**(8), e37290 (2022). https://doi.org/10.2196/37290
18. Khan, H.U., Alhusseini, A.: Optimized web design in the Saudi culture. In: 2015 Science and Information Conference (SAI), pp. 906–915. IEEE (2015). https://doi.org/10.1109/SAI. 2015.7237250
19. Keya, R.T.: Universal Design and Usability: Investigation into Carousel Interaction. Oslo Metropolitan University (2020) https://hdl.handle.net/10642/9250
20. Lewis, J.: The system usability scale: past, present, and future. Int. J. Hum. Comput. Interact., 1–14 (2018). https://doi.org/10.1080/10447318.2018.1455307
21. Marcus, A., Hamoodi, S.: The impact of culture on the design of Arabic websites. In: Aykin, N. (ed.) Internationalization, Design and Global Development, vol. 5623, pp. 386–395. Springer (2009). https://doi.org/10.1007/978-3-642-02767-3_43
22. Namoun, A., Alkhodre, A.B.: Towards usability guidelines for the design of effective Arabic websites. Int. J. Adv. Comput. Sci. Appl. (IJACSA) 10.4 (2019). http://dx.doi.org/10.14569/ IJACSA.2019.0100472
23. Oyewusi, W.: AI literacy in low-resource languages: insights from creating AI in Yoruba videos (2024). https://arxiv.org/abs/2403.04799
24. Palanichamy, N., Trojovský, P.: Overview and challenges of machine translation for contextually appropriate translations. iScience. **27**(10), 110878 (2024). https://doi.org/10.1016/j.isci. 2024.110878
25. Salah, A., Elyas, T., Alghizzi, T.: An analysis of website design and localization in Saudi Arabia: the case of Apple and Huawei. Bus. Econ. J. **1**, 43–61 (2023). https://doi.org/10. 14456/bej.2023.4
26. Shneiderman, B.: Universal usability. Commun. ACM. **43**(5), 84–91 (2000). https://doi.org/ 10.1145/332833.332843
27. Singh, N., Pereira, A.: The culturally customized website. Routledge (2005). https://doi.org/ 10.4324/9780080481333
28. Tamimi, H., Bensefia, A.: Software usability challenges for native Arab users. In: Proceedings of the 2018 International Conference on Software Reliability and Security, pp. 6–12. IEEE (2018). https://doi.org/10.1109/ICSRS.2018.8688826
29. Zemni, B., Zitouni, M., Bouhadiba, F., Almutairi, M.: On ambiguity in the Arabic language: scrutinizing translation issues through machine translation from English and French into Arabic. J. Intercult. Commun. **24**(1), 203–212 (2024). https://doi.org/10.36923/jicc.v24i1.171

Developing Community Event-Based Surveillance Technology for Disease Outbreaks in Cross-Cultural Contexts

Rogerio Luiz Araujo Carmine[1]([envelope]) [ORCID], Gilmara Oliveira Maquine[1] [ORCID],
Isaac Carlos Cid do Rosario[3] [ORCID], Patricia Paiva Pereira[1] [ORCID], Veruska Maia
da Costa Brant[1] [ORCID], Sarah Mendes D'Angelo[1] [ORCID], Hilary Bower[2] [ORCID],
Shelley Lees[2] [ORCID], William Nicholas[2] [ORCID], Gwenda Hughes[2] [ORCID],
Maria da Luz Lima Mendonça[3] [ORCID], and Jonas Lotufo Brant de Carvalho[4] [ORCID]

[1] Associação Brasileira de Profissionais de Epidemiologia de Campo (ProEpi),
Brasília, Brazil
`rogerio.carmine@ifam.edu.br`, `patricia.paiva@proepi.org.br`
[2] UK Public Health Rapid Support Team/London School of Hygiene & Tropical
Medicine, London, UK
`william.nicholas@lshtm.ac.uk`
[3] Instituto Nacional de Saúde Pública de Cabo Verde (INSP), Praia, Cape Verde
`mariadaluz.lima@insp.gov.cv`
[4] Sala de Situação de Saúde, Universidade de Brasília (UnB), Brasília, Brazil
`jonas.brant@unb.br`

Abstract. This study addresses the development of a Community Event-Based Surveillance (CEBS) digital system, focusing on cross-cultural collaboration between community leaders in Brazil and Cape Verde, as part of the Guardians of Health—Community Leaders project. CEBS utilizes community leaders as sources for monitoring public health, emphasizing its importance in situations where resources are limited. This research investigates whether involving community leaders from different countries in adapting and developing a health surveillance application impacts the usability and acceptance of these tools and identifies cross-cultural factors that must be considered for implementation in other territories. We employed a user-centered design approach that included workshops and usability testing. Our evaluation considered two phases: Phase 1 involved testing an initial version of the application and gathering feedback for improvements, while Phase 2 assessed the revised version to compare usability metrics. Substantial advancements were highlighted in the results. User satisfaction, measured by the System Usability Scale (SUS), increased from 81.6 in Phase 1 to 84.1 in Brazil and from 76.6 to 84.2 in Cape Verde. Efficiency was improved, with average completion times reduced, decreasing from 359 to 277.6 s in Cape Verde. However, cross-cultural challenges continued: in Cape Verde, the need for offline functionality, while in Brazil, improvements on accessibility for users with different levels of digital literacy. The research reinforces the importance of cross-cultural design principles and the involvement of community leaders as co-designers to create inclusive and sustainable digital solutions for global health challenges.

© The Author(s), under exclusive license to Springer Nature Switzerland AG 2026
P.-L.P. Rau and H. Krömker (Eds.): HCII 2025, LNCS 16336, pp. 18–31, 2026.
https://doi.org/10.1007/978-3-032-12798-3_2

Keywords: cross-cultural design · event-based surveillance · user-centered design · public health · digital health

1   Introduction

The timely detection and effective control of epidemics are fundamental for protecting global public health, overcoming geographical barriers and socioeconomic disparities, and having a direct and substantial impact on the social and economic stability of nations [1,2]. Infectious diseases are not confined to certain regions of the globe, although developing countries bear the brunt of the burden [1]. Negligence in controlling outbreaks can trigger pandemics of catastrophic proportions, with devastating consequences for global health, the economy, and security [3].

One of the processes carried out to control outbreaks is Event-Based Surveillance (EBS), which is a method that synthesizes data from various sources, often unstructured, to detect health threats [4]. Community Event-Based Surveillance (CEBS) is an early warning system to identify and verify rumors about public health events at the community level and then forward them to the appropriate authorities for risk assessment and response [5]. For effective implementation, the active involvement of communities is necessary. This requires the development of local capacities, creation of trust, and establishment of two-way communication channels between communities and health systems [6].

The use of technologies in CEBS includes mobile applications that can be used to report health events in real time, accelerating the detection of and response to outbreaks [7]. These applications must be adapted to local contexts and culturally appropriate if they are to be sustainable. In developing these tools, it is important to consider involving local community representatives and experts (health surveillance and information technology) from the outset, to ensure that they are easy to use, accessible, and meet the needs of communities [8]. This requires continued investment in capacity, resources, and coordination.

Usability refers to the extent to which specific users can effectively, efficiently, and satisfactorily use a product to achieve specified goals within a particular context of use. It is related to the ability of a system to respond, through its technical and ergonomic properties, to the individual characteristics of its users to perform a given task in a specific context [9]. The System Usability Scale (SUS) tool is widely used and provides an easy way for developers to measure the usability of a wide variety of products or services [10]. User-centered design (UCD) is a systematic approach to solution development that ensures that the needs and desires of end users are considered throughout the design process, which involves conducting user research, creating prototypes, and performing usability testing [11].

The use of cross-cultural design in the development of digital solutions presents an essential paradigm to ensure that these tools are appropriate and effective for users from a variety of backgrounds [12]. The exchange of cultural elements offers a valuable basis for creating digital platforms that have a positive impact in different contexts [13]. Likewise, in the Health Surveillance process, information sharing and collaboration both within countries and internationally are crucial for controlling outbreaks and epidemics.

The Guardians of Health—Community Leaders project was developed to investigate the feasibility of applying the CEBS method in Brazil and Cape Verde. The project focuses on the participation of community leaders to identify and report health events in their communities, using a mobile application developed specifically for this purpose. Since the project involves users from 2 countries with certain similarities (e.g., language and cultural proximity), but also with cultural differences, it is important to identify the cross-cultural issues that may influence the acceptance and use of the application.

This study aims to investigate whether the involvement of community leaders from different countries in the adaptation and development of a health surveillance mobile application impacts the usability and acceptance, and therefore the sustainability of this kind of tool. It also aims to identify cultural and local characteristics that need to be considered in the development process.

We believe that cross-cultural contextually relevant design is fundamental for the development of digital health surveillance tools that will be sustainably integrated by users. This will enable greater community engagement in reporting public health issues, thereby increasing the quantity and quality of data collected, positively impacting the capacity to respond to disease outbreaks.

2   Methodology

The methodological approach of this study was structured to ensure the development, adaptation, and evaluation of a mobile app for CEBS, with active participation of community leaders in Brazil and Cape Verde, considering cultural and local aspects of the communities in these countries. User-centered design, based on development and evaluation cycles, was used to verify if the mobile app was of satisfactory quality for use in the pilot study of the CEBS application. It is important to mention that the project team was formed of IT and Health Surveillance professionals native to the countries to ensure effective communication during activities, such as identifying needs, user profiles, usage scenarios, and developing the application's user interface.

2.1   Phase Structure

The study was conducted in the following phases, including participants from both countries to ensure representativeness in the definitions and assessments:

- **Initial Development:**
    - **User understanding:** Based on data from the mapping of community leaders, a user profile common to the two countries (Brazil and Cape Verde) was identified, taking into account the similarities (Portuguese language speakers, cultural proximity) and differences (especially digital literacy) between them.

- **Structuring the activity to be computerized:** A workflow and a digital form for reporting signals were defined, considering the identified user profiles, the requirements of the surveillance process, and the cross-cultural context, and addressing concerns about the effective use of the application (e.g., terminology), simplicity, and understanding of the form and process flow in both countries.
- **Defining the requirements:** Functional and non-functional requirements were identified as a basis for building the initial version of the application.
- **Development of the initial version of the application:** Based on the defined requirements for user evaluation.

– **Evaluation phase 1:** Conducting development workshops to evaluate the initial version of the mobile app.

– **Development of a new version of the mobile app:** Addition of new features based on the feedback obtained in the first workshop.

– **Evaluation phase 2:** Conducting development workshops to evaluate the new version of the app.

– **Analysis:** Analysis of the results obtained in the evaluation phases.

2.2 Development Workshops

In phases 1 and 2 of the application evaluation, on-site development workshops were held in each country, explaining the project, the EBS process, an overview of the digital solution, usability testing, and facilitating group sessions where participants discussed the EBS process and evaluated the mobile application.

In the Usability Tests, tasks were carried out on three representative usage scenarios, in which participants reported warning signals using the Guardians of Health (GoH) mobile app while being observed by moderators. Each of the three tasks corresponded to a specific scenario for reporting health warning signals. The scenarios addressed were: (1) animal mortality in a region, (2) cases of people with similar symptoms suggestive of diseases, and (3) environmental issues with potential impact on human health. In each scenario, participants were asked to record the following information in the app: type of occurrence, number, and nature of those affected, date, and location of the event. These scenarios were designed to simulate realistic health surveillance situations, including linguistic and cultural adaptations, according to the workshops held in each country (Brazil and Cape Verde).

During the execution of the scenarios, moderators observed participants and recorded quantitative metrics on an observation sheet, including: (a) task completion, (b) start and end times for each task, (c) number of operational errors, (d) deviations from the expected sequence of actions, and (e) instances in which participants requested assistance. When necessary, moderators provided non-direct prompts to enable the activity to continue. After completing the tasks, participants answered the electronic usability evaluation questionnaire.

Participants also completed an evaluation questionnaire containing sociodemographic data, questions about the subjective experience of using the mobile app based on the System Usability Scale, and a free text field for open-ended qualitative feedback to identify strengths of the system and areas for improvement.

Five development workshops were held during the period from November 2023 to April 2024, with three workshops in Brazil (one in the first phase and two in the second phase, to reach the minimum number of 8 participants in each phase) and two workshops in Cape Verde (one in each phase). In Brazil, the workshops took place in the city of Brasília (Federal District) and in Cape Verde, in the city of Praia (island of Santiago), with participants traveling from other locations to attend.

Participants. A total of 45 participants were recruited for the usability evaluations in Brazil and Cape Verde. Participants were selected from community leaders and health-related organizations, following the selection process outlined in the project (currently under publication). Inclusion criteria required that participants had basic familiarity with the use of smartphones and did not have significant visual or cognitive impairments that could hinder interaction with the application. Participants were grouped separately by evaluation phase in each country to account for cultural and contextual differences.

Table 1. Age, sex, and digital literacy of participants, Brazil and Cape Verde, 2023 and 2024 (n = 45).

Variable	Category	n
Age	< 35	13
	35–50	19
	> 50	13
Sex	Male	28
	Female	17
Digital Literacy	Basic (Internet, email, social networks)	22
	Intermediate (Office, Enterprise Applications)	18
	Advanced (IT Professional)	5

Participants consisted of 28 men and 17 women, aged 22 to 73 years, with a mean (M) of 43.15 years and a standard deviation (SD) of 12.34. Regarding digital literacy, 22 participants reported a basic level of computer skills (e.g., access to the internet, emails, social networks or WhatsApp), 18 reported an intermediate level (e.g., use of office or corporate applications), and five reported an advanced level (e.g., professional expertise in IT). Table 1 presents the demographic characteristics and digital literacy levels of the entire cohort. Table 2 details the distribution of participants (number, age, sex, and digital literacy) by country and phase for each group.

Table 2. Age, sex, and digital literacy of participants by country and phase, Brazil and Cape Verde, 2023 and 2024 (n = 45).

Country	Phase	Total	Age (M, SD)	Sex (M/F)	Digital Literacy (B/I/A)
Brazil	Phase 1	8	45.00 (12.19)	3/5	2/5/1
	Phase 2	14	50.79 (12.01)	9/5	10/4/0
Cape Verde	Phase 1	11	40.64 (9.78)	8/3	5/4/2
	Phase 2	12	35.33 (10.39)	7/5	5/5/2

All participants signed an informed consent form, as required by the ethics committees of the participating countries. The anonymity of the participants was ensured, and the use of personal data was limited to what was necessary for analysis. The study was approved by the ethics committees of the University of Brasília (Brazil), the Instituto Nacional de Saúde Pública - INSP (Cape Verde), and the London School of Hygiene & Tropical Medicine (United Kingdom).

2.3   Materials

The study used a set of materials and tools to evaluate the usability of the mobile application. The materials included: (1) the Guardians of Health mobile application (GoH), (2) smartphones and tablets, (3) the electronic evaluation questionnaire, (4) an informed consent form, and (5) an observation spreadsheet for recording quantitative metrics (e.g., task completion rates, execution time, assistance, errors and deviations) and qualitative items (e.g., perceptions of use) during task performance.

The GoH application was developed using the React Native framework technology, which allows for generating versions for both Android and iOS platforms; however, this study only considered the first. The functionality for reporting health warning signals (Fig. 1) was evaluated, including fields for type of event, number of individuals affected, identification of those affected (people, animals, or environment), as well as the date and place of occurrence.

3   Results and Discussion

The results of the Phase 1 app evaluation provided essential information to guide the development of a new version. Significant improvements were made to the signal reporting form, including: revision of terms that were difficult to understand due to cultural issues and users' familiarity with the CEBS process; improvements in the visual identification of mandatory fields; revision of the display of location and incident details fields; and improvements in the visual feedback provided to users. In Phase 2, participants reported fewer needs for improvements and no difficulties related to understanding the terms. Suggestions instead focused on aspects such as offline functionality, visual improvements (such as the use of more prominent colors on buttons), and the inclusion of

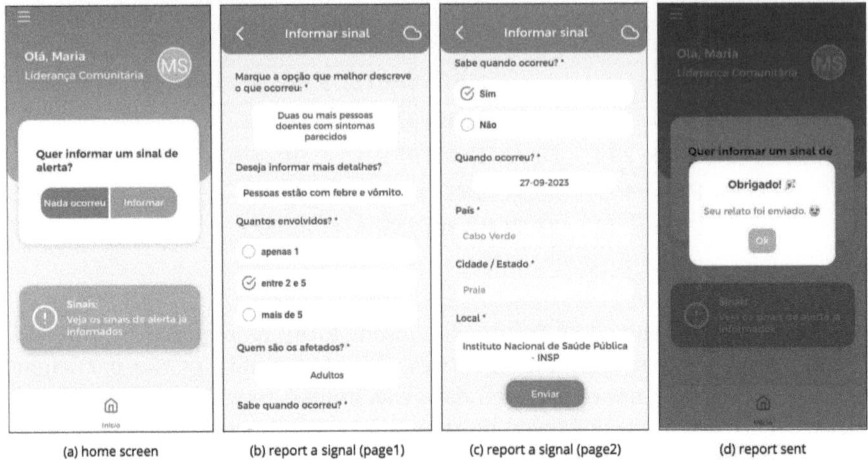

(a) home screen   (b) report a signal (page1)   (c) report a signal (page2)   (d) report sent

Fig. 1. Guardians of Health (GoH) mobile application—navigation screenshots.

tutorials to guide the first use of the app. It should be noted that to avoid evaluation being affected by familiarity, different participants were involved in Phases 1 and 2.

3.1 Quantitative Results

The means and respective standard deviations of the quantitative usability metrics were calculated based on the data collected during the participants' use of the application, and a significance test was applied to the difference in means between the two phases. The metrics evaluated included the number of tasks completed, the average time to complete the tasks, the number of assistance requests, the number of errors and deviations committed, and the SUS score. The results, presented in Table 3 provide a detailed comparison between the countries and the study phases.

The analysis of usability metrics revealed substantial changes between the two phases of the study regarding the SUS score in both countries. In Brazil, this metric increased from 81.6 (SD = 15.1) in Phase 1 to 84.1 (SD = 21.4) in Phase 2, which shows a positive perception of the improvements implemented. In Cape Verde, the increase was even more expressive, from 76.6 (SD = 13.2) in Phase 1 to 84.2 (SD = 17) in Phase 2. Although the changes between phases were not statistically significant, the SUS score observed in both countries can be considered within a good usability parameter for a system, according to acceptability scales [14].

A notable result is the very similar SUS score values in the second phase: Brazil (84.1) and Cape Verde (84.2), following the development of the new version based on participant feedback from both countries. This demonstrates that

Table 3. Usability metrics results by country and phase, Brazil and Cape Verde, 2023 and 2024.

Country	Metric	Phase 1			Phase 2			Diff	p-value	Signif.
		Mean	SD	n	Mean	SD	n			
Brazil	SUS	81.6	15.1	8	84.1	21.4	14	2.5	0.748	ns
	Tasks	3	0	8	3	0	14	0	NA	ns
	Duration	189.8	76.1	8	274.7	74.3	14	85	0.023	signif.
	Assistance	2.4	2.7	8	3.9	3	14	1.6	0.226	ns
	Errors	0.6	1.1	8	0.8	1.6	14	0.2	0.782	ns
	Deviations	0.8	0.9	8	2.4	2.3	14	1.6	0.032	signif.
Cape Verde	SUS	76.6	13.2	11	84.2	17	12	7.6	0.244	ns
	Tasks	2.6	0.8	11	2.8	0.6	12	0.2	0.513	ns
	Duration	359	154.1	11	277.6	156.6	12	-81.4	0.223	ns
	Assistance	2.7	2.6	11	3.9	4.9	12	1.2	0.469	ns
	Errors	0.8	1.8	11	2.1	1.8	12	1.3	0.113	ns
	Deviations	1.1	1.9	11	3.2	2.7	12	2.1	0.045	signif.

Note: SUS scores are on a 0–100 scale; Duration is in seconds; ns = not significant, signif. = significant at $p < 0.05$.

participants have similar perceptions of usability during a cross-cultural development process.

The analysis of usability metrics revealed differences between the countries regarding effectiveness (completed tasks). In Brazil, there was consistency in both phases, with all participants completing the three proposed tasks (mean = 3.0; SD = 0.0). In Cape Verde, Phase 1 presented a lower mean (2.6; SD = 0.8), which indicates that not all participants were able to complete all tasks. However, there was an improvement in Phase 2 (mean = 2.8; SD = 0.6), suggesting that the improvements implemented between phases contributed to greater effectiveness.

Changes in the efficiency metric (duration) also differed between countries. In Brazil there was a significant difference (p = 0.023) between phases with the duration to completion in Phase 1 considerably lower (189.8 s; SD = 76.1) compared to Phase 2 (274.7 s; SD = 74.3), indicating that changes in the application may have increased perceived complexity or introduced new elements that required more interaction time. In Cape Verde, duration to completion was higher than Brazil in both phases (Ph.1: 359.0 s; SD = 154.1; Ph.2: 277.6 s; SD = 156.6), reflecting challenges related to technological familiarity and local infrastructure (i.e., quality of internet connection), but showed an improvement between Phase 1 and 2.

The need for assistance also varied across countries and phases. In Brazil, the average number of requests for assistance in Phase 1 was 2.4 (SD = 2.7), increasing to 3.9 (SD = 3) in Phase 2, which may be explained by the introduction of new flows or functionalities in the application. In Cape Verde, requests were more frequent and varied across participants, with averages of 2.7 (SD = 2.6) in Phase 1 and 3.9 (SD = 4.9) in Phase 2. The substantial increase in the standard deviation in Phase 2 suggests that some participants faced much greater difficulties than others, possibly due to individual differences in technological familiarity.

Regarding errors and deviations, which reflect the frequency of difficulties during interactions, these were lower in Brazil in both phases compared to Cape Verde. In Phase 1, errors in Brazil were 0.6 (SD = 1.1), and deviations were 0.8 (SD = 0.9). In Phase 2, there was an increase in both metrics: errors (mean = 0.8; SD = 1.6) and deviations (mean = 2.4; SD = 2.3), with the latter being significant (p = 0.032), possibly related to the changes to the application that introduced some confusion for participants. In Cape Verde, there was a nonsignificant increase in errors between phases (Ph.1: 0.8, SD = 1.8; Ph.2: 2.1, SD = 1.8; p = 0.113) and a significant increase in deviations (Ph.1: 1.1, SD = 1.9; Ph.2: 3.2, SD = 2.7, p = 0.045), reinforcing that, although the improvements have increased effectiveness, there are still aspects that need to be refined to reduce the perceived complexity.

These results highlight the importance of cultural and technological context in system design. Participants in Brazil had greater fluidity and less effort in interactions, while those in Cape Verde faced more pronounced challenges, especially in Phase 1. The improvements made between phases were effective in both contexts, but the impact was most evident in Cape Verde, where effectiveness, satisfaction, and consistency of results increased substantially. However, the increases in errors, deviations, and assistance in Phase 2 in both countries suggest that the changes to the application added new challenges that need to be addressed.

3.2   Qualitative Results

The qualitative results were organized into four main categories: understanding and navigation, technological infrastructure, interface and visual design, and contextual relevance, and highlighted distinct perceptions and common points between participants from Brazil and Cape Verde. These were analyzed in light of cultural and technological differences between countries, as well as improvements made between phases of the study.

Although participants in both countries recognized the potential of the app as a community health tool, cultural and technological differences were notable. The changes implemented after Phase 1 contributed to substantial improvements in user experience, but specific barriers persisted, especially in Cape Verde. In Brazil, the challenges were more related to the clarity of fields and the use of technical terminology, while in Cape Verde, technological infrastructure difficulties and less digital familiarity were predominant. Table 4 shows a comparison of perceptions between countries in this phase.

Phase 1 was characterized by challenges related to navigation within the application and the clarity of its interface. In both countries, participants initially faced difficulties in understanding the flow of filling and the meaning of some fields; however, these limitations were more pronounced in Cape Verde, where limited connectivity and less digital familiarity presented additional barriers.

Table 4. Comparison of perceptions by country, collected in phase 1 development workshops, Brazil and Cape Verde, 2023 and 2024.

Category	Brazil	Cape Verde
Understanding and Navigation	Difficulty in identifying mandatory fields and technical terms, such as the distinction between "sanitary" and "environmental".	Difficulty understanding the task flow and starting to fill out the form
Technological Infrastructure	Connectivity with no reports of significant issues.	The lack of connectivity has impacted the continued use of the application
Interface and Visual Design	Overloaded interface, with too much information and unclear visual hierarchy.	Small buttons and hard-to-read fonts made interaction difficult, especially for older participants
Contextual Relevance	High relevance for community leaders, but need for adjustments in terminology and greater visual clarity in the fields.	Recognition of the app's potential as a surveillance tool but limited by technological barriers and confusing navigation

Regarding the perception highlights, in Brazil, one participant commented that the terminology was confusing, especially when related to the health and environment. Furthermore, the lack of highlighting mandatory fields resulted in incomplete filling. In Cape Verde, difficulties in understanding the initial flow of the form were recurrent.

In Phase 2, improvements were implemented based on feedback from Phase 1, such as revising terms, visually highlighting mandatory fields, and simplifying the layout. These changes resulted in a more positive experience for participants, but specific challenges remained, particularly in Cape Verde, as shown in Table 5.

Despite the improvements made, cultural and technological differences between countries continued to influence the user experience. In Brazil, participants suggested adjustments related to personalization for specific audiences (e.g., older users). In Cape Verde, limited connectivity and the need for additional support for users with less digital experience remained important challenges, and the need for an offline option was also important.

Table 5. Comparison of perceptions by country, collected in phase 2 development workshops, Brazil and Cape Verde, 2023 and 2024.

Category	Brazil	Cape Verde
Understanding and Navigation	Review of terms and highlighting of mandatory fields, reducing incorrect entries.	Perceptible improvements, but difficulties persist among users with less digital familiarity.
Technological Infrastructure	No connectivity issues, but suggestions to improve system responsiveness.	Limited connectivity persistence, with strong demand for offline functionality.
Interface and Visual Design	More intuitive layout, with buttons and required fields clearly highlighted. Suggestions for customization (seniors).	Partial improvements, but the need for larger buttons, more legible fonts, and greater visual clarity.
Contextual Relevance	Participants highlighted the positive impact of the app for community leaders, with greater acceptance after the adjustments were made.	The application has been recognized as essential for community communication, but technological barriers still limit its full adoption.

Regarding similarities, in both countries, participants recognized the relevance of the application as an essential tool for community health surveillance and improvements to the interface, such as visual highlighting of mandatory fields and revision of terminology, facilitated navigation, and reduced filling errors.

About differences, in Brazil, participants were more familiar with mobile devices and had adequate connectivity, which allowed for smoother use of the app, and emphasized suggestions for visual customization and greater accessibility. In Cape Verde, technological limitations and limited connectivity represented more significant barriers, reinforcing the need for offline functionality and additional support for users with limited digital experience.

These results reinforced the importance of adapting digital health technologies to the cultural and technological context. In order to ensure inclusion and usability in different scenarios, the application must continue to evolve, focusing on features such as offline access in Cape Verde and more accessible visual elements in Brazil.

3.3   Limitations of the Study

As noted above, to avoid evaluation being affected by familiarity (i.e., participants simply getting used to the app), different participants were involved in Phases 1 and 2. However, this also meant that the participants in the two phases did not necessarily have the same characteristics, which may explain the absence of significant change in most metrics despite substantial improvements. The characteristics of the participants, particularly their level of digital literacy and age, may have influenced the results of the usability metrics and perceptions. Although a minimum level of digital literacy was required for participation, it was not possible to achieve a completely balanced distribution of profiles in some sessions. For instance, in Brazil (Phase 2), a significant number of participants with limited digital literacy were present, which likely impacted negatively certain usability metrics.

The study focused on a population with relatively similar cultural characteristics, such as Portuguese as a common language and cultural proximity in literature and audiovisual content. However, in Cape Verde, although Portuguese is the official language, most Cape Verdeans use Crioulo as their primary language in everyday life. This linguistic distinction may have influenced the use of the application, particularly in understanding the technical terms commonly used in public health communication. Future studies could address this limitation by evaluating the usability of surveillance applications with participants from more diverse cultural and linguistic backgrounds to better understand additional factors that may affect usability and acceptance.

Regarding the project's material resources, the quality of the internet connection in Cape Verde emerged as a potential limiting factor. Poor connectivity seems to be a common challenge for the general population. Participants emphasized the importance of the offline option to ensure the application's use in remote and underconnected areas.

4   Conclusion

The study showed that the development of the GoH mobile application with community leaders was essential to ensure its usability and acceptance in different cultural and technological contexts. The use of a user-centered approach allowed us to identify specific barriers and implement improvements that promoted significant advances in the user experience between the evaluated phases.

In Brazil, participants demonstrated greater technological familiarity, which allowed a more fluid interaction with the application. The improvements made (e.g., visual representation of the fields and the simplification of the layout) resulted in more intuitive usability and minimized filling errors. However, suggestions related to customization and accessibility were identified, especially for the older audience.

In Cape Verde, the challenges were more pronounced, such as limitations in technological infrastructure and participants' lack of experience with mobile devices. Limited connectivity highlighted the importance of implementing offline functionality. Despite these barriers, the results of Phase 2 demonstrated important advances, with greater effectiveness in tasks and increased user satisfaction, reflected in high SUS scores. The similarities between the contexts reinforce the potential of the application as a community health surveillance tool. In both countries, participants valued the ability of GoH to connect communities to health systems, promoting the rapid and efficient reporting of warning signs. In addition, the review of terminology and the simplification of workflows helped to reduce initial navigation and use barriers.

The differences observed highlight the importance of adapting digital technologies to local, cultural, and technological conditions. In Brazil, technological familiarity has enabled a focus on design adjustments and customization, while in Cape Verde, improvements should prioritize connectivity and support for users with little digital experience.

This study demonstrates that User-centered Design, combined with an iterative evaluation process, is essential for the development of inclusive and effective digital health surveillance technologies. The results reinforce the importance of considering cultural diversity and local conditions to ensure the adoption and positive impact of solutions such as Guardians of Health. For the future, it is recommended to continue developing and evaluating this kind of digital solution in broader and diverse contexts to identify more requirements that can be implemented to contribute to the sustainability of processes of detecting and managing outbreaks in countries.

Acknowledgments. The Associação Brasileira de Profissionais de Epidemiologia de Campo (ProEpi) and the Instituto Nacional de Saúde Pública de Cabo Verde (INSP) would like to thank all partner institutions for their strong collaboration. In Brazil, the Superintendência da Região Leste de Saúde do Distrito Federal and the Superintendência de Vigilância em Saúde da Secretaria de Estado da Saúde de Goiás. In Cape Verde, the Comissão Multissetorial da Instância Nacional de Coordenação da Abordagem "Uma Só Saúde". In addition, the longstanding technical and financial support of the UK Public Health Rapid Support Team / London School of Hygiene & Tropical Medicine has enabled this technology to develop and contribute to epidemic prevention and response efforts. We are especially grateful to the communities and community volunteers for their ongoing engagement in community health activities and their invaluable contributions to the success of this initiative. This research study is funded within the United Kingdom Public Health Rapid Support Team (UK-PHRST) NIHR CCF award: IS-RRT-1015-00. The UK Public Health Rapid Support Team is funded by UK Aid from the Department of Health and Social Care and is jointly run by the UK Health Security Agency and the London School of Hygiene & Tropical Medicine. The views expressed in this publication are those of the author(s) and not necessarily those of the Department of Health and Social Care.

Competing interest statement. The authors have no competing interests to declare that are relevant to the content of this article.

References

1. Becker, K., Hu, Y., Biller-Andorno, N.: Infectious diseases – a global challenge. Int. J. Med. Microbiol. **296**(4–5), 179–185 (2006). https://doi.org/10.1016/j.ijmm.2005.12.015
2. Phua, K.-L., Lee, L.K.: Meeting the challenge of epidemic infectious disease outbreaks: an agenda for research. J. Public Health Policy **26**(1), 122–132 (2005). https://doi.org/10.1057/palgrave.jphp.3200001
3. De Gaetano, S., et al.: Global trends and action items for the prevention and control of emerging and re-emerging infectious diseases. Hygiene **5**(2), 18 (2025). https://doi.org/10.3390/hygiene5020018
4. Balajee, S.A., Salyer, S.J., Greene-Cramer, B., Sadek, M., Mounts, A.W.: The practice of event-based surveillance: concept and methods. Glob. Secur. Health Sci. Policy **6**(1), 1–9 (2021). https://doi.org/10.1080/23779497.2020.1848444
5. Houlihan, C.F., Whitworth, J.A.: Outbreak science: recent progress in the detection and response to outbreaks of infectious diseases. Clin. Med. **19**(2), 140–144 (2019). https://doi.org/10.7861/clinmedicine.19-2-140
6. Ramsbottom, A., O'Brien, E., Ciotti, L., Takacs, J.: Enablers and barriers to community engagement in public health emergency preparedness: a literature review. J. Community Health **43**(2), 412–420 (2017). https://doi.org/10.1007/s10900-017-0415-7
7. McMichael, T.M., et al.: COVID-19 in a long-term care facility — king county, Washington, February 27–March 9, 2020. MMWR Morb. Mortal. Wkly. Rep. **69**(12), 339–342 (2020). https://doi.org/10.15585/mmwr.mm6912e1
8. Garg, S., Bhatnagar, N., Gangadharan, N.: A case for participatory disease surveillance of the covid-19 pandemic in India. JMIR Public Health Surveill. **6**(2), e18795 (2020). https://doi.org/10.2196/18795
9. Menant, L., Gilibert, D., Sauvezon, C.: The application of acceptance models to human resource information systems: a literature review. Front. Psychol. **12**, 659421 (2021). https://doi.org/10.3389/fpsyg.2021.659421
10. Brooke, J.: SUS-a quick and dirty usability scale. Usability Eval. Ind. **189**(194), 4–7 (1996)
11. Gulliksen, J., Göransson, B., Boivie, I., Blomkvist, S., Persson, J., Cajander, Å.: Key principles for user-centred systems design. Behav. Inf. Technol. **22**(6), 397–409 (2003). https://doi.org/10.1080/01449290310001624329
12. Law, W.K., Perez, K.: Cross-cultural implementation of information system. J. Cases Inf. Technol. **7**(2), 121–130 (2005). https://doi.org/10.4018/jcit.2005040108
13. Reinecke, K., Bernstein, A.: Knowing what a user likes: a design science approach to interfaces that automatically adapt to culture. MIS Q. **37**(2), 427–453 (2013). https://doi.org/10.25300/MISQ/2013/37.2.06
14. Bangor, A., Kortum, P., Miller, J.: Determining what individual SUS scores mean: adding an adjective rating scale. J. Usability Stud. **4**(3), 114–123 (2009)

A Study on the Optimization of the Interface of a Medical Lung Function Tester Based on EEG Technology: Improvement of Cognitive Performance and User Experience

Wenjing Cao, Lang Qin[✉], Rouzi Xing, Peimeng Liu, Zhiyong Chen, Ying Zhang, and Jiang Shao

School of Architecture & Design, China University of Mining and Technology, Xuzhou, China
`laree1207@163.com`

Abstract. Medical pulmonary function testing equipment is a crucial tool for diagnosing respiratory diseases, but its interface design often suffers from information overload and complex layouts, leading to high cognitive load and poor user experience for healthcare professionals. This study employs electroencephalography (EEG) to explore the impact of different interface design factors, such as data visualization formats (single, dual, and triple combinations) and color schemes (color vs. grayscale), on cognitive performance and user experience. Using a 2×3 Oddball experimental paradigm, behavioral data (reaction time and accuracy) and EEG data (P200 and P300 components) were analyzed to evaluate the effects of interface design. Results indicate that complex visualization formats (e.g., graphs, tables, and scales) significantly increase P200 and P300 amplitudes, reflecting higher cognitive load. Color interfaces elicited significantly lower P300 amplitudes compared to grayscale, suggesting that color interfaces may enhance perceptual efficiency and decision-making. This study provides scientific evidence for optimizing pulmonary function testing equipment interfaces, recommending simplified visualization formats and color schemes to reduce cognitive load and improve user experience. The findings have significant theoretical and practical implications for the design of medical device interfaces.

Keywords: Medical Pulmonary Function Testing Equipment ·
Electroencephalography · Cognitive Performance · User Experience · Interface
Optimization.

1 Introduction

With the increasing environmental pollution, the prevalence of chronic respiratory diseases (e.g., asthma) has been increasing globally in recent years. According to the 2015 Global Burden of Disease (GBD) Study, 358 million people suffer from asthma worldwide, a 12.6% increase in prevalence from 1990 [1]. As a chronic airway disease, the diagnosis and treatment of asthma relies on pulmonary function testing devices, which

P.-L.P. Rau and H. Krömker (Eds.): HCII 2025, LNCS 16336, pp. 32–50, 2026.
https://doi.org/10.1007/978-3-032-12798-3_3

can provide healthcare professionals with accurate patient respiratory data, such as first-second exertion lung volume (FEV1) and maximal expiratory flow rate (PEF), and other key indicators, which are crucial for determining whether a patient's lung function is impaired, so the design of the interface of the pulmonary function testing device directly influences healthcare professionals' work efficiency and diagnostic accuracy [1–3] (Fig. 1).

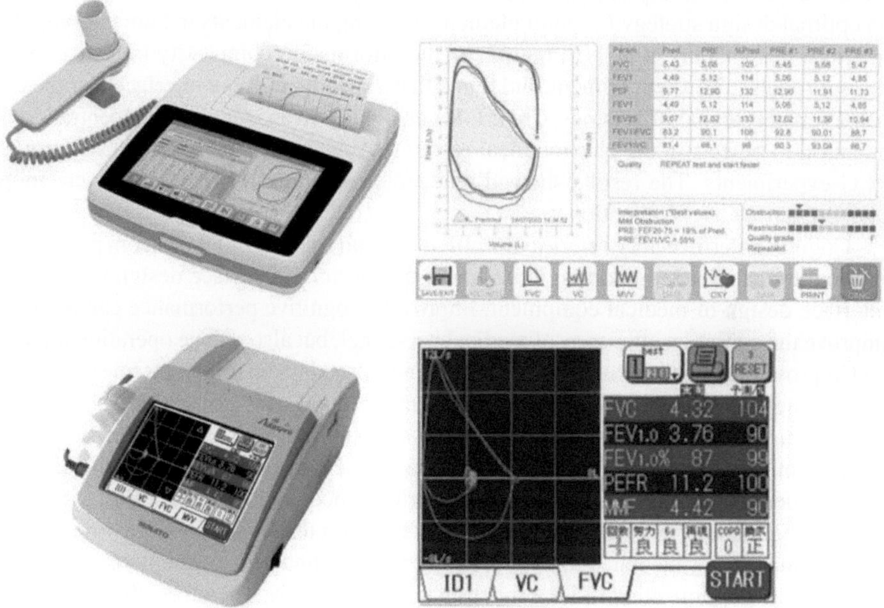

Fig. 1. Interface of some existing pulmonary function testers.

Despite the important role of pulmonary function testing devices in the diagnosis of chronic respiratory diseases such as asthma, there are relatively few studies on their interface design. Existing studies mainly focus on device performance optimization and functional improvement, while the information layout and data presentation form of interface design have not been sufficiently explored [4]. As a real-time monitoring device, the interface of the lung function tester is characterized by multiple types of information, multidimensional display of data and information, and diverse operating environments, which creates more loads on the visual cognition of healthcare workers and is prone to human factors errors [5]. Therefore, the research on the interface design of pulmonary function tester has important theoretical and practical significance. For example, Li, Y., et al. [6] conducted eye - tracking experiments and found that the impact of dynamic icons on users' attention varies with the number of dynamic icons. This finding provides crucial reference points for the design and implementation of future dynamic graphic interfaces. Li Wenjie et al. [7] identified and classified the main design factors influencing the interface consistency of responsive websites through eye -

tracking and questionnaires, and created a responsive interface across multiple terminal devices with a consistent and sustainable user experience.

Electroencephalography (EEG) technology provides a powerful tool for interface design research. By recording the EEG signals of users while they operate an interface, researchers can analyze the changes in interface interaction performance and users' cognitive performance [8]. Jin et al. [9] used the ERP component of EEG technology to analyze subjects' information perception of different colors and shapes, and based on the results of the experiment combined with cognitive mechanisms, they proposed an optimal design strategy for color elements and graphic elements in human-computer interface design.Tang et al. [10] optimized the information complexity in device interfaces through an EEG experiment, and found that a specific range of interface complexity helps subjects to make decisions. Choi, J. K., et al. [11] investigated the concentration of attention to objects in the physiological response to humans' preferred spaces through EEG experiments. The results showed that preferred and familiar images were more likely to attract users' attention.

Cognitive Performance refers to the efficiency and accuracy of the user in processing information, and is an important indicator of the merits of interface design [12]. In the interface design of medical equipment, improving cognitive performance can not only improve the operation efficiency of medical personnel, but also reduce operational errors and improve diagnostic accuracy. User Experience also plays an important role in medical device interface design. Studies have shown that a good user experience can improve the operational efficiency and satisfaction of users and reduce operational errors [13].

In summary, although existing research has achieved certain results in the areas of medical device interface design, cognitive performance, and user experience, in-depth research on the interface design of pulmonary function testers is still relatively lacking. In particular, experimental studies combining EEG technology have not yet been fully applied in the optimization of lung function tester interfaces. Therefore, this study aims to explore the effects of different interface design factors (e.g., information visualization combinations, color interfaces) on the cognitive performance and user experience of healthcare workers through EEG experiments, so as to provide a scientific basis for the interface design of lung function testers. The research results can not only improve the operation efficiency and decision-making accuracy of healthcare workers, but also provide a reference for the interface optimization of other medical devices.

2 Behavioral and Electrophysiological Indicators

In terms of behavioral indicators, reaction time and correctness are commonly used and more objective in performance evaluation, which can reflect the efficiency and quality of task completion to a certain extent. Zhang j et al. [14] investigated the interaction between semantic memory and icons in the hierarchical approach to complexity perception and found that familiarity can enhance cognitive efficiency under complex semantic stimuli. The cognitive performance of low - and high - complexity encodings is superior to that of medium - complexity encoding.Scharroo J et al. [15], in an experimental analysis of the effect of stimulus graphic complexity on visual search, found that when interference complexity was unchanged, the reaction time increased with the increase in the complexity of the target; When target complexity is constant, reaction time decreases with increasing interference complexity. Makovski T et al. [16] in target information tracking experiments, by analyzing the correctness data, found that the tracking efficiency when the target features are different is significantly higher than the tracking efficiency when the target features are the same.

Electrophysiological indicators of brain activity (P200, P300, etc.) are thought to reflect different functional event-related potential (ERP) components of many cognitive processes. The P200 generally occurs during the primary processing stage of visual stimuli, reflecting early processing of the visual input, and reflecting the assessment of internally represented or anticipated processes, including recognition and encoding processes. The amplitude of the P200 may change when an individual pays attention to a particular stimulus or task, reflecting differences in attentional processing, and previous studies have found that a higher average amplitude of the P200 indicates that the stimulus will consume more attentional resources [17]. Jin et al. [18] found that higher P200 amplitudes indicated that subjects paid greater attention to the stimulus and mobilized more attentional resources. In visual stimuli, generally the amplitude of P300 is considered to reflect the extent to which a person invests in mental factors, i.e., the amount of allocated cognitive resources. P300 is generated based on the magnitude of the probability of responding to the task, the attentional state of the subject, and other conditions, and target stimuli with low probability of appearing in Oddball's experiments underlie the generation of the P300. Polich [19] argued that the P300 represents the user's attentional resource allocation relationship between tasks and is related to the individual's arousal level, and the level of arousal determines the total amount of attentional resources in the brain. Hillyard [20] believes that P300 can reflect the subsequent stages of perceptual information processing, which embodies the selective cognition of the attentional channel and the response mechanism working together on the target stimulus. Therefore, the changes of behavioral and EEG physiological indexes in Oddball experiments of information search and decision making under different cognitive difficulty influencing factors (e.g., form of data combination, visualization presentation) are the issues explored in this paper.

3   Materials and Methods

3.1   Participants

A total of 16 male subjects were recruited for this experiment, all of these subjects were undergraduate or graduate students with a medical background, aged between 20–28 years old, and this group was chosen mainly because of their ability to quickly familiarize themselves with the experimental material, as well as the fact that the electroencephalographic component of the brain is more pronounced in males than in females. The inclusion criterion was that the subjects had to be right-handed, and the exclusion criteria were color blindness and color weakness. All subjects were trained on the background of the experiment before the experiment began, and their names, gender, age, and specialty were counted during the experiment.

3.2 Apparatus

Subjects' EEG signals were recorded by using a NeuSen W 64-channel EEG acquisition system, and the experiments were conducted in a well-lit and sound-proofed closed laboratory, with subjects 750 mm away from the computer screen on which the stimuli were presented. The experimental stimuli appeared in the center area of a 1920×1080 23-in. computer screen with an eye viewing angle of $10.5° \times 7.5°$ for the subjects. The stimulus presentation software was E-Prime, and subjects were asked to respond to a randomly presented experimental picture in the stimulus. This is shown in Fig. 2. The experiment was conducted using a 2×3 two-factor oddball experimental paradigm.

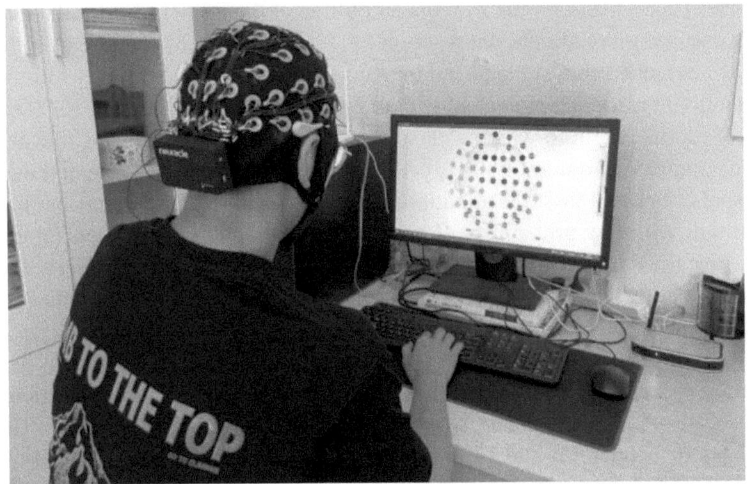

Fig. 2. EEG experiment to reduce electrical resistance.

3.3 Experimental Design

This experiment adopts a 2×3 factorial oddball experimental paradigm to explore the effects of different data visualization combination forms and different color interfaces on users' information search and decision-making abilities through behavioral data and ERP data. Here, the visualization data combination forms are mainly curve graph, curve graph and table, and curve graph table and scale, and the color interface is divided into two kinds of color and grayscale interface.

EEG signal acquisition and ERP extraction. The sampling frequency was 1000 Hz by using a NeuSen W 64-channel EEG acquisition system as shown in Fig. 3. scalp electrodes were placed using the internationally recognized 10–20 system, and the scalp resistance was set to be less than 5 kΩ. the sampling frequency of the EEG was 512 Hz. labeled target stimuli were initiated 200 ms before the stimulus onset and ended 800 ms after the stimulus onset. The EEG data collected were preprocessed and ERPs were extracted using the EEGLAB toolbox in Matlab R2015a.The main processes include: data integration, electrode removal, band-pass filtering, downsampling, re-referencing, segmentation, baseline correction, myoelectric signal removal, eye movement, and superimposed averaging. The useless electrodes were removed in the de-electrode operation, and the EEG signals from the P3, Pz, P4, F3, Fz, F4, C3, Cz, C4, CP3, CP4, and Poz electrode channels were acquired. Baseline correction was applied to all segments (200 ms before the end), and the processed EEG data segments were superimposed and averaged to obtain the P300 waveform, and the ERP waveform was extracted based on the component time-range analysis, with a time window of 500 ms–550 ms for the P300.Finally, the eigenvalues of the mean amplitude and latency of the P300 waveform were analyzed.

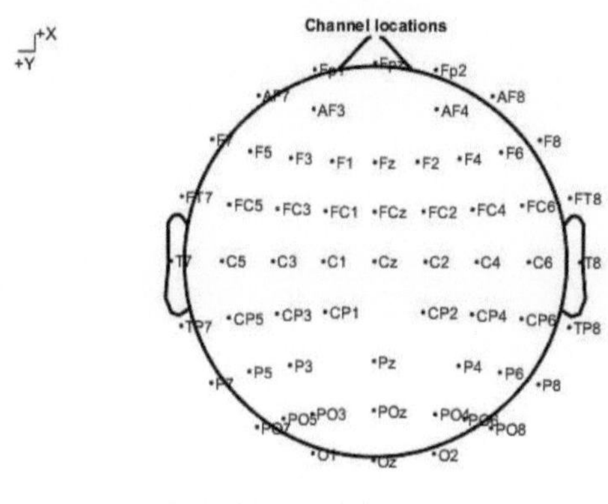

Fig. 3. NeuSen W 64-channel EEG acquisition system.

Experimental Material. Data visualization combination form, mainly including single category, double category, triple category, are real visualization combination form, including single category for a single curve graph form, double category for curve graph and table combination form, triple category for the combination of curve graph, table and scale; to ensure the authenticity of the simulation experiments, the comparison of the color interface and grayscale interface is added here, and the grayscale interface is derived from the color interface converted to RGB grayscale, the As shown in Table 1.

3.4 Experimental Design

In the Oddball experiment, subjects were required to judge the subject's respiratory effort based on the status of the FVC curve, pressing the A key for good effort and the L key for no effort to breathe. There were a total of 1200 trials in the formal experiment, of which 60% were standard stimuli, i.e., non-target stimuli, which were FVC interfaces that did not need to be judged by the subject, and 40% were target stimuli, i.e., targeted stimuli, with six interface layouts, where the subject was required to make a key-pressing response based on the curves. Each stimulus was presented randomly, with

Table 1. Experiment Interface Materials.

Visualization Portfolio	color interface	grayed-out interface
triple category	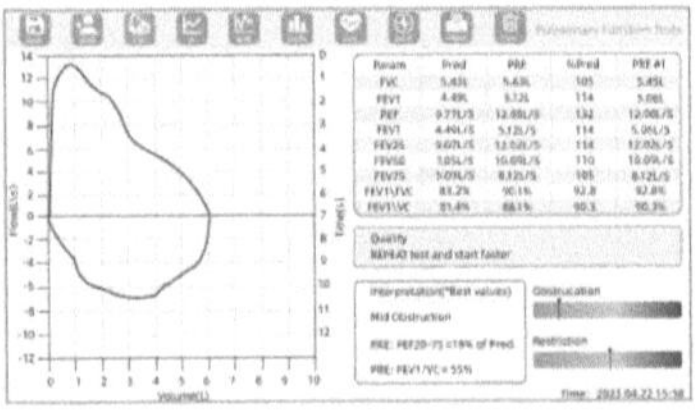	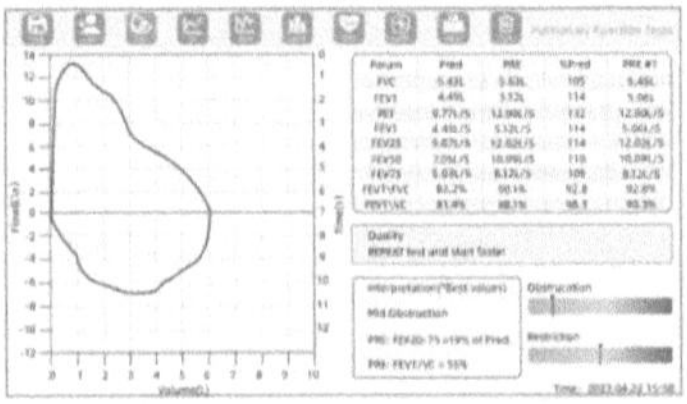
double category	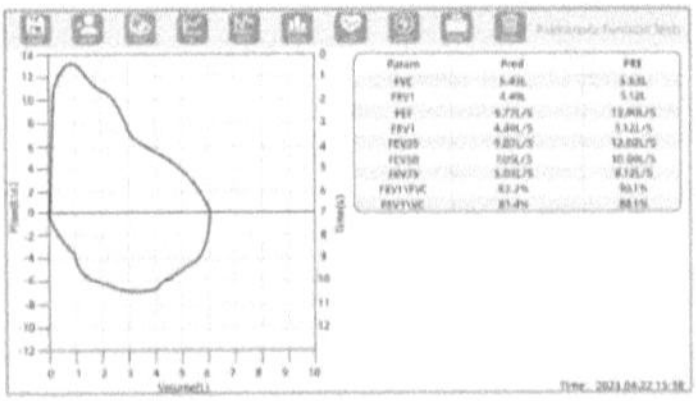	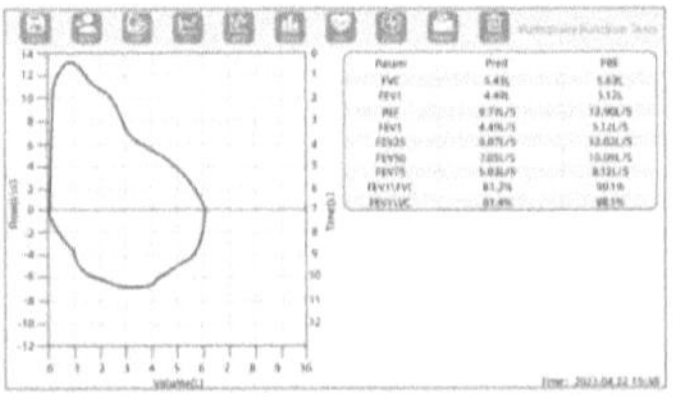
single category	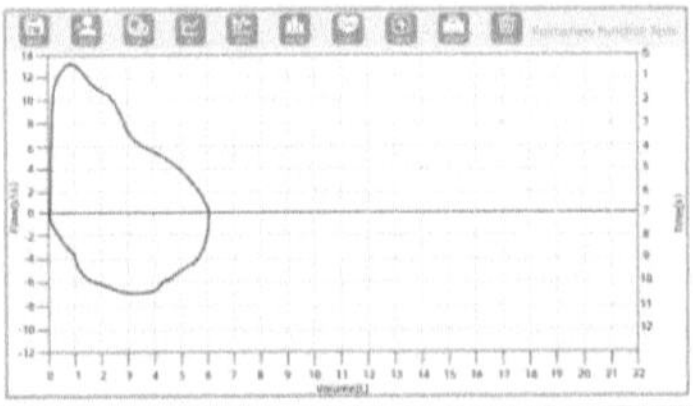	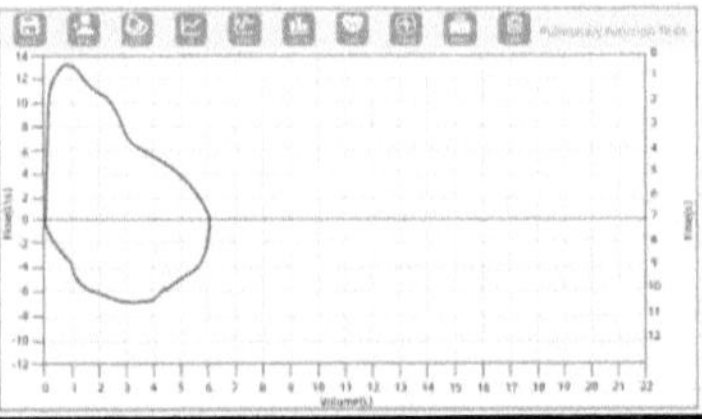

a duration of 1000 ms and a stimulus interval of 1000 ms. all subjects were asked to read the experimental instructions carefully at the beginning of the experiment and to have practice experiments before the formal experiment, which were different pictures from the formal experimental stimuli, to help subjects adapt to the experimental task. The total duration of the experiment was 10 min, and before the formal experiment began, subjects were allowed to perform practice experiments to determine the experimental flow, and EEG and eye movement signals were acquired in both normal and fatigue states. Approximately 200 trials were performed in 10 min. The experimental flow is shown in Fig. 4.

4   Results

4.1   Behavioral Data Analysis

Two-factor repeated measures analysis of the collected correctness and response time was performed using SPSS 26.0 software with an experimentally set significance level value of $p = 0.05$. The correctness results showed that color (color, grayscale) did not have a significant effect on subjects' correctness as shown in Table 2 Within-subjects

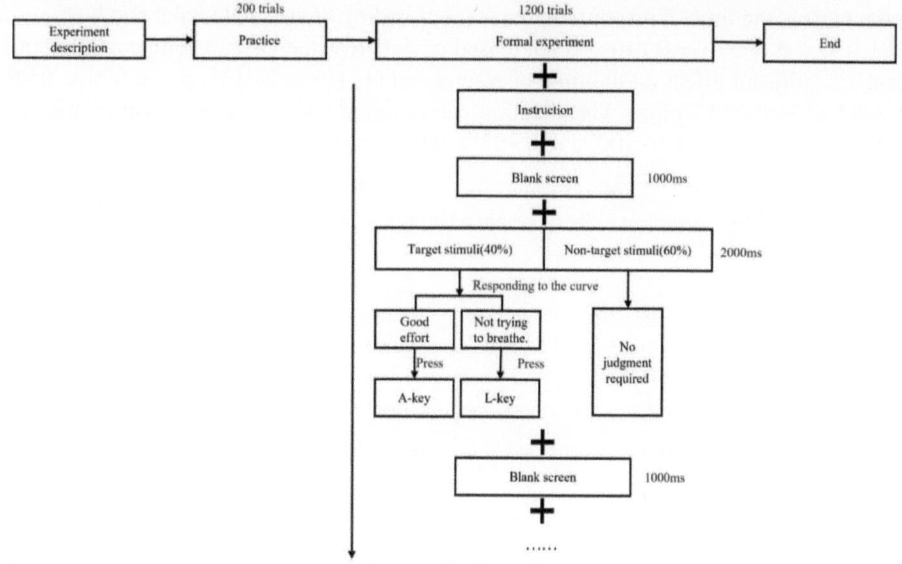

Fig. 4. Experimental Flow.

effect test for correctness under the combined coding format of size and layout, $F(1, 12) = 0.920$, $p = 0.358 > 0.05$, biased $\eta^2 = 0.077$, visualization combination format had a significant effect on subjects' correctness, $F(1.903, 20.937) = 18.122$, $p = 0.000 < 0.05$, biased $\eta^2 = 0.622$, and the interaction effect of color $\times$ visualization combination was not significant, $F(1.464, 16.105) = 0.432$, biased $\eta^2 = 0.038$.

Table 2. Intra-subject effect test for accuracy in different combinations of color and visualization.

Experimental Variable	Class III sum of squares	Degrees of Freedom	mean square	F	significance	Partial Eta Square
Color	0.001	1.000	0.001	0.920	0.358	0.077
Visual Combination	0.140	1.903	0.074	18.122	0.000*	0.622
Color*Visualization Combinations	0.001	1.464	0.001	0.432	0.596	0.038

The * in the left column of experimental variables indicates combinations of multiple experimental variables (color and visualization); The * in the right column of significance indicates that the labeled values are less than our set significance level (p=0.05), meaning the corresponding experimental variable (visualization combination) has a significant impact on accuracy or reaction time.

The results at the time of response indicated that color (color, grayscale) did not have a significant effect on the subjects' time of response as shown in Table 3 within-subjects effect test at the time of response in the form of coding of size and layout combinations, $F(1, 19) = 5.685$, $p = 0.240 > 0.05$, biased $\eta^2 = 0.169$. the visualization combinations had a significant effect on the time of response, $F(1, 19) = 24.131$, $p = 0.000 < 0.05$, biased $\eta^2 = 0.463$. color x visualization combination had a nonsignificant interaction effect, $F(1, 49.352) = 56.100$, $p = 0.493 > 0.05$, biased $\eta^2 = 0.667$.

Table 3. Tests for in-subject effects when reacting in different combinations of color and visualization.

Experimental Variable	Class III sum of squares	Degrees of Freedom	mean square	F	significance	Partial Eta Square
Color	0.003	1.000	0.003	5.685	0.240	0.169
Visual Combination	0.013	1.000	0.013	24.131	0.000*	0.463
Color*Visualization Combinations	2.236	1.000	2.236	56.100	0.493	0.667

The * in the left column of experimental variables indicates combinations of multiple experimental variables (color and visualization); The * in the right column of significance indicates that the labeled values are less than our set significance level (p=0.05), meaning the corresponding experimental variable (visualization combination) has a significant impact on accuracy or reaction time.

4.2 P200 Data Analysis

After excluding three subjects with incomplete data recording, P3, P4, Pz, CP3, CP4 and POz electrodes were analyzed using SPSS as shown in Fig. 5.

The P200 amplitude is associated with the onset of memory updating and reflects the assessment of internally represented or anticipated processes, including recognition and encoding processes. Successful performance of decision making for the onset of memory updating was demonstrated in this experiment with a time window of 200 ms–260 ms for P200, and the EEG topography during the time window is shown in Fig. 6.

The sets of data for the P200 mean amplitude obeyed a normal distribution by the S-W (Shapiro-Wilk) test. Repeated-measures ANOVA for color, data visualization combination, and electrodes, as shown in Table 4 Within-subjects effect test for P200 mean amplitude, showed that the main effect of color on P200 amplitude was not significant, $F(1, 12) = 2.117$, $p = 0.171 > 0.05$, skewed by $\eta^2 = 0.150$; and that the type of visualization combination had a significant main effect on the P200 mean amplitude $F(1.580, 18.965) = 4.590$, $p = 0.031 < 0.05$, bias $\eta^2 = 0.277$, and the type of visualization combination of graphs, tables, and scales caused larger P200 amplitudes, $M = 2.926$, $SD = 0.775$. electrodes had a significant main effect on the P200 amplitude, $F(2.253, 27.036) = 3.866$, $p = 0.031 < 0.05$, bias $\eta^2 = 0.244$, and some electrodes are shown in Fig. 7.

The data sets for P200 latency followed a normal distribution by the S-W (Shapiro-Wilk) test. Repeated-measures ANOVA for color, data visualization combinations, and

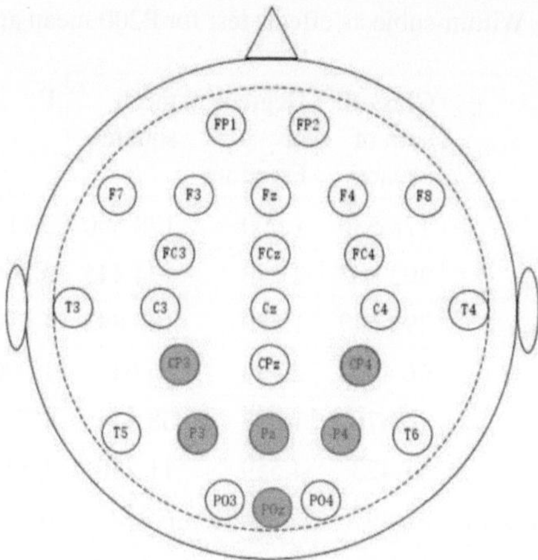

Fig. 5. P200 EEG electrode distribution.

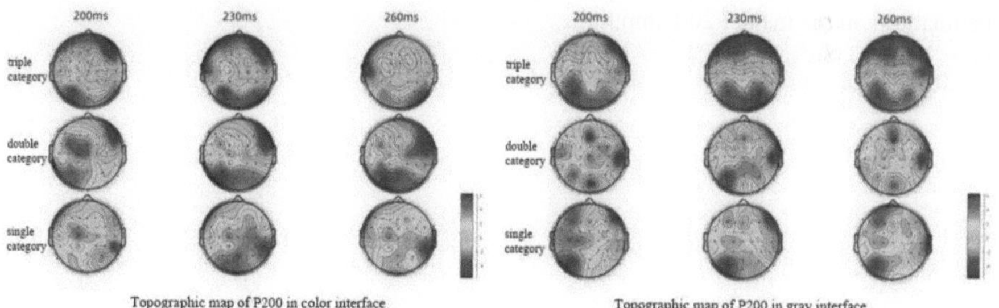

Fig. 6. Topographic map of P200 composition 200 ms–260 ms under color interface and grayscale interface.

electrodes, as shown in Tables 4, 5, 6, 7, 8 and 9 Within-subjects effect test for P200 latency, showed that the main effect of color on P200 latency was not significant, $F(1, 12) = 1.975$, $p = 0.187 > 0.05$, skewed by $\eta^2 = 0.152$, and that the main effect of the different types of visualization combinations on P200 latency was significant $F(1.961, 21.567) = 57.402$, $p = 0.000 < 0.05$, bias $\eta^2 = 0.839$; the visualization combination type of graph, table and scale caused a longer P200 latency ($M = 239.313$, $SD = 1.908$) and the graph alone caused a shorter P200 latency ($M = 224.847$, $SD = 1.778$). The main effect of electrode on P200 latency was not significant, $F(2.582, 28.400) = 1.012$, $p = 0.393 > 0.05$, partial $\eta^2 = 0.084$; the interaction effect of color and visualization combination was significant, $F(1.838, 20.216) = 4.723$, $p = 0.023 < 0.05$, partial $\eta^2 = 0.300$; the interaction effect of visualization combination and electrode had a significant interaction effect, $F(5.002, 55.019) = 6.725$, $p = 0.000 < 0.05$, partial $\eta^2 = 0.379$; color, visualization combination and electrode had a significant interaction effect, $F(4.427, 48.701) = 4.092$, $p = 0.005 < 0.05$, partial $\eta^2 = 0.271$. The color main effect, the electrode main effect and the color and electrode main effect were significant. effect and

Table 4. Within-subjects effects test for P200 mean amplitude.

Experimental Variable	Class III sum of squares	Degrees of Freedom	mean square	F	significance	Partial Eta Square
Color	178.530	1.000	178.530	2.117	0.171	0.150
Electrode	302.905	2.253	134.445	3.866	0.029*	0.244
Visualization Combination	290.547	1.580	183.843	4.590	0.031*	0.277
Color*Electrode	66.449	2.494	26.642	1.390	0.266	0.104
Color*Visualization	76.376	1.987	38.444	1.781	0.190	0.129
Electrode*Visualization	51.423	4.559	11.280	1.551	0.194	0.114
Color*Electrode*Visualization	32.497	5.218	6.228	0.844	0.528	0.066

The * in the left column of experimental variables indicates different combinations of multiple experimental variables (color, electrode, and visualization). The * in the right column of significance indicates that the labeled values are less than our set significance level (p=0.05), indicating a significant main effect of the corresponding experimental variable (electrode and visualization combination) on the mean P200 amplitude.

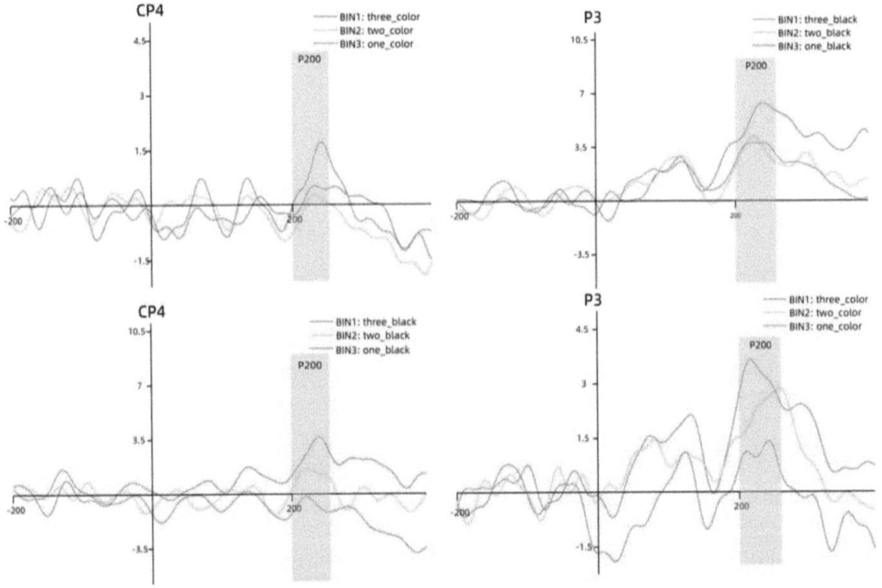

Fig. 7. Waveform diagram of different electrodes.

the interaction effect of color and electrode were not significant, p > 0.05. as shown in Table 5. Further analysis revealed that the interface with three categories of color induced the longest P200 latency at the Pz electrode (M = 246.33, SD = 12.955), and the interface with a single category of grayscale induced the shortest P200 latency at the CP3 electrode (M = 211.50, SD = 10.959).

Table 5. Intra-subject effect test for P200 latency.

Experimental Variable	Class III sum of squares	Degrees of Freedom	mean square	F	significance	Partial Eta Square
Color	2191.502	1.000	2191.502	1.975	0.187	0.152
Electrode	15261.097	1.961	7783.811	57.402	0.000*	0.839
Visualization Combination	1136.660	2.582	440.256	1.012	0.393	0.084
Color*Electrode	762.956	2.947	258.891	1.048	0.384	0.087
Color*Visualization	1280.782	1.838	696.901	4.723	0.023*	0.300
Electrode*Visualization	6663.097	5.002	1332.156	6.725	0.000*	0.379
Color*Electrode*Visualization	4971.968	4.427	1122.999	4.092	0.005	0.271

The * in the left experimental variables column indicates different combinations of multiple experimental variables (color, electrode, and visualization). The * in the right significance column indicates that the labeled value is less than our set significance level (p=0.05), signifying a significant main effect of the corresponding experimental variable (visualization combination, color and visualization combination, electrode and visualization combination) on the P200 latency.

Table 6. The mean and standard deviation of the P200 incubation period in different visualization combinations.

Experimental Variables	Mean value	standard error	95% confidence interval	
			limit	lower limit
Three categories (graphs, tables, scales)	239.313	1.908	235.113	243.512
Two-category (graphs, tables)	230.653	1.879	226.517	234.789
Single category (graphs)	224.847	1.778	220.935	228.760

4.3 P300 Data Analysis

ERP studies generally measure the P300 by amplitude and latency. Amplitude is the difference between the pre-stimulus mean baseline voltage and the maximum positive peak of the ERP waveform within a specific time window, which may be influenced by conditions such as experimental design, the subject's own factors, and the task stimulus. Latency is the length of time from stimulus onset to the point of maximum positive amplitude within a time window. The main scalp distribution of the P300 is at the midline electrodes (Fz, Cz, and Pz), and its amplitude typically increases from the forehead to the parietal electrode sites. The P3, Pz, P4, F3, Fz, F4, C3, Cz, C4 electrodes were analyzed using SPSS and these electrodes were classified into three brain regions including parietal (P3, Pz, P4), frontal (F3, Fz, F4) and central (C3, Cz, C4) as shown in Fig. 8.

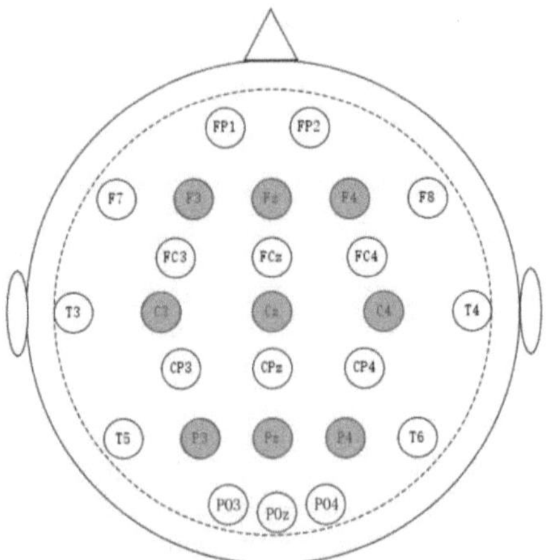

Fig. 8. P300 EEG electrode distribution.

Repeated measures ANOVA was used to analyze the EEG data, comparing the P300 components of the three different visualization forms as well as the two factors of color, and whether there were statistically significant differences in the eigenvalues of the amplitude and latency of the ERP waveforms over a time window of 500 ms–500 ms, and the EEG topography during the time window is shown in Fig. 9.

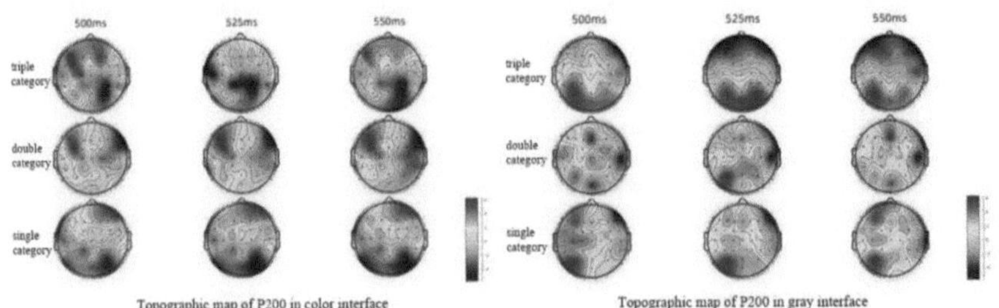

Fig. 9. Topographic map of P300 composition 500 ms–550 ms under color interface and grayscale interface.

After excluding three subjects with incomplete data recording, the data in each group obeyed a normal distribution by the S-W (Shapiro-Wilk) test, and a three-factor ANOVA repeated-measures analysis was performed on the P300 mean amplitude, which were color (color, grayscale), visualization combinations (single, double, and triple categories), and brain regions (frontal, central, and parietal lobes). The results showed a significant main effect of color (color, grayscale), $F(1, 12) = 42.714$, $p = 0.023 < 0.05$, bias $\eta^2 = 0.955$. the P300 amplitude for the color interface ($M = -0.044$, $SD = 0.550$) was lower than the P300 amplitude for the grayscale interface ($M = 0.777$, $SD = 0.648$). The main effect of data visualization combinations (single, dual, and triple categories) was significant, $F(1.130, 12.259) = 20.468$, $p = 0.036 < 0.05$, skewed $\eta^2 = 0.911$, with P300 amplitudes being significantly lower for the combined form of single categories than for dual and triple categories, and highest P300 amplitudes were found for the combined form of curved graphs, scales, and tables. The main effect of brain region was not significant, $F(1.079, 12.158) = 0.837$, $p = 0.354 > 0.05$, partial $\eta^2 = 0.295$. the rest of the interaction effects were not significant, $p > 0.05$. as shown in Tables 7 and 8.

Table 7. Within-subjects effects test for P300 mean amplitude.

Experimental Variable	Class III sum of squares	Degrees of Freedom	mean square	F	significance	Partial Eta Square
Color	9.104	1	9.104	42.714	0.023*	0.955
Brain Area	3.564	1.079	3.302	0.837	0.461	0.295
Visualization Combinations	93.966	1.130	83.109	20.468	0.036*	0.911
Color*Brain Area	4.580	1.050	4.360	0.502	0.558	0.201
Color*Complexity	3.860	1.616	2.389	1.385	0.354	0.409
Brain Area*Complexity	5.375	1.222	4.398	1.018	0.425	0.337
Color*Brain Area*Complexity	20.301	1.424	14.261	3.112	0.188	0.609

The * in the left column of experimental variables indicates different combinations of multiple experimental variables (color, brain area, and complexity). The * in the right column of significance indicates that the labeled values are less than our set significance level (p=0.05), indicating a significant main effect of the corresponding experimental variable (color, visualization combination) on the mean P300 amplitude.

In addition, as shown by the experimental data, P300 induced the maximum P300 amplitude in the central brain area ($M = 0.730$, $SD = 0.776$), in which the P300 of the Cz electrode had the largest average amplitude under the gray-scale three-category interface ($SD = 4.083$, $SD = 3.440$). Some of the electrode waveforms are shown in Fig. 10.

ANOVA repeated measures analysis of P300 latency showed that color did not have a significant effect on P300 latency, $F(1,2) = 0.866$, $p = 0.450 > 0.05$, biased $\eta^2 = 0.302$, and different brain regions had a significant effect on P300 latency $F(1.490,2.979) = 18.953$, $p = 0.021 < 0.05$, biased $\eta^2 = 0.905$ three data visualization combinations had a significant effect on P300 latency $F(1.065,2.130) = 29.185$, $p = 0.028 < 0.05$, biased $\eta^2 = 0.936$. the rest of the interaction effects were not significant, $p > 0.05$. The longest latency for P300 was the interface of the three types of visualization combinations of

Table 8. Mean and standard deviation of the average amplitude of P300 in different visualization combinations.

Experimental Variables	Mean value	standard error	95% confidence interval	
			limit	lower limit
Three categories (graphs, tables, scales)	2.052	0.336	0.607	3.498
Two-category (graphs, tables)	0.216	0.490	-1.893	2.325
Single category (graphs)	-1.168	0.987	-5.414	3.077

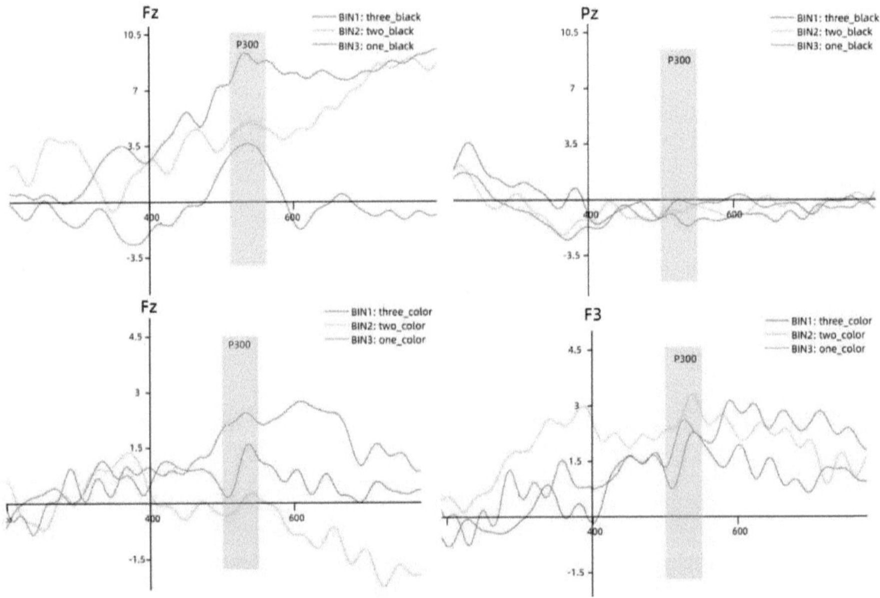

Fig. 10. P300 waveform of some electrodes.

grayscale located at the Fz electrode, and the shortest latency was the color single class visualization combination interface located at the C4 electrode. As shown in Table 9.

5   Discussion

In this study, a 2×3 two-factor Oddball paradigm EEG experiment was conducted to investigate the effects of different combination forms of color and visualization on subjects' perception and decision-making. Behavioral data showed that the color element did not have a significant effect on both correctness and response time, but the visualization combination format had a significant effect on both correctness and response time of the subjects. This suggests that color may not have a significant effect on subjects'

Table 9. Within-subjects effects test for P300 mean amplitude.

Experimental Variable	Class III sum of squares	Degrees of Freedom	mean square	F	significance	Partial Eta Square
Color	740.741	1.000	740.741	0.866	0.450	0.302
Brain Area	1973.926	1.490	1325.082	18.953	0.021*	0.905
Visualization Combinations	4673.926	1.065	4388.177	29.185	0.028*	0.936
Color*Brain Area	366.815	1.134	323.560	1.368	0.362	0.406
Color*Visualization	169.926	1.016	167.327	0.544	0.539	0.214
Brain Area*Visualization	938.519	1.272	737.746	1.946	0.286	0.493
Color*Brain Area*Visualization	325.185	1.654	196.611	2.078	0.255	0.510

The * in the left column of experimental variables indicates different combinations of multiple experimental variables (color, brain area, and visualization combination). The * in the right column of significance indicates that the labeled values are less than our set significance level (p=0.05), indicating that the corresponding experimental variable (brain area , visualization combination) has a significant main effect on P300 latency.

perception and decision making, but the different combination formats affected subjects' decision making. As shown in Fig. 11.

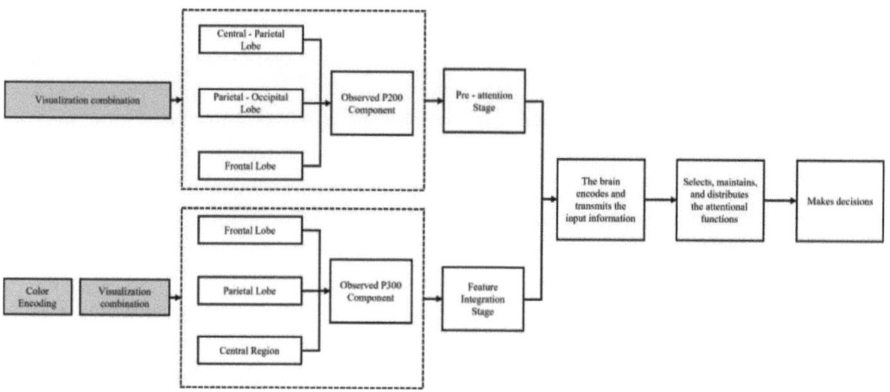

Fig. 11. Neural mechanisms of different coding forms influencing participants' decision-making.

The ERP components P200 and P300 were analyzed by EEG data, and in the experiment, there was a significant effect on the mean P200 amplitude when the interface presented different combinations of visualizations, in which the P200 amplitude was the highest when a combination of graphs, tables, and scales was presented in the FVC interface of the medical lung function tester, which may be due to the higher complexity of the interface for the combinations of the three visual graphs and charts and presumably, the more complex interfaces consumed more attentional resources of the subjects, and higher P200 amplitude represents the stage where the brain puts more mental load or mobilizes more brain resources, which corresponds to the increase of cognitive functions of selective and sustained attention, which implies that subjects need to expend more effort to make the right decision [21]. At the same time, higher P200 amplitude may be related to anxiety, negative emotions and fatigue, and when more information is presented in the interface, it may make subjects feel emotionally uncomfortable thus causing higher amplitude. Previous studies have shown that decision-making tasks mainly elicit temporal and parietal lobe activity in the brain [21], and further analyses found that the P200 elicited larger amplitudes at the P3 electrode, which is consistent with previous studies. However, the color and grayscale interfaces did not elicit significant P200 amplitude changes, suggesting that subjects' early perception of color coding was not significant. In addition, the longer P200 latency implies that the brain needs more time to parse and process the information from the interface, and may also be related to higher levels of cognitive control, as processing complex information may require more cognitive resources and advanced stages of processing, and thus the FVC interface with only the curvilinear graphs had a shorter P200 latency, but the combination of the curvilinear graphs, the tables, and the scales presented more lung function related information thus eliciting a longer P200 latency.

The P300 is an important component of the event-related potential (ERP) that typically appears about 300 ms after stimulus onset. According to the task design, subjects were required to press the A or L key in the presence of a target stimulus, but press the space bar in the presence of a non-target stimulus, and then a sufficiently salient P300 component could be induced by subjects simply by paying attention to recognizing the target stimulus. In the results of the experiment, it was found that larger P300 amplitudes and longer latencies were induced when graphs, tables, and scales appeared in the interface, which may be due to the fact that the interface displayed a larger amount of information, which attracted more intense attention and triggered more advanced cognitive processes during the cognitive task, and the larger P300 amplitudes indicated that the brain invested more attentional resources, meanwhile, longer latencies may indicate deeper processing of the task and information and more complex cognitive decision-making processes in subjects. It has been shown in previous studies [19, 20] that P300 activity is typically recorded on electroencephalographic (EEG) electrodes at the top and side of the brain. In these regions, especially the Pz (parietal) and Cz (central region) electrode locations, the P300 in the central region usually reflects the brain's attention and evaluation of a specific stimulus or task, which may include perception, discrimination, and decision-making processes of information, which is consistent with the findings of the present experiment. In addition, the interface color was found to significantly affect the mean P300 amplitude in the present experiment, and surprisingly, the color interface evoked significantly lower P300 amplitude than the grayscale interface, suggesting that the color interface may be easier for subjects to perceive and make correct decisions.

6 Conclusion

In this study, we investigated the effects of different interface design factors (e.g., information visualization combinations, color interfaces) on the cognitive performance and user experience of healthcare workers through EEG experiments. The experimental results showed that the form of information visualization combinations had a significant effect on the correct rate and response time of healthcare workers, and complex combination forms (e.g., graphs, tables, and scales) led to higher P200 and P300 amplitudes, indicating higher cognitive load and attentional resource consumption. Color interfaces had a significant effect on P300 amplitude, with color interfaces inducing significantly lower P300 amplitudes than grayscale interfaces, suggesting that color interfaces may be easier to perceive and make correct decisions.

Based on the experimental results, this study proposes the following interface optimization suggestions:

1. Simplify information visualization combinations: use concise information presentation (e.g., single-category graphs) to reduce cognitive load and enhance operational efficiency.
2. Optimize the color interface design: Use colorful interface to enhance the perceivability of information and reduce the decision-making difficulty.
3. Balance the amount of information and cognitive load: In the interface design, information overload should be avoided to ensure that healthcare workers can quickly access key information.

The results of this study provide a scientific basis for the interface design of the lung function tester, which is of great significance for improving the operational efficiency and decision-making accuracy of healthcare workers. Future research can further explore the optimization strategies of interface design for other medical devices and conduct in-depth studies by combining multimodal experimental data.

Acknowledgments. This paper is supported by the National Nature Science Foundation of China Grant No.72001202.

References

1. McDougall, S., Tyrer, V., Folkard, S.: Searching for signs, symbols, and icons: effects of time of day, visual complexity, and grouping. J. Exp. Psychol. Appl. **12**(2), 118 (2006)
2. Alejos-Palomares, R., Ramírez Cortes, J.M., Dominguez-Martinez, N.: Digital spirometer with LabView interface [C]. In: International Conference on Electronics. IEEE Computer Society (2008). https://doi.org/10.1109/CONIELECOMP.2008.31
3. Ibrahim, S.N., Jusoh, A.Z., Malik, N.A., et al.: Development of Portable Digital Spirometer Using NI sbRIO. IEEE (2017). https://doi.org/10.1109/ICSIMA.2017.8311987
4. Richar, J.C.M., Kacmarek, R.M.: ICU mechanical ventilators, technological advances vs. user friendliness: the right picture is worth a thousand numbers. Intensive Care Med. **35**(10), 1662–1663 (2009)

5. Zeitlhofer, I., Zumbach, J., Schweppe, J.: Complexity affects performance, cognitive load, and awareness. Learn. Instr. **94**, 102001 (2024). https://doi.org/10.1016/j.learninstruc.2024.102001

6. Yan, L.I., Zhou, Y.: Attention allocation of dynamic icons on mobile app interfaces. Tech. Gaz. **30**(3) (2023). https://doi.org/10.17559/TV-20221128070155

7. Li, W., Zhou, Y., Luo, S., Dong, Y.: Design factors to improve the consistency and sustainable user experience of responsive interface design. Sustainability. **14**(15), 9131 (2022). https://doi.org/10.3390/su14159131

8. Zhou, C.M., Shi, Z.Y., Huang, T., et al.: The impact of swipe direction on the interaction performance of smart home interfaces for the elderly: EEG and eye – tracking evidence. Front. Psychol. **14**, 1089769 (2023). https://doi.org/10.3389/fpsyg.2023.1089769

9. Jin, T., Zhou, S., Lang, X., et al.: Combined effect of color and shape on cognitive performance. Math. Probl. Eng. **2022**(1), 3284313 (2022)

10. Yao, J., Hu, Z., Jiang, H., et al.: Visual recognition efficiency of handheld infrared thermometer interface information under low ambient illuminance. Int. J. Ind. Ergon. **83**, 103143 (2021)

11. Choi, J.K., Kim, J.Y.: Differences activation areas using EEG (electroencephalogram) and eye – tracking experiments according to time series data in psychophysiology response for spatial preference. Korean J. Hum. Ecol. **28**(5), 527–540 (2019). https://doi.org/10.5934/kjhe.2019.28.5.527

12. Devos, H., Akinwuntan, A.E., Alissa, N., et al.: Cognitive performance and cognitive workload in multiple sclerosis: two different constructs of cognitive functioning? Mult. Scler. Relat. Disord. **38**, 101505 (2019). https://doi.org/10.1016/j.msard.2019.101505

13. Yang, F., Wang, L., Ding, X.: Why some "user-centred" medical devices do not provide satisfactory user experiences? An investigation on user information factors in new device development processes [C]. In: International Conference on Human-Computer Interaction. Springer, Cham (2022). https://doi.org/10.1007/978-3-031-05897-4_22

14. Zhang, J., Xue, C., Shen, Z., et al.: Study on the effects of semantic memory on icon complexity in cognitive domain [C]. In: International Conference on Engineering Psychology and Cognitive Ergonomics (2016)

15. Scharroo, J., Stalmeier, P.F.M., Boselie, F.: Visual search and segregation as a function of display complexity. J. Gen. Psychol. **121**(1), 5–17 (1994)

16. Makovski, T., Jiang, Y.V.: The role of visual working memory in attentive tracking of unique objects. J. Exp. Psychol. Hum. Percept. Perform. **35**(6), 1687–1697 (2009)

17. Ma, Q., Bai, X., Pei, G., et al.: The hazard perception for the surrounding shape of warning signs: evidence from an event-related potentials study. Front. Neurosci. **12** (2018). https://doi.org/10.3389/fnins.2018.00824

18. Jin, J., Zhang, W., Chen, M.: How consumers are affected by product descriptions in online shopping: event-related potentials evidence of the attribute framing effect. Neurosci. Res. **125**, 21–28 (2017)

19. Polich, J.: Updating P300: an integrative theory of P3a and P3b. Clin. Neurophysiol. **118**(10), 2128–2148 (2007)

20. Hillyard, S.A., Hink, R.F., Schwent, V.L., et al.: Electrical signs of selective attention in the human brain. Science. **182**(4108), 177–182 (1973)

21. Bai, Y., Shao, J., Zhang, Y., et al.: ERP study of mine management system warning interface under fatigue. Int. J. Environ. Res. Public Health. **19**(19), 12616 (2022)

Efficacy of Pedagogical Conversational Agents in Design Education: Perspectives from the Chinese Context

Fan Chen[1(✉)] and Renxuan Liu[2]

[1] Tongji University, Shanghai 200092, China
chenfantj@foxmail.com
[2] University of Sydney, Sydney, NSW 2006, Australia

Abstract. This study focuses on the application and effectiveness of Pedagogic Conversational Agents (PCAs) in design education, particularly within the Chinese context. It reviews the technological evolution of PCAs and explores their roles and value in student engagement, academic tutoring, computational thinking, user experience design, and cultural responsibility. Through a literature review and empirical research, the findings reveal that PCAs significantly enhance the efficiency of accessing tools and methods, promote interdisciplinary collaboration, and bridge cultural and technological gaps. However, challenges remain in achieving depth, reliability, and adaptability, especially in addressing complex academic inquiries and ethical issues. The study emphasizes the importance of designing high-quality prompts, validating PCA outputs, and integrating AI tools with human expertise to unlock their full potential. Future research will extend to more diverse cultural contexts and participants to further uncover the global impact of PCAs on design education.

Keywords: Pedagogic Conversational Agents (PCA) · Design Education · Human-AI Collaboration · Qualitative Research.

1 Introduction

Pedagogical Conversational Agents (PCAs) have undergone significant evolution over the past decades, reflecting advancements in artificial intelligence (AI) and their application in education. Early research on PCAs, rooted in rule-based expert systems during the 1980s and 1990s, focused on simulating instructional interactions through predefined scripts and rules [1]. Systems like Socratic Tutor and early versions of AutoTutor demonstrated the potential of AI to facilitate learning by employing dialogic teaching methods, though they lacked flexibility and adaptability [2].

The early 2000s marked a shift towards incorporating statistical models and emotional interaction, enabled by developments in natural language processing (NLP) and affective computing. This period saw the emergence of PCAs capable of recognizing and responding to learners' emotional states, exemplified by systems such as the Affective Learning Companion [3]. These agents not only improved user engagement but also

P.-L.P. Rau and H. Krömker (Eds.): HCII 2025, LNCS 16336, pp. 51–74, 2026.
https://doi.org/10.1007/978-3-032-12798-3_4

personalized the learning process, tailoring interactions based on learners' cognitive and emotional needs.

With the advent of deep learning in the 2010s, PCAs benefited from significant improvements in understanding and generating natural language. Neural network models, such as LSTMs and Transformers, facilitated more dynamic and coherent dialogic interactions. Large-scale language models like GPT further enhanced PCAs' ability to deliver high-quality instructional content and adaptive feedback, expanding their applications in platforms like Duolingo Bots and educational technologies integrated into MOOCs [4].

In the 2020s, the integration of generative AI models, such as GPT-3 and GPT-4, has ushered PCAs into a new era of intelligence and accessibility. These advanced systems excel in semantic understanding and interactive learning design, allowing for real-time adaptive teaching strategies and personalized educational experiences. For example, AI-powered systems like ChatGPT and Khanmigo have been widely adopted to support learners by answering questions, generating customized study plans, and fostering deeper engagement through conversation [5].

PCAs can serve as partners or mentors for students, assisting with classroom interaction and mastery of learning content [6]. Pérez-Marín [7] explored the application of PCAs in various classroom roles, highlighting their ability to enrich students' learning experiences by providing guidance both inside and outside the classroom. The study proposed several recommendations for PCA design and suggested that this technology should be widely adopted in future education to enhance learning outcomes. Based on this, the present study aims to investigate the usability of PCAs in higher design education through empirical research, identify existing issues, and propose future improvements at the practical application level.

2 Literature Review

2.1 The Role of PCAs in Student Interaction and Engagement

AI conversational agent robots play a significant role in enhancing student interaction and engagement in the classroom. Brummelen et al. [8] proposed trust-building and interaction design strategies for teaching activities, providing guidance for fostering a healthy relationship between students and AI. Similarly, Yang et al. [9] introduced the Ellie robot, showcasing its performance in language interactions within EFL (English as a Foreign Language) courses in South Korea, demonstrating its effectiveness in enhancing language learning outcomes in the classroom. Furthermore, Mageira et al. [10] developed AsasaraBot, which aids students in learning foreign languages and cultural content through interactive methods, exemplifying the diverse applications of AI robots in education.

Personalization and emotional awareness are key future directions for AI conversational agents. Kusal et al. [11] explored how machine learning and deep learning technologies enable conversational agents to develop emotional perception capabilities, simulating human behavior and enhancing human-AI interaction experiences. Winkler et al. [12] further demonstrated that voice interaction support provided by the Sara robot in online programming education can effectively improve learning outcomes. Meanwhile, the development of multi-agent systems offers new perspectives for expanding intelligent tutoring systems. Lemon [13] highlighted that multi-agent dialogue systems can achieve more complex task coordination and language communication, providing collaborative support for learners in various contexts.

Emotion perception and empathetic response are emerging fields in the design of AI conversational agents. Grosuleac et al. [14] developed a conversational agent model capable of recognizing emotions and providing appropriate responses, performing close to state-of-the-art empathy models and offering immersive emotional support in educational applications. At the same time, the potential of generative AI models, such as ChatGPT, in education is becoming increasingly apparent. Matthew et al. [15] explored strategies for optimizing student interactions using prompt engineering, allowing students to receive real-time guidance through natural language generation, thereby improving learning engagement and comprehension. Liao et al. [16] further proposed the concept of proactive conversational agents, which encourage students to actively engage in learning by expanding topics and initiating interactions, overcoming the passivity of traditional conversational agents.

The concept of "learning through teaching" is driving innovative applications of AI conversational agents. Chhibber and Law [17] designed a novel conversational agent, Curiosity Notebook, which encourages students to reinforce their own learning by teaching the AI agent. This approach not only deepens students' understanding but also provides new perspectives for instructional design research.

2.2 Application of PCAs in Academic Tutoring

The application of AI conversational agent robots in academic tutoring is becoming increasingly widespread, covering various fields and educational scenarios. Lippert et al. [18] explored the potential of multi-agent systems in intelligent tutoring, finding that these systems have advantages in science, technology, engineering, and language comprehension through simulation and interaction. By coordinating the behaviors, strategies, and social interactions of multiple agents, these systems help students gain a deeper understanding of knowledge across disciplines. Similarly, Mekni [19] designed a conversational agent system to provide round-the-clock academic information support for higher education institutions, with its effectiveness validated through experimental projects. In the context of mathematics learning, Tan et al. [20] demonstrated that AI agent robots received positive feedback from students in facilitating learning outside the classroom, indicating the potential role of this technology in autonomous learning.

In the field of language learning, AI conversational agents have also shown significant contributions. Belda-Medina and Calvo-Ferrer [21] found that AI agent robots not only enhanced learners' positive attitudes towards their use but also influenced behavioral intentions to some extent. Furthermore, research by Alfehaid and Hammami [22] revealed that the application of AI chatbots in online classrooms significantly improved student engagement, a factor especially critical in remote education. Additionally, Ji et al. [23] proposed that collaboration between human teachers and AI conversational agents can further optimize the effectiveness of language education. Mageira et al. [10]

developed AsasaraBot, which showcased a new model of Content and Language Integrated Learning (CLIL), combining foreign language teaching with cultural content to effectively enhance the comprehensive outcomes of language and cultural education. Wang [24] studied the application of AI conversational agents in Korean language education, finding that their multilingual support capabilities helped non-native learners better master the target language.

Moreover, the application of AI conversational agents has been explored in professional fields such as medical education. Dolianiti et al. [25] developed a virtual patient system that allows students to interact with virtual patients through natural language processing technology. This system not only improved the training of decision-making skills in medical education but also demonstrated the wide applicability of this technology in scenario-based simulations. These applications can also be extended to other professional education fields.

In higher education, the application of AI conversational agents is gradually increasing. Mekni [19] designed a virtual assistant platform that provides students and faculty with information on courses, instructors, and classrooms. This round-the-clock service has become an essential tool in the student support systems of higher education. Yang and Evans [26] analyzed the potential challenges and opportunities of deploying AI chatbots in higher education environments, emphasizing their role in improving academic advising and support.

2.3 Promoting Computational Thinking and Programming Learning

Penney et al. [27] pointed out that generative AI and conversational agent robots can effectively support the development of students' computational thinking and enhance programming skills through personalized guidance and interactive learning experiences. Meanwhile, the study by Wellnhammer et al. [28] demonstrated that the design features of conversational agent robots have a significant impact on the learning process and proposed a series of optimization recommendations to better support learning. In K-12 education, understanding and utilizing AI conversational agents have gradually become a critical skill. Brummelen et al. [29] developed an AI literacy curriculum to help students understand the working principles of conversational agents and their societal impacts, emphasizing the importance of mastering foundational knowledge of AI technologies and ethical issues, thus laying the groundwork for future applications of AI technologies.

2.4 Integration of Learning Analytics and Remote Teaching

With the increasing demand for remote teaching, the integration of learning analytics and AI conversational agents has shown great potential. Atif et al. [30] developed an AI conversational agent system based on learning analytics that can utilize data from Learning Management Systems (LMS) in real-time to provide personalized support for students. This system not only enhances self-exploration by anonymously addressing students' repetitive questions but also offers real-time feedback through human-like interactions, significantly improving convenience and support for online teaching. In Massive Open Online Courses (MOOCs), AI conversational agents also play an important role as learning partners for students. Caballé and Conesa [31] proposed a conversational agent model to support collaborative learning, with their research indicating that this approach significantly improves student engagement. Additionally, Krassmann et al. [32] analyzed interaction logs between MOOC students and conversational agents, discovering that students' emotional states significantly impact their learning engagement. They suggested enhancing emotional support to further improve students' satisfaction and the effectiveness of agent usage.

2.5 Design to Enhance Student Trust

Research has shown that specific design and educational strategies can effectively enhance students' trust in AI. For example, Brummelen et al. [29] pointed out that explaining to students how robots acquire and process information can reduce misunderstandings and distrust toward AI. This trust-oriented design is particularly crucial in children's educational applications to ensure that students neither overly rely on nor incorrectly trust AI systems. Additionally, to ensure that the application of conversational agents in children's education is safe and reliable, Ho et al. [33] proposed an ethical interaction model specifically designed for children. This model enhances the credibility and adaptability of conversational agents in educational settings by accommodating children's emotional and comprehension needs.

2.6 PCAs Supporting Corporate and Adult Learning

Göschlberger and Brandstetter [34] demonstrated that conversational AI holds significant potential in corporate e-learning applications. They proposed a service architecture aimed at lowering the barriers for companies to deploy conversational AI. Additionally, Kulkarni et al. [35] highlighted that deep learning-based conversational agents can drive innovation by automating complex tasks to improve learning efficiency. In vocational education, conversational agents are particularly well-suited for practice-oriented fields such as software engineering. For instance, Ciupe et al. [36] designed a conversational agent for teaching agile development methods. Through simulation-based training, the agent helps students acquire practical skills, and testing results showed that the system effectively enhanced student engagement and skill mastery levels.

2.7 The Role of PCAs in Enhancing Well-Being

Wahde and Virgolin [37], in a comprehensive review of the theory and applications of conversational agents, emphasized the broad potential of conversational agents in education and healthcare, as well as their significant role in enhancing well-being. The study summarized the functional characteristics of different types of conversational agents and their potential societal impacts, providing theoretical support for further applied research. In the field of multilingual education, AI conversational agents help students overcome language barriers, fostering cross-cultural learning and interaction, thereby enhancing learning-related well-being. Nguyen et al. [38] designed a multilingual conversational agent system to support diabetes management, which provided personalized support in various languages with natural pronunciation, significantly improving patients' health experiences and well-being. Similar design principles can be applied to multilingual educational environments, further enhancing well-being through promoting cross-language communication.

2.8 Development Principles of Deep Learning-Based PCAs

Deep learning technology provides essential support for the development of conversational systems. Su et al. [39] summarized the progress of deep learning-based conversational systems in both open-domain and task-oriented dialogue applications, highlighting how this technology significantly improves the response accuracy and adaptability of AI conversational systems, especially in multitask teaching scenarios. Gao et al. [40] further reviewed the evolution of deep learning-based conversational systems in task-oriented dialogue and social robot domains, emphasizing their broad application potential in educational settings. These systems, with enhanced precision and interactivity, not only improve intelligence levels but also play an active role in addressing complex tasks in educational environments.

2.9 Existing Challenges

Despite the significant potential of AI conversational agent robots in the field of education, the author identifies challenges in the integration of technology and education. Kulkarni et al. [35] noted that building complex AI models and natural language interfaces remains a key bottleneck in realizing the educational potential of conversational agent robots. Yang and Evans [26] emphasized both the opportunities and technical challenges of using conversational agents in higher education.

1. **Technical Limitations and Adaptability.** AI conversational agents face technical limitations in handling complex tasks and diverse user needs. For instance, neural network-driven dialogue systems still exhibit issues of precision and coherence in natural language understanding and task management, particularly in open-domain conversations where agent systems struggle to adapt to dynamic conversational scenarios [40]. Kulkarni et al. [35] pointed out that although deep learning has improved the performance of conversational systems, bottlenecks remain in multitask processing and real-time adaptability.
2. **Challenges in Human-AI Collaboration in Language Learning.** In language learning environments, effective collaboration poses a significant challenge for AI conversational agents. Studies indicate that although conversational agents can assist students in language practice, their collaboration with human teachers is still insufficient, potentially affecting the overall effectiveness of classroom teaching. Ji et al. [23] emphasized that AI agents in language education need to better support teachers to achieve the goals of intelligent teaching enhancement and workload reduction.
3. **Ethical and Privacy Issues in Children's Education.** Ensuring the ethicality and privacy of AI conversational agents in children's education is a pressing issue. Brummelen et al. [29] studied the design of AI agents in K-12 education, pointing out

that AI agents in children's education require particular attention to ethical interaction and protective measures to avoid potential privacy risks. Similar studies recommend implementing additional safeguards when deploying conversational agents in children's educational environments [33].

4. **Challenges of User Acceptance and Trust in Higher Education.** In higher education, the application of AI conversational agents faces challenges related to user acceptance and trust. Yang and Evans [26] noted that although AI conversational agents have potential in assisting students with academic support and information retrieval, limited trust among students and faculty in higher education affects their widespread adoption. Similarly, Tan et al. [20] investigated students' acceptance of conversational agents in mathematics learning and found that while students had a positive attitude, their trust in agents, particularly regarding accuracy and adaptability, was relatively low.

5. **Diverse Needs and Adaptability in Application Scenarios.** In diverse educational scenarios, such as online learning platforms (MOOCs), AI conversational agents need greater interactive adaptability to meet the varied needs of students. Caballé and Conesa [31] highlighted that AI agents in large-scale online courses require dynamic feedback and adaptability to help students better engage in the learning process, but current technological capabilities fall short of meeting these needs. Additionally, Grosuleac et al. [14] emphasized the importance of emotional understanding for AI conversational agents, though achieving this remains a technical challenge.

6. **Resource Consumption and Cost-Effectiveness.** High-quality AI conversational agent systems often require substantial computing resources and hardware support, leading to high costs in practical deployment. Su et al. [39] noted that existing conversational systems rely on complex models and large-scale datasets, posing obstacles to their practical application in educational institutions due to high computational resource demands. Balancing resource consumption and educational effectiveness remains an unresolved issue.

Additionally, through practical design education practices, the author observes that PCAs show limited support in specialized domains, such as providing case-based support for design education projects, course recommendations, transferable skill training for design research, and cultivating designer personas. Based on the aforementioned advancements and current challenges in PCA development, this study raises the following research questions: What is the effectiveness of PCAs in supporting design educational activities? What aspects of PCAs need improvement? The author aims to explore the underlying reasons for these challenges, potential solutions, and future development trends through an empirical qualitative study.

3   Methodology

3.1   Literature Review

This study investigates the current development and application of PCAs in the educational field from eight perspectives, including their development principles, interaction technologies with students, application in academic tutoring, cultivation of computational thinking, promotion of remote and continuing education, and enhancement of student trust and well-being. The author identifies a series of existing challenges and aims to explore the reasons behind these challenges, as well as potential solutions, based on the performance of PCAs in supporting design education.

3.2 Empirical Study

1. **Starting Point.** This study takes the author's doctoral dissertation, "A Study on the Five Elements of Doctoral Education in Design since the 21st Century and its Future Qualities," as its starting point. Based on the course element within the five key elements of doctoral education in design, it provides a reference for constructing the knowledge system in the following sections. This approach not only ensures that the research has a clear trajectory but also contributes to verifying the author's previous research findings and empowering future research directions.
2. **Demo Development.** The author has developed a PCA prototype based on an existing commercial operation platform, with plans to first conduct a trial run at their current workplace. Subsequently, experiments will be extended to design graduate students at multiple universities worldwide to observe the prototype's performance and investigate the academic and research status of students in this field (Fig. 1).

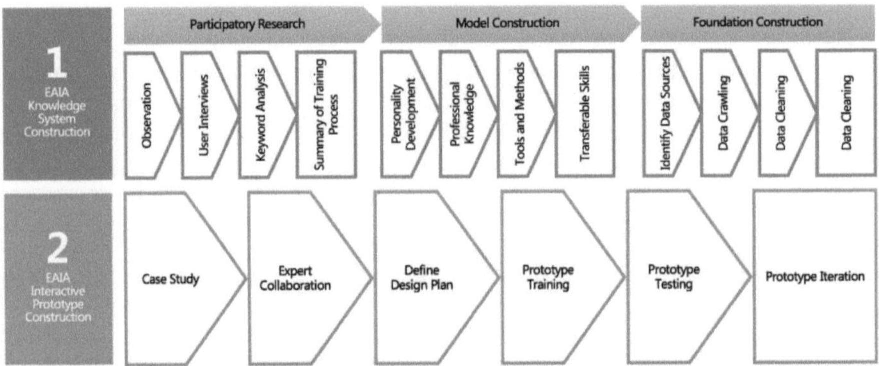

Fig. 1. Technical Roadmap for PCA Prototype Development, made by the author.

The empirical research section is mainly divided into two parts: the construction of the PCAs knowledge system and the development of the interaction prototype. The knowledge system serves as the foundation for building the interaction prototype, while the construction and testing of the interaction prototype provide the basis for iterating the knowledge system.

The construction of the knowledge system involves three main steps: participatory research, knowledge system model construction, and foundational framework development. First, the author identified relevant teaching plans and course content for design doctoral students through observation and stakeholder interviews. By extracting keywords from the interviews, the scope of the knowledge system for this study was determined. Second, based on the "Knowledge, Competence, and Character" framework [41], the author incorporated the "Tools and Methods" element to form four domains of the knowledge system for this study:

Knowledge refers to the literature essential for design students to conduct practice and research.

Competence specifically refers to transferable skills in this study, such as delivering public speeches and communicating effectively with others.

Character refers to general education knowledge beyond the professional knowledge required by design students, aiming to cultivate elements such as ethics, morals, and values.

Tools and Methods provide the means necessary for design students to conduct practice and research, bridging the gap between the design subject (designer) and the design object (artifact).

Finally, through a panoramic review of 84 doctoral programs worldwide, data collection, cleaning, and archiving were performed for the four components of the knowledge system to build a database for subsequent prototype development.

The construction of the interaction prototype consists of five parts. First, the author used a case study approach to identify cost-effective development tools and platforms. Second, the selected tools and platforms were discussed with relevant experts to determine the final design tools. Third, research on the selected tools and platforms was conducted to finalize the prototype design plan, including data format, platform computational power testing, and external connectivity. Fourth, after the prototype was built, prompts were input by diverse stakeholders, including design students, instructors, scholars, and administrators, to train and test the system to identify knowledge gaps and interaction barriers. Fifth, based on the issues identified in the previous step, the prototype was iteratively refined, accompanied by continuous testing and subsequent usage. The author ultimately chose ChatGPTs (4o version) for the customized configuration of PCAs due to the platform's wide audience reach, technological maturity, and high accessibility.

3. **Stakeholder Interviews.** The author sent out 100 research invitations to graduate students in their college via one-on-one invitations and received 1291 question-and-answer records from 89 respondents within a one-month period. By qualitatively summarizing the content of the questions, the author identified 66 typical and relatively complete Q&A records. Through semantic analysis and coding, it was found that questions related to the "Tools and Methods" domain were the most frequently asked, while questions in the "Character" domain were the least.

Additionally, for the user interview section, six graduate students and graduate advisors were selected and invited to provide insights into the user question list (Table 1). This aimed to explore the motivations behind user inquiries and identify emerging trends. The information about the interviewees is presented in the following table.

By collecting conversation records between the participants and the PCA, the author categorized and organized the dialogue content. Based on this, stakeholders were interviewed to identify current issues with PCA usage in design educational activities, explore future improvement directions, and uncover existing problems in design graduate education.

Table 1. Table captions should be placed above the tables.

Role	Gender	Font size and style	Years of Experience
Graduate A	Female	Parametric Design	9
Graduate B	Male	Service Design	7
Graduate C	Male	Material Development and Sustainable Design	2
Graduate D	Female	Human Factors Engineering and Interaction Design	5
Graduate E	Female	Chinese Traditional Culture and Sustainable Development	4
Graduate F	Male	Industrial Design and Interaction Design	1.5
Faculty 1	Male	Product Design	6
Faculty 2	Female	Interaction Design	8
Faculty 3	Female	Collaborative Design and Participatory Design Methodology Research	5
Faculty 4	Male	Landscape Design	18
Faculty 5	Male	Urban Design	10
Faculty 6	Female	Design Philosophy	12

4　Discussion

The author processed the original Q&A records as follows. First, the author read through all the Q&A texts to clean them, including removing meaningless modal particles, adjusting question syntax, and organizing the logical sequence of questions. Next, the cleaned texts were deduplicated by identifying and deleting redundant questions with similar meanings, using semantic analysis tools to assist in this process. Then, the cleaned and deduplicated Q&A texts underwent manual verification to ensure no question category was overlooked. The 1,291 unique and meaningful Q&A records were subsequently coded into four categories: Knowledge, Competence, Character, and Tools and Methods. Finally, through qualitative analysis, the author selected 66 representative questions.

In essence, during the selection process, the author retained Q&A records categorized as "information inquiry," typically led by specific question words like "What is/Why/How?", such as "What is design?". On the other hand, "task processing" questions, such as "Please translate/summarize the following text for me…", were excluded as they fall outside the scope of this study.

Below, the author showcases the 66 typical and representative questions from the 1,291 Q&A records and lists the related perspectives of stakeholders under four categories of questions.

4.1 Knowledge

4.1.1 Design Trends and Future Directions

- What are the contemporary design trends, and how can they be integrated into my project?
- What is the impact of the metaverse on the future of the design field?
- What are the most popular interior design styles of 2024?

Graduate C believes that interacting with the PCA "allows me to quickly access trend summaries, such as the latest material technologies, sustainable design, or smart product development directions. Its conversational format is very flexible, adjusting the scope of responses based on my questions, which helps me explore different possibilities more efficiently." However, the biggest challenge when using the PCA to discuss "design trends and future directions" is "the lack of reliability and depth in the information. While its responses are quick, they are sometimes not specific enough, especially in areas requiring data support. For example, it might say 'the metaverse will influence design in the future,' but it doesn't explain why or how to achieve this. In the future, it should be more aligned with design practice, even simulating design thinking to provide more specific recommendations, such as proposing practical design solutions based on contextual input rather than offering only conceptual trend analysis."

Faculty 2 believes that "this is an inevitable development of the times. It can provide students with interdisciplinary information they have not been exposed to and even help them define their research questions more clearly. However, the information it provides requires critical analysis and cannot fully replace traditional research methods. I often use it to validate some of my teaching ideas or explore new research perspectives, but ultimately it must return to core literature and theoretical analysis."

Faculty 3 points out that for doctoral students, the exploration phase requires a significant amount of information, and in this regard, the PCA is very useful. However, for faculty members, what is needed more is innovative thinking based on existing research foundations. The PCA's interpretation of professional trends "is sometimes overly broad" and may not suit specific research contexts. Moreover, "its knowledge cutoff time could lead to missing the latest research developments. This reminds us to combine multiple resources rather than rely entirely on AI. I look forward to progress in interdisciplinary integration, where it could provide more forward-looking and comprehensive analyses for the design field. However, regardless of how tools evolve, design will always be a human-centered discipline. AI's role is to assist, not replace, the creativity and critical thinking of designers."

4.1.2 Design Concepts and Principles

- What are the key principles of sustainable design?
- What is human-centered design, and how can it be practiced?
- How is design applied to social issues, such as accessible design?

Graduate E mentions that research often involves questions about design theories, such as how to combine specific design concepts with practical applications. "The PCA provides me with a platform to quickly explore ideas. For instance, when studying sustainable design, I wanted to understand how design principles are expressed across different cultural contexts. I asked the PCA, 'How is the concept of sustainable design reflected in Chinese traditional culture?' It not only provided some existing theoretical frameworks but also suggested directions I hadn't thought of, such as combining ecological design with social responsibility. This made my subsequent literature review more targeted." The student believes that while it cannot replace the in-depth guidance of advisors, "it helps think through problems more efficiently and occasionally throws out some 'out-of-the-box' ideas. Students believe that design concepts and principles are the core of design research, as they determine the direction of a project. ChatGPT's strength lies in its ability to integrate knowledge across disciplines, providing cross-disciplinary perspectives for design problems."

Faculty 6 notes that, unlike textbooks, it can respond to questions dynamically. However, "as an advisor, I remind students that the information provided by ChatGPT is only a starting point, not the final answer. Sometimes, I use it to validate whether my teaching examples have broader applicability. For instance, I might ask, 'Which cross-cultural factors are often overlooked in design principles?' Its response makes me aware of certain dimensions I had not considered. This is very helpful for guiding students in topic selection or revising papers."

Faculty 1 hopes that AI can better understand "design language," "not just textual analysis, but also multidimensional understanding, including visual and perceptual aspects. If this can be achieved, it will have a profound impact on design education and research."

4.1.3 Design Methods and Processes

- What are the differences between parametric design and traditional design methods?
- What are the core steps of design thinking?
- What is the difference between agile design and waterfall design workflows?

Graduate B believes, "For example, when I was researching 'user participation in the design process,' the way I phrased the question was crucial. Asking a broad question like 'What is a design method?' is not meaningful. Instead, questions tied to specific scenarios, such as 'How can mood boards be applied in social welfare projects?' lead to more targeted and useful responses."

Faculty 4 states, "Design research itself is interdisciplinary. When students encounter problems, the traditional approach may involve reading a large number of papers or consulting teachers, but this requires time and accumulation. Tools like ChatGPT can provide diverse references in a short amount of time, which is very valuable. Of course, the limitations of the tool must also be understood, such as its sources and the depth of information. For instance, if a student asks how to embed sustainability in complex system design, I may not immediately have specific cases to share. At that point, I use ChatGPT to quickly generate some preliminary suggestions, then filter and supplement them with my own expertise. The role of the tool is to accelerate information retrieval and broaden thinking, but creativity is fundamentally a human capability."

For doctoral students, the key is to enter the stage of deep thinking more efficiently with the help of tools. Faculty 6 "suggests using the tool with a clear goal and structuring questions in layers. First, ask for basic theoretical concepts, then inquire about practical cases, and finally request integrated suggestions for the problem. This method helps students systematically organize their research framework."

4.1.4 Tools and Skills

- What are the recommended graphic design software tools, and what are their pros and cons?
- What are some practical examples of AI tools in product design?
- What are the best resources for self-learning UI/UX design?
- What core skills should design students master?

Graduate F believes, "When conducting research, we often encounter various topics that require quick understanding, such as a new modeling software or analysis method. Traditional approaches like searching literature or watching tutorials are relatively inefficient, so I prefer tools like the PCA, which can quickly provide an overview."

Graduate C thinks, "Especially when learning a new tool, it can provide the core logic in very concise language, helping me get started quickly. However, it cannot pose thought-provoking questions like a mentor would; it serves more as a 'knowledge provider.'"

Graduate D comments, "The PCA is more like an information carrier, while the advisor serves as a guide. For example, after I quickly grasp the basic use of a tool through the PCA, I can discuss with my advisor how to apply this tool in my research, which may even lead to new research questions."

Faculty 5 says, "I remind students that the tool itself is not the goal but a means. If the content provided by the PCA is not critically analyzed, it may lead to deviations in research direction. Therefore, I encourage students to use it with a questioning mindset, diving deeper into the analysis instead of relying on it entirely."

Faculty 2 states, "Doctoral education is not just about imparting knowledge but about cultivating research thinking. The PCA can help students save time on information gathering, allowing them to focus more on thinking and practical work."

4.1.5 Cases and Inspiration

- What are some classic brand design cases worth referencing?
- Where can I find excellent design inspiration online?

Graduate F notes, "In the research process, it's often necessary to analyze classic cases and understand the factors behind their success. Using the PCA to ask questions helps me quickly compile high-quality case references and discover resources I hadn't considered before. Reliability was a concern for me at first. So, after receiving ChatGPT's suggestions, I always verify whether the cases or resources it provides are authoritative—for example, by checking the credibility of the websites or confirming the accuracy of information through cross-referencing. For me, it functions more like a 'first-step filtering tool.'"

Graduate E states, "It's important to be as specific as possible when asking questions. Instead of just asking, 'What are some classic brand design cases worth referencing?' it's better to add qualifying conditions like 'brand design cases focusing on social responsibility' or 'brand design cases targeting Gen Z consumers.' This makes the answers more targeted. Personally, it has also changed my learning habits. I used to passively acquire information, but now I focus more on actively designing questions. I think future design education might place more emphasis on the ability to ask questions because, with tools like the PCA, finding answers is no longer the hardest part—the challenge lies in asking truly valuable questions."

Faculty 1 comments, "Time and energy are extremely valuable. Using large language models like the PCA can indeed save time, especially for 'search tasks' such as gathering cases and inspiration. I recommend that advisors guide students to reflect on the logic behind their questions to ChatGPT. For example, 'Why do we need these cases?' or 'How can we extract actionable design elements from these cases?' These reflective questions help students transform the AI tool's outputs into their own academic insights."

4.2 Competence

- How can individual freedom and team consistency be balanced in multi-user collaborative tools?
- How can interdisciplinary design teams collaborate effectively?
- What are the key considerations in design reviews?

Graduate C states, "As a doctoral student in a design school, my research and work often involve interdisciplinary team collaborations, such as working with colleagues from engineering, business, or even social sciences to design solutions. In these collaborations, everyone has their own professional background and preferences, which can lead to many challenges. For example, some people want to express more individual ideas, while others emphasize team alignment. I am particularly interested in knowing if there are better tools or methods that allow teams to respect individual freedom while maintaining a common direction."

Graduate B shares, "This is actually a significant pain point in my team collaborations. Coming from different disciplines, we often have misunderstandings due to differences in terminology or perspectives. Sometimes it even feels like we are not discussing the same issue. So, I wonder if AI can serve as a 'common language' or 'translation tool' to help us quickly align our understanding while also sparking more creativity. This is why I use the PCA to simulate some dialogue scenarios, to see if it can help find suitable collaboration methods."

Graduate F notes, "I've found that design reviews heavily test communication and presentation skills. Different reviewers have completely different focuses—some look at technical implementation, others at social impact, and some at design aesthetics." As a designer, "I often struggle with how to engage their interest while accurately conveying the value of our design. I hope the PCA can generate simulated questions or suggestions to help the team prepare more effective review presentations."

Faculty 3 comments, "A core characteristic of design disciplines is balancing creativity and collaboration. This balance becomes even more complex in interdisciplinary environments, where each field has its own thinking style and working mode. This actually involves knowledge from organizational behavior, social psychology, and design management. AI can play an important role as a 'facilitator' in interdisciplinary teams. It can quickly sort and integrate information from different fields and even present it to team members in an easily understandable way. Therefore, these questions are not just about 'how to do it,' but also about 'why do it this way' and 'what is the underlying logic.'"

Faculty 6 believes, "The core issues students need to address in design reviews are 'empathy' and 'logic.' Empathy refers to a designer's ability to understand the perspectives and needs of different reviewers, while logic refers to presenting their design in a clear and persuasive manner. In this process, tools like the PCA can help students simulate multiple perspectives, anticipate different questions and feedback, and optimize their presentation in advance. This is an excellent training process."

4.3 Character

- Can generative AI completely replace traditional designers? What are its limitations and breakthroughs?
- How can a privacy-first social media experience be designed?
- How can ethical challenges of multi-user data (e.g., physiological data, behavioral data) in health device design be addressed?
- How can autonomous vehicle UI design provide ethical decision-making information in emergencies?
- In designing medical products for the elderly, how can efficiency be improved while maintaining humanity?
- Will AI-assisted design education weaken students' hand-drawing skills? How can the two be balanced?
- How can a designer grow into a design manager?

Graduate D remarks, "This question ties closely to my identity as a designer. The development of generative AI excites me but also causes some concern. On the one hand, I see its potential to improve efficiency and expand creative boundaries; on the other hand, I cannot ignore the question of whether it will marginalize the role of designers. Through the PCA, I hope to find more insightful answers to understand the relationship between this technology and the future of the design profession."

Graduate A comments, "Privacy has become an unavoidable topic in digital product design. With heightened awareness of privacy, I found in my research that many users are unaware of privacy policies but are deeply concerned about data usage. I want to explore through the PCA whether we can make a 'privacy-first' experience more intuitive and user-friendly, less abstract. My main questions are rooted in concerns about data ethics. In health device design, we handle a lot of sensitive data, such as heart rate, movement data, and even emotional states. These data enhance device intelligence but also bring risks of misuse or over-surveillance. I want to see if the PCA can suggest more forward-looking solutions."

Graduate B states, "The needs of elderly users are highly complex. They want products to be easy to use but resist overly complicated interfaces. I think such questions reflect the value systems of us as designers. We need to find a balance between technological innovation and human care. ChatGPT here acts more as a supporting tool, helping me organize design directions."

From a mentor's perspective, Faculty 4 notes, "I think students asking such questions reflects their sensitivity to technological ethics. Generative AI is a tool, but the value of designers lies not only in execution but also in a profound understanding of culture and society. By asking such questions, students are attempting to project their thoughts into a technological framework, which I find very encouraging."

When addressing the question of how to design a privacy-first social media experience, Faculty 2 comments, "This question highlights the unique approach of the design discipline in responding to technological and ethical challenges—we are not just seeking theoretical answers but aim to translate them into specific design solutions. Such questions help us in teaching students to realize that a designer's job is to bridge users and technology, rather than making technology more 'mysterious.' PCA's strength lies in quickly generating potential ideas, but we need to make students aware that solutions to ethical issues are often not technology-driven but require more interdisciplinary dialogue."

Faculty 2 further remarks, "This actually points out the responsibility of designers. The core of elderly product design is not about catering to market trends but about standing in the users' shoes and using technology to address their real pain points."

4.4 Tools and Methods

4.4.1 Integration of Technology and Design

- How can AI-generated virtual reality scenarios be incorporated into urban planning for participatory design?
- How can blockchain technology be introduced into product design to ensure user data privacy and transparency?
- In smart home device design, how can the conflict between user privacy and efficient interaction be resolved?
- How might quantum computing change the application of parametric design in architectural design?
- How can transparency and user trust be ensured when designing AI chatbots?
- How can virtual reality be integrated into design education to simulate interdisciplinary collaboration in real projects?
- How can design and data visualization be combined?
- How can realism and artistic expression be balanced in virtual scene design?
- How can deep learning optimize the visual design of product recommendation systems?

Graduate D notes, "For us doctoral students, research directions are often very focused, especially in fields combining technology and design. The amount of information is vast, and knowledge updates rapidly. The PCA's advantage lies in quickly providing a starting point, helping us determine whether certain technologies can be applied to specific design scenarios. For example, when I was researching the application of augmented reality in interaction design, the PCA helped me quickly find relevant technical keywords or reference cases. Design disciplines increasingly emphasize innovation, and technology offers more possibilities. Whether it's choosing tools or improving methods, understanding the technology itself is essential as it directly impacts the feasibility of the design solutions."

The design discipline is inherently practice-oriented, whereas technology often leans more theoretical. Faculty 1 observes, "Students' questions using the PCA reflect an important need: finding a 'bridge' at the intersection of technology and design. By using the PCA, they can quickly grasp the technical background, saving us as advisors a lot of time, especially when discussions reach the details stage, as students already have a basic understanding of the technology."

Faculty 5 states, "The core of this issue lies in 'integration.' In the past, technology and design had relatively clear boundaries. Now, with the diversification of design demands, technology has deeply penetrated design processes, such as algorithm-generated design and data-driven user research. We need to continually seek new tools and methods to achieve this integration, and the PCA is particularly helpful in clarifying ideas during the early stages."

4.4.2 User Experience and Interaction Design

- How can a global e-commerce platform be designed to meet the needs of users from different cultural backgrounds?
- How can the UI design of traffic systems in smart cities ensure a consistent experience across multi-device platforms?
- How can a data-driven approach be used to optimize the user experience of medical products?
- How can interface design help users reduce 'digital decision fatigue'?
- In social media UI design, how can the phenomenon of 'doomscrolling' be minimized?
- How can an interface based on behavioral economics theory influence user decisions?
- How can the design of online education platforms for children meet the unique needs of their cognitive development stages?
- How can A/B testing be used to improve interaction design on a real-time updated SaaS platform?
- How can mobile interfaces be optimized for better reading experiences on small screens?

Graduate F explains, "As a doctoral student, my research not only requires deep exploration of specific fields but also the constant search for new research methods or tools to support experimental design. For example, in user experience research, we need to combine quantitative analysis with qualitative insights. To me, the PCA is a helpful tool for quickly obtaining information and organizing ideas. It helps me discover tools and methods I hadn't noticed before and provides structured suggestions for my papers. When selecting user experience evaluation tools, I often face the challenge of too many options. After asking the PCA, it lists common methods, such as usability testing or sentiment analysis, and provides the scenarios in which each is applicable. This allows me to filter and conduct secondary research accordingly. Additionally, when designing interaction prototypes, it helps me find open-source tools or industry standards. During its use, I've also learned a lot from my advisor's feedback. For instance, while the

PCA's answers may seem comprehensive, my advisor reminds me to be aware of hidden assumptions or overlooked literature, helping me better understand the boundaries of human-AI collaboration."

Faculty 3 comments, "The practicality and inspiration of tools are not mutually exclusive. For instance, students conducting empirical research might use the PCA to find specific questionnaire templates, while advisors could use it to refine the theoretical framework behind the questionnaire. These two processes complement each other."

4.4.3 Culture and Social Responsibility

- How can contemporary "Guochao" (Chinese cultural trend) design avoid cultural appropriation and achieve true cultural value inheritance?
- How can public spaces in multi-ethnic regions be designed to balance the needs of different cultural groups?
- How can design reduce the accessibility barriers to smart devices for low-income populations?
- In rural revitalization, how can local materials be used to design modern buildings aligned with ecological principles?
- In architectural design addressing climate change, how can costs, efficiency, and aesthetic demands be balanced?
- How can Chinese traditional cultural elements be incorporated into modern design?
- How can landscape design integrate local cultural elements?

Graduate B observes, "For example, in socially responsible design, designers often need to balance the needs of multiple stakeholders, including communities, governments, and markets. This multidimensional complexity makes it challenging for designers to find solutions that satisfy all parties while staying aligned with social responsibility goals. The PCA can quickly provide potential ideas or point to other successful cases, which is very helpful during the initial concept development phase. For practical applications, especially in the fields of culture and social responsibility, the PCA can act as a bridge between different cultures, helping designers better understand the needs within diverse cultural contexts."

Faculty 3 remarks, "Design education and practice must keep pace with the times, particularly in the context of social responsibility. AI tools offer us new ways of understanding, but whether they can genuinely assist designers in taking on cultural and social responsibilities requires further exploration. I encourage my students to use the PCA to explore this issue, as it can provide multi-perspective insights and even break the limitations of traditional thinking. Culture and social responsibility span multiple disciplines, from anthropology to economics, and it's nearly impossible for designers to master such cross-disciplinary knowledge in a short period. The PCA's advantage lies in its ability to integrate knowledge from different fields and present it in actionable formats, helping designers quickly find entry points. On one hand, AI tools expand designers' knowledge base; on the other, designers drive these tools to be more attuned to real human needs. In the future, I hope to see more cases of AI integrated with design practice, particularly in critical areas such as social responsibility and cultural preservation."

4.4.4   Tools and Practice

- How can Figma be used for collaborative UI design?
- How can Rhino and Grasshopper be used for complex architectural modeling?
- How can a design solution be developed starting from user research?
- How can feedback and iterations be effectively managed in a design project?
- How can packaging design highlight product features?
- How can a unique logo be designed for a new brand?
- How can an outstanding design portfolio be prepared?
- How can design deliverables be efficiently converted into development-ready resources?

Graduate E hopes the PCA can better understand the language of designers. "For instance, when it comes to the use of design tools, if it could provide detailed guidance combined with specific cases or step-by-step instructions, it would be much more practical. Additionally, if interactions with it could help us generate initial design prototypes or solutions, that would be especially meaningful."

Faculty 6 believes, "For students, efficiency is indeed a key point. For me, however, it's more about organizing thoughts. Design practice methods often involve complex logical chains, such as moving from problem definition to method selection and then to actual implementation. Asking the PCA is not just about getting a direct answer, but also about validating whether one's thought process is clear or if any perspectives have been overlooked. This instant conversation model is somewhat like brainstorming with a virtual assistant."

Faculty 2 observes, "While the PCA doesn't propose original research points when answering questions, its associative ability is strong. For example, when students ask about how to use a tool, the PCA might mention relevant practices by research teams abroad or highlight some emerging design concepts. This kind of information can guide students to view problems from a broader perspective."

Faculty 1 points out, "The effectiveness of the PCA largely depends on the quality of the question. If the question is too vague, it might provide irrelevant answers. On the other hand, if the question is overly specific, its response might lose its inspirational value. Therefore, I usually advise students to think clearly about their purpose before asking, as this not only improves efficiency but also leads to more useful feedback."

4.4.5   Cutting-Edge Research and Education

- How can AI optimize the teaching of tacit knowledge (such as creativity and inspiration) in design education?
- How can brain-computer interface (BCI) technology enable fully touchless user interaction experiences?
- In mixed reality (MR) environments, how can the visualization structure of 3D information be designed?
- How can ecological models be applied to landscape design to create more efficient ecosystems?
- Based on neuroscience research, how can work environments be designed to better stimulate creativity?

- How can a big data-based user experience evaluation system be constructed in design research?
- In digital education for remote areas, how can low-bandwidth learning platforms be designed to better meet local needs?
- How can the design field adapt to the rapid development of AI and big data?

Graduate B notes, "Although the PCA's answers seem comprehensive, they are not 'personalized' enough. For example, when I ask a more specific design question, its response tends to be generic. This made me realize that the way we frame questions needs to be more precise as well."

Faculty 3 observes, "As advisors, we are not only researchers but also educators. Innovations in educational tools and methods directly impact how we train students. If these tools can help students quickly acquire research skills and even develop critical thinking, we as advisors will also adjust our guidance strategies accordingly. Such questions reflect a broader consideration of how to better link research with education."

5 Findings

5.1 Impact of Answer Quality on Users' Questioning Tendencies

Statistical analysis reveals that most questions are framed with "how", focusing on tools and methods, while fewer questions are framed with "what" or "why", which seek definitions or principles. This is closely related to the perceived accuracy of PCA's answers and users' confidence in them. One reason is that PCA organizes answers based on its existing text database, and the time lag in database updates prevents it from addressing all types of queries effectively.

On one hand, this reflects that the current database provides comprehensive support for tool- and method-related content but has limited coverage in definitions and principles. On the other hand, user interviews reveal that users tend to seek answers to "what" questions from other platforms, such as Baidu, Wikipedia, academic paper websites, or books. These are key areas that stakeholders should focus on improving.

5.2 Better Performance in Answering General Knowledge Questions

Many users report that PCA's answers lack depth, which poses higher requirements for the vertical knowledge reserves of the database. For instance, when users seek introductions to relevant research cases, PCA often fails to respond effectively. These two scenarios clarify the boundaries of human-AI collaboration. Specific recommendations for human-AI collaboration are as follows: (1) PCA is currently adept at providing task-based execution framework suggestions. Users should verify the accuracy of key information in its answers. (2) When PCA offers interpretations of professional fields or trends, users should leverage other channels to obtain more comprehensive extensions, including related concepts and practical cases.

5.3 PCA as a Communication Bridge

PCA can act as a bridge in two key ways to reduce communication costs when coordinating collaboration among members of different professional fields. First, as a language translator for international team collaboration, PCA can help overcome language barriers and improve cooperation efficiency. Its voice input functionality further enhances user inclusivity, enabling those who find keyboard input inconvenient to better participate in team collaboration. Second, as a translator of specialized terminology within same-language, cross-disciplinary teams, PCA breaks down professional barriers, ensuring that complex technical terms no longer impede collaboration. Additionally, PCA can serve as a simulated interview robot, rehearsing dialogues for various scenarios to familiarize users with potential interview questions in advance, thereby increasing their chances of success.

5.4 How to Obtain Better Answers?

Essentially, the quality of the prompt determines whether more desirable answers can be obtained. High-quality prompts help reduce ambiguity and improve model performance. Methods to improve prompt quality include adding contextual explanations, providing constraints and examples, and breaking down complex questions into guided steps. For instance, adding contextual explanations can utilize frameworks such as CARE (Context, Action, Result, Example) to refine questions and achieve more ideal responses.

6 Conclusion and Limitation

This study highlights the evolving role of Pedagogic Conversational Agents (PCAs) in design education, particularly in the Chinese context, by examining their application across multiple dimensions such as student engagement, academic tutoring, computational thinking, user experience design, and cultural responsibility. The findings reveal that PCAs significantly enhance efficiency in accessing tools, methods, and design knowledge while fostering interdisciplinary collaboration and bridging cultural and technical gaps. However, challenges persist in achieving depth, reliability, and adaptability in responses, particularly in addressing nuanced academic inquiries and ethical considerations. The empirical analysis underscores the importance of tailored prompt design, critical validation of PCA outputs, and the integration of AI tools with human expertise to maximize their potential. As PCAs continue to evolve with advancements in AI and NLP, their ability to support design education will hinge on refining their knowledge systems, improving real-time adaptability, and fostering human-AI synergy to empower creative and critical thinking in future designers.

On the other hand, this study currently focuses on testing and interviewing graduate students from a single design school in mainland China. Future research will broaden the diversity of participants by including universities from other regions in China as well as international institutions, aiming to uncover the diverse impacts of PCAs on design education across different cultural contexts.

Acknowledgments. The authors thank for the contributions from all participates and interviewees.

Authors' Contributions Conceptualization, F.C.; methodology, F.C.; formal analysis, F.C.; data curation, F.C. & R.L.; writing—original draft preparation, F.C.; writing—review and editing, R.L.; funding acquisition, F.C. All authors have read and agreed to the published version of the manuscript.

Availability of Data and Material Data and related materials can be received from corresponding author regarding reasonable requirement.

Disclosure of Interests The authors declare no competing interests.

Ethics Approval and Consent to Participate This study obtained informed consent from the participants and ensured the protection of their data privacy.

Funding. This research was funded by CHINA POSTDOCTORAL SCIENCE FOUNDATION, grant number GZC20231938.

References

1. Graesser, A.C., Person, N.K., Magliano, J.P.: Collaborative dialogue patterns in naturalistic one-to-one tutoring. Appl. Cogn. Psychol. **9**(6), 495–522 (1995)
2. Graesser, A.C.: Conversations with AutoTutor help students learn. Int. J. Artif. Intell. Educ. **26**, 124–132 (2016)
3. D'Mello, S.K., Craig, S.D., Gholson, B., Franklin, S., Picard, R.W., Graesser, A.C.: Integrating affect sensors in an intelligent tutoring system. In: Proceedings of the 5th International Conference on Intelligent Systems Design and Applications (ISDA), pp. 640–645. IEEE, Piscataway (2005)
4. Radford, A., Wu, J., Child, R., Luan, D., Amodei, D., Sutskever, I.: Language models are unsupervised multitask learners. OpenAI blog. (2019)
5. OpenAI Homepage. https://openai.com/index/teaching-with-ai/. Last accessed 15 June 2025
6. Ye, X., Zhai, W., Du, J., et al.: Authentic or artificial intelligence? Faculty's perspectives on the ChatGPT's impact on U.S. urban planning Ph.D. programs. Front. Urban Rural Plann. **2**(23) (2024)
7. Pérez-Marín, D.: A review of the practical applications of pedagogic conversational agents to be used in school and university classrooms. Digital. **1**(1), 18–33 (2021)
8. Van Brummelen, J., Kelleher, M., Tian, M., Nguyen, N.: What do children and parents want and perceive in conversational agents? Towards transparent, trustworthy, democratized agents. In: Proceedings of the 22nd Annual ACM Interaction Design and Children Conference (IDC), pp. 187–197. ACM, New York (2023)
9. Yang, H., Kim, H., Lee, J.H., Shin, D.: Implementation of an AI chatbot as an English conversation partner in EFL speaking classes. ReCALL. **34**(3), 327–343 (2022)
10. Mageira, K., Pittou, D., Papasalouros, A., Kotis, K., Zangogianni, P., Daradoumis, A.: Educational AI chatbots for content and language integrated learning. Appl. Sci. **12**(7), 3239 (2022)
11. Kusal, S., Patil, S., Choudrie, J., Kotecha, K., Mishra, S., Abraham, A.: AI-based conversational agents: a scoping review from technologies to future directions. IEEE Access. **10**, 92337–92356 (2022)

12. Winkler, R., Hobert, S., Salovaara, A., Söllner, M., Leimeister, J.M.: Sara, the lecturer: improving learning in online education with a scaffolding-based conversational agent. In: Proceedings of the 2020 CHI Conference on Human Factors in Computing Systems (CHI), pp. 1–14. ACM, New York (2020)

13. Lemon, O.: Conversational AI, natural language processing, human-robot interaction, and multi-agent communication. AI Commun. **35**(4), 295–308 (2022)

14. Grosuleac, A., Budulan, Ş., Rebedea, T.: Seeking an empathy-abled conversational agent. In: Proceedings of RoCHI 2020, pp. 103–107. ACM, New York (2020)

15. Matthew, U.O., Bakare, K.M., Ebong, G.N., Ndukwu, C.C., Nwanakwaugwu, A.C.: Generative artificial intelligence (AI) educational pedagogy development: conversational AI with user-centric ChatGPT-4. J. Trends Comput. Sci. Smart Technol. **5**(4), 401–418 (2023)

16. Liao, L., Yang, G.H., Shah, C.: Proactive conversational agents. In: Proceedings of the 16th ACM International Conference on Web Search and Data Mining (WSDM), pp. 1244–1247. ACM, New York (2023)

17. Chhibber, N., Law, E.: Using conversational agents to support learning by teaching. arXiv preprint arXiv:1909.13443 (2019)

18. Lippert, A., Shubeck, K., Morgan, B., Hampton, A.J., Graesser, A.: Multiple agent designs in conversational intelligent tutoring systems. Technol. Knowl. Learn. **25**(3), 443–463 (2019)

19. Mekni, M.: An artificial intelligence-based virtual assistant using conversational agents. J. Softw. Eng. Appl. **14**(9), 455–473 (2021)

20. Tan, C.P., Yeap, C.K., Chong, O.L., Chan, Y.S.: University students' perception on the usefulness of the incorporation of conversational agents in mathematics learning. In: Proceedings of the 4th Artificial Intelligence and Cloud Computing Conference (AICCC), pp. 229–233. ACM, New York (2021)

21. Belda-Medina, J., Calvo-Ferrer, J.R.: Using chatbots as AI conversational partners in language learning. Appl. Sci. **12**(17), 8427 (2022)

22. Alfehaid, A., Hammami, M.A.: Artificial intelligence in education: literature review on the role of conversational agents in improving learning experience. Int. J. Membr. Sci. Technol. **10**(3), 3121–3129 (2023)

23. Ji, H., Han, I., Ko, Y.: A systematic review of conversational AI in language education: focusing on the collaboration with human teachers. J. Res. Technol. Educ. **55**(1), 48–63 (2022)

24. Wang, G.: Natural language analysis of Korean texts of AI-based chatbots and exploration of Korean education utilization: focusing on ChatGPT and New-Bing. Korean Soc. Cult. Converg. **45**(5), 1–17 (2023)

25. Dolianiti, F., Tsoupouroglou, I., Antoniou, P., Konstantinidis, S., Anastasiades, S., Bamidis, P.: Chatbots in healthcare curricula: the case of a conversational virtual patient. In: Frasson, C., Bamidis, P., Vlamos, P. (eds.) Brain Function Assessment in Learning Conference, BFAL 2020, LNCS, vol. 12462, pp. 137–147. Springer, Cham (2020)

26. Yang, S., Evans, C.: Opportunities and challenges in using AI chatbots in higher education. In: Proceedings of the 3rd International Conference on Education and E-Learning (ICEEL), pp. 79–83. ACM, New York (2019)

27. Penney, J., Pimentel, J.F., Steinmacher, I., Gerosa, M.A.: Anticipating user needs: insights from design fiction on conversational agents for computational thinking. In: Følstad, A., et al. (eds.) Chatbot Research and Design. CONVERSATIONS 2023. LNCS, vol. 14524, pp. 204–219. Springer, Cham (2024)

28. Wellnhammer, N., Dolata, M., Steigler, S., Schwabe, G.: Studying with the help of digital tutors: design aspects of conversational agents that influence the learning process. In: Proceedings of the 53rd Hawaii International Conference on System Sciences (HICSS), pp. 1–10. IEEE, Piscataway, NJ, USA (2020)

29. Van Brummelen, J., Heng, T., Tabunshchyk, V.: Teaching tech to talk: K-12 conversational artificial intelligence literacy curriculum and development tools. In: Proceedings of the AAAI Conference on Artificial Intelligence, pp. 15655–15663. AAAI Press, Virtual Event (2021)

30. Atif, A., Jha, M., Richards, D., Bilgin, A.A.: Artificial intelligence (AI)-enabled remote learning and teaching using pedagogical conversational agents and learning analytics. In: Caballé, S., Demetriadis, S.N., Gómez-Sánchez, E., Papadopoulos, P.M., Weinberger, A. (eds.) Intelligent Systems and Learning Data Analytics in Online Education, pp. 3–29. Academic, Cambridge (2021)

31. Caballé, S., Conesa, J.: Conversational agents in support for collaborative learning in MOOCs: an analytical review. In: Xhafa, F., Barolli, L., Greguš, M. (eds.) Advances in Intelligent Networking and Collaborative Systems, LNDECT, vol. 23, pp. 384–394. Springer, Cham (2018)

32. Krassmann, A.L., Paz, F.J., Silveira, C., Tarouco, L.M.R., Bercht, M.: Conversational agents in distance education: comparing mood states with students' perception. Creat. Educ. **9**, 1726–1742 (2018)

33. Ho, H.-R., Hubbard, E.M., Mutlu, B.: "It's not a replacement": enabling parent-robot collaboration to support in-home learning experiences of young children. In: Proceedings of the CHI Conference on Human Factors in Computing Systems (CHI), pp. 1–18. ACM, New York (2024)

34. Göschlberger, B., Brandstetter, C.: Conversational AI for corporate e-learning. In: Proceedings of the 21st International Conference on Information Integration and Web-based Applications & Services (iiWAS), pp. 674–678. ACM, New York (2019)

35. Kulkarni, P., Mahabaleshwarkar, A., Kulkarni, M.H., Sirsikar, N., Gadgil, K.D.: Conversational AI: an overview of methodologies, applications & future scope. In: Proceedings of the 5th International Conference on Computing, Communication, Control and Automation (ICCUBEA), pp. 1–7. IEEE, Piscataway (2019)

36. Ciupe, A., Mititica, D.F., Meza, S., Orza, B.: Learning Agile with intelligent conversational agents. In: Proceedings of the 2019 IEEE Global Engineering Education Conference (EDUCON), pp. 1344–1350. IEEE, Piscataway (2019)

37. Wahde, M., Virgolin, M.: Conversational agents: theory and applications. In: Handbook of Computer Learning and Intelligence, vol. 2, pp. 497–544. World Scientific, Singapore (2022)

38. Nguyen, T.T., et al.: Designing AI-based conversational agent for diabetes care in a multilingual context. arXiv preprint arXiv:2105.09490 (2021)

39. Su, P.-H., Mrkšić, N., Casanueva, I., Vulić, I.: Deep learning for conversational AI. In: Proceedings of the 2018 Conference of the North American Chapter of the Association for Computational Linguistics: Tutorial Abstracts, pp. 27–32. Association for Computational Linguistics, New Orleans (2018)

40. Gao, J., Galley, M., Li, L.: Neural approaches to conversational AI. In: Proceedings of the 41st International ACM SIGIR Conference on Research & Development in Information Retrieval (SIGIR), pp. 1371–1374. ACM, New York (2018)

41. WUPEN Homepage. http://www.wupen.org/. Last accessed 13 June 2025

Using Augmented Olfactory Feedback to Assist Visually Impaired Students' Geography Learning

Weijane Lin[1]([✉]) [iD], Meng-Ju Lee[1], and Hsiu-Ping Yueh[2,3] [iD]

[1] Department of Library and Information Science, National Taiwan University, Taipei, Taiwan
`vjlin@ntu.edu.tw`
[2] Research Center for Digital Humanities, National Taiwan University, Taipei, Taiwan
`yueh@ntu.edu.tw`
[3] Department of Psychology/Department of Bio-Industry Communication and Development, National Taiwan University, Taipei, Taiwan

Abstract. Visually impaired students face challenges in geography learning due to traditional visual teaching methods. This study explores the use of augmented olfactory feedback to enhance their learning outcomes. By introducing scents related to debris flow, an important topic for daily life and disaster prevention, this study aims to improve memory retention and engagement. Fourteen visually impaired junior and senior high school students with normal olfactory abilities participated. The experimental group received geography lessons enriched with scents, while the control group did not. Results indicated that while olfactory feedback did not significantly enhance geography learning or olfactory imagery, interviews revealed it could boost student interest, comprehension, and memory. Additionally, scent feedback may assist students in self-study environments like libraries. This research offers insights into the potential of olfactory feedback to improve learning for visually impaired students and suggests avenues for further exploration in other subjects.

Keywords: Visually impaired · Augmented feedback · Olfactory imagery.

1 Introduction

Human beings primarily rely on five sensory modalities to acquire information from their environment. Research indicates that vision accounts for approximately 83% of cognitive information processing, with hearing constituting 11%, smell at 3.5%, touch at 1.5%, and taste at 1% [1]. This pronounced reliance on visual perception poses significant challenges for individuals with visual impairments. According to the World Health Organization (2020), an estimated 2.2 billion people globally experience some form of visual impairment. In Taiwan, the Ministry of Health and Welfare [2] reports that there are 54,088 individuals classified as visually impaired as of November 2023, which constitutes 4.5% of the total population with disabilities. While this percentage may appear relatively modest, the predominance of visual information in everyday life engenders substantial barriers to access for individuals with visual impairments.

© The Author(s), under exclusive license to Springer Nature Switzerland AG 2026
P.-L.P. Rau and H. Krömker (Eds.): HCII 2025, LNCS 16336, pp. 75–84, 2026.
https://doi.org/10.1007/978-3-032-12798-3_5

To compensate for the absence of vision, visually impaired individuals must leverage their other sensory modalities. For instance, they often employ auditory mechanisms to navigate their surroundings and to access auditory materials [3]; tactile senses to read Braille and engage with three-dimensional models [4]; and olfactory senses to assess food quality and evaluate environmental safety [5]. Recent investigations have also examined the potential for scent to enhance the museum experience for visually impaired visitors [6].

For visually impaired learners, geography learning could be challenging. Geography, as an interdisciplinary field encompassing both natural and social sciences, conventionally relies heavily on visual components, such as maps, charts, and field observations. This dependency on visual information creates specific challenges for visually impaired students. Research indicates that these students face greater difficulties in disciplines such as mathematics and the natural sciences [7]. Nevertheless, with appropriate modifications and supportive pedagogical strategies, academic objectives can still be attained.

Despite the extensively documented connection between olfactory stimuli and memory, often referred to as the "Proust phenomenon" [8], olfactory senses remain underutilized within educational contexts for visually impaired students. Given that certain odors can evoke memories and emotions more persistently than visual or auditory inputs [9], and that olfactory imagery can elicit comparable responses even in the absence of actual scent stimuli [10], there is a compelling rationale for further exploration into the incorporation of olfactory elements into pedagogical practices.

Motivated by the aforementioned issues, this study aims to design and evaluate the effectiveness of augmented olfactory feedback in teaching geography, focusing specifically on the topic of debris flow for students with visual impairments. The research investigates the learning outcomes of these students as well as their attitudes toward the teaching materials in general and the augmented olfactory feedback design in particular. Additionally, the study examines students' olfactory imagery to determine whether the augmented olfactory feedback enhances their learning abilities.

2 Literature Review

2.1 Theories of Multimedia Learning and Visually Impaired Learning

The cognitive theory of multimedia learning [11] provides the theoretical framework for this study. This theory is grounded in human information processing and comprises three stages: sensory registry, short-term memory, and long-term memory. According to Mayer [12], meaningful learning is facilitated by three essential principles: dual-channel processing, limited capacity, and active processing. Since individuals process information through distinct channels with a finite capacity, learners are encouraged to actively engage in the selection, organization, and integration of that information.

Research on multisensory stimulation indicates that engaging multiple sensory channels enables the processing of more information than relying on a single channel. This approach facilitates the transfer of information to working memory and enhances the integration of that information into long-term memory [13, 14]. Several applications of multisensory methods have been developed specifically for visually impaired individuals. These include combining tactile perception with audio guidance [15], integrating touch, sound, and smell to enrich the reading experiences of children [16], and designing gamified science learning tools that utilize voice messages and tactile graphics [17].

2.2 Odor, Emotion and Memory

Although smell is one of the five senses, it has often been undervalued in various contexts [9, 18]. The American Medical Association's "Guides to the Evaluation of Permanent Impairment" [19] assigns a mere 1–5% value to the impairment of smell and taste in terms of overall life quality, in stark contrast to the 85% attributed to vision loss. Nevertheless, olfaction plays essential roles, such as detecting danger, assessing food quality, and regulating emotions. The olfactory system is distinctive among the sensory systems due to its direct connection to brain regions associated with emotion (the amygdala) and memory (the hippocampus), bypassing the thalamus entirely [20]. This unique anatomical structure fosters stronger connections between smell, emotion, and memory compared to other senses.

Engen [21] introduced the odor-associative learning theory, which posits that when individuals first encounter an odor alongside specific contexts, emotions, and experiences, that odor evolves from being inconsequential to significant. This process clarifies how certain odors can be perceived as either pleasant or unpleasant, as well as how they can evoke emotions and influence behavior. Herz [18] highlighted two essential processes in odor-associative learning. First, odors can become linked to emotions, gaining meaning that subsequently affects our hedonic responses. Second, odors can elicit previously associated emotions, impacting our current feelings and behaviors.

2.3 Library Services for Visually Impaired Patrons

Libraries play a critical role in ensuring equal access to information for all users, including those with visual impairments. As stated in Article 7 of Taiwan's Library Law, "Libraries shall provide fair, free, timely, and convenient access to library information rights for their service recipients." Currently, library services for visually impaired users mainly focus on auditory and tactile resources [22, 23], such as audiobooks, Braille books, and assistive technologies like screen readers and magnifiers. However, the use of olfactory elements in library settings remains largely unexamined, despite their significant potential to enhance reading experiences and improve information retention.

3 Methodology

3.1 Research Design

This experimental study employed a between-subjects design with two conditions: experimental (with augmented olfactory feedback) and control (without olfactory feedback). The independent variable was the presence or absence of debris flow-related environmental odors during learning activities. Dependent variables included learning outcomes and olfactory imagery ability. The environmental odor of debris flow was created using a blend of patchouli (10 drops), vetiver (5 drops), and cedarwood (5 drops) essential oils diluted in approximately 250 mL of water, designed to simulate damp soil and woody scents associated with forest environments prone to debris flows. The control condition used odorless water mist.

3.2 Participants

Fourteen visually impaired students (4 males, 10 females) from grades 7–12 participated in the study. Participants were recruited through special schools and institutions for the visually impaired in Taiwan between July and October 2024. The experimental group consisted of 9 students (5 congenitally blind, 4 with low vision), while the control group included 5 students (3 congenitally blind, 2 with low vision).

3.3 Materials and Instruments

This study examines the learning experiences of visually impaired students in geography, using debris flows as the central theme for the educational activity. Although the term "debris flow" is introduced in elementary school within the contexts of natural science and social studies, there is currently no comprehensive curriculum specifically dedicated to teaching this topic [24]. In middle school geography, discussions of debris flows are limited to land use and natural disasters. It is only in high school that students encounter more in-depth material related to debris flow concepts, hazard assessment, and emergency response.

Teaching about debris flows serves several important purposes. It not only enhances students' geographical knowledge but also integrates disaster prevention education. By understanding the formation and hazards associated with debris flows, students can develop greater awareness of disaster prevention, enabling them to better protect themselves and others from potential risks. Therefore, "debris flows" is an apt theme that connects with real-life experiences, enriches geographical understanding, and plays a crucial role in disaster prevention education.

The teaching materials on debris flow included a short video compilation that illustrated key concepts related to debris flows, along with a news report that explored the idea of detecting debris flows through smell. Additionally, the materials featured learning handouts available in two formats: Braille and large print. As shown in Fig. 1, the content provided a comprehensive overview of debris flow definitions, factors contributing to their formation, high-risk areas, and important warning signs.

The study employed four assessment instruments. The Learning Achievement Test contained 10 items, comprising 3 true/false questions and 7 multiple choice questions, administered as both pre- and post-tests. The Vividness of Olfactory Imagery Questionnaire (VOIQ) used the original 16-item scale [25] for the pre-test and an adapted version focusing on debris flow-related odors for the post-test. The Disaster Prevention Attitude Survey consisted of a 10-item scale measuring attitudes toward debris flow prevention. Finally, semi-structured interviews were conducted to explore participants' experiences with olfactory-enhanced learning.

The experimental procedure began with consent and demographic information collection. Participants then underwent olfactory function screening using coffee and lemon scents. Following screening, participants completed the pre-tests, which included the

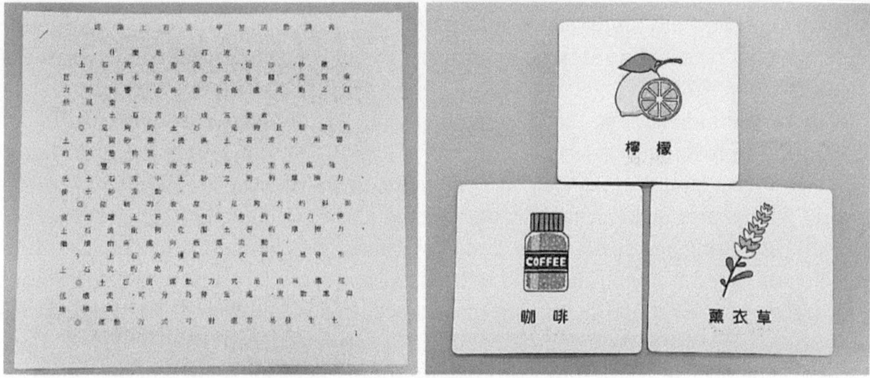

Fig. 1. Teaching materials in Braille.

VOIQ and learning achievement test. The main learning activity lasted approximately 20 min, during which the experimental group received olfactory augmentation while the control group did not. After the learning activity, participants completed the post-tests consisting of the learning achievement test and disaster prevention attitude survey. Once any odors had dissipated, participants completed the adapted VOIQ post-test. The procedure concluded with individual interviews. The total duration was approximately 60 min per participant.

4 Results

4.1 Learning Outcomes

The results of the learning achievement test revealed intriguing patterns between the experimental and control groups. In the pre-test, the experimental group recorded a mean score of 61.11 (SD = 23.15), slightly surpassing the control group, which had a mean score of 54.00 (SD = 20.74). However, this difference was not statistically significant (t = 0.570, p = .579). In the post-test, scores improved for both groups. The experimental group achieved a mean score of 65.56 (SD = 24.04), while the control group reached a mean score of 66.00 (SD = 15.17) (Table 1).

Table 1. Learning achievement test scores.

Group	Pre-test		Post-test	
	M	S.D.	Mean	S.D.
Experimental (n = 9)	61.11	23.154	65.56	24.037
Control (n = 5)	54.00	20.736	66.00	15.166

Paired t-tests demonstrated that the control group exhibited a significant improvement from the pre-test to the post-test (t = 3.21, p = .033). In contrast, the experimental group did not show any significant improvement (t = 0.61, p = .559). Additionally, independent t-tests revealed no significant differences between the groups at the post-test (t = −0.037, p = .971).

The results indicate that the learning materials were effective, as evidenced by the significant improvement observed in the control group. However, the incorporation of olfactory stimulation did not yield the anticipated enhancement in learning outcomes. Several factors may account for this unexpected finding. Firstly, individual differences in smell perception and preferences could have influenced learning effectiveness. Some participants found the environmental odor associated with debris flow to be unpleasant or distracting, potentially obstructing their concentration and overall learning process. Secondly, the relatively short duration of the intervention—approximately 20 min—may not have provided sufficient time for olfactory stimuli to generate measurable effects on learning outcomes. Lastly, the complexity of the test items, along with the abstract nature of certain concepts, may have led to ceiling effects that obscured any potential advantages of olfactory enhancement.

4.2   Olfactory Imagery Ability

The assessment of olfactory imagery ability yielded consistent results across both groups and time points. Pre-test scores were remarkably similar between the experimental group (M = 61.33, SD = 9.39) and control group (M = 60.40, SD = 11.55). Post-test scores showed slight decreases for both groups, with the experimental group scoring M = 59.89 (SD = 12.22) and the control group M = 59.20 (SD = 12.44) (Table 2).

Table 2. Olfactory imagery scores.

Group	Pre-test		Post-test	
	M	S.D.	Mean	S.D.
Experimental (n = 9)	61.33	9.39	59.89	12.22
Control (n = 5)	60.40	11.55	59.20	12.44

Statistical analyses indicated no significant differences between the groups at either the pre-test (t = 0.165, p = .872) or the post-test (t = 0.100, p = .923). The consistently high scores, approximately 60 out of a possible 80 points, across all conditions suggest that participants generally exhibited strong olfactory imagery abilities, regardless of the experimental conditions.

The absence of improvement in olfactory imagery ability following olfactory stimulation raises questions about the assumed connection between actual olfactory experience and mental olfactory representation. This finding aligns with previous research [26, 27] suggesting that olfactory imagery ability may be more closely linked to long-term olfactory memory and familiarity with specific odors rather than short-term exposure. The slight decline in scores from pre-test to post-test for both groups may be attributed to fatigue or the increased complexity of the adapted questionnaire, which focused on debris flow-related odors that were likely less familiar to participants than the everyday odors in the original version.

4.3 Disaster Prevention Attitude

Both groups displayed positive attitudes toward debris flow disaster prevention, with the experimental group achieving slightly higher scores (M = 34.33, SD = 4.82) compared to the control group (M = 31.80, SD = 5.22) on a scale of 40 points. However, this difference was not statistically significant (t = 0.916, p = .378). The uniformly positive attitudes across both groups suggest that the educational content was effective in raising awareness of disaster prevention, irrespective of the olfactory enhancement. This finding has important implications for disaster education, indicating that well-crafted educational materials about debris flows can effectively improve students' understanding of disaster prevention, whether or not additional sensory channels are employed.

4.4 Qualitative Findings

The qualitative data yielded significant insights that elucidate the quantitative findings and demonstrate the intricacies involved in implementing olfactory augmentation within educational contexts. Among the nine participants in the experimental group, eight reported the detection of odors during the learning activity, thereby confirming the successful delivery and perception of the olfactory stimulus.

Participants' characterizations of the odor displayed considerable variability, reflecting individual differences in sensory perception and interpretation. Some participants described the scent negatively, employing terms such as "rotten," "unpleasant," and "sour," with participants S2 and S7 indicating that the odor proved somewhat distracting during the learning activity. Conversely, other participants established positive environmental associations that resonated with the intended theme of debris flow, describing the scent as reminiscent of "stone," "damp soil," "rain," and "grass" (participants S1, S6, S8, and S9). Particularly noteworthy was the account of one participant (S1), who associated the scent with favorable memories from a visit to a fossil museum, underscoring the profound connection between olfactory experiences and autobiographical memory.

In regard to participants' attitudes toward olfactory-enhanced learning, a range of perspectives emerged. Eight out of the 14 total participants posited that the incorporation of odors into geography instruction could enhance memory retention, facilitate comprehension, and foster greater engagement. One participant articulated that odors "help create mental associations with abstract concepts," suggesting that olfactory cues may serve as cognitive anchors for understanding complex geographical phenomena. However, six participants expressed skepticism or concerns about potential distractions, with one individual asserting that "tactile aids are more effective" for their preferred learning style.

The impact of prior experience with scent-enhanced learning appeared to influence participants' receptiveness to this pedagogical approach. Eight participants reported previous exposure to olfactory stimuli in educational settings, including science classes, camps, or hands-on activities. Such prior experiences likely contributed to these participants' comfort level and acceptance of olfactory elements in learning environments.

Most encouraging for future applications was the considerable interest expressed in library spaces featuring scents tailored to reading materials. Thirteen of the 14 participants conveyed enthusiasm for such facilities, indicating that they could enhance comprehension, retention, and the overall enjoyment of reading. This finding suggests substantial potential for the implementation of olfactory elements in library contexts, notwithstanding the mixed outcomes observed in formal learning environments.

5 Discussion and Conclusion

The juxtaposition of quantitative and qualitative results underscores the intricacies inherent in multisensory learning interventions. While statistical analyses indicated no significant advantages associated with olfactory augmentation, qualitative data illuminated that numerous participants derived value from the experience and could foresee potential benefits applicable to various contexts or through modified implementation strategies.

Several factors likely contributed to the limitations observed in the quantitative outcomes. Notably, individual differences in odor perception and preference emerged as significant variables; some participants reported that the environmental odor facilitated the development of mental associations, whereas others found it to be a distraction. The intervention duration, approximately 20 min, may have been inadequate for the emergence of measurable effects, particularly given that odor-associative learning typically necessitates repeated exposure or emotionally impactful experiences. Moreover, although the selected scent blend was thematically congruous, it may not have been optimal for all participants, suggesting a need for more personalized or diverse olfactory stimuli. Lastly, the small sample size imposed constraints on the statistical power necessary to detect potentially subtle effects.

Despite these limitations, the study demonstrates the practical feasibility of integrating olfactory elements into educational contexts. The effective administration of controlled olfactory stimuli, the participants' capacity to establish associations between odors and academic content, and the pronounced interest in future applications collectively advocate for further exploration of this approach. The findings imply that olfactory augmentation may yield the most substantial effects when implemented as an optional enhancement rather than a compulsory element, thereby allowing learners to engage with sensory modalities in accordance with their preferences and individual learning styles.

Our ongoing works aim to rectify the limitations identified in this study by expanding sample sizes and enhancing demographic diversity, investigating longer-term interventions that facilitate the development of stronger odor-learning associations, examining various subject areas and odor types to identify optimal pairings, establishing standardized protocols for olfactory augmentation within educational settings, and exploring individual factors that predict favorable responses to olfactory enhancement.

This study examined the use of augmented olfactory feedback as a means to enhance geography learning for visually impaired students. While the quantitative data did not reveal significant improvements, the qualitative findings suggested potential benefits for certain learners. This research underscores the feasibility of integrating olfactory elements into educational settings and highlights the necessity of considering individual differences in sensory preferences. The results contribute to our understanding of multisensory learning approaches for visually impaired students, indicating that olfactory augmentation, although not universally effective, can serve as a valuable addition to an educator's toolkit. Libraries and educational institutions should consider launching pilot programs that utilize scent-enhanced materials, with careful attention to implementation details and the collection of user feedback.

As we continue to explore innovative methods for accessible education, olfactory augmentation emerges as a promising strategy among many. Its effectiveness appears to vary significantly among individuals, requiring a flexible and optional implementation rather than a uniform approach. Future research should aim to pinpoint the optimal conditions and individual characteristics that predict positive responses to olfactory-enhanced learning.

Acknowledgments. This study was supported by the Taiwan National Science and Technology Council (grant number NSTC111-2628-H-002-006-MY3).

Disclosure of Interests. The authors have no competing interests to declare that are relevant to the content of this article.

References

1. Lee, K.-L., Yen, J.: A preliminary study on the construction of the "five senses" design model – a case study of food packaging design. J. Des. Res., 156–164 (2008)
2. Ministry of Health and Welfare: In: Ministry of Health and Welfare (ed.) Disabilities Statistics, Taipei (2023)
3. Kolarik, A.J., Raman, R., Moore, B.C., Cirstea, S., Gopalakrishnan, S., Pardhan, S.: The accuracy of auditory spatial judgments in the visually impaired is dependent on sound source distance. Sci. Rep. **10**, 7169 (2020)
4. Millar, S.: Reading by touch in blind children and adults. In: Handbook of Children's Literacy, pp. 437–457. Springer, Dordrecht (2004)
5. Çomoğlu, Ş., Orhan, K.S., Kocaman, S.Ü., Çelik, M., Keleş, N., Değer, K.: Olfactory function assessment of blind subjects using the sniffin' sticks test. Otolaryngol. Head Neck Surg. **153**, 286–290 (2015)
6. Verbeek, C., Leemans, I., Fleming, B.: How can scents enhance the impact of guided museum tours? Towards an impact approach for olfactory museology. Senses Soc. **17**, 315–342 (2022)
7. Tseng, Y.-T., Liao, K.-S.: Cooperative instruction in teaching blind students during their chemistry experiment course: an action research. J. Spec. Educ. **33**, 1–28 (2011)
8. Chu, S., Downes, J.J.: Odour-evoked autobiographical memories: psychological investigations of Proustian phenomena. Chem. Senses. **25**, 111–116 (2000)
9. Herz, R.S.: Aromatherapy facts and fictions: a scientific analysis of olfactory effects on mood, physiology and behavior. Int. J. Neurosci. **119**, 263–290 (2009)
10. Stevenson, R.J., Case, T.I.: Olfactory imagery: a review. Psychon. Bull. Rev. **12**, 244–264 (2005)
11. Mayer, R.E.: Cognitive theory of multimedia learning. In: The Cambridge Handbook of Multimedia Learning, vol. 41, pp. 31–48 Cambridge University Press, Cambridge, U.K. (2005)

12. Mayer, R.E.: Learning strategies for making sense out of expository text: the SOI model for guiding three cognitive processes in knowledge construction. Educ. Psychol. Rev. **8**, 357–371 (1996)
13. Covaci, A., Zou, L., Tal, I., Muntean, G.-M., Ghinea, G.: Is multimedia multisensorial?-a review of mulsemedia systems. ACM Comput. Surv. (CSUR). **51**, 1–35 (2018)
14. Shams, L., Seitz, A.R.: Benefits of multisensory learning. Trends Cogn. Sci. **12**, 411–417 (2008)
15. Cho, J.D., Quero, L.C., Bartolome, J.I., Lee, D.W., Oh, U., Lee, I.: Tactile colour pictogram to improve artwork appreciation of people with visual impairments. Color Res. Appl. **46**, 103–116 (2021)
16. Edirisinghe, C., Podari, N., Cheok, A.D.: A multi-sensory interactive reading experience for visually impaired children; a user evaluation. Pers. Ubiquit. Comput. **26**, 807–819 (2022)
17. Chang, C.-H.S., Kuo, C.-C., Hou, H.-T., Koe, J.J.Y.: Design and evaluation of a multi-sensory scaffolding gamification science course with mobile technology for learners with total blindness. Comput. Hum. Behav. **128**, 107085 (2022)
18. Herz, R.S.: Odor-associative learning and emotion: effects on perception and behavior. Chem. Senses. **30**, i250–i251 (2005)
19. Rondinelli, R.D., et al.: AMA Guides® to the Evaluation of Permanent Impairment, Sixth Edition, 2023. American Medical Association, Illinois, U.S.A. (2023)
20. Manzini, I., Frasnelli, J., Croy, I.: Wie wir riechen und was es für uns bedeutet: Grundlagen des Geruchssinns (Leitthema). HNO. **62**, 846–852 (2014)
21. Engen, T.: Odor Sensation and Memory. Praeger Publishers, New York, U.S.A. (1991)
22. Fernandez, A., Fernandez, P., López, G., Calderón, M., Guerrero, L.A.: Troyoculus: an augmented reality system to improve reading capabilities of night-blind people. In: Ambient Assisted Living. ICT-Based Solutions in Real Life Situations: 7th International Work-Conference, IWAAL 2015, Puerto Varas, Chile, December 1–4, 2015, Proceedings 7, pp. 16–28. Springer (2015)
23. Mikułowski, D., Brzostek-Pawłowska, J.: Multi-sensual augmented reality in interactive accessible math tutoring system for flipped classroom. In: International Conference on Intelligent Tutoring Systems, pp. 1–10. Springer (2020)
24. Hsu, M.-Y., Wu, H.-W., Wang, Y.-H.: A study on a learner-centered teaching program of debris flow disaster prevention for high graders in a primary school. Curric. Instr. Q. **13**, 233–259 (2010)
25. Gilbert, A.N., Crouch, M., Kemp, S.E.: Olfactory and visual mental imagery. J. Ment. Imag. **22**(3–4), 137–146 (1998)
26. Arshamian, A., et al.: The perception of odor pleasantness is shared across cultures. Curr. Biol. **32**, 2061–2066. e2063 (2022)
27. Bensafi, M., Rouby, C.: Individual differences in odor imaging ability reflect differences in olfactory and emotional perception. Chem. Senses. **32**, 237–244 (2007)

How Interactive Contexts Affect College Students' Perceptual, Emotional, and Behavioral Tendencies Toward Social Robots

Hsiu-Ping Yueh[1,2] (iD), Yung-Ning Tsao[3], Chia-Ho Chen[1] (iD), and Weijane Lin[3(✉)] (iD)

[1] Research Center for Digital Humanities, National Taiwan University, Taipei, Taiwan
[2] Department of Psychology/Department of Bio-Industry Communication and Development, National Taiwan University, Taipei, Taiwan
[3] Department of Library and Information Science, National Taiwan University, Taipei, Taiwan
vjlin@ntu.edu.tw

Abstract. The Stereotype Content Model and Behaviors from Intergroup Affect and Stereotypes model suggest that perceptions of others' warmth and competence significantly influence emotional responses and behavioral tendencies. While these models have been successfully applied to human-robot interaction with results consistent with interpersonal interactions, the role of interactive context remains underexplored. This study examines how different interactive contexts—instrumental versus interactional—influence college students' perceptions of robot warmth and competence. Through an online experiment with 151 participants viewing video prototypes of human-robot interactions, we found that context significantly affects perception outcomes. Instrumental contexts enhanced both warmth and competence perceptions compared to interactional contexts. High-warmth, high-competence robots elicited admiration and facilitation behaviors, while low-warmth, low-competence robots evoked contempt and harm behaviors. However, ambivalent emotions (envy and pity) showed weaker effects than predicted by the original models. These findings underscore the importance of context in HRI research and provide insights for designing context-appropriate robot behaviors.

Keywords: human-robot interaction · social context · social cognition.

1 Introduction

As social robots integrate increasingly into human environments, they have evolved from simple tools to collaborators, companions, and educators that carry significant emotional weight for users. Research in social robotics aims to cultivate harmonious relationships between humans and robots, enabling meaningful human-robot interactions that align with interpersonal social norms [1, 2]. The embodied nature of social robots leads individuals to anthropomorphize them, assigning names, genders, and personality traits, which fosters emotional attachment during interactions [3]. The "Computers Are Social Actors" (CASA) paradigm [4, 5] suggests that individuals unconsciously

© The Author(s), under exclusive license to Springer Nature Switzerland AG 2026
P.-L.P. Rau and H. Krömker (Eds.): HCII 2025, LNCS 16336, pp. 85–95, 2026.
https://doi.org/10.1007/978-3-032-12798-3_6

apply social norms to robots, viewing them as social actors and allowing the application of interpersonal theories, such as social cognition theory, in human-robot interaction research.

Social cognition theory examines how individuals perceive and understand others and themselves, exploring processes like impression formation. Fiske and Neuberg [6] proposed a model where perceivers categorize individuals to facilitate understanding, leading to emotional responses and behaviors. Their Stereotype Content Model (SCM) analyzes stereotype formation along warmth and competence axes, serving as a crucial framework in social cognition and human-robot interaction [5, 7]. Furthermore, Cuddy and colleagues developed the Behaviors from Intergroup Affect and Stereotypes (BIAS) model [8, 9], which describes the relationships among stereotypes, emotions, and behaviors. This model posits that stereotypes not only trigger emotional responses but also shape interactive behaviors [10, 11]. Thus, individuals' behavioral tendencies can be predicted based on their stereotypes of others. Despite the application of stereotype formation theories to HRI empirical research [7, 12], most studies adopt only partial theoretical frameworks. Reeves et al. [5] and Mieczkowski et al. [11] are among the few to comprehensively reference SCM and BIAS models from interpersonal interaction, validating whether warmth and competence perceptions in human-robot interaction elicit emotions and behavioral tendencies consistent with interpersonal patterns. However, both studies provided participants with static robot photographs rather than actual interactions. Reeves et al. [5] confirmed that SCM and BIAS models apply not only to interpersonal interaction but also explain potential actions people take after perceiving robot warmth and competence features. They specifically described how robot appearance features, such as mechanical structure visibility, degrees of freedom, and form, influence warmth and competence perceptions. Mieczkowski et al. [11] found that robot warmth and competence features can respectively elicit admiration, contempt, pity, and envy emotions, consistent with interpersonal results. However, they noted in their limitations that participants evaluated robots without context, or participants believed robots lacked self-awareness, resulting in significantly lower tendencies toward active harm behaviors toward robots.

According to context theory, interactive contexts are crucial cues for understanding human behavior [13]. Different interaction purposes or types may make people more likely to notice or overlook certain features in others [14–16]. Without context, people may struggle to form an understanding or expectations about robot behavior due to relatively limited interaction experience with robots, thereby affecting their own behavioral tendencies. Based on this research background and gap, and considering current generative AI and robotics technology development, this study examines whether SCM and BIAS models from interpersonal interaction apply to human-robot interaction and collaboration contexts with interactive contexts present, serving as a reference for designing robot interactive features.

This study seeks to explore how human perceptions and behavioral tendencies towards robots differ across various interactive contexts during human-robot interaction. Specifically, we aim to determine whether perceptions of warmth and competence in robots vary between instrumental contexts, where robots perform tasks, and interactional contexts, focused on social engagement. Additionally, we will examine whether the emotions and behavioral tendencies that arise from these perceptions align with findings from interpersonal interactions. The expected benefits of this research include a better understanding of how context influences perception, which could enhance our ability to predict emotions and behaviors in human-robot interactions, thereby improving collaboration and interaction design.

2   Literature Review

2.1   Warmth and Competence in Interpersonal Social Cognition

When individuals encounter others, they swiftly form impressions based on prior interactions with people who possess similar traits. This ability allows them to draw on their past experiences when meeting new individuals, enhancing the efficiency of their perceptions and responses while reducing cognitive load. Consequently, they can quickly adopt the appropriate emotions and behaviors for interaction [17–19]. Research has established that two key attributes, warmth and competence, play a significant role in shaping social cognition. These characteristics are recognized as universal and vital perceptual elements that influence our perceptions, emotional responses, and behaviors toward others.

The notions of warmth and competence in social cognition were first articulated by Asch [17], who conducted a study in which participants were asked to form personality impressions based on lists of character traits. The participants were divided into two groups: one received a list that included the trait "warm," while the other received a list with the trait "cold," while all other traits remained identical across both groups and included a mix of positive and negative features. The results revealed that individuals characterized by warmth-related traits received more favorable evaluations, demonstrating that the contrast between warm and cold traits has a profound impact on overall perceptions of individuals. This underscores that personal traits possess varying levels of significance when forming impressions, with warmth and coldness serving as central traits that shape our overall judgments of others. Building on Asch's theoretical foundation, Kelley [20] studied how people form first impressions of others. The study introduced speakers to students using warm or cold descriptors before class to create expectations about speaker characteristics. The research included speaker-led student discussions, recording verbal interaction frequency between students and speakers. Post-class, students were asked about their impressions of the speaker. Results showed that speakers introduced as having warm qualities were better liked by students and elicited more interaction. Even though students had opportunities for actual interaction to reassess speaker characteristics during class, their final impressions remained consistent with initial introductions. This research confirmed that first impressions of others' warmth or coldness substantially influence perceivers' overall evaluations.

Rosenberg and his colleagues [19] argued that personality traits encompass multiple dimensions. Their study involved 120 college students categorizing 64 personality traits into a maximum of ten groups, revealing that these traits could be effectively described along the axes of good versus bad sociality and intellectual ability. Traits associated with good sociality included warmth, sociability, and kindness, while good intellectual ability was marked by intelligence, determination, and skill. They also emphasized the relevance of Asch's [17] warm versus cold research, which indicated that consistent intellectual representations led to reliable trait perceptions. Furthermore, Bales [21] employed interaction process analysis to examine problem-solving behaviors within small groups, categorizing behaviors into social and task orientations. Social-oriented behaviors were divided into positive responses (e.g., solidarity, tension release) and negative responses (e.g., rejection, pressure). Task-oriented behaviors involved goal-directed interactions, which included providing suggestions and asking for guidance. On the other hand, Wojciszke [22] identified morality and competence as key dimensions influencing social cognition. Morality, closely tied to good sociality, elicits stronger emotional responses from perceivers. This was evident in participants' tendencies to describe others in moral terms more frequently than in competence terms, indicating that moral traits significantly affect interpersonal approaches.

To sum up, the framework of warmth and competence in social cognition, established by Asch [17] and supported by ongoing research, indicates that these dimensions heavily influence perceptions of others. Despite variations in terminology across studies, such as warmth being referred to as "good-social" or "morality," the concepts remain consistent. Warmth involves prosocial traits, while competence pertains to ability traits [23]. This research adopts the terminology proposed by Fiske [4] for clarity.

2.2   The BIAS Model: From Perception to Behavior

Cuddy and colleagues developed the BIAS (Behaviors from Intergroup Affect and Stereotypes) model [9], which explores the relationships among stereotypes, emotions, and behavior. This theoretical framework posits that stereotypes elicit distinct emotional responses that influence individuals' interactions [8, 10, 11, 24]. As a result, one's behavioral tendencies can be anticipated based on their stereotypes of others. In 2007, Cuddy et al. [9] extended the Stereotype Content Model (SCM) by proposing that perceptions of warmth and competence, alongside the emotions they generate, significantly impact behavior. Behaviors can be classified in terms of intensity (active vs. passive) and valence (facilitative vs. harmful). The idea of intensity differentiates between active behaviors, which are effortful and goal-directed, such as harassment, and passive behaviors, which are incidental and demand minimal effort. Although passive actions may not aim for specific outcomes, they can result in neglect or exclusion. On the other hand, valence refers to the positive or negative impact of behaviors. Facilitative behaviors yield benefits for others, while harmful behaviors have detrimental effects.

The BIAS model identifies four behavioral tendencies: active facilitation (intentional help), active harm (deliberate harm), passive facilitation (tolerating others for personal gain), and passive harm (devaluing or excluding others). Cuddy et al. [9] analyzed 31 behaviors to illustrate these tendencies, and they proposed three hypotheses: Hypothesis One asserts that stereotypes regarding warmth and competence predict behaviors. Warmth is a more salient indicator and influences both active and passive actions. Hypothesis Two suggests that emotions also predict behavior: admiration and contempt drive helping and harming behaviors, respectively. Emotions like envy and pity can lead to ambivalent reactions, resulting in both active helping and passive harm. Hypothesis Three posits that emotions take precedence in predicting behavior and act as mediators between perception and action. The BIAS model and its hypotheses have been adopted in subsequent research to validate not only interpersonal interactions but also human-robot interactions.

2.3 Applying Warmth and Competence Theory in Human-Robot Interaction

Interpersonal interaction patterns are often unconsciously applied to human-robot interactions (HRI), leading to extensive research on perceptions of warmth and competence in this field. Studies involving both physical social robots [25, 26] and virtual robots [27–29] have shown that humans can discern these characteristics and that these perceptions significantly influence interaction experiences. Although warmth and competence are frequently studied, only Reeves et al. [5] and Mieczkowski et al. [11] have validated specifically the Stereotype Content Model (SCM) and Beliefs, Information, Attitudes, and Stereotypes (BIAS) theories together in the context of HRI. These studies confirmed the universal applicability of these theories. Reeves et al. [5] demonstrated that individuals primarily perceive robots through warmth and competence, establishing that robot appearance correlates with these perceptions. Mieczkowski et al. [11] revised existing scales to affirm that perceptions of warmth and competence are integral to the human evaluation of robots, consistent with interpersonal interactions. High-warmth robots evoked active assistance and correlated with admiration and pity, while high-competence robots elicited passive help and linked to admiration and envy. However, low warmth or competence did not predict aggressive behaviors.

Despite these insights, both studies relied on static robot photographs, overlooking the impact of interactive contexts. According to context theory [13], this omission may affect research outcomes. Notably, Mieczkowski et al. [11] found that while positive behavioral tendencies were consistent with interpersonal findings, aggressive tendencies showed no correlation with warmth and competence. This discrepancy may arise from the lack of an interactive context, as retributive justice theory suggests individuals do not retaliate against robots absent prior harm. Therefore, this study aims to explore whether SCM and BIAS theories can replicate interpersonal interaction outcomes within contextualized HRI and how varying contexts influence perceptions of warmth and competence. Insights from this research may enhance predictions of human-robot interaction results based on contextual factors, thus improving future design and interaction experiences in HRI.

3 Methodology

3.1 Research Design

This study followed previous research design [5, 9, 11, 23], but replaced static photographs with video prototypes to present complete interactive contexts and conducted large-scale usability testing online. We employed a 2x2 factorial design exploring how interactive context (instrumental vs. interactional) and robot warmth characteristics (high warmth / low warmth) influence participants' perceptions of robots.

To prevent overly dispersed conversations, we set three interaction scenarios (restaurant sharing, group project, internship application). Each online participant was randomly assigned to instrumental or interactional context groups and asked to watch interaction performances of high-warmth and low-warmth social robots across these three scenarios before answering robot perception questionnaires. Because videos can provide sufficient information richness with interactive context for participants to generate perceptions [30], while also standardizing research and more easily reaching more participants, and because on-site and video experimental results show high consistency in single-person HRI scenarios [31], this research adopted video prototyping with participants watching videos and responding based on their own perceptions, emotions, and behavioral tendencies.

3.2 Participants

The majority of social cognition theories concerning perceptions of warmth and competence have primarily utilized college students as research participants. Given that warmth and competence are understood to be universal and cross-cultural constructs, and that previous studies have found no significant differences in perceptions between college students and the general public [8, 9, 23, 32], this study chose to include college students and graduate students for the online usability testing. This decision aimed to reduce participant variability compared to earlier research. We crafted conversation topics based on familiar life scenarios relevant to this demographic, such as sharing meals at restaurants, collaborating on group projects, and applying for internships. These relatable scenarios were designed to facilitate greater participant engagement. Additionally, participants were required to be enrolled in college and possess the ability to read and comprehend Chinese independently.

3.3 Apparatus – Robot and Operating System

This research used the small humanoid robot Kebbi® (see Fig. 1) as the platform to implement our conversation design. This robot has partial humanoid features suitable for our research design. Robot verbal dialogue was generated by connecting to the large language model GPT-3.5, allowing robot responses based on participant utterances for free conversation between participants and robots.

Since warmth perception carries higher weight [4, 9, 17], and considering that dialogue generated by large language models inherently varies in quality, with participants perceiving competence as high or low based on whether robot dialogue content meets their expectations, this research primarily manipulated warmth verbal representations (including ingratiation behaviors, encouraging speech) as dialogue strategies without manipulating competence representations.

To design the robot's contextual behaviors, the theoretical models of SCM and BIAS were adopted to set the social roles and response strategies of the GPT model through prompt engineering. These instructions covered various scenarios for GPT to judge participant utterances and provide appropriate responses with warmth differences. Since voice volume and pitch affect competence perception [33], we did not adjust robot voice volume and pitch, keeping them as control variables.

The scales for warmth and competence perception, emotional responses, and behavioral tendencies from Mieczkowski et al. [11] were adopted. Each scale used a 6-point

Fig. 1. Kebbi the robot adopted in this study.

Likert scale ranging from 1 (very low) to 6 (very high). Emotional responses gauged the feelings participants experienced when interacting with robots, including admiration, contempt, envy, and pity. Behavioral tendencies were restructured based on context to evaluate active and passive helping and harming tendencies, with one item assigned to each behavior type, as identified by Cuddy et al. [9].

4 Preliminary Findings

4.1 Participant Profile

The study included 151 participants after excluding non-college students, consisting of 35% male, 65% female, with a mean age = 23.05, SD = 4.95. 72% of the participants are undergraduates, and 28% are graduate students. Participants' negative attitudes toward robots averaged 45.90 (SD = 7.85, scale maximum = 84), and self-efficacy averaged 42.35 (SD = 6.64, scale maximum = 60). Regression analysis showed neither negative attitudes nor self-efficacy significantly influenced warmth or competence perceptions ($p > 0.001$). This finding suggests that participants' pre-existing attitudes toward robots did not bias their perception results, supporting the robustness of our experimental manipulation.

4.2 Context Effects on Participants' Perceptions

Independent samples t-tests were conducted to investigate how context influences perceptions of warmth and competence. The findings revealed significant differences in both warmth ($t = 5.774$, $p < .001$) and competence ($t = 6.982$, $p < .001$), with participants exhibiting higher perceptions in instrumental contexts compared to interactional ones. These results support our hypothesis, highlighting that the type of context significantly affects perception outcomes.

A noteworthy finding was that instrumental contexts enhanced perceptions of both warmth and competence, likely due to participants' emphasis on task completion and problem-solving. In settings characterized by instrumental interactions, robots that offered helpful suggestions were perceived as both warmer and more competent, potentially because task-oriented interactions made their contributions more prominent and valuable. This observation diverges from the initial hypothesis that instrumental contexts would primarily enhance perceptions of competence, while interactional contexts would focus on warmth.

The results suggest that when robots successfully assist with specific problems, they are evaluated more favorably across both fundamental dimensions of social perception. This underscores the active role of context in shaping social cognition, rather than merely serving as background. The context dependency indicates that perception outcomes can vary significantly based on the interaction type, with instrumental contexts potentially activating different evaluation criteria than interactional contexts. For designers of HRI, these insights imply that robots should adapt their expressions of warmth and competence to align with the goals of the interaction. In instrumental contexts, a balanced presentation of both dimensions may yield particularly positive results.

4.3 Perception-Emotion-Behavior Relationships

Warmth-Competence Correlation. The results of the correlation analysis indicated a significant positive relationship between perceptions of warmth and competence ($r = 0.725$, $p < .001$). This suggests that participants who perceived robots as warmer also regarded them as more competent. This finding stands in contrast to the typical trade-off mechanism observed in interpersonal perception, where warmth and competence tend to be negatively correlated [23, 24]. This positive correlation corresponds with the halo effects noted when only one aspect is manipulated [34], indicating that participants tend to generalize from prominent cues of warmth to infer competence levels. When warm robots offered more suggestions and supplementary information, they were perceived as more competent, despite having similar response accuracy to less warm robots. This variation in attribution processes for robots compared to humans may stem from limited experience with robots or the influence of anthropomorphism. As individuals gain more exposure to a range of robots, this halo effect could diminish, potentially leading to more refined distinctions in perceptions of warmth and competence.

Perceptions Predicting Emotions. Regression analyses revealed that both warmth ($b = 0.447$, $SE = 0.08$, $p < .001$, $\beta = 0.878$) and competence ($b = 0.427$, $SE = 0.13$, $p < .001$, $\beta = 0.746$) positively predicted positive emotions. Higher perceptions of warmth or competence were linked to stronger positive emotional responses. When examining specific emotions, competence was a significant predictor of admiration ($b = 0.455$, $SE = 0.011$, $p < .001$, $\beta = 0.805$) and negatively predicted contempt ($b = -0.261$, $SE = 0.18$, $p < .001$, $\beta = -0.433$). Furthermore, competence displayed weak positive correlations with both envy ($b = 0.096$, $SE = 0.15$, $p < .001$, $\beta = 0.211$) and pity ($b = 0.107$, $SE = 0.17$, $p < .001$, $\beta = 0.207$). Similarly, warmth strongly predicted admiration ($b = 0.416$, $SE = 0.09$, $p < .001$, $\beta = 0.828$) and negatively predicted contempt ($b = -0.259$, $SE = 0.16$, $p < .001$, $\beta = -0.483$). The relationship between warmth and envy was weak ($b = -0.068$, $SE = 0.13$, $p < .001$, $\beta = -0.167$), while it demonstrated a positive but weak association with pity ($b = 0.105$, $SE = 0.15$, $p < .001$, $\beta = 0.229$).

The attenuated ambivalent emotional responses likely reflect fundamental differences between robots and humans. Interpersonal competence perceptions involve status and resource implications central to envy and pity [8–10, 24]. Since robots lack status and resources, participants have lower tendencies to experience these complex emotions toward them. This suggests modifications to SCM when applied to artificial agents, where clear emotions (admiration, contempt) remain robust, but ambivalent emotions requiring status considerations are diminished.

Behaviors Predicted by Perceptions and Emotions. Competence positively predicted both active facilitation (b = 0.372, SE = 0.013, p < .001, β = 0.679) and passive facilitation (b = 0.417, SE = 0.013, p < .001, β = 0.735), while negatively predicting active harm (b = −0.261, SE = 0.018, p < .001, β = −0.442) and passive harm (b = −0.296, SE = 0.017, p < .001, β = −0.500). Standardized coefficients indicated that competence had a more significant impact on helping behaviors, especially passive facilitation. Warmth demonstrated similar effects, positively predicting active facilitation (b = 0.368, SE = 0.011, p < .001, β = 0.756) and passive facilitation (b = 0.378, SE = 0.011, p < .001, β = 0.747), while negatively predicting both active harm (b = −0.274, SE = 0.015, p < .001, β = −0.521) and passive harm (b = −0.273, SE = 0.015, p < .001, β = −0.519). Warmth's influence was stronger than that of competence, contrary to the BIAS model predictions. Regarding emotions, admiration positively predicted both types of facilitation while negatively predicting harms. In contrast, contempt positively predicted harm and negatively predicted facilitation. Ambivalent emotions like envy and pity had weaker effects, with pity showing positive predictions mainly for active and passive facilitation but a weak association with active harm and no significant relationship with passive harm.

5   Conclusion

This study provides evidence that interactive context significantly influences how people perceive and respond to social robots, addressing a gap in the literature that has relied on static evaluations. By applying the SCM and the BIAS model within instrumental and interactional contexts using video prototypes, we identify both consistencies and critical departures from established interpersonal patterns.

Key findings reveal that instrumental contexts enhance perceptions of warmth and competence compared to interactional contexts, challenging the assumptions about task-focused versus social interactions. The correlation between warmth and competence (r = 0.725) suggests different attribution processes for robots, possibly due to halo effects or limited experience. While clear emotions aligned with theoretical predictions, ambivalent emotions showed weakened effects, indicating that robots may not fully engage the status and resource dynamics present in human interactions.

Notably, contextualized video-based interactions enabled a broader range of behavioral responses, including harmful behaviors absent in static evaluations. This highlights that context is an active factor in shaping social cognition in human-robot interactions. The mediation effects of emotions between perceptions and behaviors confirm that social psychological processes are relevant within HRI, necessitating theoretical adaptations.

These findings have important implications. Theoretically, they suggest modifications to the SCM and BIAS models for artificial agents, particularly regarding emotional responses and warmth-competence dynamics. Practically, robots should adjust their behaviors to match interaction contexts, as instrumental settings may benefit from a balanced display of warmth and competence.

As social robots increasingly interact with humans, understanding these contextual influences is essential for designing effective robotic behaviors. This research bridges social psychological theory with HRI practice, laying the groundwork for developing robots that can navigate complex human social expectations. Future work should explore how perceptions evolve, vary across cultures, and inform the creation of adaptive robotic systems tailored for specific contexts and goals.

Acknowledgments. This study was supported by the Taiwan National Science and Technology Council (grant number NSTC112-2927-I-002-509; NSTC112-2410-H-002-121-MY3).

Disclosure of Interests. The authors have no competing interests to declare that are relevant to the content of this article.

References

1. Bartneck, C., Belpaeme, T., Eyssel, F., Kanda, T., Keijsers, M., Šabanović, S.: Human-Robot Interaction: An Introduction. Cambridge University Press, Cambridge, U.K. (2020)
2. Leite, I., Pereira, A., Mascarenhas, S., Martinho, C., Prada, R., Paiva, A.: The influence of empathy in human-robot relations. Int. J. Hum. Comput. Stud. **71**, 250–260 (2013)
3. Young, J.E., et al.: Evaluating human-robot interaction. Int. J. Soc. Robot. **3**, 53–67 (2010)
4. Fiske, S.T., Cuddy, A.J.C., Glick, P.: Universal dimensions of social cognition: warmth and competence. Trends Cogn. Sci. **11**, 77–83 (2007)
5. Reeves, B., Hancock, J., Liu, S.X.: Social robots are like real people: first impressions, attributes, and stereotyping of social robots. Technol. Mind Behav. **1**, 1–14 (2020)
6. Fiske, S.T., Neuberg, S.L.: A continuum of impression formation, from category-based to individuating processes: influences of information and motivation on attention and interpretation. Adv. Exp. Soc. Psychol. **23**, 1–74 (1990)
7. Carpinella, C.M., Wyman, A.B., Perez, M.A., Stroessner, S.J.: The robotic social attributes scale (RoSAS) development and validation. In: Proceedings of the 2017 ACM/IEEE International Conference on Human-Robot Interaction, pp. 254–262, ACM (2017)
8. Cuddy, A.J., Fiske, S.T., Glick, P.: When professionals become mothers, warmth doesn't cut the ice. J. Soc. Issues. **60**, 701–718 (2004)
9. Cuddy, A.J., Fiske, S.T., Glick, P.: The BIAS map: behaviors from intergroup affect and stereotypes. J. Pers. Soc. Psychol. **92**, 631–648 (2007)
10. Fiske, S.T.: Stereotype content: warmth and competence endure. Curr. Dir. Psychol. Sci. **27**, 67–73 (2018)
11. Mieczkowski, H., Liu, S.X., Hancock, J., Reeves, B.: Helping not hurting: applying the stereotype content model and bias map to social robotics. In: 2019 14th ACM/IEEE International Conference on Human-Robot Interaction (HRI), pp. 222–229. IEEE, New York, U.S.A. (2019)
12. Liu, X.S., Yi, X.S., Wan, L.C.: Friendly or competent? The effects of perception of robot appearance and service context on usage intention. Ann. Tour. Res. **92**, 103324 (2022)
13. Dervin, B.: Given a context by any other name: methodological tools for taming the unruly beast. Inf. Seek. Context. **13**, 38 (1997)
14. Castellano, G., Leite, I., Pereira, A., Martinho, C., Paiva, A., McOwan, P.W.: Detecting engagement in HRI: an exploration of social and task-based context. In: 2012 International Conference on Privacy, Security, Risk and Trust and 2012 International Conference on Social Computing, pp. 421–428. IEEE, New York, U.S.A. (2012)
15. Gilmartin, E., Saam, C., Vogel, C., Campbell, N., Wade, V.: Just talking-modelling casual conversation. In: Proceedings of the 19th Annual SIGdial Meeting on Discourse and Dialogue, pp. 51–59. Association for Computational Linguistics, Melbourne, Australia (2018)

16. Yokozuka, T., Miyamoto, H., Kasai, M., Miyake, Y., Nozawa, T.: The relationship between turn-taking, vocal pitch synchrony, and rapport in creative problem-solving communication. Speech Comm. **129**, 33–40 (2021)
17. Asch, S.E.: Forming impressions of personality. J. Abnorm. Soc. Psychol. **41**, 258–290 (1946)
18. Fiske, S.T.: Attention and weight in person perception: the impact of negative and extreme behavior. J. Pers. Soc. Psychol. **38**, 889–906 (1980)
19. Rosenberg, S., Nelson, C.E., Vivekananthan, P.S.: A multidimensional approach to the structure of personality impressions. J. Pers. Soc. Psychol. **9**, 283–294 (1968)
20. Kelley, H.H.: The warm-cold variable in first impressions of persons. J. Pers. **18**, 431–439 (1950)
21. Bales, R.F.: A set of categories for the analysis of small group interaction. Am. Sociol. Rev. **15**, 257 (1950)
22. Wojciszke, B.: Multiple meanings of behavior: construing actions in terms of competence or morality. J. Pers. Soc. Psychol. **67**, 222–232 (1994)
23. Fiske, S.T., Cuddy, A.J.C., Glick, P., Xu, J.: A model of (often mixed) stereotype content: competence and warmth respectively follow from perceived status and competition. J. Pers. Soc. Psychol. **82**, 878–902 (2002)
24. Cuddy, A.J., Glick, P., Beninger, A.: The dynamics of warmth and competence judgments, and their outcomes in organizations. Res. Organ. Behav. **31**, 73–98 (2011)
25. Kim, S.Y., Schmitt, B.H., Thalmann, N.M.: Eliza in the uncanny valley: anthropomorphizing consumer robots increases their perceived warmth but decreases liking. Mark. Lett. **30**, 1–12 (2019)
26. Scheunemann, M.M., Cuijpers, R.H., Salge, C.: Warmth and competence to predict human preference of robot behavior in physical human-robot interaction. In: 2020 29th IEEE International Conference on Robot and Human Interactive Communication (RO-MAN), pp. 1340–1347. IEEE, New York, U.S.A. (2020)
27. Bergmann, K., Eyssel, F.A., Kopp, S.: A Second Chance to Make a First Impression? How Appearance and Nonverbal Behavior Affect Perceived Warmth and Competence of Virtual Agents over Time. Lecture Notes in Computer Science, pp. 126–138, Springer, Berlin, Heidelberg (2012)
28. Chattaraman, V., Kwon, W., Gilbert, J.E., Ross, K.: Should AI-Based, conversational digital assistants employ social- or task-oriented interaction style? A task-competency and reciprocity perspective for older adults. Comput. Hum. Behav. **90**, 315–330 (2019)
29. Roy, R., Naidoo, V.: Enhancing chatbot effectiveness: the role of anthropomorphic conversational styles and time orientation. J. Bus. Res. **126**, 23–34 (2021)
30. Harley, D., Fitzpatrick, G.: Creating a conversational context through video blogging: a case study of Geriatric 1927. Comput. Hum. Behav. **25**, 679–689 (2009)
31. Woods, S., Walters, M., Koay, K.L., Dautenhahn, K.: Comparing human robot interaction scenarios using live and video based methods: towards a novel methodological approach. In: 9th IEEE International Workshop on Advanced Motion Control, 2006, pp. 750–755. IEEE, New York, U.S.A. (2006)
32. Fiske, S.T., Juan, X., Cuddy, A.C., Glick, P.: (Dis)respecting versus (dis)liking: status and interdependence predict ambivalent stereotypes of competence and warmth. J. Soc. Issues. **55**, 473–489 (1999)
33. Ko, S.J., Judd, C.H., Stapel, D.A.: Stereotyping based on voice in the presence of individuating information: vocal femininity affects perceived competence but not warmth. Pers. Soc. Psychol. Bull. **35**, 198–211 (2009)
34. Judd, C.H., James-Hawkins, L., Yzerbyt, V., Kashima, Y.: Fundamental dimensions of social judgment: understanding the relations between judgments of competence and warmth. J. Pers. Soc. Psychol. **89**, 899–913 (2005)

Cross-Cultural and Creative Design Futures

End-Side AI Application Maturity Index System Construction and Measurement Analysis

Xuefang Chai[✉], Qi Peng, Jingdong Liu, and Qiaohui Jiang

Research Institute of China Telecom Corporation Ltd., Guangzhou 510630, China
chaixf@chinatelecom.cn

Abstract. With the generative AI big model gradually moving from the technology base to product application, AI big model capability has been successively integrated into all kinds of major terminals, and the end-side AI application has become a hot spot of attention in the industry. This paper focuses on the actual application of 5 types of end-side AI on the user side, draws on the existing maturity assessment models of various types, and constructs the end-side AI application maturity evaluation index system from the industry, market, and brand dimensions, and implements the evaluation based on the index system and carries out evaluation and analysis. Ultimately, we put forward suggestions for advancing the rapid development of end-side AI applications from four aspects: market cultivation, scenario integration, focus on personalization, and cultivation of explosive applications.

Keywords: end-side AI · AI applications · application maturity · metrics system

1 Introduction

At the end of 2022, ChatGPT products set off a wave of generative AI industry driven by the technology of big models, and pre-trained big models became the focus of AI industry development again. In 2023, the "big model fever" intensified. Various types of domestic large model companies, including Internet vendors, startups, universities, have deeply cultivated the iterative technology base and modeling capabilities, laying a good foundation for the large-scale outbreak of large model applications. In 2024, the big model from the technology base to the product ecology, the big model capabilities one after another from the cloud to the edge and the terminal side of the transfer, the end-side devices gradually become the core entrance of the big model application interaction, but also various vendors to obtain the market resources, the user and the product ecosystem of the key carrier. As a result, cell phones, computers, smart homes, wearable, automotive and other categories of terminals ushered in product changes in the era of the big model, end-side AI applications into the era of commercialization, each terminal category manufacturers have launched terminal products with AI functions, in order to reverse the downward trend of terminal product sales since the epidemic through the support of AI and layout of the terminal competition in the era of the big model.

P.-L.P. Rau and H. Krömker (Eds.): HCII 2025, LNCS 16336, pp. 99–117, 2026.
https://doi.org/10.1007/978-3-032-12798-3_7

This paper expects to analyze the AI functions provided by major terminal categories with AI functions in the current market, as well as users' cognition, usage, and evaluation by establishing a relatively complete, objective, scientific, and operable evaluation system. Thereby, providing a referenceable direction for experience improvement and development of end-side AI applications across categories.

2 Scope Definition and Theoretical Foundations

2.1 Scope Definition

2.1.1 Scoping of the "End-Side"

End-side refers to the terminal side. This paper focuses on AI functions or applications that can be realized on the endpoints, without making a strict distinction between whether they are realized through cloud-side or end-side capabilities. The scope of terminals evaluated by the index system focuses on five categories of terminal products, namely, cell phones, computers, smart home devices, wearable devices, and automobiles, which are equipped with AI functions.

2.1.2 Conceptualization of Five Categories of End-Side AI Applications

The above five types of terminals with AI functions have relatively consistent calls in the industry, namely: AI phone, AI PC, AI home device, AI wearable device and smart car.

AI Phone. It refers to smartphones that integrate artificial intelligence technology. Compared with traditional smartphones, AI phones have more powerful intelligent processing capabilities in addition to basic functions such as communication and multimedia, and are able to realize intelligent features such as environment perception and learning, voice assistant, image recognition and processing through AI hardware modules.

AI PC. is a personal computer configured with an AI chip that can run large models locally and has a good energy balance, which has rudimentary AI capabilities? In terms of product form, the research scope of this paper is limited to desktop and laptop computers.

AI Home Device. Applying artificial intelligence technology to the home field, it organically combines various application subsystems related to family life by integrating advanced computer, network communication, automatic control and other technologies. Through integrated management, it makes home life more comfortable, safe, effective and energy efficient. Compared with the traditional smart home single product and Internet smart home, AI home can realize complex semantic understanding, fuzzy command recognition and active decision-making, and has the ability of automatic identification, self-learning, and autonomous decision-making to provide more intelligent services for the family.

AI Wearable Device. It refers to a portable smart device that can be worn on the body or integrated into the user's clothing or accessories. Its applications include smart watches, smart earrings, smart headphones, smart necklaces, smart glasses, fitness trackers and wearable medical devices. AI wearable devices realize user information interaction, human health monitoring, health relaxation and life entertainment functions through built-in sensors, wireless communication, integrated chips, multimedia technology, etc., and are able to learn from user behaviors and make corresponding adjustments, with five basic features: wearability, mobility, sustainability, interactivity, and simplicity of operation.

Smart Car. Composed of single-vehicle intelligence and vehicle networking, it refers to the fusion of new technologies such as information communication, Internet of Things, big data, cloud computing and artificial intelligence by carrying advanced sensors, controllers, actuators and other devices, realizing the intelligent information exchange and sharing of the in-vehicle network, out-of-vehicle network and inter-vehicle network, and possessing the function of collaborative control of information-sharing and complex environment sensing intelligent decision-making automation. Currently, the "smart ca" is composed of three main elements, namely, smart interaction, smart driving and smart services. 1) Intelligent driving refers to vehicle control and driving functions, including assisted driving, intelligent safety, intelligent vehicle control, intelligent maps, etc. 2) Intelligent interaction refers to demand input or active recognition, including voice interaction, gesture/facial recognition and biometric monitoring. 3) Intelligent services refer to services related to people and life, including aftermarket services, travel services, social and life services.

2.1.3 Scoping the Study of End-Side AI Function

The five types of end-side AI functions applied by the AI application maturity evaluation index system in this paper are all based on the AI functions available in the listed terminals, while the AI functions in the laboratory stage and pilot stage are not included in the research scope.

The research perspective of this paper is the user and the market, focusing on analyzing and evaluating the cognitive and experiential status of the five types of end-side AI functions from the perspective of user perception, and the evaluation system does not involve the industry's value chain, the enterprise organization itself, and its production and manufacturing technologies and processes, but focuses mainly on its external market performance.

2.2 Theoretical Foundations

The research in this paper draws on the main theories and models related to maturity at home and abroad, and applies the user behavior theory and brand loyalty theory in the design process of the index system, and the Kano model used for the analysis of the importance of the product in the research and analysis process.

2.2.1 An Overall Overview of Maturity Theory and Modeling

The current maturity models in the industry are divided into five categories: industry maturity models, manufacturing maturity models, enterprise maturity models, software capability maturity models, and product maturity models.

Industry Maturity Models. Typical of this is the Industry 4.0 Readiness Scale proposed by the Verband Deutscher Maschinen und Anlagenbau (VDMA) in October 2015, which analyzed the questionnaire and distilled a readiness scale model with six levels, six dimensions, and 18 domains. the six levels are The six levels are: Unplanned, Initial, Intermediate, Skilled, Expert, and Top Demonstration; and the six dimensions are: Strategy and Organization, Smart Factory, Efficient Operations, Smart Products, Data-Driven Services, and Employees.

Manufacturing Maturity Model. Originated from the Smart Manufacturing System Readiness Level (SMSRL) of the National Institute of Standards NIST. Derived from two models in China: one is the Capability Maturity Model launched by the Electronic Standards Research Institute, which takes the smart manufacturing system architecture in the "National Smart Manufacturing Standard System Construction Guidelines (2015 Edition)" as a reference model and proposes three dimensions of life cycle, system hierarchy, and smart functions; and refines and summarizes the core features and elements of smart manufacturing, which are summarized as The core features and elements of intelligent manufacturing are refined and summarized into two dimensions of "intelligence + manufacturing", and finally presented in a one-dimensional form, from design, production, all the way to 10 categories of core capabilities, such as resource elements and emerging industries, as well as 27 domains of refinement. Another is the intelligent manufacturing evaluation model "Reference Framework for Enterprise Intelligent Manufacturing Core Competency Measurement" launched by the China Software Evaluation Center, which, from the perspectives of product competitiveness and supply chain competitiveness, deconstructs a manufacturing enterprise into three basic dimensions: enterprise organization, supply chain, and product, of which, for the industry dominated by the 2C mode, it needs to be oriented by the user's experience of use.

Software Capability Maturity Models (SW-CMM). Released in 1987 by the Software Engineering Institute at Carnegie Mellon University, the SW-CMM is a process improvement maturity model for developing software products, covering the entire life cycle of a product from conception to delivery. The SW-CMM proposes 18 process domains that require attention and continuous improvement in the software development process, based on the maturity of an organization's software development capabilities, which are divided into five levels, namely, Initial, Managed, Defined, Quantitative and Continuous Optimization. The SW-CMM proposes 18 process domains in the software development process that need to be focused on and continuously improved; according to the maturity of the organization's software development capability, it is divided into five levels, which are Initial, Managed, Defined, Quantitatively Managed, and Continuously Optimized.

Industrial Internet Application Maturity Assessment Model. Jointly released by the Industrial Internet Industry Alliance (AII), Huawei, PTC and IDC in 2019. Establishes five assessment modules for industrial Internet-driven basic support upgrading, strategic organizational reshaping, product and service innovation, production and operation optimization, and business model change, and further subdivided into 22 core assessment elements.

Product Maturity Assessment-Product Readiness Index (PRI). is an assessment system constructed from five dimensions: capital support, measured by the scale of investment and financing, and the attention of the capital market, etc.; market applicability, the estimation of the subsequent market volume of the product, mainly measured by the number of users, applicable fields, and the evaluation of the audience, etc.; technological maturity, measured by the application of high-end technology, etc. Product completeness is mainly measured by the degree of completeness of the product's construction in a certain field; media expectations are mainly measured by the number of online media reports, search indexes, etc.

This paper draws on the design ideas of different types of maturity models, while focusing on the three dimensions of industry, market (user) and brand. Modeling specifics will be developed in detail in the research design section.

2.2.2 Kano Model

The Kano model is a tool for categorizing and prioritizing user needs and reflects the nonlinear relationship between individual product attributes and user satisfaction.

The KANO model defines five types of requirements: five types of required attribute requirements (M), expected attribute requirements (O), attractive attribute requirements (A), undifferentiated attribute requirements (I), and reverse attribute requirements (R). Research is conducted through standardized questionnaires, and attribute categorization of different product functions is performed according to the research results to solve the positioning problem of product functions in order to improve customer satisfaction. The relationship between different attribute needs and user satisfaction is shown in Fig. 1.

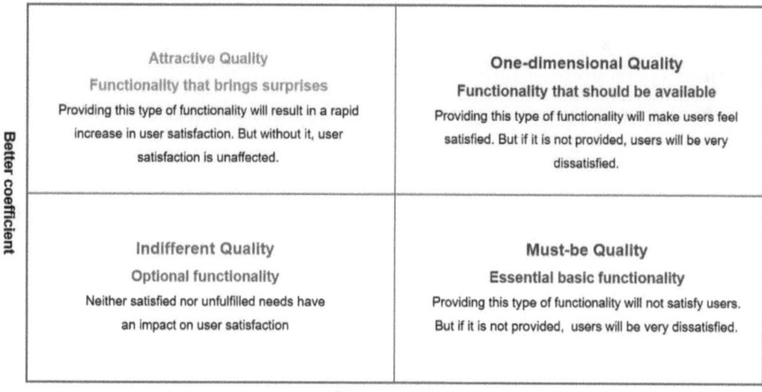

Fig. 1. Kano Model Product Attribute Categorization Quadrant.

In this paper, the experience satisfaction of Kano product attributes and AI functions are combined and analyzed, and through the comparison of the experience satisfaction of AI functions with different attributes, it provides a reference for the enhancement direction of end-side AI applications.

3 Research Design

3.1 Indicator System Construction

This paper constructs an end-side AI application maturity model (IMB) that includes three dimensions: industry maturity, market recognition, and brand influence. The three dimensions are progressive and comprehensively consider the main aspects that can comprehensively assess the maturity of end-side AI applications.

Industry Maturity. The external market performance and internal innovation ability of the industry development are both emphasized. It mainly measures the number of vendors that have launched terminals integrating AI technology in a certain category of terminals, market penetration rate, market growth rate and innovation ability, in order to objectively react to the current situation of the development of AI technology in this category of terminals and the potential space.

Market Recognition. Using the theory of user behavior, we set up indicators through the four stages of users' interaction with the product, and evaluate users' attitudes towards AI functions in a certain type of terminal in the whole process. User behavior theory believes that the user's behavior towards a certain product generally goes through 5 stages: cognition, familiarity, trial, use, and loyalty. In this paper, we simplify it into four stages: cognition, use, evaluation and loyalty, which correspond to four indicators: market awareness, function use, experience satisfaction and function recommendation.

Brand Influence. Focuses on the role of mainstream brands in the industry in cultivating and pulling the market. Drawing on the theory of brand loyalty, it is subdivided into two indicators, namely, brand recognition and brand recommendation, in order to assess users' recognition and willingness to recommend brands related to AI terminals (Table 1).

Based on the evaluation results of the above index system, the maturity of end-side AI applications is categorized into five levels, L1-L5.

Cultivation period (L1, below 5 points): The market is still in the primary exploration stage, with fewer participating vendors, innovation capability to be improved, relevant AI functions and brands are in the early stage of promotion, and the overall penetration rate is not high.

Growth period (L2, 5–6 points): The market size and market penetration rate are steadily increasing, and with the increase in the number of participating vendors and the enhancement of innovation capability, relevant AI functions and brands are beginning to be promoted and applied on a large scale, and the user's experience is also improving.

Explosion period (L3, 6–7 points): the market size and market penetration rate are growing at a high speed, the number of participating vendors and technical innovation capability are showing explosive growth, and the related AI functions and brands are also rapidly popularizing, which may bring disruptive use experience to users.

Maturity period (L4, 7–8 points): the industry has a high degree of maturity, is in a stable and saturated stage, the relevant AI functions are rich and diverse and can fully meet the needs of users, bring users a good experience, the brand has a good degree of awareness and wide dissemination.

Table 1. Components of the end-side AI application maturity metrics system and the meaning of the metrics.

Tier 1 indicators	Tier 2 indicators	Indicator Meaning
Industry maturity (I)	Number of vendors	Number of terminal vendors in the category that have launched terminals incorporating AI technology.
	Market penetration rate	Proportion of AI terminals in this category in the total number of terminals in the category.
	Market growth rate	Compound annual growth rate of AI terminals in this category in the next five years.
	Innovation ability	Scoring by industry experts to assess the ability of functional application innovation brought about by the fusion of the category's terminals with AI technology.
Market recognition (M)	Functional Recognition	Consumers' awareness of the AI functions of each category of terminals.
	Function utilization	Users who have already used the AI terminals in the category, and their use of the AI functions of the AI terminals in the category.
	Experience satisfaction	The degree of satisfaction of users who have already used the AI terminals in this category with the AI functions of the AI terminals in this category.
	Function Recommendation	The willingness of users who have used this type of AI terminal to recommend the AI functions of this type of AI terminal to others.
Brand influence (B)	Brand Recognition	Consumers' awareness of common brands of various types of AI terminals
	Brand Recommendation	The willingness of users who have purchased a certain brand of AI terminal to recommend that brand to others

Recession period (L5, below 5 points): the industry begins to decline, vendors gradually withdraw, technological innovation stagnates, and the degree of use and usage experience of users of relevant AI features and brands declines significantly.

3.2 Research Methodology and Data Sources

This study mainly applies three major research methods: desk research, expert rating, and consumer survey:

1. Objective data such as the number of vendors, market penetration rate, market growth rate, etc. in the industry are collected through desk research, and the data sources are mainly research reports from authoritative organizations such as IDC and Canalys.
2. Fifteen industry experts from terminal vendors, consulting organizations, and research institutes are invited to score some of the indicator data and indicator weight allocation through the Delphi method. The expert scoring is mainly divided into two parts, one is to evaluate the indicator data of "innovation ability" of each end-side AI application, and the other is to score the weight allocation of all primary and secondary indicators, so as to determine the weight of the indicator system.
3. Online consumer research was conducted in May 2024, using qualitative interviews and quantitative questionnaires to invite consumers to evaluate the real experience and needs of various end-side AI applications. The consumer research is mainly divided into three parts: first, the evaluation of the market recognition of each end-side AI function, including the evaluation of the recognition, use, satisfaction and recommendation of the function; second, the evaluation of the brand influence of each brand of AI terminals, including the brand's recognition and recommendation; and third, the information related to the demographic characteristics, which mainly contains the age, gender, city, income level, and household structure, etc. . The research collected a total of 10 qualitative samples and 1,818 quantitative samples, with the sample range covering the whole country, and the distribution is in line with the demographic characteristics and is representative (Tables 2 and 3).

Table 2. End-side AI application maturity metrics system weights.

Tier 1 indicator	Tier 1 indicator weights	Tier 2 indicator	Tier 2 indicator weights
Industry maturity (I)	30%	Number of vendors	28.8%
		Market penetration rate	25.3%
		Market growth rate	24.5%
		Innovation ability	21.4%
Market recognition (M)	40%	Functional Recognition	36.3%
		Function utilization	24.0%

(continued)

Table 2. (*continued*)

Tier 1 indicator	Tier 1 indicator weights	Tier 2 indicator	Tier 2 indicator weights
		Experience satisfaction	21.7%
		Function Recommendation	18.0%
Brand influence (B)	30%	Brand Recognition	50.0%
		Brand Recommendation	50.0%

Table 3. Consumer Research Sample.

	Quantitative questionnaire sample size	Qualitative interviews sample size
AI phone	316	2
AI PC	309	2
AI home device	394	2
AI wearable device	394	2
Smart car	405	2
Total	1818	10

4 Results Analysis

This paper applies the above index system to the evaluation of AI application maturity of five types of terminals, namely, AI phone, AI PC, AI home device, AI wearable device, and smart car, and conducts comparative analysis.

4.1 Overall Evaluation of End-Side AI Application Maturity

Comprehensively evaluating the three dimensions of industry maturity, market recognition, and brand influence, the maturity of five categories of end-side AI applications are, in descending order: AI phone (6.65), smart car (6.55), AI PC (6.53), AI wearable device (6.06), and AI home device (6.03) (Table 4).

At this stage, the number of vendors and their brand influence are the two factors that most affect the maturity of end-side AI applications, and they will ultimately affect the market's perception and use of end-side AI, which are indicators that play a key role (Table 5).

Table 4. Overall Comparison of the Maturity of AI Applications on the End Side of the Five Categories.

	AI phone	AI PC	AI home device	AI wearable device	Smart car
Industry maturity (I)	8.65	6.54	4.70	4.30	6.62
Market recognition (M)	6.49	6.59	6.67	7.61	6.69
Brand influence (B)	6.28	7.28	4.84	4.26	7.21
Total	**7.07**	**6.78**	**5.53**	**5.61**	**6.82**

4.2　End Side AI Industry Maturity Comparison and Influential Factors Analysis

The performance of different types of end-side AI in terms of industry maturity and its four secondary metrics varies significantly. The AI phone has the highest level of maturity, followed by AI PC and smart car, while the AI home and AI wearable have relatively weaker levels of maturity (Table 6).

4.2.1　Indicator Scoring Methodology

Number of vendors: It is mainly based on whether domestic mainstream vendors have launched AI terminals of the category, and whether dominant vendors with favorable market share have emerged for AI terminals of the category. Recognized mainstream vendors that have launched AI terminals are assigned 8 points or more, and the rest are assigned according to the proportion of vendors that have launched AI terminals of a certain category.

Market penetration rate: The value is assigned according to the penetration rate in the domestic market: below 5% is assigned 0–2.5 points, 6%–20% is assigned 2.6–5 points, 21%–50% is assigned 5.1–7.5 points, and above 50% is assigned 7.6–10 points.

Market Growth Rate: Segmented and assigned according to the compound annual growth rate (CAGR) forecast of the domestic market for the next 5 years. CAGR below 5% is assigned 0–2.5 points, 6%–20% is assigned 2.6–5 points, 21%–50% is assigned 5.1–7.5 points, and above 50% is assigned 7.6–10 points.

Innovative capacity: Using industry expert scoring method.

4.2.2　Indicator Scoring Basis

AI Phone. Mainstream cell phone manufacturers have launched AI cell phones embedded with large models or AI chips, such as Huawei, Apple, Honor, Xiaomi, OPPO, VIVO, etc., and some other niche cell phone manufacturers, such as Yiga, Nubia, Realme, etc. have also launched AI cell phones one after another in hopes of occupying a place in the wave of the new wave of cell phone revolution. As a result, AI phones scored the highest in the "number of vendors" indicator. From the point of view of market size and growth rate, according to Canalys statistics, AI cell phone shipments of 11.9 million units in mainland China in 2024Q1, and the annual shipments will be close to 50 million units;

Table 5. Five categories of end-side AI application maturity levels.

	AI application maturity levels	Instruction
AI phone	L3+, Explosion period	The industry has a high degree of maturity, a large market size and high growth rate, and a high market penetration rate. There are more niche brands and the overall brand influence is relatively weak, which affects the market recognition.
AI PC	L3-, Explosion period	The industry maturity is a little lower, but mainstream manufacturers have participated in the industry and have a strong innovation ability. AI functions are widely used in the market, and the market recognition and brand influence indicators are strong.
AI home device	L2, Growth period	Influenced by the dual impact of low industry maturity and weak brand influence; fewer participating vendors and lack of leading vendors, and innovation ability needs to be improved.
AI wearable device	L2, Growth period	Influenced by the dual impact of low industry maturity and weak brand influence; fewer participating vendors and lack of leading vendors, and innovation ability needs to be improved.
Smart car	L3-, Explosion period	Industry maturity is high, the number of participating vendors is increasing, innovation ability is strong, and the application of AI functions on the ground is more optimistic.

Table 6. Comparison of industry maturity of end-side AI applications.

	AI phone	AI PC	AI home device	AI wearable device	Smart car
Number of vendors	8.50	8.00	5.60	5.00	6.00
Market penetration rate	6.00	5.20	7.60	7.80	6.50
Market growth rate	7.00	5.50	3.80	3.90	7.00
Innovation ability	6.90	6.30	5.20	4.90	6.00
Industry maturity	**7.07**	**6.54**	**4.70**	**4.30**	**6.62**

from 2023 to 2028, the compound annual growth rate (CAGR) of China's AI cell phone market will reach 56.67%, and the penetration rate of AI cell phones will exceed 50%.

AI PC. 2024 is the first year of AI PC, at present, domestic mainstream computer manufacturers including Huawei, Lenovo, Honor, Asus, Acer, etc. have launched AI PC. the industry believes that the penetration iteration of AI PC in the Chinese market is expected to be completed in about two years. According to IDC forecast, AI PC (excluding AI tablets) shipments in the Chinese market will reach 21 million units in 2024, and the penetration rate is expected to reach 55% in 2024 from 8% in 2023. However, IDC forecasts a CAGR of 26% for AI PCs from 2024 to 2027, thus experts take a reserved view of the market penetration forecast for 2024, scoring it slightly lower.

AI Home Device. A number of vendors in the industry have already launched smart home devices that incorporate AI, including TVs, refrigerators, washing machines, camera surveillance, and smart home control. However, from the perspective of the overall development of the industry, the problems of fewer entry vendors, especially those with high brand awareness, fewer products, and the lack of a close combination of AI and home scenarios are more prominent, resulting in a lower growth rate of its market. In addition, the home involves many terminal categories, and the development is not ideal, and there is a lack of authoritative statistics in the industry. Combining the above, the overall maturity of the industry of AI home is low.

AI Wearable Device. Although domestic and foreign technology companies have explored a variety of forms of terminals, such as AI headphones, AI necklaces, AI rings, AI glasses, etc., and even launched AI Pin, Rabbit R1 and other "native AI devices", but its market response is dismal. And from a global perspective, the market shipments and growth of the lack of authoritative statistics, the existing data is still stuck in the traditional "smart wearable device" category. Therefore, the industry maturity of AI wearable is low.

Smart Car. At present, domestic mainstream automobile manufacturers have developed and listed smart cars, especially the new forces represented by Ideal, Future, Xiaopeng, etc. However, there are still many automobile manufacturers have not launched smart cars with AI functions. According to Guotai Junan forecast, the domestic smart car sales scale is expected to be 18.53 million units in 2024, with a CAGR of 51.1% from 2024–2028.

4.3 End Side AI Market Recognition Comparison and Influential Factors Analysis

The performance of different types of AI terminals on the four secondary indicators of market recognition has a common feature: the degree of functional awareness is relatively low, and none of them exceeds 5 points except for AI wearable. In terms of the degree of function usage, the users who know about the AI function have a high degree of usage, and the users who have already used it show a high degree of satisfaction and recommendation for the AI function. It shows that real users basically hold a positive attitude towards the AI functions that AI terminals have, and that functional awareness is a key factor in improving the overall market recognition of end-side AI at this stage. Various industries also need to continuously cultivate the market to further improve the market's recognition of AI terminals and their AI functions, so as to expand the market scale (Table 7).

Table 7. Comparison of market recognition of end-side AI applications.

	AI phone	AI PC	AI home device	AI wearable device	Smart car
Functional Recognition	4.69	4.47	5.00	5.88	3.93
Function utilization	7.06	7.19	7.85	7.83	8.28
Experience satisfaction	8.44	8.54	7.76	7.93	8.53
Function Recommendation	8.04	8.41	7.58	7.76	8.33
Market recognition	**6.49**	**6.59**	**6.67**	**7.61**	**6.69**

4.3.1 Indicator Scoring Methodology

Functional Recognition, Experience Satisfaction, Functional Recommendation. These three indicators take the same scoring method: based on the awareness/satisfaction/recommendation of each specific AI function, the functional awareness/satisfaction/recommendation of the AI function of the terminal in this category is calculated by arithmetic average method.

Function Utilization Degree. Based on the usage of each AI function of the terminals in this category, the usage degree of each AI function in this category is calculated using the "user's usage frequency of each AI function" as the weight; then the overall AI function usage degree of this category is calculated using the arithmetic average method. Empowerment of "Users' Frequency of Use of Detailed AI Functions": Users' frequency of use of detailed AI functions is categorized into 4 grades and empowered respectively: used every day (empowered by 1), used weekly (empowered by 0.75), used 1–2 times per month (empowered by 0.5), and used only once very recently (empowered by 0.25).

4.3.2 Evaluation and Analysis of Functional Perception

Users' awareness of end-side AI is low, and the overall degree of understanding is shallow.

First of all, from the user's overall understanding of the market of various types of AI terminals, the user's understanding of various types of end-side AI is not deep, and nearly half of the users only sporadically understand some information. As commonly used terminals, cell phones and PCs have a relatively deep understanding; the proportion of users who have "never heard of" AI home, AI wearable and smart car is about twice as high as that of AI phones and AI PCs; and the proportion of users who have "a better understanding of and specifically inquired about" is also higher than that of AI phones and AI PCs. The proportion of users who "know more about and have specifically inquired about"is also significantly higher for AI phones and AI PCs, indicating that users are relatively more concerned about the AI applications of cell phones and PCs, which are two types of daily-use terminals (Table 8).

Table 8. Comparison of overall understanding of AI end-side applications.

	AI phone	AI PC	AI home device	AI wearable device	Smart car
Never heard of it.	1.9%	1.3%	3.3%	2.8%	3.2%
I've heard of it but don't know exactly what it accomplishes.	31.3%	20.1%	30.5%	34.5%	29.9%
Know a little, occasionally read related articles or news.	42.4%	49.5%	47.0%	46.2%	48.2%
Know more about it, and have specifically inquired about the relevant introductions.	24.4%	29.1%	19.3%	16.5%	18.8%

Second, AI functions that are close to users' lives and have a high potential usage rate are widely recognized, such as the photo/picture beautification function of AI cell phones, the text-based function of cell phones and PCs, the portrait recognition function of AI homes, the voice interaction function of AI wearables, and the in-vehicle comfort adjustment function of smart cars. The new AI functions provided after the AI capabilities are integrated into the end-side have relatively low recognition, such as the real-time translation function for calls on AI cell phones, the system auto-tuning function for AI PCs, the AI mural function for AI homes, the intelligent assistant function for AI wearables, and the cockpit entertainment function for smart cars (Table 9).

4.3.3 Evaluation and Analysis of Functional Utilization

The usage degree of end-side AI functions depends on the degree of user reliance on them. The AI functions on the cell phone and PC side are not just needed by users, and they are only used in specific scenarios, thus the degree of use of AI functions is relatively low. As for the AI functions of smart cars, users' car habits will make them rely on certain functions to a certain extent, such as the Bluetooth door opening function, the distance and driver status monitoring function, the voice Q&A function, the intelligent parking function, and the in-vehicle comfort adjustment function, etc., with a utilization rate of around 90% and above. And from the analysis of the characteristics of the AI function with high usage, the AI upgrade of the original function and the enhancement of the efficiency of these two types of AI functions have relatively high usage (Table 10).

Table 9. Top 3 and Least Recognized AI Functions in terms of Functional Recognition.

	AI phone	AI PC	AI home device	AI wearable device	Smart car
Top 3 Recognized AI Functions	Photo/image beautification (62.6%)	Text-based AI functions (67.1%)	Portrait recognition (65.1%)	Voice interaction (68.4%)	In-vehicle comfort adjustment (62.0%)
	Copy generation (61.6%)	Image-based AI functions (59.7%)	Whole-house AI IoT (63.3%)	AI meeting assistant (67.6%)	Intelligent assisted driving (48.0%)
	Notes assistant (60.7%)	AI mini assistant voice Q&A (54.7%)	Sound quality optimization (60.6%)	AI Translation (60.1%)	Voice Q&A with Smart Recommendations (48.0%)
Least Recognized AI Functions	Text summary (39.7%)	Video call audio and video noise reduction (35.8%)	Automatic optimization settings for games (42.8%)	Image Recognition (51.2%)	Cockpit entertainment features (28%)
	Create hybrid images (38.1%)	Intelligent conference class (35.0%)	AI mural (35.4%)	AI intelligent assistant (47.3%)	Bluetooth automatic door opening feature (28%)

Table 10. Top 3 AI functions in terms of functional utilization

	AI phone	AI PC	AI home device	AI wearable device	Smart car
Top 3 AI functions in terms of functional utilization	AI phone answering (80.8%)	Text-based AI features (73.7%)	Picture quality optimization (59.5%)	Behavior monitoring and alerts (69.3%)	Distance and driver status monitoring (100%)
	Finding files (76.7%)	Video call audio and video noise reduction (73%)	Voice Interaction (59.1%)	Data monitoring and suggestion (64.3%)	Bluetooth door opening (92.5%)
	AI voice assistant conversation (75%)	Speech to text (72.6%)	Whole-house AI IoT (57.7%)	AI meeting assistant (62.9%)	Voice Q&A and Smart Recommendations (91.3%)

4.3.4   Evaluation and Analysis of Experience Satisfaction

In addition to evaluating the overall experience satisfaction of AI functions of each terminal category, this paper also combines the Kano model to analyze the experience satisfaction of AI functions with different attributes, in order to provide the industry with a direction for optimizing AI functions in the future. The analysis found that: 1) the AI functions of cell phones and PCs do not fit well with user needs. As intelligent terminals with strong personal attributes, AI cell phones and AI PCs have fewer AI functions with essential attributes and some redundant AI functions ("undifferentiated attribute" functions), and users' demand for these functions is not obvious at present; in addition, the experience satisfaction of the "undifferentiated attribute" AI functions of the two types of terminals is not enough to meet users' needs; the experience satisfaction of the "undifferentiated attribute" AI functions of the two types of terminals is not enough to meet users' needs. In addition, the experience satisfaction of these two types of terminals' "undifferentiated attribute" AI functions is higher than that of the "essential attribute" and "desired attribute" AI functions. 2) AI home and AI wearable basically have no redundant functions, but the satisfaction is relatively low, with an average experience satisfaction of 7.76, 7.7, 7.7, and 7.8 respectively. (2) AI Home and AI Wearable are basically free of redundant functions, but their satisfaction is relatively low, with an average experience satisfaction of 7.76 and 7.93 respectively, which is lower than that of the remaining three categories. (3) Intelligent automobiles lack AI functions with "charismatic attributes", i.e., there is a lack of breakout functions that can excite users, and the scenario value of AI functions needs to be explored (Fig. 2).

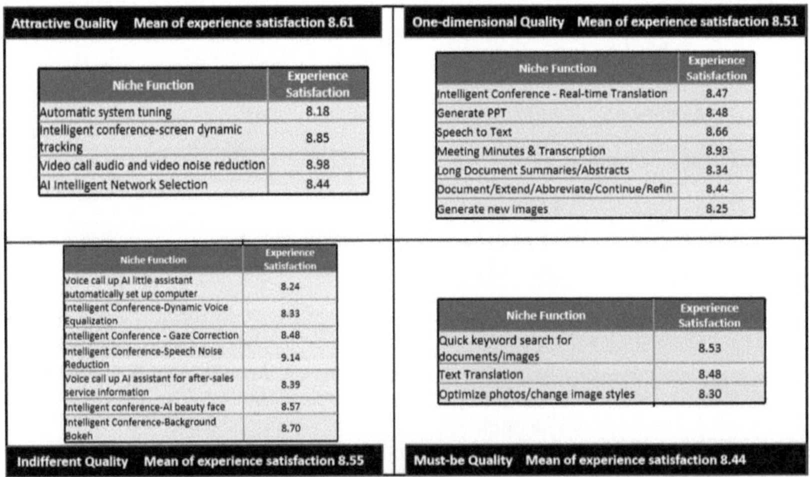

Attractive Quality   Mean of experience satisfaction 8.61

Niche Function	Experience Satisfaction
Automatic system tuning	8.18
Intelligent conference-screen dynamic tracking	8.85
Video call audio and video noise reduction	8.98
AI Intelligent Network Selection	8.44

One-dimensional Quality   Mean of experience satisfaction 8.51

Niche Function	Experience Satisfaction
Intelligent Conference - Real-time Translation	8.47
Generate PPT	8.48
Speech to Text	8.66
Meeting Minutes & Transcription	8.93
Long Document Summaries/Abstracts	8.34
Document/Extend/Abbreviate/Continue/Refin	8.44
Generate new images	8.25

Indifferent Quality   Mean of experience satisfaction 8.55

Niche Function	Experience Satisfaction
Voice call up AI little assistant automatically set up computer	8.24
Intelligent Conference-Dynamic Voice Equalization	8.33
Intelligent Conference - Gaze Correction	8.48
Intelligent Conference-Speech Noise Reduction	9.14
Voice call up AI assistant for after-sales service information	8.39
Intelligent conference-AI beauty face	8.57
Intelligent Conference-Background Bokeh	8.70

Must-be Quality   Mean of experience satisfaction 8.44

Niche Function	Experience Satisfaction
Quick keyword search for documents/images	8.53
Text Translation	8.48
Optimize photos/change image styles	8.30

Fig. 2. Satisfaction with AI functions for different attributes of AI PCs.

4.3.5 Evaluation and Analysis of Functional Recommendations

The real users all have a high degree of recommendation for the AI features they use. Functions with distinctive AI features, communication and interaction, and scenario-based features are especially highly recommended, such as the instant circle search function of AI cell phones, the intelligent meeting function of AI PCs, the spatial/gesture control and voice interaction function of AI homes, the AI intelligent assistant function of AI wearable device, and the automatic reversing and voice Q&A/intelligent recommendation function of smart cars. In addition, the highly recommended functions of AI home are security-related, such as "portrait recognition", followed by convenient operation-related functions, such as "touch control and voice interaction" (Table 11).

Table 11. Top 3 AI functions in terms of functional recommendation

	AI phone	AI PC	AI home device	AI wearable device	Smart car
Top 3 AI functions in terms of functional recommendation	Instant Circle Search (8.93)	Intelligent meeting (8.84)	Portrait Recognition (7.91)	AI intelligent assistant (8.23)	Auto Reverse (8.58)
	Video editing (8.72)	Video call audio/video noise reduction (8.67)	Spaced touch/gesture control (7.9)	Data monitoring and recommendation (8.01)	In-vehicle comfort adjustment (8.52)
	Real-time translation for calls (8.72)	Picture-based AI function (8.46)	Voice Interaction (7.76)	Behavior monitoring and reminders (7.86)	Voice Q&A and Intelligent Recommendation (8.5)

4.4 End-Side AI Brand Influence Comparison and Influence Factor Analysis

4.4.1 Indicator Scoring Methodology

Different types all have the contrasting phenomenon of low brand recognition and high recommendation, which limits the overall influence of end-side AI brands. Among them, AI PC and smart car have relatively high brand influence, and AI wearable has the lowest. the brand recommendation of AI cell phone is high, but due to its high number of niche brands, it pulls down the overall brand influence. the brand recognition of AI PC is much higher than other categories, but it has not been transformed into a high degree of recommendation, and it needs to be combined with the demand scenarios to deeply cultivate the user experience (Table 12).

The contrast between brand awareness and brand recommendation is more prominent in the categories of AI phones and AI home devices (Fig. 3).

Table 12. Comparison of brand influence of end-side AI applications.

	AI phone	AI PC	AI home device	AI wearable device	Smart car
Brand Recognition	3.77	5.18	3.26	3.05	4.30
Brand Recommendation	8.42	7.81	7.78	7.52	8.64
Brand influence	**6.28**	**7.28**	**4.84**	**4.26**	**7.21**

AI phone

Brand	Recognition	Recommendation
Huawei	55.5%	8.82
Xiaomi	42.9%	8.38
OPPO	30.3%	8.20
vivo	30.3%	8.19
Apple	27.7%	8.11
Honor	18.4%	8.00
Samsung	17.7%	10.00
One Plus	12.9%	8.67
Meizu	10.7%	10.00
Red Magic	7.4%	8.00
Nubia	7.1%	7.00

AIPC

Brand	Recognition	Recommendation
Huawei	54.4%	7.68
Apple	47.3%	7.66
Lenovo	41.1%	7.61
Dell	35.9%	7.87
HP	28.5%	7.80
Asus	26.9%	7.69
Honor	26.5%	7.99
Acer	16.2%	8.20

Smart car

Brand	Recognition	Recommendation
BYD	76.0%	8.77
Tesla	71.4%	8.25
Xiaomi	55.8%	9.00
NIO	50.9%	9.00
Xiaopeng	45.4%	10.00
Li Auto	44.9%	9.00
Changan	22.0%	8.80
Link	16.3%	7.50
Sallis	10.9%	9.00
Leapmotor	10.9%	8.00
Chery	10.4%	8.00

AI home device

Brand	Recognition	Recommendation
Xiaomi	74.3%	7.79
Huawei	68.0%	8.21
Hisense	30.0%	7.41
Samsung	26.5%	7.97
Alibaba	20.5%	7.17
Changhong	20.2%	7.39
360	20.0%	7.05
TCL	17.9%	7.63
Konka	15.8%	8.00

AI wearable device

Brand	Recognition	Recommendation
Xiaomi	69.5%	7.86
Huawei	67.1%	8.06
iFLYTEK	34.7%	7.62
Samsung	29.8%	7.64
Google	23.5%	6.93
VIVO	22.2%	7.40
OPPO	18.3%	7.30
LAWK	9.4%	7.38

Fig. 3. Comparison of brand recognition of various types of AI terminals.

5   Conclusion

Although there is a certain gap in the application of AI in different terminal categories, the whole is still in the growth stage or even an earlier start. The performance of different categories in the three dimensions of industry maturity, market recognition, and brand influence each has its own characteristics. From the analysis results of the end-side AI application maturity evaluation system, there are several prominent problems: 1) the market recognition of all types of AI terminals is low. 2) the degree of fit between the launched AI functions and user needs is insufficient. 3) the AI home and AI wearable categories lack the lack of explosive functions to ignite the market. 4) the market for AI terminals is still in the growth stage or even early start-up stage.

Users have a high degree of acceptance of terminals with AI functions. In order to promote the end-side AI application towards rapid development, this paper puts forward the following suggestions: 1) pay attention to market cultivation, improve user awareness of end-side AI functions. 2) AI functions do not fit well enough with user demand, and we need to deeply excavate and analyze the potential use scenarios of users' AI functions of terminals of various categories, and tightly combine the functions with the application scenarios, and launch the pop-up AI functions to ignite the market. 3) improve the compatibility and intelligent interconnection of end-side AI functions, and improve the compatibility and intelligent interconnection of end-side AI functions. Function compatibility and intelligent interconnection, improve ecological inclusiveness. Cross-device intelligent interconnection and collaboration is the future trend, requiring terminal category manufacturers to plan ahead to form a strong inclusive ecology to promote industry prosperity.

References

1. Zhang, W.: Smart manufacturing capability maturity assessment trilogy. Knowl. Autom. (2018)
2. Global Intelligent Industry Readiness Index Initiative: 2022 Global Intelligent Industry Insight Report, China Electronic Information Industry Development Research Institute (2015)
3. Industrial Internet Consortium: Industrial Internet Application Maturity Assessment White Paper (2019)
4. Huawei & Tsinghua University: AI Collaborating with People, Serving People – AI Terminal White Paper (2024)
5. Avery Consulting & Mechanical Revolution: China AI PC Industry Research Report (2024)
6. IDC&Lenovo: AI PC Industry (China) White Paper (2024)
7. IDC&OPPO: AI Mobile Phone White Paper (2024)
8. GFK: China Personal Smart Wearables Market Analysis (2023)
9. Facecar: Smart Cockpit Trend Insight Report for Beijing Auto Show (2024)
10. Haitong International: AI-Enabled Industry Opportunities in the Automotive Industry (2024)

Users' Experience and Satisfaction of Intelligent Assistants Based on Sentiment Analysis of Online Reviews

Hanjing Huang(✉) ⓘ and Zhen Zeng ⓘ

School of Economics and Management, Fuzhou University, Fuzhou 350108, China
hhj@fzu.edu.cn

Abstract. Intelligent assistants are becoming increasingly important for controlling devices, providing social companionship, and assisting people with everyday life. Despite their increasing use, the user experience of intelligent assistants still needs to be improved. This research investigates users' experience and satisfaction with intelligent assistants, using topic analysis, sentiment analysis, regression analysis, and the KANO model to analyze online reviews. The results show that, in terms of users' experience, users pay attention to the device attributes (hardware features, functions, and connectivity), and the experience attribute (shopping experience) of the intelligent assistants. Comments related to device attributes contain more user sentiment than comments related to experience attribute. Emotions expressed in reviews related to hardware features and functions are more positive, while emotions expressed in reviews related to connectivity are more negative. In terms of satisfaction, emotional expressions related to hardware features and shopping experience had the greatest impact on users' satisfaction. Improvements in hardware features and functions are prioritized the highest. The results of this study have implications for the design of intelligent assistants.

Keywords: Intelligent assistants · Users' experience · Sentiment analysis · Satisfaction · Online reviews

1 Introduction

Intelligent assistants play a crucial role in social entertainment, health management, life assistance, and device control [1, 2]. For instance, they can provide reminders and answer questions about the weather [3–5]. They can also meet users' social needs and reduce loneliness by providing entertainment and companionship [6–8]. Intelligent assistants have become increasingly popular in recent years. However, users still have concerns about privacy risks, security vulnerabilities, and devices' inability to understand their needs when using intelligent assistants [9, 10]. Therefore, more research is needed to understand the user experience with intelligent assistants and the future direction of product development.

Previous research has mainly used questionnaires, interviews or laboratory methods to investigate consumers' willingness to buy and use intelligent assistants [6, 11, 12].

P.-L.P. Rau and H. Krömker (Eds.): HCII 2025, LNCS 16336, pp. 118–134, 2026.
https://doi.org/10.1007/978-3-032-12798-3_8

However, these approaches do not fully reflect consumers' real experiences and behaviors with intelligent assistants [13, 14]. Because these approaches mainly rely on pre-designed research models for hypothesis testing [13]. On the other hand, online reviews can reflect the actual user experience and help to understand people's concerns, feelings and opinions [15, 16]. Online review mining has become increasingly important in recent years as a new method for investigating the user experience. Evaluating user experience based on online reviews involves two steps. First, the product attributes affecting user experience are extracted from the reviews. Second, the impact of users' emotions towards these attributes on user experience (especially satisfaction) is analyzed. This provides suggestions for improving the user experience. Specifically, Topic analysis can be used to extract the product attributes that users are interested in [17–19], and sentiment analysis can be used to uncover users' emotional responses [5, 20]. The regression analysis and the KANO model can further investigate the complex relationship between user experience and product attributes [13, 21, 22].

This study aims to extract user requirement attributes and analyze emotional responses to them. The study then analyzes the impact of these emotional responses on satisfaction ratings, obtaining a prioritized classification of the attributes to improve the user experience. In particular, we employed topic analysis, sentiment analysis, linear regression and the KANO model, based on online reviews, to investigate users' experience and satisfaction with intelligent assistants.

2 Methods

2.1 Data Collection and Pre-processing

JD.com (https://www.jd.com), recognized as one of China's leading e-commerce platforms specializing in consumer electronics retail, was selected as the data source for this study. We used 'home intelligent assistant' as the keyword. We then crawled the online reviews of the top 50 home intelligent assistants in terms of sales from the 37 products of brands such as 'Xiaomi', 'Baidu' and 'Tmall Genie' (e.g. 'Xiaodu Intelligent Screen x10', 'Xiaodu Speaker Ultimate', 'Xiao Ai Speaker Pro', 'Xiaodu Sound'). The online reviews included review text, satisfaction rating, device type, purchase time, review time, and membership level. After removing stop words and duplicates, 28,837 reviews were used for further analysis.

2.2 Topic Clustering of Online Reviews Based on LDA Model

To decode latent user experiences of intelligent assistants from consumer feedback, we implemented a topic modeling approach using Latent Dirichlet Allocation (LDA) to analyze the online reviews [23]. Through parameter optimization, the number of topics (K) was systematically varied across the range 1–15, with model performance quantified through coherence score analysis. Quantitative evaluation demonstrated maximum semantic consistency at $K = 5$ (Fig. 1), establishing this configuration as optimal for subsequent pattern recognition tasks. Ultimately, we extracted five requirement attributes, each of which was associated with ten keywords.

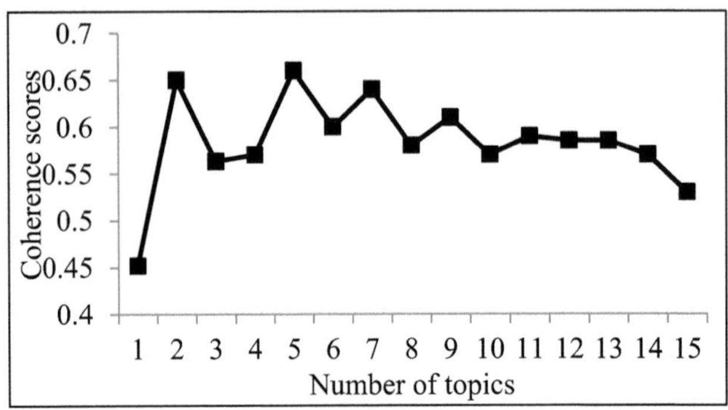

Fig. 1. Coherence scores under different numbers of topics.

2.3 Sentiment Analysis of Online Reviews Based on SKEP Model

The SKEP model [24] and the SnowNLP library (v0.12.3) [25] were used in this study to systematically decode emotional valence and arousal patterns in user reviews of intelligent assistants. Firstly, We used the SKEP model to extract feature words, sentiment words, and sentiment tendencies of comments. After that, it is mapped to requirement attributes.

The set of attributes extracted from the online reviews is denoted by $F = \{f_1, f_2, ..., f_J\}$, where f_j denotes the jth attribute and $j = 1, 2, ..., J$. The set of I online reviews is denoted by $R = \{r_1, r_2, ..., r_I\}$, where r_i denotes the ith review in R and $i = 1, 2, ..., I$. For each comment r_i, we evaluate its emotional presence toward a requirement attribute as follows:

- If r_i contains a feature word that is a keyword of f_j and the sentiment is positive, then $EP_{ij} = Pos.$
- If r_i contains a feature word that is a keyword of f_j and the sentiment is negative, then $EP_{ij} = Neg.$
- If r_i contains a feature word that is a keyword of f_j but the sentiment word is not recognized, then $EP_{ij} = Neu.$
- Otherwise, $EP_{ij} = Mv.$

Each comment r_i is represented as a vector $r_i = (EP_{i1}, EP_{i2}, ..., EP_{ij}, ..., EP_{iJ})$, where J is the total number of requirement attributes, and each EP_{ij} is derived from the above rules.

Secondly, we used the SnowNLP library to calculate the sentiment score of each statement comprising a feature word and a sentiment word. Sentiment scores range from -1 to 1. The closer the score is to 1, the more positive the sentiment. the closer the score is to -1, the more negative the sentiment. For each comment r_i, we calculate a sentiment score EI_{ij} for requirement attributes f_j using the following rules:

- If r_i contains a feature word that is a keyword of f_j and a sentiment word is detected, then EI_{ij} be the corresponding sentiment score.
- If r_i contains a feature word that is a keyword of f_j but no sentiment word is detected, then $EI_{ij} = 0.$
- Otherwise, $EI_{ij} = Mv.$

Each comment r_i is represented as a vector $r_i = (EI_{i1}, EI_{i2},...,EI_{ij},...,EI_{iJ})$, where J is the total number of requirement attributes, and each EI_{ij} is derived from the above rules.

Define the number of online reviews with $EP_{ij} = Pos$ as E_{j_pos}, the number of online reviews with $EP_{ij} = Neg$ as E_{j_neg}, and the number of online reviews with $EP_{ij} = Neu$ as E_{j_neu}. Let S_{ij} denote the sentiment score of online review r_i on attribute f_j, where $i = 1,2,...,I$ and $j = 1,2,...,J$. The total emotional presence (EP_j), positive emotional presence (EP_{j_pos}) and negative emotional presence (EP_{j_neg}) of attribute f_j can be calculated using eqs. (1), (2) and (3), respectively. Similarly, the total emotional intensity (EI_j), positive emotional intensity (EI_{j_pos}) and negative emotional intensity (EI_{j_neg}) of attribute f_j can be calculated using eqs. (4), (5) and (6), respectively.

$$EP_j = \frac{E_{j\_pos} + E_{j\_neg}}{E_{j\_pos} + E_{j\_neg} + E_{j\_neu}}, j = 1, 2, \cdots, J \tag{1}$$

$$EP_{j\_pos} = \frac{E_{j\_pos}}{E_{j\_pos} + E_{j\_neg}}, j = 1, 2, \cdots, J \tag{2}$$

$$EP_{j\_neg} = \frac{E_{j\_neg}}{E_{j\_pos} + E_{j\_neg}}, j = 1, 2, \cdots, J \tag{3}$$

$$EI_j = \frac{\sum_{i=1}^{I} |S_{ij}|}{E_{j\_pos} + E_{j\_neg} + E_{j\_neu}}, j = 1, 2, \cdots, J \tag{4}$$

$$EI_{j\_pos} = \frac{\sum_{i=1}^{I} S_{ij}}{E_{j\_pos}}, S_{ij} > 0, j = 1, 2, \cdots, J \tag{5}$$

$$EI_{j\_neg} = \frac{\sum_{i=1}^{I} |S_{ij}|}{E_{j\_neg}}, S_{ij} < 0, j = 1, 2, \cdots, J \tag{6}$$

2.4 Analysis of the Relationships Between User Satisfaction and Emotional Expressions Based on Linear Regression

We employed linear regression to quantify the effects of emotional expressions on satisfaction ratings, and to determine whether the relationship between the two was statistically significant. Categorical emotion codes (Pos, Neg, Neu, Mv) were transformed into numerical values through the operations (Eqs. 7 and 8). Two regression models (Eqs. 9 and 10) were constructed. *Satisfaction_rating* is the dependent variable, *Attirbute_ep_j* indicates the emotional presence of reviews on attribute f_j in eq. (9), and *Attirbute_ei_j* indicates the user's emotional intensity of reviews on attribute f_j in eq. (10).

$$EP_{ij} = \begin{cases} 1 & EP_{ij} = Pos \text{ or } EP_{ij} = Neg \\ 0 & EP_{ij} = Neu \text{ or } EP_{ij} = Mv \end{cases}, i = 1, 2, \cdots, I; j = 1, 2, \cdots, J \tag{7}$$

$$EI_{ij} = \begin{cases} EI_{ij} & EI_{ij} > 0 \\ |EI_{ij}| & EI_{ij} < 0, i = 1, 2, \ldots, I; j = 1, 2, \ldots, J \\ 0 & EI_{ij} = Mv \text{ or } EI_{ij} = 0 \end{cases} \tag{8}$$

$$Satisfaction\_rating = \alpha_0 + \alpha_1 Attribute\_ep_1 + \alpha_2 Attribute\_ep_2 + \cdots + \alpha_J Attribute\_ep_J \tag{9}$$

$$Satisfaction\_rating = \beta_0 + \beta_1 Attribute\_ei_1 + \beta_2 Attribute\_ei_2 + \cdots + \beta_J Attribute\_ei_J \tag{10}$$

2.5 Analysis of the Nonlinear Relationships Between User Satisfaction and Emotional Expressions Based on ENNM and KANO Model

Previous research has shown that the requirement attributes of the products and satisfaction ratings obtained from online reviews may have more complex correlations (e.g., multiple covariance, non-linear relationships, etc.). To explore the complex relationship between requirement attributes and user satisfaction ratings, this study further used the ENNM and KANO models to analyze the data [13]. For each comment r_i, if $EP_{ij} = Pos$, let $EP_{ij}^+ = 1$; if $EP_{ij} = Neg$, let $EP_{ij}^- = 1$; otherwise 0. The independent variable can be denoted as $\left(EP_{i1}^+, EP_{i1}^-, EP_{i2}^+, EP_{i2}^-, \cdots, EP_{iJ}^+, EP_{iJ}^- \right)$ and the dependent variable is satisfaction rating. For intelligent assistant reviews, the algorithm starts to converge when the number of iterations is 200. The weights of the user's positive sentiment (negative sentiment) towards the attributes on the satisfaction rating $\overline{W}_j^+$ $(\overline{W}_j^-)$ are finally obtained.

Based on the weights $\overline{W}_j^+$ and $\overline{W}_j^-$ obtained from the ENNM training, this study categorizes and prioritizes the improvement of requirement attributes. The specifics are as follows:

- If $| \overline{W}_j^+ | < \tau$ and $| \overline{W}_j^- | < \tau$, it is an indifferent attribute. This means that the attribute has little impact on the satisfaction rating. There is a predefined threshold, $\tau = (1/10 \times J)$.
- If $| \overline{W}_j^+ | \le 0$ and $| \overline{W}_j^- | < 0$, it is a must-be attribute and is located in the third quadrant. Fulfilling these attributes will not increase satisfaction rating, but lacking them will decrease satisfaction rating.
- If $| \overline{W}_j^+ | \le 0$ and $| \overline{W}_j^- | \ge 0$, it is a reverse attribute and is located in the second quadrant. Satisfaction rating will decrease with the fulfillment of these attributes, but increase with their absence.
- If $| \overline{W}_j^+ | > 0$ and $| \overline{W}_j^- | < 0$, it is a performance attribute and is located in the fourth quadrant. The fulfillment of these attributes will increase the satisfaction rating, while their absence will decrease the satisfaction rating.
- If $| \overline{W}_j^+ | > 0$ and $| \overline{W}_j^- | \ge 0$, it is an excitement attribute and is located in the first quadrant. Fulfilling these attributes will increase satisfaction rating, but their absence will not decrease them.

According to these principles, must-be attributes in the third quadrant should be prioritized for improvement because they have the greatest potential to increase satisfaction ratings. Next are the excitement attributes in the first quadrant and the performance attributes in the fourth quadrant. Reverse attributes in the second quadrant should be given the lowest priority.

3   Results

3.1   Topic Clustering of Online Reviews Based on LDA Model

Table 1 shows the LDA topics, frequency, keywords and examples of comments. The second column shows the clustered topics labeled according to the meaning of the keywords. The first column of the table provides a summary of the categories to which the topics belong.

The following topics are listed in order of frequency: Device control (40.56%), Connectivity (17.54%), Entertainment companionship (14.83%), Hardware features (13.76%) and Shopping experience (13.30%). Device control and Entertainment companionship belong to the category of Functions. Therefore, the requirement attributes of intelligent assistants are Connectivity, Functions, Hardware features and Shopping experience. The device attributes include Connectivity, Functions and Hardware features, and the experience attribute include Shopping experience.

For Device control attributes, users mentioned the keywords 'intelligent', 'control' and 'recognition', indicating their interest in the intelligent control functions of home assistants, particularly voice recognition and smart home integration. Some comments regarding the device control function are as follows: (1) 'It is easy to control home appliances by voice, and the voice recognition is very sensitive.' (2) 'The sensitivity of voice control is very high. It can execute commands quickly and is easy to use for managing smart home devices.'

With regard to Connectivity, users raised issues relating to Bluetooth connectivity, network support and device compatibility. Some of the comments regarding connectivity are as follows: (1) 'The connection with the phone is smooth and Bluetooth is stable.' (2) 'There are network delays with the intelligent assistant.' These comments indicate that users are particularly concerned about connection stability and device compatibility.

With regard to Entertainment companionship attributes, users commented on the intelligent assistant's performance in these areas. Some comments regarding these functions are as follows: (1) 'Children like to use the device to listen to music and stories.' (2) 'Elderly people in the family have a bad memory. The intelligent assistant has a reminder service and can listen to the news and tell stories.' (3) 'The intelligent assistant can listen to the news and tell stories, which is useful for elderly people with a bad memory.' These comments suggest that users are concerned about the entertainment and companionship functions of intelligent assistants in the home environment.

For Hardware features, users highlighted the characteristics of the intelligent assistant's hardware. Keywords such as 'appearance', 'workmanship', 'texture' and 'color' indicate that users pay high attention to the product's appearance and quality of workmanship. Users' comments are as follows: (1) 'The appearance is compact, the color is correct, and the workmanship feels good.' (2) 'The appearance design is very atmospheric, and it looks good in the home.' In addition, users expressed concerns about the ease of use of the intelligent assistant, believing that the operating process should be simplified to make it more convenient.

When it came to Shopping experience, users mentioned product quality, logistics speed, and packaging services. Some comments regarding the shopping experience are as follows: (1) 'The product packaging is very good, and shipping is fast.' (2) 'The customer service is very patient and helpful.' This suggests that users have high expectations for the shopping experience, including the communication of information before making a purchase, the transaction experience during the purchase, and the logistics and after-sales service after the purchase.

Table 1. Topics and keywords in reviews.

Category	Topic	Frequency	Keywords	Example
Functions	Device control	40.56%	Intelligent, Control, Smart, Home, Recognize, Sensitive, Devices, Play, Smart Home, Appliances	Devices can be easily controlled by intelligent assistants. Intelligent detection is very responsive.
Connectivity	Connectivity	17.54%	Connectivity, Bluetooth, Cell phone, Sound, Network, Support, Charging, Songs, Networking, Latency	The Bluetooth connection is stable and charges very quickly.
Functions	Entertainment companionship	14.83%	Kids, Like, Music, Sound quality, Membership, Stories, Listening, Singing, Alarm clock, Seniors	The child enjoys using the device to listen to music and stories.
Hardware features	Hardware features	13.76%	Sound quality, Appearance, Sound, Workmanship, Texture, Shape, Installation, Difficulty, Color, Pretty	The appearance is compact, the color is beautiful.
Shopping experience	Shopping experience	13.30%	Quality, Logistics, Received, quickly, Purchase, Packaging, Shopping, Speed, Shipping, Service	Good quality product, packaged with care and shipped quickly.

3.2   Sentiment Analysis of Online Reviews Based on SKEP Model

This study uses the SKEP model to calculate the degree to which requirement attributes are expressed emotionally in online reviews. The results, expressed as emotional presence and emotional intensity, are shown in Table 2.

Table 2. Emotional expression of requirement attributes.

Emotion	Number of Comments	Emotional Presence	Emotional Intensity	Requirement attributes
Total	6770	90.9%	0.52	Device control
Positive	5494	89.3%	0.54	
Negative	658	10.7%	0.37	
Total	338	91.1%	0.42	Connectivity
Positive	203	65.9%	0.37	
Negative	105	34.1%	0.44	
Total	7307	90.9%	0.52	Entertainment companionship
Positive	5881	88.5%	0.54	
Negative	763	11.5%	0.39	
Total	4177	91.6%	0.81	Hardware features
Positive	3691	96.5%	0.82	
Negative	134	3.5%	0.19	
Total	3256	87.9%	0.44	Shopping experience
Positive	2632	92.0%	0.45	
Negative	230	8.0%	0.41	

Figure 2 shows the emotional presence of requirement attributes of intelligent assistants. First, the positive emotional presence of the requirement attributes is higher than the negative emotional presence, suggesting that users are generally satisfied with intelligent assistants. Second, comments about Hardware features, Connectivity, and Functions have more emotional presence. This suggests that consumers are more likely to make emotive comments about hardware features, connectivity, and functions than about the shopping experience. Overall, there is more positive emotional presence and less negative emotional presence regarding hardware features, the shopping experience, and functions.

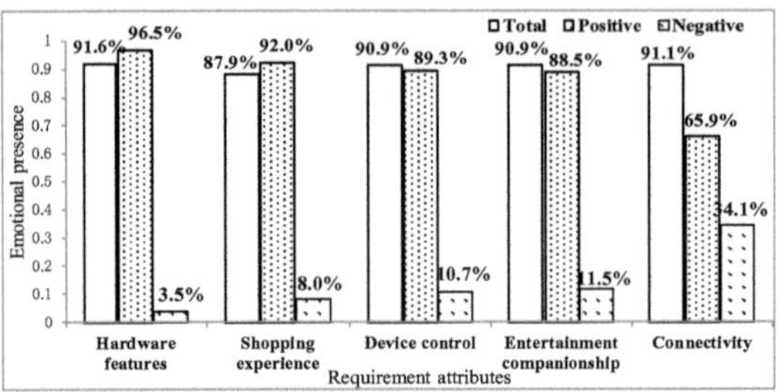

Fig. 2. Emotional presence of requirement attributes.

In terms of emotional intensity, Fig. 3 shows the emotional intensity of the requirement attributes. First, comments about hardware features and functions expressed more positive feelings. Accordingly, users are more satisfied with the hardware features and functions of intelligent assistants. Second, the positive emotional intensity associated with hardware features, functions, and the shopping experience is greater than the negative emotional intensity associated with them. However, the positive emotional intensity associated with connectivity is lower than the negative emotional intensity associated with it. This suggests that users may be dissatisfied with intelligent assistants' connectivity. Current connectivity may not meet users' expectations, resulting in more negative emotions expressed in related reviews.

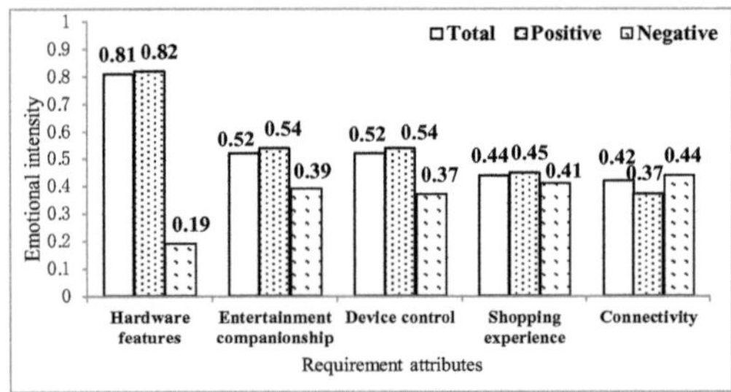

Fig. 3. Emotional intensity of requirement attributes.

3.3 Analysis of the Relationships Between User Satisfaction and Emotional Expressions Based on Linear Regression

This study explores the possible effects of the emotional presence and intensity of requirement attributes on satisfaction ratings based on the calculated emotional presence and intensity. The satisfaction rating is the dependent variable in this study, while the emotional presence and intensity of the attributes are the independent variables. A number of control variables that have been associated with reviews in previous research [16, 26, 27] are also introduced in this paper. These variables include interval, membership level, device type, anonymity and text length. Table 3 lists the descriptions of the variables.

Table 3. Descriptions of variables in linear regression.

Variable	Description
Satisfaction ratings	User satisfaction ratings of intelligent assistants.
Device_control_ep	Whether the user expressed emotion about the device control attribute in the comment, 1 for yes, 0 for no.
Connectivity_ep	Whether the user expressed emotion about the connectivity attribute in the comment, 1 for yes, 0 for no.
Entertainment_companionship_ep	Whether the user expressed emotion about the entertainment companionship attribute in the comment, 1 for yes, 0 for no.
Hardware_features_ep	Whether the user expressed emotion about the hardware features attribute in the comment, 1 for yes, 0 for no.
Shopping_experience_ep	Whether the user expressed emotion about the shopping experience attribute in the comment, 1 for yes, 0 for no.
Device_control_ei	Intensity of user's emotion towards device control attributes, where 1 is strongest and 0 is weakest.
Connectivity_ei	Intensity of user's emotion towards connectivity attributes, where 1 is strongest and 0 is weakest.
Entertainment_companionship_ei	Intensity of user's emotion towards entertainment companionship attributes, where 1 is strongest and 0 is weakest.
Hardware_features_ei	Intensity of user's emotion towards hardware features attributes, where 1 is strongest and 0 is weakest.
Shopping_experience_ei	Intensity of user's emotion towards shopping experience attributes, where 1 is strongest and 0 is weakest.
Interval	Number of days between date of purchase and date of review.
Membership level	The user's membership level on the platform.
Device type	The type of device used by the user.
Anonymity	Whether the comment is posted anonymously by the user, yes is 1, no is 0.
Text length	Length of the comment in Chinese characters.

Regression analysis was performed using SPSS 24.0 software to investigate the relationship between emotional presence and satisfaction ratings. In this study, the satisfaction ratings of intelligent assistants are used as dependent variables and control variables as independent variables for regression analysis to create model 1. Model 2 is then created by adding *Device_control_ep, Connectivity_ep, Entertainment_companionship_ep, Hardware_features_ep* and *Shopping_experience_ep* to the independent variables. Table 4 shows the results.

Table 4. The effect of emotional presences of requirement attributes on satisfaction ratings.

Predictive variables	User satisfaction ratings of intelligent assistants	
	Model 1	Model 2
Control variables		
Interval	0.014*	0.019**
Membership level	0.021**	0.013*
Device type	0.088***	0.090***
Anonymity	0.197***	0.188***
Text length	0.092***	0.068***
Independent variables		
Device_control_ep		0.064***
Connectivity_ep		−0.037***
Entertainment_companionship_ep		0.090***
Hardware_features_ep		0.155***
Shopping_experience_ep		0.108***
R^2	0.062	0.119
Adjusted R^2	0.061	0.119
F	322.539***	331.711***

Notes. ***$p < 0.001$; **$p < 0.01$; *$p < 0.05$

The Variance Inflation Factor (VIF) values for all independent and control variables were between 1 and 3, which is within the acceptable range of 1 to 10. As a result, there is no significant multicollinearity between the variables in this regression.

The regression coefficients were all positive and significant at the $p < 0.001$ level, and the standardized coefficients of the independent variables *Device_control_ep*, *Entertainment_companionship_ep*, *Hardware_features_ep*, and *Shopping_experience_ep* on satisfaction ratings were 0.064, 0.090, 0.155, and 0.108 respectively. The more positive people feel about the hardware features, shopping experience, and functions of the intelligent assistant, the higher the satisfaction ratings. Second, there is a negative regression coefficient and a standardized coefficient of *Connectivity_ep* on satisfaction rating of −0.037, which is significant at the $p < 0.001$ level. Users' satisfaction ratings are lower when they have negative feelings about the connectivity of the intelligent assistant. Finally, the regression coefficients of *Hardware_features_ep* and *Shopping_experience_ep* on satisfaction ratings are higher compared to other variables. Users' satisfaction ratings are more likely to increase when they feel positive about the hardware features and shopping experience. Furthermore, *Entertainment_companionship_ep* has a higher regression coefficient than *Device_control_ep*. This suggests that an emotional presence in the entertainment companionship function of the intelligent assistant is more likely to increase satisfaction ratings than in the device control function.

This study also investigates the relationship between the emotional intensity of attributes and user satisfaction ratings. Using the satisfaction rating as the dependent variable and the control variables as the independent variables for regression analysis, Model 3 is obtained in this paper. Model 4 is then obtained by adding *Device_control_ei*, *Connectivity_ei*, *Entertainment_companionship_ei*, *Hardware_features_ei* and *Shopping_experience_ei* to the independent variables. Table 5 shows the results.

Table 5. The effect of emotional intensity of requirement attributes on satisfaction ratings.

Predictive variables	User satisfaction ratings of intelligent assistants	
	Model 3	Model 4
Control variables		
Interval	0.014*	0.019**
Membership level	0.021**	0.013*
Device type	0.088***	0.090***
Anonymity	0.197***	0.188***
Text length	0.092***	0.068***
Independent variables		
Device_control_ei		0.070***
Connectivity_ei		−0.031***
Entertainment_companionship_ei		0.102***
Hardware_features_ei		0.158***
Shopping_experience_ei		0.097***
R^2	0.062	0.123
Adjusted R^2	0.061	0.123
F	322.539***	345.903***

Notes. ***$p < 0.001$; **$p < 0.01$; *$p < 0.05$

The Variance Inflation Factor (VIF) values for all independent and control variables were between 1 and 2, which is within the acceptable range of 1 to 10. As a result, there is no significant multicollinearity between the variables in this regression.

The independent variables *Device_control_ei*, *Entertainment_companionship_ei*, *Hardware_features_ei*, and *Shopping_experience_ei* were found to have standardized coefficients of 0.070, 0.102, 0.158, and 0.097 on satisfaction ratings, respectively. The regression coefficients were also found to be positive and significant at the $p < 0.001$ level. This suggests that, with the exception of *Connectivity_ei*, there is a strong positive correlation between the independent variables and satisfaction ratings, i.e., the stronger the user's emotions about the functions, hardware features, and shopping experience, the higher the satisfaction ratings. Secondly, there is a negative regression coefficient and a significant $p < 0.001$ level for the standardized coefficient of *Connectivity_ei* on user satisfaction rating, which is −0.031. This suggests a strong negative correlation between *Connectivity_ei* and satisfaction ratings, i.e., the stronger the user's emotion towards connectivity, the lower the satisfaction ratings. Furthermore, compared to *Connectivity_ei* and *Device_control_ei*, the regression coefficients of *Hardware_feature_ei*, *Shopping_experience_ei*, and *Entertainment_companionship_ei* on satisfaction ratings were higher. This implies that the impact of *Hardware_features_ei*, *Shopping_experience_ei*, and *Entertainment_companionship_ei* on satisfaction ratings is comparatively higher. Compared to connectivity and device control function, the stronger the user's emotion towards hardware features, shopping experience, and entertainment companionship function, the higher the satisfaction ratings.

3.4   Analysis of the Nonlinear Relationships Between User Satisfaction and Emotional Expressions Based on ENNM and KANO Model

The values of $\overline{W_j^-}$ converge when the number of ENNM iterations is 200. Therefore, the values of $\overline{W_j^+}$ and $\overline{W_j^-}$ corresponding to the number of iterations of 200 are selected as the experimental results, which are shown in Table 6.

Table 6. The effect of positive and negative emotional weights of requirement attributes on satisfaction ratings.

Requirement attributes	$\overline{W_j^+}$	$\overline{W_j^-}$
Device control	−0.0268	−0.1533
Connectivity	0.0432	−0.1301
Entertainment companionship	−0.0529	−0.1882
Hardware features	−0.0016	−0.1570
Shopping experience	0.0329	−0.1830

The KANO classification of the requirement attributes can be determined by the quadrant in which the attributes are located, as shown in Fig. 4. None of the five required attributes were found to be indifferent or reverse attributes. It is possible that the lack of indifferent attributes is due to the fact that online reviews typically contain both positive and negative comments from users, and individuals are unlikely to highlight attributes that aren't important to them. Must-be attributes include Device control, Entertainment companionship and Hardware features that are critical to satisfying users' requirements, and the absence of these attributes significantly reduces users' satisfaction ratings. Performance attributes include Connectivity and Shopping experience, and the fulfillment of these attributes is linearly related to satisfaction ratings. Fulfillment of these attributes significantly increases user satisfaction ratings, while the absence of these attributes significantly decreases user satisfaction ratings.

It was also shown that Hardware features and Functions (such as Device control and Entertainment companionship) were given the highest priority, followed by Connectivity and Shopping experience. This suggests that consumers have higher expectations for hardware features (such as appearance and audio) and functions of intelligent assistants. Improving the hardware features and functions of intelligent assistants should be a top priority in the future.

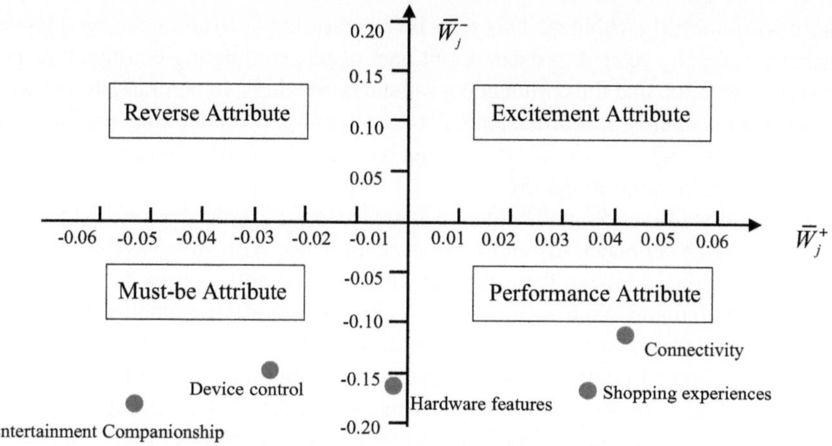

Fig. 4. Improvement prioritization of requirement attributes.

4   Discussions and Conclusion

The results of this study indicate that users' requirements for intelligent assistants include functions (device control, entertainment companionship), hardware features, connectivity, and shopping experience. On the one hand, users want intelligent assistants to be functional and provide social entertainment and device control services [3]. On the other hand, users are concerned about the appearance design of intelligent assistants, including the morphology and level of anthropomorphism [28, 29]. In addition, users have a high concern about the connectivity of intelligent assistants, which is reflected in device interconnection, Bluetooth pairing, and network connection. Existing research confirms that connectivity failures reduce the user experience [12]. As many users often use intelligent assistants to build smart home systems, it is important to improve the connectivity of intelligent assistants [30].

In terms of emotional responses, hardware features, functions, and connectivity inspire users to post more emotional comments than the shopping experience attribute. Among them, the emotions in the comments related to hardware features and functions are more positive, while the emotions in the comments related to connectivity are more negative. This may be related to the fact that connectivity currently does not meet the needs of users and makes them feel uncomfortable [12].

With the exception of connectivity, all attributes were significantly and positively correlated with satisfaction ratings when it came to emotional expression. The emotional expression of hardware features and shopping experience had the greatest impact on satisfaction ratings. This may be related to first impressions: appearance and shopping experience are the initial aspects of a product or service with which users engage, and these attributes are more likely to elicit emotional responses from users, which in turn affect satisfaction [31]. Regarding functions, users' emotional expression of entertainment companionship attributes is more likely to influence satisfaction ratings than device control attributes. This may be because the entertainment companionship attribute is directly related to users' emotional needs, stimulating emotional responses through interaction and thus influencing satisfaction ratings. In contrast, the device control attribute is mainly utilitarian, aimed at completing tasks rather than emotional interactions. It may play a lesser role in eliciting user emotions and have a relatively limited impact on satisfaction ratings [5].

Furthermore, functions and hardware features were the highest priorities for improvement, followed by connectivity and shopping experience. This suggests that users expect as much from the hardware features of intelligent assistants as they do from the functions. Although many manufacturers have focused on improving functional attributes to increase the intelligence of intelligent assistants [5]. However, this study found that the hardware features of intelligent assistants are just as important as the functions.

This study also has some limitations. On the one hand, this study extracts the attributes of users' requirements for an intelligent assistant using the LDA model. According to a related study, the LDA model requires the intervention of the researcher to interpret the extracted topics, which could lead to a biased interpretation of the topics [32]. In addition, the extracted topics contain some noise words [23]. In the future, methods such as questionnaires, interviews and logs can be combined to observe the interaction process between users and intelligent assistants in home scenarios. On the other hand, this study only collected online reviews of intelligent assistants from the Chinese e-commerce platform "JD.com". To validate the results of this study, future research should take cultural considerations into account and use the same methodology to collect reviews of intelligent assistants in different cultural contexts.

Acknowledgments. This research was supported by the National Natural Science Foundation of China (No. 72301073), the Major Science and Technology Special Project of Fujian Province (No. 2024HZ022013), and the Natural Science Foundation of Fujian Province of China (No.2022J05018).

References

1. Zhong, R., Ma, M., Zhou, Y., Lin, Q., Li, L., Zhang, N.: User acceptance of smart home voice assistant: a comparison among younger, middle-aged, and older adults. Univ. Access Inf. Soc. **23**(1), 275–292 (2024). https://doi.org/10.1007/s10209-022-00936-1
2. Pal, D., Arpnikanondt, C., Funilkul, S., Varadarajan, V.: User experience with smart voice assistants: the accent perspective. In: 2019 10th International Conference on Computing, Communication and Networking Technologies (ICCCNT), pp. 1–6 (2019). https://doi.org/10.1109/ICCCNT45670.2019.8944754
3. Bentley, F., Luvogt, C., Silverman, M., Wirasinghe, R., White, B., Lottridge, D.: Understanding the long-term use of smart speaker assistants. Proc. ACM Interact. Mobile Wearable Ubiquitous Technol. **2**(3), 1–24 (2018). https://doi.org/10.1145/3264901
4. Tabassum, M., Kosiński, T., Frik, A., Malkin, N., Wijesekera, P., Egelman, S., et al.: Investigating users' preferences and expectations for always-listening voice assistants. Proc. ACM Interact. Mobile Wearable Ubiquitous Technol. **3**(4), 1–23 (2019). https://doi.org/10.1145/3369807

5. Kim, S., Choudhury, A.: Exploring older adults' perception and use of smart speaker-based voice assistants: a longitudinal study. Comput. Hum. Behav. **124**, 106914 (2021). https://doi.org/10.1016/j.chb.2021.106914

6. Cheng, Y., Jiang, H.: How do AI-driven chatbots impact user experience? Examining gratifications, perceived privacy risk, satisfaction, loyalty, and continued use. J. Broadcast. Electron. Media. **64**(4), 592–614 (2020). https://doi.org/10.1080/08838151.2020.1834296

7. Liu, M., Wang, C., Hu, J.: Older adults' intention to use voice assistants: usability and emotional needs. Heliyon. **9**(11), e21932 (2023). https://doi.org/10.1016/j.heliyon.2023.e21932

8. García-Méndez, S., De Arriba-Pérez, F., González-Castaño, F.J., Regueiro-Janeiro, J.A., Gil-Castiñeira, F.: Entertainment chatbot for the digital inclusion of elderly people without abstraction capabilities. IEEE Access. **9**, 75878–75891 (2021). https://doi.org/10.1109/ACCESS.2021.3080837

9. Ziefle, M., Calero Valdez, A.: Domestic robots for homecare: a technology acceptance perspective. In: Zhou, J., Salvendy, G. (eds.) Human Aspects of IT for the Aged Population. Aging, Design and User Experience, pp. 57–74. Springer (2017). https://doi.org/10.1007/978-3-319-58530-7_5

10. Huxohl, T., Pohling, M., Carlmeyer, B., Wrede, B., Hermann, T.: Interaction guidelines for personal voice assistants in smart homes. In: 2019 International Conference on Speech Technology and Human-Computer Dialogue (SpeD), pp. 1–10 (2019). https://doi.org/10.1109/SPED.2019.8906642

11. Fernandes, T., Oliveira, E.: Understanding consumers' acceptance of automated technologies in service encounters: drivers of digital voice assistants adoption. J. Bus. Res. **122**, 180–191 (2021). https://doi.org/10.1016/j.jbusres.2020.08.058

12. Jain, S., Basu, S., Ray, A., Das, R.: Impact of irritation and negative emotions on the performance of voice assistants: netting dissatisfied customers' perspectives. Int. J. Inf. Manag. **72**, 102662 (2023). https://doi.org/10.1016/j.ijinfomgt.2023.102662

13. Bi, J.-W., Liu, Y., Fan, Z.-P., Cambria, E.: Modelling customer satisfaction from online reviews using ensemble neural network and effect-based Kano model. Int. J. Prod. Res. **57**(22), 7068–7088 (2019). https://doi.org/10.1080/00207543.2019.1574989

14. Javdan, M., Ghasemaghaei, M., Abouzahra, M.: Psychological barriers of using wearable devices by seniors: a mixed-methods study. Comput. Hum. Behav. **141**, 107615 (2023). https://doi.org/10.1016/j.chb.2022.107615

15. Chen, K., Jin, J., Luo, J.: Big consumer opinion data understanding for Kano categorization in new product development. J. Ambient. Intell. Humaniz. Comput. **13**(4), 2269–2288 (2022). https://doi.org/10.1007/s12652-021-02985-5

16. Yang, T., Zhang, C.J., Wu, J., Zhang, J.: The hidden gems in online reviews: unraveling how the expressions of affective needs impact review usefulness. J. Hosp. Market. Manag. **34**(2), 234–256 (2025). https://doi.org/10.1080/19368623.2024.2413189

17. Kumar, A., Bala, P.K., Chakraborty, S., Behera, R.K.: Exploring antecedents impacting user satisfaction with voice assistant app: a text mining-based analysis on alexa services. J. Retail. Consum. Serv. **76**, 103586 (2024). https://doi.org/10.1016/j.jretconser.2023.103586

18. Han, M., Lee, S., Kim, J.: A hybrid approach to discern customer experience for facilitating the adoption of smartwatches. Tech. Anal. Strat. Manag. **34**(5), 535–549 (2022). https://doi.org/10.1080/09537325.2021.1912318

19. Yoon, S.-H., Park, G.-Y., Kim, H.-W.: Unraveling the relationship between the dimensions of user experience and user satisfaction: a smart speaker case. Technol. Soc. **71**, 102067 (2022). https://doi.org/10.1016/j.techsoc.2022.102067

20. Li, Y.-H., Yue, S.-T., Zheng, J., Wang, W.: Customer-oriented product design: an integrated decision framework with sentiment analysis and optimisation model. J. Control Decis. **11**(2), 165–179 (2024). https://doi.org/10.1080/23307706.2022.2146607

21. Xie, Z., Li, W., Xie, Y., Wang, L.: Demand and satisfaction analysis of short health videos among Chinese urban youth: a mixed-methods study based on the KANO model. Humanit. Soc. Sci. Commun. **11**(1), 740 (2024). https://doi.org/10.1057/s41599-024-03266-0

22. Shi, Y., Peng, Q.: Enhanced customer requirement classification for product design using big data and improved Kano model. Adv. Eng. Inform. **49**, 101340 (2021). https://doi.org/10.1016/j.aei.2021.101340

23. Blei, D.M., Ng, A., Jordan, M.: Latent Dirichlet allocation. In: J. Mach. Learn. Res., vol. 3, pp. 993–1022 (2003). https://doi.org/10.7551/mitpress/1120.003.0082

24. Tian, H., Gao, C., Xiao, X., Liu, H., He, B., Wu, H., et al.: SKEP: Sentiment knowledge enhanced pre-training for sentiment analysis. In: Jurafsky, D., Chai, J., Schluter, N., Tetreault, J. (eds.) Proceedings of the 58th Annual Meeting of the Association for Computational Linguistics, pp. 4067–4076. Association for Computational Linguistics (2020). https://doi.org/10.18653/v1/2020.acl-main.374

25. He, D., Yao, Z., Zhao, F., Feng, J.: How do weather factors drive online reviews? The mediating role of online reviewers' affect. Ind. Manag. Data Syst. **120**(11), 2133–2149 (2020). https://doi.org/10.1108/IMDS-02-2020-0121

26. Rice, R.E., Pearce, K.E., Calderwood, K.J.: W(h)ither the device divide? Changing relationships between personal computer or mobile device with online activities. Mobile Media Commun. **11**(3), 484–506 (2023). https://doi.org/10.1177/20501579221142134

27. Zhang, Z., Zhang, Z., Zhang, Z.: Why do online reviewers seek anonymity? Empirical evidence on the effects of prior anonymous reviews and focal reviews. Aslib J. Inf. Manag. **76**(3), 498–521 (2024). https://doi.org/10.1108/AJIM-08-2022-0369

28. Sasser, J.A., McConnell, D.S., Smither, J.A.: Investigation of relationships between embodiment perceptions and perceived social presence in human–robot interactions. Int. J. Soc. Robot. **16**(8), 1735–1750 (2024). https://doi.org/10.1007/s12369-024-01138-w

29. Lv, X., Liu, Y., Luo, J., Liu, Y., Li, C.: Does a cute artificial intelligence assistant soften the blow? The impact of cuteness on customer tolerance of assistant service failure. Ann. Tour. Res. **87**, 103114 (2021). https://doi.org/10.1016/j.annals.2020.103114

30. Shlega, M., Maqsood, S., Chiasson, S.: Users, smart homes, and digital assistants: impact of technology experience and adoption, A. Moallem, ed., vol. 13333, pp. 422–443. Springer (2022). https://doi.org/10.1007/978-3-031-05563-8_26

31. Liu, W., Guo, F., Ye, G., Liang, X.: How homepage aesthetic design influences users' satisfaction: evidence from China. Displays. **42**, 25–35 (2016). https://doi.org/10.1016/j.displa.2016.02.004

32. Park, J., Yang, D., Kim, H.Y.: Text mining-based four-step framework for smart speaker product improvement and sales planning. J. Retail. Consum. Serv. **71**, 103186 (2023). https://doi.org/10.1016/j.jretconser.2022.103186

Mapping the Future of Mobility Through Crowd Innovation Workshops: Integrating Strategic Foresight with Design Innovation

Tiantian Li[1,2], Kaiqi Yin[3], Yue Gu[2], and Yiyu Li[4(✉)]

[1] Hubei Institute of Fine Arts, Wuhan 430205, China
tiantianli@hifa.edu.cn

[2] Academy of Arts & Design, Tsinghua University, Beijing 100085, China
tiantianli@mail.tsinghua.edu.cn, y-gu20@mails.tsinghua.edu.cn

[3] TCL Design Innovation Center (DIC), Shenzhen 518055, China
yinkq@tcl.com

[4] School of Politics and Law, Zhejiang Sci-Tech University, Hangzhou 310018, China
lilysmoke@foxmail.com

Abstract. Smart mobility, as a complex socio-technical system, has an evolutionary path determined by multiple interwoven factors. However, current mainstream paradigms for foreseeing mobility trends operate in silos, leading to several gaps that urgently need bridging: between expert experience and collective intelligence, between quantitative analysis and qualitative insight, and between strategic foresight and design thinking. Simultaneously, the expanding role of designers requires them to possess multiple literacies, including data, futures, and design literacy, yet traditional education often cultivates these in isolation. To address these challenges, this study proposes an integrative framework to bridge these paradigmatic gaps, validated through a two-stage crowd innovation workshop. In the first stage, 'Strategic Foresight,' a systematic refinement from cases to trends is achieved through a 'Case-Signal-Feature-Trend/Motif' process. In the second stage, 'Design Innovation,' the transition from trends to Product-Service System (PSSD..) solutions is realised through 'Trend/Motif-Opportunity-Vision-Solution' steps. The application of this methodology in a five-day workshop involving 36 design students demonstrated its procedural coherence and effectiveness. This research not only provides an integrative framework for foresight and design innovation in the field of future mobility but also offers an effective model for cultivating the integrative literacies required by the next generation of innovators.

Keywords: Smart Mobility · Scenarios · Foresight Paradigms · Strategic Foresight · Design Innovation · Integrative Literacies

1 Introduction

Smart mobility can be understood as a complex socio-technical system [1], whose evolutionary path is shaped by the interplay of technological innovation, user behaviour, business models, policy regulations, and even socio-cultural factors [2]. This high degree

P.-L.P. Rau and H. Krömker (Eds.): HCII 2025, LNCS 16336, pp. 135–151, 2026.
https://doi.org/10.1007/978-3-032-12798-3_9

of complexity means that any effective foresight of future mobility forms must rely on an integrative framework capable of unifying multidimensional elements to avoid partiality in analysis. Consequently, constructing insightful future scenarios is widely regarded as a key tool for integrating various factors and driving innovation. However, in practice, foresight methodologies exhibit significant fragmentation. Specifically, current mainstream future foresight methods belong to three paradigms, each with its own strengths and limitations: the quantitative-predictive paradigm, the qualitative-critical paradigm, and the design-generative paradigm. These three paradigms operate largely independently, resulting in several gaps that urgently need bridging: between expert experience and collective intelligence, between quantitative analysis and qualitative insight, and between strategic foresight and design thinking. Therefore, constructing and validating an integrative methodology capable of bridging these gaps to serve foresight in the complex field of future mobility became the primary motivation for this research.

A current phenomenon is that the role of designers is expanding from executing specific tasks to encompassing other areas, including strategic foresight and design innovation. This requires them to possess more composite capabilities and literacies, such as Data Literacy, Futures Literacy, Design Literacy, and so on. However, traditional education often cultivates these literacies in isolation, failing to meet the demands of the new era. Thus, exploring a pedagogical framework that can effectively integrate and cultivate designers' integrative literacies constitutes another motivation for this study.

Building on this, this paper proposes and validates a Two-Stage Crowd Innovation Workshop. By guiding participants through the entire process from evidence analysis to PSSD.. solution generation, this method not only bridges the gap between strategic foresight and design innovation at a methodological level but also, at an educational level, provides participants with a training ground to cultivate their comprehensive ability to integrate data, futures, and design literacies.

This paper is divided into five sections. Section 1 is the introduction. In Sect. 2, we first elaborate on the key role of scenarios in addressing complexity in the mobility domain, then investigate the strengths and limitations of the three mainstream foresight paradigms, and argue for the necessity of integration. In Sect. 3, we detail the integration strategies, objectives, and specific implementation steps of the proposed two-stage crowd innovation workshop. In Sect. 4, we report on a workshop themed 'Contextual Integration and Mobility Forms,' showcasing the application process and outcomes of the method. Finally, we discuss the theoretical contributions, limitations, and future directions of this research, and conclude the entire paper.

2   Related Works

2.1   Smart Mobility Scenarios

The concept of smart mobility has been proposed as a broad, organic system [3–5]. Furthermore, smart mobility can be understood as a typical complex socio-technical system [1]. Sheller et al. [6] introduced the 'new mobilities paradigm', exploring how mobility reshapes social relations and daily life practices, emphasising the interaction between technology and social space. In social sciences, automobility is considered to affect not only local public spaces and opportunities for assembly but also the formation of gender subjectivity, family and social networks, spatially segregated urban neighbour-hoods, national image and aspirations for modernity, and even global relations ranging from transnational migration to terrorism and oil wars [7]. In summary, smart mobility involves multi-layered interactions, including technological factors, societal needs, and policy governance dimensions.

Given this intricate complexity, any single-dimensional analysis is likely to be partial. Therefore, academia and industry have adopted scenarios at various levels as a core analytical framework or design driver [8, 9], valued for their integrative power. In design innovation, scenario-based design originates from human-computer interaction and software engineering disciplines and is continually applied in product development to provide imagination and visualisation capabilities [10, 11]. In futures studies, scenarios can help organisations prepare for potential eventualities, making them more flexible and innovative [12]. Scenarios can weave seemingly isolated elements—from the technical parameters of autonomous driving to ethical considerations of data privacy, and the potential impacts of shared mobility on urban form—into a logically coherent and understandable overall narrative. They are a key tool for integrating diverse factors and driving innovation.

The utility of scenarios heavily depends on their organisation and classification. Scenarios can be categorised along multiple axes, such as time scale (short, medium, long-term) [13], task and functional purpose (exploratory, normative), or technology penetration rate (e.g., high automation vs. low automation) [14]. Lyons et al. [15] proposed the Triple Access System (TAS) concept, which posits that land use, transport, and telecommunication systems are enablers of economic and social activity, corresponding respectively to spatial proximity, physical mobility, and digital connectivity. In urban planning, the link between transport and land use is crucial [16]. Schwanen [17] discussed urban form policies and their impact on travel based on Dutch experiences. In essence, discussing mobility based on geographical attributes (e.g., urban, intercity, rural) is another important method of categorisation. Its potential advantage lies in the fact that geographical space is the physical medium for all travel activities and the most concentrated intersection of social, economic, and technological factors. This classification method firmly 'anchors' the analysis in specific physical and social contexts, naturally integrating variables such as population density, infrastructure, lifestyles, and individual/household attributes. This avoids vague discussions and helps to advance research in depth.

In summary: (i) Smart mobility is a typical complex socio-technical system, and scenarios are a key tool for integrating various elements and driving innovation. (ii) Effective scenario classification is a strategic choice. Scenario division based on geographical attributes can serve as a foundational framework and analytical basis, upon which variables such as technology and social factors can be overlaid as tags.

2.2 Three Key Paradigms for Foreseeing Mobility Trends

To construct insightful future scenarios, it is first necessary to foresee future trends. Reviewing existing research, this paper categorises methods for foreseeing trends in the mobility sector into three paradigms that are interconnected yet have distinct focuses (Table 1).

138   T. Li et al.

The Quantitative-Predictive Paradigm. This paradigm is based on historical data and mathematical models and aims to predict the 'most likely' deterministic outcomes of the future through logical deduction [18]. Its core lies in the belief that the future is an extension of the past and can be inferred through rigorous algorithms. Representative methods include System Dynamics, discrete choice models, Bayesian networks, simulation models, and machine learning methods, among others. Among these, System Dynamics simulates the long-term dynamic behaviour of complex systems by establishing causal feedback loops between variables [19]. As System Dynamics methods increasingly adopt a hierarchical approach, allowing systems and policies to interact across time and space, the overall approach is well-suited to the transport problems we currently face [20]. Its application areas are extensive, including the use of alternative fuel vehicles, supply chain management affecting transport, highway maintenance, strategic policy, airport infrastructure and airline business cycles, and a range of emerging application areas [20]. In the transport sector, Bayesian Network (BN) models are used to predict the overall performance of unmanned aerial vehicle technology and quantitatively assess the resilience of urban transport systems [21, 22]; they are important tools within the quantitative-predictive paradigm. Simulation models, such as microscopic traffic simulation, are widely used to predict traffic flow and congestion, providing theoretical and practical support for quantitative prediction [23]. In the broad field of Intelligent Transport Systems (ITS), the intersection of emerging technologies like machine learning with transport systems also brings unprecedented possibilities for transformation [24, 25].

While the strengths of this paradigm lie in its rigour, repeatability, and quantitative capabilities, its limitations are also significant: (i) It heavily relies on historical data, which makes it perform poorly when predicting discontinuous changes (such as 'black swan' events) or disruptive innovations [26]. (ii) Complex models can appear as a 'black box' to non-experts, leading to an opaque decision-making process. Human intuition, experience, and qualitative insights play a minor role, making it difficult to stimulate genuine innovative thinking.

The Qualitative-Critical Paradigm. This paradigm originates from futures studies and social sciences. Its aim is not to predict a single future, but rather to explore 'possible futures' or advocate for 'preferable futures', and to offer critical reflections on prevailing technological and societal assumptions. Representative methods include Scenario Planning [27], Causal Layered Analysis (CLA), and Speculative Design. Among these, Scenario Planning involves identifying key uncertainties and combining them to construct multiple logically coherent and mutually independent future scenarios. It encourages decision-makers to explore the characteristics, uncertainties, and boundaries of the future landscape and to engage with other perspectives. For 40 years, Shell has used scenario planning to help deepen its strategic thinking. Its scenarios extend beyond traditional energy outlooks to consider long-term trends in the economy, energy supply and demand, geopolitical shifts, and social change [28]. In summary, scenario planning helps in considering how the future might unfold and is particularly important when understanding uncertainty is necessary – a point highly relevant to the transport sector today [2]. For instance, recognising the significant uncertainties it faced, the New Zealand Ministry of Transport undertook a major strategic initiative in 2014 centred on the use of scenario planning to demonstrate how diverse futures could emerge and to challenge conventional wisdom [15]. Causal Layered Analysis (CLA) is a deep analytical tool that uncovers the underlying factors driving the future by deconstructing issues at the surface, systemic, worldview, and myth/metaphor levels. Its purpose is not to predict the future, but to create transformative space for an alternative future [29]. Speculative Design goes further by creating thought-provoking 'design fictions' to stimulate public debate on technological, ethical, and social issues [30].

The great strength of this paradigm lies in its intellectual liberation and critical nature; it can help us break free from conventional thinking and open up entirely new possibilities for innovation. However, its limitations are also apparent: (i) The process of identifying 'driving forces' often relies on small-scale, top-down expert workshops, which can lead to limited and closed perspectives. The resulting future visions, while potentially intellectually stimulating, are often disconnected from the real-life situations, tacit needs, and cultural values of the wider user base, sometimes even devolving into self-referential discourse. (ii) The paradigm focuses on constructing grand, macro-level scenarios and lacks a clear pathway to translate these into concrete, actionable product or service solutions.

The Design-Co-Creation Paradigm. This paradigm centres on design thinking and participatory design, emphasising the exploration and expression of the future through 'learning by making' and multi-stakeholder collaboration. It posits that the future is not predicted, but designed and created. Representative methods include design thinking, participatory design, and Product/Service System Design (PSSD..), among others. Among these, Design Thinking is a human-centred innovation process (empathise – define – ideate – prototype – test) [31]. Viviani et al. [32] utilised the Double Diamond design thinking model, through interdisciplinary design research, to successfully develop an efficient micro-vehicle and propose an urban transport innovation model, demonstrating the model's effectiveness in solving sustainable transport problems and guiding interdisciplinary practice. Co-design/Participatory Design emphasises inviting end-users, designers, engineers, and other stakeholders to jointly participate in the design process. For example, in the public transport sector, a 'Living Lab' was established in Sweden, composed of a wide range of stakeholders such as national and local transport authorities, bus operators, private and non-governmental organisations, and academia [33]. They assessed public transport conditions and drafted policy guidelines. Ciasullo et al. [34] engaged stakeholders through telephone calls, online surveys, and focus group discussions to identify mobility needs and design an information exchange platform to guide transport mode decisions. Furthermore, Product/Service System Design (PSSD..) focuses on creating sustainable value by integrating products, services, and systems [35, 36]. One of Ran et al.'s [37] research areas focuses on smart product-service system design for human mobility based on medium-sized autonomous vehicles. Beckmann-Dobrev et al. [38] brought together scientists from diverse fields such as engineering and arts to jointly explore new methods for developing and testing Product/Service Systems (PSS). Through interdisciplinary collaboration, they proposed three use cases based on urban bicycle mobility (bicycle rental, mobile device services, new types of transport) to define the main requirements for an urban hybrid bicycle simulator.

The strengths of this paradigm lie in its human-centred approach, emphasis on empathy, and its ability to rapidly produce tangible, iterative, and concrete solutions that place human perception and experience at their core. However, its limitations include: (i) Design thinking emphasises 'doing things right' (how to solve problems), but may lack sufficient critical reflection on the premise of 'doing the right things' (what problems to solve). This can lead to 'local optimisation' of solutions. (ii) Although methods like PSSD.. are adept at system integration, in practice, their starting point for innovation is often 'present-day' observable user pain points or immediate commercial opportunities, rather than being based on a systematic foresight of 'future' social, technological, and cultural trends. Consequently, there is a lack of systematic, evidence-based strategic input (Fig. 1).

Table 1. Comparative Analysis of the Three Paradigms for Foreseeing Mobility Trends.

Paradigm	Philosophical Stance	Representative Methods	Key Strengths	Key Limitations
Quantitative-Predictive	The future is an extension of the past and can be predicted	System Dynamics [20] Bayesian Networks [22] Simulation Models [23] Machine Learning [24]	• Rigorous, objective; • Highly repeatable; • Adept at handling complex variable relationships;	• Reliant on historical data; • 'Black box' effect;
Qualitative-Critical	The future is diverse and can be explored and critiqued	Scenario Planning [15] CLA [29] Speculative Design [30]	• Stimulates disruptive thinking; • Possesses strategic depth;	• Expert-centric bias; • Difficult to translate into concrete solutions;
Design-Co-Creation	The future can be jointly designed and created	Design Thinking [31] Co-design [33] PSSD.. [38]	• Human-centred, emphasises empathy; • Produces tangible, concrete solutions;	• Prone to local optimisation; • Lack of strategic input;

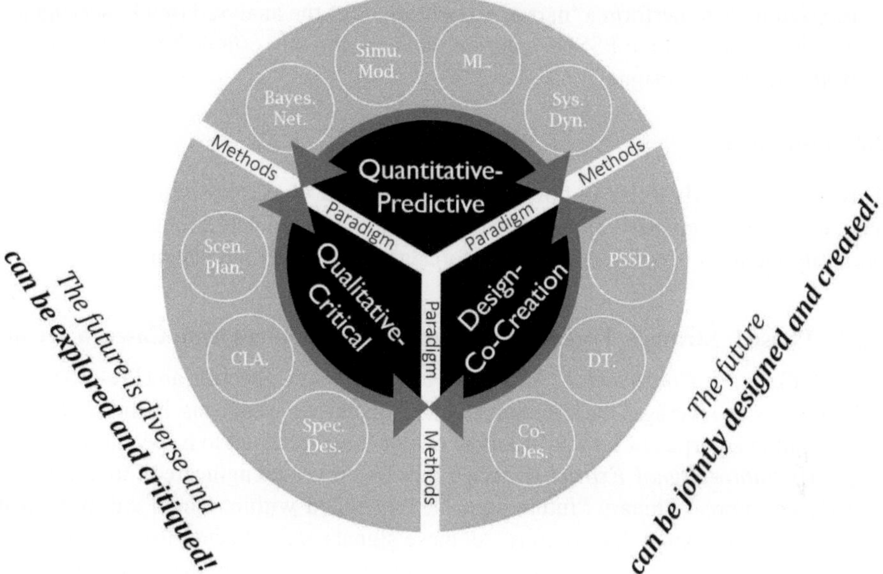

Fig. 1. The Three Paradigms for Mobility Trends Forecasting: Quantitative-Predictive, Qualitative-Critical and Design-Co-Creation.

3   Methodology

3.1   Strategies and Objectives

Building on the key strengths and limitations of the three aforementioned paradigms, this paper proposes three integration strategies, focusing respectively on sources of insight, analytical methods, and design translation, to guide the development of foresight methodology for future mobility.

- **Integration Strategy 1: Expert-Driven + Collective Intelligence:** This strategy primarily addresses the limitations of expert-centric bias and the 'black box' effect (Table 1). Its objective, regarding sources of insight, is to shift the knowledge generation model from an 'experience-driven' approach reliant on a few experts to an 'evidence-emergence' process dependent on collective observation, interpretation, and induction of cases in the smart mobility domain.
- **Integration Strategy 2: Quantitative Data + Qualitative Insight:** This strategy primarily addresses the limitations of reliance on historical data and the 'black box' effect (Table 1). Its objective, for analytical methods, is to leverage the rigorous logical framework of quantitative analysis, but to replace its processor—algorithms dependent on historical data—with human participants capable of intuitive judgement and disruptive thinking. This emphasises the role of human intuition and experience to stimulate innovative and disruptive thought.

- **Integration Strategy 3: Strategic Foresight + Design Thinking:** This strategy addresses the limitations of absent strategic input, falling into local optimisation, and difficulty in translating into concrete solutions (Table 1). Its objective, for design translation, is to perform a 'narrative translation' of the analysed trends, serving as a creative motif to drive PSSD.. solution ideation, thereby establishing a clear bridge from strategy to design.

3.2 Procedure

This section intends to break down the strategies and objectives into a set of actionable, logically progressive implementation steps, to be executed through workshops. It primarily includes two phases: strategic foresight and design innovation.

3.2.1 Phase I: Strategic Foresight – Systematic Refinement from Cases to Trends.

Step (i): Case-lab. Construction. Analogous to Document Collection and Pre-processing in NLP, this step leverages the structured logic of quantitative analysis. Participants begin by compiling a corpus of forward-looking design cases relevant to a specific scenario.

Step (ii): Future Signal Extraction. Each case is "reverse-engineered" to extract the underlying, more visionary "future signals" embedded within, which are then documented through textual descriptions. As these signals are extracted from cases within a specific mobility context, they possess a stronger contextual relevance. This method is superior to the decontextualised collection of signals, which may yield insights less pertinent to the field of mobility.

Step (iii): Feature Extraction. This step mirrors Feature Engineering and Co-occurrence Analysis in NLP. The "signals" from the previous step are distilled into more concise "feature" keywords. Subsequently, hundreds of these features are inductively grouped (e.g., using a collective affinity diagramming method) to identify latent patterns and co-occurrence relationships hidden within the data.

Step (iv): Trend Synthesis. Comparable to Topic Generation and Naming in Topic Modelling (e.g., LDA), multiple related features are further clustered to form a "trend" – a synthesised insight with far-reaching impact and the potential for systemic change.

Step (v): Narrative Encapsulation. To transform a trend into a powerful conceptual tool, it undergoes narrative encapsulation, which comprises three components: Naming, Description, and Reality Anchoring. Naming involves assigning the trend a memorable, narrative title, such as 'Her' or 'The Minority Report'. Description involves crafting a concise, objective core definition. Reality Anchoring, based on the principle of Triangulation [39], involves finding corroborating evidence for each synthesised trend from current technology news, industry reports, or market data (Fig. 2).

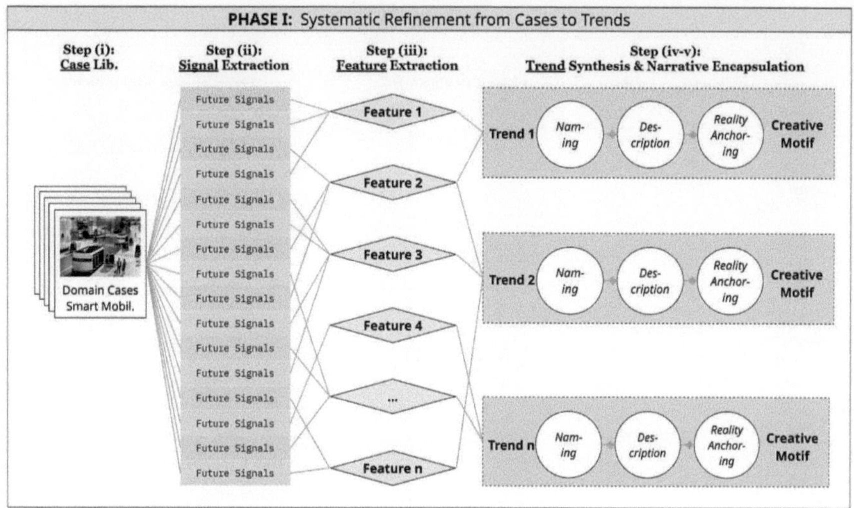

Fig. 2. Systematic Refinement Process from Cases to Trends from Phase I.

3.2.2 Phase II: Design Innovation – Transitioning from Trends to PSSD.. Solutions

Step (i): Opportunity Framing. Each group first undertakes an in-depth interpretation of the narratively encapsulated 'creative motifs' formulated in Phase 1. For each selected trend motif, the team deliberates and translates it into several specific, actionable 'Opportunity Points'. The essence of this step is the product/service-isation of trends.

Step (ii): Vision Establishment. The team reviews all translated 'Opportunity Points,' identifying combinations that are logically related, mutually complementary, or collectively point towards a more valuable future mobility landscape. Subsequently, these Opportunity Points are thematically aggregated, and from this aggregation, one or more clear PSSD.. 'Solution Visions' are distilled and sublimated, establishing the core value of each vision. In essence, this involves consolidating multiple 'actionable starting points' into an 'ideal blueprint'.

Step (iii): PSSD.. Solution Exploration. For each established 'Solution Vision,' the team employs PSSD.. methodologies and tools to design concrete solutions. This primarily comprises three components: Scenario (storyboards), Design (product and experience design), and Blueprint (system maps or user journey maps). Through this process, new 'cases' are generated, which can, in turn, serve as input for future trend derivation (Fig. 3).

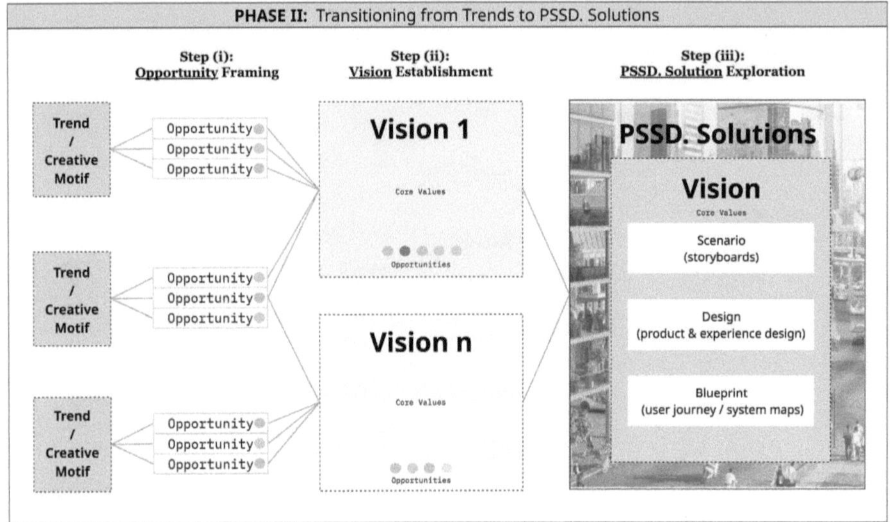

Fig. 3. Transition from trends to PSSD.. Solutions in Phase II.

4 Application: Collective Intelligence Innovation Workshop

4.1 Process and Results

To apply the methodology proposed in this study, we designed and conducted a five-day, two-phase innovation workshop titled "Contextual Integration and Future Mobility Forms". A total of 36 students with design backgrounds participated in the workshop. The execution of the workshop strictly followed the aforementioned methods. Furthermore, we embedded a series of mechanisms aimed at stimulating and deepening collective intelligence. Firstly, at key junctures in each phase, representatives from each group were required to report their results and analytical logic to all members. Through extensive exchange and discussion, groups were prompted to examine their blind spots, thereby achieving collective iteration of knowledge. Secondly, thematic sharing sessions by senior experts from consulting firms were arranged at opportune moments. Unlike the conventional approach of scheduling guest presentations before the workshop begins, we interspersed these presentations within the workshop's procedural intervals. These external stimuli and professional case studies helped to stimulate and encourage participants to further iterate their insights and solutions.

In the first phase, "Strategic Foresight", participants were divided into five groups, each focusing on mobility themes in urban, intercity, rural, uninhabited, and special scenarios. On a customised online collaborative platform, each group began by collecting smart mobility cases and translating signals, then proceeded through feature identification, and finally, collectively completed the assessment of future mobility trends. These trends were then narratively encapsulated, yielding over 20 cross-validated trends. For example, in the Rural Mobility group, members collected over 50 mobility cases. After signal extraction, these cases were re-clustered to form 19 features, including "multi-scenario applicable sightseeing vehicles", "mobile rapid medical care", "vehicles finding people to provide services", "relocatable living parks", and "natural disaster rescue scenarios". Subsequently, these features were clustered into 4 trends, which were narratively encapsulated and described as follows: "New" – New Agricultural Posture: Technology is reshaping traditional agriculture into a new, intelligent industrial ecosystem closely interconnected with cities. "Reverse" – Urban Service Transfer: High-quality urban resources (such as healthcare, education, culture) are flowing back into and reshaping rural life in a mobile manner. "Return" – Return to the Countryside: Rural areas are transforming into new living and cultural tourism spaces that cater to modern people's desires for natural integration, emotional experiences, and diverse leisure needs. "Segment" – Segmentation of Rural Mobility Users: Rural mobility services are shifting from an "integrated" to a "refined" approach, providing tailor-made solutions for specific groups with different needs. Participants had a genuine and intuitive understanding of these narratively encapsulated trends, which will help them to identify opportunities and devise solutions around these themes (Fig. 4).

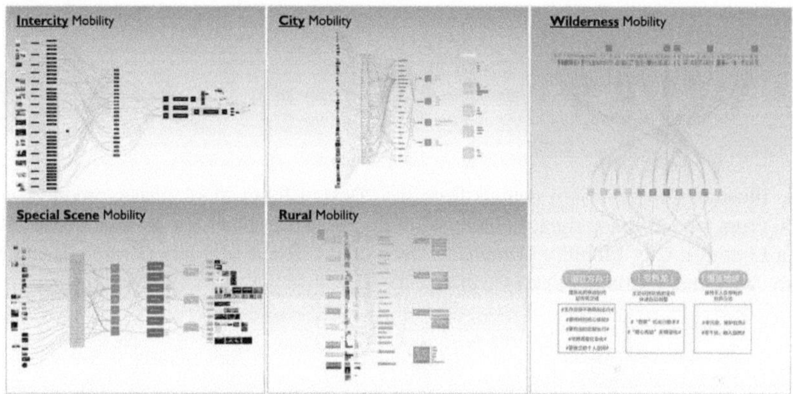

Fig. 4. The deduction process of five groups in the "Strategic Foresight" phase (case-signal-feature-trend/motif). Top Left: Intercity Mobility (Wenxing Jia et al.); Bottom Left: Special Scene Mobility (Angfu Li et al.); Middle Left: City Mobility (Yanghang Deng et al.); Middle Right: Rural Mobility (Bowen Zhang et al.); Right: Wilderness Mobility (Yixi Gu et al.).

In Phase 2, 'Design Innovation,' each group then used these trends as strategic input to construct design opportunity points, establish and articulate a vision, ultimately delivering five complete Product-Service System (PSSD.) solutions. Let us take the urban mobility group as an example. Firstly, in the opportunity identification stage, the research team delved deeply into the trend motifs to formulate several specific opportunity points, such as 'the emergence of smart detection poles,' 'personalised, customisable, and scenario-based vehicle experiences,' and 'private exoskeletons that are foldable and auto-follow.' These opportunity points then collectively shaped a future-oriented vision for smart urban mobility for the elderly in 2035. Its core lay in leveraging technology integration to grant elderly users unprecedented travel autonomy and an enhanced quality of life. Finally, the team designed and presented a specific PSSD. solution. This solution integrated smart foldable exoskeletons, a personalised mobility service app, and synergistic operation with smart road infrastructure and autonomous shuttle systems. Through vivid user journeys – such as app-based service selection, automatic vehicle collision avoidance, personalised vehicle interiors, and automated charging and payment – the team comprehensively depicted a safe, convenient, and comfortable door-to-door travel experience for elderly users in future urban environments. This fully demonstrated how macro-trends and opportunity points can be transformed into tangible and valuable innovative designs. Originating from the identified trends, this solution not only depicted a vision but also culminated in a concrete solution (Figs. 5 and 6).

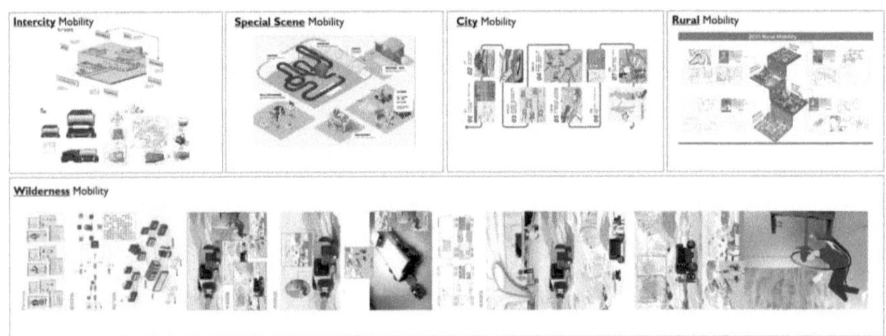

Fig. 5. Illustrates some design outputs from the "Design Innovation" phase, produced by five groups. From top left to top right: Intercity Mobility (Wenxing Jia et al.); Special Scene Mobility (Angfu Li et al.); City Mobility (Yanghang Deng et al.); Rural Mobility (Bowen Zhang et al.); Bottom: Wilderness Mobility (Yixi Gu et al.).

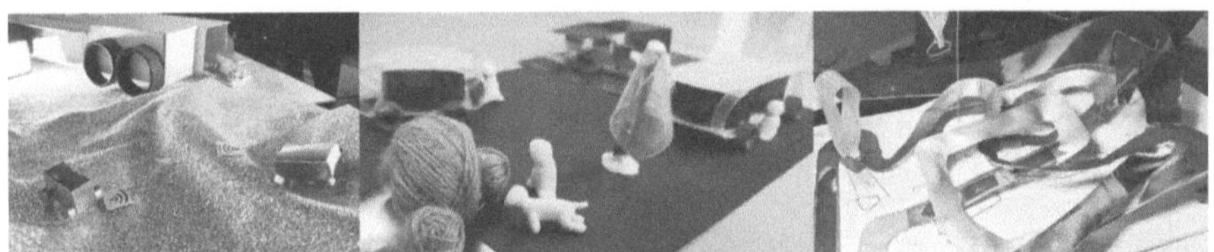

Fig. 6. Some prototypes from the "Design Innovation" phase. From left to right: Wilderness Mobility (Yixi Gu et al.); Rural Mobility (Bowen Zhang et al.); Special Scene Mobility (Angfu Li et al.).

4.2 Evaluation and Feedback

Due to the exploratory nature of this study, the evaluation did not employ quantitative metrics. Instead, the validity of this qualitative research framework was assessed through process observation, participant interviews, and output analysis, from the two dimensions of methodological effectiveness and capability enhancement.

Regarding methodological effectiveness, the process demonstrated several key advantages. In the first phase, through the "case-signal-feature-trend/motif" workflow, the workshop transformed unstructured brainstorming into a traceable process of collective insight generation. For instance, the "Rural Mobility" group converged from over 50 cases to 4 core trends. Furthermore, encapsulating trends as narrative motifs successfully converted detached analytical conclusions into engaging creative starting points. In the second phase, the "trend/motif-opportunity-vision-solution" workflow ensured a systematic and logical translation of strategic insights into concrete design concepts, underscoring the pivotal role of vision. For example, the "Urban Mobility" group, starting from trend-derived opportunities, progressively developed a coherent "2035 Urban Elderly Smart Mobility Vision" and a detailed PSSD.. solution, clearly illustrating the effectiveness of this structured pathway.

In terms of participant capability enhancement, we observed significant improvements in three competencies: (i) 'Translational' Data Literacy: Participants learned to examine qualitative cases with structured thinking. As one participant noted, their focus shifted from "collecting cases" to "exploring the invariant features behind the cases." This indicates that the method successfully 'translates' the structured thinking of data science into an analytical capability that designers can manually operate and from which they can derive inspiration. This may hold profound value for novices and design education, particularly in the context of design's shift towards interdisciplinarity. (ii) Deepened Strategic Thinking: Through mechanisms of cross-group critique and cross-validation, participants discovered that their identified trends were not based on mere guesswork, thereby building confidence in their insights. (iii) Solution-Oriented Systems Innovation: Through the construction of a vision, isolated opportunity points naturally led to systemic PSSD.. solutions.

It can be considered that the methodology proposed in this study is logically coherent and effective in its procedures. More importantly, it holds significant practical value and educational meaning in cultivating the integrative competencies required for future-oriented design talent.

5 Discussion and Conclusion

Smart mobility is a typical complex socio-technical system, its evolutionary path determined by the interplay of multiple factors including technology, users, business, and policy. Therefore, any foresight into future mobility should rely on an integrative framework capable of unifying multidimensional elements. However, reviewing existing research, future foresight methods are categorised into three paradigm, each with its own strengths, weaknesses, and operating independently. To bridge these paradigmatic gaps, this study, through literature review and theoretical deduction, proposes a methodology aimed at integrating the strengths of these three approaches, and applies it to a collective intelligence innovation workshop focused on future mobility.

It can be argued that the greatest theoretical contribution of this study lies in providing an "integrative framework" that bridges paradigmatic gaps. Its contributions and reflections are as follows:

(i) Integration of Expert-Driven and Collective Intelligence: Unlike traditional methods (such as the Delphi method) that rely on the experience of a few experts, this method is based on an "evidence-emergence" model. Knowledge generation stems from the collective interpretation and induction of a large number of external cases (evidence) by the group. Research has indicated that forecasts made by experts are no more accurate than those of knowledgeable individuals [26]. We hope this helps to reduce expert-centric bias and empower a wider range of participants with future exploration capabilities. Its performance still awaits further validation.

(ii) Integration of Quantitative Thinking and Qualitative Insight: Traditional quantitative models are often criticised for their "black box" nature. This method cleverly "translates" their structured thinking (such as NLP processes) and relies on human collective intelligence and information processing capabilities to analyse data. We hope this enables participants to benefit from the rigour of structured analysis while also injecting unique human intuition, experience, and critical reflection, thereby opening the "black box" and achieving a unity of rigour and inspiration. While this might lead to a waste of manpower, it could perhaps help train participants in structured thinking. We maintain reservations on this point.

(iii) Integration of Strategic Foresight and Design innovation: Through the key mechanism of "narrative encapsulation", this study builds a solid bridge between abstract strategic trends and concrete design solutions. It transforms a high-level analytical conclusion (Trend) into an emotionally and culturally resonant "Creative Motif", directly driving the ideation of PSSD.. solutions. This effectively addresses the classic challenges of strategic foresight being "difficult to implement" and design thinking "lacking strategic input". We hope to develop more tools to refine this step.

As exploratory research, the main limitations and future directions of this study are as follows:

(i) Homogeneity of Participant Backgrounds: The participants in this workshop were all design students. Although this thoroughly validates the method's significant potential in design education—especially in cultivating interdisciplinary integrative competencies—its applicability within multidisciplinary teams comprising senior industry experts, engineers, policymakers, etc., remains to be further verified. Scholars have emphasised that scenario analysis processes should have clear participation to achieve good results [40]. However, the scope of participants mainly includes stakeholders and experts. Therefore, results obtained with design students as participants have considerable limitations. Future research should test this method among more diverse participant groups to observe how different knowledge backgrounds affect the emergence process of collective intelligence.

(ii) Scalability of the Method: A workshop with 36 people can be managed with human guidance. However, if the scale expands to hundreds, effectively collecting, clustering, and synthesising vast amounts of qualitative information will become a huge challenge. Future research should explore combining this method with Artificial Intelligence (AI) technologies. For example, using models like NLP to assist in the initial extraction of signals and clustering of features, followed by human participants conducting higher-order trend synthesis and narrative encapsulation, to build a human-AI collaborative, more scalable collective intelligence system.

(iii) Challenges in Outcome Evaluation: This paper employed qualitative evaluation. However, assessing the quality of a "future scenario" is itself a difficult problem. Future research could focus on developing new evaluation frameworks, for example, by tracking the impact of solutions generated by this method on subsequent decision-making, product iteration, or organisational strategic adjustments, to measure their true value over a longer period.

In summary, the proposed method not only provides an operational toolkit for effectively translating macro-trends into concrete PSSD.. (Product/Service System) design solutions but, more importantly, it offers an effective paradigm for design education and practice aimed at systematically cultivating the integrative competencies (i.e., blending structured analysis, critical foresight, and systemic creative capabilities) of the next generation of innovative talent. We hope this research can inspire researchers and practitioners.

Acknowledgements. We would like to express our gratitude to all the participants who took part in this workshop.

References

1. Righi, A.W., Saurin, T.A.: Complex socio-technical systems: characterization and management guidelines. Appl. Ergon. **50**, 19–30 (2015). https://doi.org/10.1016/j.apergo.2015.02.003
2. Lyons, G., Rohr, C., Smith, A., Rothnie, A., Curry, A.: Scenario planning for transport practitioners. Transp. Res. Interdiscip. Perspect. **11**, 100438 (2021). https://doi.org/10.1016/j.trip.2021.100438
3. Bazzan, A.L., Klügl, F.: Introduction to Intelligent Systems in Traffic and Transportation. Springer Nature, London (2022).
4. Nallur, V., Elgammal, A., Clarke, S.: Smart route planning using open data and participatory sensing. In: Damiani, E., Frati, F., Riehle, D., Wasserman, A.I. (eds.) Open Source Systems: Adoption and Impact, pp. 91–100. Springer International Publishing, Cham (2015). https://doi.org/10.1007/978-3-319-17837-0_9
5. Bıyık, C., Abareshi, A., Paz, A., Ruiz, R.A., Battarra, R., Rogers, C.D.F., et al.: Smart mobility adoption: a review of the literature. J. Open Innov. Technol. Mark. Complex. **7**, 146 (2021). https://doi.org/10.3390/joitmc7020146
6. Sheller, M., Urry, J.: The new mobilities paradigm. Environ. Plan. A. **38**, 207–226 (2006). https://doi.org/10.1068/a37268
7. Sheller, M.: Automotive emotions: feeling the car. Theory Cult. Soc. **21**, 221–242 (2004). https://doi.org/10.1177/0263276404046068
8. Gall, T., Hörl, S., Vallet, F., Yannou, B.: Integrating future trends and uncertainties in urban mobility design via data-driven personas and scenarios. Eur. Transp. Res. Rev. **15**, 45 (2023). https://doi.org/10.1186/s12544-023-00622-0
9. Vallet, F., Puchinger, J., Millonig, A., Lamé, G., Nicolaï, I.: Tangible futures: combining scenario thinking and personas-a pilot study on urban mobility. Futures. **117**, 102513 (2020)
10. Anggreeni, I., van der Voort, M.C.: Tracing the Scenarios in Scenario-Based Product Design: A Study to Support Scenario Generation. (2007).
11. Eilouti, B.: Scenario-based design: new applications in metamorphic architecture. Front. Archit. Res. **7**, 530–543 (2018)
12. Hiltunen, E.: Scenarios: process and outcome. J. Futures Stud. **13**, 151–152 (2009)

13. Eggink, W., Reinders, A.H.M.E., van der Meulen, B.: A practical approach to product design for future worlds using scenario development. In: 11th International Conference on Engineering and Product Design Education: Creating a Better World, E and PDE 2009. Creating a Better World: Proceedings of the 11th International Conference on Product Design Education, 10th–11th September 2009, pp. 538–543. University of Brighton, Brighton (2009)

14. Inagaki, T., Sheridan, T.B.: A critique of the SAE conditional driving automation definition, and analyses of options for improvement. Cogn. Tech. Work. **21**, 569–578 (2019). https://doi.org/10.1007/s10111-018-0471-5

15. Lyons, G., Davidson, C.: Guidance for transport planning and policymaking in the face of an uncertain future. Transp. Res. A Policy Pract. **88**, 104–116 (2016). https://doi.org/10.1016/j.tra.2016.03.012

16. Rode, P., Floater, G., Thomopoulos, N., Docherty, J., Schwinger, P., Mahendra, A., Fang, W.: Accessibility in cities: transport and urban form. In: Meyer, G., Shaheen, S. (eds.) Disrupting Mobility, pp. 239–273. Springer International Publishing, Cham (2017). https://doi.org/10.1007/978-3-319-51602-8_15

17. Schwanen, T., Dijst, M., Dieleman, F.M.: Policies for urban form and their impact on travel: the Netherlands experience. Urban Stud. **41**, 579–603 (2004). https://doi.org/10.1080/0042098042000178690

18. Orrell, D., McSharry, P.: System economics: overcoming the pitfalls of forecasting models via a multidisciplinary approach. Int. J. Forecast. **25**, 734–743 (2009)

19. Forrester, J.W.: Industrial dynamics: a major breakthrough for decision makers. In: Klaus, P., Müller, S. (eds.) The Roots of Logistics, pp. 141–172. Springer Berlin Heidelberg, Berlin, Heidelberg (2012). https://doi.org/10.1007/978-3-642-27922-5_13

20. Shepherd, S.P.: A review of system dynamics models applied in transportation. Transportmetrica B Transp. Dyn. **2**, 83–105 (2014). https://doi.org/10.1080/21680566.2014.916236

21. Hossain, N.U.I., Sakib, N., Govindan, K.: Assessing the performance of unmanned aerial vehicle for logistics and transportation leveraging the Bayesian network approach. Expert Syst. Appl. **209**, 118301 (2022)

22. Tang, J., Heinimann, H., Han, K., Luo, H., Zhong, B.: Evaluating resilience in urban transportation systems for sustainability: a systems-based Bayesian network model. Transp. Res. Part C Emerg. Technol. **121**, 102840 (2020). https://doi.org/10.1016/j.trc.2020.102840

23. Treiber, M., Kesting, A.: Traffic Flow Dynamics: Data, Models and Simulation. Springer Berlin Heidelberg, Berlin, Heidelberg (2013). https://doi.org/10.1007/978-3-642-32460-4

24. Chen, G., Zhang, J.w.: Intelligent transportation systems: machine learning approaches for urban mobility in smart cities. Sustain. Cities Soc. **107**, 105369 (2024). https://doi.org/10.1016/j.scs.2024.105369

25. Boukerche, A., Wang, J.: Machine learning-based traffic prediction models for intelligent transportation systems. Comput. Netw. **181**, 107530 (2020)

26. Makridakis, S., Hogarth, R.M., Gaba, A.: Forecasting and uncertainty in the economic and business world. Int. J. Forecast. **25**, 794–812 (2009). https://doi.org/10.1016/j.ijforecast.2009.05.012

27. Amer, M., Daim, T.U., Jetter, A.: A review of scenario planning. Futures. **46**, 23–40 (2013). https://doi.org/10.1016/j.futures.2012.10.003

28. Bentham, J.: The scenario approach to possible futures for oil and natural gas. Energy Policy. **64**, 87–92 (2014)

29. Inayatullah, S.: Causal layered analysis: poststructuralism as method. Futures. **30**, 815–829 (1998)

30. Dunne, A., Raby, F.: Speculative Everything: Design, Fiction, and Social Dreaming. The MIT Press, Cambridge (2013)

31. Miller, P.N.: Is "design thinking" the new liberal arts? In: The Evolution of Liberal Arts in the Global Age
32. Viviani, S., Gulino, M.-S., Rinaldi, A., Vangi, D.: An interdisciplinary double-diamond design thinking model for urban transport product innovation: a design framework for innovation combining mixed methods for developing the electric microvehicle "leonardo project". Energies. **17**, 5918 (2024)
33. Pettersson, F., Westerdahl, S., Hansson, J.: Learning through collaboration in the Swedish public transport sector? Co-production through guidelines and living labs. Res. Transp. Econ. **69**, 394–401 (2018)
34. Ciasullo, M.V., Palumbo, R., Troisi, O.: Reading public service co-production through the lenses of requisite variety. Int. J. Bus. Manag. **12**, 1–13 (2017)
35. van Halen, C.J., te Riele, H.R.: Product Service Systems, Ecological and Economic Basics. (1999).
36. Sakao, T., Lindahl, M.: Introduction to Product/Service-System Design. Springer Science & Business Media, London (2009)
37. Ran, B., Qin, J.: Smart product-service system design based on human mobility with the medium autonomous vehicles. In: Rau, P.-L.P. (ed.) Cross-Cultural Design. Product and Service Design, Mobility and Automotive Design, Cities, Urban Areas, and Intelligent Environments Design, pp. 228–247. Springer International Publishing, Cham (2022). https://doi.org/10.1007/978-3-031-06053-3_16
38. Beckmann-Dobrev, B., Kind, S., Stark, R.: Hybrid simulators for product service-systems – innovation potential demonstrated on urban bike mobility. Procedia CIRP. **36**, 78–82 (2015). https://doi.org/10.1016/j.procir.2015.01.049
39. Blaikie, N.W.: A critique of the use of triangulation in social research. Qual. Quant. **25**, 115–136 (1991)
40. Banister, D., Hickman, R.: Transport futures: thinking the unthinkable. Transp. Policy. **29**, 283–293 (2013). https://doi.org/10.1016/j.tranpol.2012.07.005

Cultural Radar: A Design Method for Identifying Weak Signals by Integrating Media Anthropology and Futures Studies

Qing Xia, Zhengqi Lin, and Jiaqi Wang[✉]

Luxun Academy of Fine Arts, Dalian, Lioaning, China
`1092216908@qq.com`

Abstract. In today's highly mediatized and culturally fluid society, identifying weak signals of future trends has become a key challenge for design futures research and practice. Traditional forecasting tools often overlook micro-practices and heterogeneous narratives embedded in everyday cultural life, making it difficult to detect early signs of emerging issues. This paper integrates methodologies from media anthropology and futures studies to propose a Cultural Radar method for detecting weak signals. Two case studies—youth emotional hunger and the deconstruction of "Deng" as a cultural power holder—demonstrate how design can function as cultural laboratories. This research expands the cultural dimension of weak signal theory and offers a practical paradigm for future-oriented design inquiry.

Keywords: Design Futures · Media Anthropology · Futures Studies · Weak Signals

1 Introduction

In an age marked by uncertainty and complexity, the ability to detect early-stage issues that have not yet taken shape but may profoundly impact the future is a core challenge for design futures. Envisioning futures should not rely solely on macro trends or explicit technologies; rather, it requires attention to the subtle movements and cultural clues emerging from the margins.

Media anthropology, a discipline focused on media practices and cultural expressions, has recently demonstrated strong observational capabilities. It excels in uncovering non-mainstream behaviors and heterogeneous expressions in everyday media interactions [1, 2]. With its emphasis on field-based cultural perception, media anthropology explores media content, user behavior, and participation structures, making it well-suited to identifying cultural signals not yet captured by dominant ideologies [3].

Meanwhile, the concept of weak signals—first proposed by Igor Ansoff in 1975—has become central to futures studies [4]. Weak signals are ambiguous, dispersed phenomena that have not yet entered the mainstream but may signal the early stages of significant change. Compared to trends or drivers, weak signals are more elusive and often lie

P.-L.P. Rau and H. Krömker (Eds.): HCII 2025, LNCS 16336, pp. 152–166, 2026.
https://doi.org/10.1007/978-3-032-12798-3_10

hidden in daily life, subcultures, technological margins, or linguistic peripheries. Yet, they are regarded as crucial early indicators for discovering new issues [5]. In design futures research and practice, weak signal identification is increasingly incorporated in early-stage exploration, with methodologies like Ethnographic Experiential Futures and Speculative Scenarios encouraging the extraction of potential signals from social peripheries and cultural gaps to inspire new directions in design [6, 7].

Therefore, this paper proposes a method that combines the observational depth of media anthropology with the structural models of futures research to create a cultural weak signal discovery method aimed at design practice. This approach expands the cultural sources of signals and provides critical and imaginative materials for agenda-setting and concept exploration in the early stages of design.

This method attempts to answer several key questions: In an age when media plays a central role in shaping society, how can design anticipate emerging issues through cultural perception? Can the discovery of future signals move beyond expert knowledge to originate from everyday life? Can design become a kind of cultural radar that actively engages in the identification and construction of future issues?

This study seeks to build a bridge between media anthropology and futures studies by developing a cultural weak signal discovery method tailored for early-stage design exploration. The research offers both theoretical innovation and practical value, especially in design education and practice. Through this method's formulation and validation, the paper aims to address the often-overlooked question of how design discovers problems and further advance a culturally sensitive, methodologically structured, and translatable pathway for recognizing the future through culture.

2   Literature Review and Theoretical Framework

In the digital era, where media deeply permeates daily life, cultural trends are no longer shaped solely by mainstream narratives or centralized discourse. Instead, they increasingly emerge through fragmented expressions from marginal communities, grassroots cultures, and micro-practices. Media anthropology—a discipline examining the relationship between media practices and cultural formations—offers both theoretical foundations and field methods for recognizing these emerging patterns [8–11]. A central concept in media anthropology is media practices, which refers to how people "use," "create," and are "shaped by" media content within specific social and cultural contexts. Unlike media studies that often focus on the macro functions of media technologies, media anthropology emphasizes media as a platform for social interaction, identity construction, and meaning negotiation [12].

In terms of identifying cultural trends, media anthropologists employ several strategies: Close reading of micro-expressions and unconventional behaviors in media content, such as the use of niche slang, memes, emojis, and the visual aesthetics of short videos; Observation of the contextual and creative nature of media use, such as the replication of memes or collective "bullet comment" cultures during livestreams; Documentation of marginalized group expressions, including identity performances and cultural creations among youth, subcultural communities, or regional groups. These approaches not only reveal how cultural trends are generated, but also provide clues to future shifts in values and public attention [13, 14].

Media anthropology pays attention to "marginality" and "everydayness"—those expressions that have not yet entered the mainstream but reflect underlying cultural tensions. For instance, Downey, Mihelj and Peter Bajomi-Lázár have examined Eastern European television cultures during the post-socialist transition to understand how ordinary people participated in social change through media [15, 16]. In the Chinese context, scholars like Yuhuan Zhong, Lijun Guo, etc., have explored the media practices of elderly TikTok users, revealing structural cultural demands behind their atypical expressions [17, 18].

In design research, these marginal expressions are often overlooked, yet they may signal the emergence of future societal concerns. Incorporating a media anthropological lens into weak signal research can expand the cultural dimension of future signals—not only attending to technology or policy shifts, but also tracking energy accumulations within micro-cultural spheres. Many societal changes originate not from top-down interventions but from the slow build-up of everyday practices, becoming visible only after reaching a tipping point. Thus, this study advocates for replacing macro-level scanning with micro-level cultural observation, and expert-led filtering with field-based signal collection. This provides a more culturally sensitive entry point into future design practice.

In the field of futures studies, weak signals are regarded as early indicators of major societal transformation—still hidden, ambiguous, and not yet fully formed. Compared with more prominent elements like trends or drivers, weak signals are scattered, subtle, and often overlooked. However, this very elusiveness makes them valuable entry points for detecting emerging issues and envisioning alternative futures [19].

The concept of weak signals was first introduced by Igor Ansoff in 1975, who described them as "early, imprecise, and incomplete" but potentially important pieces of information [4]. Hiltunen later refined this definition in 2008, identifying three defining characteristics of weak signals, novelty, marginality and ambiguity [5]. Signals often come from unfamiliar domains or unknown behavioral patterns; They lack dominance in current mainstream narratives or discourses; Their meaning is unclear, potentially multi-layered, and difficult to classify. Due to these traits, the process of identifying weak signals is inherently uncertain—but also crucial for unlocking possibilities that lie beyond the visible horizon [20].

In practice, futures researchers have developed various tools and methods to detect and analyze weak signals, such as Environmental Scanning [21], Horizon scanning [22], Trend and impact analysis [23], etc. However, these approaches also present limitations: Over-reliance on expert-driven scanning can exclude insights from marginalized communities and non-institutional voices; Content bias toward technological, market, or institutional signals may result in blind spots when it comes to everyday cultural phenomena; Standardized tools may filter out irrational, emotional, or non-linear expressions that often carry rich cultural significance. In the Chinese context, particularly, weak signals rooted in youth culture, rural transformation, or ironic online discourse often remain invisible to traditional foresight systems.

In recent years, design futures practice has increasingly adopted weak signal methodologies in early-stage ideation and trend exploration. For instance, in scenario building, tools such as Ethnographic Experiential Futures encourage designers to draw inspiration from edge cases and social margins [6]; In workshop formats, trend cards and future headlines are used to guide speculative thinking [24]; In speculative design outputs, weak signals often serve as seeds for design fictions and provotypes [25]. This indicates that such integration is needed in the field of design, and this integration has formed good practical examples in some certain specific fields

In light of this, we maintain that weak signal methods should evolve beyond rationalist, expert-centric models to embrace cultural sensing mechanisms—where signals are viewed not merely as data points but as emerging fields of meaning shaped by sociocultural contexts. Identifying such signals demands both fine-grained observation and cross-cultural interpretation. Moreover, weak signals should not only be tools for seeing the futures but also raw materials for constructing it. Designers can cultivate cultural radaring capabilities: not only responding to existing problems but actively discovering and defining future issues by engaging with emerging cultural expressions.

This study therefore proposes the integration of weak signal theory with media anthropology as a foundation for developing a weak signal discovery method tailored for design futures practice. The resulting framework—Cultural Radar—aims to serve as a new theoretical model for surfacing potential design issues and inspiring socially meaningful innovation.

3   Methodology

This study is grounded in the epistemological framework of constructivism, which views the future not as a fixed outcome to be predicted, but as a collective imagination shaped by different social groups within specific cultural contexts. The researcher is not seen as a neutral observer but as a co-creator and interpreter. We also adopt a reflexive practice approach, emphasizing the dynamic relationship between the researcher, the data, participants, and methods. This orientation makes weak signal identification more culturally sensitive and provides a richer foundation for inclusive design inquiry.

The methodology follows a three-phase structure of Observation – Analysis – Translation, forming the Cultural Radar method. We use media anthropological tools to collect heterogeneous narratives and marginal expressions from Chinese youth media environments (data collection methods shown as Table 1). The materials serve as potential signal sources for analysis.

This study focuses on two cultural phenomena as case examples. The first is emotional hunger in youth, expressed through social media behaviors and symbolic digital rituals to seek connection or recognition. The second is the deconstruction of "Deng" as a cultural power marker, where youth use irony and parody to challenge dominant aesthetic and identity norms.

To balance cultural sensitivity and design applicability, this study introduces two mechanisms. First, integrating multi-modal material. We analyze not only text but also images and video to deepen the contextual interpretation and capture subtle affective cues. This enhances the richness and accuracy of signal recognition. Second, introducing signal iteration mechanism. Rather than fixing signals at first recognition, we enable recursive questioning, group validation, and reconstruction. This iterative approach improves flexibility and robustness in signal selection and supports the transformation of cultural insight into design-relevant issues.

Table 1. Data collection methods.

Method	Tools	Content
Heterogeneous Narrative Sampling	Screenshots, video, field notes	Youth language, symbolic use, metaphorical expressions
Co-creation Workshops	Post-it tools, keyword cards	Collaborative signal recognition and interpretation

Despite these efforts, we acknowledge the limitations of the methodology: First, the identification and interpretation of weak signals rely heavily on the researcher's cultural lens and judgment, which introduces subjectivity and limits generalizability; Second, the study is grounded in specific observation contexts (e.g., co-creation workshop and youth social platforms), which may result in sample bias and exclude other cultural groups or fringe voices; Third, due to the short time frame of the study, it is difficult to track the long-term evolution or societal impact of the identified signals. Future research should expand cross-regional sampling, enable longitudinal tracking, and incorporate multi-researcher perspectives to enhance robustness and scope.

4 Cultural Radar: A New Method for Discovering Weak Signals in Design Futures

The Cultural Radar method is a framework for early-stage design exploration, aimed at identifying emerging future issues. It integrates the deep observation of media anthropology with signal modeling techniques from futures studies, ultimately generating design-relevant insights from weak cultural signals. This method not only provides a structured pathway for recognizing emerging trends within everyday culture, but also offers designers a workflow of Observation-Analysis-Translation.

The method consists of three interconnected stages: Fist stage, using media anthropology to surface cultural material for analysis; Second stage, applying structured signal modeling to analyze and cluster the material; Third, translating the results into weak signal insights for design (as Fig. 1).

The Cultural Radar tool emphasizes visual thinking and interdisciplinary collaboration. If we model the structure of these three stages, it resembles a set of concentric rings: The inner layer shows primary cultural signals (inspiration fragments); On the middle layer, there are signal clustering and inductive inference (issues, signals, interpretations); On the outer layer, visual narrative forms (signal cards, conceptual maps, prototypes) are distributed.

This concentric model helps express complex cultural trends systematically, and can be used in teaching, design research, or cultural policy formulation.

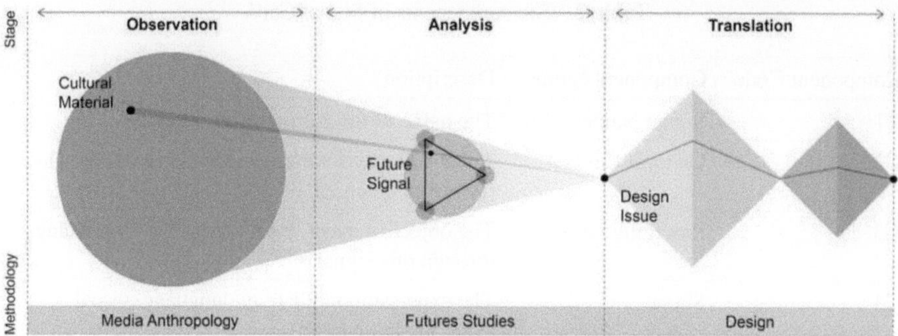

Fig. 1. The three stages of Cultural Radar.

4.1 The Stages of Cultural Radar

Phase 1: Ethnographic Signal Surfacing. In this first phase, researchers use techniques such as media behavior observation, informal interviews, and symbolic documentation to conduct micro-ethnographic fieldwork. The goal is to capture expressions that are occurring within cultural groups but not yet mainstream. These materials are treated as potential signal sources with the traits: subtle but frequent occurrences (e.g., youth repeatedly expressing "emotional hunger" online), local cultural traits or subcultural aesthetics (e.g., the ironic use of the word "Deng"), unstable forms, drifting semantics.

Through the methodological lens of media anthropology, these heterogeneous cultural fragments are systematically collected and recorded to provide the foundation for later signal identification.

Phase 2: Structured Signal Analysis. The second phase involves analyzing the collected material using Future sign model from futures studies. The model was proposed by Hiltunen in 2007 [26], which organizes analysis into three core dimensions of issues, signals and interpretation. The issues are that what we see and feel is truly happening around us and is an objective fact. The signals come from some information in newspapers or news, and have a certain quantity and visibility. Interpretation is the understanding of future signs by those who receive signals and questions, tending towards subjective inference. These three dimensions can also be visualized as a three-dimensional space, from which potential trends can be inferred. Potential trends indicate whether future signals may be amplified and transformed into important issues in the future, or whether it can be connected with certain macro trends such as technology, society and ecology.

Through this structured process, vague cultural phenomena are transformed into primary signal units, each with potential paths of future development.

Phase 3: Design-Oriented Signal Translation. In the third phase, cultural signals are no longer just research data—they are translated into design-relevant insights. These insights help guide design problem framing, scenario construction, or speculative prototyping. The core tool for this translation is the Signal Card, which organizes each signal into eight analytical components, including signal name, Cultural Context, Emerging Issue, signal, Interpretation, Emerging Trend, Design Implication and Note (as Table **2**).

Table 2. The components of Signal Card.

Component Code	Component Name	Description
C1	Signal Name	The name of the cultural phenomenon
C2	Cultural Context	The media environment and social group in which the signal emerged
C3	Emerging Issue	The objective event, trend, or problem surfacing through this signal
C4	Signal	The expression mode (e.g., language, visual, symbolic interaction)
C5	Interpretation	Subjective interpretation of the signal (e.g., cultural meaning, boundaries)
C6	Emerging Trend	The possible future directions of social and cultural development
C7	Design Implication	How this signal could inspire new design topics, methods, or strategies
C8	Note	Background information, references, related resources, etc.

The cards can be used in brainstorming workshops or scenario-building activities to create signal maps that may reveal deeper underlying themes. They also serve as inputs for diegetic prototypes, which embedding the signals into speculative future scenarios, or as trigger topics for co-creation workshops, facilitating participants to carry out design concepts based on real cultural insights.

The method of three stages enables researchers designing the future to identify problems more acutely, trigger imagination, and intervene in the construction process of potential future cultural issues in advance through the perception mechanism of culture.

4.2 Cultural Radar Toolkit

The Cultural Radar Toolkit is a practical implementation of the above method. It is composed of three core modules, which are Heteroglossia Scanner, Weak Signal Analyzer and Future Signal Generator (as Table 3). Each module addresses a different step in the weak signal discovery process.

The application of the Cultural Radar follows a three-step methodology of Scanning-Analyzing-Translating.

In M1, the primary task is the scanning process, which employs methods and tools from media anthropology to conduct broad observation and collection: information is gathered within cultural fields through interviews, observations, visual documentation, and other means, with a focus on heterogeneous expressions, semantic shifts, and everyday non-mainstream rituals. Researchers perform preliminary coding and categorization from an anthropological perspective, identifying cultural fragments that appear "seemingly unrelated yet frequently recurring", thereby compiling a primary signal list.

Table 3. The modules of Cultural Radar Toolkit.

Module Code	Module Name	Function	Card Component
M1	Heteroglossia Scanner	Capture narrative differences in marginal groups and media behaviors; co-label signals with participants	C2, C8
M2	Weak Signal Analyzer	Use signal structure frameworks to analyze and cluster material	C3, C4, C5, C6
M3	Future Signal Generator	Generate signal cards and creative design prompts	C1, C7

In M2, the main procedure is analysis, utilizing futures research tools—specifically, the Future Sign—as the analytical framework. Through methods such as Card Mapping, Affinity Diagram and AI-assisted summarization, participants collaboratively cluster similar signals to form preliminary weak signal clusters.

In M3, the translation process is executed, refining Signal Card content using images, text, and other mediums. Multiple signal cards are created to establish a future signals library, which serves to inspire subsequent design innovation.

4.3   Case Study and Method Application

This section presents two case studies to empirically apply the Cultural Radar method, aiming to showcase how this method operates in cultural observation, signal extraction, and design translation. Both cases are based on real field scenarios and teaching practices, highlighting expressions from youth culture that are not yet mainstream but possess future potential.

In these case studies, in addition to using the three core modules of the Cultural Radar tool, an additional module, Future Interactive Space Prototypes, was introduced to better connect with the subsequent design inspiration process (as Table 4).

Case 1: Emotional Hunger in Youth Media Culture.   In the daily use of social media, an increasing number of young people are seeking a sense of existence and validation through like-counting, limited-time follows, random anonymous remarks, and similar behaviors. These actions are no longer casual entertainment-driven interactions but rather conceal a collective expression of "emotional hunger". Behind this lies a desire for stable relationships, visibility, and emotional dependency on algorithmic feedback mechanisms (see Table 5).

Table 4. Application process of the case studies.

Module Code	Operation	Tools & Materials
M1-1	Micro-ethnographic observation, screenshots of social platform behavior, keyword public opinion analysis. Participants are asked to widely search for non-mainstream forms related to youth on online media.	Screenshots or screen recordings from TikTok, Weibo, Redbook, Douban observation records
M1-2	Coding cultural expression patterns, preliminary semantic categorization.	Obsidian, NVivo
M2	Reorganizing and analyzing materials using the Future Signals tool template.	Future Signals tool template
M3	Forming signal cards.	Signal card tool template
Additional Module	Creating future envisioning prototypes	AI image generation

Case 2: Deconstructing "Deng" as Cultural Power Holder. In the Chinese online context, the term "Deng" originally meaning lowbrow or out of bounds, has been repurposed by youth culture in ironic, self-deprecating, and parodic ways. This process challenges traditional power structures, mocking authority and questioning the dominant aesthetic and identity standards (see Table 6).

Through two case studies, the Cultural Radar tool has been preliminarily validated to possess the following capabilities: (1) Identifying latent issues, capturing cultural signals with evolutionary potential from non-mainstream subcultures; (2) Translating cultural materials into design materials, structuring cultural observations into analyzable signals for design application; (3) Enabling proactive design intervention, assisting designers in framing problems and selecting value orientations before trends fully crystallize. The cases also reveal that design is not merely a problem-solving tool—it can also serve as a frontline mechanism for discovering issues and constructing cultural imaginaries.

Table 5. Signal Card for Emotional Hunger in Youth Media Culture.

Component Name	Description
Signal Name	Emotional Hunger in Youth Media Culture
Cultural Context	Youth media environment formed by short video platforms, bullet comment culture, emoji remakes, anonymous forums, and algorithmic recommendation mechanisms. Cultural context of weakened family support and diminished offline social interaction.
Emerging Issue	Growing internal demand among youth for being seen and being understood, expressed as a continuous reliance on immediate emotional responses, attention feedback, and companionable content.
Signal	Ritualistic "like" behavior: "The 6th person who likes my post, I'll treat you to milk tea", Collective "+1" in bullet comments. Content fragments spreading feelings of loneliness: "Post a moment to see if anyone cares" "Today's mood check-in" "Drinking coffee alone". AI talk as emotional substitute conversations: Heart-to-heart talks with ChatGPT, Screenshot-sharing of AI chat, Custom virtual lover interfaces
Interpretation	Emotional hunger is not a psychological disorder, but a tension between attention demand and empathy void in the digital media environment. It is a mediated emotional solicitation behavior, showing characteristics of high immediacy, anonymity, and symbolism.
Emerging Trend	Emotion will become one of the central axes of media interaction: future AI companionship, virtual empathy communities, anonymous psychological broadcasts, and digital emotional products may see explosive growth. Emotions may evolve into new dimensions of social participation.
Design Implication	These signals point to an emerging yet non-mainstream future issue: the design of "emotional infrastructure" in the technological era, where emotions are no longer maintained through interpersonal relationships but captured, managed, and reproduced through algorithms and media. Ideas: developing "Emotional Resonance" Service Products (e.g., public mood calendars, collective emotion theaters), exploring Digital Emotional Visualization Formats (e.g., emotional terrain mapping, interactive ritual design), Enhancing AI's Ability to Detect and Respond to Subtle Emotional Cues, building an "Experience of Being Understood" Mechanism
Note	Related to emotional internet, AI companionship product design, and loneliness economy. Typical cases include the documentary Emotional Harvesters, Soul App's emotional squares, and Bilibili's bullet-comment interactive AI livestreams. Keywords: empathy economy, emotional visualization, psychosocial media.

Table 6. Signal Card for Deconstructing "Deng" as Cultural Power Holder.

Component Name	Description
Signal Name	Deconstructing "Deng" as Cultural Power Holder
Cultural Context	Online discourse in communities such as Douban, Weibo, Bilibili, Zhihu, and Hupu, expressing collective resistance and satire against mainstream elite cultures and hierarchical social systems.
Emerging Issue	Youth use the "Deng" label to deconstruct success narratives and its symbolic expressions (e.g., Academic flexing, Neijuan speech), forming a kind of desacralization and dissection of cultural capital and elite authority discourse.
Signal	Deconstructing existing power structures: Old Deng movie rankings, New Deng literary elements analysis. Low aesthetic = new identity politics: Deng-exclusive fashion challenge, Deng-style emoji. Reversing algorithmic control by using "being looked down upon" to gain platform recommendation flow: Deng leader's imitation video.
Interpretation	Deng label points to the old-age power. Its deconstruction is symbolic protest for cultural capital redistribution, reflecting youth's ironic resistance and silent opposition to structural inequalities.
Emerging Trend	Future network culture may continue to resist and parody existing hegemonies, promoting greater legitimacy for diverse, non-elite, emotional expressions. The digital space will become a new battleground for discourse power.
Design Implication	These signals suggest an important future design issue: the decentralization and redistribution of cultural power, and how design can intervene in media taste formation, social identity shaping, and the flow of cultural symbolic rights. Ideas: Anti-Elitist discourse-Driven community interaction design (e.g., collaboration platforms that de-emphasize KPIs), social products featuring De-Performatized expression (e.g., satirical narrative templates, anti-Deng meme packs), identifying cultural resistance mechanisms in linguistic symbols and translating them into inputs for pluralistic design.
Note	Related to self-optimization anxiety, middle-class disguise. Derivative contexts include middle-class fashion, POA check-ins and professional identity scripts. Relevant issues: Bilibili anti-workplace videos, cultural events of Kong Yiji literature.

5   Discussion

This study aims to construct a weak signal identification method—Cultural Radar—that integrates media anthropology with futures studies, in order to address the tension in design futures research between early issue detection and design applicability. This chapter discusses the research outcomes from three perspectives: (1) the theoretical contribution and boundaries of the Cultural Radar method; (2) the design implications of the signal card; and (3) the strategic significance of design as a trigger for future issues.

Traditional futures research often emphasizes structured data analysis, expert consensus modeling, and trend synthesis. In contrast, the Cultural Radar method which grounded in constructivism and media anthropology, advocates entering future-oriented inquiry through cultural perception. This approach emphasizes the idea that the future is incubated within culture, and treats micro-cultural shifts, semantic mutations, and media rituals as valid sources of signals. This offers a new possibility of what counts as a signal in futures research and enables a more sensitive identification of emerging issues than conventional trend forecasting. The proposed Observation–Analysis–Translation three-phase process highlights the function of Cultural Radar as a front-end discovery tool, especially useful in design education, social innovation, and cultural policy, the fields where the redefinition of problems is essential. The concentric-circle structure of "material layer-interpretive layer -translational layer" also provides a logical analysis for multimodal signal construction. This mechanism shows that future design does not need to begin solely with user needs; it can also generate topics from cultural differences, emotional tensions, and marginal expressions. The culture-to-design pathway provided by Cultural Radar offers a practical vocabulary for engaging with deeper social issues in design.

The two cases in this study demonstrate that cultural observation is not an endpoint, but a gateway for design intervention. In the "emotional hunger in youth" case, the mediation of emotional needs led to the imagination of emotional infrastructure - a form of empathy maintenance no longer dependent on intimate relationships, but on media systems. In the "Deng" culture deconstruction case, marginalized identities use ironic expressions to reshape cultural symbols, suggesting a possible design path toward redistributing cultural power. These topics are typically non-technological; their core concerns are not system optimization or technical invention, but rather emotional politics, symbolic power, and social identity. Yet it is precisely the visual, prototypical, and narrative capabilities of design that allow these implicit and unstructured cultural signals to become tangible, modelable, and translatable into specific scenarios and societal imaginaries. Therefore, designers should not only be responders to technological trends, but also discoverers and definers of cultural transformations. The anticipatory function of design lies not in predicting what will happen, but in asking how should we interpret what is happening now, and in constructing negotiable future narratives through form, language, and participation.

However, this approach is not applicable to all design futures contexts. It is not a traditional predictive tool but rather a cultural condensation device, capable of inspiring designers to construct and re-narrate emerging issues. The value of weak signals here lies not in the accuracy of trend prediction, but in how they reveal signs of cultural fissures, guiding us to sense early stress, shifts, and to realigning value. Therefore, this method is more suited to open-ended inquiries with high cultural relevance and early-stage design uncertainty, rather than clearly defined and quantifiable forecasting tasks. at the methodological level, the Cultural Radar is influenced by constructivism and reflexive practice. It emphasizes the interaction and interpretation between the researcher and the signal, which means its effectiveness relies heavily on the researcher's cultural intuition and analytical framework. This can lead to observer bias, and interpretations may vary subjectively. Practically, the study's data sources are relatively concentrated (e.g., Chinese urban youth and specific social media platforms), with limited platform diversity and contextual breadth. Also, due to the study's short time frame, it could not trace whether the signals truly evolved into long-term social trends or resonated with other cultural groups. Further research is needed to expand regional coverage, extend temporal observation, and include multi-researcher collaboration for validation.

6 Conclusion

This study proposes the Cultural Radar as a new design methodology that integrates media anthropology and futures research. It introduces a practical framework capable of identifying weak signals within everyday cultural life and translating them into design issues. Compared with models that rely on macro variables, this method emphasizes extracting future clues from subtle, non-mainstream cultural practices, thus offers the new possibilities of weak signal identification in design futures. The structural advantages of this method are twofold: first, it provides a standardized process of Observation-Analysis-Translation, allowing cultural materials to be processed systematically; second, it uses the signal card as a core translation unit, making abstract cultural insights tangible as design materials.

Through two empirical cases, Emotional Hunger in Youth Media Culture and Deconstructing "Deng" as Cultural Power Holder, this study demonstrates how the Cultural Radar method can identify non-mainstream issues, anticipate cultural trends and inspire design ideation. The method enables the discovery and re-organization of cultural signals, acting as a generator of new agendas. Especially when dealing with non-technological, non-rational, or unstructured social phenomena, Cultural Radar serves as a mechanism for early-stage design intervention, guiding designers to sensitively engage with "as-yet-unnamed" social problems and generate diverse and socially imaginative design responses.

However, this study also has limitations. First, cultural interpretation is highly subjective, and the researcher's experience and perspective can influence the identification and categorization of signals. Second, the data sample is limited to specific age groups and social media platforms, which may introduce contextual bias. Third, due to time constraints, the study lacks long-term tracking of signal evolution, and the validation of future trends requires ongoing observation and supplementation.

Future research may deepen this method in the following directions: (1) Cross-cultural comparative analysis to explore how Cultural Radar performs across different national and cultural contexts; (2) Integration of AI-assisted analysis mechanisms to improve the efficiency and diversity of signal filtering and card generation; (3) Embedding the method into real policy-making processes to test its practical value as a cultural foresight tool for early-stage social insight.

Overall, Cultural Radar is a tool both for designing and paradigm shifting. It advocates for design research not only to begin with existing needs and problems, but also to proactively identify unseen issues. It uses culture as a perceptual interface to engage in the semantic construction and future negotiation of society.

Acknowledgments. This study was funded by the 2024 Basic Scientific Research Project (Special Project) of Luxun Academy of Fine Arts, Youth Talent Team Project, project number 2024-JBZX-QNRCTD-05.

Disclosure of Interests The authors have no competing interests to declare that are relevant to the content of this article.

References

1. Coleman, E.G.: Ethnographic approaches to digital media. Annu. Rev. Anthropol. **39**, 487–505 (2010)
2. Hampton, K.N.: Studying the digital: directions and challenges for digital methods. Annu. Rev. Sociol. **43**, 167–188 (2017)
3. Tolbert, J.A., Johnson, E.D.M.: Digital folkloristics: text, ethnography, and interdisciplinarity. West. Folk. **78**(4), 327–356 (2019)
4. Ansoff, H.I.: Managing surprise and discontinuity: strategic response to weak signals. Calif. Manag. Rev. **18**(2), 18–35 (1975)
5. Hiltunen, E.: Good sources of weak signals: a global study of where futurists look for weak signals. J. Futures Stud. **12**(4), 21–44 (2008)
6. Candy, S., Kornet, K.: Turning foresight inside out: an introduction to ethnographic experiential futures. J. Futures Stud. **23**(3), 3–22 (2019)
7. Chen, Y., Fu, Z.: Speculative scenarios: the exhibition as a new space of thinking. In: Rau, P.L.P. (ed.) Cross-Cultural Design. Applications in Arts, Learning, Well-Being, and Social Development. HCII 2021 Lecture Notes in Computer Science, vol. 12772, pp. 191–204. Springer, Cham (2021)
8. Spitulnik, D.: Anthropology and mass media. Annu. Rev. Anthropol. **22**, 243–265 (1993)
9. Ginsburg, F.D., Abu-Lughod, L., Larkin, B.: Media Worlds: Anthropology on New Terrain. University of California Press, Berkeley/Los Angeles/London (2002)
10. Coman, M., Rothenbuhler, E. (eds.): Media Anthropology. Sage, London (2005)
11. Coman, M.: Media anthropology: an overview. J. Media Anthropol. **1**(1), 1–10 (2005)
12. Boyer, D.: From media anthropology to the anthropology of mediation. Anthropol. Med. **41**, 411–422 (2012)
13. Tkhorzhevska, T.: Experience of media anthropology in the research of media influence. Obraz. **23**, 45–60 (2023)
14. Jakubowicz, A.: Media and marginalized groups. Media Stud. J. **7**(4), 111–130 (2006)
15. Downey, J., Mihelj, S.: Central and Eastern European Media in Comparative Perspective: Politics, Economy and Culture. Ashgate Publishing, Ltd., Surrey (2012)
16. Bajomi-Lázár, P.: Manipulál-e a média? Médiakutató, 61–79 (2017)
17. Zhong, Y.: The image of elderly web celebrities on TikTok. Lect. Notes Educ. Psychol. Public Media. **11**, 112–125 (2023)
18. Guo, L., Xu, J., Zhu, R., Peng, L., Wang, S.: Self-presentation of grey-haired influencers on TikTok: active ageing in China. Continuum. **38**(2), 137–150 (2024)
19. Schoemaker, P.J.H., Day, G.S.: How to make sense of weak signals. MIT Sloan Manag. Rev. **50**(1), 1–9 (2009)
20. Holopainen, M., Toivonen, M.: Weak signals: Ansoff today. Futures. **44**(3), 198–205 (2012)
21. Hambrick, D.C.: Environmental scanning and organizational strategy. Strateg. Manag. J. **3**(1), 21–36 (1982)
22. Cuhls, K.E.: Horizon scanning in foresight-why horizon scanning is only a part of the game. Futures Foresight Sci. **1**(2), 65–79 (2020)

23. Gordon, T.J.: Trend Impact Analysis. In: Futures Research Methodology, pp. 34–46. Foresight.pl, Poland (1994)
24. Fu, Z., Li, J.: Design Futurescaping: interweaving storytelling and AI generation art in world-building. In: Rau, P.L.P. (ed.) Cross-Cultural Design Lecture Notes in Computer Science, vol. 12772, pp. 194–207. Springer, Cham (2023)
25. Zhu, L., Fu, Z.: New space narrative: responding to multiple futures with design perspective. In: Rau, P.L.P. (ed.) Cross-Cultural Design, Lecture Notes in Computer Science, vol. 12772, pp. 331–345. Springer, Cham (2023)
26. Hiltunen, E.: The future sign and its three dimensions. Futures. **40**, 247–260 (2008)

Exploring Design Strategies for Brand Visual Innovation in Cross-Cultural Contexts: A Case Study of the Guangdong-Hong Kong-Macao Greater Bay Area

Zekai Xu[1]([✉]), Yichuang Zhao[2], and Xu Zhao[1]

[1] Beijing Normal University, 19 Xinjiekouwai Street, Haidian District, Beijing, China
`202222089019@mail.bnu.edu.cn`
[2] Shanghai University, No.149, Yanchang Road, Jing'an District, Shanghai, China

Abstract. As economic globalization intensifies and cross-cultural exchanges proliferate, brand visual design in cross-cultural regions confronts critical challenges: the pronounced limitations of conventional methodologies, inadequate expression of multicultural integration, and constrained participation among diverse ethnic communities. This investigation seeks to construct innovative brand visual design methodologies tailored to cross-cultural regional characteristics, utilizing the Guangdong-Hong Kong-Macao Greater Bay Area as an exemplar to explore dynamic brand visual expression strategies within contexts characterized by multicultural diversity and rapid development. The research employs a mixed-method paradigm that synthesizes literature review, case analysis, and in-depth interviews. Through systematic examination of brand design practices in renowned cross-cultural cities and regions, alongside comprehensive assessment of contemporary dynamic brand design paradigms, this study conducts rigorous analysis of exemplary cases to identify innovative characteristics while delineating design constraints. Subsequently, by collecting brand design cases from the Greater Bay Area and conducting in-depth interviews with nine participants representing diverse backgrounds, the research extracts core requirements for brand design within this cross-cultural context. Building upon these findings, the study develops a dynamic brand design methodology framework encompassing "landscape → imagery → data → familiar territorial texture → visual text → brand carriers → co-creation and sharing," thereby establishing a cross-cultural dynamic brand visual expression system that integrates multicultural landscapes while facilitating evolutionary development. Furthermore, a collaborative brand visual co-creation platform is constructed to facilitate meaningful participation from diverse communities in brand design processes. The research successfully transcends the limitations inherent in traditional cross-cultural regional brand design by establishing an open-ended brand visual design system that synthesizes diverse landscapes with dynamic evolution. This achievement represents a paradigmatic shift from complex contextual approaches toward dynamic integration in brand visual design. Consequently, this methodology provides both a systematic theoretical framework and practical pathway for cross-cultural regional brand visual design.

P.-L.P. Rau and H. Krömker (Eds.): HCII 2025, LNCS 16336, pp. 167–192, 2026.
https://doi.org/10.1007/978-3-032-12798-3_11

Keywords: Cross-cultural regions · Brand visual design · Dynamic branding · Guangdong-Hong Kong-Macao Greater Bay Area · Co-creation design

1 Introduction

In the aftermath of deepening economic globalization and the conclusion of the large-scale COVID-19 pandemic, global human mobility has become increasingly liberalized, consequently intensifying intercultural exchanges and encounters across continents, ethnicities, and nationalities. Concomitant with regional economic agglomeration development, escalating urbanization rates worldwide—particularly in third-world nations—and major economies' intensified demand for talent acquisition, distinguished metropolitan regions have progressively emerged. The evolution of these metropolitan areas inevitably catalyzes convergence among intra-ethnic sub-groups, inter-ethnic communities, transnational populations, and diverse racial constituencies, thereby gradually constituting cross-cultural cities or urban clusters—substantively representing cross-cultural regions.

Contemporary cross-cultural regions are predominantly constituted by individual cities or urban agglomerations. Archetypal cross-cultural regions such as the New York Bay Area and Tokyo Bay Area comprise principal cross-cultural cities, whereas the San Francisco Bay Area and Guangdong-Hong Kong-Macao Greater Bay Area are characterized by cross-cultural urban clusters. Given that residents with disparate ethnic, economic, and—critically—cultural backgrounds must negotiate a shared identity, coherent regional branding becomes indispensable. Echoing Mumford's assertion that "a city is a theater, a stage" [1], city and regional brands serve as dramaturgical devices that align plural identities. Keller observes that logos not only project brand imagery but also transform inhabitants' emotions and viewpoints into tangible symbols [2]. Place branding, as Sarbiat Sanchez, Cerda-Bertomeu, and Kalandides contend, is inseparable from public governance; authorities must safeguard local identity while orchestrating stakeholder collaboration [3]. Yet, Zenker and Braun note that many city-brand managers impose top-down strategies, overlooking the audience's diverse perceptions [4]. Rodriguez et al. further criticizes the concentration of logo-design decisions in executive hands, neglecting the public-relations dimension of visual identity [5]. Ashworth and Kavaratzis add that city symbols ought to articulate intrinsic cultural traits, achieving competitive distinction through cultural depth [6]. Traditional city-branding processes, however, seldom prioritize local heterogeneity or dynamic cultural evolution. A genuinely cross-cultural brand must visualize multicultural fusion, champion inclusivity, and invite co-creation—capabilities largely absent from conventional practice.

With the rapid evolution of the Information Age and Internet Era, the continuous emergence of newly emergent and diversified media appears to provide a promising solution to this challenge. Zhang observes that under pervasive digitization and ever-expanding multimedia channels, brand visual values are shifting toward dynamism and pluralism [7]. Negroponte likewise anticipates a migration from one-way to dialogic media, wherein recipients actively seek and generate content [8]. Yuan asserts that during the traditional media era, brand communication was received by audiences through a linear process following this sequence: Attention → Interest → Cultivated Desire → Memory Formation → Purchase Action, where audiences passively absorbed brand messages unidirectionally. In the contemporary digital media landscape, audiences access richer, multimodal information and engage with brands through interactive experiences, transforming the pathway into Attention → Interest → Search → Action → Sharing. Through audience search behaviors and social sharing, brands achieve real-time interaction and dissemination, enabling consumers' active participation in brand co-creation and communication [9]. Gobe therefore insists that brands must be "activated" online, providing multi-sensory experiences that enliven their social relevance [10]. Fu argues that dynamic branding—leveraging versatile formats and flexible aesthetics—deepens emotional resonance and strengthens value recognition among the culturally diverse public [11]. As Arnheim postulated, active selection constitutes an innate characteristic of human visual perception, whereby dynamically changing elements within an environment invariably become the predominant objects of conscious focus during perceptual engagement [12], Hsu's analysis of 44 cases demonstrates that kinetic identities significantly enhance brand recognition, aesthetic appeal, functional clarity, and affective engagement, particularly when varying media and artistic styles are deployed. Dynamic systems further embed "customization," "personalization," and "modularity," thereby reinforcing loyalty [13].

Consequently, dynamic visual branding—characterized by multimodal media, participatory mechanisms, bidirectional communication, and co-creative expression—offers rich cultural signification and heightened sensory impact. Such qualities are crucial for cross-cultural regions that must integrate multiple cultures, facilitate plural expressions, and accommodate diverse emotional registers. The Guangdong–Hong Kong–Macao Greater Bay Area, a complex and vibrant Asia-Pacific nexus, thus requires innovative dynamic branding strategies to articulate it's evolving regional identity.

2 Literature Overview

2.1 Research on City Brand Design and Cross-Cultural Regional Brand Design

The study of city branding gained momentum in the 1990s, initially drawing on the branding theories of David Ogilvy and Kevin Lane Keller to conceptualize urban brand images. Scholars generally contend that a credible city brand must synthesize both tangible attributes and intangible qualities, thus shaping a holistic image in the minds of its target audience. Diverse perspectives exist on the essential design elements of an urban or regional brand. Zinaida et al. argue that a compelling city logo must be persuasive, harmonious, and explicitly reflective of local culture—though they regard these traits as merely foundational [14]. Urbanist Gilbert famously asserted that "everything seen in the city is an element" [15]; hence, historical memory, civic activity, natural environment, and cultural heritage collectively constitute a city's visual identity system. In contemporary practice, this view implies that urban or regional brands must embed local culture within their visual language. Echoing this premise, Ashworth, Kavaratzis, and Cozmiuc maintain that a city brand distills distinctive historical, cultural, humanistic, geographic, and industrial features, integrates them during urban development, and projects them as core concepts to the public [16]. In China's Urban Competitiveness Report, Pengfei

Ni further distinguishes conceptual, behavioral, industrial, humanistic-landscape, and natural-landscape cultures as integral strata of the urban cultural system [17]. Physical artifacts thus map cultural attributes outwardly, while their reinterpretation conveys a deeper "cultural temperament." Wheeler likewise positions city brands at the intersection of tangible signifiers—built form, landscape, art—and intangible facets such as collective viewpoints, civic personality, strategic positioning, and policy orientation [18].

These insights imply that urban visual identity should be multidimensional—an imperative accentuated in cross-cultural contexts. Peng Duan therefore proposes an evaluative framework that merges media communication and public-management perspectives with urban planning, culture, and social identity. Adapting Simon Anholt's Competitive Advantage Recognition System and his six-dimension brand indicator model, Duan recommends assessing a city's digital-era visual identity across seven facets: attractiveness, humanistic appeal, vitality, inclusiveness, economic development, public image, and communicative reach [19]. Consequently, this study argues that cross-cultural brand design cannot rely on a limited subset of factors; rather, it must deliberately integrate the full spectrum of urban attributes through innovative visual strategies. Such comprehensiveness is indispensable given the complexity and diversity inherent in cross-cultural regions.

With respect to concrete visual practice, Kevin Lynch identifies three sources from which urban images derive: "identity and character," "structure and associations," and "meaning and implication" [20]. A city brand therefore abstracts shared memories into symbols that represent the whole. Brand familiarity—"share of mind"—as defined by Alba, Hutchinson, Kent, and Allen, arises from accumulated direct and indirect experiences [21, 22]. Designing from the most familiar cityscapes can forge enduring visual memories. Kavaratzis notes that iconic skylines, such as New York's with the Statue of Liberty and the Empire State Building, are powerful communicative tools [23]. Likewise, Kyoto's Kinkaku-ji both epitomizes Japanese tradition and anchors Kyoto's global brand. Bowen Zhang, Yucheng Wang, Zhimin Zhou, and Xiaohui Sun find that emblematic landmarks and cultural landscapes profoundly shape brand perception [24]. Analyzing multiple cases, Yang Liu and Ling Wang distill three traits common to strong city brands—specificity, entertainment, and plasticity—and advocate first articulating a city's style and temperament, then identifying or reframing its core imagery [25]. Empirical work by Burns et al. (1993) and Unnava & Agarwal (1996) further demonstrates that image-rich stimuli are recalled more readily than text-heavy equivalents [26, 27]. Accordingly, this study explores translating landmark and cultural landscapes into visual forms that encapsulate a cross-cultural region's multicultural content.

Addressing methodological considerations, Jiuyang Lu and Geng Zhang outline three representational strategies for urban branding: resemblance, indication, and convention [28]. Resemblance relies on imitation and reproduction, transforming iconic architecture or cultural motifs into figurative symbols. Indication establishes a causal or proximal link between image and referent, enabling audiences to associate them through perceptual memory, as illustrated by contemporary Hong Kong's brand. Convention deploys socially agreed rules or conceptual associations to signify meaning; the classic "I Love NY" logo exemplifies this approach.

Beyond the core principles that urban branding and cross-cultural branding must pursue, scholarly consensus has emphasized the pivotal role of urban populations— or more comprehensively, stakeholders—in shaping brand designs for both cities and cross-cultural contexts. Compte-Pujol and Kavaratzis highlight residents' indispensable contributions [29]. Hereźniak and Florek regard urban populations as custodians of authenticity [30], while Demirbag, Yurt, Güneri, and Kurtuluş (2010) urge that branding be grounded in residents' and visitors' values, behaviors, and traits [31]. Braun et al. identify indigenous inhabitants as pivotal ambassadors, alongside other citizen groups whose voices warrant attention [32]. Insch and Walters (2018) describe co-creation as complex, given evolving cultural and emotional identities, yet deem it essential for meaningful brands [33]. Strategically engaging residents as co-producers and co-consumers not only legitimizes the process but also fosters favorable evaluations.

Building on these principles, this study contends that the visual branding of cross-cultural regions must holistically integrate historical heritage; cultural, humanistic, and natural landscapes; industrial dynamism; urban landmarks and characteristics; artistic particularities; and collective memories. We propose translating landmark, characteristic, and symbolic landscapes into unified yet distinctive visual forms that encapsulate this plurality. Equally critical is recognizing the identities and emotions of diverse stakeholders, forging affective and mnemonic bonds, and enabling active participation through innovative branding mechanisms, thereby nurturing a cohesive social identity.

2.2 Research on Dynamic Brand Design

In brand logo design, Wheeler (2009) argues that a comprehensive brand-identity process must address visual dimensions such as primary and secondary colour combinations, size, proportion, typeface, imagery, motion, form, style, photography, illustration and iconography. Audience-related factors include experience and emotion, media texture, tactile response, packaging structure, as well as auditory and olfactory cues. In the era of digital media, dynamic brand visual design entails additional considerations. Specifically, Yali Zhang notes that dynamic logos—often termed Dynamic Logos or Dynamic Symbols—typically integrate graphics, colour, typography, motion and sound [7]. Wen Zhu contends that dynamic city brand identity design transcends conventional two-dimensional representations, rejecting static forms and fixed color schemes. Guided by specific design principles, it enables evolutionary and adaptable implementations conveyed through sequenced still frames—or more holistically—via spatiotemporal and acoustic dimensions. Such methodologies morphologically transform 2D visual identifiers, amplifying urban brands' multifaceted richness and dissemination efficacy [34].

Among the earliest and most comprehensive treatments of dynamic branding, Irene van Nes's 2012 monograph collates cases, presents design strategies and analyses methods. She identifies six approaches to creating dynamic brand identities—container, wallpaper, gene, formula, customised and generative methods—yet acknowledges a theoretical lacuna regarding dynamic brand generation [35]. Krasner offers a detailed account of dynamic logo design, tracing its development and contemporary practice while analysing its impact on visual communication, particularly in heightening sensory awareness; this work provides valuable insights for future research [36]. Reviewing the field, Ruox-uan Lu and Xia Li observe that most studies focus on non-interactive dynamic brand imagery. They group these studies into three categories: (1) investigations of the origin, concept and significance of dynamic branding that justify its inevitable rise; (2) critiques of designs whose visual language is overly simple or literal, leading to more system-atic design guidelines; and (3) compilations of morphology-centred cases from which methodologies are distilled and reapplied [37].

Research on the construction, transformation and foundational frameworks of dynamic brand design has advanced from several perspectives. Through visual experi-mentation, Pedro Matos Chaves explores flexible visual treatments—rotation, positional shift, morphological change and content substitution—that enable dynamic brand recog-nition [38]. Wen Zhu summarises common visual-construction techniques for dynamic branding: (1) repetition, in which identical elements recur to enhance unity and legibility; (2) rotation, whereby elements pivot around a central axis in mirrored configurations; and (3) gradation, in which elements systematically vary by size, orientation or figure–ground relation. She further stresses that dynamic branding can leverage video for new media while remaining compatible with traditional media in static form, thereby reflecting communicative diversity [34]. Using time as the primary frame, MING-CHIEH HSU classifies dynamic brand identities into four motion types—fixed-interval, rotational, non-fixed rotational and motionless dynamic images—corresponding respectively to linear, rotational, nonlinear and static time structures [13]. Drawing on Norman and related scholarship, HSU also delineates three evaluative dimensions: (1) cognitive—recognisability, familiarity and memorability; (2) functional—personalisation, usabil-ity, motivational effect and support for creativity; and (3) affective—identity, pleasure, playfulness, aesthetic enjoyment, emotional fulfilment and entertainment [13].

Through a detailed examination of motion-graphics techniques applicable to dynamic branding, Zeng Jin distils four construction principles: (1) temporality—modu-lating speed and rhythm; (2) spatial variation—altering size, position and angle; (3) tonal rhythm—adjusting light/dark values and colour temperature; and (4) logical mapping—converting information or data into visual sequences. These principles, applied indi-vidually or in combination, generate diverse motion graphics and, ultimately, dynamic brand designs [39]. Achieving the intended effects relies on coherent association, concise information delivery, complete creative expression and diversified forms, all underpinned by motion-graphic conventions. Zeng also catalogues generative and transformational techniques, including movement, colour, shape, interaction, typographic and graphic variations.

Yan Zhang characterises dynamic branding as delivering three-dimensional visual impact, diversified emotional interaction and integrated information transmission. She argues that dynamic branding (1) conveys more complete brand messages, (2) dissemi-nates information more efficiently and (3) enhances brand recognition and visual engage-ment [40]. Complementing this view, Ruiwen Jiao highlights the chief advantage of dynamic branding: key frames extracted from a dynamic logo can constitute a series of individual marks that function independently or in combination [41]. Each configura-tion thus adapts to distinct contexts, media and even temporal settings, while remaining traceable to the same dynamic logo and maintaining intrinsic coherence.

Synthesising definitions, cases and construction methods reveals several developmental constraints in current dynamic branding: (1) designs that repeat motion at fixed intervals resemble perpetually looping "movies"; (2) designs that employ fixed linear transformations—such as combination, rotation, gradation or mirroring—amount to repetitive motion and are better described as motion-brand designs (e.g., Swisscom and Brooklyn Museum dynamic identities); and(3) Regarding the remaining dynamic brand designs that appear to manifest shape-based transformations: they primarily undergo 'dynamic' morphological alterations. Such alterations essentially entail the liberation of inherent attributes—e.g., color and form—from static graphics (termed static brand design); alternatively, they evolve according to predetermined configurations, combinatorial arrangements, or other stochastic rules to achieve visually pseudo-dynamic progression (e.g., dynamic brand design by Mit-media lab; dynamic brand identity for Norway's Nordkyn tourism region by Neue Design Studio; dynamic branding for Polish telecommunications provider Netia by White Cat Studio).Although these examples exhibit certain dynamic traits, they lack a genuinely dynamic visual system. In summary, the design of the aforementioned three types of dynamic brands fails to: randomly extract and generate dynamic elements from multimodal, dynamically evolving source materials; subsequently form dynamic visual expressions; and ultimately manifest through kinetic media vectors. They do not create a multimodal, dynamically transforming brand visual environment nor establish a genuinely dynamic visual system.

For cross-cultural regions with complex backgrounds and multifaceted tasks, dynamic branding must integrate diverse, evolving contexts. It should employ novel methodologies to generate, express and deploy dynamic visuals that function authentically in fluid environments, ultimately enabling stakeholders from different communities to participate in shaping the region's cross-cultural brand identity.

3 Research Method and Case Analysis

3.1 Traditional Dynamic Brand Generation Methods

Based on theoretical research and practical case studies, this study categorizes traditional dynamic brand design generation into eight core types: (1) Graphics generation: As the main application category of dynamic brand visual design, the logo and supporting graphics are the most prominent. For example, the Copenhagen Climate Change Conference (COP15) logo, which is 192 lines long, symbolizes the United Nations member states and its generation software to support dynamic speed, focus, and other ten parameters; (2) Composition generation: focus on the overall planning of visual layout, covering the arrangement of elements, location, size, and angle. For example, the dynamic branding system designed by Pentagram for the UNESCO Literacy Summit uses 3D geometric shape algorithms that emulate the laws of physics; (3) Typography: Dynamic visual design utilizes text messaging and morphological plasticity to enhance the recognition system's adaptability. For example, the brand designed by Studio Dumbar for the DEMO Festival uses a grid system to slice up the letters and adjust the ratio of the units; (4) Color Generation: Based on the brand's existing standard color selection and combination, usually used in conjunction with graphics, fonts, and other elements; (5) Material Generation: The visual contrast of materials, such as metal, liquid, plush, etc., triggers the viewer's attention. For example, M-seen, a sustainable material brand, creates a concept of material that divides and grows like a biological cell; (6) Dimension Generation: This refers to the dynamic transformation of a two-dimensional plane into a three-dimensional one. For example, as the first example of dynamic brand visual design, the Hanover World Expo emblem realized a visual breakthrough through such changes; (7) Element shape generation: of key significance in the era of digital media, including segmentation and reorganization, and overall deformation of two forms; (8) Interaction Generation: Mainly applied to digital media, it refers to the instantaneous dynamic changes generated by human face, gesture tracking, or mouse interaction. For example, the logo system designed by FormlessTwins for the Busan Museum of Modern Art uses the circle as the fundamental element, creating variable samples by including the letter 'O' and spreading the circle (Fig. 1).

Fig. 1. Case of Traditional Dynamic Brand Generation Methods.

3.2 Research Strategy and Methodology (Fig. 2)

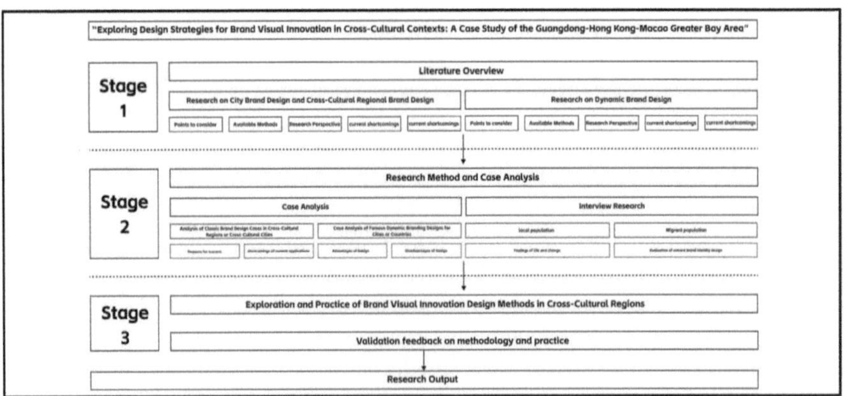

Fig. 2. Research Flowchart.

This study adopts a case study method, relevant population interviews, and focus group tracking evaluation to conduct analysis and methodological practice assessment. Firstly, through the dual analysis of classic brand design cases in cross-cultural regions and dynamic brand design cases in cities or countries, we summarize their strengths, weaknesses, and success factors. Secondly, we collect brand design cases from the Guangdong, Hong Kong, and Macao Greater Bay Area and major cities and conduct interviews with residents, various immigrants, and their descendants to evaluate the above brand design cases and collate their experiences and feelings of change in the Greater Bay Area, to provide research perspectives, contextual focuses and design key points for the construction of the methodology. Finally, after completing the construction and practice of the cross-cultural regional brand visual innovation design methodology, the methodology was verified, and feedback was provided through focus groups.

3.3 Relevant Case Analysis

Analysis of Classic Brand Design Cases in Cross-Cultural Regions or Cross-Cultural Cities. Many successful city brand designs in the world are characterized by diversity, tolerance, openness, and freedom, among which New York City's brand identity and Madrid's city-tourism brand identity are the most renowned.

1. New York City brand image design

New York's brand image, propelled to global fame by Milton Glaser's "I Love NY," has become the most successful city brand visual identity worldwide and one of the discipline's classic cases. The design comprises a capital "I," a red heart symbol, and the letters "N" and "Y" rendered in a rounded, bold, serif American typewriter font. As a core visual symbol, "I Love NY" is celebrated for its simplicity, boldness, and directness, communicating with the global public in English—the world's lingua franca—and establishing an open, inclusive, and welcoming "social pact" that embodies the city's spirit. Moreover, "love" is an abstract, polyvalent concept that encompasses virtually all human emotions, which grants the word formidable appeal and inclusiveness, making the design an iconic emblem of New York and earning worldwide recognition. It has become a model of diversity and tolerance, inspiring emulation by numerous cities. However, over time several issues have emerged: first, the design's fixed visual form limits diverse applications and multimedia adaptations; second, the original design provided no scope for co-creation or participatory adaptation, rendering it less compatible with today's interactive information age; and third, its inherently static nature hampers adaptation to new dynamic media.

For these reasons, New York City introduced a new identity featuring a simple, variable "NYC" typeface that facilitates multiple uses, crowd co-creation, and dynamic morphing. A dedicated website was also launched to support co-creation, life-sharing, and online interaction, aiming to cultivate a multicultural, open, and inclusive cross-cultural brand image for the digital era. In addition, to retain the influence of "I Love NY," the design team introduced the slogan "We Love NYC" and applied the heart symbol dynamically across various materials. Nonetheless, because the underlying "NYC" typeface lacks standardized fonts, colors, and visual structures, the brand's visual consistency and impact remain limited, and its generative context is still insufficiently rich (Fig. 3).

2. Madrid City Tourism Brand Identity Design

Fig. 3. New York Old and New City Brand Identity Design Case.

The new Madrid City Tourism Brand Identity, introduced in 2018, comprises two broad sets of motifs—basic and extended. The Spanish word "Madrid" serves as the main textual element; however, the six letters are arranged not symmetrically but in a randomly "leaning" manner, imparting dynamism and facilitating diverse applications. The most striking element is a pair of outstretched hands, reminiscent of a mother embracing every visitor and delivering the clear message: "Madrid embraces you." The space between the arms is reserved for co-creation and varied text-and-graphic collaboration. This brand identity presents Madrid as warm, welcoming, open, inclusive, and diverse and has become a recent exemplar of inclusivity and co-creation through its variable hand shapes and randomly positioned text. Nevertheless, practical issues persist: first, because the text and arms do not share a unified visual language, co-created text, and graphics appear visually disjointed from the fixed elements; second, the font and arm forms are limited in variation, failing to elicit a strong visual response.

From the above well-known city brand design cases, it is evident that their common characteristics are inclusiveness, openness, and diversity. These qualities are manifested in the spirit conveyed by their visual design, the co-creation space intentionally reserved within the brand system, the foresight to accommodate diversified applications, and the dedicated community portals established for co-creation and sharing. At the same time, when emphasizing co-creation, diversity, and inclusiveness, city brand design must maintain a unified visual language, a simple yet powerful visual image, and an underlying design language that is both variable and evolvable. Only by meeting these criteria can communication remain effective while still embodying tolerance and openness (Fig. 4).

Fig. 4. Madrid City Brand Identity Design Case.

Case Analysis of Famous Dynamic Branding Designs for Cities or Countries. Under the wave of digital media, many countries and cities have begun to explore the dynamization of their brand identities, including the Melbourne city brand, the Porto city visual identity, the Norway national brand, and the London White City brand. Among these, the Melbourne identity created by Landor Design is the most celebrated.

(1) Melbourne city brand image design

In 2009, Landor Design produced a new identity for Melbourne, taking the initial letter "M" as the point of departure for dynamic expression. The brand mark leverages the letter's rich, three-dimensional tangents as a dynamic origin, incorporating diverse visual shapes and color variations that represent Melbourne while also providing space for residents to co-create and collaborate around the "M." As a pioneer of dynamic branding for a diverse and inclusive city, the scheme successfully exploits dynamization to saturate each viewpoint with fresh, animated visuals, thereby reflecting Melbourne's internationally recognized image of diversity, innovation, livability, and ecological awareness. Nevertheless, as noted in the preceding literature review, the design remains insufficiently open from the perspective of cross-cultural, inclusive dynamism. It predominantly operates through confined transformations within its internal brand elements—such as chromatic or typographic components—wherein ostensibly dynamic alterations essentially constitute the liberation of static intrinsic attributes (e.g., color and form). Melbourne's city branding persists as variations upon fixed paradigms, failing to comprehensively integrate all visual properties into culturally diverse districts, nor to genuinely randomly extract, generate, and form fully open dynamic visual expressions within stochastically dynamic environments, or to manifest through kinetic media vectors—ultimately preventing the establishment of an authentically dynamic visual system (Fig. 5).

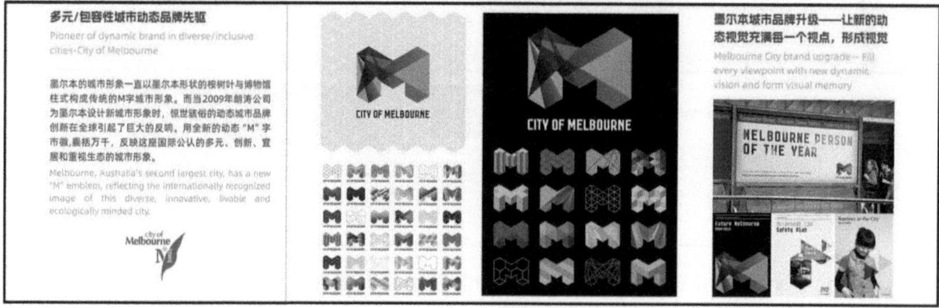

Fig. 5. Melbourne Dynamic City Brand Identity Design Example.

3. Porto city brand visual identity design

Introduced in 2013, Porto's identity is an early exemplar of open, co-creative city branding. Inspired by the city's blue-and-white azulejo tiles, the core visual language comprises 74 interconnected icons that form a single visual whole. These icons can be recombined endlessly, allowing citizens to create new compositions collaboratively. Because

Porto is continually evolving, the icon set remains open to updates, enabling the city's visual identity to grow in a dynamic environment. However, practical issues persist. Foremost, the profusion of icons dilutes communicative clarity; the absence of a direct, simple, and unified symbol prevents Porto from establishing a strong emblem comparable to New York's. Moreover, icon clusters constructed from numerous thin lines appear visually fragmented, hindering recognition and recall.

4. Norway's national branding design

Scandinavian Design's national brand for Norway reconfigures the flag into dynamic graphics, recombining points, lines, and planes in the flag's red, blue, and white palette, supplemented by scaling, rotation, and movement. Yet the scheme merely rearranges fixed flag elements into superficially dynamic sequences and remains overly singular. It neither reflects Norwegian culture nor integrates national stakeholders in co-creation or collaboration.

5. White City London

White City's identity, rooted in the concept of "Networking Creative Thinking," presents the district as a creative melting pot and nexus for transport, social interaction, intellect, and technology. Infinite line combinations form paths that merge and transform at intersections, while gradient color spectrums strengthen the identity's dynamic quality. Nonetheless, like Norway's scheme, the design merely animates lines along random rules and fails to convey a multifaceted character.

From these city- and nation-level cases, current dynamic brand image design still lacks openness. As summarized in the literature review, dynamic traits often remain superficial—limited to animated presentation or media carriers—without constructing a diversified dynamic visual environment or a systematic dynamic ecosystem. Conversely, where shape shifts occur, they often release static attributes in predefined reorganizations and lack essential dynamism (Fig. 6).

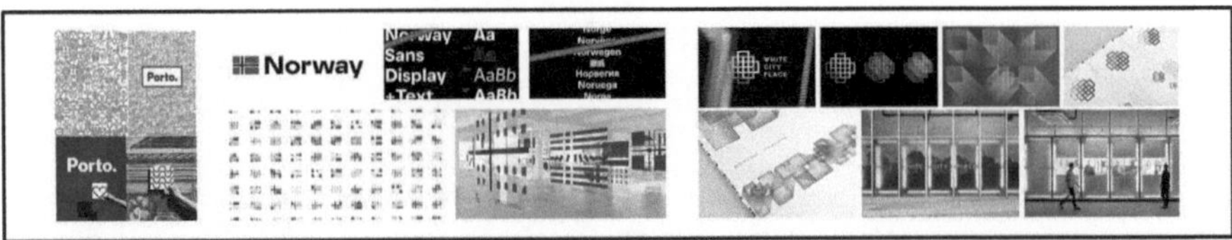

Fig. 6. Porto Band Design, ;Norway Band Design; London White CityBand Design.

3.4 Interview Research

Collection of Brand Design related to Guangdong, Hong Kong and Macao Bay Area. Given that the Guangdong-Hong Kong-Macao Greater Bay Area lacks a unified official regional brand image, this study collects brand design cases of key regional events and core cities, including the official city brands of the Guangdong-Hong Kong-Macao Greater Bay Area National Games, the four official node cities (Guangzhou,

Shenzhen, Hong Kong, and Macao), the important node of Guangfu culture Foshan, and the emerging city of Zhuhai, as well as the related designs of the Guangzhou Asian Games and the Shenzhen Universiade.

The case study reveals that the Guangdong-Hong Kong-Macao Greater Bay Area Universiade brand uses three ceremonial flowers to symbolize the mingling and rotation of the iconic flowers of Guangdong, Hong Kong, and Macao, implying synergistic development of the region. The Hong Kong city brand utilizes the dynamic element of the "flying dragon" and skillfully blends Chinese and English characters, highlighting the characteristics of the East-West cultural convergence and urban development momentum. Shenzhen's brand design has gone through a change from the figurative expression of the "roc spreading its wings" shape echoing the nickname 'Pengcheng' combined with the composition of the azalea flower in 2011 to the abstract transformation of the new version that takes the English letters as the main body and combines the "S" shape with the petals of the azalea flower, thus realizing the evolution from the regional logo to the simplification of the symbols. Guangzhou's design reflects the inheritance from traditional to modern landmarks: the Asian Games design originated from the city's symbol of the five-goat statue constituting the torch shape, and the new version of the city's image continues the use of iconic landscaping methods by using the word "Guangzhou" in Chinese to outline the contemporary landmark of the Canton Tower jointly. Foshan directly adopts the classic style of the Guangfu lion, emphasizing the status of cultural heritage. Zhuhai shows the city's characteristics through the sculpture of a fisherwoman, the Hong Kong-Zhuhai-Macao Bridge, and the abstract combination of mountain and sea elements.

Comprehensive analysis shows that the existing brand design mainly presents static visual characteristics, and a few dynamic applications are also based on the motion processing of static design. The visual expression strategy is divided into two paths: a direct sampling of figurative iconic landscapes and abstract allegorical expression, reflecting the limitations of the current design in terms of dynamics and expression (Fig. 7).

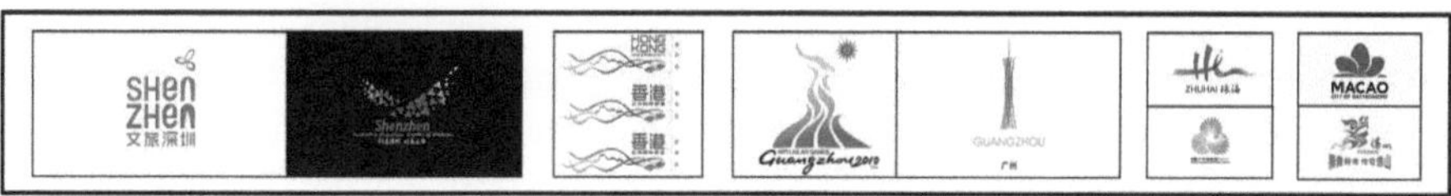

Fig. 7. Collection of Brand Design related to Guangdong, Hong Kong and Macao Bay Area.

Selection of Interview Population and Interview Results. As a model of cross-cultural integration in East Asia, the Guangdong-Hong Kong-Macao Greater Bay Area brings together the three major Han Chinese ethnic groups, namely the Guangfu, Hakka and Chaoshan, and carries the dual cultural imprints of the Anglo-Portuguese colonial legacy and their immigrant descendant groups, as well as accommodating Southeast Asian immigrants represented by Vietnam and the Philippines, and the business people from South Asia, the Middle East, Africa and other Third World countries engaged in cross-border trade. As a result, the region has developed a unique composite heritage of local cultural landscapes, diverse dialectal and linguistic systems, and the collision of Chinese and Western cultures and systems. In addition, the new industrial clusters of high-tech, Internet, and drones represented by Shenzhen have attracted many new immigrants from provinces such as Jiangxi, Hunan, and Sichuan, constituting a typical cross-cultural region that is vibrant and diverse yet maintains its local heritage. It is worth emphasizing that this region is also one of the most rapidly urbanizing areas in the world, with cities such as Shenzhen and Zhuhai achieving a leapfrog transformation from fishing villages to cities in the past four decades, and the region's urban and cultural landscapes are characterized by a continuous dynamic evolution.

Based on the complexity of these cultural components, this study precisely targeted nine interviewees: three local Guangfu aborigines of different ages, two representatives of the Hakka and Chaoshan ethnic groups who have moved in from outside the region, one British immigrant, one Macao resident of Portuguese descent, and two interviewees of Jiangxi and Hunan origins who have moved in due to industrial opportunities, in order to ensure cultural representativeness of the sample and the validity of the study (Fig. 8).

Fig. 8. Summary of findings from interviews with relevant populations.

This interview study followed a dual methodology, with the first part of the interviews aiming to gain insights into the backgrounds of the interviewees, the populations they belonged to, as well as their migration or residency status in the Guangdong-Hong Kong-Macao Greater Bay Area and the cities they lived in. The second part of the interviews had two focuses, the first focus was to understand the feelings of the interviewee group about the life and changes in the Guangdong-Hong Kong-Macao Greater Bay Area in recent years, and the second focus was to understand the evaluation and feelings of the interviewee group about the eight cases of branding design in the Guangdong-Hong Kong-Macao Greater Bay Area collected in this study. The interviews were conducted in a semi-structured interview format, and a total of nine valid data were collected, with participants coded as P1, P2, P3, etc. The results of the collected interviews were coded and presented in Fig. 1. In the first question about what feelings the respondent group had about the life and changes in the Guangdong-Hong Kong-Macao Greater Bay Area in recent years? The majority of respondents generally felt that life in the Greater Bay Area is fast-paced, efficient, and full of opportunities (especially in terms of industry and wealth mobility), as well as the trend of "co-location" brought about by the increasingly close transportation and economic ties. At the same time, the openness, inclusiveness and diversity of this cross-cultural region, as well as the rapid emergence of new things and the fusion of Chinese and Western cultures, have also been mentioned many times.

However, significant barriers to cultural integration, a general lack of cultural identity and sense of belonging to newcomers, the feeling of being "out of place" due to the movement of people, the impact of foreign cultures on the local population, and the imbalance of development between regions were also highlighted as challenges and complexities in the respondents' feedback. In the second question, what are the comments and feelings of the respondents about the eight branding cases in the Guangdong-Hong Kong-Macao Greater Bay Area collected in this study? Respondents' evaluations of the current Guangdong-Hong Kong-Macao Greater Bay Area brand design cases were generally on the negative side. The core criticism focuses on the general lack of distinctiveness and diversity in the designs, which fail to effectively reflect the core qualities of vitality, innovation and diversified integration of the Greater Bay Area. Most of the cases were found to be ambiguous in terms of expression, such as P2: "I can recognize the English and the architecture, but I don't understand the rest", P4: "I don't understand some of the unexplained words"; and P7: "Several of them are not readable, and those that are readable don't really understand them". The direction of the brand design is either too straightforward and figurative or too abstract, for example, P1 pointed out that the design is fragmented into "either a city logo or colorful", and P6 added: "both straightforward or abstract", and both ends of the spectrum fail to successfully convey the connotations of the Bay Area. In addition, respondents generally felt that the design was weakly related to their own experiences or perceptions of the fast-changing and new phenomena in the Bay Area, e.g., P8 stated, "It doesn't feel like it has anything to do with us", and P9 emphasized that the design was "fragmented and not connected to the fast-changing and new things in the Bay Area". Some comments, such as P5, also pointed out that the design style is traditional and monotonous. Based on the results of the interviews, this study extracted keywords such as urban culture, inclusiveness, population influx, vitality, and rapid change, as well as keywords for the population such as youth, identity, sense of belonging, and heterogeneity, and finally came up with the focus of the current design of the brand image of the Guangdong-Hong Kong-Macao Greater Bay Area.

Through the results of the interviews, we can firstly conclude that when designing the brand image of the cross-cultural region of Guangdong, Hong Kong and Macao, we should pay attention to the expression of a diversified, tolerant, integrated and innovative culture and the ever-changing and energetic face of the region, and we should also pay attention to solving the problems of the newly migrated people's general feeling of a lack of cultural identity and a sense of belonging, as well as the discomfort of the locals in the face of the impacts of foreign cultures. In addition, it should also focus on solving the problem of the lack of cultural identity and sense of belonging of the newly immigrated people and the discomfort of the local people in the face of the impact of foreign culture, so as to carry out the interaction and integration between the people by means of soft visual expression and co-creation. Secondly, in terms of specific brand visual design methods, we should avoid the content singularity formed by static brand design or dynamization based on static brand design, and at the same time, it can be found that using the city's iconic architecture or cultural symbols as visual presentation forms can effectively improve the communication efficiency, but we should also pay attention to avoiding the problems of being too abstract so that the viewers can not be recognized and being too concrete so that the viewers can understand the problems of bias, and try to find a brand design style between the abstract and the concrete. However, we should also pay attention to avoid the problems of too abstract so that the viewers cannot recognize and too concrete so that the viewers' understanding will be biased, and try to find a way to design the brand between abstract and concrete (Fig. 9).

Fig. 9. Case Study Summary/Summary of interviews.

4   Exploration and Practice of Design Methods

Based on a comprehensive review of the literature, case analyses, and interview data, branding design in cross-cultural regions must embody characteristics of multicultural and multi-ethnic integration while synthesizing multi-dimensional content holistically. Dynamic branding, through the use of diverse media, bidirectional communication, and co-creative expression, effectively addresses the complex demands of integrating multiple cultural identities and emotional resonances across groups. As previously discussed, the incorporation of familiar landmarks or cultural motifs can significantly enhance brand recognition, cultural identification, and audience engagement. Image-based visual translation techniques can be employed to convert iconic architecture and humanistic landscapes into specific visual forms, thereby establishing a unified visual language alongside a concise yet adaptable design vocabulary that balances clarity of communication with inclusiveness. In such regions, cross-cultural branding must foster both identity-based and emotional resonance among stakeholders, necessitating novel branding strategies that actively invite participation from various population segments. These approaches aim to generate emotional, mnemonic, and social connections. Interviews further reveal that core challenges in the brand image design of the Guangdong-Hong Kong-Macao Greater Bay Area include the articulation of cultural hybridity, the construction of identity across demographic groups, the negotiation of visual strategies between abstraction and representation, and the depiction of the region's rapid development and evolving urban-cultural landscape.

Therefore, it is imperative to construct a genuinely dynamic visual system capable of randomly extracting and generating content from diverse, continuously evolving visual materials. Such a system should be capable of real-time visual generation, articulation, and application within dynamic environments, while also encouraging broad-based participation in brand visual development.

In response to these demands, this study explores and further proposes an innovative methodology for cross-cultural brand visual design. This study found that the diverse and rapidly evolving dynamic landscapes of cross-cultural territories represented by the Guangdong, Hong Kong, and Macao Greater Bay Area are usually recorded by people in static pictures in the current digital media era, while the static pictures of the most popular cross-cultural territories' landscapes in the information media are probable to be the most popular and fastest-changing dynamic landscapes of cross-cultural territories in the current time (Fig. 10).

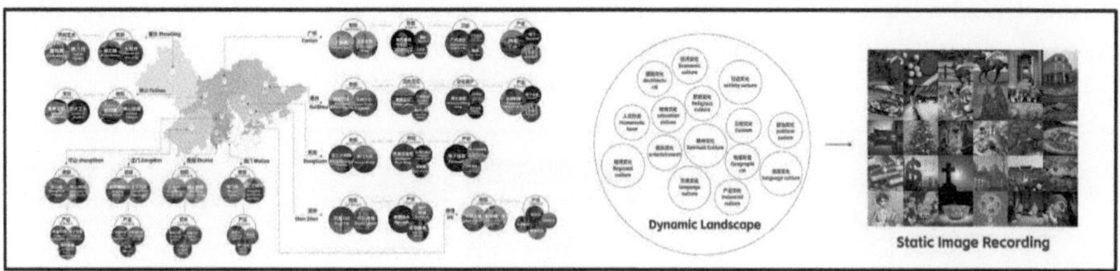

Fig. 10. Transformation of a flowing cityscape into a static picture schematic

Therefore, color data is extracted from the images using Processing code and subsequently transformed to generate a new visual language. Specifically, the color proportions and distributions in the images are pre-analyzed and translated into continuously varying data streams that generate dynamic, evolving color blocks. This process enables the transformation of dynamic landscapes into static images, which are then used to simulate and document the trajectory of multicultural evolution. This, in turn, informs a dynamic visual transformation process for brand identity and supports the construction of a foundational visual language for cross-cultural regional branding. As a result, a diversified and continuously evolving brand visual environment is established, where visual content is dynamically extracted and generated from multifaceted and dynamic materials and expressed through dynamic visual forms—ultimately realizing a truly dynamic visual system (Fig. 11).

Fig. 11. Schematic illustration of dynamic visual transformation of static images.

Familiar regional elements can enhance brand recognition, cultural identification, and audience engagement in cross-cultural contexts. Consequently, many static city branding projects translate landmark architecture, iconic features, and cultural symbols into specific visual forms to evoke memory and unify diverse content within a coherent visual language. With this in mind, this study conducted an image collection of popular core cities in the Guangdong-Hong Kong-Macao Greater Bay Area, which document the rapid changes in urban contours from the time of China's reform and opening up to recent years. This reflects the rapid development and change of this cross-cultural region over the years, as well as the hyper-vitality of the territory, as shown in the interviews.

This study applies a blurring technique to these static images to extract evolutionary data related to city contours. It then integrates this contour data with flowing, color-shifting block data, converting the result into a dynamically changing urban texture. This method simultaneously activates cultural memory among viewers while enabling differentiated visual outputs from multiple perspectives and achieving unified brand expression across diverse visual content (Figs. 12 and 13).

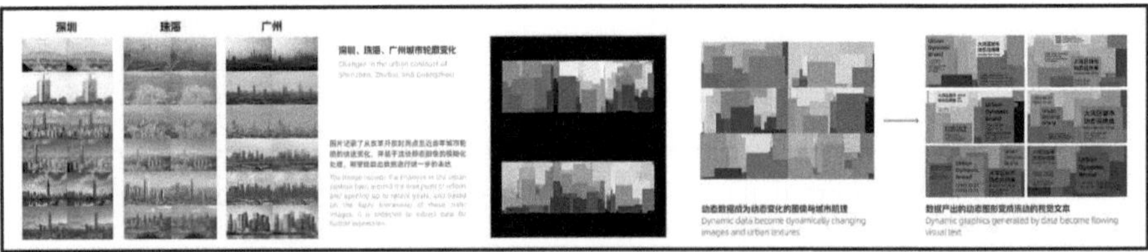

Fig. 12. Schematic illustration of dynamic visual transformation of urban silhouette texture.

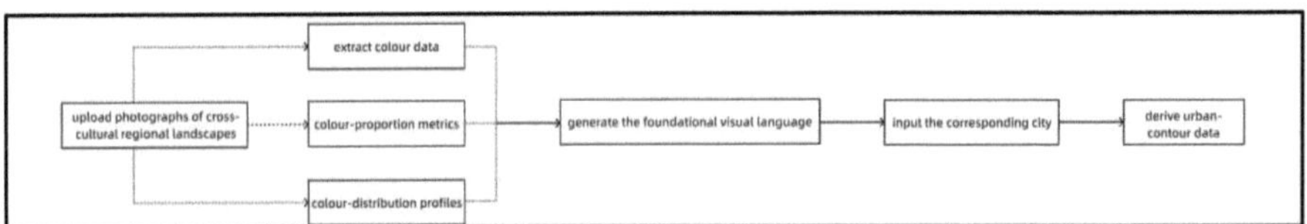

Fig. 13. Schematic workflow of the method.

Through this approach, the study enables individuals and groups from different cultural backgrounds within cross-cultural regions to upload images of familiar or favored landscapes and collectively participate in the design of city branding visuals. Following the design of the primary visual elements representing the Greater Bay Area, the study further developed both Chinese and English typefaces using a unified modular square system. These typefaces were standardized and encoded to support open-ended co-creation by people across the region. Ultimately, a dedicated co-creation website was established for the Guangdong-Hong Kong-Macao Greater Bay Area. The visual language system and bilingual typefaces produced by this research were uploaded to the platform, making them accessible as open, co-creatable brand assets and a participatory branding platform (Figs. 14 and 15).

Eventually, a visual innovation methodology tailored for cross-cultural regional branding was formulated. This method follows the sequence: landscape → image → data → familiar regional texture → visual text → brand carrier → co-creation and sharing. Through this approach, the study effectively addresses both the design imperatives

Fig. 14. Examples of design outputs

Fig. 15. Example of co-creation participation.

of cross-cultural branding and the contextual needs specific to the Guangdong-Hong Kong-Macao Greater Bay Area (Fig. 16).

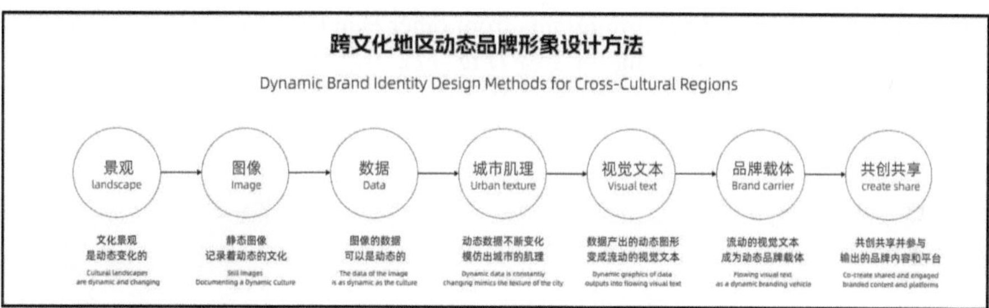

Fig. 16. Schematic of the path of Dynamic Brand Identity Design Methods for Cross-Cultural Regions.

5   Verification and Results

The validation of the cross-cultural brand visual innovation design methodology proposed in this investigation is oriented toward satisfying the dynamic brand design requirements for cross-cultural regions summarized in the preceding section and addressing the authentic needs of brand image design within the Guangdong-Hong Kong-Macao Greater Bay Area. In verifying whether the methodology proposed in this study meets the requirements for dynamic brand design in cross-cultural regions, this research adopts the evaluative framework developed by Ming-Chieh Hsu, which is grounded in Norman's theoretical foundations and contributions from multiple scholars, encompassing three analytical dimensions: cognitive level, functional level, and affective experience level [13], These three levels of progression also progressively fulfill the basic requirements of brand design, the design requirements of cross-cultural regional brands, the requirements of cross-cultural regional audiences, and the actual needs of the Guangdong-Hong Kong-Macao Greater Bay Area. The interview insights from the preceding section provide crucial reference points for validating the alignment between the methodology proposed in this study and the practical requirements of brand image design in the Guangdong-Hong Kong-Macao Greater Bay Area. Therefore, the validation assessment instrument comprises twelve evaluative criteria across four domains: cognitive dimension (recognizability, visual consistency, memory familiarity), functional dimension (personalization, applicability, co-creation support), affective experience dimension (identity recognition, engagement, aesthetic perception, emotional support), and regional characteristic presentation dimension (manifestation of dynamism and vitality, manifestation of multiculturalism). The assessment scale employs a five-point Likert scale format: 1 (highly unsatisfactory), 2 (unsatisfactory), 3 (neutral), 4 (satisfactory), and 5 (highly satisfactory). The evaluation cohort for this validation exercise consisted of twelve participants, comprising the nine interview subjects who continued in the follow-up phase and three migrants working within the Bay Area. The demographic composition included three women accounting for 25% and nine men accounting for 75%, with participants representing: three individuals from the local indigenous population accounting for 25%, four immigrants from Chinese provinces outside Guangdong Province accounting for 33%, one British immigrant accounting for 8%, one individual of Portuguese heritage accounting for 8%, and three immigrants from other Han Chinese ethnic groups within Guangdong Province accounting for 25% (Fig. 17).

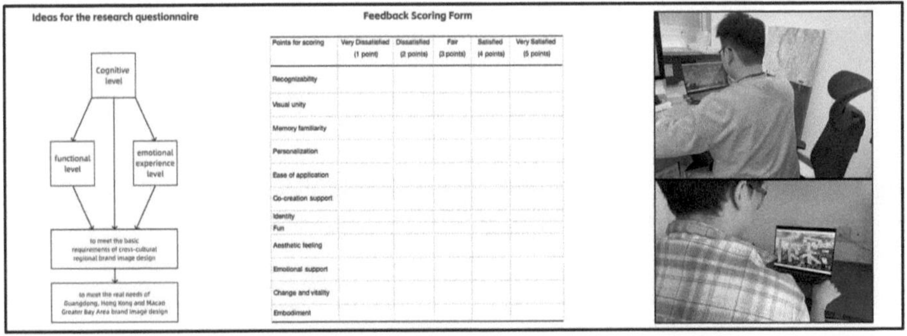

Fig. 17. Feedback validation ideas, questionnaires and photos.

Analysis of the feedback score data from the cross-cultural brand visual innovation design methodology for the Guangdong-Hong Kong-Macao Greater Bay Area demonstrates that the average dimensional scores range from 2.92 to 4.75 (five-point scale, n = 12), with the majority of indicators exceeding the median threshold of 3.0, indicating that the methodology receives a relatively positive overall evaluation.

The cognitive dimension encompasses three indicators: recognizability, visual consistency, and memory familiarity. Results demonstrate that both recognizability and visual consistency achieved high evaluative scores of approximately 4.5, confirming that the methodology effectively constructs a highly distinctive brand visual identity while maintaining robust visual coherence across cross-media applications. This characteristic holds substantial significance for cross-cultural communication, ensuring effective recognition among audiences from diverse cultural backgrounds. The memory familiarity score of 3.42 represents a moderate-to-high level, demonstrating that the methodological design has established foundational visual anchor points, though opportunities for enhancement remain.

The functional dimension encompasses personalization, applicability, and co-creation support, with significant performance variations across these indicators. Co-creation support achieved the highest score with an average of 4.75, indicating that the methodology effectively facilitates multi-stakeholder participation in collaborative creative construction, demonstrating excellent openness and adaptability that promotes brand adaptation and integration across diverse cultural contexts. Applicability received an average score of 3.67, confirming that the design solution possesses strong versatility within multimedia environments. However, the personalization dimension achieved only an average score of 2.92, representing the sole indicator below the median threshold, reflecting methodological limitations in cultivating brand distinctiveness. This deficiency may stem from the inherent contradiction whereby co-creation-oriented design pursues inclusivity while simultaneously diluting brand recognition.

The affective experience dimension incorporates four indicators: identity recognition, engagement, aesthetic perception, and emotional support. Identity recognition demonstrated exceptional performance with an average score of 4.58, indicating that the brand visually successfully integrates regional cultural elements and resonates with audiences within the multicultural and integrated Greater Bay Area environment. The average scores for aesthetic perception at 3.50 and emotional support at 3.58 both achieved moderate levels, satisfying fundamental requirements. The engagement dimension received a comparatively low average score of 3.0, exposing design limitations in generating novel experiential dimensions, potentially attributable to excessive emphasis on standardization and procedural systematization.

The regional characteristic presentation dimension comprises two indicators: manifestation of dynamism and vitality, and manifestation of multiculturalism. The manifestation of dynamism and vitality achieved a high average score of 4.50, confirming that the brand visual effectively communicates the dynamic developmental characteristics of the Greater Bay Area and demonstrates the methodology's efficacy in reflecting regional practices. The manifestation of multiculturalism received an average score of 3.75, indicating that the design successfully incorporates the diverse cultural elements within the Guangdong-Hong Kong-Macao Greater Bay Area, though opportunities remain for optimization in exploring nuanced cultural specificities (Fig. 18).

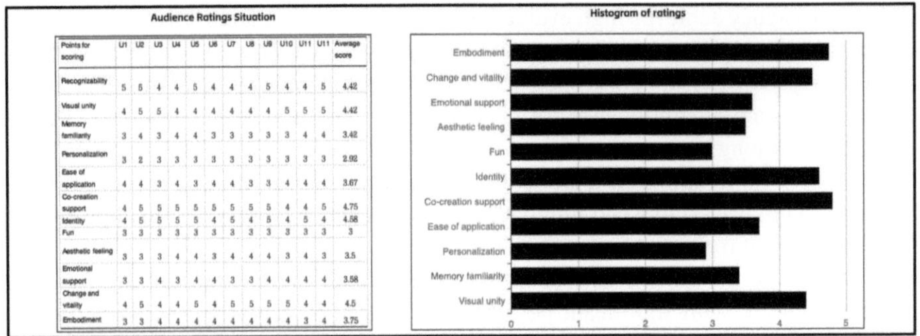

Fig. 18. Feedback on the results of the validation.

6 Discussion and Conclusion

6.1 Discussion

This investigation examines innovative paradigms for visual innovation in cross-cultural brand design contexts. Following a comprehensive literature synthesis that establishes research parameters and theoretical foundations, the study employs case study analysis and structured interviews to assess contemporary challenges and practices in cross-cultural brand design. Utilizing the Guangdong-Hong Kong-Macao Greater Bay Area as an exemplary case study, this research advances a dynamic, multidimensional, and participatory framework for brand visual design that integrates methodological rigor with practical application. The proposed approach successfully achieves a dynamic generation of diversified design assets while establishing a coherent visual expression taxonomy. Subsequent validation through feedback-driven assessment confirms the methodology's efficacy in synthesizing multicultural elements and diverse landscape contexts, thereby enhancing brand recognition and audience engagement through collaborative creation processes. The framework maintains visual coherence across multimedia platforms while reinforcing regional cultural identity and fostering connectivity among heterogeneous communities within cross-cultural environments. Nonetheless, opportunities for advancement persist in brand personalization and experiential engagement dimensions. This research contributes substantively to methodological discourse in cross-cultural brand visual design, providing novel theoretical insights and significant exploratory contributions while establishing a foundational framework for the dynamic generation and expression of visual content from heterogeneous source materials.

The empirical findings corroborate several theoretical propositions articulated in the literature review. Specifically, the strategic integration of indigenous landmarks and cultural signifiers into visual design substantially amplifies brand recognition and identity formation—a conclusion that aligns with established scholarship asserting that effective place-based branding must evoke authentic geographical identity. Furthermore, the research validates that dynamic, multimedia visual presentations effectively address the participatory expectations of multicultural constituencies, thereby reinforcing scholarly arguments regarding the strategic advantages of adaptive brand systems.

Through its collaborative co-creation platform, this investigation strengthens the emotional nexus between brands and their target audiences, resonating with the audience-centric paradigm emphasized in contemporary urban branding scholarship. Concurrently, the study reveals significant departures from extant research trajectories. While prevailing dynamic brand designs predominantly rely on predetermined configurations or static-derived variations that merely simulate dynamism, this investigation constructs an authentically fluid and temporally responsive visual ecosystem through data-driven visual language generation. This methodological innovation transcends conventional constraints of static-to-dynamic conversion, enabling real-time visual content synthesis from diversified material sources. These divergent outcomes emanate from the study's distinctive cross-cultural analytical lens and its deployment of innovative methodological and technological frameworks. Anchored in the rapidly evolving cultural milieu of the Greater Bay Area, the research incorporates generative visual components and participatory co-creation mechanisms, yielding results that diverge substantively from conventional branding research paradigms.

Several methodological constraints circumscribe this investigation's scope and generalizability. Geographically, the research remains confined to the Guangdong-Hong Kong-Macao Greater Bay Area, precluding extrapolation to alternative cross-cultural contexts and thereby limiting the universal applicability of its conclusions. Regarding sample demographics, the study inadequately controls for potential confounding variables including participants' educational backgrounds and cultural socialization patterns. In terms of analytical scope, the investigation primarily examines the nexus between visual symbolism and cultural semantics while providing limited consideration of macro-level determinants such as economic development trajectories or policy frameworks. Additionally, the methodology relies predominantly on qualitative interviews and short-term evaluative measures, lacking both large-scale quantitative validation and longitudinal monitoring, which constrains the depth of temporal analysis. In response to these limitations, future scholarly endeavors should expand along three critical dimensions. Primarily, adopting a mixed-methods research paradigm that incorporates large-scale surveys, experimental designs, and longitudinal studies would yield multidimensional analytical insights and enhanced empirical robustness. Secondly, integrating analyses of interactive effects among economic, technological, and contextual variables would facilitate the construction of a comprehensive theoretical framework for cross-cultural brand visual design. Finally, given the accelerating digital transformation landscape, subsequent investigations should examine how emerging technologies—particularly artificial intelligence applications—reshape visual cognition processes and transnational communicative practices.

Despite its practical contributions, the proposed methodology requires refinement in two specific domains: personalization capabilities and experiential engagement mechanisms. To enhance personalization, incorporating distinctive brand elements and stylistic characteristics while preserving cross-cultural accessibility would improve visual identity recognition. To augment experiential engagement, integrating dynamic and interactive visual components into the design process would elevate user participation and satisfaction levels.

In conclusion, this investigation, employing the Guangdong-Hong Kong-Macao Greater Bay Area as a representative case study, successfully conceptualizes and validates a dynamic brand visual system that synthesizes multiculturalism, multidimensional dynamic generation, and collaborative creation strategies. The research provides a replicable and sustainable framework for brand identity development within cross-cultural contexts.

6.2 Conclusion

This study focuses on the investigation of dynamic branding design methods and strategies within cross-cultural regions, using the Guangdong-Hong Kong-Macao Greater Bay Area as a representative example. It centers on two primary research themes: brand image design and dynamic brand design in cross-cultural contexts. To this end, the study first undertakes a literature review on theoretical frameworks related to cross-cultural brand image design and dynamic brand design. This is followed by empirical research employing case studies and interviews, structured in three parts. First, it analyzes representative brand visual cases from typical cross-cultural cities and synthesizes their design characteristics, emphasizing diversity and inclusivity. Second, it examines dynamic brand design cases from various cities and countries, identifying both the strengths and limitations of their dynamic performance. Third, it collects and analyzes existing brand visual design cases from the Guangdong-Hong Kong-Macao Greater Bay Area and its core cities, complemented by interviews and surveys with diverse population groups. This enables a deeper investigation into the evolving challenges and transformations in brand design within the complex cultural milieu of the region. On this foundation, a dynamic brand visual design methodology tailored for cross-cultural regions is proposed and practically implemented.

The main research contributions of this study are manifested in the following aspects: First, it proposes a dynamic brand design methodology mapped as a sequential path—"from landscape → image → data → familiar regional texture → visual text → brand carrier → co-creation and sharing"—thereby constructing an open, multifaceted system of dynamic brand visual expression that integrates cross-cultural landscapes with generative mechanisms. Second, it establishes a co-creative framework for cross-cultural brand design, facilitating collaborative content creation by audiences from diverse cultural backgrounds. Third, the study underscores the pivotal role of brand visual systems in shaping regional identity. It highlights the capacity of visual design to foster cultural resonance and identity among heterogeneous ethnic groups, thus contributing to the emergence of cultural consensus.

These findings extend existing theories and methodologies in both cross-cultural regional brand design and dynamic brand design while introducing applicable case-based insights. They not only transcend the inherent limitations of traditional branding paradigms but also explore how brand image design can articulate the nuances of multicultural integration and dynamic development. Moreover, by embedding co-creation as a core mechanism, the study enhances audience identification and participatory engagement, thereby offering theoretical significance and practical value to the field.

References

1. Mumford, L.: The City in History. China Architecture & Building Press, Beijing (2005)
2. Campbell, M.C., Keller, K.L.: Brand familiarity and advertising repetition effects. J. Consum. Res. **30**(2), 292–304 (2003)
3. Sarabia-Sanchez, F.J., Cerda-Bertomeu, M.J.: Expert stakeholders' expectations of how the public sector should act in place branding projects. J. Place Manag. Dev. **11**(1), 78–96 (2018)
4. Zenker, S., Braun, E., Petersen, S.: Branding the destination versus the place: the effects of brand complexity and identification for residents and visitors. Tour. Manag. **58**, 15–27 (2017)
5. Rodriguez, L., Asoro, R.L., Lee, S., Sar, S.: Gestalt principles in destination logos and their influence on people's recognition and intention to visit a country. Online J. Commun. Media Technol. **3**(1), 91–107 (2013)
6. Ashworth, G., Kavaratzis, M.: Beyond the logo: brand management for cities. J. Brand Manag. **16**(8), 520–531 (2009)
7. Zhang, Y.: Dynamic development in brand visual identity design and promotion: taking MB (moving brands) as an example. Art Des. (03), 88–89 (2016)
8. Negroponte, N.: Being Digital. Hainan Publishing House, Haikou (1997)
9. Yuan, J.: Dynamic brand identity design and promotion in new media context. Packag. Eng. **37**(10), 13–16 (2016)
10. Gobé, M.: Emotional Branding. People's Fine Arts Publishing House, Shanghai (2011)
11. Fu, M.: Expression of aesthetic appeal and formal performance in brand image under new media environment. Journal. Knowl. (02), 82–84 (2018)
12. Arnheim, R.: Visual Thinking: Aesthetic Intuition Psychology. Sichuan People's Publishing House, Chengdu (2010)
13. Hsu, M.C.: Visual expression and design principles for dynamic brand identities. Int. J. Vis. Des. **7**(2), 7–12 (2014)
14. Zinaida, R.S., Sunarto, S., Sunuantari, M.: City branding of Palembang: understanding cultural identification through logo and tagline. Int. J. Commun. Soc. **2**(1), 30–40 (2020)
15. Guo, E.: Several issues in the construction of urban public space in the United States. World Archit. (06), 7–8 (1989)
16. Cozmiuc, C.: City branding-just a compilation of marketable assets? Econ. Transdiscipl. Cogn. **14**(1), 428–434 (2011)
17. Ni, P., Ma, H.: International comparative study on sustainable competitiveness of China's urban system. Soc. Sci. Dig. (07), 49–51 (2021)
18. Wheeler, A.: Designing Brand Identity: An Essential Guide for the Whole Branding Team, 4th edn. Wiley (2014)
19. Duan, P.: Perception and management of urban brand image in a mediatized society: based on public perception and urban management dimensions. Modern Communication. **43**(2), 17–23 (2011)
20. Lynch, K.: Reconsidering the image of the city. In: Rodwin, L., Hollister, R.M. (eds.) Cities of the Mind, pp. 151–161. Springer, Boston (1984)
21. Alba, J.W., Hutchinson, J.W.: Dimensions of consumer expertise. J. Consum. Res. **13**(4), 411–454 (1987)
22. Kent, R.J., Allen, C.T.: Competitive interference effects in consumer memory for advertising: the role of brand familiarity. J. Mark. **58**(3), 97–105 (1994)
23. Kavaratzis, M.: Cities and their brands: lessons from corporate branding. Place Brand. Public Dipl. **5**(1), 26–37 (2009)
24. Zhang, B., Wang, Y., Zhou, Z., Sun, X.: The effect of logo design elements on city brand knowledge and awareness. Mark. Intell. Plan. **43**, 1424–1442 (2025)

25. Liu, Y., Wang, L., Xie, Z., Hua, X.: Innovative design method for city brand image. Packag. Eng. **41**(10), 235–241 (2020)
26. Burns, A.C., Biswas, A., Babin, L.A.: The operation of visual imagery as a mediator of advertising effects. J. Advert. **22**(2), 71–85 (1993)
27. Unnava, H.R., Agarwal, S.: Interactive effects of presentation modality and message-generated imagery on recall of advertising information. J. Consum. Res. **23**(1), 81–91 (1996)
28. Lv, J., Zhang, G.: Cultural character design of urban brand image from the perspective of semiotics. Archit. Cult. (08), 137–139 (2022)
29. Compte-Pujol, M., Eugenio-Vela, J.D.S., Frigola-Reig, J.: Key elements in defining Barcelona's place values: the contribution of residents' perceptions from an internal place branding perspective. Place Brand. Public Dipl. **14**(4), 245–259 (2017)
30. Kavaratzis, M.: The participatory place branding process for tourism: linking visitors and residents through the city brand. In: Pasquinelli, C., Bellini, N. (eds.) Tourism in the City: Towards an Integrative Agenda on Urban Tourism, pp. 93–107. Springer, Cham (2017)
31. Hereźniak, M., Florek, M.: Citizen involvement, place branding and mega events: insights from Expo host cities. Place Brand. Public Dipl. **14**(2), 89–100 (2018)
32. Braun, E., Kavaratzis, M., Zenker, S.: My city – my brand: the different role of residents in place branding. J. Place Manag. Dev. **6**(1), 18–28 (2013)
33. Insch, A., Walters, T.: Challenging assumptions about residents' engagement with place branding. Place Brand. Public Dipl. **14**(3), 152–162 (2018)
34. Zhu, W.: Research on dynamic design of city brand image in the "converged media" era. Packag. Eng. **43**(18), 334–340 (2022)
35. Nes, I.V.: Dynamic Identities: How to Create a Living Brand. BIS Publishers (2012)
36. Krasner, J.: Motion Graphic Design: Applied History and Aesthetics, 3rd edn. Routledge (2013)
37. Lu, R., Li, X.: Interactive design of dynamic brand image based on context awareness. Design. **35**(11), 65–67 (2022)
38. Cunha, J.M., et al.: Dynamic visual identities: exploring variation mechanisms to achieve flexibility. In: Raposo, D. (ed.) Perspectives on Design and Digital Communication Springer Series in Design and Innovation, vol. 8, pp. 91–104. Springer, Cham (2021)
39. Zeng, J.: Analysis of fundamentals in motion graphics design. Art Des. (08), 90–92 (2013)
40. Zhang, Y.: Application research of motion design in brand visual design. Design. **35**(18), 141–143 (2022)
41. Jiao, R.: From Static to Dynamic: Research on Dynamic Design of Brand Visual Identity.

Enhancing Fidelity of Text-to-Image AI Generation: A Natural Language Prompt Framework for Non-experts

Yining Ye, Pei-Luen Patrick Rau, and Liang Ma[✉]

Department of Industrial Engineering, Tsinghua University, Beijing 100084, China
`liangma@tsinghua.edu.cn`

Abstract. Generative text-to-image AI tools allow users to generate images based on keywords, known as prompts, enabling users to create high-quality images. However, current research mainly focuses on professional prompt settings for text-to-image generation, with limited exploration of natural language prompts used by non-expert users. Therefore, this study aims to understand how non-expert users describe images using natural language and the challenges they face in the process, and then construct a prompt framework to help them more accurately generate expected images. Twenty non-expert users without art backgrounds were recruited to participate in an exploratory experiment, in which they were instructed to use natural language prompts to reproduce two types of given images using Midjourney. Based on the textual content of the collected prompts, effective prompts were extracted and subjected to hypothesis testing and directed content analysis. The results showed that participants tend to overestimate the similarity between the images they generated and the original images, suggesting that individuals tend to overlook certain aspects subjectively when unguided, which underscores the necessity for a systematic prompt framework. A natural language prompt framework containing five main themes (composition and proportion, color and tone, subject description, thematic expression, and details) was proposed, providing sub-entries and example prompts for each theme. The effectiveness of the prompt framework has been preliminarily verified. This framework can help users more effectively utilize text-to-image AI tools and improve the user experience of generative AI.

Keywords: Prompt engineering · Text-to-image generation · Generative AI

1 Introduction

Since 2022, Large Language Modeling (LLM) technology and Artificial Intelligence (AI) tools, have made rapid progress and the user community has expanded rapidly. With the enhancement and differentiation of functionality, AI tools have developed several branches with different functions despite text-based conversation, such as drawing and making videos [1]. Generative AI tools such as Midjourney and DALL.E support users to generate images based on keywords, also known as prompts [2–5].

P.-L.P. Rau and H. Krömker (Eds.): HCII 2025, LNCS 16336, pp. 193–209, 2026.
https://doi.org/10.1007/978-3-032-12798-3_12

However, the performance of generative AI depends heavily on the accuracy of the prompts. In the absence of a systematic understanding of the prompts, the use of natural language to generate prompts often fails to produce the desired output [6,7]. To help users prompt more efficiently and get AI outputs that better meet their expectations, prompt engineering has been developed, and LLM developers, researchers, and experienced users have written tutorials, manuals, and other references for AI prompts to help users improve prompts from various perspectives, such as structure describing, parameter definition and setting, and accurate terminology [3,8–10]. These tutorials and manuals emphasize the necessity of structured prompts, guiding the user towards style switching and theme setting, helping users to get more professional creations.

For users with a background in art, photography, or other artistic disciplines, the parameters defined in these guidelines, such as "style: Renaissance" and "film type: color splash", are clear and easy to understand. However, compared to professional users who use AI tools only to get creative inspiration and have independent drawing ability, for ordinary users who lack professional knowledge, referred to as "non-expert users", one of the purposes of using text-to-image AI may be that they have an established need for an image, but due to the lack of professional drawing skills, they need to use AIs as "appointment painters" to realize what they've got in mind. In this type of task, ensuring high fidelity of images is an important objective. Fidelity refers to the degree to which an electronic device's output reproduces the input signal; similarly, we use "fidelity" here to denote the similarity between the images output by the text-to-image AIs and the intended input targets. To achieve high fidelity without obstacles, the key need of such non-expert users is to get an image that meets their expectations through simple, intuitive, and plain natural language descriptions, rather than through repeated debugging of complex, indistinguishable, and specialized parameters. Therefore, it's important and valuable to understand how users would characterize given images through natural language from the average user's perspective, contributing to better construction of an intuitive and universally applicable prompt framework.

The current study expects to understand the natural language structure of image descriptions by non-expert generative AI users, find out the obstacles and challenges they face during the description process, and construct a prompt framework to help users more accurately generate the expected images through the method of exploratory experimental research. These user-centered explorations are essential to improve the ease of use and user acceptance of generative AI tools, and provide insights to the optimization and improvement of generative AI tools for user experience.

In this paper, we recruited 20 users who do not have a professional background in the art to conduct an exploratory experiment using Midjourney. Using hypothesis testing, this study analyzes whether there is a significant difference between participants' subjective perceptions of similarity, human similarity scores guided by professional rating criteria, and automated Structural Similarity Index Measure (SSIM) scores. Based on the professional rating criteria, a natural language prompt framework for text-to-image AI generation was derived through directed content analysis. Our contributions are as follows:

- We generalize the five prompt categories used by participants when writing prompts in Midjourney based on the structure of the evaluation criteria of the Chinese Art College Entrance Examination.
- Based on the textual content of the prompts collected from the experiments, we extracted the prompt scheme with a better generation effect, and based on the categorization framework, with the help of NVivo 15, we encoded the sub-entries contained in each of the five categories of prompts and formulated examples of prompts under each sub-entry.
- We obtained each participant's perception of the problems that could not be solved by the improved description strategy through open-ended questioning of them after the experiment, and organized and summarized the feedback based on the collected content.
- Based on our findings, we propose a prompt framework with general applicability for all users.

2   Related Work

2.1   Brief Introduction to Text-to-Image AI

Generative Artificial Intelligence (AI) is a technology capable of producing new and meaningful content, such as text, images, or audio. Unlike traditional discriminative models, generative models create new data samples by learning the distribution of input data [11]. The core of this technology lies in its generative capability, enabling a wide range of applications across various fields, including artistic creation, content generation, and programming assistance [1].

A typical application of generative AI is Large Language Models (LLMs), such as OpenAI's ChatGPT, which is trained on extensive text data using deep learning techniques to generate coherent and logical text [12]. However, while generative AI holds significant potential for enhancing efficiency and creativity, it also presents challenges and risks, such as issues with the accuracy and reliability of generated content, as well as potential copyright and ethical disputes [13].

Text-to-Image AI is a technology that utilizes deep learning and Natural Language Processing (NLP) to convert textual descriptions into images. In recent years, advancements in technologies such as Generative Adversarial Networks (GANs), autoregressive models, and diffusion models have significantly improved the capabilities of text-to-image generation [14]. These models analyze textual data to produce high-quality images that match the descriptions, finding extensive applications in artistic creation, content generation, and digital marketing [4].

For instance, models like Midjourney, DALL-E, and Imagen can generate realistic or abstract images based on textual prompts, providing new creative tools for artists and designers. These models not only enhance creative efficiency but also lower the technical barriers to artistic creation, allowing more people to engage in creative expression [5].

In summary, generative AI, represented by text-to-image AI, is a powerful tool that is transforming various aspects of our work and life. On the other hand, the powerful capabilities of AI technology also determine the richness and complexity of its usage methods. Therefore, further comprehensive and in-depth exploration and research are needed to help users better utilize this technology.

2.2   Prompt Engineering for Text-to-Image AI

In the field of text-to-image AI, prompt engineering is a critical research direction that involves effectively constructing and optimizing text prompts to guide generative models in producing high-quality image outputs. Developers of large language models (LLMs) and experienced online users have created AI prompt tutorials, manuals, and other reference materials to assist a broad user base in crafting prompts from various perspectives, such as descriptive structure, parameter definition and settings, and precise language use [3,8–10]. For instance, the "DALL.E 2 Prompt Book" provides a comprehensive guide covering a range of prompt strategies from aesthetics and emotional language to photography, film styles, illustration styles, art history, and 3D art. It emphasizes the need to consider multidimensional factors when constructing prompts, such as how to use specific vocabulary and phrasing to guide the generative model to produce images with particular styles and emotions [3].

In recent years, significant progress has been made in the field of prompt engineering for text-to-image AI, with researchers proposing innovative insights and methods from various perspectives. The Promptify system developed by Brade et al. [2] represents a major breakthrough in the automation of prompt engineering. By integrating the capabilities of LLMs, this system provides users with innovative features such as automatic prompt expansion, optimization suggestions, and image layout and clustering, significantly enhancing the efficiency of prompt construction and the quality of generated images. This system has laid an important technical foundation for subsequent research.

In terms of the expressive dimensions of prompt engineering, Liu [15] broke through the limitations of traditional text prompts and proposed an innovative approach using multimodal prompts. Her research emphasizes the importance of incorporating visual language and multimodal interactions into prompt engineering, offering new perspectives to meet the creative needs of artists and designers. This research perspective complements the user interaction study conducted by Mahdavi Goloujeh et al. [8], who, through empirical research, revealed the core challenges users face in the prompt construction process, particularly in aligning AI intentions and acquiring prompt-related knowledge, providing critical insights for optimizing user interaction experiences.

In the theoretical framework of prompt engineering, the research by Oppenlaender [16] has made a systematic contribution. His proposed taxonomy of prompt modifiers, which identifies six distinct types of modifiers—including subject terms, image prompts, and style modifiers—provides a clear conceptual framework for understanding and analyzing prompt engineering practices. This taxonomy not only synthesizes previous research findings but also offers an extensible theoretical foundation for future studies in prompt engineering.

These studies have advanced the development of prompt engineering for text-to-image AI from multiple dimensions, including technical implementation, user interaction, and theoretical frameworks, providing comprehensive theoretical support and practical guidance for building more intelligent and user-friendly prompt engineering systems. However, existing prompt engineering primarily focuses on technical and tool-based approaches, emphasizing diverse prompting methods or exploring users' prompting processes and challenges; prompt guides tend to focus on a wide range of parameters and their definitions, which can be complex for novice users. For non-expert users lacking professional knowledge, they prefer to obtain images that largely meet their expectations through simple, intuitive, and plain natural language descriptions, rather than through repeated adjustments of complex and difficult-to-distinguish professional parameters. To address this gap, understanding how non-expert users naturally describe images from their perspective can help construct an intuitive and universally applicable prompting framework.

Therefore, this study aims to explore the natural language structure of image descriptions used by non-expert generative AI users, as well as the obstacles and challenges they face during the description process, to construct a prompt framework that helps users more accurately generate expected images. With this goal in mind, we formulated the following research questions:

- RQ1: What is the way that non-expert users (i.e., users who don't have specialized knowledge of art) describe an image?
- RQ2: By what prompt structure does generative AI produce image results that better match user expectations?
- RQ3: What are the challenges in using generative AI that cannot be fully overcome by improving prompt descriptions?

3 Methods

This study employed an exploratory experimental research method. In this section, we introduce details about participant recruitment, experimental design, and criteria setting methods used in this study.

3.1 Participants

A total of 20 participants were recruited for the experiment, all from Tsinghua University, with a female:male ratio of 1:1, and the age range of the participants was within 22-30 (mean = 24 years old, SD = 3). All participants are proficient in the use of computers, to ensure that they were able to learn and adapt to the experimental platform during the experimental process.

A recruitment information sheet and a pre-experiment questionnaire were prepared to collect basic information of the participants. According to the questionnaire, 60% of the participants had experience in the use of text-generated image AI. Among the participants with usage experience, DALL.E and Midjourney had the highest percentage of usage, accounting for 41.7% and 33.3%, respectively, while other commonly used AIs included New Bing, ChatGLM, and ERNIE Bot, with a total of 41.7% of participants having used at least one of them. All recruited participants completed the experiment successfully and received a basic payment and a performance-based incentive.

3.2   Experimental Task

We designed an exploratory experimental task to find out what kind of prompt strategy participants would use when they want to generate a given image with the help of Midjourney. In the experiment, participants were required to use Midjourney to describe two given images in as much detail as possible, with a time limit of 10 minutes for each task. The task requirement was that at the end of the timer, the AI-generated images should be as similar as possible to the original ones, which was linked to participants' performance rewards.

The two images were thematically different, one scene-oriented (labeled task s-scenario) and one character-oriented (labeled task p-person), to explore the effect of different image styles on participants' prompting strategies. As observed through social media, AI is commonly used to generate two types of tasks, portrait and landscape, which are also quite common and representative of the fine art field. We want to cover as much as possible the user's requirement goals through these two images. The complexity of the description between the two images mainly comes from the type and number of tuples in them, so as to make a certain degree of difficulty (that Task S is more complex than Task P), in order to ensure that the summarizing framework has a certain degree of applicability for various types of difficulty in the generation of images. Both images were generated using generative AI tools to ensure that the capabilities of AI tools can meet the technical requirements for generating these two images.

Midjourney is highly recognized in the field of generative text-to-image AI, known for its powerful capabilities and high-quality outputs. Therefore, it was chosen as the model for this experiment. To meet the conversational convenience needs of participants whose native language is Chinese, the Midjourney model was accessed via Niji Bot on the Discord platform, allowing participants to conduct the experiment in Chinese.

3.3   Experimental Procedure

Firstly, as the experiment consisted of two subtasks, before the start of the experiment, we randomly divided the participants into two groups, controlling for a female: male ratio of 1:1 in each group, with different order of subtasks in the two groups, and the rest of the conditions were identical.

Before the start of the experiment, participants were required to sign an informed consent form, which included basic information such as the purpose of the study, the content of the study, the criteria for recruiting participants, the time and place of the experiment, the remuneration for the experiment, and the potential risks of the experiment, etc. Participants were required to confirm that they fully understood the information and volunteered to participate in the experiment. At the beginning of the experiment, participants were asked to fill out a basic information questionnaire to understand their demographic information and history of using text-to-image AI tools. After completing the questionnaire, we introduced Discord to the participants, and they were given 5 minutes of practice time to familiarize themselves with the steps and commands required in the experiment. After the practice session, the formal experiment began: participants were required to describe two given images in as much detail as possible to generate images as similar as possible to the original ones, with a time limit of 10 minutes for each task. All of the input prompts and their corresponding generated images would be fully documented by video recording, and the chat logs were kept by the platform, Discord.

At the end of each experimental task, participants were required to fill out the NASA-TLX scale, which was used to measure the task load of the participants. At the end of the formal experiments, participants were asked to fill out a post-experiment questionnaire, which consisted of three types of questions: the first question asked participants to rate (in percent) their degree of completion, i.e., how well the images were reproduced, in both experiments; the second question asked the participants to summarize their prompt strategies; and the third question asked participants to suggest difficulties they encountered in reproducing the images that could not be artificially overcome.

The total duration of the experiment was approximately 30 minutes per person. At the end of the experiment, the performance of all participants was calculated and ranked, and the appropriate experimental payment was issued according to the criteria.

3.4 Scoring Criteria

Evaluating the output results of text-to-image generation models requires a combination of quantitative and qualitative methods [17]. This is the same for assessing the output image fidelity of text-to-image AI. In this study, for the scoring of image similarity, automated scoring for quantitative scoring combined with manual scoring for qualitative scoring was used.

For automated scoring, Structural Similarity Index Measure (SSIM) was used for the similarity assessment between the participant-generated image and the original image. SSIM is a full-reference image quality evaluation metric that measures image similarity in terms of brightness, contrast, and structure [18,19]. SSIM takes values in the range of $[-1,1]$, the larger the value, the smaller the image distortion, and greater than 0 represents the existence of image similarity. In practical application, the image can be chunked using a sliding window, so that the total number of chunks is N. Considering the effect of window shape on the chunks, Gaussian weighting is used to calculate the mean, variance, and covariance of each window, and then the structural similarity of the corresponding chunks is calculated as SSIM, and finally, the mean value is used as the structural similarity measure of the two images, i.e., the average structural similarity MSSIM.

The manual scoring criteria are derived from the evaluation criteria of the Chinese Art College Entrance Examination, mainly referring to the guidelines of the Shanghai and Tianjin Art Examinations, the examination requirements of the two guides are identical, and both are formulated in accordance with the standards of the Ministry of Education, which are representative. The examination includes three parts: drawing, color and sketching, and the examination form is to provide references for the candidates to draw works that meet the requirements according to the references, which is in line with the task set in this experiment in which the reference image is given and the participant describes the image, so the evaluation criteria of the art examination is of reference value to this experiment. According to the evaluation criteria of the art exam, five scoring items were summarized: *composition and proportion, color and tone, subject description, thematic expression,* and *details. Composition and proportion* evaluate the degree of similarity between the two images in terms of screen layout, spatial allocation, and element location relationships. *Color and tone* evaluate the similarity of the two images in terms of color usage, hue matching, saturation, brightness, etc. *Subject description* evaluates the similarity between two images in the depiction and presentation of the main representational objects (e.g., people, objects, scenes). *Thematic expression* evaluates the similarity of the two images in terms of conveying core ideas, emotions, story content, etc. *Detail* evaluates the similarity of two images in terms of detail depiction [20, 21]. For each scoring item, five scoring rules were formulated based on the specific details of the original image, e.g., "Color and tone-people's tops are bright yellow", and the item was scored one point for each rule met, with a single score value of 0–5 points and a total score of 25 points, and the score of each participant was the standardized total score, which is the total score scored by the scoring. Each participant's score was standardized by dividing the total score by 25 so that the scores were distributed in the range of [0,1] to keep the manual score and the SSIM score consistent. The specific definition of the manual scoring criteria is shown in Table 1.

For each image generated by a participant, the final score for fidelity, i.e., similarity to the original image, is taken as the mean of the manual score and the SSIM score, with the values range of [0,1]. For a weighted score obtained, being closer to 1 indicates a higher degree of similarity between the image produced by the participant and the original image, reflecting higher fidelity; conversely, a total score closer to 0 indicates lower fidelity.

Table 1. The scoring themes and evaluation criteria for manual scoring

Aspects	Definitions
Composition and proportion	Evaluate the degree of similarity between two images in terms of screen layout, spatial allocation, and element location relationships.
Color and tone	Evaluate the similarity of the two images in terms of color usage, hue matching, saturation, brightness, etc.
Subject description	Evaluate the similarity between two images in the depiction and presentation of the main representational objects (e.g., people, objects, scenes).
Thematic expression	Evaluate the similarity of two images in terms of conveying core ideas, emotions, story content, etc.
Detail	Evaluate the similarity of two images in terms of detail depiction.

4 Results

In this section, we present the process and results of the data analysis in this study and summarize the findings of the experiment.

4.1 Scoring of Images

From all the generated images, the image with the highest fidelity completed by each participant in each group was selected for analysis, resulting in a total sample comprising ratings for 40 images.

Based on the manual similarity scoring results, the SSIM scoring results, and the post-experiment questionnaire results, we obtained six sets of experimental data categorized according to the two types of tasks (task S, task P), i.e., SSIM_S, SSIM_P, Manual_S, Manual_P, Perceived_S and Perceived_P. Where the Perceived_S and Perceived_P represent the subjective ratings that participants gave to their image reproduction in the post-experiment questionnaire. The basic statistics for the six sets of data are shown in Table 2 and Fig. 1.

Firstly, the correlation between the participants' self-ratings and the objective ratings of SSIM was analyzed to explore the discrepancy between users' subjective ratings and actual fidelity. For the four data groups, SSIM_S, SSIM_P, Perceived_S and Perceived_P, the Kolmogorov-Smirnov normality test was used to test normality respectively. The results showed that the p-values of the four data groups were: SSIM_S: p-value > 0.150, SSIM_P: p-value = 0.031, Perceived_S: p-value = 0.101, and Perceived_P: p-value > 0.150, indicating that

Table 2. The basic statistics of the six scoring items

Variables	Mean	S.E. of Mean	S.D.	Minimum	Median	Maximum
SSIM_S	0.276	0.003	0.013	0.252	0.277	0.297
SSIM_P	0.526	0.011	0.049	0.370	0.531	0.589
Manual_S	0.418	0.019	0.083	0.200	0.420	0.560
Manual_S	0.496	0.027	0.123	0.280	0.460	0.760
Perceived_S	0.651	0.036	0.160	0.200	0.675	0.870
Perceived_S	0.700	0.035	0.156	0.320	0.705	0.950

only the data of SSIM_P is not normally distributed, and the other three data groups are normally distributed.

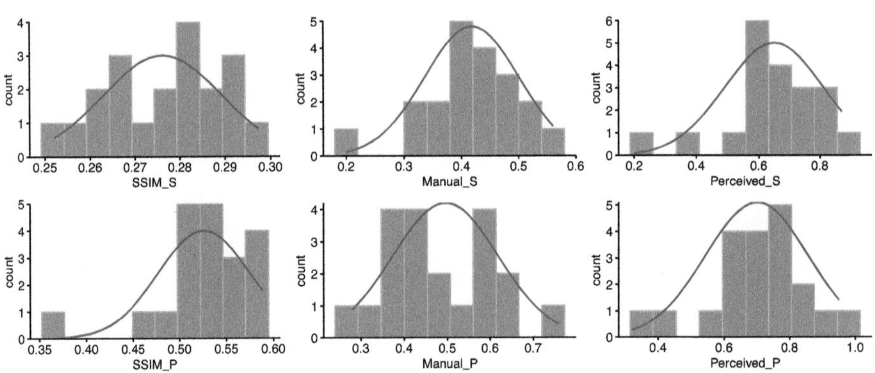

Fig. 1. The histograms of the six scoring items

Based on the results of the normality test, comparisons were made among different task groups. For Group S, a two-sample t-test was conducted. When the alternative hypothesis was that the mean of SSIM_S is less than the mean of Perceived_S, the resulting p-value < 0.001, indicating that participants' self-ratings were significantly higher than the objective ratings obtained from SSIM. For Group P, the Mann-Whitney non-parametric test, suitable for comparing means between two groups, was utilized. When the alternative hypothesis was that the mean of SSIM_P is less than the mean of Perceived_P, the resulting p-value < 0.001, indicating that participants' self-ratings were also significantly higher than the objective ratings obtained from SSIM in Group P. The common pattern observed in both Group S and Group P suggests that individuals tend to overlook certain aspects subjectively when unguided, which supports the notion that having a framework can assist users in providing more accurate descriptions. This underscores the necessity for a systematic prompting framework.

Secondly, the correlation between manual scores and SSIM scores was compared to validate the rationality of the proposed manual scoring criteria. Pearson correlation analysis was employed to calculate the correlation coefficients between SSIM_S and Manual_S, as well as between SSIM_P and Manual_P. The correlation scatters are shown in Fig. 2. For Group S, the paired Pearson correlation yielded a p-value of 0.057, which is marginally significant. Upon examining the scatter plot, two significant outliers were identified (ID = 10, 13). After removing these two outliers, the paired Pearson correlation was re-evaluated, resulting in a p-value of 0.015, indicating a significant correlation between SSIM_S and Manual_S. The two outlier points (ID = 10, 13) were analyzed for potential causes of their deviation: The image for ID = 10 had significant differences in composition and color tone compared to the original image, leading to a very low manual score according to the established criteria, thus becoming an outlier. The image for ID = 13 had a composition and details that closely matched the original image, resulting in a high manual score. However, its main shortcomings were high brightness and color contrast, which did not align with the original image's color tone (also reflected in the manual score for color tone). The SSIM algorithm, which assesses image similarity based on brightness, contrast, and structure, is highly sensitive to brightness and contrast, hence resulting in a lower SSIM score and a discrepancy with the manual score. Therefore, both outlier points can be reasonably explained. For Group P, the paired Pearson correlation yielded a p-value of 0.016, indicating a significant correlation between SSIM_P and Manual_P. The significant results of the correlation tests between manual scores and SSIM scores in both groups validate the rationality of the manual scoring framework.

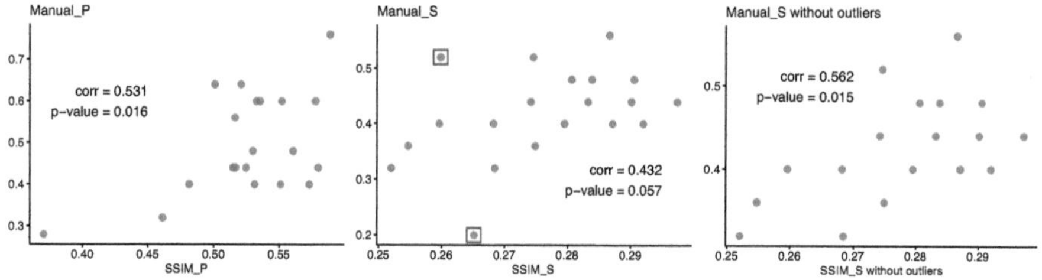

Fig. 2. The correlation scatters

4.2 The Natural Language Prompt Framework

In Sect. 4.1, we have already validated the rationality of the established manual scoring criteria. From another perspective, this manual scoring framework can serve as the primary basis and structure for developing a prompt framework. Therefore, we employed the method of directed content analysis [22], using the five major themes of the manual scoring criteria—Composition and Proportion, Color and Tone, Subject Description, Thematic Expression, and Details—as the main structure to further develop the prompt framework. For the creation of sub-codes, NVivo 15 was utilized as the coding tool, and traditional conventional content analysis was applied to directly derive coding categories from all the prompt texts collected in the experiment. A total of 173 prompts were included in the analysis. Among them, the minor differences arising from slight adjustments and supplements in the prompts of the same participant were considered negligible. The 40 prompts corresponding to the 40 images with the highest fidelity selected from each participant were analyzed in detail. The content analysis results are shown in Table 3.

Table 3. The content analysis results

Aspects	Sub-items	Amount of points encoded
Composition and proportion	Objects and elements	21
	Position and direction	13
	Proportion	4
Color and Tone	Color descriptions	16
	Light	4
	General mood or Tone	6
Subject description	Character description	42
	Environment description	17
	Item description	6
Thematic expression	Art style	7
	Atmosphere	6
Detail	Buildings and structure	11
	Human features	7
	Nature and landscape	34
	Objects and items	25

The summarized prompt framework includes five major themes: Composition and Proportion, Color and Tone, Subject Description, Thematic Expression, and Details, with sub-themes categorized under each theme according to details. Based on the results of the qualitative content analysis, the final prompt framework is shown in Table 4.

4.3 User Prompt Challenges

During the experiment, while exploring how to craft prompts for better results, some issues that cannot be resolved through improvements in prompt words were also revealed. In the post-experiment questionnaire, the following two issues were frequently mentioned by participants:

Table 4. The natural language prompt framework

Aspects	Sub-items	Example prompt
Composition and proportion	Objects and elements	A book; A desk
	Position and direction	The book is in the middle of the table, with its cover facing left
	Proportion	The person makes up 70% of the picture
Color and tone	Color descriptions	Orange sweater
	Light	High brightness
	General mood or tone	Warm/Cool tone
Subject description	Character description	The subject is a tall guy in a blue denim jacket
	Environment description	The subject is a snow-capped mountain soar into the sky
	Item description	The subject is a red train
Thematic expression	Art style	Animation style
	Atmosphere	Quiet, warm atmosphere
Detail	Buildings and structure	Warm yellow lights shone from every window of the tall building
	Human features	A small round black stud is on her left ear
	Nature and landscape	There are scattered flowers on the grassland
	Objects and items	Inside the book was a maple leaf

1. AI has a significant degree of randomness and cannot accurately implement the described details, leading to discrepancies between the details and those explicitly mentioned in the prompts. The more detailed the description, the more likely the result may deviate from expectations (mentioned 15 times).
2. The inherent style of the AI differs significantly from the target image, making it difficult to achieve accurate corrections through prompts (mentioned 6 times).

The above two categories of issues explain why participants cannot achieve a perfect reproduction of the given images. They are also common and significant challenges for all users of generative AI, greatly affecting user satisfaction.

5   Discussion

This section discusses the results of the experimental analysis, emphasizing how our findings can help construct a prompt framework that assists users in generating images more accurately, thereby enhancing the usability and user acceptance of generative AI tools. Also, limitations of this study are discussed.

Through the exploratory experimental study, we addressed the research questions proposed. First, through the experiment, non-expert users were found to prefer using complete natural language paragraphs to describe images. Their descriptions centered on five themes: Composition and Proportion, Color and Tone, Subject Description, Thematic Expression, and Detail. Under each theme, the specific content of user prompts followed more detailed patterns, which were summarized into sub-themes within the natural language prompt framework we proposed.

Based on the prompts written according to the proposed framework, generative AI can produce images that better match user expectations. To verify the effectiveness of the framework, we guided the creation of images containing prompts for each item according to this framework and used SSIM scores for validation. The images generated from a single prompt had lower SSIM scores compared to most of the highest-fidelity images completed by participants during the experiment. However, they significantly exceeded the SSIM scores of images generated by participants in just a single attempt. The comparison of images generated based on the prompt framework with the original images is shown in Fig. 3. This demonstrates the usability and efficiency of the prompt framework for inexperienced users, indicating that using this prompt framework can help users generate higher-fidelity images in a shorter time and with fewer iterations. When applying the prompt framework, one can either fill in each item according to the framework or write in natural paragraphs and then check if all the items are met.

(a) Person -
Original Image

(b) Person -
New Generation

(c) Scenario -
Original Image

(d) Scenario -
New Generation

Fig. 3. Comparison of images generated by midjourney in a single conversation based on the prompt framework with the original images

Beyond prompt engineering, we summarized common issues encountered by users when using text-to-image AI, namely the randomness of AI and the differences in artistic styles. These challenges, which cannot be addressed by prompts, are related to the characteristics of the AI model itself. The issue of details stems from the inherent uncertainty of the AI, while the style issue arises partly from the lack of diversity in the inherent style of the model, and partly from the complexity of describing the style. Since the participants recruited for this experiment do not have a background in art, particularly in fine arts, describing style in a professional manner may be challenging for them. Therefore, to address these issues, it is necessary to focus more on improving the technology of AI for text-to-image generation. From the perspective of optimizing AI models, enhancing their ability to understand prompt content can align the AI's cognitive foundation with that of the user. This can effectively improve the stability of the generated results, making them more aligned with user expectations, thereby increasing user satisfaction and the willingness of potential users to use the tool.

There are some limitations to this study. First, the effectiveness of the framework has only been superficially demonstrated through the researcher's own trials and has not been validated through experiments with a sufficient sample size to confirm its broad applicability. Second, all participants in this study were from China, with Chinese as their native language. Therefore, the prompt framework developed is based on Chinese prompts and may yield different results when applied in English or other language contexts. Another possible reason for the ineffectiveness of prompts emphasizing certain detail corrections is that Midjourney was developed by native English speakers, and its Chinese conversation capabilities were only implemented in later generations of the model. Thus, its understanding of Chinese prompts may not be as sensitive as its understanding of English. This could be one of the reasons why participants in this study could not achieve satisfactory results. This potential factor also suggests that language and cultural differences can significantly impact the user experience of models and the effectiveness of prompt engineering.

6   Conclusion

This study focuses on developing a natural language prompt framework for non-expert users utilizing AI tools as "commissioned artists" to fulfill their specific image needs. Through exploratory experimental research, we gained insights into the natural language structure of generative AI users' image descriptions, emphasizing the descriptive themes and considerations frequently mentioned by users when generating images with AI, such as composition and proportion, color and tone, etc. Based on this understanding, we proposed a prompt framework that can effectively help users efficiently and comprehensively obtain high-fidelity target images using text-to-image AI tools. This framework aligns with users' natural language habits for image description from their own perspective, requiring no extensive professional knowledge and being simple to use. The effectiveness of the framework for portrait and landscape images has been partially validated. Additionally, the study summarized the obstacles and challenges users face in crafting prompts that cannot be resolved through prompts alone. These user-centered explorations contribute to enhancing the usability and user acceptance of generative AI tools and even promote optimizations and improvements in user experience.

In summary, this work provides a guiding solution to help users better utilize text-to-image AI and offers suggestions for improving the user experience of generative AI from the perspective of user language habits.

Acknowledgments. This study was supported by the National Natural Science Foundation of China with the Research Project on Human-Machine Collaborative Decision-Making (No. 72192822).

References

1. Nah, F.F.-H., Zheng, R., Cai, J., Siau, K., Chen, L.: Generative AI and ChatGPT: applications, challenges, and AI-human collaboration. J. Inform. Technol. Case Appl. Res. **25**(3), 277–304 (2023). https://doi.org/10.1080/15228053.2023.2233814

2. Brade, S., Wang, B., Sousa, M., Oore, S., Grossman, T.: Promptify: text-to-image generation through interactive prompt exploration with large language models. In: Proceedings of the 36th Annual ACM Symposium on User Interface Software and Technology, pp. 1–14. Association for Computing Machinery, New York, NY, USA (2023).https://doi.org/10.1145/3586183.3606725

3. A traveler's guide to the latent space. https://sweet-hall-e72.notion.site/A-Traveler-s-Guide-to-the-Latent-Space85efba7e5e6a40e5bd3cae980f30235f. Accessed 05 Jan 2025

4. Singh, A.: A survey of AI text-to-image and AI text-to-video generators. In: 2023 4th International Conference on Artificial Intelligence, Robotics and Control (AIRC), pp. 32–36. IEEE, Cairo, Egypt (2023). https://doi.org/10.1109/AIRC57904.2023.10303174

5. Singh, T.: The influence of AI text-to-image technologies on modern creative practices. IOSR J. Comput. Eng. (IOSR-JCE) **26**(5), 01–06 (2024)

6. Reynolds, L., McDonell, K.: Prompt programming for large language models: beyond the few-shot paradigm. In: Extended Abstracts of the 2021 CHI Conference on Human Factors in Computing Systems, pp. 314:1–7. Association for Computing Machinery, New York, NY, USA (2021). https://doi.org/10.1145/3411763.3451760

7. Rezwana, J., Maher, M.L.: Designing creative AI partners with COFI: a framework for modeling interaction in human-AI co-creative systems. ACM Trans. Comput.-Human Interact. **30**(5), 67:1–28 (2023). https://doi.org/10.1145/3519026

8. Mahdavi Goloujeh, A., Sullivan, A., Magerko, B.: Is it AI or is it me? Understanding users' prompt journey with text-to-image generative AI tools. In: Proceedings of the 2024 CHI Conference on Human Factors in Computing Systems, pp. 1–13. Association for Computing Machinery, New York, NY (2024). https://doi.org/10.1145/3613904.3642861

9. Sanchez, T.: Examining the text-to-image community of practice: Why and how do people prompt generative AIs?. In: Proceedings of the 15th Conference on Creativity and Cognition, pp. 43–61. Association for Computing Machinery, New York, NY (2023). https://doi.org/10.1145/3591196.3593051

10. The DALL.E 2 Prompt Book. https://dallery.gallery/the-dalle-2-prompt-book/. Accessed 05 Jan 2025

11. Feuerriegel, S., Hartmann, J., Janiesch, C., Zschech, P.: Generative AI. Bus. Inform. Syst. Eng. **66**(1), 111–126 (2024). https://doi.org/10.1007/s12599-023-00834-7

12. Stokel-Walker, C., Van Noorden, R.: What ChatGPT and generative AI mean for science. Nature **614**(7947), 214–216 (2023). https://doi.org/10.1038/d41586-023-00340-6

13. Epstein, Z., Hertzmann, A.: The investigators of human creativity: art and the science of generative AI. Science **380**(6650), 1110–1133 (2023). https://doi.org/10.1126/science.adh4451

14. Zhang, N., Tang, H.: Text-to-image synthesis: a decade survey. http://arxiv.org/abs/2411.16164. https://doi.org/10.48550/arXiv.2411.16164. Accessed Jan 2025

15. Liu, V.: Beyond text-to-image: multimodal prompts to explore generative AI. In: Extended Abstracts of the 2023 CHI Conference on Human Factors in Computing

Systems, pp. 1–6. Association for Computing Machinery, New York, NY (2023). https://doi.org/10.1145/3544549.3577043

16. Oppenlaender, J.: A taxonomy of prompt modifiers for text-to-image generation. J. Behav. Inform. Technol. **43**(15), 3763–3776 (2024). https://doi.org/10.1080/0144929X.2023.2286532

17. Vinothkumar, S., Varadhaganapathy, S., Shanthakumari, R., Dhanushya, S., Guhan, S., Krisvanth, P.: Utilizing generative AI for text-to-image generation. In: 2024 15th International Conference on Computing Communication and Networking Technologies (ICCCNT), pp. 1–6. IEEE, Kamand, India (2024). https://doi.org/10.1109/ICCCNT61001.2024.10725454

18. Sampat, M.P., Wang, Z., Gupta, S., Bovik, A.C., Markey, M.K.: Complex wavelet structural similarity: a new image similarity index. IEEE Trans. Image Process. **18**(11), 2385–2401 (2009). https://doi.org/10.1109/TIP.2009.2025923

19. Wang, Z., Bovik, A. C., Sheikh, H. R.: Image quality assessment: from error visibility to structural similarity. IEEE Trans. Image Process. **13**(4) (2004)

20. Shanghai Municipal Commission of Education's Guide to the Unified Examination for Fine Arts and Design Majors in Shanghai's General Colleges and Universities. https://www.shmeea.edu.cn/page/08000/20231103/17950.html. Accessed 06 Jan 2025

21. Tianjin Municipal Educational Recruitment and Examination Institute's Guide to the Unified Examination for Art Majors in General Colleges and Universities. http://www.zhaokao.net/gkck/system/2024/10/29/030007849.shtml. Accessed 06 Jan 2025

22. Hsieh, H.-F., Shannon, S.E.: Three approaches to qualitative content analysis. Qual. Health Res. **15**(9), 1277–1288 (2005). https://doi.org/10.1177/1049732305276687

Quantitative Analysis of the Use of "Oriental" Design Elements in VOGUE Covers: Using a Visual Grammar Analysis Framework

Lejia Zhang[1], Lili Zhang[1], Shanguang Chen[2(✉)], and Jingyu Zhang[3,4]

[1] Jiangsu University, Zhenjiang 212013, China
[2] National Key Laboratory of Human Factors Engineering, Beijing 100101, China
shanguang_chen@126.com
[3] National Key Laboratory of Behavioral Science, Chinese Academy of Sciences, Beijing 100864, China
zhangjingyu@psych.ac.cn
[4] Department of Psychology, University of Chinese Academy of Sciences, Beijing 100101, China

Abstract. Under the background of globalization and cross-cultural communication, fashion magazine covers are not only the wind vane of trends, but also the key carrier of cross-cultural visual symbols translation. In this study, the covers of VOGUE magazine from 1909 to 1932 are selected as subjects, and the significance differences of 9 visual features among 113 covers are analyzed through nonparametric Friedman tests and post hoc tests with multiple corrections. These findings are further combined with Kress and Van Leeuwen's visual grammar theory to reveal the priority of core visual symbols in cross-cultural translation. The results show that color, lines and shapes, compositional layout are the most important features affecting the perception of artistic style, indicating that the cross-cultural translation of "Oriental" design elements is highly dependent on the symbolic appropriateness of core visual features. Adopting a multimodal framework, the study analyzes "Oriental" design elements from the dimensions of image, color and composition, and explores how they convey cultural messages through Representational Meaning, Interaction Meaning and Compositional Meanings. It is found that "Oriental" design elements are not only introduced as cultural symbols in cover design, but also form a unique cross-cultural visual language through symbolic translation and aesthetic reconstruction (e.g., cultural symbols of colors, cross-contextual translation of symbols such as folding fan). These findings validate the explanatory power of Visual Grammar Theory in cross-cultural design and provide new historical and theoretical perspectives on symbolic adaptation in cross-cultural design.

Keywords: Cross-cultural visual design · Visual grammar · Magazine cover design · "Oriental" design elements

P.-L.P. Rau and H. Krömker (Eds.): HCII 2025, LNCS 16336, pp. 210–226, 2026.
https://doi.org/10.1007/978-3-032-12798-3_13

1 Introduction

During the late 19th and early 20th centuries, Western societies, propelled by colonial expansion and international trade, exhibited a pronounced fascination with Eastern cultures. This interest manifested in literary and artistic works and progressively influenced the fashion industry, where "Oriental" design elements emerged as significant sources of inspiration across fashion, art, and design. As an authoritative publication within the fashion sector, VOGUE magazine's covers, characterized by their distinctive illustration styles, served as pivotal platforms for the convergence of Eastern and Western aesthetics during this era. These covers encapsulated the visual translation process of cross-cultural symbols. Through the appropriation and reconstruction of motifs such as folding fans, screens, and traditional oriental attire, the cover designs exemplified the unique transformation of Eastern elements within the context of Western fashion. Critically, the term "Oriental" in this study is deliberately enclosed in quotation marks to problematize its colonial connotations, recognizing the diversity of Asian, Middle Eastern, and Islamic design traditions reduced to a monolithic 'Eastern' fantasy."

In the context of globalization, the introduction of "Oriental" design elements is not only a simple appropriation of cultural symbols, but also a reshaping of the aesthetic image of non-Western culture through "symbolic translation" and "cross-cultural reconstruction". Based on Kress and Van Leeuwen's theory of visual grammar, this study uses Friedman's test [1] to analyze the differences in visual features, identify the core visual features of cross-cultural design, and quantitatively analyze the visual features of "Oriental" design elements on the covers of VOGUE magazine between 1909 and 1932. In order to break through the limitations of subjective interpretation, the introduction of the significance difference test in the study quantifies the differences in the importance of visual features, reveals the role of different visual symbols in cross-cultural communication, and analyzes in-depth how these elements can promote the fusion of Eastern and Western cultures and innovation through the transformation of Representational Meaning, Interaction Meaning and Compositional Meaning.

The significance of this study lies in the fact that it systematically reveals how "Oriental" design elements realize cross-cultural meaning reconstruction through visual grammar, which provides important insights for understanding the interaction between Eastern and Western cultures in modern fashion design. The results of this study will provide theoretical references for fashion design in the context of contemporary globalization and promote the paradigm shift from "cultural borrowing" to "cultural dialogue".

2 Theoretical Context

By applying the multi-modal framework of Visual Grammar Theory, this study breaks down "Oriental" cross-cultural design into three levels of Representational Meaning, Interaction Meaning and Compositional Meaning, revealing how visual symbols work in synergy to convey multiple messages about "Oriental" culture, and to promote cross-cultural integration in fashion design. The 'Oriental' visual language in VOGUE covers reflects a Eurocentric synthesis of diverse Asian traditions, perpetuating colonial-era exoticization.

2.1 Extension of Visual Grammar Theory and Application in Cover Design

Multimodal Discourse Analysis (MDA), which originated in the 20th century, analyzes the interaction of symbolic elements such as images, sounds, and behaviors through the use of various human sensory modalities such as audiovisual and tactile senses, in order to investigate how multiple symbols convey meanings [2]. Based on this framework, Kress and Van Leeuwen (1996/2006) extended the three-dimensional function of Systemic Functional Linguistics (SFL) to the visual level and constructed a multimodal visual grammar system centered on the Representational Meaning, Interaction Meaning, and Compositional Meaning [3], which emphasizes the social and functional nature of visual symbols, and reveals the roles of visual expressions in multimodal contexts through the analysis of visual meanings. This study extends it to cross-cultural design contexts in order to analyze the symbolic reconstruction mechanism of "Oriental" design elements in VOGUE covers. The extensibility of visual syntax is fully reflected in the cover design of VOGUE. The visual symbols in the cover are not only a simple combination of images and colors, but also convey specific cultural information through the construction and reshaping of symbols (see Fig. 1).

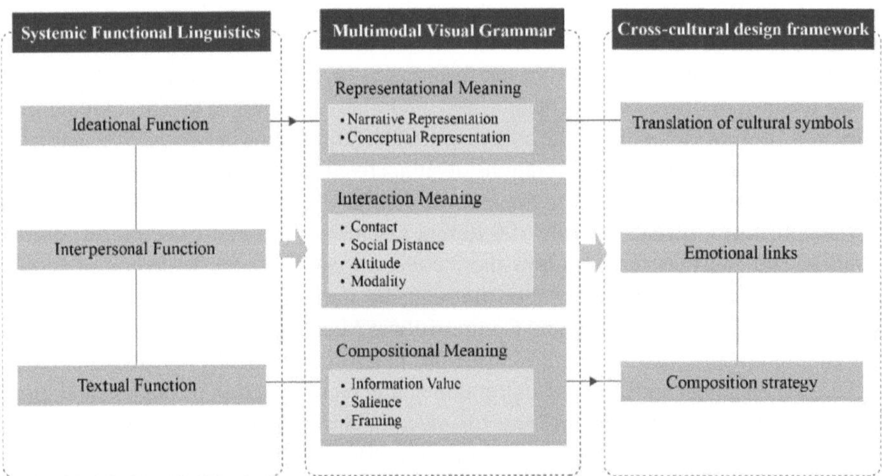

Fig. 1. Visual Grammar Theory Framework Diagram.

Within the framework of cross-cultural design, the three core levels of visual grammar correspond to cultural symbol translation, emotional connection, and layout strategy. First, Representational Meaning pertains to the cross-cultural adaptation of symbols, particularly the transformation of Eastern cultural elements into recognizable motifs within Western fashion contexts. For instance, the incorporation of image-based symbols such as folding fans and screens on magazine covers serves as both a visual representation of Eastern culture and an integration with Western fashion aesthetics. Second, Interactive Meaning focuses on the emotional engagement between the image and the viewer. The cover design fosters a sense of cultural resonance through elements such as color contrasts, the direction of a character's gaze, and compositional perspective. For example, saturated red conveys joy and authority in Eastern culture while simultaneously exerting a strong visual impact in Western society. The dual symbolism of this hue enables viewers to perceive deeper cultural narratives across different cultural contexts. Finally, Compositional Meaning reflects cultural synthesis within layout strategies. The spatial arrangement and emphasis on information hierarchy in cover design illustrate the interplay between Eastern and Western visual expressions. For instance, the strategic placement of white space and the balance of visual weight contribute to a sense of subtlety and harmony, reinforcing the restrained elegance characteristic of "Oriental" aesthetics.

2.2   History and Cross-Cultural Communication of "Oriental" Design Elements

Between the 17th and early 20th centuries, Eastern culture was progressively integrated into the Western visual system through international trade, art exhibitions, and colonial activities, emerging as a vital source of inspiration for art and fashion. During this period, Chinese handicrafts—celebrated for their intricate patterns and motifs—gained favor among court nobles and significantly influenced Western fashion. In the 18th century, the French fashion magazine "Happer's Magazine" introduced the term "Chinoiserie" (Chinese style), marking the evolution of respect for "Oriental" aesthetics into a widely popular trend. With the rise of Art Deco in the early 20th century, "Oriental" design elements influenced both the creative approaches of artists and designers as well as the public's visual perception of Eastern culture. Notably, the prevalence of VOGUE magazine covers featuring "Oriental" design elements reached its zenith during this period, while the Panama-Pacific Exposition in 1915 further accelerated the symbolization of these elements (see Fig. 2).

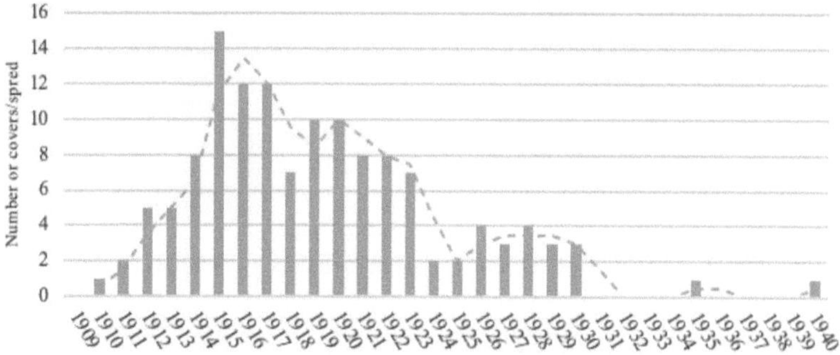

Fig. 2. Statistics of VOGUE covers with "Oriental" design elements between 1909–1940.

"Oriental" design elements on covers from this period are primarily defined by two features: decorative qualities and symbolic significance. Nevertheless, the concept of the "Orient" is molded by diverse cultural and historical influences, rendering its precise definition elusive due to differing perspectives. Early interpretations of "Oriental" style extended beyond a mere geographical label. Rather, it signified an amalgamation of influences—Middle Eastern patterns, Japanese ukiyo-e lines, South Asian religious symbols, among others—that coalesced into a mixed pan-oriental visual language. This "Oriental visual language" represents an idealized, abstracted portrayal of Far Eastern civilization, as interpreted by Western artists with limited geographical knowledge and cultural insight. Consequently, the design elements of this period often embodied a synthesis of Eastern and Western cultures. On one hand, these elements were extensively employed in art design, fashion illustration, and various decorative contexts due to their distinctive patterns and forms; on the other, the symbols underwent reinterpretation to satisfy the aesthetic demands of the Western market. For example, the July 1919 cover of VOGUE adopted a Ukiyo-e thematic framework, synthesizing elements such as Persian miniature-inspired headdresses, Mughal-style ornamental turbans, kimono-derived silhouettes with obi sash detailing, and East Asian parasol iconography, thereby exemplifying the colonial-era homogenization of diverse Asian aesthetics into a singular "Oriental" visual trope under Western gaze.(see Fig. 3).

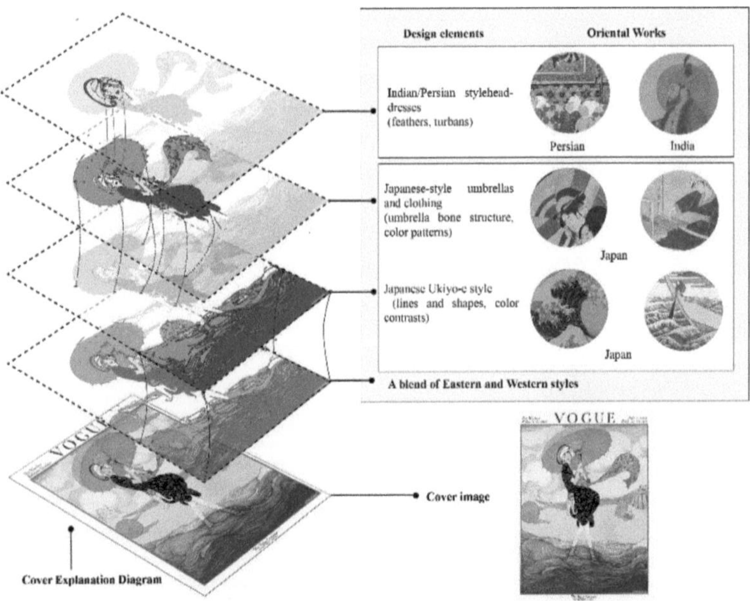

Fig. 3 . Analysis of "Oriental" design elements in VOGUE covers.

Cross-cultural communication has made "Oriental" design elements not only become decorative symbols in the fashion world, but also given these symbols new cultural meanings. In western fashion magazines, these elements are transformed and fused through symbols, and "Oriental" culture is reconstructed in the western context, becoming an important bridge between cultural exchange and fashion design.

3   Magazine Cover Art Style Perception Research Design

To examine the influence of visual syntax on the perception of artistic style, this study draws on a sample of VOGUE covers from 1909 to 1932. It incorporates interviews with art professionals to identify key measurement variables that distinguish artistic styles. A questionnaire is then developed to quantify the relative importance of each visual feature, and the analysis focuses on their impact on the perception of artistic style in cover images.

3.1   Hierarchy of Visual Information in Magazine Covers

The multi-layered nature of visual information processing provides a theoretical basis for parsing the perceptual logic of cross-cultural design elements. This study combines David Marr's theory of hierarchical visual processing to categorize the visual communication of magazine covers into multiple levels: extraction of basic features, integration of feature information, selection and attention to visual elements, emotional response, and advanced cognitive processing of visual information [4]. Therefore, the process of identifying the artistic style of magazine covers is divided into three main layers in the questionnaire design; primary information perception layer, intermediate visual structure organization layer, and advanced visual semantic expression layer, which helps users to understand the question items and improves the scientific validity of the research results (see Fig. 4).

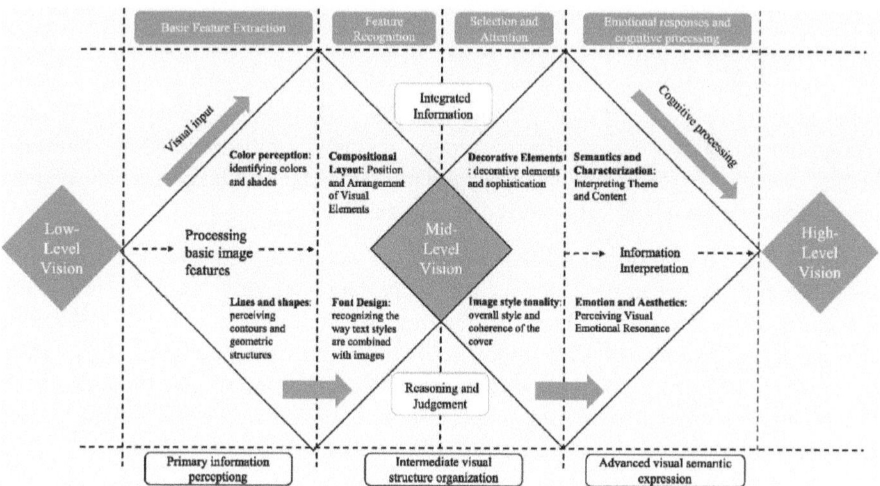

Fig. 4. Hierarchy of visual information processing for magazine covers.

The primary information perception layer covers the basic image features that are directly captured and processed by the human eye at the initial stage of visual perception, such as colors, lines and shapes, etc., and these visual elements have different symbolic meanings in different cultures. The intermediate visual structure layer involves the integration and organization of visual elements, which influences the order of visual information and the overall visual balance. Different cultures have different preferences for visual layout, for example, "Oriental" design pays more attention to white space and asymmetry. The advanced visual semantic expression level emphasizes visual semantic understanding and emotional resonance, including advanced cognition and judgment of the overall style, theme and emotional expression of the cover, and people may have different emotional responses and cultural identities to the same symbols. Based on the visual hierarchy analysis and visual syntax theory, this study extracts nine visual features that may affect the perception of cover style: color, lines and shapes, compositional layout, font design, decorative elements, image representation, image style tonality, and representation of Cover Subjects. The study analyzes the priority of these visual features in the perception of artistic style by quantifying the frequency, distribution, and significance differences of the visual features.

3.2   Analysis of Measurements Influencing Perceptions of Cover Art Style

For non-normally distributed data (Kolmogorov-Smirnov test, $p < 0.05$) [5], this study used Friedman's test (non-parametric repeated-measures ANOVA) to determine the significance of differences in the medians of the nine visual features. This method circumvents the normality assumption restriction through rank order comparisons and is suitable for paired designs in which the same subjects rate multiple features (e.g., evaluation of visual features on magazine covers). Post-test two-by-two comparisons by Wilcoxon signed rank test [6] with Holm-Bonferroni correction [7] further clarified the source of differences.

Data Preprocessing and Normality Tests. In order to ensure the scientific and objective nature of the research results, the survey participants chose the group with professional education experience in art. At the same time, taking into account the differences in cognitive characteristics of different groups, the gender ratio and age distribution of the participants were basically balanced, and more than half of the group indicated that they had knowledge about magazine cover design.

In this study, a total of 101 valid questionnaires were collected using a 5-point Likert scale format (1 = not important, 5 = very important) to rate 9 visual features. After deletion of suspected invalid data, the final retained sample was N = 95. The sample size met the requirements of the study (at least 5 times the number of items asked for measurement) [8]. For non-normally distributed data, the results showed that the data deviated significantly from normal distribution (absolute value of skewness >0.5, significant kurtosis), therefore the study used non-parametric tests (Table 1).

Overall Difference: Friedman Test. In order to investigate the differences in the importance of the nine visual features, data were analyzed using Friedman's test. The results showed that there was a significant difference in the median scores of the features ($\chi^2(8)$ = 56.502, $p < 0.001$),and the effect size Kendall's W = 0.074, indicating a small but statistically significant degree of variation (Table 2).

Comparative analysis of the box-and-line plots shows that color has the highest median score and a concentrated distribution, indicating that its importance is widely

Table 1. Normality test results of visual features (Kolmogorov-Smirnov).

Visual feature	Average	Standard deviation	Skewness	Kurtosis	Kolmogorov-Smirnov test	
					Statistic D-value	P
C	4.474	0.770	−1.769	4.072	0.353	0.000**
L	4.253	0.812	−0.863	0.110	0.274	0.000**
CL	4.263	0.802	−1.148	1.917	0.263	0.000**
FD	4.211	0.837	−0.862	0.129	0.259	0.000**
DE	3.874	0.866	−0.353	−0.546	0.242	0.000**
IMR	3.968	0.831	−0.622	0.052	0.284	0.000**
IST	4.063	0.836	−0.791	0.884	0.249	0.000**
RCS	3.905	0.912	−0.756	0.361	0.278	0.000**
STH	3.895	1.005	−1.005	1.060	0.257	0.000**

Table Note: *p < 0.05, **p < 0.01.
C=Color, L = Lines and Shapes, CL = Compositional Layout, FD=Font Design, DE = Decorative Elements, IMR = Image Representation, IST = Image Style Tonality, RCS = Representation of Cover Subjects, STH=Scene Theme.

Table 2. Results of multi-sample Friedman analyses.

Visual feature	Q1	Q2	Q3	χ^2	p
C	4.000	5.000	5.000	56.502	0.000**
L	4.000	4.000	5.000		
CL	4.000	4.000	5.000		
FD	4.000	4.000	5.000		
DE	3.000	4.000	4.500		
IMR	4.000	4.000	5.000		
IST	4.000	4.000	5.000		
RCS	3.000	4.000	5.000		
STH	3.000	4.000	5.000		

recognized. In contrast, scene theme scores were scattered with a low 25th percentile, and some subjects perceived its importance as weak (see Fig. 5).

Ex Post Facto Testing and Multiple Corrections. Two-by-two comparisons of 36 pairs of features were performed by the Wilcoxon signed rank test and the Holm-Bonferroni method was used to correct for multiple comparison error rates ($\alpha = 0.05$). The results showed that 10 pairs of features were statistically significantly different (corrected p < 0.05). Abbreviations are used in the figure to represent the feature names: C

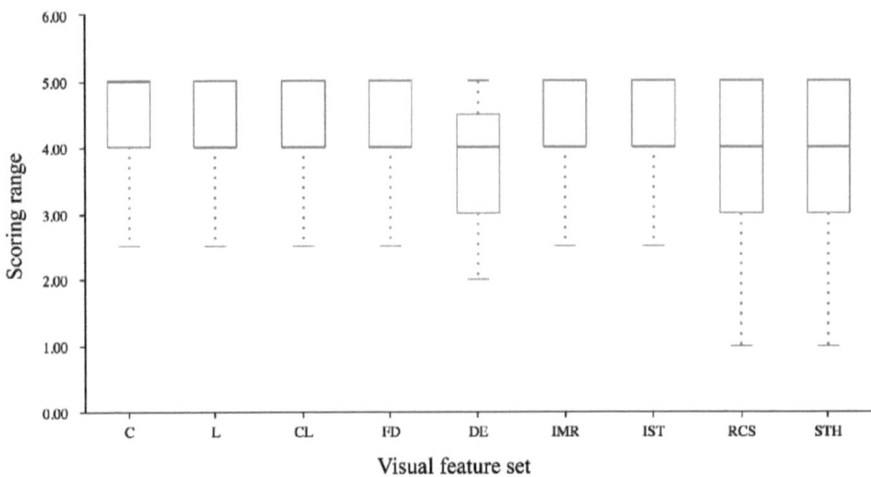

Fig. 5. Boxplot of Friedman test results for visual features.

= Color, L = Lines and Shapes, CL = Compositional Layout, FD = Font Design, DE = Decorative Details, IMR = Image Representation, IST = Image Stylistic Tone, RCS = Representation of Cover Subjects, and STH = Scene Theme, as follows (Fig. 6):

	C	CL	DE	FD	IMR	IST	L	RCS	STH
C		0.4568	0.0001035	0.1038	0.0002435	0.01004	0.2111	0.0001892	0.002477
CL	0.4568		0.006084	1	0.03235	0.6852	1	0.03181	0.03235
DE	0.0001035	0.006084		0.06102	1	0.8978	0.01601	1	1
FD	0.1038	1	0.06102		0.2668	1	1	0.116	0.3699
IMR	0.0002435	0.03235	1	0.2668		1	0.1387	1	1
IST	0.01004	0.6852	0.8978	1	1		1	1	1
L	0.2111	1	0.01601	1	0.1387	1		0.1693	0.1386
RCS	0.0001892	0.03181	1	0.116	1	1	0.1693		1
STH	0.002477	0.03235	1	0.3699	1	1	0.1386	1	

Fig. 6. Contrastive heat map of visual feature saliency.

The Hedges' g effect size heatmap (Fig. 7) can be used to further visualize and compare the direction and intensity of the difference in the ratings of each visual feature ($|g| > 0.5$ is a large effect, $0.3 \le |g| < 0.5$ is a medium effect, and $|g| < 0.3$ is a small effect). The comparison follows an X-axis: Y-axis schema, where a positive g for feature

A (X-axis) compared to feature B (Y-axis) indicates a higher mean rating for A, and a negative value implies the opposite.

The findings reveal that among the ten pairs with significant differences, color exhibits substantially higher ratings than the other features with a large effect size, affirming its status as a core visual element in the perception of artistic style. In contrast, Composition Layout, Lines and Shapes show minimal differences within a group of highly rated features, suggesting medium importance that should be prioritized according to the context. Although Decorative Details achieved a median rating of 4.0, its ratings are considerably lower than those for Color, Lines and Shapes, indicating a relatively weak influence on artistic style perception.

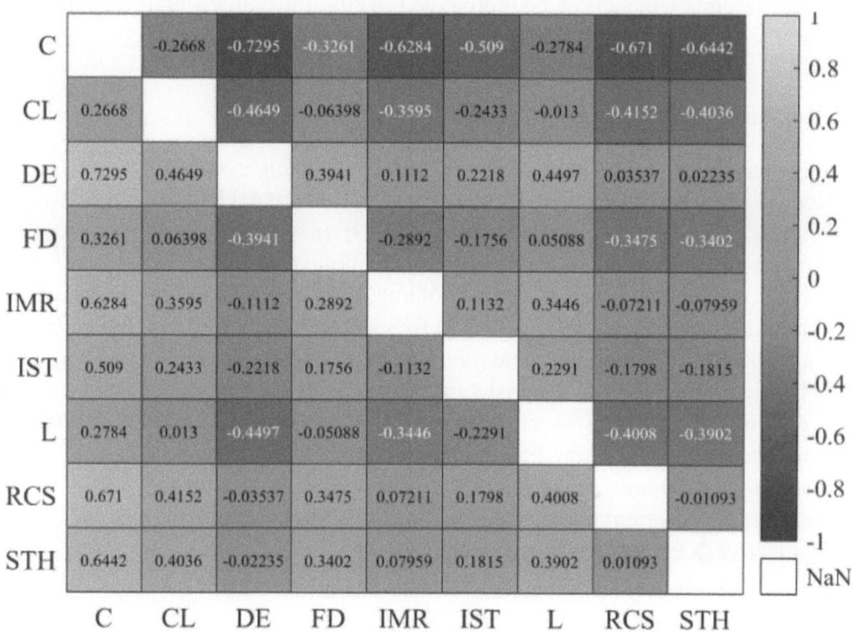

Fig. 7. Hedges' g effect size heatmap for visual feature comparisons.

3.3 Results and Discussion

Based on the comparison of median scores and effect sizes, the nine visual features were ranked in the following order of importance: color (C), lines and shapes (L), compositional layout (CL), typography (FD), image representation (IMR), image style tonality (IST), cover subject representation (RCS), decorative detailing (DE), and scene theme (STH). Under the framework of visual grammar theory, these features collectively contribute to the Representation, Interaction, and Compositional Meanings of images. The findings validate the applicability of visual grammar theory in cover design analysis, while the use of non-parametric methods reinforces the scientific rigor of the visual data analysis. This approach provides a methodological foundation for quantifying the visual translation of cultural symbols.

4 Multimodal Representation of "Oriental" Design Elements in Covers

Through the framework of Visual Grammar Theory, this study separately explores how visual elements such as color, lines and shapes, and compositional layout work together at different levels to convey the symbolic, emotional interaction and visual structure of Eastern culture. Through a specific case study of a VOGUE cover, it further reveals how "Oriental" design elements can be reproduced as cultural symbols in a western fashion cover and convey the visual message of "Oriental" culture.

4.1 Representational Meaning Analysis

In the analysis of Representational Meaning, image meaning is subdivided into Conceptual Reproduction and Narrative Reproduction, and Conceptual Reproduction's involves image kinds, analysis and symbolization process [9]. Images reproduce the semantics of Eastern cultures to Western societies through symbolic translation. In the cover design of VOGUE, symbolic elements (such as folding fans, screens, kimonos and other typical "Oriental" cultural symbols) appeared frequently in 113 covers between 1909 and 1932, and these design elements were transformed from functional tools to recognizable decorative symbols in the visual translation, which conveyed the visual message of "Oriental" culture to the Western society. The parasol motifs in the covers hybridize Chinese oil-paper parasols, symbolizing literati elegance, and Japanese wagasa, associated with traditional tea ceremonies, epitomizing the colonial-era conflation of distinct cultural symbols into a pan-oriental visual trope. After counting, umbrellas, fans and screens with distinctive "Oriental" styles accounted for a total of 28, 8 and 5 times respectively in these cover designs (Table 3).

Table 3. Distribution of symbolic image symbols in VOGUE covers.

Time		1909–1919		1920–1929		1930–1932	
Symbolic Elements		Number and percentage		Number and percentage		Number and percentage	
	Umbrellas	34	1.15	10	0.4	0	0
	Fans	8	0.27	4	0.16	0	0
	Screens	1	0.03	4	0.16	0	0

Aside from these common visual symbols, the covers also incorporate other elements with "Oriental" flavor, such as Oriental-style clothing and furniture. For example, on the cover of the November 1918 issue, the figure's shawl costume features elements of Chinese blue-and-white porcelain patterns, and the red-framed dressing mirror is in the shape of the Ruyi pattern; the cover of the April 1921 issue depicts a woman with a feathered headdress seated under an East Asian style screen, checking her makeup in a red-lacquered dressing mirror. The decorative detailing demonstrates how "Oriental" design elements were reinterpreted to suit the aesthetic needs of Western fashion.

In addition, the philosophical thinking of "Oriental" aesthetics is based on the concept of animism and sympathy for all things, which arises from the practical activities of human beings interacting with all things in nature. The beauty is based on the embodiment of the fullness of life's energy, and the beauty is based on what shows exuberant vitality [10]. East Asian aesthetics (e.g., Chinese literati ink-wash traditions) are often are often expressed through smooth lines and botanical patterns, giving the work a strong romanticism. American illustrator Helen Dryden, who was deeply influenced by "Oriental" culture, often used natural elements such as plants and flowers to present "Oriental" romanticism style when creating for VOGUE magazine. For example, on the covers of the April and June 1917 issues, the characters are dressed in kimonos, with flowers, vines and tree branches in the background; on the cover of the March 1919 issue, willow-like cherry blossoms occupy a large area of the picture, emphasizing the visual impact of natural aestheticism. The muted colors and lines and shapes in the illustrations work together to create Oriental-style scenes (see Fig. 8).

Fig. 8. VOGUE Cover Group 1.

Narrative Reproduction emphasizes how the cover image interacts with the viewer through actions or events that constitute visual vectors and build cross-cultural narratives. For example, on the cover of the February 1923 issue, a short-haired woman in a long white and green striped dress holds a red vessel and reaches out to interact with a divine dragon; on the cover of the September 1929 issue, a modern woman gazes at an "Oriental" theater statue held up in her hands. These actions not only reflect Western society's interest in and exploration of "Oriental" culture at the time, but also create an "Oriental context" by using visual symbols as vectors to guide and reinforce the viewer's sense of participation, setting off and reproducing "Oriental" style. These cases show how Eastern design elements are reproduced and reconstructed in Western fashion design through multimodal syntax, promoting the interaction and fusion of Eastern and Western cultures (see Fig. 9).

Fig. 9. VOGUE Cover Group 2.

4.2 Interactive Meaning Analysis

Interactive Meaning focuses on revealing the complex interaction between the image communicator, the information carried by the image, and the image viewer. Visual images show diverse modes of contact, social distance and affective tendencies according to different themes and meanings.

Contact is usually expressed as a virtual association between the image and the receiver when their eyes meet, while the visual language of fashion magazine covers pays more attention to the viewer's interpretation of the image. Social distance refers to the relative relationship between the image and the viewer, and the image often establishes this relationship through the change of the character's point of view and angle, such as the cover of the June 1919 issue, which shows a woman dressed in costumes filled with East Asian aesthetics, holding an umbrella and gazing forward at a horizontal angle to interact with the viewer, and the image focuses on the character's upper body, building a personal proximity to enhance the sense of cultural intimacy. Mood is shown through the synergy of color elements, and Kress and Van Leeuwen point out that the important potential of color's significance in the visual syntax is its associative significance [11]. Color not only conveys emotion through its visual impact, but also helps the cover establish an emotional connection between the viewer and the design content. Different cultures often have deep emotional preferences for specific colors. In the Chinese aesthetic concept of color, saturated red is regarded as the most symbolic color, representing joy, authority and prosperity. Therefore, the use of Chinese red as a core color is crucial in a cover with a strong "Oriental" style.

This study uses the Image Color Summarizer tool [12] to analyze images of VOGUE magazine covers with "Oriental" colors, extracting the percentage of different colors in the images and helping to determine the dominance of red in these cover designs (Table 4).

The analysis results show that red not only occupies a large area in the image, but also contrasts sharply with other colors (e.g., black, gold). Most of the cover colors related to Chinese red show the triangular combination of "red-black-gold", whose color suitability stems from the commonality between the Eastern metaphor of "richness" and the Western aesthetic culture of "luxury". Its color suitability stems from the commonality between the metaphor of "richness" in the East and "luxury" aesthetic culture in the West. In the Western context, red is associated with passion and danger, and the semantic duality of Eastern and Western colors in the VOGUE cover achieves the emotional adaptation

Table 4. An analysis of color clustering in selected VOGUE covers.

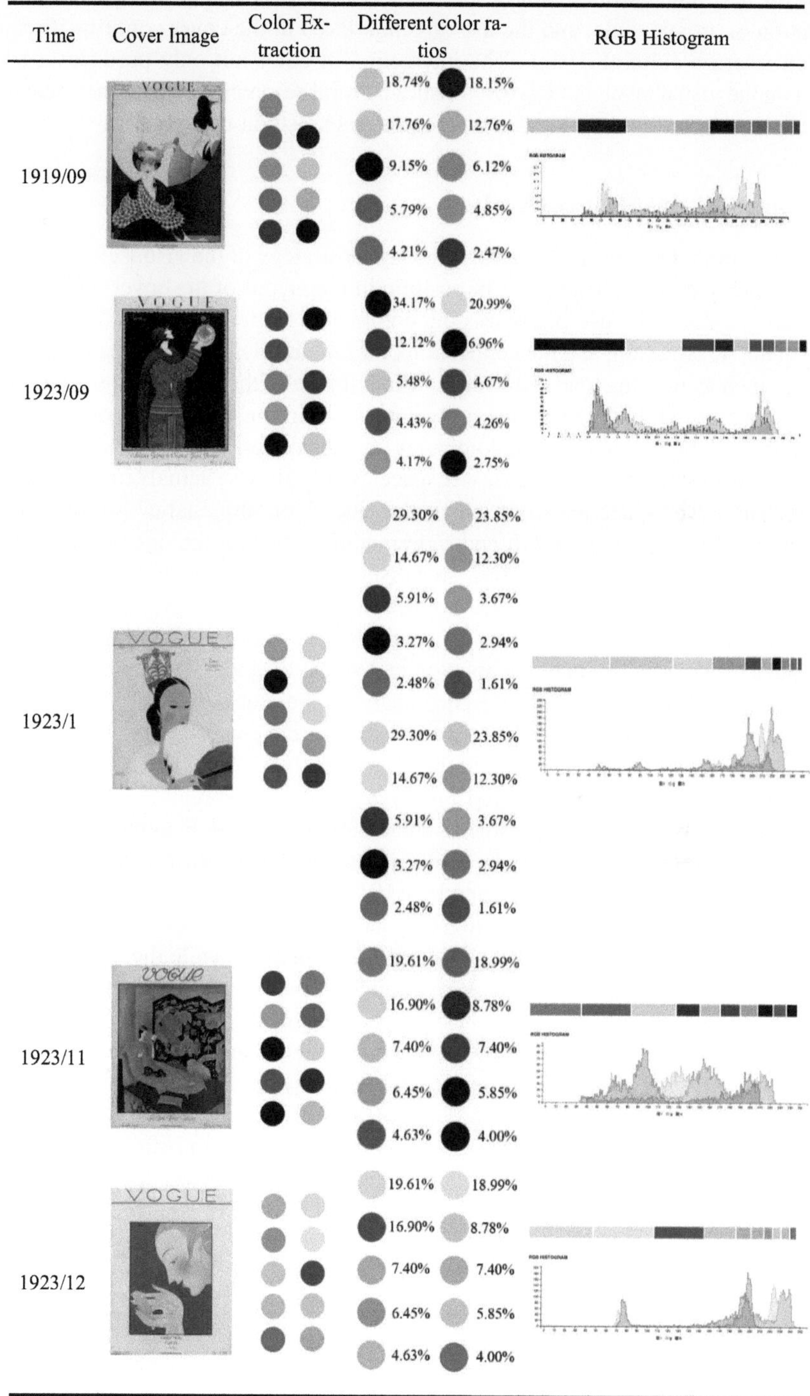

Time	Cover Image	Color Extraction	Different color ratios		RGB Histogram
1919/09			18.74%	18.15%	
			17.76%	12.76%	
			9.15%	6.12%	
			5.79%	4.85%	
			4.21%	2.47%	
1923/09			34.17%	20.99%	
			12.12%	6.96%	
			5.48%	4.67%	
			4.43%	4.26%	
			4.17%	2.75%	
1923/1			29.30%	23.85%	
			14.67%	12.30%	
			5.91%	3.67%	
			3.27%	2.94%	
			2.48%	1.61%	
			29.30%	23.85%	
			14.67%	12.30%	
			5.91%	3.67%	
			3.27%	2.94%	
			2.48%	1.61%	
1923/11			19.61%	18.99%	
			16.90%	8.78%	
			7.40%	7.40%	
			6.45%	5.85%	
			4.63%	4.00%	
1923/12			19.61%	18.99%	
			16.90%	8.78%	
			7.40%	7.40%	
			6.45%	5.85%	
			4.63%	4.00%	

of cross-cultural design through color matching. At the same time, the results of the significance difference in the study show that color has the highest importance in the perception of artistic style, and the use of Chinese red in the cover confirms its central position in cross-cultural design. The interaction of color not only produces a strong impact on the visual level, but also establishes cultural resonance on the emotional level, promoting cross-cultural dialogue and integration in fashion design.

4.3 Compositional Meaning Analysis

The compositional meaning emphasizes the layout strategy of the visual elements of the image, which includes: differences in position in the layout of the cover with different information values, the use of contrasting colors and shapes to emphasize the prominence of the information, and the connection of the visual elements by means of framing methods such as lines or spatial divisions. The left side of the image layout symbolizes known elements, while the right side represents novel or non-traditional content. For the vertical dimension, the upper area dominates the visual hierarchy and tends to be "idealized" or "generalized", while the lower space usually shows "actual" or "generalized" content. The lower space usually presents "practical" or "pragmatic" information [3]. In addition to the top, bottom, left and right modules, the "center" area usually carries the core information, while the "edge" area displays subsidiary or supplementary information. The meaning of the overall composition may change according to the specific theme and content, and it is important to coordinate the spatial relationship of the design elements to realize the semantic adaptation and visual balance of the cultural symbols. In the results of the significant difference analysis, the compositional layout plays an important role in the perception of the artistic style of the cover.

In the context of "Oriental" aesthetics, Hegel defines "Oriental" art as "symbolic art" in Aesthetics, which is centered on revealing the inner realm, emphasizing the beauty of subtlety and unique aesthetic characteristics. As an example of "Oriental" aesthetics, white space on the screen subtly embodies this characteristic. For example, the cover design of the March, April and June 1915 issues of VOGUE uses a large area of white space to take in the scene, highlighting the main body of the character image and strengthening the design theme through simple composition, while the area underneath the cover utilizes a large area of dark color blocks, guiding the viewer to focus their attention on the core area of the cultural symbols. The characters on the cover are dressed in "Oriental" style, and the details of the natural elements and contrasting colors in the scene, together with the overall layout, show the unique beauty of "Oriental" culture. This composition not only reflects the unique pursuit of space and implicit aesthetics in "Oriental" culture, but also realizes the reproduction and reconstruction of culture in the cover design through the layout arrangement of visual elements, conveying the deep cultural symbols (see Fig. 10).

Fig. 10. VOGUE Cover Group 3.

5   Conclusion and Future Work

This study reveals the cross-cultural translation mechanism of "Oriental" design elements in VOGUE covers between 1909 and 1932 through the combination of visual grammar theory and quantitative analysis methods. It is found that core visual features such as color, lines and shapes, and compositional layout work together through the three levels of Representational Meaning, Interaction Meaning, and Compositional Meaning to convey "Oriental" cultural information and artistic style, which verifies the applicability of visual grammar theory in cover design analysis, and at the same time, through the significance difference test, the quantitative analysis provides an actionable reference of priorities for cross-cultural design. Through the multimodal expression of these visual features, the "Oriental" design elements realize the semantic reconstruction of symbols, which not only enhances the visual attractiveness of the cover but also improves the cross-cultural appropriateness, and facilitates the integration and reproduction of East Asian, South Asian, and Middle Eastern and Western cultures.

Although this study reduces subjective bias through quantitative analysis methods, there are still limitations: the breadth of cultural coverage is limited to Western perspectives during the period of 1909–1932, failing to include cases of Eastern media's translation of Western culture during the same time period; the depth of technology is limited, and future research can combine big data analysis and deep learning techniques to further study cultural symbols in visual design and extend the study to other fashion design media (e.g. advertising, brand packaging). Designers can draw on the expression of cross-design elements, especially in the use of color, composition and symbolization, to create fashion cover designs with cultural depth and visual appeal. Meanwhile, how to convey multicultural messages through visual design in the context of globalization, the cross-cultural communication and dynamic evolution of visual symbols can be explored in depth in the future.

Acknowledgments. This study was supported by the National Natural Science Foundation of China (Grant No. T2192932, T2192933).

Disclosure of Interests The authors have no competing interests to declare that are relevant to the content of this article.

References

1. Brown, I., Mues, C.: An experimental comparison of classification algorithms for imbalanced credit scoring data sets. Expert Syst. Appl. **39**(3), 3446–3453 (2012)
2. Zhang, D.: A comprehensive theoretical framework for multimodal discourse analysis. Foreign Lang. China. **6**(1), 24–30 (2009). https://doi.org/10.3969/j.issn.1672-9382.2009.01.006
3. Kress, G., Van Leeuwen, T.: Multimodal Discourse: The Modes and Media of Contemporary Communication. Bloomsbury Academic, London (2017)
4. Acock, M.: Review of 'vision: a computational investigation into the human representation and processing of visual information' by David Marr. Mod. Sch. **62**(2), 141–142 (1985)
5. Drezner, Z.: A modified Kolmogorov-Smirnov test for normality. Commun. Stat. Theory Methods. **39**, 693 (2009)
6. Rosner, B., Glynn, R.J., Lee, M.T.: Incorporation of clustering effects for the Wilcoxon rank sum test: a large-sample approach. Biometrics. **59**(4), 1089–1098 (2015)
7. Holm, S.: A simple sequentially rejective multiple test procedure. Scand. J. Stat., 65–70 (1979)
8. Nunnally, J.C., Bernstein, I.H.: Psychometric theory. Am. Educ. Res. J. **5**(3) (1994)
9. Kress, G., Van Leeuwen, T.: Reading Images: The Grammar of Visual Design. Routledge, London (1996)
10. Qiu, Z., Xi, C.: The unique aesthetic thinking system and poetic aesthetic theory: the general characteristics of eastern aesthetics. J. Nanjing Univ. **1**, 106–116 (2003). https://doi.org/10.3969/j.issn.1007-7278.2003.01.014
11. Zheng, Q., Zhang, B.: A multimodal discourse analysis of China-themed covers in the economist. J. Xi'an Int. Stud. Univ. **23**(1), 47–50 (2015). https://doi.org/10.16362/j.cnki.cn61-1457/h.2015.01.012
12. Image Color Summarizer. https://mk.bcgsc.ca/color-summarizer/. Last accessed 15 Jan 2025

Design and Engineering of Mobility Experiences

When Technology Becomes a Barrier: The Accessibility Issue in Mobility Interfaces

Flavia De Simone[(✉)], Martina Casillo, and Roberta Presta

Suor Orsola Benincasa University, Naples, Italy
`flavia.desimone@unisob.na.it,`
`roberta.presta@docenti.unisob.na.it`

Abstract. Recent advancements in Human-Machine Interfaces (HMIs) have transformed in vehicle experiences through visual displays and infotainment systems. While these technologies enhance usability, they often exclude users with visual impairments by prioritizing sighted interaction models. Current HMI design guidelines rarely account for the needs of elderly or disabled individuals.

This paper presents a critical review of literature on HMIs with a specific focus on visual accessibility. It highlights the persistent challenges faced by blind and low-vision users, identifies gaps in current design practices, and outlines strategies for more inclusive interfaces. Visual-centric systems remain inherently inaccessible to those with reduced acuity or contrast sensitivity. Despite the promise of autonomous vehicles (AVs) to expand independent mobility, their interfaces often replicate the same exclusions found in conventional vehicles.

Multimodal feedback—integrating audio and haptics with visual cues—remains uncommon, despite being essential for equitable interaction. Voice interfaces, tactile prompts, and simplified visual elements are key to enabling access. Yet, these features are rarely implemented systematically.

Although user-centered design is broadly advocated, real-world implementation often neglects the input of disabled users. Participatory co-design remains limited, and AV systems continue to reflect sighted norms. Inclusive design benefits all users, not only by ensuring access but also by improving overall usability. This review offers theoretical and practical insights by synthesizing cross-disciplinary findings and proposing a framework for embedding accessibility throughout the design lifecycle. Inclusivity must be treated as a foundational principle, integrated from the outset of interface development rather than added post hoc as a correction.

Keywords: Accessibility · Human-Machine Interfaces · Visually Impaired Users · Autonomous Vehicles · Inclusive Design.

1 Introduction

The progressive integration of Human-Machine Interfaces (HMIs) in modern vehicles has significantly transformed user-vehicle interactions, substituting physical controls with digital displays, touchscreens, and voice commands.

P.-L.P. Rau and H. Krömker (Eds.): HCII 2025, LNCS 16336, pp. 229–246, 2026.
https://doi.org/10.1007/978-3-032-12798-3_14

These interfaces optimize usability, customization, and safety by offering real-time feedback, navigation assistance, and entertainment options. However, their development has predominantly favored users without perceptual or cognitive limitations, systematically excluding individuals with diverse access needs. Current HMI design guidelines inadequately address the physical and mental limitations of elderly or disa- bled drivers [1].

This issue is especially evident in the context of autonomous vehicles (AVs), frequently presented as solutions to improve mobility for marginalized user groups.

Nevertheless, infrastructural and interface-level assumptions in AVs perpetuate exclusionary practices seen in conventional vehicle designs. Indeed, while AVs could potentially remove transportation barriers for visually impaired individuals, current technology design often overlooks the specific requirements of disabled users [2].

Systems are predominantly designed around present-day drivers, who are invariably sighted, rather than future operators who may have visual impairments or other disabilities [2]. This paper critically reviews existing literature on HMIs, focusing specifically on accessibility challenges experienced by visually impaired users. Although HMIs can support multiple interaction modalities, their current designs predominantly rely on visual outputs. Dedicated research and targeted design strategies are essential to guarantee safe, intuitive, and equally usable interactions for individuals with visual impairments [3].

Visually impaired users continue to encounter significant obstacles with standard vehicle interfaces, including challenges related to blurred vision, reduced contrast sensitivity, and difficulty interpreting icons or on-screen text in varied lighting conditions [3]. According to WHO and W3C guidelines, common impairments affecting screen usage include visual acuity issues, blur, light sensitivity, contrast sensitivity, field of vision limitations, and color vision deficiencies [4].

Multimodal systems could offer practical alternatives through auditory and haptic feedback; however, such systems are not yet standard practice in automotive HMI design. Multimodal interactions, integrating visual enhancements and visual substitutions through compensatory sensory methods, could significantly improve usability for visually impaired users [5]. Research indicates tactile or auditory feedback supports the perception and communication of visual information effectively, yet these channels require structured and user-tailored integration [5].

Furthermore, the lack of inclusive interface strategies in automated driving system development, coupled with the limited capacity of driving automation alone, fails to address user diversity comprehensively [6]. Automated mobility solutions could alleviate the social isolation and loneliness experienced by visually impaired individuals, significantly enhancing their sense of independence and quality of life [6].

Nonetheless, automation of driving tasks alone is insufficient. Effective and inclusive interface designs that enable meaningful interactions between passengers and systems are essential components for successful inclusive driving automation [6].

Insufficient adoption of participatory and user-centered design principles further compounds accessibility issues. Despite increased attention to user-centered approaches, disabled users continue to experience frustration with emerging technologies [7]. Genuine inclusion demands shifting from superficial user testing to authentic co-design processes centered on the lived experiences of people with disabilities. Inclusion must originate from informed design decisions that actively engage potential users and address their unique requirements.

Literature also highlights systemic challenges, including the absence of regulatory mandates and industry standards for accessible HMI design. For instance, the blind and visually impaired community identifies essential accessibility needs for AVs, such as the requirement for visual information to be provided via alternative sensory formats, like auditory or tactile channels, both within the vehicle and across transportation infrastructures to aid navigation [8]. This deficiency in comprehensive accessibility frameworks reflects broader institutional and industry shortcomings, further widening the accessibility divide and limiting the potential of AVs to serve as inclusive mobility solutions [8]. Additionally, broader societal and infrastructural barriers continue to restrict equal mobility access, rendering transportation inaccessible or unreliable for many within the disability community [9].

For blind and low-vision individuals, the lack of accessible personal vehicles, as well as the inadequacy of alternative transportation modes, significantly hinders their independence and participation in daily life. These users are disproportionately reliant on public and third-party transport and frequently face navigation and wayfinding challenges exacerbated by urban environments and vehicle design limitations [9]. Automated vehicles hold great potential to transform mobility for this population, but only if critical design elements such as multimodal feedback, non-visual interfaces, and clear orientation cues are addressed early in development [9].

While inclusive design has often been treated as a benefit for minority populations, evidence suggests broader benefits. Indeed, it has been shown that adoption of inclusive design tools and processes during the development of mainstream products improves uptake not only for those with capability impairment but also for those who do not consider themselves impaired [10]. Given this landscape, it is no longer sufficient to treat visual accessibility as a secondary concern in automotive design.

This paper reframes it as a central design challenge, calling for research and industry to coalesce around inclusive principles that account for the perceptual limitations of visually impaired users across the entire HMI development lifecycle.

To structure this investigation, we conducted a scoping review of the scientific literature, following the PRISMA-ScR guidelines [11]. This review was designed to systematically map the current body of knowledge concerning HMI accessibility for visually impaired users in the context of autonomous mobility, and to identify critical gaps in research and design practices.

In summary, this review study aims to answer the following questions:

1. What are the main accessibility barriers faced by visually impaired users when interacting with vehicle Human-Machine Interfaces (HMIs)
2. What inclusive design strategies have been proposed to support visual accessibility in the context of automated or assistive mobility systems?

2 Methodology

To achieve the objectives of this work, a scoping review of the scientific literature was conducted in accordance with the PRISMA-ScR guidelines [11]. This methodological approach was chosen to systematically explore the accessibility barriers and inclusive strategies relevant to visually impaired users interacting with HMIs in the context of automated mobility systems.

The literature search was carried out across four major scientific databases: Scopus, Web of Science, IEEE Xplore, and Google Scholar. These platforms were selected for their comprehensive coverage of studies in the fields of human-computer interaction, engineering, and assistive technologies. The search strategy was constructed by combining terms related to user conditions—visual impairment, blind, low vision, visual disability, accessibility—with terms related to the technological context—human-machine interface, automated vehicle, autonomous car, driverless, in-vehicle system, mobility interface.

The final list of keywords was adapted for each database according to its syntax requirements. After the removal of duplicates, a two-step screening process was conducted, beginning with the analysis of titles and abstracts, followed by full-text reading of the selected documents. Publications were included if they addressed HMIs or in-vehicle technologies in relation to visual accessibility in the mobility domain, and if they were written in English and published in peer-reviewed journals or conference proceedings. Studies that did not explicitly consider users with visual impairments, or that focused exclusively on unrelated disability categories, were excluded.

Data from the selected publications were analyzed by identifying relevant qualitative features such as the type of HMI studied, the forms of visual impairment considered, the accessibility barriers reported, and the design strategies proposed. The synthesis was conducted thematically, with the aim of highlighting recurring patterns, open challenges, and under explored areas of research.

The literature search was finalized in May 2025, and additional relevant contributions may be integrated in future updates through citation tracking and database alerts configured on the primary keywords.

3 Results

Through a systematic filtering process 22 articles met the criteria for full-text review and were included in this scoping review. Hence, all included studies satisfied four predefined eligibility criteria: they (i) focused on human–machine interfaces (HMIs) or autonomous mobility technologies; (ii) directly involved or addressed the needs of individuals with visual impairments; (iii) were published in peer-reviewed journals or presented as scientifically validated preprints; and (iv) were accessible in full text through open-access platforms.

This evidence base was selected with the aim of ensuring both conceptual alignment and methodological transparency. The final set of studies spans a range of approaches, from experimental evaluations and participatory design to systematic reviews and policy-oriented analyses, yet all converge on the shared objective of understanding and improving the accessibility of autonomous systems for blind and visually impaired users.

To enhance clarity what follows is a synthesis of the findings, structured to reflect the key conceptual and empirical insights that emerged across the included studies. Rather than grouping results by methodological type, the synthesis is organized around recurring themes that collectively describe the current state of knowledge in the field. Each theme integrates evidence from multiple sources and serves as a foundation for the subsequent critical discussion.

3.1 Perceived Accessibility Barriers

Visually impaired users face a spectrum of accessibility barriers when interacting with autonomous vehicle systems. A fundamental challenge is the inability to perceive visual feedback from vehicles and interfaces that are designed with sighted users in mind. Many current HMIs rely on screens, lights, or visual cues that blind and low-vision users cannot detect.

As a result, essential information, from vehicle status to navigation prompts, may not reach the user in any perceivable form.

It is therefore imperative that any visually conveyed information must be provided through alternative modalities, audio or haptics, to ensure accessibility [8].

Unfortunately, this multimodal parity is often absent in today's AV prototypes. For example, external vehicle-to-pedestrian communication concepts frequently use visual displays or light signals, which exclude blind pedestrians who cannot see them [12]. Likewise, in-vehicle interfaces such as touch-screen panels or digital dashboards typically lack auditory or tactile counterparts, rendering them effectively unusable to a blind rider [1]. Studies confirm that introducing voice feedback or haptic indicators can dramatically improve usability for visually impaired people, underlining how the absence of multimodal interaction is a critical barrier in current designs [13].

The implementation of universal design by default, including the integration of auditory and haptic outputs with visual displays, has been identified as essential to prevent the exclusion of blind users from important feedback [14].

The lack of such inclusive design features today leaves blind passengers without situational cues that sighted users take for granted, undermining both usability and safety.

Another widely reported barrier is the lack of orientation cues and difficulty locating vehicles during pick-up and drop-off. Without the benefit of sight, blind travelers cannot rely on visual spotting of their ride or surrounding landmarks. Participants in multiple studies raised concern about finding the vehicle in complex, dynamic environments.

For instance, blind users also users expressed concerns about how they would identify the correct self-driving car and orient themselves to its door, especially in crowded areas like parking lots or busy curbs, absent any driver assistance [15]. Orientation upon arrival is equally problematic, for example users fear being dropped off amidst the expanse of a parking, with no cues as to which direction to go for their actual destination [15].

Traditional ride-sharing drivers often help visually impaired passengers by verbally confirming locations or physically guiding them, but an AV has no human to fulfill this role. Autonomous shuttles will need built-in solutions for boarding and disembarking assistance because tasks like guiding a blind passenger to the door, securing their seating, or escorting them off the vehicle are no longer handled by a human driver [16].

Early design studies highlight these gaps, for instance, blind riders strongly desire AV systems to provide the same kinds of assistance that human drivers do, for example, help with confirming the right drop-off spot and guidance to the destination's entrance, through intuitive audio or tactile interfaces [17].

When such orientation supports are missing, users are left disoriented and dependent on others, participants thus stressed the need for features to verify their arrival at the correct location, given the anxiety of not knowing where an autonomous car has let them off [18].

Without accessible cues like audible announcements of stops or tactile markers, a blind passenger may have no confirmation of the right destination, which is a clear safety and comfort concern [8]. Overall, the literature indicates that orientation and wayfinding in the context of AV travel remains an unsolved challenge, and its absence is a perceived barrier to independent use of these vehicles.

Beyond locating the vehicle and one's destination, participants also report a pervasive lack of situational awareness during the ride. Inside a moving autonomous vehicle, blind and low-vision riders cannot glance out windows or at instrument panels to gauge their progress, nearby traffic, or unexpected events. This loss of environmental awareness leads to feelings of vulnerability. Indeed, not having access to critical information during a trip was described by users as severely diminishing their sense of control [19].

Visually impaired users consistently ask for real-time updates about what the vehicle is doing and what is happening around it [18]. A targeted investigation into conveying traffic information to blind passengers confirmed that gaining knowledge of the surrounding traffic is challenging with today's AV interfaces [20].

These usability barriers are tightly intertwined with psychological factors such as user confidence and trust in the technology. A recurring theme is that when blind users cannot obtain information or feel oriented, their trust in the autonomous system erodes. Numerous studies document low trust in AV systems among people with visually impairments, often linked to safety anxieties and the lack of transparency.

For example, safety and reliability were among the strongest determinants of unwillingness to ride [21]. Similarly, AV development still centers on sighted drivers, thus risking systematic exclusion of non-sighted users [15].

Moreover, elevated initial stress among blind passengers during AV trials has been observed [22]. Because perceived control significantly influences comfort and trust [23], trust in automation strongly correlates with a blind user's perceived ability to interact with the vehicle [24]

In summary, blind and low-vision individuals have reported numerous difficulties and limitations in using autonomous vehicles as currently envisioned. Key barriers include an inability to perceive purely visual displays or signals, lack of orientation and wayfinding support for locating vehicles and destinations, insufficient multimodal communication leading to reduced situational awareness, and the anxiety or low trust that these shortcomings engender. The convergence of evidence across studies makes it clear that, without significant improvements in inclusive design, autonomous vehicles may fail to deliver on their promise of independent mobility for those who are blind or visually impaired. These perceived barriers set the stage for a critical discussion on how future AV systems can be made accessible, intuitive, and trustworthy for users of all visual abilities.

Consequently, each challenge identified points toward design opportunities to better support blind and low-vision travelers [15, 17].

3.2 Proposed Inclusive Interface Strategies

Across the literature, auditory interfaces consistently emerge as a cornerstone of accessible AV design. Studies report that visually impaired users overwhelmingly prefer voice output for receiving navigation information and status updates, as well as voice input for issuing commands, given its natural and eyes-free interaction style [15, 19].

Several projects have accordingly prototyped voice-driven HMIs to allow passengers to set destinations, adjust in-vehicle features like climate or audio, and query the vehicle's status through speech [18, 25]. Researchers emphasize leveraging familiar personal devices: smartphone-based interfaces offer a flexible platform for accessible interaction, as they can integrate the screen reader, voice control, and vibration features that visually impaired users already rely on daily [14]. Consistent with this rationale, a proof-of-concept mobile application has been implemented that enables passengers with heterogeneous sensory and motor impairments to summon on autonomous vehicle and adjust on board settings entirely through the phone's native accessibility services [26].

Haptic feedback represents another key modality frequently proposed to augment or substitute for visual cues. Tactile signals, as vibrations through a handheld device or seat, can discreetly convey alerts and directional guidance, and they have been shown to reinforce user confidence when used alongside audio prompts.

Many authors therefore argue for multimodal HMIs that combine auditory, tactile, and simplified visual outputs, rather than relying on any single channel [14, 27]. Recent experimental interfaces exemplify this principle: for instance, a mid-air gesture control system for blind passengers was designed with synchronized audio and haptic feedback to help users perform and confirm gesture commands [27].

Furthermore, inclusive design extends beyond the vehicle interior to its external signals: autonomous cars must also communicate effectively with visually impaired pedestrians. Evidence indicates that supplementing visual displays with audio cues significantly improves pedestrians' comprehension of vehicle intentions and trust in roadway interactions [12].

Another recurring theme is personalization and adaptability of interfaces to accommodate the diversity of visual impairments. Rather than a one-size-fits-all solution, it's recommended to give users the ability to tailor interaction modes and information presentation to their own needs and preferences [14]. For example, individuals with residual vision may benefit from optional high-contrast visual displays or large-print text in the vehicle, whereas those who are blind might rely exclusively on speech output and Braille or vibratory feedback; an ideal HMI would support multiple modalities in parallel so that each user can utilize their preferred channels [14, 15].

Providing flexibility in how information is received and how controls are enacted is also seen as crucial for fostering a sense of agency. Visually impaired riders express a strong desire to remain informed about their journey and to exert some level of control over the vehicle's behavior, even in fully autonomous settings [19].

Interface designs that address this need include features like real-time route progress updates, the ability to request stops or adjust the route via accessible commands, and clear feedback to confirm that the vehicle has acknowledged a passenger's input [18, 19].

The importance of participatory design methods that actively involve individuals with visual impairments in the development and evaluation of AV interfaces is widely recognized. In practice, several studies have employed co-design workshops to elicit novel interface ideas directly from visually impaired users, resulting in solutions such as voice-controlled assistants and tactile feedback prototypes that reflect users' real needs and preferences [19, 20].

High-level frameworks have been proposed to structure inclusive design approaches. One model recommends embedding an intuitive virtual co-pilot, implemented as an embodied agent, within the vehicle interface to deliver guidance and reassurance akin to a human driver's presence [28]. Frameworks also emphasize addressing the social dimensions of accessibility by designing assistive features that empower users without inducing feelings of self-consciousness or stigma [29].

3.3 User Experience Evaluation

People with visual impairments generally voice cautious optimism about autonomous vehicles, anticipating significant gains in independent mobility and access to transportation. Across the literature, a recurrent theme is hope for greater autonomy, with many expecting that AVs could restore a sense of freedom to travel without sighted assistance [21].

In surveys, a majority of visually impaired respondents predicted positive outcomes from AV adoption, such as fewer accidents and improved road safety, indicating a baseline of trust in the technology's potential [15]. First-hand exposure tends to reinforce this optimism: blind and low-vision users who participated in real or simulated AV rides reported high levels of comfort and enjoyment. Their self-reported emotional responses (predominantly excitement and happiness) and feelings of safety during these trials were comparable to those of sighted passengers, with minimal anxiety or fear [22]. Such findings suggest that direct experience can significantly increase trust, alleviating some of the initial uncertainty among visually impaired users.

At the same time, safety and reliability concerns are prominent in user experience evaluations. Many individuals harbor reservations about the trustworthiness of an AV's decisions and the robustness of its technology. Common worries include the risk of equipment failures, navigation errors in unexpected situations, and the vehicle's ability to safely interact with pedestrians and other traffic [30]. For some, these safety-related anxieties translate into a desire for greater transparency from the vehicle: users want the car to clearly convey what it is doing and any hazards it detects. Indeed, studies emphasize the importance of continuous feedback to reassure blind passengers that the AV is functioning correctly and making safe choices. Researchers note that clear communication of vehicle intent can help mitigate fear, thereby fostering a sense of security and control for the passenger [12, 30].

Notably, affordability has also been identified as a pragmatic concern influencing user attitudes, some blind participants worry that AV technology may be prohibitively expensive initially, potentially tempering their enthusiasm [21]. Overall, however, perceived safety and trust in the system emerge as far more critical determinants of acceptance than cost considerations in the current literature.

Another central theme is the balance between independence and perceived control. On one hand, fully autonomous vehicles are attractive to many visually impaired users precisely because they eliminate the need for a human driver, offering an experience of independence that was previously unattainable [24]. In general, trust in the AV tends to increase with higher levels of automation, participants often expressed greater confidence in a car that can drive itself unassisted, as it reduces reliance on any human actions that they themselves cannot perform [24].

On the other hand, some users, particularly those with residual vision or prior driving experience before losing sight, voice a desire for some degree of control or oversight during the journey. Qualitative studies reveal nuanced preferences: for instance, experienced drivers who are now visually impaired sometimes favor a semi-autonomous mode that would allow them to intervene or make certain driving decisions [19]. These individuals often associate the act of driving with personal agency and thus feel uneasy relinquishing full control. By contrast, people who have never driven a car (e.g., those blind from birth) tend to be less comfortable with any scenario that might require their intervention; they are more inclined to trust a fully autonomous vehicle to handle all driving tasks, thereby avoiding situations where they might be expected to take the wheel [19].

This divergence highlights a key user experience consideration: perceived control is highly personal, and an optimal design might offer flexible interaction levels.

Thus, the consensus in the literature is that AV interfaces should, where feasible, provide options for user input or overrides without making such input mandatory for those who do not wish to engage.

Because of these needs, interface accessibility and modality preferences are a focal point of user experience research. It is well established that blind and low-vision users overwhelmingly prefer auditory interfaces for vehicular interaction.

Voice output and spoken feedback are seen as essential for conveying navigational information in real time. In nearly all studies, participants ranked speech-based interaction as their top choice for both receiving information and issuing commands to an AV [24].

Voice recognition and speech commands offer an intuitive and hands-free way to communicate with the vehicle, aligning with how visually impaired users interact with other assistive technologies. Tactile modalities, like vibrations through the seat or a handheld device, are generally viewed as useful supplements to audio, but not as a primary channel for complex information. Users appreciate haptic cues for drawing attention or providing confirmation, yet purely tactile displays were typically the least preferred option for detailed feedback [24].

For those with low vision, visual displays can still play an important complementary role: interfaces that present high contrast, enlarged text or simple graphics are valued by partially sighted individuals who wish to leverage their remaining vision [24]. In fact, research indicates that a significant subset of low-vision users wants to use the visual interfaces when available, even as they rely on audio for most interactions, hence, designers are encouraged to support multimodal output that can flexibly cater to different impairment levels.

A consistent recommendation is that AV HMIs should integrate redundant cues to maximize clarity and accommodate diverse user preferences. Indeed, the emphasis on multimodal interaction reflects a core insight of these studies: providing information through multiple senses not only ensures accessibility but also reinforces user confidence by keeping the passenger well-informed of the vehicle's actions and surround- ings.

Accessible design and user-centered development are paramount for delivering a positive user experience. Many visually impaired participants are acutely aware that current transportation systems have often overlooked their needs, and there is skepticism in some quarters about whether AV developers will fully address accessibility [21].

This skepticism manifests as concern that if interfaces are not thoughtfully designed then the promise of autonomous mobility will not be realized for blind users.

Correspondingly, by involving end-users in prototyping and usability testing, developers can identify accessibility gaps before the vehicles hit the market [14]. The reviewed studies collectively highlight features that make AVs more usable and trustworthy for visually impaired riders: these include straightforward voice-command systems, haptic locators to find buttons or seatbelts, consistent audio updates about trip status, and smartphone apps that seamlessly interface with the vehicle for tasks like summoning the car or setting destinations [15]. When such features are in place, users report significantly greater confidence in their ability to ride independently.

Perceived ease of use is therefore a key mediator of user experience, many blind users are willing to embrace autonomous mobility if they feel the vehicle is truly designed for them.

The literature therefore converges on a clear recommendation: designing AV systems with the nuanced needs of blind and low-vision individuals in mind is not only feasible, but it markedly improves user acceptance, confidence, and overall ride experience [19, 24]. By fostering trust and safety through accessible interfaces and empowering interactions, autonomous vehicles can truly become a life changing technology for people with visual impairments, enabling them to travel with a level of independence and ease that was previously unattainable.

3.4   Control, Autonomy, and Metaphors of Interaction

Visually impaired users consistently express a strong desire for control over autonomous vehicles to ensure personal safety and reassurance. Across multiple studies, participants report wanting the ability to intervene or override the vehicle when necessary, reflecting underlying trust concerns with fully automated systems [15].

In one survey, 94.5% of visually impaired respondents indicated that a self-driving car should still be equipped with manual driving controls, like steering wheel, pedals, specifically so that a human could take control in an emergency [15].

Likewise, focus group findings show unanimous sentiment that being able to take control at will is essential, many blind and low-vision participants cited safety fears and lack of trust in automation as reasons for wanting an emergency stop or other direct control options available [15, 19]. Even individuals who cannot legally drive often voiced that simply knowing some form of control is possible greatly increases their confidence and comfort in an autonomous vehicle [19]. Ensuring users feel safe and in command has thus been identified as a key design consideration for accessible autonomous mobility.

At the same time, preferences regarding vehicle autonomy levels and the ideal balance of control vary widely among visually impaired users, influenced by factors such as prior driving experience and degree of vision loss. Those with little or no driving experience often prefer a fully autonomous mode, trusting the vehicle to handle all driving functions because they feel unqualified to intervene in traffic scenarios [19].

In contrast, visually impaired individuals with past driving experience tend to favor semi-autonomous operation or at least the option for human input. Participants who had previously driven a car express interest in maintaining a driver role, they want the ability to oversee the system and to take over if something goes wrong, highlighting features like manual overrides or shared-control modes [19]. This divergence aligns with recent survey results showing that severity of impairment also impacts autonomy preferences: users with residual vision exhibit higher trust in lower levels of automation and wish to be more involved in driving, whereas those with total blindness are generally more inclined toward full automation for practicality and safety reasons [24].

Notably, users with some usable vision often still desire visual feedback in addition to audio, while fully blind users rely on non-visual modalities, underscoring that interaction needs are not monolithic in the blind low-vision community [24].

Overall, the literature suggests a need for flexible, user-adjustable autonomy in accessible HMI design, accommodating a spectrum of control preferences to suit different comfort levels.

Finally, researchers have documented how visually impaired individuals conceptualize their interaction with autonomous vehicles through familiar metaphors, revealing preferred roles for the human–vehicle relationship. One common perspective is to treat the AV as a co-navigator or partner in travel. In this view, users imagine an interaction dynamic where they actively collaborate with the vehicle, for example, conversing with the car to set destinations, plan routes, and make real-time decisions, much like working with a human co-pilot [19].

Studies report that participants often compare the vehicle's interface to voice assistants or GPS navigation systems, expecting a conversational agent they can query for navigation updates and instruct about their preferences, rather than a silent machine [19]. This co-navigator metaphor emphasizes mutual communication: the user provides goals or adjustments while the AV continuously informs the user of its actions and any situational changes.

Alternatively, some participants frame the AV as an assistant or chauffeur, essentially a service-oriented entity that should reliably handle the driving tasks and proactively look out for the passenger's needs [17]. In this assistant role, the vehicle is expected to behave akin to a helpful human driver: announcing important events, guiding the passenger through complex maneuvers like pick-ups or drop-offs, and generally providing the reassurance and courtesy a sighted driver might offer to a blind passenger [18]. Whether envisioned as a cooperative co-navigator or a dependable personal driver, these metaphors highlight a shared priority of user-centered interaction, the AV should engage with the passenger in a human-like, dialogic manner.

In summary, findings coalesce into a cohesive narrative: blind and low-vision individuals do not seek a passive, one-dimensional ride in autonomous vehicles; rather, they envision a travel experience defined by user empowerment, choice, and trust. They favor designs that allow them to configure their experience, stay informed of the vehicle's status, and exert influence when desired. Control, in this context, is not about literally steering the car, it is about having autonomy within autonomy, the freedom to direct one's journey even when a machine is at the wheel. By integrating familiar interaction metaphors and offering multiple avenues for input and feedback, AV designers can craft interfaces that treat visually impaired users not as simply passengers, but as active co-navigators of their own mobility. This thematic insight emphasizes that the future of accessible autonomous transportation lies in shared control: the vehicle and the user each have vital roles, working in tandem to ensure not only a safe arrival, but an empowering and inclusive journey for the rider [6, 15].

3.5 Policy and Systemic Constraints

Accessible HMI development for AVs is further impeded by broad policy gaps and systemic barriers. The literature consistently highlights the absence of clear and inclusive regulatory mandates to ensure accessibility in autonomous vehicle design

Existing legal and policy frameworks often reflect assumptions rooted in traditional models of vehicle operation, where active visual supervision is a prerequisite. This creates uncertainty regarding whether individuals with visual impairments can be formally recognized as legitimate operators of fully autonomous vehicles.

Moreover, disability rights frameworks have yet to explicitly address the specific accessibility requirements of AV interfaces and services. This lack of regulatory alignment has been described as indicative of a fragmented and non-compulsory approach to AV accessibility [14], in which no enforceable standards or institutional incentives ensure that manufacturers systematically incorporate the needs of blind and low-vision users. As a result, accessibility features often remain peripheral or experimental rather than structurally embedded, delaying the equitable realization of AVs' potential benefits for visually impaired populations.

Another recurring barrier identified in the literature is the absence of standardized frameworks and authoritative guidelines for inclusive HMI in autonomous vehicles for visual impaired users. Indeed, existing design norms in the automotive industry have historically overlooked users with disabilities, effectively embedding exclusionary assumptions into interface systems [1].

Unlike in the domains of web or software accessibility, no unified regulations currently ensure that AV interfaces systematically provide non-visual feedback mechanisms, such as speech output or tactile controls. This regulatory void leads to inconsistent implementations across manufacturers, producing variability that generates confusion, and increased learning demands for blind and low-vision users [14].

Several sources emphasize that the integration of universal design principles into HMI policy is essential to establish a minimum standard of accessibility across the AV ecosystem. Standardizing auditory cues, haptic feedback, and multimodal information delivery is not only seen to guarantee functional equity, but also as a foundation to drive broader innovation by ensuring that inclusive solutions are not treated as exceptional cases [31].

However, in the current landscape, such principles remain largely absent, and this regulatory inertia reflects a broader pattern of systemic exclusion in the governance and development of autonomous vehicle technologies.

In the absence of formal pressure from regulatory institutions, industry practices tend to prioritize general marketability over inclusive design, repeating patterns of marginalization seen in earlier transportation systems [1].

Disabled stakeholders, including blind and low-vision user, remain underrepresented in design standards, regulatory frameworks, and strategic industry planning [15], highlighting a critical disconnection between accessibility needs and current AV development trajectories.

The literature underline that the lack of accessibility in AV systems is not only the result of market dynamics but rather reflects a deeper absence of regulatory accountability and institutional commitment. In the absence of frameworks that prioritize inclusive design and actively involve disabled stakeholders, accessibility risks being relegated to a secondary concern, treated as an optional enhancement rather than a foundational requirement.

Bridging this gap and translating technical innovation into tangible, equitable outcomes for visually impaired users requires deliberate efforts to overcome the standardization and governance challenges consistently identified in the literature.

4 Discussion

Fully autonomous vehicles (AVs) hold significant potential to improve mobility and independence for individuals who are blind or have low vision [15]. To realize this promise, however, AV HMIs must be designed with accessibility as core requirement, since traditional visually oriented displays and controls inherently exclude these users [19].

This scoping review systematically maps the key interaction challenges and design needs of blind and low-vision users in autonomous vehicles, offering a comprehensive overview of an emerging research area. The literature highlights several common concerns that can undermine trust and comfort—difficulties obtaining situational information, fears about safety, and only preliminary design considerations to mitigate these issues [21].

Visually impaired users face several recurring accessibility barriers when interacting with current AV interfaces. A fundamental challenge is the lack of situational awareness due to inaccessible visual displays, hence blind or low-vision passengers often cannot obtain critical real-time information about their journey, nearby obstacles, or vehicle status, which leaves them feeling vulnerable and out of control [17, 20].

Users consistently report difficulty orienting themselves and locating vehicles or destinations without appropriate non-visual cues, and they lack alternative sensory feedback for events that sighted riders take for granted.

Safety and trust concerns are pervasive: without accessible feedback, blind travelers experience anxiety about what the vehicle is doing and whether it is safe.

Empirical studies confirm that safety and reliability issues can deter visually impaired people from accepting or riding in AVs [21]. Furthermore, much of AV technology development still implicitly assumes a sighted driver or passenger, leading to design biases that systematically exclude blind users [15].

Notably, elevated stress levels have been observed among blind passengers during initial autonomous ride trials [22]. Prior research suggests that increasing a visually impaired user's sense of control and interactivity can improve comfort and trust – for example, riders report greater confidence when they can actively engage with the HMI or influence the ride [19].

In summary, key obstacles include the inability to perceive visual-only information, insufficient orientation and wayfinding support, limited multimodal communication, and the anxiety or low trust that these deficiencies produce. Without significant advances in inclusive design, autonomous vehicles may fall short of their promise of independent mobility for individuals who are blind or have low vision.

To address these challenges, researchers have begun evaluating inclusive HMI strategies. A central theme is the adoption of multimodal interfaces that extend beyond vision. Audio-based interaction is crucial: studies show that blind users strongly prefer auditory feedback for navigation updates and system status, as well as voice input for commands. Accordingly, many prototypes feature voice-driven HMIs that let passengers set destinations, control in-vehicle functions, and query the vehicle's status via speech [25, 26]. Personal smart devices provide a flexible alternative interface, allowing visually impaired users to interact through familiar touchscreen or voice apps.

Beyond audio, researchers highlight the value of haptic and tactile feedback as a complement to auditory cues – for example, using vibrational alerts or tangible guides to help users locate controls [3]. Some innovative solutions even explore novel sensory channels, such as mid-air gesture controls that provide tactile feedback and illustrate how touchless haptic interactions might convey information to a blind passenger [27]. Emotion-aware interfaces offer a promising approach to improve the autonomous travel experience for visually impaired and other vulnerable users by actively managing their emotional states. For example, in-vehicle emotion regulation techniques, using digital nudging strategies coupled with soothing media like music or calming voice interactions can effectively mitigate passenger stress and prevent emotional overload during autonomous trips [32].

Such approaches recognise that reducing anxiety through the HMI itself can be as important as providing information, especially for first-time or hesitant users. Collectively, these inclusive strategies constitute a growing toolkit that can make AV travel more intelligible, comfortable, and empowering for visually impaired individuals.

The evidence base, however, remains limited. Only a small number of empirical studies have examined AV HMI accessibility for visually impaired users, and most proposed solutions are still in prototype or conceptual stages.

Further research and development are needed to translate these ideas into mature, real-world systems. The literature also underscores the necessity of involving end-users at every stage: participatory design and co-creation with visually impaired people are strongly recommended to ensure that accessibility features truly meet user needs [2].

Genuine inclusion requires engaging blind and low-vision individuals as co-designers and decision-makers in the HMI development process.

Another overarching finding is the gap in standards and policy: current automotive guidelines and regulations offer little direction on accessible HMI requirements, thus without formal accessibility mandates, accessibility may remain a secondary concern in AV design [14]

Bridging this gap will require not only technical innovation but also updated governance and sustained collaboration among industry, regulators, and the visually impaired community.

By addressing the identified barriers with inclusive, multimodal, and usercentered HMI designs, autonomous vehicles can become truly accessible, trustworthy, and empowering for users of all visual abilities. Such advancements would enable blind and low-vision individuals to travel with unprecedented independence and confidence, fulfilling the transformative promise of autonomous mobility for this population.

5 Conclusion

Autonomous vehicles (AVs) hold significant potential to revolutionize mobility for blind and low-vision individuals. However, the current design of Human–Machine Interfaces (HMIs) remains largely inaccessible, relying on visual modalities that exclude a substantial user base. This review has outlined critical barriers—including limited situational awareness, lack of orientation support, and low system transparency—that undermine user trust, comfort, and safety.

Multimodal interaction strategies, particularly those combining voice and haptic feedback, emerge as promising pathways for enabling more inclusive AV experiences. Inclusive interfaces not only address immediate functional challenges but also foster confidence and autonomy—key elements for independent travel. Participatory and co-de- sign practices must become standard, positioning visually impaired users not as passive recipients but as active contributors in HMI development.

Moreover, accessibility should not be treated as an afterthought or a secondary feature. Regulatory standards must evolve to embed inclusive principles into automotive design norms, ensuring equity and consistency across systems. Without such shifts, the promise of AVs will remain incomplete—leaving behind those who could benefit most.

Truly accessible mobility is not merely a technological objective; it is a societal imperative. Building autonomous vehicles that empower users of all visual abilities will help redefine transportation as a domain of inclusion, independence, and dignity.

Acknowledgments. This work was funded by EU Horizon KDT JU Research and Innovation Programme under Grant Agreement 101139769 (DistriMuSe - Distributed Multi-Sensor Systems for Human Safety and Health)

Disclosure of Interests The authors have no competing interests to declare that are relevant to the content of this article.

References

1. Wirtz, L., Sever, E., Eckstein, L.: Adaptive human-machine interfaces and inclusivity in the automotive field: a review. In: Accessibility, Assistive Technology and Digital Environments, vol. 121(121) (2024)
2. Huff Jr, E.W., Lucaites, K.M., Roberts, A., Brinkley, J.: Participatory design in the classroom: exploring the design of an autonomous vehicle human-machine interface with a visually impaired co-designer. In: Proceedings of the Human Factors and Ergonomics Society Annual Meeting, vol. 64, no. 1, pp. 1921–1925. SAGE Publications, Sage/Los Angeles (2020)
3. Angeleska, E., Aleksovska, A., Avramov, N., Sidorenko, S., Rizov, T., Jankovic, A.: Design and evaluation of an inclusive autonomous vehicle user interface developed for persons with visual acuity loss. Proc. Des. Soc. **2**, 2035–2044 (2022)
4. World Health Organization: World Report on Vision. World Health Organization (2019). https://www.who.int/publications/i/item/9789241516570
5. Zhang, W., An, C.: Research on multimodal interaction design patterns for visually impaired people under sensory compensation theory. In: Design Studies and Intelligence Engineering, pp. 799–808. IOS Press (2024)
6. Arfini, S., Bellani, P., Picardi, A., Yan, M., Fossa, F., Caruso, G.: Design for inclusivity in driving automation: theoretical and practical challenges to human-machine interactions and interface design. In: Connected and Automated Vehicles: Integrating Engineering and Ethics, pp. 63–85. Springer Nature Switzerland, Cham (2023)
7. Brinkley, J.: Using personas with visual impairments to explore the de- sign of an accessible self-driving vehicle human-machine interface. In: Proceedings of the Human Factors and Ergonomics Society Annual Meeting, vol. 65, no. 1, pp. 337–341). SAGE Publications, Sage/Los Angeles (2021)
8. Golbabaei, F., et al.: Enabling mobility and inclusion: designing accessible autonomous vehicles for people with disabilities. Cities. **154**, 105333 (2024)
9. Bayless, S.H., Davidson, S.: Driverless cars and accessibility: designing the future of transportation for people with disabilities (2019)
10. Bradley, M., Langdon, P.M., Clarkson, P.J.: An inclusive design perspective on automotive HMI trends. In: Universal Access in Human-Computer Interaction. Users and Context Diversity: 10th International Conference, UAHCI 2016, Held as Part of HCI International 2016, Toronto, ON, Canada, July 17–22, 2016, Proceedings, Part III 10, pp. 548–555. Springer International Publishing (2016)
11. Tricco, A.C., et al.: PRISMA extension for scoping reviews (PRISMA-ScR): checklist and explanation. Ann. Intern. Med. **169**(7), 467–473 (2018)
12. Colley, M., Walch, M., Gugenheimer, J., Askari, A., Rukzio, E.: Towards inclusive external communication of autonomous vehicles for pedestrians with vision impairments. In: Proceedings of the 2020 CHI Conference on Human Factors in Computing Systems, April, pp. 1–14 (2020)
13. Angeleska, E., Lü, L., Pretto, P.: Evaluation of an autonomous vehicle user interface for sensory impaired users. J. Transp. Technol. **14**(4), 570–589 (2024)
14. Fink, P.D., Holz, J.A., Giudice, N.A.: Fully autonomous vehicles for people with visual impairment: policy, accessibility, and future directions. ACM Trans. Access. Comput. (TACCESS). **14**(3), 1–17 (2021)
15. Brinkley, J., Huff Jr., E.W., Posadas, B., Woodward, J., Daily, S.B., Gilbert, J.E.: Exploring the needs, preferences, and concerns of persons with visual impairments regarding autonomous vehicles. ACM Trans. Access. Comput. (TACCESS). **13**(1), 1–34 (2020)
16. Kanjilal, S., Ray, S.: Intelligent automated vehicles for passengers with visual disability. In: 2024 IEEE International Conference on Smart Internet of Things (SmartIoT), pp. 382–383. IEEE (2024)

17. Fink, P.D., Alsamsam, M., Brown, J.R., Kindler, H.D., Giudice, N.A.: Give us something to chauffeur it: exploring user needs in traditional and fully autonomous rides- haring for people who are blind or visually impaired. Transport. Res. F: Traffic Psychol. Behav. **98**, 91–103 (2023)
18. Brinkley, J., Posadas, B., Woodward, J., Gilbert, J.E.: Opinions and preferences of blind and low vision consumers regarding self-driving vehicles: results of focus group discussions. In: Proceedings of the 19th International ACM SIGACCESS Conference on Computers and Accessibility, October, pp. 290–299 (2017)
19. Brewer, R.N., Kameswaran, V.: Understanding the power of control in autonomous vehicles for people with vision impairment. In: Proceedings of the 20th International ACM SIGACCESS Conference on Computers and Accessibility, October, pp. 185–197 (2018)
20. Meinhardt, L.M., et al.: Hey, what's going on? Conveying traffic information to people with visual impairments in highly automated vehicles: introducing OnBoard. Proc. ACM Interact. Mob. Wearable Ubiquitous Technol. **8**(2), 1–24 (2024)
21. Bennett, R., Vijaygopal, R., Kottasz, R.: Willingness of people who are blind to accept autonomous vehicles: an empirical investigation. Transport. Res. F: Traffic Psychol. Behav. **69**, 13–27 (2020)
22. Kempapidis, T., Castle, C.L., Fairchild, R.G., Hussain, S.F., Cash, A.T., Gomes, R.S.: A scientific evaluation of autonomous vehicle user experience on sighted and visually impaired passengers based on FACS (Facial Analysis Coding System) and a user experience questionnaire. J. Transp. Health. **19**, 100906 (2020)
23. Hayton, P.A.: Visually impaired people's perceptions on how autonomous vehicles will impact everyday life
24. Beran, R., Wu, Y.H., Lei, Q.: Preferences of individuals with different levels of visual impairment for autonomous vehicles. In: Proceedings of the Human Factors and Ergonomics Society Annual Meeting, vol. 68, no. 1, pp. 1718–1719. SAGE Publications, Sage/Los Angeles (2024)
25. Brinkley, J., Posadas, B., Sherman, I., Daily, S.B., Gilbert, J.E.: An open road evaluation of a self-driving vehicle human–machine interface designed for visually impaired users. Int. J. Hum.-Comput. Interact. **35**(11), 1018–1032 (2019)
26. Martelaro, N., Carrington, P., Fox, S., Forlizzi, J.: Designing an inclusive mobile app for people with disabilities to independently use autonomous vehicles. In: Proceedings of the 14th International Conference on Automotive User Interfaces and Interactive Vehicular Applications, September, pp. 45–55 (2022)
27. Fink, P.D., et al.: Autonomous is not enough: designing multisensory Mid-Air gestures for vehicle interactions among people with visual impairments. In: Proceedings of the 2023 CHI Conference on Human Factors in Computing Systems, April, pp. 1–13 (2023)
28. Gluck, A., Huff, E.W., Boateng, K., Brinkley, J.: Toward a framework for embodiment in emerging transportation technologies for facilitating in-vehicle experiences for vulnerable and disabled road users. In: 2022 IEEE 3rd International Conference on Human-Machine Systems (ICHMS), pp. 1–5. IEEE (2022)
29. Shinohara, K., Wobbrock, J.O.: Self-conscious or self-confident? A diary study conceptualizing the social accessibility of assistive technology. ACM Trans. Access. Comput. (TACCESS). **8**(2), 1–31 (2016)
30. Miller, K., Chng, S., Cheah, L.: Understanding acceptance of shared autonomous vehicles among people with different mobility and communication needs. Travel Behav. Soc. **29**, 200–210 (2022)

31. Bastola, A., Wang, H., Boroujeni, S.P.H., Brinkley, J., Moshayedi, A.J., Razi, A.: Driving towards inclusion: a systematic review of AI-powered accessibility enhancements for people with disability in autonomous vehicles. IEEE Access. (2025)
32. Presta, R., De Simone, F., Tancredi, C., Chiesa, S.: Nudging the safe zone: design and assessment of HMI strategies based on intelligent driver state monitoring systems. In: International Conference on Human-Computer Interaction, pp. 166–185. Springer Nature Switzerland, Cham (2023)

Conception and Prototyping of an Adaptive Dispatcher Station to Control Delivery Robots

Melanie Kirchkesner[(✉)], Blanche Schoch[iD], Waldemar Titov[iD], and Thomas Schlegel[iD]

Institute for Intelligent Interactive Ubiquitous System (IIIUS), Furtwangen University, Furtwangen im Schwarzwald, Germany
iiius@hs-furtwangen.de
https://iiius.de/

Abstract. The increasing interest in sustainable logistics solutions calls for new concepts that simultaneously consider ecological factors, are user-friendly and compatible with the existing infrastructure. In urban areas, a significant proportion of traffic congestion and environmental impact is attributable to delivery vehicles. One such sustainable solution that addresses both the last mile and transport from the depot is the integration of delivery robots into the transportation of goods and people. For the integration to succeed, the delivery robots need to be integrated into the same control center as the transporting public transport system for being controlled and monitored. However, the development of such a control center poses a challenge, as existing control center systems already have weaknesses in terms of user-friendliness and functionality and do not offer a suitable basis—apart from the novel integration of public passenger and goods traffic. In addition, the high volume of information and the pressing need for immediate action can result in cognitive and emotional stress for dispatchers, which is exacerbated by the overloaded and inflexible applications. The aim of our contribution is to address these problems and close the gap between a possible logistics solution and busy dispatchers. The objective of sustainable transport is addressed through the use of delivery robots. Furthermore, a user-centred and efficient control station system for dispatchers is developed from scratch. Our focus is on the development of an adaptive system. Users are supported in their day-to-day work with the help of flexible customisation in various scenarios and with individual requirements. The practical implementation and functionality of the concept are implemented as prototypes and evaluated with test persons from the domains of mobility and user experience.

Keywords: Adaptive and personalized interfaces · Future transportation systems · User research · UX (User experience) and Usability · Delivery robots · Autonomous systems · Multi-device

P.-L.P. Rau and H. Krömker (Eds.): HCII 2025, LNCS 16336, pp. 247–260, 2026.
https://doi.org/10.1007/978-3-032-12798-3_15

1 Introduction

1.1 Background and Problem Description

The prototype and our study are focused on the challenges and difficulties of a dispatcher's role in a control center, utilizing group discussions with experts. Qualitative usability tests were conducted to gather individual perceptions, needs, and experiences, enabling suggestions for improvement. The concept was developed as a prototype to showcase ideas quickly and collect initial feedback. The usability tests were conducted to assess usability, user interface, and comprehensibility, enabling further literature research and existing projects.

A group discussion with an expert revealed the underlying issues in the work of dispatchers. Dispatchers in public transportation systems are unable to take breaks or move from their workstations for brief periods while working at the control center. This can be attributed to the sheer volume of information, the pressing need for immediate action, and the profound stress that accompanies such situations. Furthermore, the findings of our research indicate that it is not uncommon for a single dispatcher at a given workstation to be assigned up to eight monitors. This finding suggests that the quantity of information being processed is substantial, resulting in elevated levels of cognitive and emotional stress (cf. Ferreira et al. [4]: 173; Schwarz et al. [11]: 99).

Moreover, the work carried out at the control station has the possibility of becoming monotonous. This additional challenge can result in a reduction in vigilance when working purely observationally (cf. Schwarz et al. [11]: 94). This has the effect of reducing the already limited attention and responsiveness of dispatchers. As a result, disruptions cannot be recognized and addressed in a timely manner (cf. Evers et al. [3]: 113; Schwarz et al. [11]: 94).

The integration of parcel robots into the transportation of goods and people is a concept with relevance in even more aspects. First, it has the potential to offset the anticipated deficit of personnel in courier services (cf. Wolf et al. [12]: 75). Secondly, the impact on road traffic and the environment is considered (cf. Giuffrida et al. [6]: 1321). Parcels that are delivered by van use road traffic which leads to pollution, traffic jams and accidents (cf. ibid.). An alternative approach is also desirable due to higher fuel prices (cf. Giuffrida et al. [6]: 1320). The integration of parcel robots within the supply chain facilitates the realization of sustainable transportation goals (cf. IIIUS [8]).

1.2 Research Objectives

It is clear that there are some deficits and problems that need to be addressed. The initial objective is to establish a control center that is user-friendly, efficient and a pleasant working environment. Secondly, there is a need to further develop the concept of parcel robots in the context of goods and passenger transportation.

The purpose of this study is to develop a detailed control center concept that is responsible for the control and rescheduling of parcel robots. This system is utilized by dispatchers and other control center operators. The parcel robots contain parcels that must be delivered via sidewalks and trams. In addition to monitoring the location of individual parcels, dispatchers are responsible for the planning of delivery routes and the management of parcels in transit. The application shows whether the daily schedule is running according to plan or whether disruptions and errors have occurred. Another area of focus is the integration of an adaptive system. The platform's adaptability to diverse scenarios and individual requirements in everyday working life is a key strength. Such automatic suggestions lead to quick and efficient solutions and are tailored to the needs and wishes of the target group.

Considering the above mentioned problems and objectives, the following research questions arise:

- RQ1: How can user experience and user interface design principles be applied to visualise information with high usability in a control station for delivery robots?
- RQ2: What adaptive features can the delivery robot control center use to respond to different user needs and situations while improving the user experience?
- RQ3: Can multi-device-use support work at the control center with delivery robots?

2   Conception

This work is derived from the ongoing research projects 'regioKArgoTramTrain' and 'IADAPT' of the Institute for Intelligent Interactive Ubiquitous Systems (IIIUS). In 'regioKArgoTramTrain' the combination of passenger and goods transport, utilizing delivery robots on existing public transport system, will be researched and implemented (cf. IIIUS [8]). In the future, goods are to be transported in trams, which will make transport more efficient and sustainable (cf. ibid.). In the 'IADAPT' project, an interactive and adaptive control center is being developed for local public transport (cf. IIIUS [9]).

The following concept descriptions explain the approach to developing a control station for parcel robots. The idea is presented through a detailed description of the structure, components and functionality.

Parcel Robot. Each parcel robot is assigned a unique identification number, which is displayed alongside the abbreviation 'PR'. For instance, 'PR-22'. The parcel robot is designed to accommodate a maximum of 13 parcels. Six of these are size S, a further six parcels are size M and one is size L, as shown in Figure 1. The design of the parcel robots and the compartments they contain was adopted from the 'regioKArgoTramTrain' project.

Transportation and Navigation. Parcel robots utilize sidewalks for navigation. These devices travel at a speed of 5 km/h, a rate selected to ensure the

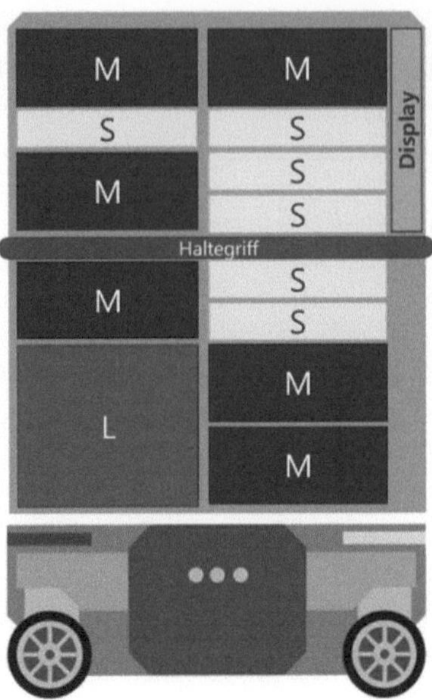

Fig. 1. Design prototype of an autonomous delivery robot with 13 parcel compartments. Source: Lars Münster; SEW-Eurodrive GmbH & Co KG

safety of other road users and to match the average walking pace of pedestrians. To get to their destination faster, they can take the trams. Special platforms are installed on the platform for transferring to the tram. The route is followed with the assistance of a built-in navigation system. This makes it possible to take the shortest route and automatically avoid road closures or other obstacles.

Handover of Parcels. Parcels that necessitate alternative delivery methods can be transferred in a variety of ways. On the one hand, there is the option of transferring the item to a different parcel robot in the area. In the event that a technician is present at the site while the defective robot is being repaired, they are able to collaborate with the dispatcher to facilitate this process. For instance, the technician may elect to either drive to the location where the other robot is positioned or to wait for the robot's arrival while the technician packs up his things. Beyond that, the option of bicycle courier services is available upon request. The courier has the option of collecting the parcel directly from the parcel robot or via an intermediate step from the warehouse or pick-up station. The dispatcher can also hand the parcel over to a delivery van if it is traveling in the same direction. They can hand it over to the recipient or at a pick-up station. Another option is crowdsourcing. This allows deliveries to be carried out as a service by people who use their own means of transportation (cf. Castillo et al. [2]: 8). In the event that the parcel is located within the warehouse, it is also feasible to dispatch it from that location via drone. For handovers, the weight of the parcel, possible signature requirements, registered returns or shipping parcels should be taken into account.

Degree of the Adaptive System. The degree of adaptivity can be set, so actions can be performed automatically or suggested. How much should be automated depends on the user's preferences, profession and experience. If the user is a beginner, the adaptive system makes fewer suggestions. This is due to the fact that new users should possess a comprehensive understanding of the application. If routine tasks and background checks are taken over by the adaptive system, the user lacks a deep understanding. The actions on which the complex processes are based must be internalized. As an experienced user, adaptivity can take over these actions. A distinction is made between four levels of adaptivity:

Level 1—No adaptivity: Users work without adaptive functions.

Level 2—Minimal adaptivity: This is aimed at beginners. Only suggestions for personalization are made. Content recommendations for tasks are not given. The following suggestions are provided as illustrative examples: "Taking into account your frequency of use, the system suggests adding the 'Call supervisor' function to the menu bar", "The system suggests saving your favorite views to open them immediately after the next login".

Level 3—Medium adaptivity: Experienced users benefit from partial automation. Routine tasks or suggestions for standardized processes are suggested and checked by the user, carried out, rejected or adapted if necessary. This is predicated on the nature of the tasks that the user typically performs. For instance, the checklist is executed, and recommendations are provided, such as "Should the report 'Error BS-01 Workshop repair' be generated based on the same parameters as previously utilized?" and "A template has been created based on your standard workflow. Should this template be saved for future tasks?"

Level 4—High adaptivity: The system takes over more complex processes. A suggestion is made, whereby the routine tasks have already been completed. These advanced suggestions for action can also be accepted, adapted or rejected. This increases efficiency without losing control of the process. Suggestions could be: "The system suggests solving problem BS-03 before fault VS-01, due to urgency and availability of resources. Should this suggestion be accepted or changed?", "Parcel robot PR-82 has the same technical malfunction as two days ago. Should the parcel robot be collected for workshop repair, or should the checklist be run through from the beginning?".

Calendar. Events, roadworks and closures are documented in the calendar. This capability enables parcel robots to circumvent obstructions or routes that are overloaded with activity, thereby ensuring efficient navigation. Spontaneous events and obstacles can be avoided by the parcel robots themselves using the navigation system. If a detour is not feasible, a notification is transmitted to the designated dispatcher. The dispatcher can search for an alternative route. This new obstacle is then documented in the calendar by the dispatcher or the adaptive system.

Progress Display of the Day. The application tracks the parcels delivered so far during the day. The progress is displayed as a percentage and in various colors, indicating the degree to which today's delivery deadlines are being met. It makes it easier to decide whether and when intervention is required. If the planned minimum quantity of parcels is being processed according to plan, the figure is displayed in green. If progress is behind due to many delays or other problems, the number turns orange or red, depending on the situation. The goal is to ensure that the figure displays 100% at the end of the day. Recommendations for action are suggested for orange or red numbers. These measures are implemented to avert critical consequences. For instance, the activation of additional parcel robots can be executed, thereby compensating for any delays in progress. It is also possible for the dispatcher to accept fewer parcels for the next parcel delivery to the warehouse.

Tablet Version for Technicians. The tablet version, utilized by technicians, contains a modified range of information and functions. Assignments are viewed and processed. As with the dispatcher, the technicians' assignments are displayed and prioritized. Once an assignment has been processed, a report is created, and if necessary, a new action is taken. Communication and the map remain central functions. If a technician is on the way to the defective parcel robot, he can activate navigation on the tablet.

Adaptive Functions

Recommender: The day-to-day work and challenging moments of dispatchers should be supported by a recommender. This feature offers assistance or, if authorized, executes tasks autonomously in the background. If unnecessarily long work processes or hectic situations are identified, the adaptive system can suggest improvements to make the processes shorter and more organized. Incident reports are stored and used as a reference for recurring incidents. This results in checklists and suggested measures with a sequence. Measures that demand minimal effort and demonstrate a degree of success are prioritized and executed first. This prevents the problem from being solved at great expense, even though it could be done with just a few clicks. For instance, in the context of parcel robots, the system is capable of recognizing a pattern of frequent occurrences of the acceleration sensor becoming inactive. It also recognizes that the problem usually had to be repaired on site, but that a restart was sufficient a few times. The dispatcher therefore first restarts the parcel robot system. If this is unsuccessful, a technician is sent out.

Personalization: Suggestions for personalization can be made that are tailored to the user, should the user not personalize the appearance themselves (cf. Gajos et al. [5]: 202). These recommendations are customized to align with the user's working style, thereby fostering a more conducive work environment (cf. ibid.). For instance, windows dispersed across multiple screens can be consolidated into more compact groups, facilitating faster identification and access. Other ideas would be a personalized menu bar and other arrangements of windows after logging in to the application.

Decision support: The adaptive system also intervenes in determining the optimal delivery method for rescheduling parcels. Given the availability of six distinct delivery methods, numerous options and combinations for rescheduling are at one's disposal. These differ in the following aspects: arrival time, schedule, battery, environment, returns or shipping parcel registration, weight, free space, CO_2 emissions, and the weather.

3   Requirements

The functional and non-functional requirements address key challenges that emerged from a group discussion with an expert and literature research. The personas that were developed as a component of this project also made contributions.

The functional requirements encompass a range of essential tasks, including the oversight of parcel robots, the adjustment of scheduling for parcels and communication. The number and weight of current problems should be immediately visible so that the user knows which critical problems should be tackled first. Given the potential for a range of faults and problems, these are classified into two distinct colors. The color yellow is used to indicate faults that are functioning properly but have been held up by an external factor and are, as a result, behind schedule. These issues are less pressing for resolution in comparison to the red parcel robots. The color red is used to indicate technical issues that prevent the delivery of parcels. In terms of adaptability, it is essential to provide adapted functions and suggestions to mitigate the impact of stress in challenging situations. The actions of the adaptive system must be elucidated and presented in a comprehensible and transparent manner. It is imperative that users feel in control and be able to follow the provided suggestions.

The non-functional requirements of the dispatcher station include performance requirements such as user-centricity, digital accessibility and intuitive user guidance.

Furthermore, the application is therefore not branched and does not contain any deep levels. Users can navigate between the main functions in the tab. The components can be pulled apart and put back together again.

Personalization with role-, function-, and device-specific access ensures that users can work in a targeted manner without being overwhelmed by irrelevant information (cf. Hussain et al. [7]: 1). The group discussion with an expert emphasizes the importance of avoiding long and long-winded workflows. Functions should therefore be quickly accessible depending on the situation or problem.

Also, it is essential for users to determine the actions to be carried out. The effects that the user's actions produce should be apparent. This heightened transparency promotes trust, enhanced security measures and elevated user satisfaction.

As there is potentially little need for training, a help system is built in so that users can get to know the application on their own and need as little support as possible. The question mark icon provides explanations in many places. Definitions, meanings, possible actions and legends are included and can be accessed at any time.

Computers have the capacity to collect, store, and process large volumes of data (cf. Blair-Early/Zender [1]: 103). Humans have to exert a great deal of cognitive effort to do this (cf. ibid.). Consequently, it is logical to process the data in a manner that it can be absorbed by human capabilities (cf. ibid.). Humans can scan, recognize and remember images (cf. ibid.). They can also detect patterns and changes in size, shape, color, movement and texture (cf. ibid.). Blair-Early/Zender ([1]: 103) summarized: "As a result, the visualization of large quantities of information takes on great significance, transforming incomprehensible data into understanding". Therefore, it is imperative to present the data in a manner that aligns with human capabilities.

In today's multi-device environment, the use of different devices for different tasks is common (cf. Levin [10]). Individuals frequently alternate between multiple devices, including computers, smartphones and tablets, to accomplish a single goal (cf. ibid.). A significant number of products offer the same application for all other devices (cf. ibid.). A potential challenge arises when uniform design and content are visible on every device, yet the context is not taken into account, although this influences user satisfaction and experience (cf. ibid.). The context of use is a critical factor in determining the suitability of these devices, given the varied purposes and situations for which they are employed (cf. ibid.). Rather than emphasizing convenient access to content across devices, a more critical consideration is the timing of content delivery (cf. ibid.). As Levin ([10]) asserts, "the greater benefit would come from people getting the right thing, at the right time, on the best (available) device." Michal Levin's quote underlines the importance of relevance and context in a multi-device environment.

As indicated in a survey of contextual design data, the preference for a multi-device environment was identified (cf. Schwarz et al. [11]: 98). The majority of 12 respondents, including operators and shift supervisors, expressed a desire to work with mobile devices (cf. ibid.). The utilization of multi-touch systems is regarded as beneficial by 50% of the respondents, and collaboration is expected to be enhanced as a consequence (cf. ibid.).

Conversely, a group discussion with a former dispatcher indicated that working at a control center in public transportation involves numerous and occasionally complex tasks. This finding suggests that the utilization of a mobile application, such as those found on smartphones or smartwatches, does not necessarily result in an enhancement of work efficiency. The reason for this is that these devices lack the requisite functionality and comprehensive overview that is essential for effective task management.

It is conceivable that the reason for the contrary results of the contextual design data is that these additional functions are beneficial for the shift supervisors mentioned in the paper. They have responsibilities such as administration and managing shift schedules. The control center work can be different in certain areas and accordingly involve varying levels of effort. One solution involves enabling dispatchers to continue utilizing the desktop version while concurrently developing a tablet version for technicians, workshop workers and supervisors. The scope of information is adapted, offering a flexible solution for individuals engaged in repairing or collecting parcel robots. A tablet is characterized by its user-friendly touchscreen interface, which facilitates seamless interaction with the device. Its portability allows for convenient use in various settings and contexts. Users of the tablet version of the control center can accept and place orders, read information and communicate. Since most of the working time is not spent on the screen, a tablet is suitable.

4   Use Case

The chosen use case illustrates the daily tasks faced by dispatchers, focusing on addressing issues with the desktop application and troubleshooting. The actors' names were derived from the personas. The actors in this scenario include the dispatcher Josef Maier, the technician Alex Novak, a parcel robot, and a bicycle courier. This scenario necessitates the utilization of the desktop version for dispatchers and the adaptivity level 3 setting.

Dispatcher Josef Maier is shown two problems on the desktop application. The higher-priority problem, a defective PR-98 parcel robot, is focused on by the adaptive system. This process is initiated automatically, and the relevant checklist is executed in the background. The system then issues a recommendation to restart the parcel robot system. Josef carries this out. After a short time, the restart is completed, however, the underlying issue persists. Josef therefore clicks on "Troubleshooting" and opens the collection of measures that match the corresponding error. He runs through the recommendations that have proven successful in the past. He then compares the various solutions and initiates the next step in the checklist. The order for an on-site repair is sent to the responsible technicians. The technician, Alex Novak, accepted the order after a brief period. While Alex takes care of the faulty parcel robot, Josef waits and turns his attention to another problem.

After some time has passed, Josef receives a message from Alex. Josef has to reschedule the parcels because the robot has to be taken to the workshop because he cannot repair the robot on site. Josef accesses the rescheduling function and sees that two out of four parcels have been prioritized. Parcel #5363 is designated as an express delivery, while #7764 is prioritized due to the constrained time frame. The time window to receive the parcel closes in 52 minutes and after that the parcel cannot be received that day. The parcel robot requires, in this case, a 45-minute delivery time. This is a problem because the parcel robot has a defect, cannot drive and there is less time. A checklist is presented to facilitate the rescheduling process. These steps enable the dispatcher to quickly understand the process. The process commences with the configuration of the handover. The adaptive system recognizes that the technician is already on site and sets the options in advance. If necessary, Josef can make changes. He is satisfied and clicks on the arrow button. This opens the map with all the delivery drivers in the area. The user can observe the specific packages and transfer mechanisms through which a solution is being filtered. Various proposals also appear, which Josef compares with each other. After a thorough evaluation of the pros and cons of each proposal, he opts for the first option to avoid significant delays in the project schedule. He then examines the rescheduling window once more. In this section, Josef is able to view the implemented changes and make changes to them. For instance, it is possible to reset or notify the recipients.

The described use case was designed to address the workflow and order management of some critical moments. It covers the main functions of the application and fulfills key objectives such as efficient processes, intuitive operation and traceability. Repair processes can be designed flexibly and offer immediate communication between technician and dispatcher.

5   Evaluation

A usability test was conducted with four researchers in the fields of HCI and mobility, examining their relationships with control centers and delivery robots. A questionnaire was created to address key points. The first part involved a think-aloud scenario on the prototype, while the second part involved an A/B test for layout and navigation to assess comprehensibility and usability. The results helped identify weak points and ideas for further development.

One of the key findings is the difficulty in deciding in favor of one of the suggestions given. For instance, which delivery method or which parcel handover option should be selected. The possible routes are not yet visualized and cannot be compared. Furthermore, the map presenting suggestions for rescheduling was found to be uninteresting by two of the test subjects. They choose the first suggestion without detailed consideration. Instead, the recommender must provide enhanced support. This should clearly highlight and visualize all options and their advantages and disadvantages.

Secondly, it was emphasized that every click is too many for dispatchers. The application should be designed to require as few steps as possible to complete the main functions. For instance, a space-saving, collapsible menu bar is irrelevant because the menu will be permanently open.

Furthermore, there was a prevalence of misinterpretations regarding certain terminology. Terms were interpreted differently than intended. This experience underscores the importance of incorporating either icons, a legend, or a tooltip to enhance user comprehension.

The evaluation provided valuable insights into the effectiveness of the application and how users perceive it. These emphasize the importance of simplifying complex decisions and the need for precise terminology and interactive elements. Key problems were identified through interviews and observations. This resulted in possible suggestions for action, which ultimately led to an improved version of the prototype.

6   Results

The research questions have been designed to address the identified problems and solve them to the greatest extent possible. The focus was on the desire for an elaborate concept and a user-centered control station that relieves the user and makes the workflow efficient. To this end, the typical information density of a control station was examined, leading to a solution with defined processes and clear solution paths.

RQ1 is answered by the prototype developed, which represents a possible solution for integrating UXD and UID principles such as user centricity, personalization, intuitive user guidance, uniformity and controllability. It serves as a practical example and was further developed in light of the UCD. The iterative testing phase led to several optimizations and improved the user-friendliness. In Fig. 2, the developed application's dashboard provides an overview of all current issues and notifications. Furthermore, additional details are visualized in a map view, alongside other information.

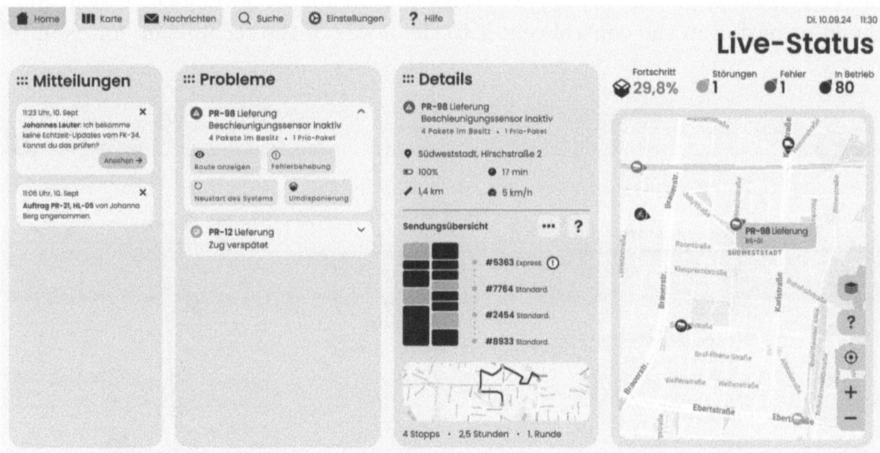

Fig. 2. Dashboard of the control center

To answer RQ2 and respond to user needs and situations, an adaptive function such as the recommender can be installed. This offers the user various suggestions depending on the situation. The user experience is improved by pre-defined views, suggested actions and ideas for personalization. Figure 3 shows the map view that is used to reschedule parcels. The application calculates alternative routes to deliver parcels using other delivery methods.

In relation to RQ3, multi-device use was only supported to a limited extent, as control centers generally require multiple screens with a high information

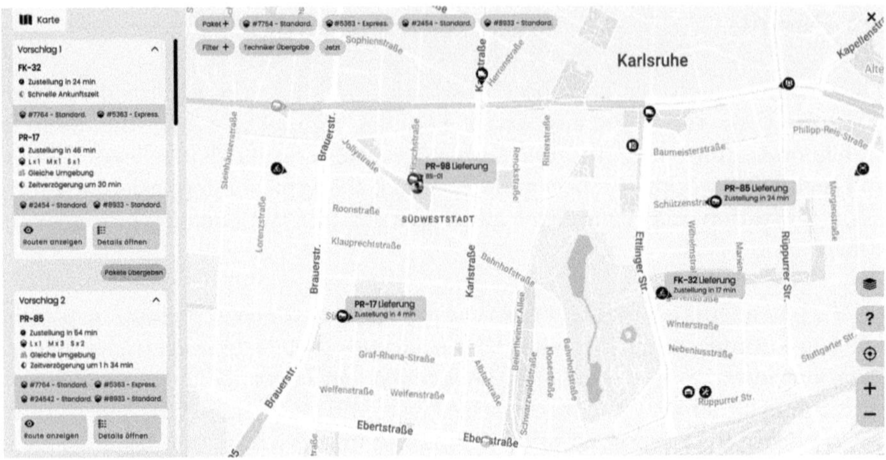

Fig. 3. Map visualizes all delivery staff in the area

density. Nevertheless, a mobile version is useful for technicians, for example. A tablet version with customised functions was therefore developed, which tailors the information in the control center to the needs of the technician, for example,

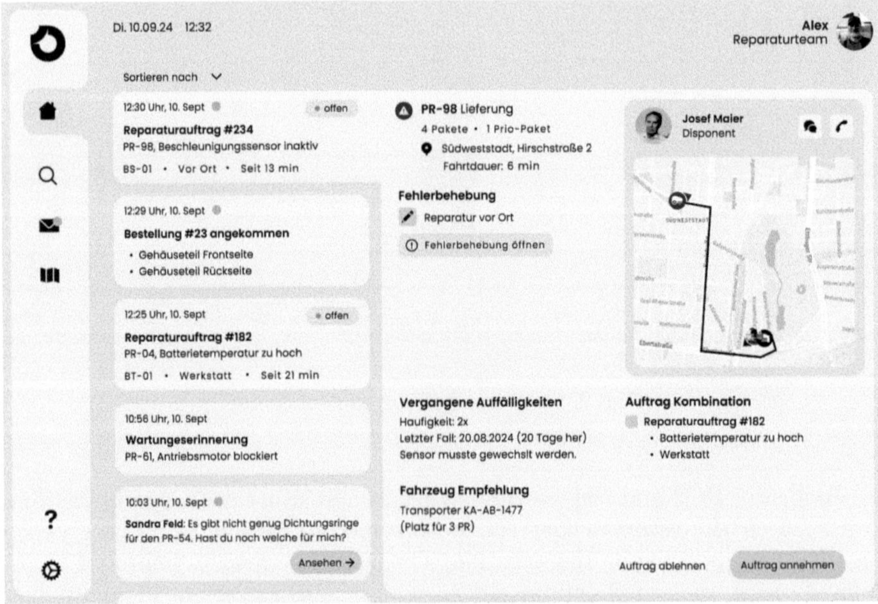

Fig. 4. Tablet version for the technician

in the event of a defective robot. In this case, the technician is shown various options for rectifying the issue, as shown in Fig. 4.

The scope of multi-device use can be further expanded. For instance, a visualization of control center information can be developed for a large display on the wall. The development of communication between delivery staff and the relevant control center information can be further advanced through the utilization of smartphone or smartwatch applications. If bicycle couriers, delivery vans and drones are not part of an external service, they can be connected to the system via their own application. This allows the delivery staff to receive all the necessary information along the way and be navigated.

7 Discussion and Conclusion

The primary success of the study lies in the fact that initial optimizations could be made without the necessity of conducting interviews with the dispatchers. Conducting a subsequent study with the participation of dispatchers could yield novel insights, as individuals with specialized expertise can evaluate the efficacy and practicality of the functions. A further step would be to test the concept or the application in operation. The evaluation under real-world conditions could provide further insights and show how the system proves itself in practical performance.

Furthermore, the development of adaptive user interfaces is not supported by any usability principles. Therefore, a research approach could be to develop missing specific guidelines that facilitate the development of user-friendly adaptive applications. These principles should clarify questions such as, which types of adaptive applications are more helpful than others and in which context? How much and how deeply should adaptive functions intervene so that there is no loss of control from the user's perspective? When should the user interface be allowed to adapt to individual user habits without causing confusion? Conceivable principles could be: simplicity, transparency and traceability of changes or reactions, context-related, consideration of the user experience, customizable adjustments and feedback.

Acknowledgements. This work is connected to the project regioKArgoTram-Train (Funding ID: RegioInn-24577775), which is funded by the European Regional Development Fund (ERDF) in Baden-Württemberg. Another component of this study is derived from the IADAPT project (grant number 13FH056KA2), which is funded by the Federal Ministry of Education and Research. **Disclosure of Interests.** The authors have no competing interests to declare that are relevant to the content of this article. Thomas Schlegel is a member of the MobiTAS program committee.

References

1. Blair-Early, A., Zender, M.: User interface design principles for interaction design. Des. Issues **24**(3), 85–107 (2008)

2. Castillo, V.E., Bell, J.E., Rose, W.J., Rodrigues, A.M.: Crowdsourcing last mile delivery: strategic implications and future research directions. J. Bus. Logist. **39**(1), 7–25 (2018)
3. Evers, C., Kniewel, R., Geihs, K., Schmidt, L.: The user in the loop: Enabling user participation for self-adaptive applications. Futur. Gener. Comput. Syst. **34**, 110–123 (2014)
4. Ferreira, Y., Aygün, M., Vogt, J., Zweck, B.M.: Informationsmenge als Indikator psychischer Belastung. Z. Arbeitswissensch. **77**(2), 173 (2023)
5. Gajos, K.Z., Czerwinski, M., Tan, D.S., Weld, D.S.: Exploring the design space for adaptive graphical user interfaces. In: Proceedings of the working conference on Advanced visual interfaces (2006), pp. 201–208
6. Giuffrida, M., Perotti, S., Tumino, A., Villois, V.: Developing a prototype platform to manage intelligent communication systems in intermodal transport. Transp. Res. Proc. **55**, 1320–1327 (2021)
7. Hussain, J., Ul Hassan, A., Muhammad Bilal, H.S., Ali, R., Afzal, M., Hussain, S., Lee, S.: Model-based adaptive user interface based on context and user experience evaluation. J. Multimod. User Interfaces **12**, 1–16 (2018)
8. IIIUS. regioKArgoTramTrain (2025). https://iiius.de/laufende-projekte/regiokargotramtrain/. Accessed 24 Feb 2025
9. IIIUS. IADAPT (2025). https://iiius.de/laufende-projekte/iadapt/. Accessed 24 Feb 2025
10. Levin, M.: Designing multi-device experiences: an ecosystem approach to user experiences across devices. O'Reilly Media, Inc. (2014)
11. Schwarz, T., Kehr, F., Oortmann, H., Reiterer, H.: Die Leitwarte von heute verstehen-die Leitwarte von morgen gestalten!. In: MuC (2010), pp. 94–99
12. Wolf, J., Schneider, D., Tjaden, S., Ziegenbein, J.: Konzeption einer Leitstelle für einen kombinierten Personen-und Gütertransport im ÖPNV mit autonomen Shuttles und Transportrobotern. J. Mobilität Verkehr **21**, S.75–83

Development of Transport Control Systems: Impact of Communication Barriers

Joshua Kopp[1]([envelope]) [iD], Finn Schiedner[1], Marie Güntert[2] [iD], Ann-Kristin M. Jaros[1],
Hanna Schumm[1] [iD], Jonathan Rissler[2], Thomas Schlegel[2] [iD],
and Verena Wagner-Hartl[1] [iD]

[1] Department of Industrial Technologies, Campus Tuttlingen, Furtwangen University,
Tuttlingen, Germany
{joshua.kopp,hanna.schumm,verena.wagner-hartl}@hs-furtwangen.de,
{fsc46108,aja49071}@stud.hs-furtwangen.de
[2] Institute for Intelligent Interactive Ubiquitous Systems, Furtwangen University, Furtwangen,
Germany
{marie.guentert,jonathan.rissler,
thomas.schlegel}@hs-furtwangen.de

Abstract. Intermodal Transport Control Systems (ITCS) are critical for managing dynamic public transport operations. Communication between drivers and dispatchers is essential, especially during disruptions caused by construction, accidents, or delays. Language barriers which nowadays become more and more relevant due to the shortage of domestic skilled workers and the influx of international staff, can elevate stress levels and hinder effective communication. Therefore, the aim of the presented exploratory study was to investigate the impact of communication barriers on the efficiency and workload of drivers and dispatchers. Overall, 36 participants participated in the experiment. Three language conditions (German, English, AI translation from English to German) and the presence or absence of background noise during radio communication were examined as independent variables. Furthermore, all participants completed tasks in both roles: (tram) driver and dispatcher. The findings highlight the significant influence of language barriers and noise on communication efficiency and workload. In summary, the results provide valuable insights to optimize ITCS user interfaces, especially in multilingual and high-stress environments.

Keywords: Transport Control Systems · Communication Barriers · Human Factors.

1 Introduction

Disruptions to local public transport are a recurring phenomenon, often precipitated by factors such as construction work, accidents or personal injury [1]. These disruptions can result in delays or cancellations. In order to resolve these disruptions quickly and with as little impact on passengers as possible, it is important to ensure a proper communication between the drivers of the respective vehicles and the dispatchers in the control center. If

P.-L.P. Rau and H. Krömker (Eds.): HCII 2025, LNCS 16336, pp. 261–274, 2026.
https://doi.org/10.1007/978-3-032-12798-3_16

this is not possible, this may cause stress, especially if language barriers between drivers and dispatchers do exist [2].

With demographic changes and increasing attention on climate objectives, leading to an expansion of public transportation systems, German public transportation faces a shortage of skilled labor that is projected to increase in the near future [3]. For this reason, skilled migrant labor from non-German European (EU) countries is becoming increasingly important in this sector [4]. Nonetheless, the presence of a more diverse range of nationalities and linguistic capabilities can result in challenges pertaining to effective communication. To overcome these possible language barriers, commercial real-time translators like "Microsoft Translator" [5] are already available for public use. Furthermore, tools like "EA TONI" [6] utilize AI to improve detection of languages and live translation as well as transcription in a more specific manner. Other sections such as healthcare have already shown that AI translators can be used to overcome language barriers [7, 8]. For example, AI can be used in clinical environments to help medical staff communicate with patients [7]. Panayiotou et al. [8] demonstrated the efficacy of translation applications in facilitating communication between healthcare professionals and non-native patients. However, it is important to note that these applications are not capable of replacing professional interpreters. A significant concern in the domain of AI translation pertains to the presence of background noise, which has the potential to disrupt the voices detected by microphones.

Additionally, the role of traffic noise should be considered, especially in urban areas a traffic noise level of 55 db(A) and much higher is not uncommon, with public transport representing a large contributor to this noise [9]. Furthermore, a public transport bus driving at 50 km/h can reach noise levels of 75–80 db(A), which is comparable to the combined noise of four passenger cars going the same speed [10]. It was also shown that perceived disturbance of communication increases with higher noise pollution [11]. Moreover, it is not possible to block out noise, as hearing is a permanent process during which the brain absorbs, filters and interprets acoustic information in order to be able to react to it [12–14]. Furthermore, background noise, even of moderate intensity, can lead to an increased workload and negatively affect cognitive performance as well as well-being, especially when they are exposed to the human auditory system for an extended period (e.g. [15–17]).

In general, cognitive, emotional or social processes are typically linked to physiological reactions [18]. Such psychophysiological responses like cardiovascular or electrodermal activity can reveal valuable information about otherwise hidden processes, such as workload while driving and communicating. According to Gaillard et al. [19] psychophysiological measurement methods are highly effective for assessing workload because they provide objective, direct insight into physiological responses. Furthermore, these responses are associated with emotional and mental demands in the workplace. Xie et al. [20] already showed that bus drivers are often confronted with a high amount of workload during a normal workday.

The aim of the presented study was to investigate the effect of communication barriers between drivers and dispatchers on the efficiency and effectiveness of public transport services. Therefore, the following research questions should be answered: Is there an influence of the type of communication (German / English / AI translation English-to-German) on the (1) communication time / (2) number of communication errors / (3) number of steps required to achieve the goal / (4) subjectively perceived workload / (5) psychophysiological responses of the cardiovascular (ECG) and electrodermal (EDA) activity of the participants depending on the role assumed (driver/dispatcher) and the interference caused by background noise (with/without)?

2   Method

2.1   Participants

Overall, 37 participants took part in the exploratory study. One participant had to be excluded due to technical problems, so that the final sample consists of 36 participants (23 male, 13 female) aged between 19 and 38 years ($M = 24.08$, $SD = 4.24$). With regard to the participants' educational background, 8.3% had undergone vocational training, apprenticeship 55.6% had completed secondary education (i.e. the German Abitur), and 36.1% had obtained a university degree. Most of the participants were students (86.1%), 8.3% were employees, or seeking for employment (5.4%). Regarding sensory impairments, 61.1% of the participants were vision corrected (short-sightedness) and one participant was hearing impaired with a hearing aid. Pure tone audiometry (MAICO ST 20 audiometer) was used to screen participant's hearing abilities. Following WHO guidelines [21] and the recommendations of the European Working Group on Genetics of Hearing Impairment (EUWG, [22]), pure-tone average (PTA) of 0.5, 1, 2, and 4 kHz was calculated. Participants' hearing loss (HL) ranged from 5.75 to 26.00 pure tone average (PTA) dB HL ($M = 11.79$, $SD = 4.37$) for their poorer hearing ear. In former research [23, 24] regarding mild hearing impairment on working performance as well as other work-related effects, the criterion to be included in the hearing impaired group was a worse ear hearing loss of 15 dB or more on a minimum of two out of the four (speech relevant) frequencies 0.5, 1, 2, and 4 kHz. Following this criterion, 8 of the 36 participants (22.22%) were (mild) hearing impaired. All participants provided their informed consent at the beginning of the study and participated in the study voluntarily. The study was approved by the ethical committee of Furtwangen University (24 - 082).

2.2   Study Design and Materials

The exploratory study used a 2x2x3 mixed design. The study design is shown in Fig. 1. The following independent variables were used: IV1 type of communication was operationalized via three different language resp. communication scenarios resulting in three different groups: German, English and English-to-German AI translation. The participants were randomly assigned to each group. No significant differences were shown neither for the three groups regarding hearing impairment, $F(2, 32) = .34$, $p = .717$, $\eta_{part.}^2 = .021$, nor regarding age, $F(2, 33) = 2.76$, $p = .078$, $\eta_{part.}^2 = .143$. The second independent variable (IV2) background noise was operationalized with two different levels during radio communication, one with (white noise, 64 dB) and one without background noise. Again, the participants were randomly assigned to a group. Both groups were not significantly different in terms of hearing impairment, $t(33) = -.62, p = .542$, and age, $t(34) = -.12, p = .908$. Furthermore, all participants completed tasks in both roles: (tram) driver and dispatcher (IV3, measurement repetition factor).

Noise		Dispatcher/Driver		
	Yes	6	6	6
	No	6	6	6
		German	English	AI-Translation
		Different ways of communication		

Fig. 1. Study design.

To answer the research questions presented in Sect. 1, the following dependent variables were measured: DV1 communication time was measured as the duration time (in minutes) between the initial fault report given by the driver and the identification of the correct position of the affected public transportation by the dispatcher. The second dependent variable (DV2) was the number of communication errors operationalized as frequency of errors in determining the location by the dispatcher. Furthermore, the number of attempts needed to reach the location respectively number of steps required to achieve the goal (DV3) was counted. DV4 represented the subjective perceived workload of the participants measured assessing the NASA Task Load Index (NASA-TLX; [25, 26]), which was assessed after each trial (driver, dispatcher). Additionally, objective psychophysiological parameters of the cardiovascular (ECG; DV5) and electrodermal activity (EDA; DV6) were measured while the participants performed the different tasks. Both were recorded using the respective movisens move4 sensors [27, 28]. Regarding the cardiovascular responses heart rate (HR) and heart rate variability (HRV) were used (measured using a chest strap). For EDA, measured on the left hand of the participants to prevent interference from mouse usage during the study, the parameters skin conductance level (SCL), NS.SCR, and mean sum amplitude (sum amplitude/NS.SCR) were analyzed. All psychophysiological parameters were baseline-corrected.

2.3 Study Procedure

The exploratory study was conducted in a laboratory at Campus Tuttlingen of the Furtwangen University. The laboratory was divided into two rooms, with a soundproof acoustic cabin being utilized for this purpose. The cabin was used to simulate the public transportation system in which the participants sat when they were in the experimental role of a driver. To be as near as possible to the real situation of a driver and a dispatcher, the participant and the investigator communicated only through an intercom system during the tasks. Therefore, the dispatchers' simulated workplace was outside the soundproof acoustic cabin.

At the beginning of the exploratory study, the participants were welcomed and informed about the study procedure. Afterwards they gave their informed consent and were asked about their sociodemographic data. As the presented results were part of a greater study, different questionnaires and psychological tests like the Recovery Stress Questionnaire (RESTQ; [29, 30]), the Big-Five Structure Inventory (BFSI; [31]), and the Visual Memory Test (VISGED; [32]) were completed using the Vienna Test System [33], a computer-based diagnostic tool developed by SCHUHFRIED GmbH. Afterwards the participants assessed their subjectively perceived workload using the NASA-TLX [25]. Participants were then equipped with the psychophysiological measures to record cardiovascular and electrodermal activity [27, 28]. The next step was to enter the sound-proof acoustic cabin, followed by the pure tone audiometry (MAICO ST 20 audiometer) for both ears. Next, the investigator informed and guided the participants through the study, first having them assume the roles of a driver in public transportation. The participants always started with the drivers' role which was used to stay as close as possible on the real conditions. For instance, during a standard dispatcher training the employees are required to work first as drivers before they can begin dispatcher training. A baseline measurement of three minutes was conducted before the first scenario. Afterwards, the first scenario started in which the participants were asked to act like a tram driver who was experiencing a technical breakdown in the greater Zurich area. The location of the breakdown was displayed via a Google Street View-based web application, and the participants had to describe the scene verbally to the dispatcher (experimental assistant who played this role) to gain help and more information regarding their next steps. Depending on the group they were randomly assigned to, they had to explain their problem and help the dispatcher to locate the tram using German, English, or the English-to-German translation provided by the AI translator using the intercom system depending on their assigned group with or without background noise which was played by an extra speaker. They were allowed to use the Google Street View-based web application to get more information about their location. This application provided a lot of details about the scenery, and they could use the zoom function to help improve location identification. The task was finished when the dispatcher was able to locate the tram. Afterwards the participants had to assess their perceived task load via NASA-TLX [25], followed by another resting period of 90 s before the start of the second scenario. In the second scenario, roles were reversed: participants acted as dispatchers while the experimental assistant played the tram driver. When the second task was accomplished, the participants had to assess their perceived task load via NASA-TLX [25] again, followed by a resting measurement of 90 s. Then the measurement equipment was removed, and as a last step, the study concluded with a post-interview and the participants were thanked and dismissed. Overall, each participant needed about 60–75 min to complete the study.

2.4 Statistical Analyses

IBM SPSS statistics and JASP were used to calculate the results. The statistical analyses were based on a significance level of 5%. Mixed ANOVAs were analyzed to answer the research questions.

3   Results

3.1   Communication Time

To examine the effects of the type of communication (German / English / AI translator) as well as background noise on the duration of communication (research question 1) depending on the role assumed (driver, dispatcher), a mixed ANOVA was analyzed. Following the results (see also Fig. 2), a significant interaction role x type of communication x background noise, $F(2, 30) = 3.74$, $p = .035$, $\eta^2_{part.} = .200$, a significant interaction role x type of communication, $F(2, 30) = 4.83$, $p = .015$, $\eta^2_{part.} = .244$, as well as significant effects of role, $F(1, 30) = 25.89$, $p < .001$, $\eta^2_{part.} = .463$, and type of communication, $F(2, 30) = 5.43$, $p = .010$, $\eta^2_{part.} = .141$, were shown. All other effects did not reach the level of significance. Post-hoc analyses (Tukey) revealed that participants acting as a tram driver who used an AI translation during the situation with background noise needed significantly longer than in the same condition using German or English (both $p < .001$), and significantly longer than all three types of language groups without background noise ($p < .001$, except for German – $p = .009$) as well as significantly longer than all six dispatcher groups ($p < .001$).

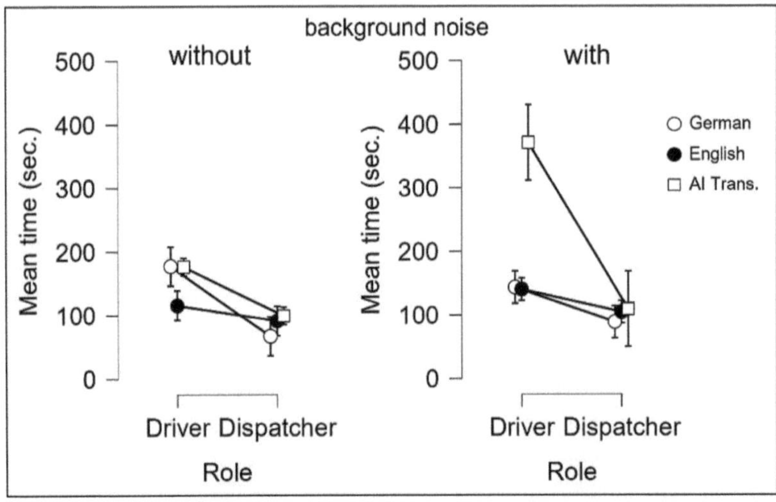

Note. I ... standard error of mean

Fig. 2. Communication time in seconds - significant interaction role x type of communication x background noise.

3.2   Communication Errors

To answer research question 2 regarding the effects of the type of communication (German / English / AI translator), background noise and role on the communication errors made during performing the task, the results of a mixed ANOVA showed a significant effect of the role the participants assumed, $F(1, 30) = 20.47, p < .001, \eta^2_{part.} = .406$. As presented in Fig. 3 significantly more communication errors were made during the task while the participants took the drivers' role than while he/she worked in the role of a dispatcher. All other effects did not reach the level of significance.

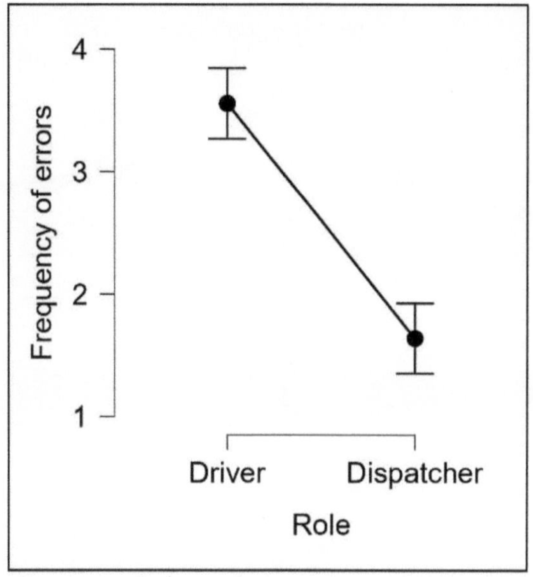

Note. I ... standard error of mean

Fig. 3. Communication Errors (frequency) by assumed role.

3.3 Steps to Accomplish the Task

Regarding the steps to achieve the goal respectively accomplish the task successfully (research question 3) a mixed ANOVA showed that none of the effects reached the level of significance of $\alpha = .05$.

3.4 Subjectively Perceived Workload

Following the results of a mixed ANOVA (research question 4), a significant interaction role x background noise, $F(1, 30) = 5.41, p = .027, \eta2part. = .153$, and a significant effect type of communication, $F(2, 30) = 4.04, p = .028, \eta2part. = .212$, was shown regarding the perceived workload of the participants (NASA-TLX; [25]; see Fig. 4). All other effects did not reach the level of significance.

Following post-hoc analyses (Sidak) there was a significant difference between the background noise condition and the condition without additional background noise for the role of dispatcher ($p = .031$). The Group without background noise perceived a significant higher workload than the group with background noise. Furthermore, communication in English resulted in a significantly higher perceived workload than communication in German ($p = .041$).

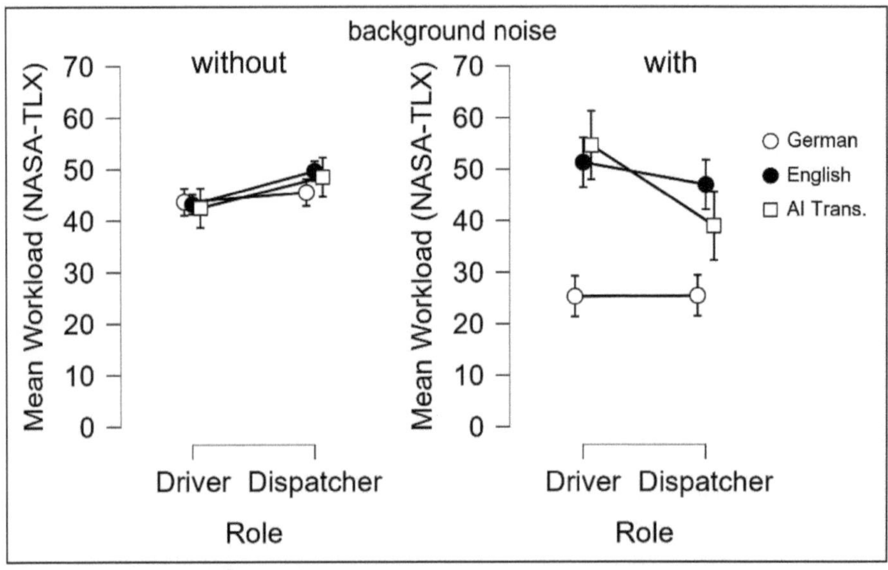

Note. I … standard error of mean

Fig. 4. Subjectively perceived Workload (NASA-TLX; [25]) by assumed role, type of communication and noise condition.

3.5 Psychophysiological Parameters

To answer the fifth research question psychophysiological responses of the cardiovascular (ECG) and electrodermal (EDA) activity of the participants were analyzed. Mixed ANOVAs showed for the cardiovascular parameter heart rate (HR) a significant interaction type of communication x background noise, $F(2, 30) = 3.94$, $p = .030$, $\eta^2_{part.} = .208$ (Fig. 5). Following post-hoc analyses (Sidak), in the German ($p = .036$) as well as in the English ($p = .043$) language condition the HR of the participants was significantly higher during the condition without background noise than when performing the task with background noise.

In addition, a mixed ANOVA showed significant differences for the role (repeated measurement factor) regarding the heart rate variability (HRV) of the participants while performing the different task, $F(1, 30) = 4.94$, $p = .034$, $\eta^2_{part.} = .141$ (Fig. 6). Following the results, the participants showed significantly higher heart rate variability while performing a task in the role of a driver than while performing the task in the role of a dispatcher. All other effects did not reach the level of significance.

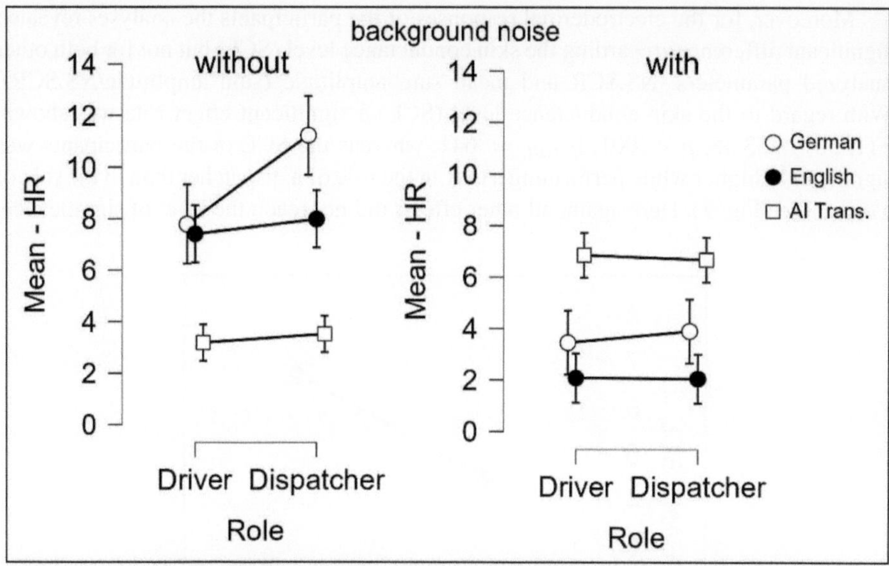

Note. I ... standard error of mean, all values were baseline-corrected

Fig. 5. Cardiovascular parameter heart rate (HR) by assumed role, type of communication and noise condition.

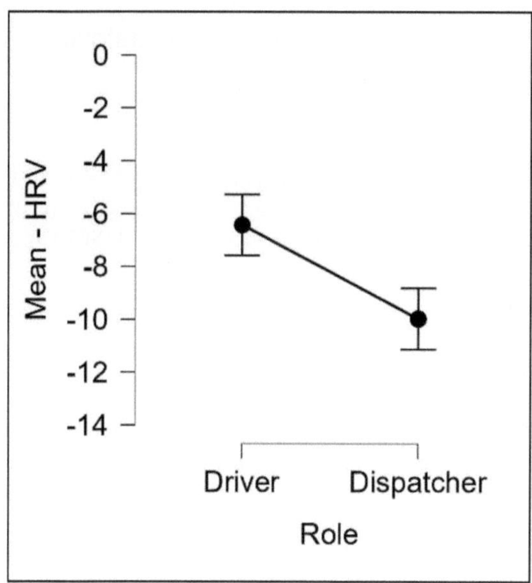

Note. I ... standard error of mean,
all values were baseline-corrected

Fig. 6. Cardiovascular parameter heart rate variability (HRV) by assumed role.

Moreover, for the electrodermal responses of the participants the analyses revealed significant differences regarding the skin conductance level (SCL) but not for both other analyzed parameters, NS.SCR and mean sum amplitude (sum amplitude/NS.SCR). With regard to the skin conductance level (SCL) a significant effect role was shown, $F(1, 30) = 53.48$, $p < .001$, $\eta^2_{part.} = .641$, whereas the SCL of the participants was significantly higher while performing a task in the role of a dispatcher than in the role of a driver (see Fig. 7). Here again, all other effects did not reach the level of significance.

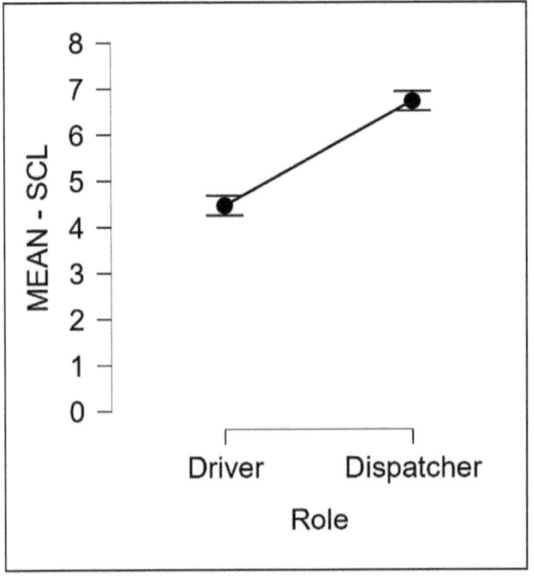

Note. I … standard error of mean,
all values were baseline-corrected

Fig. 7. Electrodermal parameter skin conductance level (SCL) by assumed role.

4 Discussion

The objective of the present study was to examine the impact of communication barriers on the efficiency and workload of drivers and dispatchers in public transport. It is posited that the results of the study will facilitate enhanced communication between drivers and dispatchers in the future, thereby overcoming any existing communication barriers.

In order to respond to the initial research question, the statistical analyses revealed that participants acting as a tram driver who used an AI translation during the situation with background noise needed significantly longer than in the same condition using English or German, and significantly longer than all three types of language groups without background noise as well as significantly longer than all six dispatcher groups. It is hypothesized that this may be due to the voice-based interaction with the AI translator. It is important to note that background noise may have interfered with the microphones, resulting in issues with speech recognition by the AI. Similarly, to white noise, disturbing background noise can occur in road traffic, which could also interfere with the microphones. It is conceivable that alternative instruments for artificial intelligence translation might employ noise cancellation techniques analogous to those utilized by Nvidia's RTX Voice [34].

Furthermore, a significantly higher number of errors had to be posed when the subjects assumed the role of the driver. The elevated number of errors necessitated in the initial scenario (driver) might be attributable to the learning effects of both the test subjects and the test supervisor. The latter were able to optimize their explanation strategies in the course of the tests, e.g., by focusing on street names, prominent buildings or shops. The post interview revealed that most of the participants tried to focus on these landmarks.

The third research question does not demonstrate statistical significance for the steps to accomplish the task, since none of the tests reached the level of statistical significance required for the study.

The analysis of the subjectively perceived workload data showed that the group without background noise in the role of the dispatcher perceived a significant higher workload compared to the condition with background noise. A further finding was a significant effect for the type of communication, with a significantly lower perceived workload in German compared to English. Without further information about the mother tongue of the participants, this could be due to the setting of a German university as main recruitment place. Studies by Wu et al. [35] demonstrate that communication in a non-native language led to an increased workload due to word-finding difficulties and a lower degree of automatization of speech production. These effects could also have occurred in the English and AI-Translated conditions.

The psychophysiological data demonstrated that additional noise exposure was associated with higher heart rate in the conditions German and English without noise in comparison with the condition with noise. A higher heart rate could indicate physical, mental or emotional strain [36]. In this case, the cognitive exercise caused mostly mental and emotional strain. In the post interview the participants have noted that the noise was not disturbing after a short period of time. As the participants began to concentrate on their exercise, they blocked out the noise.

In addition, significantly higher heart rate variability was observed in drivers compared to dispatchers. Decreased heart rate variability in both conditions may indicate (marked) less mental strain [37]. In this case, during performing the task in the role of a driver the participants experienced less mental strain because his heart rate variability decreased than in the dispatcher role. This could be attributed to the complexity of the tasks, which encompassed decision-making, prioritizing information, and multitasking. Furthermore, the participants had a significantly higher SCL in the dispatcher role than in the driver condition. According to Boucsein and Backs [37], a higher SCL indicates higher strain. This could be due to the before mentioned multitasking involved in the dispatcher role combined with the new and unusual exercise.

This study is subject to the same limitations as any other study: the sample is not fully representative or technical limitations like the interference of the microphones by

AI-Translations. Other limitations are the sequential effect of the roles and the difference between the locations of the participants in the role as driver.

Another interesting approach could be implementing trainings for driver and dispatcher to improve their communication. Based on procedures used in aviation the efficacy of standardized communication phrases could be implemented and tested further studies should takes this in account.

Another impressing approach could be to develop an AI that will start the conversation with the driver with the goal to get the most critical information like location, reason for call or what intervention is needed. This could be combined with the standardized phrases to get the needed information as fast as possible.

To sum it up the results can be seen as an important basis for the further development of the future user interfaces of Transport Control Systems. They can provide initial indications of the influence of communication between driver and dispatcher. Building on this, the results can help to improve existing systems and shall be used to support future developments and optimizations of user interfaces used within the important field of public transportation.

Acknowledgments. This work was funded by the Federal Ministry of Education and Research (BMBF) as part of the project IADAPT [FH-Kooperativ 1-2023: Intelligente User Interfaces für adaptive Leitstand-Systeme im öffentlichen Personenverkehr (IADAPT); 13FH056KA2]. We would like to thank Katharina Gleichauf, Jonas Birkle, and Valentin Wunsch for their support and all participants for their time and willingness to contribute to our study.

Disclosure of Interests The authors have no competing interests to declare that are relevant to the content of this article. An informed consent was obtained from all subjects involved in the study. The study was approved by the ethical committee of Furtwangen University (24 - 082).

References

1. Bachmann, F.R., Briem, L., Busch, F., Vortisch, P.: Dynamics and processes in operations control centers in urban public transport: potentials for improvement. IEEE Trans. Intell. Transp. Syst. **23**(10), 17819–17834 (2022)
2. Briem, L., Buck, H.S., Magdolen, M., Lange, L., Vortisch, P.: Incident Management in public transport – surveying dispatchers' actions. In: Association for European Transport (AET) (ed.) EUROPEAN TRANSPORT CONFERENCE 2020, pp. 1–10. AET (2020)
3. Verband Deutscher Verkehrsunternehmen (VDV) [Association of German Transport Companies], Personal- und Fachkräftebedarf im ÖPNV [Staff and skilled labour requirements in public transport]. https//www.vdv.de/personal-und-fachkraeftebedarf-im-oepnv.aspx. Last accessed 30 May 2025
4. Verband Deutscher Verkehrsunternehmen (VDV) [Association of German Transport Companies]. Maßnahmen gegen den Personalmangel im Fahrbetrieb. Für einen qualitativ hochwertigen ÖPNV [Measures against staff shortages in transport operations. For high-quality public transport]. Position paper/Jan 2023, VDV, Cologne (2023)
5. Microsoft translator. https://translator.microsoft.com. Last accessed 12 Feb 2025
6. WTG, EA-TONI. https://www.wtg.com/ea-toni. Last accessed 30 May 2025
7. Bahrami, S., Rubulotta, F.: Artificial intelligence-driven translation tools in intensive care, units for enhancing communication and research. Int. J. Environ. Res. Public Health. **22**(95), 1–7 (2025)

8. Panayiotou, A., et al.: Language translation apps in health care settings: expert opinion. JMIR Mhealth Uhealth. 7(4), e11316 (2019)
9. Laib, F., Braun, A., Rid, W.: Modelling noise reductions using electric buses in urban traffic. A case study from Stuttgart, Germany. Transp. Res. Procedia. 37, 377–384 (2019)
10. Annecke, R., et al.: Silence. Noise reduction in urban areas from traffic and driver management. A toolkit for city authorities. In: Ellebjerg, L. (ed.) WP H.1 Methods for Noise Control by Traffic Management, pp. 1–61. European Commission DG Research (2008)
11. Öhrström, E., Skånberg, A., Svensson, H., Gidlöf-Gunnarsson, A.: Effects of road traffic noise and the benefit of access to quietness. J. Sound Vib. 295, 40–59 (2006)
12. Babisch, W.: Noise and health. Environ. Health Perspect. 113(1), 14–15 (2005)
13. Genuit, K., Fiebig, A.: Prediction of psychoacoustic parameters. J. Acoust. Soc. Am. 118, 1874 (2005)
14. Overath, T., et al.: An information theoretic characterisation of auditory encoding. PLoS Biol. 5(11), 2723–2732 (2007)
15. Grenzebach, J., Romanus, E.: Quantifying the effect of noise on cognitive processes. A review of psychophysiological correlates of workload. Noise Health. 24(115), 199–214 (2022)
16. Ising, H., Babisch, W., Guski, R., Kruppa, B., Maschke, C.: Exposure and Effect Indicators of Environmental Noise. WHO, Berlin (2002)
17. Ramirez, J.M., Alvarado, J.M., Santisteban, C.: Individual differences in anger reaction to noise. Individ. Differ. Res. 2(2), 125–136 (2004)
18. Boucsein, W.: Psychophysiologische Methoden in der Ingenieurspsychologie [Psychophysiological methods in engineering psychology]. In: Sonderdruck aus Enzyklopädie der Psychologie: Themenbereich D Praxisgebiete: Serie III Wirtschafts-, Organisations- und Arbeitspsychologie, pp. 317–358. Hogrefe, Göttingen (2006)
19. Gaillard, A.W., Boucsein, W., Stern, J.: Psychophysiology of work-load. Biol. Psychol. 42(3), 245–247 (1996)
20. Xie, L., Zhang, J., Cheng, R.: Comprehensive evaluation of freeway driving risks based on fuzzy logic. Sustainability. 15(1), 810 (2023)
21. Mathers, C., Smith, A., Concha, M.: Global Burden of Hearing Loss in the Year 2000. Global Burdon of Disease. World Health Organization, Geneva (2000)
22. European Working Group on Genetics of Hearing Impairment [EUWG] (1996)
23. Wagner-Hartl, V., Kallus, K.W.: Investigation of psychophysiological and subjective effects of long working hours– do age and hearing impairment matter? Front. Psychol. 8, 2167 (2018)
24. Wagner-Hartl, V., Grossi, N.R., Kallus, K.W.: Impact of age and hearing impairment on work performance during long working hours. Int. J. Environ. Res. Public Health. 15(1), 98 (2018)
25. Hart, S.G., Staveland, L.E.: Development of NASA-TLX (Task Load Index): results of empirical and theoretical research. In: Hancock, P.A., Meshkati, N. (eds.) Human Mental Workload, vol. 198, pp. 139–183. North Holland Press, Amsterdam/London (1988)
26. Hart, S.G.: NASA-TASK LOAD INDEX (NASA-TLX); 20 years later. Proc. Hum. Factors Ergon. Soc. 50(9), 904–908 (2006)
27. ECG and Activity Sensor. EcgMove 4. Movisens. https://www.movisens.com/en/products/ecg-sensor/. Last accessed 31 May 2025
28. EDA and Activity Sensor. EdaMove 4. Movisens. https://www.movisens.com/en/products/eda-and-activity-sensor/. Last accessed 31 May 2025
29. Kallus, K.W.: Erholungs-Belastungs-Fragebogen [Recovery-Stress Questionnaire] EBF [RESTQ] – Manual. In: B. Bogner. Handanweisung, Wiener Test System [Manual, Vienna Test System]. SCHUHFRIED, Mödling (1999)
30. Kellmann, M., Kallus, K.W. (eds.): The Recovery-Stress Questionnaires: A User Manual. Routledge, London/New York (2025)
31. Arendasy, M.: Big-Five Struktur Inventar [Big-Five Structure Inventory] BFSI– Manual. Wiener Test System [Manual, Vienna Test System]. SCHUHFRIED, Mödling (2018)

32. Etzel S., Hornke, L.F.: Visueller Gedächtnistest [Visual Memory Test], VISGED – Manual. Wiener Test System [Manual, Vienna Test System]. SCHUHFRIED, Mödling (2018)
33. SCHUHFRIED: Vienna Test System. https://www.schuhfried.com/en/. Last accessed 31 Oct 2025
34. Nvidia: Nvidia Broadcast App. https://www.nvidia.com/de-de/geforce/broadcasting/broadcast-app/. Last accessed 10 June 2025
35. Wu, Y., et al.: Mental workload and language production in non-native speaker IPA interaction. In: Proceedings of the 2nd Conference on Conversational User Interfaces, pp. 1–8. ACM, Bilbao (2020)
36. Boucsein, W., Backs, W.R.: Engineering psychophysiology as a discipline: historical and theoretical aspects. In: Backs, W.R., Boucsein, W. (eds.) Engineering Psychophysiology: Issues and Applications, pp. 3–16. LEA, Mahwah (2000)
37. Boucsein, W., Backs, W.R.: The psychophysiology of emotion, arousal, and personality: methods and models. In: Duffy, V.G. (ed.) Handbook of Digital Human Modelling: Research and Applied Ergonomics and Human Factors Engineering, pp. 35.1–35.13. CRC, Boca Raton (2009)

Towards the Design of Model-Based Path Tracking Vehicle Control Aware of Tyres' Thermal and Wear State

Lorenzo Ponticelli$^{(\boxtimes)}$, Gianluca Pagano , Francesco Timpone ,
Gonçalo Sousa Torres , and Aleksandr Sakhnevych

University of Naples Federico II, Naples, Italy
`lorenzo.ponticelli@unina.it`

Abstract. Current Autonomous Vehicles (AVs) guidelines require increasingly stricter safety standards and aim towards developing sophisticated control logics to achieve multiple objectives in various scenarios. Indeed, major attention has been oriented towards meeting safety standards in high-velocity profile contexts where the reduction of accidents is closely related to the design of more accurate vehicle control logics. However, as the vehicle represents a intrinsically dynamic mechanical system, its operating (mass, tyre thermal and wear state) and external (weather) conditions continuously change and the performance of the controller can rapidly degrade, leading to increased safety-related risks and decreased comfort perception. This is mainly due to standard controllers not sharing their parameters with the vehicle since their calibration is usually performed in pre-defined conditions. To assess the impact of varying tyre and vehicle-related conditions, the path tracking scenario has been considered as it currently represents one of the most representative objectives when designing AVs control logics. For that purpose, a standard five-states lateral bicycle vehicle model with a Magic Formula (MF) model for tyre forces evaluation, has been employed in a Model Predictive Controller (MPC) framework with front steering as control signal. To the purpose of describing tyre wear state, a dedicated model considering the necessary working and boundary conditions, developed by the research group, has been considered. Various highway trajectories, at different speeds and road curvatures, have been simulated on a high-fidelity reference model of the real vehicle, employed as plant model. Simulations have been carried out by means of primary and secondary metrics: the former with the aim of evaluating path tracking performance through vehicle dynamics safety- and comfort-related indexes; while the latter employing tyre wear model to assess the degradation and overall environmental impact of the designed control logic.

Keywords: Vehicle sensing and control · Tyre thermal and wear state · Path tracking · Model-based control · Comfort perception

P.-L.P. Rau and H. Krömker (Eds.): HCII 2025, LNCS 16336, pp. 275–293, 2026.
https://doi.org/10.1007/978-3-032-12798-3_17

1 Introduction

In the complex scenario of future smart mobility, current research aims at defining more sophisticated control logics able to deliver automation along with safety requirements. The path tracking task [56,77] has represented a major research trend in the latest years, given the necessity of guiding the vehicle along a predefined path. A great number of studies and review articles [55,56,63,77] have been proposed on this subject. Different control strategies can be leveraged to effectively track a reference trajectory, including: Pure Pursuit [47,48,75,80], PID [1,23,50], Model-free control [43,69], LQR [29,40], Feedforward and Feedback [37,39], MPC [11,22,42,64–67], H_∞ [26,32,36] and SMC [9,25,53]. Among them, Model Predictive Control indeed appears as one of the most employed methodologies, given its ability of handling constraints and predict projected dynamics within a finite time horizon. As underlined by [56] a key point when designing an effective control logic is the definition of evaluation indexes, able to portray the accuracy and the effects of the controller's action on the vehicle system. However, in the context of Autonomous Vehicles (AVs), there is a clear need of pursuing performance along with safety and comfort. To this purpose, evaluation metrics often neglect the importance of the passengers, thus accepting solutions that may increase the occurrence of perceived discomfort up to motion sickness phenomenon [12,28,49,79]. Moreover, in a multi-objective context, mutual interactions between vehicle and human-centered factors [12,14] may appear and lead to intrinsically conflicting control objectives. This concept becomes crucial when looking towards the design of future vehicles, indeed being able to shape human perception through the knowledge of passenger's state is a challenging task. Furthermore, controller's calibration is often performed within standard operating ranges, not accounting for variation of parameters due to the external environment, vehicle's nature and operating conditions (i.e. tyres' thermal and wear states, mass, inertia, fuel consumption). Parameters are either considered to be constant within the controller's model or can be provided through parameters' observers. These methodologies mainly aim at vehicle's mass, inertia [54,68,78], tyre parameters [10,35,45,57] and road characteristics [2,24,34,68,70]; while employing Kalman filtering techniques [2,10,45] or data driven approaches (i.e. Recursive Least Squares RLS or Neural Networks [17,52,68]). However, recent works underlined the necessity of tyre thermal, pressure and wear states' knowledge [16] to improve estimation accuracy compared to traditional state observers [5,58]. To the best of authors' knowledge, there is a noticeable lack in solutions that take into account those aspects both in the vehicle sensing and control field of study. Based on the above considerations, this paper aims at analysing the influence of tyres' thermal and wear states on MPC controller for path tracking with fixed internal parameters (calibrated within normal operating ranges). The authors will employ a tyre wear model developed by their research group [59] to accurately assess tyres' performance degradation. To demonstrate the research objectives, various high-velocity profile testing scenarios will be simulated within co-simulation framework with a high-fidelity model of the real vehicle. The contribution of this paper can be summarized as:

- Evaluate the impact of tyres' thermal and wear state on path tracking accuracy and comfort perception with the aid of specific metrics. The study is oriented towards underlining the cross-domain interactions that may appear with a particular eye on passenger's comfort.
- Pave the road towards the integration of tyres' thermal and wear knowledge within advanced control logics to ensure adaptive responses aimed at mitigating discomfort and increasing road safety.

Therefore, the current work is structured as follows: the introduction of mathematical models is presented in Sect. 2, the MPC-based design of the control logic is discussed in Sect. 3 while the definition of evaluation metrics and the results can be found in Sect. 4. Finally, the conclusions are presented in Sect. 5.

2 Mathematical Modeling

2.1 Controller Model Description

The theory of Model Predictive Control introduces the need for a prediction model able to represent the dynamics of the controlled system. The path tracking task is here investigated through a simplified bicycle vehicle model [74] and Pacejka MF tyre model [46], whose equations are now summarized. The employed symbols and notation are described in Table 1. Besides the classical assumptions on bicycle model [21], here the longitudinal velocity is assumed to be constant and it is considered as an input for the model. The equilibrium equations can, therefore, be written as:

$$m\,\ddot{y} = (2\,Fy_f\,cos(\delta) + 2\,Fy_r) - \dot{\psi}\,Vx \tag{1}$$

$$I_z\,\ddot{\psi} = (2\,l_f\,Fy_f\,cos(\delta) - 2\,l_r\,Fy_r) \tag{2}$$

The lateral forces Fy_f, Fy_r are evaluated through the use of Pacejka formulation [46].

$$F_0 = D\,sin(C\,atan[B\,x_s - E(B\,x_s - atan(B\,x_s))]) + S_v \tag{3}$$

where

$$x_s = X_s + S_h \tag{4}$$

The independent variable X_s identifies the tyre slip angle, which can be evaluated as:

$$\alpha_f = atan\frac{(V_y + \dot{\psi}\,l_f)\,cos(\delta) - V_x\,sin(\delta)}{|V_x\,cos(\delta) + (V_y + \dot{\psi}\,l_f)sin(\delta)|} \tag{5}$$

$$\alpha_r = atan\frac{V_y - \dot{\psi}\,lr}{|V_x|} \tag{6}$$

The vertical loads are supposed constant and obtained from the mass distribution between front and rear axle. The described formulation refers to the pure condition F_0. The parameters are now introduced:

- B: stiffness factor;
- C: shape factor;
- D: peak value;
- E: curvature factor;
- S_v, S_h: shifts from Cartesian axes center.

Their value is derived from the tyre property file (.tir) microparameters using Pacejka's formulation. Finally, the conversion from body-fixed coordinate system to global inertial frame is performed to provide the path tracking controller with the global longitudinal and lateral positions of the vehicle [72]:

$$\dot{X} = V_x\,cos(\psi) - V_y\sin(\psi) \tag{7}$$

$$\dot{Y} = V_x\,sin(\psi) + V_y\cos(\psi) \tag{8}$$

Table 1. Vehicle model symbols and definition

Symbol	Definition
m	Vehicle mass
I_z	Moment of inertia about the z-axis
δ	Front steering angle
l_f	Distance from front axle to center of gravity
l_r	Distance from rear axle to center of gravity
Fy_f	Lateral force at front axle
Fy_r	Lateral force at rear axle
V_y	Lateral velocity of vehicle's CoG
V_x	Longitudinal velocity of vehicle's CoG
ψ	Yaw angle
X	x position of vehicle's CoG in the global inertial frame
Y	y position of vehicle's CoG in the global inertial frame

2.2 Wear Model Description

An accurate representation of tyres' behavior requires a multi-physical approach [59]: thermodynamic, structural and viscoelastic properties as well as speed and road roughness should be taken into account. Within the present work, the tyre wear model is derived from the research of Sakhnevych et al. [59]. The considered approach starts from the knowledge of relative velocity defined at the contact patch and the road roughness expressed in terms of macro parallel $\xi_{||}(m)$ and perpendicular $\xi_{\perp}(m)$ correlation lengths to define the excitation frequency f (Hz). The viscoelastic properties of the tyre are expressed with the definition of the storage modulus $\nabla E'(Pa)$ and the loss factor $\nabla tan(\delta)(-)$ for each node. Leveraging the temperature distribution $\nabla T(K)$, acquired through the adoption of a proper tyre thermal model [15,60] and the excitation frequency f from the compound master curve data [18,20] after applying the time-temperature superposition principle [61,73], instantaneous viscoelastic properties can be evaluated. Moreover, these quantities are then used to derive the $\nabla S - N$ damage curves for each node, which will be, subsequently, fed into the damage accumulation formulation. On the other hand, the generalized force vector $\overline{F} = [Fx, Fy, Fz]\ (N)$ defined at the contact patch and the viscoelastic properties are fed into the contact mechanism block to evaluate indentation levels and the stress-strain distribution curves. From those, the equivalent stress $\nabla \sigma_{eq}$ can be evaluated per each node. The last step employs Miner's methodology to define the cumulated damage, the value of which, for a selected material volume, can be expressed as:

$$D = \int_0^N \frac{dN}{Nf}(T, f) \tag{9}$$

where N refers to the number of non-identical cycles with a different temperature T and frequency level f. Therefore, the material removal depends on the damage level within the thread compound thickness. The overall functional scheme is proposed in Fig. 1.

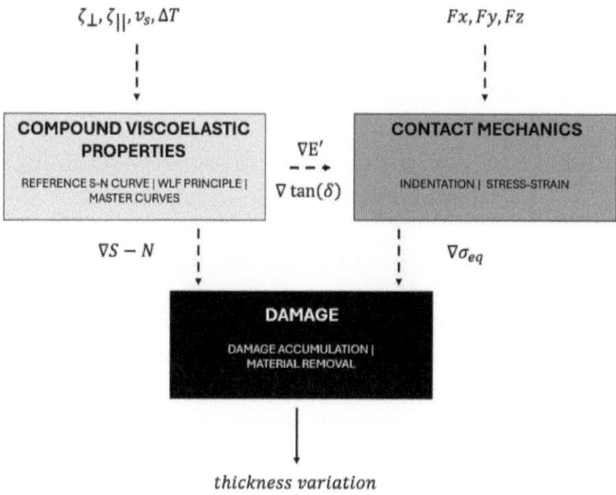

Fig. 1. Tyre wear model functional description

3   Design of Path Tracking Controller

Although linear MPC strategies [51,72] are normally preferred since computation load can be minimized, the present section aims at defining the NMPC (Nonlinear Model Predictive Control) strategy to track a reference trajectory. The objective is to compute a reliable sequence of control inputs: in this case the front steering angle δ has been chosen as control variable within the control horizon Nc (which is lower than the total prediction horizon). The control sequence should be chosen such that the error between the predicted behavior of the vehicle (obtained with the prediction model, see Sect. 2) and the reference trajectory ($X_{ref}, Y_{ref}, \psi_{ref}$) can be minimized. In CasADi [8], an open-source software in MATLAB environment, a non-linear programming problem (NLP) is formulated at sampling instant i by applying direct multiple shooting [6] to an optimal control problem (OCP) over the prediction horizon S. This is further divided into N shooting intervals $[s_0, s_{Nc}, \ldots, s_N]$, therefore the control problem aims at minimizing the cost function J, defined as:

$$J = \sum_{k=0}^{Nc} \frac{1}{2}||h_k(\xi_{k|i}, u_{k||i})||^2\, W + \sum_{k=Nc+1}^{N} \frac{1}{2}||h_k(\xi_{k|i}, u_{Nc||i})||^2\, W \tag{10}$$

$$s.t.\ 0 = \xi_{0|i} - \xi_0, \tag{11}$$

$$0 = \xi_{k+1|i} - \phi_k(\xi_{k|i}, u_{k|i}; p_{k|i}), k \in [0, N], \tag{12}$$

$$\underline{r}_{k|i} \leq r_k(\xi_{k|i}, u_{k|i}) \leq \overline{r}_{k|i}, k \in [0, N] \tag{13}$$

where ξ_0 represents the vehicle's state measurement, $\xi_{k|i}$ the systems states and $u_{k|i}$ are the control inputs. The vector p_k identifies the parameters which are fed as inputs to the model.

$$\xi = [X, Y, \psi, Vy, r]^T \tag{14}$$

$$u = [\delta]^T \tag{15}$$

Equation 12 refers to the continuity constraint and ϕ_k is a numerical integration operator which is able to solve system dynamics equation and evaluate the solution at s_{k+1}. The cost function for the controller:

$$h_k(\xi_k, u_k) = [e_X, e_Y, e_\psi]^T \tag{16}$$

where e_X, e_Y and e_ψ are the errors between the predicted states and the reference trajectory. Lastly, r_k express the constraints based on vehicle states, they are bounded by the values of $\underline{r}_k$ and $\overline{r}_k$. The values of N and Nc are chosen according to literature on path tracking control problem, considering the timestep $dt = 0.01s$. Once those values are set, an optimization strategy based on surrogateopt MATLAB function has been performed to find the value of each weight W such that, within a fixed period of time, the path tracking error can be minimized.

4   Simulation

4.1   Plant Model Description

Firstly, it is necessary to describe the vehicle's plant model: it includes 14 DoFs with 5 rigid parts (6 DoF chassis + 4 2DoF wheels). It was developed within the VI-CarRealTime [71] environment to ensure high-fidelity real-time vehicle dynamics simulation. A test vehicle was chosen as a reference for the validation of the digital twin, further details can be found in previous works by the authors' research group [58]. For sake of completeness, some of the relevant parameters, are summarized in Table 2.

Table 2. Vehicle parameter

Parameter name	Value	Units
Vehicle mass	1197.5	kg
Unsprung mass	200	kg
Wheelbase	2.31	m
Front wheelbase	1.088	m
Front track width	1.495	m
Rear track width	1.505	m
CG height	0.489	m
Front roll center height	0.0767	m
Rear roll center height	0.2084	m
Moment of inertia about the z-axis	950	$kg\,m^2$
Nominal steer ratio	14.2	–

For the purpose of describing tyres' thermodynamic state variation within the plant model, the *.tir* property file (which includes all the parameters able to describe tyre-road interaction characteristics [58,62]) has been modified accordingly. In particular, the lateral grip and cornering stiffness have been adapted through scaling coefficients, whose values can be obtained using pre-calibrated three-dimensional maps (Figs. 2 and 3). These maps are evaluated leveraging a tyre thermal model [15] whose calibration has been performed through an identification routine based on non-destructive test methodologies [3,19].

4.2   DOE

Given the nature of the wear degradation phenomenon, it is known that major effects can be associated to cornering maneuvers with moderate/high velocity. Emergency scenarios are not considered throughout the present work as they rarely occur during the life cycle of a passenger tyre. The proposed scenario is represented by high-velocity turning maneuvers, mainly reproducing the vehicle's behavior in highways.

To properly design a reference trajectory, the geometric road curvature has to be chosen within the adherence limits to ensure that the vehicle remains safe during its operation. Different authors refer to this issue [27,33,44], however the general approach derives from AASHTO 2011 [4] where the minimum radius of curvature R_{min} is evaluated as:

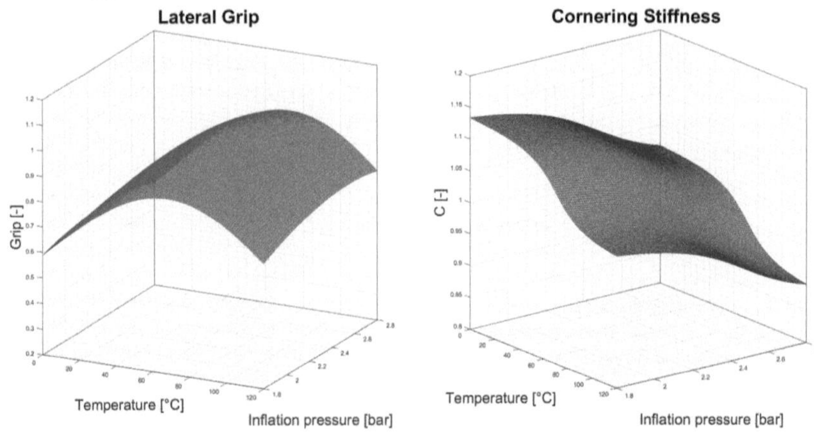

Fig. 2. Tyre's lateral grip dependencies on temperature and pressure

Fig. 3. Tyre's cornering stiffness dependencies on temperature and pressure

$$R_{min} = \frac{V^2}{15(0.01e_{max} + f_{max})} \tag{17}$$

where V is the design speed, e_{max} the maximum rate of roadway superelevation and f_{max} the maximum side friction factor. This latter parameter can be associated with the vehicle velocity (i.e. for $V = 60\,\text{km/h}, f_{max} = 0.17$, for $V = 80\,\text{km/h}, f_{max} = 0.13$)

Three vehicle velocities have been chosen ($V = [60, 80, 100]\,\text{km/h}$), the superelevation level is set to $e_{max} = 0.07$ and, considering m_{ref} as the nominal value of vehicle mass (see Table 2), three values are investigated ($m = [m_{ref}, m_{ref} + 80, m_{ref} - 80]\,\text{kg}$). These three conditions are chosen to include either the introduction or removal of a passenger. Additionally, for the tyres' thermal and pressure states, five conditions have been considered:

- (T_{nom}, P_{nom}) where both temperature and pressure are considered at their nominal levels.
- (T_{min}, P_{nom}) where the temperature is lowered to represent colder weather conditions.
- (T_{min}, P_{min}) where both temperature and pressure are at their minimum value.
- (T_{max}, P_{nom}) where the temperature is increased to represent warmer weather conditions.
- (T_{max}, P_{max}) where both temperature and pressure are at their maximum value.

4.3   Metrics definition

To quantitatively identify the impact of different working conditions on both path tracking accuracy, comfort and tyre wear, primary and secondary metrics have been chosen. The primary ones aim at identifying the accuracy of the path tracking task and the comfort level perceived by the passenger; to the first objective, literature works [38,74] suggest a combination of lateral and orientation error between the reference path and the actual vehicle position and orientation. In the current paper, the following indexes have been considered:

- Total euclidean distance *dist*: the sum of the euclidean distances between each point of the reference trajectory with respect to the actual trajectory of the vehicle subjected to the control action
- Maximum orientation error between the reference and the actual vehicle e_ψ
- Maximum and mean value of the vehicle sideslip angle $\beta_{max}, \beta_{mean}$
- Maximum and mean value of the vehicle yaw rate r_{max}, r_{mean}

On the other hand, comfort perception has been shown to be related with lateral acceleration and its change [7]. Vehicle motion is translated into a system of inputs applied to human body, ultimately representing a major factor that can abruptly modify the overall driving experience. More generally, in complex manoeuvres, the effects of combined motion along x-axis and z-axis cannot be neglected, leading to the necessity of a three-axial measurement of the vehicle's acceleration and angular velocity vector to develop advanced passengers' prediction models [41]. Although simplified, a classical approach is based on the standard ISO 2631 [31] which evaluates the level of exposure of the human body to external vibrations by means of weighted root-mean-square RMS acceleration. Other studies [13,30] mention the importance of lateral jerk using the peak value or the RMS and the correlation with perceived comfort. For these reasons, the considered metrics are here summarized:

- Maximum and mean value of lateral acceleration ay_{max}, ay_m
- Maximum and RMS lateral jerk j_{max}, j_{RMS}
- Weighted acceleration [31] $a_w = (\frac{1}{T} \int_0^T a_w^2(t) \, dt)^{1/2}$

Lastly, within the secondary metrics, the wear effect is considered; here the amount of material removed W is evaluated at each wheel $W_{FL}, W_{FR}, W_{RL}, W_{RR}$, for each side of the vehicle W_L, W_R and as mean between all the tyres W_m. This quantity can be easily identified from the knowledge of the tread thickness $thickness = (1 - W) \, thickness_{nominal}$.

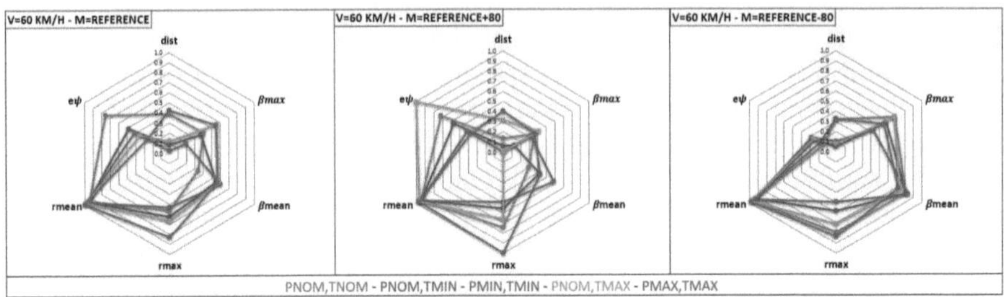

Fig. 4. Simulation results, primary metrics on path tracking performance, V = 60 km/h with varying mass conditions.

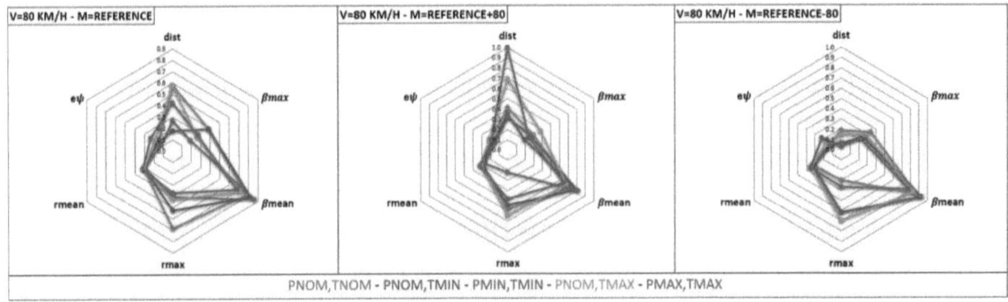

Fig. 5. Simulation results, primary metrics on path tracking performance, V = 80 km/h with varying mass conditions

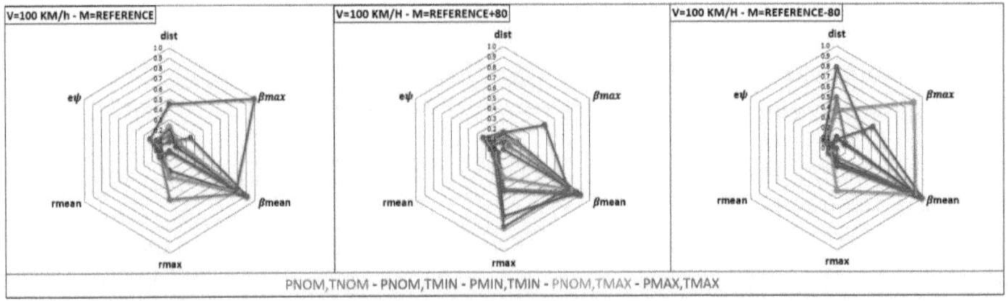

Fig. 6. Simulation results, primary metrics on path tracking performance, V = 100 km/h with varying mass conditions

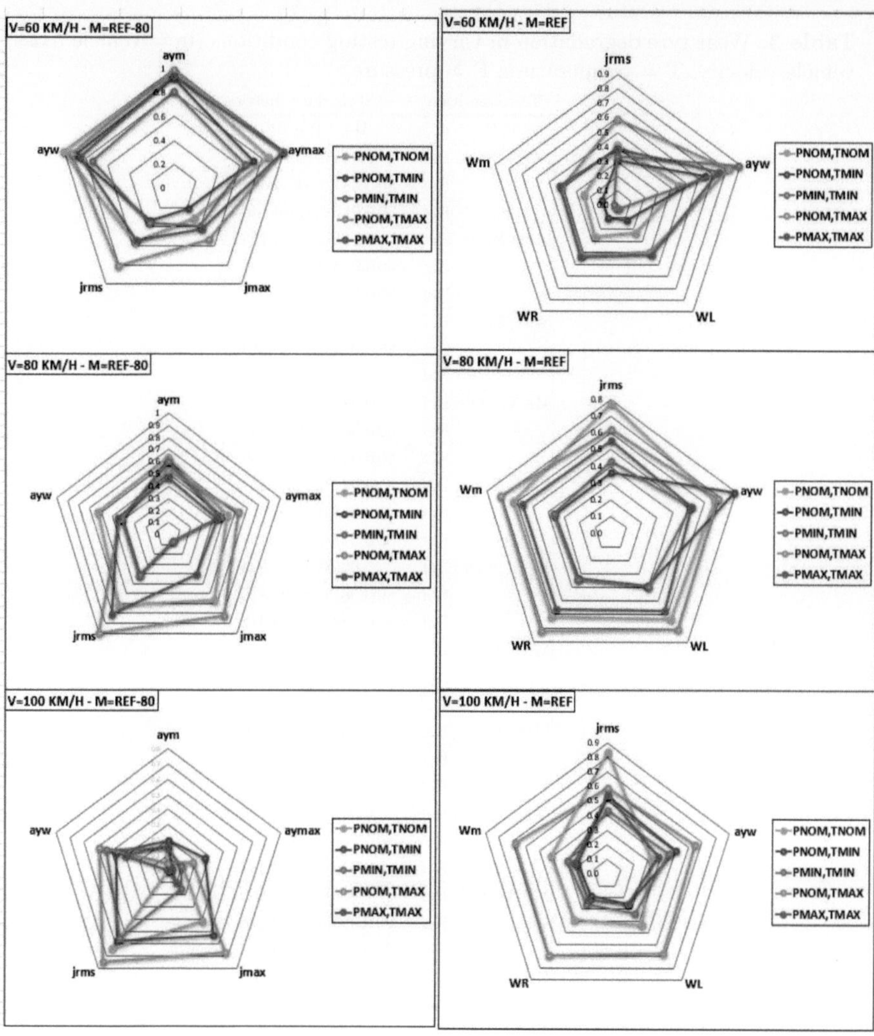

Fig. 7. Simulation results, primary metrics on comfort, m = ref-80 kg and varying velocity

Fig. 8. Interactions between different metrics. Different T,P conditions, same vehicle mass and varying velocity

4.4   Results and Discussion

Simulations were performed within MATLAB/Simulink environment on a PC employing WINDOWS 11 with a 13th Gen Intel(R) Core(TM) i7-1370P @1.90 GHz. Primary and secondary metrics have been scaled through min-max methodology to be able to compare them. For primary metrics, path results of tracking performance are summarized in Fig. 4, 5 and 6. The major remarks

Table 3. Wear tyre degradation in varying testing conditions (m = vehicle mass, V = vehicle velocity, T = temperature, P = pressure)

Test conditions			Secondary metrics		
V	T/P	m	W_L	W_R	W_m
60	NOM/NOM	Ref	0.024	0.926	0.245
		Ref + 80	0.041	0.942	0.401
		Ref − 80	0.017	0.921	0.186
	MIN/NOM	Ref	0.013	0.911	0.115
		Ref + 80	0.025	0.923	0.233
		Ref − 80	0.002	0.902	0.021
	MIN/MIN	Ref	0.008	0.905	0.060
		Ref + 80	0.024	0.919	0.210
		Ref − 80	0.000	0.900	0.000
	MAX/NOM	Ref	0.042	0.942	0.410
		Ref + 80	0.054	0.962	0.567
		Ref − 80	0.023	0.926	0.239
	MAX/MAX	Ref	0.044	0.944	0.427
		Ref + 80	0.058	0.956	0.556
		Ref − 80	0.022	0.925	0.227
80	NOM/NOM	Ref	0.066	0.962	0.624
		Ref + 80	0.087	0.979	0.813
		Ref − 80	0.038	0.938	0.372
	MIN/NOM	Ref	0.041	0.933	0.361
		Ref + 80	0.067	0.954	0.591
		Ref − 80	0.019	0.918	0.181
	MIN/MIN	Ref	0.042	0.934	0.369
		Ref + 80	0.061	0.949	0.534
		Ref − 80	0.021	0.918	0.192
	MAX/NOM	Ref	0.074	0.972	0.713
		Ref + 80	0.105	1.000	1.000
		Ref − 80	0.050	0.950	0.484
	MAX/MAX	Ref	0.060	0.956	0.568
		Ref + 80	0.093	0.987	0.878
		Ref − 80	0.028	0.929	0.279
100	NOM/NOM	Ref	0.045	0.939	0.409
		Ref + 80	0.084	0.971	0.756
		Ref − 80	0.008	0.906	0.068
	MIN/NOM	Ref	0.027	0.918	0.221
		Ref + 80	0.068	0.954	0.591
		Ref − 80	0.010	0.907	0.081
	MIN/MIN	Ref	0.035	0.925	0.295
		Ref + 80	0.064	0.948	0.547
		Ref − 80	0.008	0.903	0.051
	MAX/NOM	Ref	0.070	0.970	0.684
		Ref + 80	0.102	0.993	0.951
		Ref − 80	0.024	0.925	0.239
	MAX/MAX	Ref	0.027	0.923	0.240
		Ref + 80	0.088	0.978	0.808
		Ref − 80	0.002	0.900	0.008

are: (i) the maximum dist value is generally associated with maximum temperature and pressure condition; (ii) the changes in r_{mean} can be neglected despite the varying thermodynamic conditions; (iii) the change of e_ψ is noticeable at lower vehicle speeds (i.e. 60 km/h); (iv) P_{min}, T_{min} is the condition where most of the indexes' values are low (despite the various mass, velocity and thermodynamic conditions); (v) the change in β_{max} are more noticeable at high speed (100 km/h) with the maximum value being associated with higher level of temperature (T_{max}). Furthermore, tyre's degradation has been evaluated and summarized in Table 3. Since the simulation time is short (a single turning maneuver is considered) and the vehicle velocity is kept constant, the tyre wear metrics have been scaled.

Some intuitive considerations can be made: (i) the wear at right wheels is always larger compared to the value at left wheels as the simulated maneuver is always a left turn; (ii) the wear is always bigger when the mass is increased ($W_{m_{ref}+80} > W_{m_{ref}} > W_{m_{ref}-80}$). Higher values of W_m are associated with T_{max}, P_{nom} independently from the vehicle velocity. On the other hand, an overview on comfort-related metrics is proposed in Fig. 7. A single mass condition has been considered due to the constraint on the number of pages of the current work, however same considerations can be made with other mass conditions. Firstly, as the vehicle velocity is increased, the total area of the spider chart decreases, mainly due to the reduction of ay_m, ay_w and ay_{max}; moreover, at low temperature/pressure values most of the comfort indexes are reduced (i.e. less perceived discomfort). High temperature seems to affect the RMS value of the jerk; more generally the chart area increases as the temperature is increased (this is particularly evident when looking at 60 km/h, see top of Fig. 7). Furthermore, the cross-domain effects between both primary and secondary metrics are considered in Fig. 8, at moderate or high vehicle speed the thermodynamic condition (P_{MIN}, T_{MIN}) at which the discomfort value is lower, is associated with less tyre wear. The above considerations lead to interesting opportunities when analyzing the design of future controllers' objective function. They will, indeed, present conflicting objectives and the attention will be towards insuring better user's experience in all the possible working conditions. The modeling and the augmented knowledge of tyres' states can lead to more situational awareness not only in the context of single-vehicle optimal decision but also when the information can be translated between different ecosystems [76] (i.e. other vehicles, infrastructures, ...). Moreover, by embedding real-time feedback related to comfort, safety and vehicle integrity, future interfaces can become more supportive with the possibility to adapt their behavior based on internal vehicle states. This changes can be communicated to human drivers, thus enhancing both trust and reducing risk factors (reduced grip level due to high temperature). Ultimately providing safer and predictable human-machine interactions.

5   Conclusion

In the current article, based on a MPC control architecture, a path tracking algorithm has been proposed. The strategy has been designed employing fixed parameters referred to standard working conditions; the authors leveraged a high-fidelty digital twin of the real vehicle to assess the controller's performance in varying scenarios. Simulations include three high-velocity profile turning maneuvers with five conditions representing tyres' thermodynamic and pressure states. In addition, three vehicle mass conditions have been tested; the results have been compared by means of primary (path tracking/comfort) and secondary metrics (wear). To the latter, a wear model developed by the authors' research group, has been employed. Firstly, the results on path tracking performance have been presented, demonstrating: (i) the effects of both high temperature leading to worse tracking accuracy, (ii) change in velocity affecting the orientation error (low velocity) and the maximum value of the vehicle sideslip angle (high velocity). Furthermore, secondary metrics were evaluated, underlining the effect of various vehicle mass and high temperature was associated with overall higher values of tyre wear. Moreover, comfort perception was assessed by showing: (i) at high vehicle velocities the reduction of three indexes related to lateral acceleration (i.e. more perceived comfort); (ii) the indexes values are dependent on the tyres' thermal and pressure states as they can lead to increased discomfort when the temperature rises. In addition, specific tyres' conditions can be related to both higher comfort perception and less tyre wear, indicating an optimal window for future controllers' design. This work has the potential of unveiling crucial effects between cross-domain variables and increase user experience within future vehicle's cockpits. Although traditionally associated with vehicle behaviour, the tyre has also been shown to influence the way occupants interact with the vehicle. Further developments will include the design of controllers with conflicting objectives (i.e. comfort and tracking accuracy) to insure effective driving while improving user's experience.

Funding. This work was partly supported by the project "Homo-AD: Vehicle and Passenger oriented holistic motion planning for Autonomous Driving" funded by the Italian MUR "Progetti di Ricerca di Rilevante Interesse Nazionale (PRIN)" cup E53D23017110001.

Disclosure of Interests. The authors have no competing interests to declare that are relevant to the content of this article.

References

1. Al-Mayyahi, A., Wang, W., Birch, P.: Path tracking of autonomous ground vehicle based on fractional order PID controller optimized by PSO. In: 2015 IEEE 13th International Symposium on Applied Machine Intelligence and Informatics (SAMI), pp. 109–114. IEEE (2015)
2. Alamdari, A., Sovizi, J., Krovi, V.N.: Enhanced full-state estimation and dynamic-model-based prediction for road-vehicles. In: International Design Engineering Technical Conferences and Computers and Information in Engineering Conference, vol. 46346, p. V003T01A018. American Society of Mechanical Engineers (2014)
3. Allouis, C., Farroni, F., Sakhnevych, A., Timpone, F.: Tire thermal characterization: test procedure and model parameters evaluation. In: Proceedings of the World Congress on Engineering, vol. 2, pp. 1–6 (2016)

4. American Association of State Highway and Transportation Officials. A policy on geometric design of highways and streets, 6th edn. AASHTO, Washington, D.C. (2011), commonly referred to as the "Green Book"

5. Barbaro, M., Romagnuolo, F., Farroni, F., Timpone, F., Sakhnevych, A.: Necessity of the tire temperature-dependant parameters in vehicle virtual sensing. In: International Tribology Symposium of IFToMM, pp. 296–305. Springer (2024)

6. Bock, H.G., Plitt, K.J.: A multiple shooting algorithm for direct solution of optimal control problems. IFAC Proc. **17**(2), 1603–1608 (1984)

7. Boztaş, A.E., Özen, H.: Evaluation of the lateral acceleration on highway comfort: a case study with university students. Sigma J. Eng. Nat. Sci. **41**(1), 49–56 (2023)

8. CasADi Developers. Casadi documentation (2025). https://web.casadi.org/docs/. Accessed 21 Jun 2025

9. Chen, T., Chen, L., Xu, X., Cai, Y., Jiang, H., Sun, X.: Passive fault-tolerant path following control of autonomous distributed drive electric vehicle considering steering system fault. Mech. Syst. Signal Process. **123**, 298–315 (2019)

10. Cheng, C., Cebon, D.: Parameter and state estimation for articulated heavy vehicles. Veh. Syst. Dyn. **49**(1–2), 399–418 (2011)

11. Cheng, S., Li, L., Chen, B., Wang, X.: An autonomous vehicle path tracking controller via active steering and differential brake. J. Tongji Univ. Nat. Sci. (2017)

12. Dam, A., Jeon, M.: A review of motion sickness in automated vehicles. In: 13th International Conference on Automotive User Interfaces and Interactive Vehicular Applications, pp. 39–48 (2021)

13. De Winkel, K.N., Irmak, T., Happee, R., Shyrokau, B.: Standards for passenger comfort in automated vehicles: acceleration and jerk. Appl. Ergon. **106**, 103881 (2023)

14. Dell'Annunziata, G.N., Maglione, R., Genovese, A., Sakhnevych, A., Timpone, F., Farroni, F.: Sport driving skills: a preliminary comparative study from outdoor testing sessions. Transp. Res. Interdiscip. Perspect. **25**, 101105 (2024)

15. Farroni, F., Russo, M., Sakhnevych, A., Timpone, F.: TRT EVO: advances in real-time thermodynamic tire modeling for vehicle dynamics simulations. Proc. Inst. Mech. Eng. Part D J. Autom. Eng. **233**(1), 121–135 (2019)

16. Farroni, F., Sakhnevych, A.: Tire multiphysical modeling for the analysis of thermal and wear sensitivity on vehicle objective dynamics and racing performances. Simul. Model. Pract. Theory **117**, 102517 (2022)

17. Feng, S., Li, X., Zhang, S., Jian, Z., Duan, H., Wang, Z.: A review: state estimation based on hybrid models of Kalman filter and neural network. Syst. Sci. Control Eng. **11**(1), 2173682 (2023)

18. Genovese, A., Maiorano, A., Russo, R.: A novel methodology for non-destructive characterization of polymers' viscoelastic properties. Int. J. Appl. Mech. **14**(03), 2250017 (2022)

19. Genovese, A., Pagliarulo, V., Gloria, A., Speranza, D., Farroni, F., Martorelli, M.: Optical methodologies for the overall characterizations of non-pneumatic tires. Opt. Lasers Eng. **186**, 108829 (2025)

20. Genovese, A., Pastore, S.R.: Development of a portable instrument for non-destructive characterization of the polymers viscoelastic properties. Mech. Syst. Signal Process. **150**, 107259 (2021)

21. Guiggiani, M.: The science of vehicle dynamics: handling, braking, and ride of road and race cars. Springer, Berlin (2018)

22. Guo, J., Luo, Y., Li, K., Dai, Y.: Coordinated path-following and direct yaw-moment control of autonomous electric vehicles with sideslip angle estimation. Mech. Syst. Signal Process. **105**, 183–199 (2018)

23. Han, G., Fu, W., Wang, W., Wu, Z.: The lateral tracking control for the intelligent vehicle based on adaptive PID neural network. Sensors **17**(6), 1244 (2017)
24. Hashemi, E.: Full vehicle state estimation using a holistic corner-based approach (2017)
25. He, X., Liu, Y., Lv, C., Ji, X., Liu, Y.: Emergency steering control of autonomous vehicle for collision avoidance and stabilisation. Veh. Syst. Dyn. **57**(8), 1163–1187 (2019)
26. He, X., Liu, Y., Yang, K., Wu, J., Ji, X.: Robust coordination control of AFS and ARS for autonomous vehicle path tracking and stability. In: 2018 IEEE International Conference on Mechatronics and Automation (ICMA), pp. 924–929. IEEE (2018)
27. Hong, S.J., Oguchi, T.: Evaluation of highway geometric design and analysis of actual operating speed. J. East. Asia Soc. Transp. Stud. **6**, 1048–1061 (2005)
28. Htike, Z., Papaioannou, G., Siampis, E., Velenis, E., Longo, S.: Minimisation of motion sickness in autonomous vehicles. In: 2020 IEEE Intelligent Vehicles Symposium (IV), pp. 1135–1140. IEEE (2020)
29. Hu, C., Wang, R., Yan, F., Chen, N.: Should the desired heading in path following of autonomous vehicles be the tangent direction of the desired path? IEEE Trans. Intell. Transp. Syst. **16**(6), 3084–3094 (2015)
30. Huang, Q., Wang, H.: Fundamental study of jerk: evaluation of shift quality and ride comfort. Technical report, SAE Technical Paper (2004)
31. ISO I.: 2631-1: Mechanical vibration and shock-evaluation of human exposure to whole-body vibration-part 1: general requirements. ISO **42**, 43–4 (1997)
32. Jing, H., Hu, C., Yan, F., Chadli, M., Wang, R., Chen, N.: Robust h∞ output-feedback control for path following of autonomous ground vehicles. In: 2015 54th IEEE Conference on Decision and Control (CDC), pp. 1515–1520. IEEE (2015)
33. Kanellaidis, G., Vardaki, S.: Highway geometric design from the perspective of recent safety developments. J. Transp. Eng. **137**(12), 841–844 (2011)
34. Kim, B., Yi, K.: Probabilistic and holistic prediction of vehicle states using sensor fusion for application to integrated vehicle safety systems. IEEE Trans. Intell. Transp. Syst. **15**(5), 2178–2190 (2014)
35. Li, C., Liu, Y., Sun, L., Liu, Y., Tomizuka, M., Zhan, W.: Dual extended Kalman filter based state and parameter estimator for model-based control in autonomous vehicles. In: 2021 IEEE international intelligent transportation systems conference (ITSC), pp. 327–333. IEEE (2021)
36. Li, S.E., Gao, F., Li, K., Wang, L.Y., You, K., Cao, D.: Robust longitudinal control of multi-vehicle systems-a distributed h-infinity method. IEEE Trans. Intell. Transp. Syst. **19**(9), 2779–2788 (2017)
37. Li, X., Sun, Z., Cao, D., Liu, D., He, H.: Development of a new integrated local trajectory planning and tracking control framework for autonomous ground vehicles. Mech. Syst. Signal Process. **87**, 118–137 (2017)
38. Li, Y., Fan, J., Liu, Y., Wang, X.: Path planning and path tracking for autonomous vehicle based on MPC with adaptive dual-horizon-parameters. Int. J. Automot. Technol. **23**(5), 1239–1253 (2022)
39. Li, Y., Ni, J., Hu, J., Pan, B.: The design of driverless vehicle trajectory tracking control strategy. IFAC-PapersOnLine **51**(31), 738–745 (2018)
40. Lin, F., Ni, L., Zhao, Y., Zhuang, H., Zhang, H., Wang, K.: Path following control of intelligent vehicles considering lateral stability. J. South China Univ. Technol. Nat. Sci. Ed. **46**(1), 78–84 (2018)

41. Liu, H., Inoue, S., Wada, T.: Subjective vertical conflict model with visual vertical: predicting motion sickness on autonomous personal mobility vehicles. IEEE Trans. Intell. Transp. Syst. **25**(8), 9878–9894 (2024)
42. Liu, K., Chen, H., Gong, J., Chen, S., Zhang, Y.: A research on handling stability of high-speed unmanned vehicles. Automot. Eng. **41**(5), 514–521 (2019)
43. Liu, S., Hou, Z., Tian, T., Deng, Z., Li, Z.: A novel dual successive projection-based model-free adaptive control method and application to an autonomous car. IEEE Trans. Neural Netw. Learn. Syst. **30**(11), 3444–3457 (2019)
44. Miaou, S.P., Lum, H.: Modeling vehicle accidents and highway geometric design relationships. Accident Anal. Prev. **25**(6), 689–709 (1993)
45. Mosconi, L., Farroni, F., Sakhnevych, A., Timpone, F., Gerbino, F.S.: Adaptive vehicle dynamics state estimator for onboard automotive applications and performance analysis. Veh. Syst. Dyn. **61**(12), 3244–3268 (2023)
46. Pacejka, H.B., Bakker, E.: The magic formula tyre model. Veh. Syst. Dyn. **21**(S1), 1–18 (1992)
47. Park, J.B., Bae, S.H., Koo, B.S., Kim, J.H.: When path tracking using look-ahead distance about the lateral error method and the velocity change method tracking comparison. In: 2014 14th International Conference on Control, Automation and Systems (ICCAS 2014), pp. 1643–1647. IEEE (2014)
48. Park, M.W., Lee, S.W., Han, W.Y.: Development of lateral control system for autonomous vehicle based on adaptive pure pursuit algorithm. In: 2014 14th international conference on control, automation and systems (ICCAS 2014), pp. 1443–1447. IEEE (2014)
49. Pereira, E., Macedo, H., Lisboa, I.C., Sousa, E., Machado, D., Silva, E., Coelho, V., Arezes, P., Costa, N.: Motion sickness countermeasures for autonomous driving: trends and future directions. Transp. Eng. **15**, 100220 (2024)
50. Potluri, R., Singh, A.K.: Path-tracking control of an autonomous 4ws4wd electric vehicle using its natural feedback loops. IEEE Trans. Control Syst. Technol. **23**(5), 2053–2062 (2015)
51. Raffo, G.V., Gomes, G.K., Normey-Rico, J.E., Kelber, C.R., Becker, L.B.: A predictive controller for autonomous vehicle path tracking. IEEE Trans. Intell. Transp. Syst. **10**(1), 92–102 (2009)
52. Rajamani, R., Piyabongkarn, D., Tsourapas, V., Lew, J.Y.: Parameter and state estimation in vehicle roll dynamics. IEEE Trans. Intell. Transp. Syst. **12**(4), 1558–1567 (2011)
53. Ren, D., Zhang, J., Zhang, J.: Sliding mode control for vehicle following with parametric uncertainty. Electr. Mach. Control **14**(1), 73–78 (2010)
54. Rezaeian, A., Zarringhalam, R., Fallah, S., Melek, W., Khajepour, A., Chen, S.K., Litkouhi, B.: Cascaded dual extended Kalman filter for combined vehicle state estimation and parameter identification. Technical report, SAE Technical Paper (2013)
55. Rokonuzzaman, M., Mohajer, N., Nahavandi, S., Mohamed, S.: Review and performance evaluation of path tracking controllers of autonomous vehicles. IET Intell. Transp. Syst. **15**(5), 646–670 (2021)
56. Ruslan, N.A.I., Amer, N.H., Hudha, K., Kadir, Z.A., Ishak, S.A.F.M., Dardin, S.M.F.S.: Modelling and control strategies in path tracking control for autonomous tracked vehicles: a review of state of the art and challenges. J. Terrramech. **105**, 67–79 (2023)
57. Ryu, J.: State and parameter estimation for vehicle dynamics control using GPS. Stanford University (2005)

58. Sakhnevych, A.: Multiphysical MF-based tyre modelling and parametrisation for vehicle setup and control strategies optimisation. Veh. Syst. Dyn. **60**(10), 3462–3483 (2022)
59. Sakhnevych, A., Genovese, A.: Tyre wear model: a fusion of rubber viscoelasticity, road roughness, and thermodynamic state. Wear **542**, 205291 (2024)
60. Sakhnevych, A., Genovese, A., Luongo, G., Farroni, F.: An analytical 3d thermal model for the analysis of the rolling dissipative phenomena of the airless tyres. In: Mechanics Based Design of Structures and Machines, pp. 1–27 (2025)
61. Sakhnevych, A., Maglione, R., Suero, R., Mallozzi, L.: Nonlinear mathematical modeling of frequency–temperature dependent viscoelastic materials for tire applications. Nonlinear Dyn. **112**(24), 21729–21750 (2024)
62. Sakhnevych, A., Pasquino, N., Sperlì, G.: Design of a machine learning approach to anomaly detection in tyre-road interaction. IEEE Access (2025)
63. Samuel, M., Hussein, M., Mohamad, M.B.: A review of some pure-pursuit based path tracking techniques for control of autonomous vehicle. Int. J. Comput. Appl. **135**(1), 35–38 (2016)
64. Sun, C., Zhang, X., Xi, L., Tian, Y.: Design for the steering controller of autonomous vehicles at the limits of handling. J. South China Univ. Technol. Natural Sci. Ed. **46**(3), 78–85 (2018)
65. Sun, C., Zhang, X., Zhou, Q., Tian, Y.: A model predictive controller with switched tracking error for autonomous vehicle path tracking. IEEE Access **7**, 53103–53114 (2019)
66. Tan, Q., Dai, P., Zhang, Z., Katupitiya, J.: MPC and PSO based control methodology for path tracking of 4ws4wd vehicles. Appl. Sci. **8**(6), 1000 (2018)
67. Tang, Z., Xu, X., Wang, F., Jiang, X., Jiang, H.: Coordinated control for path following of two-wheel independently actuated autonomous ground vehicle. IET Intell. Transp. Syst. **13**(4), 628–635 (2019)
68. Tian, D., Jin, L., Zhang, Z., Li, H.: Vehicle state estimation based on multidimensional information fusion. IEEE Access **10**, 76220–76232 (2022)
69. Tian, T., Hou, Z., Liu, S., Deng, Z.: Model-free adaptive control based lateral control of self-driving car. Acta Autom. Sin. **43**(11), 1931–1940 (2017)
70. Tsunashima, H., Murakami, M., Miyataa, J.: Vehicle and road state estimation using interacting multiple model approach. Veh. Syst. Dyn. **44**(sup1), 750–758 (2006)
71. VI-grade GmbH: Vi-carrealtime (2025). https://www.vi-grade.com/en/products/vi-carrealtime/. Accessed 19 May 2025
72. Wang, H., Liu, B., Ping, X., An, Q.: Path tracking control for autonomous vehicles based on an improved MPC. IEEE Access **7**, 161064–161073 (2019)
73. Williams, M.L., Landel, R.F., Ferry, J.D.: The temperature dependence of relaxation mechanisms in amorphous polymers and other glass-forming liquids. J. Am. Chem. Soc. **77**(14), 3701–3707 (1955)
74. Xu, S., Peng, H.: Design, analysis, and experiments of preview path tracking control for autonomous vehicles. IEEE Trans. Intell. Transp. Syst. **21**(1), 48–58 (2019)
75. Yang, J., Bao, H., Ma, N., Xuan, Z.: An algorithm of curved path tracking with prediction model for autonomous vehicle. In: 2017 13th International Conference on Computational Intelligence and Security (CIS), pp. 405–408. IEEE (2017)
76. Yang, K., Huang, Y., Qin, Y., Hu, C., Tang, X.: Potential and challenges to improve vehicle energy efficiency via v2x: literature review. Int. J. Veh. Perform. **7**(3–4), 244–265 (2021)

77. Yao, Q., Tian, Y., Wang, Q., Wang, S.: Control strategies on path tracking for autonomous vehicle: state of the art and future challenges. IEEE Access **8**, 161211–161222 (2020)
78. Zhang, F., Wang, Y., Hu, J., Yin, G., Chen, S., Zhang, H., Zhou, D.: A novel comprehensive scheme for vehicle state estimation using dual extended h-infinity Kalman filter. Electronics **10**(13), 1526 (2021)
79. Zhang, Y., Zhao, H., Hu, C., Tian, Y., Li, Y., Jiao, X., Wen, G.: Mitigation of motion sickness and optimization of motion comfort in autonomous vehicles: systematic survey. IEEE Trans. Intell. Transp. Syst. (2024)
80. Zhao, J., Zhang, X., Shi, P., Liu, Y.: Automatic driving control method based on time delay dynamic prediction. In: International Conference on Cognitive Systems and Signal Processing, pp. 443–453. Springer (2016)

From Space Crew to Road Vehicles: Supporting Designers in Human Factor-Aware Design to Improve Experience and Safety

Laura Succini[(✉)] and Raffaele Montemurro

Department of Architecture, Alma Mater Studiorum, University of Bologna, Bologna, Italy
`{laura.succini,raffaele.montemurro2}@unibo.it`

Abstract. Designing a space habitat means not only conceiving an environment with extremely high functionality, capable of ensuring crew safety and supporting operational and scientific activities, but above all, imagining an extreme space designed for the everyday life of each crew member. The challenge in the context of space habitats, where access to space is becoming increasingly inclusive and diverse, is to develop design methods that improve the onboard experience and crew well-being, while respecting the environment and collective experience. Designers in this field must address a high degree of complexity, balancing the individual needs of crew members with technical constraints.

The approach proposed here combines Responsible Advanced Design (RAD) with Human System Integration (HSI) to address both functional and experiential needs in the design of future space habitats. The applied methodology brings forth several operational tools. Of particular relevance to this contribution is the design process underlying the habitat configurator, structured in two phases: in the first, needs are identified and clustered, distinguishing between common needs and those specific to particular activities; subsequently, the design model enables the development of a habitat concept by transforming those needs into design tags, which guide the adaptive and personalized definition of spatial, product, and service solutions based on both individual and collective profiles. Although originally developed for orbital modules, this design approach shows promising applications in terrestrial contexts such as autonomous mobility, where vehicle interiors are becoming multifunctional environments with characteristics similar to space habitats. This contribution illustrates how the integration of the methodology and tools developed for space habitat design can enhance the configuration of vehicle interiors and improve the travel experience, both individual and collective, according to user characteristics and specific needs.

Keywords: Human Factors · Responsible Advanced Design · Interdisciplinarity · Automotive · Space Design.

1 Introduction

Designing habitats for extreme environments is considered as a complex field of inquiry and interaction. This is not only due to the confrontation with unknown and hostile environments - where humans live in conditions never experienced elsewhere - but also

© The Author(s), under exclusive license to Springer Nature Switzerland AG 2026
P.-L.P. Rau and H. Krömker (Eds.): HCII 2025, LNCS 16336, pp. 294–308, 2026.
https://doi.org/10.1007/978-3-032-12798-3_18

because the designer must engage with a setting that cannot be observed directly, and where commonly used tools are neither accessible nor easily understood by a broad spectrum of designers. Furthermore, contact with the few people who have lived in such environments is not guaranteed, and innovation remains anchored in certain linear and still highly sectoral design processes and practices [1–3].

These challenges raise the question of how to activate forms of learning and design that support, through interdisciplinary and systemic approaches, more dynamic and adaptable design processes both to the backgrounds of designers and to the latent needs of future users [4].

In 2023, the Advanced Design Unit (ADU) of the University of Bologna launched a two-year research initiative within the framework of project 1.10 *Beyond the Space Life. Digital Living Lab for Human Life*, part of Spoke 1 of the national program *Made in Italy Circolare e Sostenibile* (MICS). One of the objectives of the research is to develop a conceptual model for the design of new in-orbit habitat configurations, integrating factors such as sustainability, well-being, and care from the early stages of conceptualization. The project is carried out in collaboration with Thales Alenia Space Italia, the Department of Mathematics at the University of Bologna, and other scientific and industrial partners from the region.

The first part of this paper analyzes the specificities of designing for Space, starting from the reflection of Häuplik-Meusburger and Bishop (2021) [5], who argue that "What any successful habitat must achieve is the experience of safety, support and sustainment." (p. 13). This implies a shift in perspective: not only do design constraints and parameters change, but there is also an opportunity to involve new types of knowledge and disciplines. The experience of living in orbit cannot be based only functionality or maintaining physical performance; rather, the relational and cultural dimension becomes central, responding to more latent needs tied to personality and individual identity [6].

To address this complexity, the ADU has adopted the Responsible Advanced Design [7, 8], a multidisciplinary, anticipatory, and inclusive approach that considers both material (e.g., cross-sector industrial integration, circularity, energy consumption) and immaterial (e.g., ethics, care, inclusion) dimensions in both the analysis and development of new strategies. This approach has enabled the construction of a different design and knowledge model that is more accessible to a wider range of designers and more attentive to the human factors of future crews. Thanks to its characteristics, this model can also be adapted to other contexts marked by isolation, confinement, physical constraints, and high levels of stress, as found in various terrestrial industrial sectors mobility being one such sector, currently undergoing profound paradigm shifts.

The final part of this paper will analyze the points of convergence and divergence between space design and automotive design, highlighting how certain strategies tested in the former context can help renew the design experience in the latter.

2 Designing for New Space Economy: Theoretical Framework

The New Space Economy, as evident from recent international developments, is currently a complex ecosystem both geopolitically and in terms of the technological advances required to rethink the configuration and structure of future orbiting stations and exploration and research programs [9]. With the planned decommissioning of the International

Space Station (ISS) in 2030, more articulated collaborative ecosystems are emerging, involving government agencies working alongside private companies and opening the door to future synergies with SMEs and start-ups [10–12], alongside the growing rise of private initiatives such as Axion Space, SpaceX, Virgin Orbit, and Blue Origin. This paradigm shift, rooted in the idea of space democratization [13], is enabling the development of new low Earth orbit (LEO) infrastructure projects designed to host more diverse human profiles.

The very notion of the space explorer is diversifying. The traditional focus on individuals from highly specialized fields - selected through stringent criteria and subjected to years of rigorous physical and psychological training - is now being complemented by the possibility of commercial explorations and by participants with different backgrounds and goals. This is increasing attention to the quality of bodily and spatial experience [14, 15].

Moreover, such an extreme environment introduces hostile conditions that cannot be experienced anywhere on Earth, such as microgravity. This condition brings with it major physiological effects on the human body - from disorientation to physical stress on limbs - alongside loss of the day/night cycle, radiation exposure, and confinement.

This shift in perspective directly impacts the design of space habitats [16]. Designing a space habitat means not only envisioning a highly functional environment capable of ensuring crew safety and supporting their operational and scientific tasks but, more importantly, imagining a confined space designed for the daily lives of each crew member, where relationships between self, crew, and environment become critical to mission success [17, 18].

This also entails creating a more accessible and responsive design, adaptable to users with diverse life stories, skills, and cultural backgrounds. It implies a reconfiguration of the habitat as a relational, identity-forming, and learning space, where well-being is no longer just ergonomic or performance-based, but also cognitive, emotional, and cultural [19, 20].

This requires identifying the macro-components to consider in designing space habitats that simultaneously address mission safety and success, as well as crew well-being. To better analyze the field, we began with the dimensions proposed by Häuplik-Meusburger and Bishop (2021) [5]: the *Setting*, the *individual*, *Micro-society*, and *Time*. These were integrated with constraints, challenges, and needs related to future scenarios, and with the difficulties a non-expert designer faces in approaching this kind of environment and managing interdependencies among these design macro-components:

- **The Setting.** This is a non-conventional context for both those who live in it and those who design it. Its current purposes make it highly technical, practical, and at times chaotic. However, the conditions of microgravity, confinement, isolation, and mental confusion redirect focus toward safety [21]. At the same time, emerging scenarios call for a broader view of needs: we now speak of *experiencing safety* [5], where the environment must convey trust and comfort not only in ergonomic terms, but through the psycho-perceptual experience of space and its personalization, thereby nurturing both interpersonal relationships and individuality [22].

  From a design perspective, significant challenges emerge around gaining open and comprehensive knowledge of the context. It is also difficult to experiment using conventional methods such as direct observation, prototyping, or field validation. This highlights the need for more accessible tools to support the early design stages of environments and to foster better understanding of space and reference projects.

- **The Individual.** As previously noted, astronauts have historically had specific characteristics defined by governmental standards. In recent years, these directives have expanded, allowing civilians to participate in space experiences. Future missions are expected to see a shift in objectives and collaboration among the various stakeholders involved [1]. This scenario will open Space exploration to users with heterogeneous physical and emotional profiles, coming from different professional backgrounds and undergoing limited training. This leads to the emergence of new needs intrinsic to the individual experience of space, as well as interpersonal dynamics. Among these are the need for spaces dedicated to physical care, environments for sharing memories, and places for entertainment and social interaction [23].

  Designers are also faced with changes in users' bodies and sensory perceptions, which they will need to understand and incorporate during the phases of analysis, design, and macro-component integration.

- **The Micro-society.** Inside a Space Station, a unique social group with specific characteristics develops unlike anything experienced on Earth. Due to confinement and the overlap of life spheres [24], social relationships are particularly delicate and can give rise to coexistence issues [25]. This underscores the need to create more flexible environments that are attentive to the emotional and cultural dimensions of users.

  From the designer's perspective, it is essential to observe extreme contexts and understand their experiential dynamics in order to inform interventions. Equally important is identifying the social and cultural characteristics that may lead to shifts within the habitat spheres.

- **Time.** The temporal dimension is undoubtedly transversal. It relates to the timeline of future missions that will be open to a broader public, the duration of such missions, varying user stays, adaptation periods, and the continuous time needed to build a sense of community. Additionally, it refers to how time is perceived differently in Space than on Earth.

  In design terms, time becomes crucial in determining the combination of functional areas to better support activities, and in guiding the choice of product-service systems that enhance users' psychological well-being.

  To integrate these macro-components, their characteristics, and their associated needs, an anticipatory and systemic approach is necessary one capable of constructing future scenarios [26, 27].

3 Responsible Advanced Design and Human System Integration for Space Habitat Design

To investigate in an interdisciplinary and advanced manner the macro-components of space habitats (environment, individual, group, time), their interdependencies, and to propose new design strategies that are more accessible, focused on open innovation processes, and attentive to user well-being, the applied research methodology was *Responsible Advanced Design (RAD)* [7]. This approach promotes **Responsible Innovation** [28] driven by **Advanced Design** [29], through its dimensions: anticipation, reflexivity, inclusiveness, responsiveness, care, and transparency [30]. In this research direction, RAD is used as a design framework to:

- Address the uncertainty typical of space conditions, by promoting a more inclusive and adaptive design capable of responding even to the needs of future users;
- Construct advanced scenarios in which to experiment with new actions and more sustainable needs, attentive to crew well-being;
- Enable collaboration among multiple professional figures in the systemic development of product and service innovation;
- Activate responsible knowledge that takes into account the social, cultural, and technical impacts of the project within a complex context such as Space;
- Generate design tools adaptable to research objectives and mission constraints.

The high degree of complexity that every Space designer faces requires informed and conscious choices, supported by a deep understanding of the specific needs of the crew and its individual members, as well as by the often-stringent technical constraints defined by NASA regulations. In this framework, stress and user well-being emerge as critical factors in determining the success of an activity, a relationship, an interaction, and ultimately of the mission itself. To these, further relevant human factors are added such as adaptability, interaction with the environment, and cultural and cognitive traits that can guide design toward responsible innovation solutions [28].

To include these factors in the design process, the *Human System Integration* (HSI) approach has been integrated with RAD. Human factors, in fact, "involve the analysis of psychological, physiological, and cognitive conditions that influence the interactions between users and complex systems"(p. 2) [23]. The HSI approach, already adopted by NASA in its design standards [31], "aims to make interactive systems more usable by focusing on the use of the system and applying human factors/ergonomics and usability knowledge and techniques" (p. 53) [32].

The integration of these two approaches allows the design process to broaden its focus on human factors and well-being, and to anticipate changes in use contexts.

4 Designing Adaptive Space Habitats Through Needs-Based Configuration

Within this integrated methodological framework, the need clearly emerges for operational tools capable of supporting designers in managing complexity, acquiring knowledge in a more accessible and integrated way, and including human factors in the decision-making process. While RAD provides strategies and tools (e.g., co-design workshops, peer-to-peer focus groups, scenario building, user research, etc.) that help orient the project toward an anticipatory, inclusive, and responsible vision, HSI offers a methodological framework for analyzing and integrating psychological, cognitive, and physiological factors into human-environment interactions (e.g., task analysis, ergonomic procedures, etc.). This is essential to inform more conscious design decisions that are responsive to various crew configurations, user-habitat interactions, and mission variability.

The design system developed, which underpins the entire research project, is articulated into three macro-areas of interaction with future designers - *Learn*, *Explore*, and *Create* - each of which is associated with a specific operational tool. In the first area, the tool is a digital platform that aggregates preliminary knowledge about the domain from the designer's perspective. The second area is characterized by an "Observatory", a repository of in-domain and out-of-domain case studies, useful for understanding sector trends. Finally, in the *Create* area, access is granted to the Demonstrator, a tool that enables the application of acquired or pre-existing knowledge to develop initial concepts for modules and Space Stations in Low Earth Orbit (LEO), in line with the research objectives.

This contribution focuses specifically on the configurator and the methodological process through which user needs are identified, classified, and employed as design tags to guide decision-making in all stages of space habitat development.

The objective of the proposed environmental configuration model is to provide designers, from the early stages of the project, with a support tool for defining optimal spatial and functional conditions for habitats intended for Space life. In particular, the configurator aims to respond to the heterogeneous needs of crew members by accounting for user variability and the constant reconfiguration of groups rotating through habitat modules on Space Stations.

To ensure a design process that is both aware and adaptable to different scales - from module configuration to interior outfitting - it is necessary to identify precise and flexible design drivers: user needs that dynamically guide the spatial and service definition process on board. In accordance with the most recent literature on human factors and Space Architecture, needs have been adopted as the unit of classification and design guidance, treated as *tags* that can provide specific indications during the design phase regarding products and solutions suited to each environment.

These needs, conceptualized as design tags, offer the advantage of condensing and harmonizing heterogeneous contributions from various sources and stages of the process: from preliminary human factors analyses, to design solutions already implemented to mitigate known issues, to synthesized recommendations, standards, and best practices established by international Space agencies.

To enable these needs to be transformed into flexible and operational tools for designing environments with varying functions, users, and usage moments, it is crucial to associate them with a spatial and temporal dimension. In this regard, the literature highlights the effectiveness of *task analysis* [33], a widely used technique in the design of complex environments, which allows modeling of the different moments of life on board and analyzing dynamics, spatial relationships, and specific needs tied to each activity.

Through the precise definition of activities, broken down into individual actions, and the phases that structure daily life in Space, it becomes possible to position identified needs within the task analysis framework, thereby determining the spatio-temporal coordinates in which these needs emerge and demand a design response. Subsequently, the analyzed activities are grouped into functional areas [5] that can be associated with specific zones or entire modules of the Space Station.

One of the main advantages of this approach is that it allows needs to be treated as independent design modules, which can be flexibly arranged within the space environment, adapting both to the activities to be performed and the individual characteristics of the inhabitants.

It is therefore possible to conceive a highly adaptive and dynamic model, capable of configuring the presence or absence of certain spaces and activities based on the crew members and their composition. Once it is established that needs are the core elements of the model, and that their processing relies on the definition of actions to determine their spatial and temporal manifestation, it is important to highlight the existence of a category of transversal needs. These refer to conditions and requirements that must be ensured for all users and across all onboard activities, regardless of their specific spatial or temporal location.

The integration between task analysis and needs analysis makes it possible to structurally identify actions, such as eating, sleeping, or reading, that define the functional areas of the station. This provides the designer with a foundation for identifying what should remain stable and high-performing over time within each module, and what, instead, should be reconfigurable in response to variations in crew composition and specific individual needs that may arise during the station's operational life, such as performing hygiene-related activities (see Fig. 1).

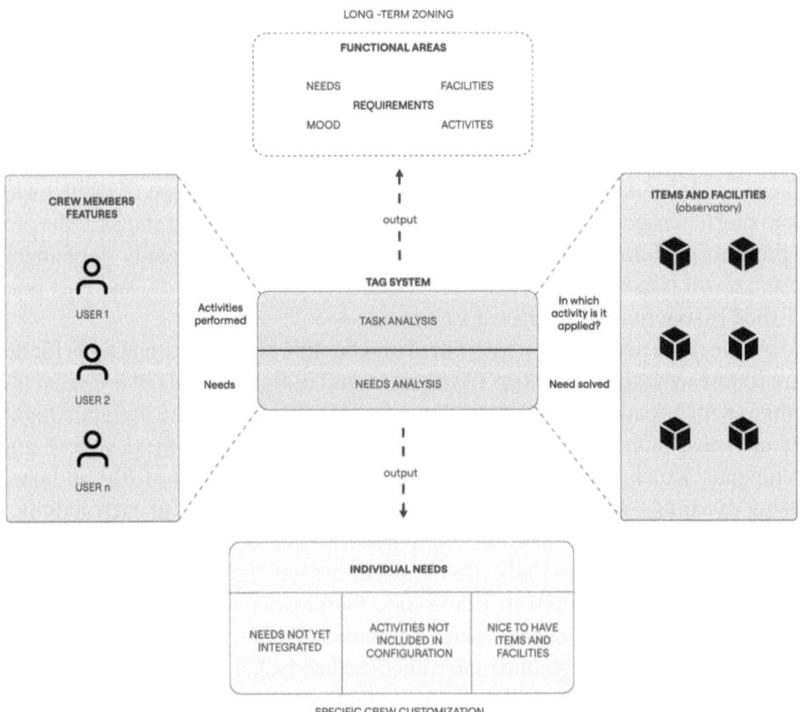

Fig. 1. Diagram illustrating the processing model for user profiles and product features within the observatory, aimed at characterizing functional areas through task analysis and needs analysis.

This approach allows for a dual objective: on the one hand, ensuring highly standardized and stable environments that maintain required performance levels for primary activities and operational safety; on the other, enabling the adaptation of certain activities and configurations to the contingent needs of the users present on board during each mission for instance, cultural, dietary, religious, or disability-related needs.

Operationally, the configuration process within the configurator unfolds in two main phases:

Definition and Allocation of Functional Areas. In this initial phase, a dedicated algorithm supports the assignment of activities to the respective functional areas by evaluating environmental, operational, and relational compatibility criteria. For example, acoustic isolation or privacy needs are considered, avoiding the juxtaposition of activities with conflicting requirements (such as noisy workspaces adjacent to rest zones).

Another sorting criterion concerns the sphere of life to which activities belong, ensuring separation among work, collective leisure, and private or individual domains. The outcome is a rational distribution of common macro-activities, including areas for meal preparation and consumption, sleeping pods, and spaces for personal care or private communication.

Detailed Design and Module Customization. Once functional areas have been defined and allocated, the process continues with the detailed design of individual environments. At this stage, materials derived from the task analysis and needs analysis are organized into a checklist of needs and actions that guides the designer in identifying the most appropriate solutions to meet the specified requirements (see Fig. 2).

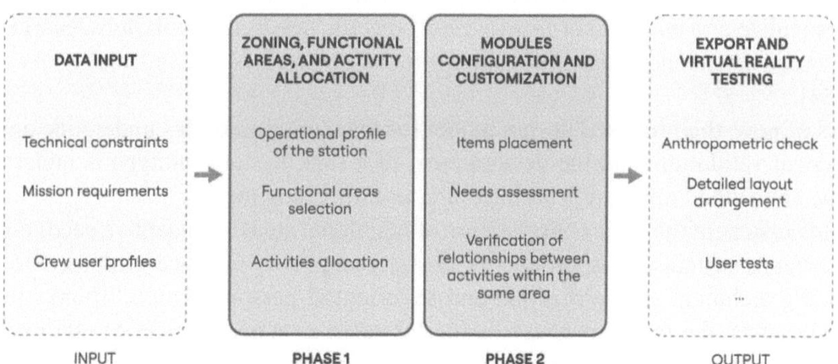

Fig. 2. Phases of the space habitat configuration process, from the definition of user needs and design constraints to the customization of interior layouts and the validation of proposed solutions through testing in virtual environments.

Through the configurator, it is also possible to integrate specific needs derived from crew composition for example, dietary restrictions, spaces for religious practices, or custom equipment to support users with temporary or permanent disabilities (see Fig. 3).

Simultaneously, the system manages an inventory of products, equipment, and furnishings, named the *"Observatory of Sustainable Innovation for Life Beyond Earth"*

Fig. 3. Representative example of the relationship between users' specific characteristics and the needs to be addressed in the design process.

[7] which are tagged according to the needs they satisfy, the actions they relate to, and, where applicable, the user categories they are intended for. This inventory is continuously recalled and updated during the design phase, ensuring consistency and traceability among needs, activities, and onboard provisions.

At the end of the configuration process, each functional area includes:

- a description of the activities performed therein;
- a list of needs to be addressed;
- a selection of compatible products and equipment, validated against operational conditions and specific requirements.

A key feature of this model is its ability to dynamically manage reconfigurations resulting from crew composition changes. When necessary, the system allows for rapid updates to spatial layouts and onboard provisions, including the possibility of sending supplementary or replacement materials during upcoming launch windows.

In summary, the proposed approach enables the structuring of highly functional and stable environments for the station's operational life, while maintaining the flexibility to personalize and adapt according to users' specific needs and evolving scenarios. This ensures consistent and updatable standards for safety, well-being, and quality of onboard life [34].

As of now, the proposed design model for the configurator has undergone an initial theoretical validation, and the development of a first digital prototype is underway to test the envisioned interaction architecture, usability, and logic.

This system of dynamic configuration of functional areas and adaptive needs management offers a structured response to the design complexity of space habitats, effectively balancing technical standardization and experiential personalization. Thanks to these characteristics, the model is also suitable for adaptation and transfer to other confined and high-variability user contexts, such as next-generation autonomous vehicles. The following chapter explores the potential transfer of this space-derived design approach to the automotive sector, analyzing the points of convergence, challenges, and opportunities associated with applying such a methodology to the design of vehicular environments for autonomous and shared mobility.

5 Discussion

The application of the proposed methodology to the field of Space Design has made it possible to systematize tools and strategies capable of dynamically and individually managing user needs within highly constrained and isolated environments. However, alongside its strengths, this experimentation is also revealing some critical issues related to the specific nature of the Space context and the limited accessibility of such environments for direct field validation. Some of these challenges are being addressed through a subsequent design phase conducted in virtual reality.

Among the main limitations, the difficulty of conducting tests in real environments stands out: Space Stations are extremely complex and scarcely accessible contexts, inhabited by a small number of users operating under strict protocols that limit the ability to verify the long-term effectiveness of adaptive configurations and personalized systems. In addition, the slow integration of innovations in the aerospace sector - due to the high safety and certification standards required - significantly hampers the iterative experimentation typically associated with design processes. Moreover, the possibility of sending objects or solutions into orbit for non-operational purposes remains limited, reducing the scope of action and restricting design interventions to only a few components. Another constraint lies in the difficulty of designing more interactive and personalized interfaces: within space habitats, these interfaces must remain standardized and offer minimal flexibility for reasons of safety, interoperability, and crew training.

Many of the critical issues observed in space habitat design can also be found, albeit in different forms, in other extreme contexts and in industrial sectors closer to us—such as mobility. In particular, the *automotive* sector provides a significant point of comparison: like space habitats, it is governed by strict safety regulations and constraints. Furthermore, innovation in this sector is not always open or continuous, as it is typically accessible only to designers with highly specialized technical backgrounds. Another commonality lies in the confined space where social interactions take place and where user well-being becomes a key design driver, both from the perspective of safety and travel experience.

In this context as well, we find the four dimensions that characterize the design of a space habitat: *setting, individual, micro-society, and time* (Häuplik-Meusburger & Bishop, 2021). In a vehicle cabin, the *setting* must respond to ergonomic principles and the psychological needs of the user, while also conveying a sense of *experienced safety*. The *individual* dimension must account not only for physical but also emotional characteristics, along with the effects of confinement. The *micro-society* dimension reflects a paradigm shift: the cabin is no longer merely a space for transportation, but a multifunctional and relational environment where it is possible to live, work, and interact in new ways. Finally, the *temporal* dimension plays a central role, as it relates both to the duration of the journey and to the quality of the time spent within the cabin.

For these reasons, the Space and automotive domains share multiple points of contact, revealing an **affinity of objectives** and the potential for transferring the design approach from an extreme environment to a consolidated yet rapidly evolving industrial context.

Within the automotive field, the most relevant area for research and innovation is the **interior design of next-generation autonomous vehicles.** The gradual transition toward self-driving cars is redefining the concept of the cabin: from a functional driving space to a multifunctional and relational environment, inhabited by users with diverse backgrounds and needs. In this scenario, the functional clustering logic, adaptive needs management, and dynamic configuration strategies tested in space habitats could be transferable and effective.

Both domains involve the management of closed environments with limited resources, designed for the coexistence or alternation of users with different roles, timeframes, and activities, where psychological well-being and the quality of social interactions directly impact both **safety and overall experience.**

In this scenario, as Sundar et al. (2022) [35] highlight, it is essential to move beyond "one-size-fits-all" HMI logic and adopt proactive systems capable of learning and adapting to individual passenger preferences.

The anthropometric and behavioral datasets collected during the experimentation of the space-based design model could be integrated into automotive design processes, enhancing predictive models for personalized use. Such digital tools would enable the development of dynamic interfaces that evolve with the user, improving the fluidity and coherence of the user experience. This may involve adjusting environmental conditions (e.g., lighting, sound, spatial arrangement) and, most importantly, implementing flexible, adaptive, and context-aware interfaces.

This real-time adaptability can reduce functional conflicts between onboard activities (e.g., work, relaxation, social interaction) and ensure user well-being by safeguarding not only physical protection but also the **quality of perceived experience.**

The potential effectiveness of applying the methodological approach developed in this research to vehicle cabin conditions - to improve travel experience and perceived safety - is confirmed by recent studies.

DeCastro et al. (2024) [36] demonstrated that personalized safety interfaces, tailored to the driver's cognitive profile, are more effective at reducing risky behavior than standard interfaces. Similarly, Popp et al. (2024) [37] showed that adaptive cabin lighting systems enhance alertness without compromising sleep, thus improving safety and well-being. From a UX standpoint, Braun et al. (2020) [38] emphasized the benefits of integrating regenerative mental activities (e.g., meditation, guided breathing) during autonomous travel, increasing both comfort and psychophysical well-being.

These trends highlight the need to design **modular, reconfigurable, and adaptive vehicular environments** capable of flexibly responding to changing scenarios and diverse user profiles. In this perspective, the approach developed for the Space domain - based on associating needs, activities, and products with user-centered situations and profiles attentive to human factors - offers a valuable reference for configuring automotive interiors designed for autonomous and shared mobility.

An additional strength lies in the adoption of the ***Responsible Advanced Design*** (RAD) approach integrated with ***Human Systems Integration*** (HSI) as an enabling framework. The capacity of this approach to integrate **material and immaterial dimensions** of design - promoting a systemic and anticipatory vision focused on human factors and the well-being of the user, community, and environment - accelerates the continuous innovation of systems, products, and vehicular experiences. It also enables the development of **multi-level learning and collaboration models** [39].

6   Future Developments: Application in the Automotive Field

The application of this design model, originally developed for Space habitat design, and its adaptation to the automotive sector could generate multidimensional benefits: reduction of human error, mitigation of travel-related stress, enhancement of both actual and perceived safety, improvement of the user experience, and the creation of adaptive environments. This strategy of integrating individual needs could enable the design of spaces that value user heterogeneity, thanks to the early incorporation of human factors and the needs of individuals and crews in the conceptual phases of design [40].

In summary, the current evolution of both human Space exploration and autonomous terrestrial mobility is converging around a shared principle: user-centered design aimed at maximizing safety and experience.

From the Space crew to the everyday automotive user, the need emerges to account for individual characteristics, promoting adaptive and personalized design. The models developed within the proposed design tools were conceived to support designers in the customization of environments, in attending to psychophysical well-being, and in enhancing the flexibility of the habitat.

The strategies applied represent a body of design knowledge that can be effectively transferred to the terrestrial mobility sector.

Looking ahead, the reverse integration is also of great interest: research in autonomous mobility is introducing technologies such as artificial intelligence, VR/AR, and biometric sensors, which could be implemented in future space modules to improve comfort and human-environment interaction [41].

We believe that an interdisciplinary approach to design, and the transfer of knowledge and competencies between contexts, will be essential for developing innovative solutions that place the human being, the environment, and the community at the center of the design process analyzing and enhancing the relationships among them, regardless of the domain of application.

Acknowledgments. This study was carried out within the MICS (Made in Italy – Circular and Sustainable) Extended Partnership and received funding from the European Union Next-GenerationEU (PIANO NAZIONALE DI RIPRESA E RESILIENZA (PNRR) – MISSIONE 4 COMPONENTE 2, INVESTIMENTO 1.3 – D.D. 1551.11-10-2022, PE00000004). This manuscript reflects only the authors' views and opinions, neither the European Union nor the European Commission can be considered responsible for them.

The project "Beyond the Space Life. Digital Living Lab for human life in space" is within Spoke 1 of the extended partnership 'Made in Italy Circolare e Sostenibile' (MICS).

This paper was translated with the support of artificial intelligence tools, and subsequently reviewed and verified by a human for accuracy and consistency.

The paper is the result of a joint effort of all two Authors. However, "1.Introduction", "2. Designing for New Space Economy: Theoretical Framework" and "Responsible Advanced Design and Human System Integration for Space Habitat Design" is attributed to L. Succini; "4. Designing Adaptive Space Habitats through Needs-Based Configuration" is attributed to R. Montemurro and L. Succini; "5. Discussion is attributed to R. Montemurro; "6. Future Developments: Application in the Automotive Field" is attributed to all Authors.

References

1. Slane, F.A., et al.: Evolving space architecture – opening the door for the space industry. In: AIAA SCITECH 2022 Forum. American Institute of Aeronautics and Astronautics, San Diego/Virtual (2022)

2. Dominoni, A., Quaquaro, B.: Le città dell'universo: come sarà abitare nello spazio. Il saggiatore, Milano (2023)

3. Orlova, A., Nogueira, R., Chimenti, P.: The present and future of the space sector: a business ecosystem approach. Space Policy. **52**, 101374 (2020). https://doi.org/10.1016/j.spacepol.2020.101374

4. Häuplik-Meusburger, S., Bannova, O.: Space Architecture Education for Engineers and Architects: Designing and Planning Beyond Earth. Springer International Publishing, Cham (2016)

5. Häuplik-Meusburger, S., Bishop, S.: Space Habitats and Habitability: Designing for Isolated and Confined Environments on Earth and in Space. Springer International Publishing, Cham (2021)

6. Raybeck, D.: Proxemics and privacy: managing the problems of life in confined environments. In: Harrison, A.A., Clearwater, Y.A., McKay, C.P. (eds.) From Antarctica to Outer Space, pp. 317–330. Springer New York, New York (1991)

7. Succini, L., Ciravegna, E., Celaschi, F., Pasini, V.: Responsible advanced design: achieving sustainability through collaborative processes. TdD, 92–111 (2024). https://doi.org/10.46467/TdD40.2024.92-111

8. Succini, L.: Leggere l'Innovazione Responsabile attraverso l'Advanced Design. In: Formia, E., Gianfrate, V., Succini, L. (eds.) Design per l'innovazione responsabile: guida per processi formativi in trasformazione, pp. 21–36. FrancoAngeli, Milano (2023)

9. OECD ed: The space economy in figures: how space contributes to the global economy. OECD Publishing, Paris (2019)

10. European Investment Bank.: The future of the European space sector: how to leverage Europe's technological leadership and boost investments for space ventures. Publications Office, LU (2019). https://doi.org/10.2867/399837

11. European Space Policy Institute, Copenhagen Institute for Future Studies: Future of Space Exploration: Strategic Scenarios for European Space Exploration 2040–2060. CIFS (2023). https://www.espi.or.at/wp-content/uploads/2025/02/Future-of-European-Space-Exploration_final-version-7.pdf. Last accessed 12 June 2025

12. Zancan, V., Paravano, A., Locatelli, G., Trucco, P.: Evolving governance in the space sector: from legacy space to new space models. Acta Astronaut. **225**, 515–523 (2024). https://doi.org/10.1016/j.actaastro.2024.09.005

13. Russo, G., et al.: Cislunar city: the outpost of humankind expansion into space. In: Gambardella, C. (ed.) For Nature/With Nature: New Sustainable Design Scenarios, pp. 999–1038. Springer Nature Switzerland, Cham (2024)

14. Häuplik-Meusburger, S., Maiwald, V., Perino, M.A., Bannova, O., Patarin-Jossec: The multidisciplinary world of space habitation design. Room Space J. Asgardia. (33). Austria (2023). https://room.eu.com/article/the-multidisciplinary-world-of-space-habitation-design. Last accessed 12 June 2025

15. Peng, K.-L., Kou, I.E., Chen, H.: Space Tourism Value Chain: When East Meets West. Springer Nature Singapore, Singapore (2024)

16. Sherwood, B.: Decadal opportunities for space architects. Acta Astronaut. **81**, 600–609 (2012). https://doi.org/10.1016/j.actaastro.2012.07.021

17. Mohanty, S., Imhof, B.: Microcosmic getaways aboard space habitats. Thresholds. **30**, 42–49 (2005). https://doi.org/10.1162/thld_a_00284

18. Bannova, O.: Space Architecture: Human Habitats beyond Planet Earth. DOM publishers, Berlin (2021)
19. Dominoni, A.: Design of Supporting Systems for Life in Outer Space: A Design Perspective on Space Missions Near Earth and Beyond. Springer, Cham (2021)
20. NASA: NASA spaceflight human-system standard, volume 2: human factors, habitability, and environmental health (Rev. D) (2023). https://www.nasa.gov/wp-content/uploads/2023/11/nasa-std-3001-vol-2-rev-d-with-signature.pdf. Last accessed 12 June 2025
21. Cohen, M.M., Junge, M.K.: Space Station crew safety: human factors model. Proc. Hum. Factors Soc. Annu. Meet. **28**, 908–912 (1984). https://doi.org/10.1177/154193128402801016
22. Van Ellen, L., Bridgens, B., Burford, N., Crown, M., Heidrich, O.: Adaptability of space habitats using the rhythmic buildings strategy. Acta Astronaut. **211**, 764–780 (2023). https://doi.org/10.1016/j.actaastro.2023.06.045
23. Zakoyan, N., et al.: Sustainable life beyond the earth. How to enhance habitat comfort for space travellers. In: 35th IAA Symposium on Space and Society. pp. 548–563. International Astronautical Federation (IAF), Milan (2024)
24. Succini, L. Bastoni, G.: Space Design sperimentations. Il Responsible Advanced Design a supporto della progettazione di soluzioni plurali per contesti Spaziali. In: DesignPlurale. National Conference Sid, Naple, Italy (in press)
25. Vakoch, D.A. (ed.): Psychology of Space Exploration: Contemporary Research in Historical Perspective. National Aeronautics and Space Administration, Office of Communications, History Program Office, Washington, DC (2011)
26. Celi, M.: Advanced Design Cultures. Springer, New York (2015)
27. Celaschi, F., Formia, E., Iñiguez Flores, R., León Morán, R.: Design processes and anticipation. In: Poli, R. (ed.) Handbook of Anticipation, pp. 773–793. Springer International Publishing, Cham (2019)
28. Stilgoe, J., Macnaghten, P., Gorman, M., Fisher, E., Guston, D., Guston, D.: A framework for responsible innovation. In: Owen, R., Bessant, J., Heintz, M. (eds.) Responsible Innovation, pp. 27–50. Wiley, Chichester (2013)
29. Celaschi, F.: Non Industrial Design: Contributi al discorso progettuale. Sossella, Rome (2016)
30. Succini, L., Ciravegna, E., Giardina, C.: Fostering regenerative processes through responsible advanced design and circularity. In: Cobreros, C., Giorgi, E., Cattaneo, T. (eds.) Regenerative Design, pp. 69–93. Springer Nature Switzerland, Cham (2025)
31. NASA: Human Integration Design Handbook (HIDH) (NASA/SP-2010-3407/REV1). NASA (2014). https://www.nasa.gov/wp-content/uploads/2015/03/human_integration_design_handbook_revision_1.pdf. Last accessed 12 June 2025
32. Boy, G.A., Doule, O., Kiss, D.V.M., Mehta, Y.: Human–Systems Integration Verification Principles for Commercial Space Transportation. New Space. **6**, 53–64 (2018). https://doi.org/10.1089/space.2017.0040
33. Häuplik-Meusburger, S.: Architecture for Astronauts: An Activity-Based Approach. Springer Praxis Books, Wien/New York (2011)
34. Smith, L.: Space station and spacecraft environmental conditions and human mental health: specific recommendations and guidelines. Life Sci. Space Res. **40**, 126–134 (2024). https://doi.org/10.1016/j.lssr.2023.10.001
35. Sundar, S.M., et al.: Personalization – exploring concepts and guidelines for AI-driven personalization of in-car HMIs in fully automated vehicles. Adv. Transp. **60**, 423–431 (2022). https://doi.org/10.54941/ahfe1002474
36. DeCastro, J., et al.: Personalizing driver safety interfaces via driver cognitive factors inference. Sci. Rep. **14**, 18058 (2024). https://doi.org/10.1038/s41598-024-65144-8
37. Popp, R.F.J., Ottersbach, J., Wetter, T.C., Schüler, S.: Multimodal in-vehicle lighting system increases daytime light exposure and alertness in truck drivers under Arctic winter conditions. Sci. Rep. **14**, 9925 (2024). https://doi.org/10.1038/s41598-024-60308-

38. Braun, F., Stegmüller, S., Agola, D., Hamel, C., Gerlach, P., Edel, F.: The vehicle as an immersive device to enhance the mental health to a peak state. In: Advances in Human Factors and Systems Interaction (AHFE Conference Proceedings) (2020)
39. Celaschi, F., Succini, L., Zannoni, M. (eds.): Digital Advanced Design. Transitional Industrial Approaches for Sustainable Innovation. Bologna University Press. Bologne (2025)
40. Juliá Nehme, B., Rodríguez, E., Yoon, S.: Spatial user experience: a multidisciplinary approach to assessing physical settings. J. Inter. Des. **45**, 7–25 (2020). https://doi.org/10.1111/joid.12177
41. Presta, R., Tancredi, C., De Simone, F., Iacono, M., Mancuso, L.: Improving time to take over through HMI strategies nudging a safe driving state. In: Krömker, H. (ed.) HCI in Mobility, Transport, and Automotive Systems, pp. 27–43. Springer Nature Switzerland, Cham (2024)

A Service Improvement Approach for Autonomous Taxi Based on Kansei Engineering and the Kano Model: A Case Study of Robo Taxi

Meiyu Zhou[✉], Hai Liu, and Jing Peng

School of Art Design and Media, East China University of Science and Technology, No. 130, Meilong Road, Xuhui District, Shanghai, People's Republic of China
1045074225@qq.com, Y81230087@mail.ecust.edu.cn

Abstract. The objective of this study is to develop or enhance a Kansei engineering-based service improvement methodology previously employed in related research. By integrating Kansei Engineering, text mining, service blueprinting, SERVQUAL, the Kano model, and Quality Function Deployment (QFD), this study proposes a comprehensive approach tailored to service optimization for autonomous ride-hailing platforms.Text mining is employed to extract Kansei-related vocabulary from online customer reviews. The service blueprint is utilized to identify key service attributes, while SERVQUAL is applied to assess the current service quality. The Kano model is used to classify these service attributes into Kano categories, and QFD is adopted to translate customer needs into technical characteristics and operational specifications. The proposed approach is validated through a case study of Robo Taxi, a leading autonomous ride-hailing service platform in China. Beyond autonomous ride-hailing platforms, the methodology is also applicable to broader service industries.

Keywords: Kansei Engineering · Kano Model · Service Design · Autonomous Taxi · Service Blueprint

1 Introduction

1.1 Research Background

With the rapid advancement of technology, the transportation industry has undergone a profound transformation—from traditional taxi services to ride-hailing platforms, and now to autonomous ride-hailing services. This evolution reflects the accelerated pace of digitalization and its far-reaching impact on the industry. At the forefront of this transformation is "Robo Taxi," an autonomous ride-hailing service platform under Baidu. Officially launched on August 18, 2021, Robo Taxi, known as "Luobo Kuaipao" in Chinese, is built upon Baidu's Apollo autonomous driving platform and operates at Level 4 autonomy. It features high-precision perception, intelligent decision-making, and accurate control systems to deliver driverless taxi services. Passengers can use the

P.-L.P. Rau and H. Krömker (Eds.): HCII 2025, LNCS 16336, pp. 309–320, 2026.
https://doi.org/10.1007/978-3-032-12798-3_19

Robo Taxi app on their smartphones to locate a nearby designated pickup point and a fixed drop-off point near their destination, enabling them to book a ride. On average, users wait approximately ten minutes before boarding.

Currently, Robo Taxi is conducting pilot operations in multiple cities across China. As of April 19, 2024, the platform has completed over six million autonomous ride orders for the public. This milestone not only demonstrates Robo Taxi's rapid development in the autonomous mobility sector but also reflects the growing public acceptance of this emerging form of transportation. However, during its pilot phase, several challenges have surfaced—including technical limitations, suboptimal user experiences, and operational inefficiencies.

Addressing these issues effectively and allocating limited resources toward the most critical areas of service improvement have become pressing concerns. Doing so is essential not only for optimizing Robo Taxi's service model but also for facilitating the broader deployment of autonomous mobility services in the future. To assess whether the proposed methodology in this study is suitable for service improvement in autonomous ride-hailing platforms, an in-depth case study was conducted on the Robo Taxi platform. Through this empirical research, we aim to provide valuable insights and recommendations for Robo Taxi and the autonomous mobility industry at large, thereby contributing to its sustainable development and advancement.

1.2 Theoretical Background

Service quality is generally regarded as a key metric of service success and serves as an important indicator for enterprises to evaluate their service performance. A positive relationship exists between service quality and customer satisfaction: the higher the service quality, the greater the level of customer satisfaction [1]. Delivering high-quality services ensures customer satisfaction, making service quality a primary determinant of customer satisfaction. High service quality can help enterprises build a favorable corporate image, enhance customer satisfaction, and foster customer loyalty.

Previous studies have primarily focused on the cognitive relationship between service quality and customer satisfaction, often overlooking the role of customers' emotional responses [2]. Riadh confirmed that emotional satisfaction significantly influences behavioral intentions, and that service quality can also indirectly affect behavioral intentions through emotional satisfaction [3]. Therefore, emotional factors, as direct influencers of emotional satisfaction, should be incorporated into the evaluation framework of service quality and become integral to the entire service design process.

Kansei Engineering is an interdisciplinary field that integrates psychology, engineering, and design, aiming to understand and apply human emotional responses in the design and development of products, services, and environments. It seeks to fulfill users' emotional needs and enhance their experience by translating consumers' feelings and impressions into specific design elements [4]. Originally applied in product design, Kansei Engineering has gradually been adopted in the field of service design.

Existing studies that apply Kansei Engineering for service improvement have mostly followed the methodological framework proposed by Schütte, which provides a systematic approach for designing and evaluating products and services to meet users' emotional and affective needs [5]. The semantic space mapping process comprises three stages:

collecting Kansei words, selecting relevant Kansei words, and compiling data. Traditional studies have relied on questionnaires and interviews to identify Kansei words; however, these methods are time-consuming and may fail to objectively capture users' genuine emotional responses. In recent years, researchers have increasingly utilized online customer reviews and text mining techniques to extract Kansei words. Compared to surveys and interviews, online reviews better reflect customers' authentic emotional experiences.

The attribute space mapping process also consists of three steps: collecting service attributes, evaluating current service quality, and categorizing service attributes. Prior studies often collected service attributes from the literature, without considering the complete service process experienced by customers. In contrast, the service blueprint is a tool that provides a comprehensive and structured depiction of service processes, detailing all necessary activities—both visible and invisible to the customer. Therefore, service blueprints are suitable for identifying relevant service attributes.

In the service quality assessment phase, the SERVQUAL model is employed. SERVQUAL is a widely used instrument for evaluating service quality. For instance, Hartono used SERVQUAL in combination with the Kano model to assess service attributes [6]. Tumsekcali proposed an innovative P-SERVQUAL 4.0 model based on the traditional SERVQUAL framework and combined it with the interval-valued intuitionistic fuzzy AHP-WASPAS method to evaluate public transportation service quality during the COVID-19 pandemic [7]. Jonkisz conducted a literature review that explored the applications of SERVQUAL in the healthcare sector, highlighting its importance and practicality in improving medical service quality [8].

The Kano model is used to classify service attributes, identifying those that most significantly affect customer satisfaction. Developed by Japanese scholar Noriaki Kano in 1984, the Kano model analyzes the relationship between customer needs and satisfaction. In this study, the Kano model is employed to classify service attributes, enabling the identification of those with the greatest impact on customer satisfaction. The service improvement design method proposed in this study, based on Kansei Engineering, is expected to be applicable to service optimization in the operation of autonomous ride-hailing platforms.

2 Methodology

The methodological framework adopted in this study is based on the Kansei Engineering model proposed by Schütte et al. Building upon this foundation, the study integrates additional methods and tools including text mining, service blueprinting, SERVQUAL, the Kano model, and Quality Function Deployment (QFD) to enhance the analysis and application process.

The Semantic Space Domain consists of three main steps: Kansei word collection, Kansei word selection, and the measurement of Kansei word importance. In this study, Kansei words were collected through text mining of online customer reviews. The Affinity Diagram method was then used to cluster and refine these Kansei words. Finally, a questionnaire survey was conducted to evaluate the importance of each selected Kansei word. The Domain of Attribute Space also comprises three parts: service attribute collection, evaluation of current service quality, and classification of service attributes into Kano categories. Service attributes were gathered through service blueprinting and literature review. The SERVQUAL model was used to assess the current level of service quality, while the Kano model was applied to categorize each service attribute based on its ability to fulfill customer needs. Lastly, QFD was employed to identify customer requirements and translate them into technical characteristics, thereby providing actionable directions for service improvement.

3 Experimental Procedure

3.1 Selection of Service Domain

Ride-hailing has become an integral part of daily transportation. With the advancement of artificial intelligence technologies, autonomous ride-hailing services have entered commercial operation, exemplified by platforms such as Waymo in the United States and Robo Taxi in China. In order to enhance customer satisfaction and loyalty, these platforms must deliver high-quality services. As a pilot autonomous ride-hailing service, Robo Taxi urgently needs to identify and address shortcomings in its current service process. Therefore, this study selects the user experience of Robo Taxi as the service domain. The target customer group comprises users who have used Robo Taxi at least once within the past year.

3.2 Collection of Kansei Words

Previous studies employing Kansei Engineering to design or improve services have primarily used questionnaires or interviews to collect Kansei words. However, these methods are time-consuming and typically involve small sample sizes. With the rise of the internet and online consumption, consumers now leave abundant reviews and feedback across e-commerce platforms, social media, and online forums. These comments reflect users' perceptions and evaluations of products, services, and experiences, offering rich sources for Kansei word extraction. Compared to traditional methods, online reviews are more timely, voluminous, cost-effective, and more objectively reflective of customers' true impressions and emotions, making them a valuable resource for identifying affective needs.

In this study, due to the limited number of user reviews on app stores for the Robo Taxi mobile application, we used Python 3.9 to scrape all posts related to "Robo Taxi" from the Chinese social media platform REDnote, resulting in a total of 5,248 posts. The main content and first-level comments were extracted and preprocessed through deduplication, cleaning, word segmentation, stop word removal, and part-of-speech tagging. This process yielded 234 adjectives. After further screening, 125 adjectives were identified as relevant to describing customer impressions and emotions.

Next, using the Affinity Diagram Method, two design experts assisted in grouping semantically similar Kansei words. This process resulted in 10 final Kansei descriptors: intelligent, efficient, safe, convenient, innovative, environmental, comfortable, reliable, accurate, and enthusiastic.

3.3 Kansei Response and Importance Questionnaires

Two separate questionnaires were administered to collect users' genuine emotional responses: a Kansei Response Questionnaire and a Kansei Importance Questionnaire (Tables 1 and 2). Participants were instructed to complete a 6-point semantic differential scale based on their past experiences with Robo Taxi. The scale ranged from 1 to 6, corresponding to increasing intensities of each Kansei response.

Table 1. Kansei response questionnaire used in this study.

Negative Kansei	Kansei Score						Positive Kansei
Stupid	1	2	3	4	5	6	Intelligent
Inefficient	1	2	3	4	5	6	Efficient
Dangerous	1	2	3	4	5	6	Safe
Inconvenient	1	2	3	4	5	6	Convenient
Traditional	1	2	3	4	5	6	Innovative
Pollutional	1	2	3	4	5	6	Environmental
Uncomfortable	1	2	3	4	5	6	Comfortable
Unreliable	1	2	3	4	5	6	Reliable
Inaccurate	1	2	3	4	5	6	Accurate
Pococurante	1	2	3	4	5	6	Enthusiastic

3.4 Collection and Evaluation of Service Attributes

This study identified service attributes through a combination of service blueprinting and literature review. A service blueprint is a visual tool that details the entire service delivery process, which facilitates the identification of necessary service attributes. In total, sixteen service attributes were collected and categorized into the five dimensions of SERVQUAL: reliability, responsiveness, assurance, empathy, and tangibles. To assess both the actual performance and customer expectations of each service attribute, a SERVQUAL questionnaire was developed (Table 3) and administered to respondents who had previously completed the Kansei questionnaire. Instead of calculating the traditional gap score between expectation and perception, this study employed the direct comparison method, where respondents directly evaluated each service attribute. Brown found that the direct comparison approach offers superior psychometric properties and reduces both questionnaire complexity and respondent burden [9].

To gain a deeper understanding of customer need hierarchies and thereby optimize resource allocation, the Kano model was applied to classify service attributes based on their impact on customer satisfaction. Accordingly, a Kano questionnaire was administered using a five-point Likert scale, in which customers evaluated both functional and dysfunctional statements for each service attribute (Table 4). Traditional Kano classification relies on a fixed evaluation table, but this can introduce certain biases. Therefore, this study utilized the method proposed by Madzík, which more accurately determines the Kano category and assigns a weight to each service attribute [10]. In this approach, the number of responses in each Kano category—Attractive (A), One-dimensional (O), Must-be (M), Indifferent (I), Reverse (R), and Questionable (Q)—is multiplied by corresponding coefficients, then summed and divided by the total number of responses to calculate a Kano weighted score for each attribute. The coefficients used in this study were A = 3, O = 2, M = 1, I = 0, and R = –2; attributes categorized as Questionable (Q) were excluded from the analysis.

Table 2. Kansei importance questionnaire used in this study.

Emotional Needs	Importance Score					
I hope that the driverless ride-hailing service provided by RoboTaxi is intelligent	1	2	3	4	5	6
I hope that the driverless ride-hailing service provided by RoboTaxi is efficient	1	2	3	4	5	6
I hope that the driverless ride-hailing service provided by RoboTaxi is safe	1	2	3	4	5	6
I hope to conveniently take the driverless ride-hailing service provided by RoboTaxi	1	2	3	4	5	6
I hope that the driverless ride-hailing service provided by RoboTaxi is innovative	1	2	3	4	5	6
I hope that the driverless ride-hailing service provided by RoboTaxi is environmental	1	2	3	4	5	6
I hope that the driverless ride-hailing service provided by RoboTaxi is comfortable	1	2	3	4	5	6
I hope that the driverless ride-hailing service provided by RoboTaxi is reliable	1	2	3	4	5	6
I hope the driving route of the RoboTaxi driverless ride-hailing service is accurate	1	2	3	4	5	6
I hope the service of the Robotaxi driverless ride-hailing service provided by RoboTaxi is enthusiastic	1	2	3	4	5	6

The procedure involved first calculating descriptive statistics such as the minimum, maximum, mean, and standard deviation for each service attribute based on Kano questionnaire responses. Next, the number of responses falling into each Kano category was tallied, multiplied by their respective coefficients, and summed. This total was then divided by the total number of valid responses to yield the Kano weighted score. The Kano category of each service attribute was determined according to this score: scores between −2 and 0 indicated a Reverse attribute, scores between 0 and 1 indicated Indifferent, scores between 1 and 2 indicated Must-be, scores between 2 and 3 indicated One-dimensional, and scores greater than 3 indicated Attractive. Descriptive statistics for the SERVQUAL questionnaire combined with Kano classifications are presented in Table 5. he Kano classification results for each service attribute can also be seen in Table 5. Based on the Kano classification results, there were 2 service attributes that belong to the attractive (A) category, 7 service attributes that belong to the one-dimensional (O) category, and 7 service attributes that belong to the must-be (M) category.

Table 3. An example of SERVQUAL questionnaire used in this study.

Assurance	Service Quality Score				
Robo Taxi protect the privacy of users	1	2	3	4	5
The technology of Robo Taxi autopilot is very mature	1	2	3	4	5
Robo Taxi vehicle security is high	1	2	3	4	5

Table 4. An example of Kano questionnaire used in this study.

Assurance	Score				
Robo Taxi protect the privacy of users	1	2	3	4	5
Robo Taxi do not protect the privacy of users	1	2	3	4	5
The technology of Robo Taxi autopilot is very mature	1	2	3	4	5
The technology of Robo Taxi autopilot is not very mature	1	2	3	4	5
Robo Taxi vehicle security is high	1	2	3	4	5
Robo Taxi vehicle security is low	1	2	3	4	5

Table 5. Descriptive statistics of SERVQUAL questionnaire incorporated with Kano category.

Variables	Min	Max	Mean	Std. Dev.	Kano Weight	Kano Category
AL1 Vehicle arrive on time	1	5	3.938	0.525	2.144	O
AL2 Accurate route	1	5	3.019	0.472	2.125	O
AL3 Service remains excellent	1	5	2.938	0.471	1.661	M
AL4 Reasonable charging	1	5	3.106	0.439	1.423	M
AL5 Order response is fast	1	5	2.971	0.506	2.009	O
AL6 System remains stable	1	5	3.005	0.432	1.634	M
AL7 Actively handle complaints	1	5	2.947	0.516	1.182	M
AL8 Provide personalized services	1	5	3.029	0.440	2.009	O
AL9 Mature technology	1	5	2.889	0.492	1.625	M
AL10 High vehicle safety	1	5	2.923	0.496	1.355	M
AL11 Protecting user privacy	1	5	2.957	0.457	1.817	M
AL12 Provide accessibility services	1	5	3.038	0.464	2.148	O

(continued)

Table 5. (*continued*)

Variables	Min	Max	Mean	Std. Dev.	Kano Weight	Kano Category
AL13 Offer customized itineraries	1	5	3.976	0.485	3.023	A
AL14 The car is clean inside	1	5	3.954	0.477	3.016	A
AL15 The car is attractive	1	5	3.011	0.516	2.074	O
AL16 Attractive interface	1	5	3.465	0.507	2.175	O

3.5 Questionnaire Collection and Processing

The online questionnaires were developed and distributed using the Wenjuanxing platform. A total of 350 responses were collected for each questionnaire. After excluding responses from participants who had not used the Robo Taxi autonomous ride-hailing service within the past year and those with excessive duplicate selections, 330 valid responses were retained for subsequent analysis, resulting in a response rate of 94.29%. Among the respondents, 194 were male and 136 were female, with 49% falling within the age group of 21–25.

To assess the reliability of the questionnaires shown in Tables 1, 2, 3, and 4, Cronbach's alpha was calculated using IBM SPSS Statistics 27. The results indicated high internal consistency: the Kansei Response Questionnaire yielded a reliability coefficient of 0.976, the Kansei Importance Questionnaire 0.898, the SERVQUAL questionnaire 0.894, and the Kano questionnaire 0.948—all exceeding the commonly accepted threshold of 0.7, thereby demonstrating high questionnaire reliability.

3.6 Multiple Linear Regression Analysis

Multiple linear regression analysis was conducted to examine the relationships between service attributes classified as Attractive (A), One-Dimensional (O), or Must-be (M) under the Kano model and the Kansei responses. The aim of this analysis was to understand the correlations between Kansei words and service attributes. In this process, Kansei words were treated as dependent variables, while service attributes served as independent variables. The analysis was performed using IBM SPSS Statistics 27, and the statistically significant regression models are presented in Table 6.

As shown in Table 6, four significant linear regression models were identified. Among the 16 service attributes included as independent variables, 13 were found to be significantly associated with specific Kansei words. The R^2 values of the regression models ranged from 0.136 to 0.214, indicating moderate levels of model fit. According to Falk and Miller, an R^2 value above 0.1 is considered acceptable in exploratory studies. Hence, all four regression models in this study are deemed valid [11].

Table 6. Significant linear regression model for each Kansei word.

Kansei Words	Significant Linear Regression Model	R^2	p-value
K3 Safe	0.266AL9 + 0.231AL10 + 0.108AL11	0.136	$\leq$0.001
K7 Comfortable	0.116AL1 + 0.163AL14 + 0.108AL15	0.175	$\leq$0.001
K8 Reliable	0.190AL2 + 0.247AL3 + 0.138AL4 + 0.179AL6	0.214	$\leq$0.001
K10 Enthusiastic	0.186AL5 + 0.163AL7 + 0.224AL12 + 0.181AL13	0.145	$\leq$0.001

3.7 Solution Analysis

A House of Quality (HOQ) matrix was constructed to prioritize service improvements for the Robo Taxi platform. Following the method proposed by Pawitra and Tan, the HOQ matrix was developed to identify and prioritize customer requirements [12]. Customer needs were derived from the results presented in Table 5. Among the 16 service attributes analyzed, 14 were found to be associated with Kansei words and were thus regarded as the customer requirements in the HOQ.

The priority or importance of each customer requirement was determined by multiplying three factors: the service quality score, the Kano weight, and the Kansei word score. The service quality score was calculated as the reciprocal of the mean evaluation score from the SERVQUAL questionnaire, such that a lower average SERVQUAL score corresponds to higher importance. Kano weights were taken from the results of the Kano questionnaire (Table 4), and the Kansei word scores were derived as the mean importance ratings across 14 Kansei descriptors.

Once the customer requirements and their relative importance were established, the next step was to assess the strength of the relationships between customer requirements and technical requirements. The HOQ matrix developed in this study is illustrated in Fig. 1. Relationship strength was represented using three symbols: (●) for strong (assigned a value of 9), (●) for moderate (assigned a value of 6), and (○) for weak (assigned a value of 3). Based on this matrix, the importance level of each technical requirement was computed. The average importance weight across all technical requirements was found to be 32.16 (14.29%). As such, service improvement efforts will prioritize technical requirements with weights above this average, namely: Advanced Autonomous Driving System (22.32%), High-Precision Maps (19.43%), and Remote Operations and Monitoring Platform (16.72%).

Customer Requirements	Technical Requirements							Importance Weight of Customer Requirements	Percentage
	Advanced autonomous driving system	High-precision maps	Remote operations and monitoring platform	Vehicle-end redundant safety architecture	HMI	Privacy protection and data security	Vehicle interior cleaning management system		
AL1 Vehicle arrive on time	●	●	○					2.144	6.14%
AL2 Accurate route	●	●						2.125	6.08%
AL3 Service remains excellent	◎	◎	◎				●	1.661	4.76%
AL4 Reasonable charging	◎	◎	○					1.423	4.07%
AL5 Order response is fast		◎						2.009	5.75%
AL6 System remains stable	◎			●				1.634	4.68%
AL7 Actively handle complaints			●					1.182	3.38%
AL9 Mature technology	●	◎						2.889	8.27%
AL10 High vehicle safety	●	●		●				2.923	8.37%
AL11 Protecting user privacy			●			●		2.957	8.47%
AL12 Provide accessibility services	○	◎				○		3.038	9.47%
AL13 Offer customized itineraries	○	○			●			3.976	11.38%
AL14 The car is clean inside			◎				●	3.954	11.32%
AL15 The car is attractive					◎		◎	3.011	8.62%
Importance Weight of Technical Requirements	50.24	43.75	37.62	26.25	16.34	28.73	22.18		
Percentage	22.32%	19.43%	16.72%	11.66%	7.26%	12.76%	9.85%		
Priority	1	2	3	5	7	4	6		

Fig. 1. House of quality (HoQ) matrix.

In the future development of Robo Taxi, targeted service improvements will be carried out for the three high-priority technical requirements. First, regarding the Advanced Autonomous Driving System, Robo Taxi should focus on enhancing the robustness and adaptability of its L4-level driving algorithms. This includes improving performance under complex real-world scenarios such as adverse weather, construction zones, and unpredictable urban conditions. Decision-making modules should be optimized using advanced AI techniques like deep reinforcement learning or V2X cooperative perception, enabling smoother vehicle behavior in mixed traffic environments. Moreover, better path planning and dynamic dispatch can reduce wait times and inefficient routing, directly improving customer perceptions of reliability, intelligence, and efficiency.

Second, improvements to High-Precision Maps are crucial for ensuring both safety and user comfort. Robo Taxi can accelerate the update frequency of its high-definition maps, especially in rapidly changing urban areas. Integrating real-time sensor data or crowdsourced information can further enhance map accuracy and responsiveness. Additionally, the user-facing experience can be improved by offering more intuitive visualizations of pick-up/drop-off points and route previews within the mobile application. These enhancements directly contribute to positive emotional responses such as feelings of convenience, accuracy, and control.

Third, the Remote Operations and Monitoring Platform plays a critical role in building user trust in an unmanned mobility experience. Robo Taxi should strengthen the responsiveness and intelligence of its remote support system, enabling human operators to intervene promptly in emergency or uncertain situations. Establishing a clear and accessible communication interface between passengers and remote personnel—such as in-vehicle voice assistance linked to real-time human support—can alleviate anxiety and provide reassurance. Moreover, predictive maintenance and intelligent alert systems can help preempt potential failures, further enhancing perceptions of safety, empathy, and reliability.

By strategically prioritizing these three technical areas, Robo Taxi can better align its service offerings with users' emotional and functional expectations. This not only enhances customer satisfaction and loyalty but also strengthens the platform's competitive positioning in the rapidly evolving autonomous mobility market.

4 Conclusions

4.1 Research Contributions and Methodological Advancements.

Kansei Engineering can be effectively integrated with other methodologies and technologies to develop more efficient, user-centered, and comprehensive solutions for service design and improvement. By capturing and responding to the emotional and perceptual needs of users, Kansei Engineering enables service providers to deliver experiences that go beyond functional performance. In this study, we proposed an innovative Kansei-based methodological framework specifically tailored for service improvement, particularly in the context of autonomous ride-hailing platforms. This integrated approach combines Kansei Engineering with text mining, service blueprinting, SERVQUAL, the Kano model, and Quality Function Deployment (QFD) to systematically identify, evaluate, and translate customer needs into actionable technical requirements.

Text mining was employed to extract Kansei-related descriptors from online customer reviews, offering a data-driven, authentic, and scalable method to capture emotional vocabulary. Compared to traditional survey-based approaches, this method allows for richer insights into user sentiments and expectations. The service blueprint provided a visual and structured representation of the entire service delivery process, allowing researchers to identify key service attributes across the frontstage and backstage of customer interaction. To assess the existing service performance, the SERVQUAL model was utilized, providing a quantitative evaluation of service gaps across five core dimensions: reliability, responsiveness, assurance, empathy, and tangibles.

The Kano model was instrumental in classifying service attributes according to their contribution to customer satisfaction, distinguishing between must-be, one-dimensional, and attractive qualities. This classification helped to prioritize attributes that not only meet basic expectations but also have the potential to delight users. The final stage of the methodology involved QFD, which served as a structured mechanism to transform customer voice into technical specifications. The House of Quality (HOQ) matrix was employed to establish the strength of relationships between customer needs and technical solutions, guiding resource allocation and strategic decision-making in service development. The HOQ further provided a clear prioritization of improvement areas, ensuring that enhancement efforts are aligned with user expectations and business goals.

4.2 Limitations and Future Work

Despite the effectiveness of the proposed framework, the study has some limitations. A complete QFD process consists of four progressive phases, but this research only implemented the first phase, which maps customer requirements to technical requirements.

Future studies should consider extending the framework to include subsequent phases of QFD, such as component deployment, process planning, and production planning, to provide a more complete service engineering solution. Moreover, while the framework was validated through an empirical case study involving the Robo Taxi autonomous ride-hailing service, further validation across different industries—such as healthcare, hospitality, public transportation, and smart retail—would enhance its generalizability and robustness.

In summary, the integration of Kansei Engineering with quantitative and qualitative service design tools presents a promising approach to address the complex and emotional nature of customer experience in the era of intelligent services. As autonomous technologies continue to evolve and permeate service environments, the need for emotionally intelligent and experience-driven service design will become increasingly critical. This research contributes a structured, scalable, and human-centered methodology that not only supports service improvement in current autonomous mobility systems but also lays the groundwork for future innovations in emotionally responsive service ecosystems.

References

1. Getty, J.M., Getty, R.L.: Lodging quality index (LQI): assessing customers' perceptions of quality delivery. Int. J. Contemp. Hosp. Manag. **15**(2), 94–104 (2003)
2. Wong, A.: The role of emotional satisfaction in service encounters. Manag. Serv. Qual. Int. J. **14**(5), 365–376 (2004)
3. Ladhari, R.: Service quality, emotional satisfaction, and behavioural intentions: a study in the hotel industry. Manag. Serv. Qual. Int. J. **19**(3), 308–331 (2009)
4. Nagamachi, M.: Kansei engineering: a new ergonomic consumer-oriented technology for product development. Int. J. Ind. Ergon. **15**(1), 3–11 (1995)
5. Schütte, S.T.W., Eklund, J., Axelsson, J.R.C., Nagamachi, M.: Concepts, methods and tools in Kansei engineering. Theor. Issues Ergon. Sci. **5**(3), 214–231 (2004)
6. Hartono, M.: The modified Kansei Engineering-based application for sustainable service design. Int. J. Ind. Ergon. **79**, 102985 (2020)
7. Tumsekcali, E., Ayyildiz, E., Taskin, A.: Interval valued intuitionistic fuzzy AHP-WASPAS based public transportation service quality evaluation by a new extension of SERVQUAL model: P-SERVQUAL 4.0. Expert Syst. Appl. **186**, 115757 (2021)
8. Jonkisz, A., Karniej, P., Krasowska, D.: SERVQUAL method as an "old new" tool for improving the quality of medical services: a literature review. Int. J. Environ. Res. Public Health. **18**(20), 10758 (2021)
9. Brown, T.J., Churchill, G.A., Peter, J.P.: Improving the measurement of service quality. J. Retail. **69**(1), 127–139 (1993)
10. Madzík, P.: Increasing accuracy of the Kano model – a case study. Total Qual. Manag. Bus. Excell. **29**(34), 387–409 (2016)
11. Falk, R.F., Miller, N.B.: A primer for soft modeling. University of Akron Press, Akron (1992)
12. Pawitra, T.A., Tan, K.C.: Tourist satisfaction in Singapore – a perspective from Indonesian tourists. Manag. Serv. Qual. Int. J. **13**(5), 399411 (2003)

Human Factors, Safety, and Driver Assistance

Towards Enhanced Driver Awareness: Designing an In-Vehicle Visual Interface for a Pedestrian Protection ADAS

Manuel Andruccioli[(✉)] , Kelvin Olaiya , Giovanni Delnevo , Silvia Mirri , and Roberto Girau

Department of Computer Science and Engineering, University of Bologna, Bologna, Italy
{manuel.andruccioli,kelvin.olaiya,giovanni.delnevo,silvia.mirri, roberto.girau}@unibo.it

Abstract. Pedestrian safety remains a critical concern in urban environments, with vulnerable road users accounting for a significant portion of traffic fatalities worldwide. This study presents the design, implementation, and evaluation of a human-centered in-vehicle visual interface integrated into a Pedestrian Protection Advanced Driver-Assistance System (ADAS). Leveraging the CARLA simulator, the system incorporates sensor fusion between RGB and depth cameras, alongside a YOLOv8-based detection pipeline, to enhance real-time pedestrian recognition. A participatory design process, including mockups and focus group sessions, guided the development of the interface, which uses multimodal alerts and intuitive visual cues to convey risk levels and improve driver situational awareness. The interface divides the driving scene into safe, warning, and danger zones, dynamically updating alert information based on estimated time-to-collision. Evaluation through user testing and the User Experience Questionnaire (UEQ) demonstrated strong usability, particularly in terms of perspicuity and efficiency, confirming the system's effectiveness in supporting timely and informed driver responses without causing cognitive overload.

Keywords: Pedestrian Safety · User-Centered Design · Human-Machine Interface · ADAS · YOLOv8 · CARLA Simulator

1 Introduction

As autonomous and semi-autonomous vehicle technologies continue to advance, the interaction between drivers and in-vehicle systems remains a critical factor in ensuring road safety [30]. One key aspect of this interaction is the protection of vulnerable road users, such as pedestrians, through Advanced Driver-Assistance Systems (ADAS). According to the World Health Organization [20], traffic accidents are one of the leading causes of death and injuries worldwide, accounting for an estimated 1.2 million fatalities and 50 million injuries annually. Pedestrians represent a significant proportion of these fatalities, particularly in low-income countries, where they make up 65% of traffic-related deaths, according to the World Bank [32]. In developed nations, pedestrian fatalities are lower but still pose a major societal and economic burden. For example, in USA, there were 7,522 pedestrian fatalities in 2022, accounting for 18% of total traffic-related deaths [12]. In Great Britain, the most common factors for pedestrians fatalities, between 2019 and 2023, were "failed to look properly" (8,832), "careless, reckless, or in a hurry" (3,279), and "failure to judge vehicle's path or speed" (2,912) [29]. The issue is even more severe in developing countries like India and China, where pedestrian and cyclist fatalities are alarmingly high due to inadequate infrastructure and mixed road usage [26]. With rapid urbanization and increasing vehicle numbers, these statistics highlight the urgency of developing effective ADAS technologies to enhance pedestrian safety. However, their effectiveness largely depends on how well they integrate with human cognitive processes and decision-making in real-time driving scenarios. This study investigates the effectiveness of an in-vehicle driver alerting system aimed at enhancing pedestrian protection.

Ensuring pedestrian safety requires a multifaceted approach that combines infrastructure improvements with advancements in vehicle technology. Modifying streets and walkways to enhance pedestrian safety includes measures such as dedicated pedestrian zones, high-visibility crosswalks, traffic calming techniques to reduce vehicle speeds, and improved lighting in high-footfall areas. Meanwhile, vehicle manufacturers are continuously improving designs to minimize pedestrian injuries in collisions by incorporating softer front-end structures, energy-absorbing materials, external airbags, and automatic pop-up hoods. These passive safety features are complemented by active safety systems aimed at preventing accidents altogether. Advanced pedestrian detection technology, automatic emergency braking, and real-time warning systems are key components of modern ADAS, working together to alert drivers and mitigate risks before a collision occurs [8]. By integrating these infrastructure-based and vehicular safety advancements, we can create safer environments for pedestrians and significantly reduce accident rates.

Despite the promising potential of ADAS in improving road safety, several challenges hinder their widespread adoption and effectiveness. User acceptance remains a critical issue [6], as drivers may either overly rely on the system, leading to complacency, or distrust its capabilities, reducing its intended impact [13,27]. Additionally, behavioral adaptation can result in unintended consequences, such as risk compensation, where drivers engage in riskier behaviors due to perceived safety improvements. Another significant challenge lies in the regulatory landscape, as government policies and regulations for ADAS implementation vary widely, creating barriers to standardization and deployment [31]. The lack of a unified framework complicates the integration of these systems into commercial vehicles, potentially delaying adoption. Furthermore, in-vehicle alerting systems, if not properly designed, may introduce cognitive overload, increasing the risk of driver distraction and leading to unintended negative consequences

[3]. Technological limitations, including sensor inaccuracies, poor performance in adverse weather conditions, and processing delays, also pose challenges to real-time pedestrian detection and warning mechanisms [10]. Additionally, the absence of comprehensive behavioral theories and empirical evidence to guide the design of these systems [24] hinders their usability and effectiveness in real-world driving conditions.

In this work, we propose and evaluate a pedestrian protection system that employs an ADAS-based in-vehicle driver alerting system. Our approach leverages the Carla Simulator to model realistic driving scenarios and assess driver interactions with the system. The ADAS integrates a sensor fusion technique combining an RGB camera and a depth camera to enhance pedestrian detection accuracy. This fusion approach improves perception in varying lighting and environmental conditions, reducing false positives and enhancing object recognition. Additionally, a YOLOv8-based detection algorithm processes sensor data in real-time to identify pedestrians with high-speed and high-accuracy detection. To ensure a human-centered design, the in-vehicle alerting system was iteratively developed through focus group sessions and experience prototyping. User testing during development allowed for refinements in alert modality, timing, and frequency, balancing cognitive load while maximizing driver awareness.

The remainder of paper goes as follows. Section 2 presents some related works. Section 3 describes the design process while Sect. 4 details the implemented system. The participants' tests and evaluation of the system are reported in Sect. 5. Finally, Sect. 6 concludes the paper, paving the way for future works.

2   Related Works

This Section reviews existing literature on active safety systems for pedestrian protection, human factors influencing ADAS acceptance and use, and the role of simulation in ADAS evaluation.

Active Safety Systems for Pedestrian Protection. Early efforts to address pedestrian crashes relied on forward collision warning and Automatic Emergency Braking (AEB). Volvo's third-generation *Collision Warning with Full Auto Brake and Pedestrian Detection* system (CWAB-PD) combined radar and vision sensors to avoid or mitigate impacts at closing speeds up to 35 km/h [5]. Field data confirm real-world benefits: pedestrian-detecting AEB reduces police-reported pedestrian crash risk by roughly 25–27% and injury crash risk by 29–30% [4].

Modern pedestrian detection pipelines increasingly build on single-stage deep networks such as YOLO. The seminal YOLO framework unified detection into a single pass through a convolutional network, enabling real-time performance [25]. Subsequent work emphasises domain generalisation; Hitke et al. [11] conducted a comprehensive review of domain adaptation approaches that aim to adapt existing detectors to new domains. Sensor–level fusion complements these advances: depth, radar or event cameras augment RGB imagery to improve detection in low-illumination and adverse-weather scenarios [9].

In Brazil, the rising number of motorcycle accidents due to blind spots prompted the development of an ADAS alerting system using visual and haptic feedback, designed with user experience in mind [21]. This system, conceived through co-design and evaluated by end-users, demonstrated that simple, easily interpretable interfaces are crucial for ADAS, ensuring drivers' primary focus remains on the road.

Human Factors: Trust, Workload and Acceptance. While technical performance is necessary, overall effectiveness depends on human–system integration. Over-trust and complacency have long been recognised pitfalls in driver assistance [13]. Ranney's taxonomy of driving tasks highlights how cognitive and motivational factors condition driver responses to automation [24]. Recent survey data show that trust in partially automated systems varies systematically with driver mental models, age and brand experience [27]. A systematic review by Damsara and de Barros identifies fifteen distinct constructs that shape user acceptance of ADAS, calling for acceptance models tailored to Level-2/3 automation [6]. Interface load is another concern: Bosurgi et al. [3]demonstrate that poorly tuned driver–vehicle interfaces can turn supportive ADAS cues into cognitive overload, degrading situation awareness in complex traffic.

ADAS Evaluation in Simulation. Because naturalistic crash data accumulate slowly, high-fidelity simulation is indispensable for rapid prototyping and controlled experimentation. The open-source CARLA simulator enables repeatable, photorealistic testing with plug-and-play sensor suites and driver-in-the-loop capabilities. Studies combining CARLA with eye-tracking and secondary-task paradigms have quantified how alert modality, timing and frequency affect driver reaction times, workload and compliance [30]. Such simulation platforms also support the end-to-end evaluation of perception pipelines (e.g. YOLOv8), sensor-fusion strategies and human–machine interfaces before costly on-road trials.

Taken together, prior work establishes (i) the scale of pedestrian risk, (ii) the technical feasibility of real-time pedestrian AEB, and (iii) the behavioural complexities of driver interaction with assistance systems. Yet open questions remain on how best to *calibrate* multimodal alerts so that drivers maintain appropriate trust under varying environmental and system-performance conditions. Few studies explore adaptive alerting that exposes graded reliability information, and even fewer couple this with sensor-fusion pipelines validated against adverse-weather edge cases. The present study addresses this gap by integrating RGB–depth fusion and YOLOv8 detection in CARLA, and by systematically varying alert modality, timing and confidence cues to optimise both detection accuracy and driver situational awareness.

3   Design Process

In this Section, we describe the design process of the in-vehicle alerting system, guided by the principles of human-centered design. Subsequently, we present the questionnaire used to assess the system's effectiveness in improving driver awareness and understanding of pedestrian detection.

3.1   Collaborative User-Centered Design

This Subsection outlines the user-centered design approach employed in developing the in-vehicle alerting system. The process began with mockup creation to explore initial design concepts, followed by focus group sessions to gather user feedback and refine the system iteratively.

Mockup Design. Prior to conducting the focus group sessions, we developed a set of mockups to explore different design concepts for the in-vehicle driver alerting system. These mockups were created based on a preliminary review of the literature on ADAS User Interfaces (UIs), common alert modalities, and known issues related to cognitive load and trust in automation. The goal was to generate concrete interface concepts that could facilitate discussion and elicit informed feedback from participants during the co-design process.

(a) Mockup of default driving state with vehicle positioned.

(b) Mockup of pedestrian detected and marked in the interface.

Fig. 1. Mockup of the user interface during default driving state and when a pedestrian is detected.

Mockups were intentionally limited in scope and focused solely on the tablet-based interface intended for in-vehicle use. Rather than presenting full interaction flows or alert mechanisms, the mockups illustrated two interface states: one showing the vehicle positioned within the interface during normal driving conditions, and another depicting the presence of a detected pedestrian in the environment. The aim was to provide participants with a minimal yet contextually grounded visual reference that could stimulate discussion around spatial layout, information relevance, and situational awareness. By introducing these mockups early in the design process, we were able to guide participants' attention toward key design aspects–such as visibility of elements, clarity of the interface, and potential distractions–without biasing them with assumptions about the final behavior of the system.

The mockups were produced using Balsamiq [2], a tool well-suited for early-stage interface design, which emphasizes layout and structural clarity over visual fidelity. This choice allowed for rapid prototyping and easy modification based on user feedback. The first mockup, shown in Fig. 1(a), presented the default driving state with only the vehicle positioned on the interface, while the second mockup, in Fig. 1(b), showed a scenario in which a pedestrian was detected and marked within the same spatial frame.

The mockups were printed on paper to facilitate hands-on interaction during the focus group, enabling participants to annotate them freely and visually explore alternative design ideas. This format encouraged creative engagement and made it easier to compare and discuss different interface concepts. These prints served as a reference point for structured discussion, grounding participant feedback in realistic design scenarios and enabling them to respond to concrete examples rather than abstract concepts. This approach helped participants reflect on the interface's potential effectiveness and usability in real-world conditions, stimulating discussion on aspects such as layout clarity, perceived usefulness, and the risk of driver distraction. Insights gathered through this process informed subsequent iterations of the design, particularly with respect to the visual organization of elements and the interface's ability to support pedestrian detection awareness.

Focus Group Sessions. Following the development of the initial mockups, two participatory focus group were conducted to elicit user-centered insights and co-design ideas regarding the proposed in-vehicle interface.

Exploratory Session. The first focus group consisted of eight participants aged between 19 and 26 (one female, seven male), all of whom had driving experience but limited familiarity with ADAS. Prior to the session, participants were informed about the objectives of the study. The goal was to gather insights on user expectations and preferences for an in-vehicle alerting system designed to enhance pedestrian safety. The session was structured to encourage open discussion and collaborative design, allowing participants to share their experiences and ideas freely.

The session began with a brief welcome and introduction, during which the moderators presented the objectives of the study and clarified the use of the tablet interface as a support tool for enhancing pedestrian safety. To foster engagement and establish rapport, an initial icebreaker activity invited participants to share their prior experiences with ADAS technologies and to sketch–freely and informally–their vision of an ideal interface for pedestrian safety.

Participants were then guided through a discussion on driving experiences and critical pedestrian-related scenarios. Using short narratives and visuals, the moderators encouraged reflections on the kinds of information that would be most useful in such situations, such as the direction of pedestrian movement or the urgency of warnings. This discussion laid the groundwork for identifying essential interface elements and interaction patterns.

The focus group outcomes revealed important user expectations for the design of the in-vehicle alert system. Participants consistently emphasized the value of multimodal alerts, combining visual and auditory cues to ensure timely driver awareness. However, they also stressed that these alerts should remain non-disruptive, avoiding excessive noise or visual clutter that could interfere with driving. Also notable, when the system performs automatic actions, such as braking or issuing warnings, participants expected a clear visual explanation of the reason behind the intervention. This was seen as essential to foster driver trust and maintain situational awareness. Finally, users were particularly wary of false positives. Repeated or unnecessary alerts were viewed as a major potential drawback, with the risk of diminishing trust in the system and causing drivers to ignore genuine warnings. These insights underscored the need for a carefully balanced interface that communicates clearly without overwhelming the user.

Co-design Session. The second focus group session, with a subset of four participants from the first group, aged from 19 and 26 (one female, three male), was structured to build on the insights gathered in the exploratory session. The goal was to collaboratively design an in-vehicle interface that effectively communicates pedestrian-related information to drivers while minimizing cognitive load and distraction.

Two mockups described in Sect. 3.1 were presented to the participants as a starting point for discussion. The first mockup (Fig. 1) illustrates the default driving condition. Starting from this baseline, participants were asked to reflect on how key information was displayed and to critique the clarity, layout, and perceived usefulness of the interface. Also, they were encouraged to reason aloud and suggest improvements, focusing on elements such as the spatial arrangement of visual cues, the use of color and symbols, the potential role of audio feedback, and the possibility of dividing the driving view into different areas, where each area could represent different levels of alertness or urgency. The discussion emphasized the importance of making alert information immediately understandable without overwhelming the driver. Participants also expressed preferences for more intuitive visual indicators when the system detects a pedestrian or takes automatic actions.

Subsequently, the second mockup (Fig. 1b) was presented, depicting a scenario in which a pedestrian was detected and marked within the interface. Participants were asked to evaluate the effectiveness of this representation in conveying critical information about the pedestrian's position and movement. Several concerns emerged during the discussion: participants expressed skepticism about the usefulness of the circular marker placed on the pedestrian, finding it visually uninformative and potentially distracting. Moreover, the indication of the pedestrian's distance in meters was not considered helpful, as it did not intuitively support quick decision-making while driving. These critiques highlighted the need for alternative visual cues that more clearly communicate urgency, relevance, and spatial context.

To address these concerns, participants proposed a revised approach to representing pedestrian-related information. They suggested dividing the road ahead

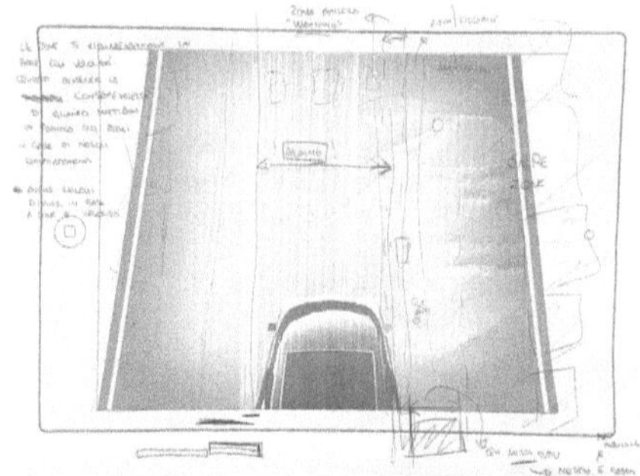
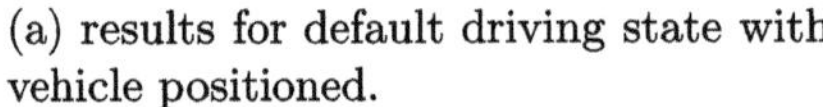

(a) results for default driving state with vehicle positioned.

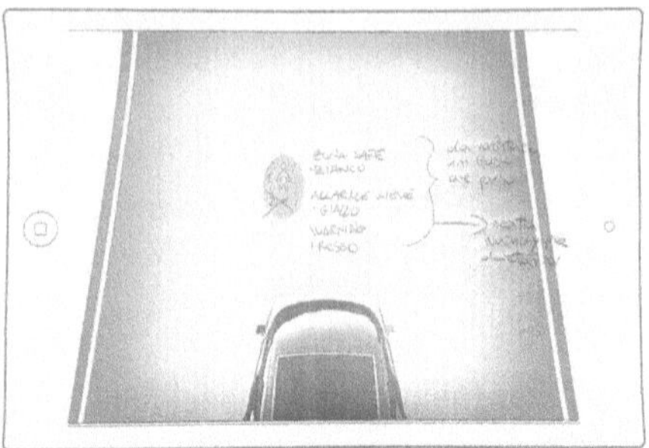

(b) results for pedestrian detected and marked in the interface.

Fig. 2. Co-design session results. The notes are presented in Italian, as the activity was conducted in that language.

into three distinct zones–safe, warning, and danger–based on the proximity and relevance of the detected pedestrian. Each zone determines the appearance change of the pedestrian icon accordingly when entering a specific area. This approach was considered more intuitive, as it could immediately convey the level of urgency without relying on precise distance measurements. Additionally, participants recommended introducing a contextual banner at the top or bottom of the interface to provide concise information about the nature of the potential danger. Results of the session could be observed in Fig. 2a and b. These additions were intended to improve situational awareness while avoiding cognitive overload, supporting faster and more informed decision-making by the driver.

3.2   Evaluation Questionnaire

The questionnaire is planned to be administered after participants engage in hands-on testing with the system implementation. In line with Nielsen et al. [19], which suggest that testing with five users typically uncovers the majority of usability issues, the number of participants has been selected to balance practical constraints with the need for meaningful qualitative and quantitative insights. The questionnaire for the evaluation is designed to be completed anonymously and includes a combination of closed-ended and open-ended questions. The closed-ended questions are primarily intended to gather quantitative data related to participants' previous experiences with similar in-vehicle or alerting systems. Moreover, it includes the User Experience Questionnaire (UEQ) [16], a standardized tool designed to measure users' impressions of an interactive product across key dimensions such as attractiveness, perspicuity, efficiency, dependability, stimulation, and novelty.

   Then, open-ended questions are also included to give participants the opportunity to elaborate on the most effective aspects of the interface and propose improvements. This qualitative feedback is intended to complement the quantitative data, offering a richer understanding of user needs and expectations. Overall, the questionnaire will serve as a comprehensive tool for evaluating the usability and user experience of the proposed alerting system in realistic driving conditions.

4 Proposed System

This Section details the implementation of the ADAS system and the in-vehicle interface. The overall system architecture is depicted in Fig. 3.

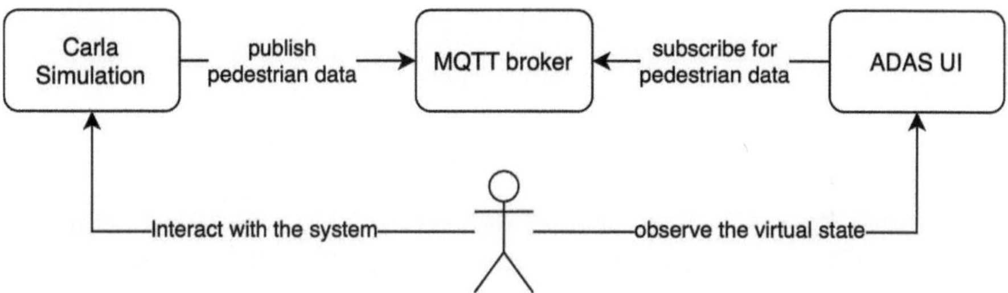

Fig. 3. System architecture for the pedestrian protection ADAS evaluation using CARLA simulator. The CARLA simulation publishes real-time pedestrian detection data via MQTT, which is subscribed to by the ADAS UI for visualization. Users interact with the simulation and observe system feedback through the UI, enabling human-in-the-loop testing.

4.1 ADAS Implementation

To develop and evaluate our Pedestrian Protection ADAS, we utilize **CARLA** [7], an open-source simulator tailored for autonomous driving research. CARLA offers realistic urban environments, configurable pedestrian and vehicle actors, and high-fidelity sensor simulation – including RGB cameras, LiDAR, and RADAR. It also features a Traffic Manager for dynamic traffic control and a ROS bridge for integration with perception and control systems. These capabilities make CARLA an ideal testbed for evaluating safety-critical interactions between vehicles and pedestrians in diverse conditions.

Sensor Simulation. To provide perception capabilities, we simulate two key sensors:

- **RGB Camera**: Captures real-time visual data.
- **Depth Camera**: Measures distance to objects within the scene.

CARLA's support for accurate sensor configuration and dynamic pedestrian modeling enables robust testing of the system's perception and decision-making logic.

Perception Pipeline. We implement a computer vision module that processes RGB frames using the **YOLOv8n** model for real-time object detection. Detected objects are filtered to retain only pedestrians with a confidence score above a threshold of 0.4.

Distance and Collision Risk Estimation. For each detected pedestrian, the system estimates the **distance** to the centroid of their bounding box using depth data. We then compute the **Time to Collision (TTC)** to assess the risk of impact. The TTC is calculated using the formula:

$$TTC = \frac{\text{distance (m)}}{\text{vehicle speed (m/s)}}$$

This provides a context-aware measure of collision risk, more informative than raw distance alone.

Driver Interaction. Users can operate the system using a keyboard or physical driving controls, such as a steering wheel and pedals. This allows realistic human-in-the-loop testing within the simulation.

Event Messaging. All critical events–such as pedestrian detections and TTC assessments–are published via an **MQTT message broker**, allowing real-time interaction with external systems. Events are serialized using the following JSON schema:

Listing 1.1. MQTT Event Schema

```
{
    "x": number,
    "distance": number,
    "time_to_collision": number,
    "camera_width": number
}
```

- x: horizontal coordinate of the pedestrian in the image frame
- distance: estimated distance to the pedestrian (meters)
- time_to_collision: time to collision estimate (seconds)
- camera_width: horizontal resolution of the camera

4.2   In-Vehicle Interface

For the in-vehicle interface, we developed a web-based application inspired by modern automotive infotainment systems–particularly those used by manufacturers like Tesla. The interface aims to present critical pedestrian-related information in an intuitive and visually engaging manner. The main section of the display features a stylized representation of the road. At the bottom-center of this visual, a vehicle icon represents the user's car. Directly beneath this, a dynamic message area communicates the current driving status:

- Normal driving: *"DRIVE SAFE – Stay Alert!"*
- Pedestrian detected: *"SLOW DOWN – Pedestrian detected ahead – <d> m – Estimating <t> s to collision", where <d> is the distance and <t> is the estimated TTC*

The road visualization is segmented into three zones: safe, warning, and danger, as illustrated in Fig. 4.

Fig. 4. Safety zones around a vehicle, illustrating proximity-based risk levels. The red zone directly in front of the vehicle represents the danger area, indicating a high-risk region where immediate action is required. The adjacent yellow zones signify caution or warning areas, where obstacles may become hazardous if approached further. The green zones denote safe areas with minimal risk.

For each pedestrian detection, an icon resembling a pedestrian is rendered on the road visualization at a horizontal position corresponding to the pedestrian's real-world location. The icon's color changes depending on the urgency of the situation, determined by TTC and the zone in which the pedestrian is detected:

$$color = \begin{cases} \text{RED} & \text{If pedestrian is in the danger zone and } TTC < 5\,s \\ \text{YELLOW} & \text{If pedestrian is in the warning zone and } TTC < 10\,s \\ \text{WHITE} & \text{Otherwise} \end{cases}$$

To enhance alert mechanisms, additional warnings can be triggered based on user preferences: flashing red lateral lights when a pedestrian is detected in a critical position and audible warning sound to draw attention to imminent danger.

These settings can be configured via a dedicated Settings Page, accessible through a button in the top navigation bar. Available options include:

- Enable/disable warning sound on pedestrian detection
- Enable/disable flashing lights on pedestrian detection

All pedestrian detections are received in real-time via MQTT from the perception module, ensuring immediate rendering and timely feedback on the UI.

5 Evaluation Methodology and User Testing

5.1 Experimental Setup for User Evaluation

To evaluate the usability and effectiveness of the proposed pedestrian alerting system, a realistic user testing environment was deployed using a desktop-based simulation platform integrated with an external display device. The testing setup was designed to support interactive and immersive evaluation sessions, enabling participants to experience the system under realistic driving conditions.

The main simulation environment runs on a workstation equipped with an AMD Ryzen Threadripper PRO 5965WX 24-core processor (3.80 GHz), 256 GB of RAM, and two Nvidia RTX 6000 Ada Generation GPUs. The system operates on Windows 11 Enterprise and hosts all core components of the ADAS prototype.

A local MQTT broker, implemented using Eclipse Mosquitto, is deployed on the workstation to allow real-time messaging between system modules. The frontend interface is a React application developed with Next.js, containerized via Docker (v28.0.4) using a dedicated Dockerfile. Both the MQTT broker and the frontend service are deployed via Docker Compose (v2.34.0). These services expose the necessary ports to the local network, allowing external devices–such as the user interface tablet–to connect seamlessly.

For the driving simulation, the CARLA server is used deployed on the same workstation, running CARLA 0.9.15, to create immersive urban environments. The simulation uses the "Town10" map, chosen for its realistic urban layout, with 50 pedestrians navigating the scene autonomously through AI-controlled behaviors, providing dynamic and unpredictable traffic scenarios. The CARLA client, responsible for user control, is implemented in Python (v3.7.16), utilizing the CARLA Python API, within a Conda virtual environment (v24.9.1). This client enables real-time control of a virtual vehicle via a physical Logitech PRO Racing Steering Wheel, offering a realistic driving experience. The complete source code for the system [14], including both the client and supporting services, is openly available for reproducibility and further development.

The in-vehicle interface is deployed on a separate device: an iPad Pro 13" with the M4 chip. The iPad connects to the React-based frontend over the local network and serves as the primary display through which users receive real-time visual and auditory alerts during the simulation. This configuration ensures a responsive, low-latency interaction between the simulated vehicle environment and the user interface.

Fig. 5. User testing setup.

An overview of the physical environment used during the testing session is shown in Fig. 5, illustrating the workstation setup with the steering wheel and pedals. Overall, the setup offers a controlled yet dynamic test environment that closely approximates real-world usage scenarios, enabling comprehensive user evaluation of the system's interaction design and situational responsiveness.

5.2   User Testing and Results Analysis

A total of 8 people participated in the user testing sessions, which were conducted in the controlled environment described in Sect. 5.1 to ensure consistency and reliability of the results. As part of the evaluation, each participant was asked to perform a 15-min free-driving session, where they were encouraged to drive naturally while actively engaging with the vehicle's ADAS UI as much as possible.

The participants comprise six men and two women, with ages ranging from 24 to 29 years. All of them were Italian and completed the evaluation questionnaire in their native language to ensure clarity and comprehension. Each participant held a valid driving license and the group showed a diverse range of driving experience: 1 participant had more than ten years, 2 had been driving for 1 to 5 years, while the remaining participants reported between 6 and 10 years of experience.

Regarding the in-vehicle display setup, the vast majority of participants reported having access to both a cockpit display and a central display in their personal vehicle. Only one participant indicated that their car was equipped solely with a central display. Regarding the usage habits, half of the group stated that they make regular use of both displays during driving, while 3 participants indicated that they primarily or exclusively use the cockpit display. Instead, in terms of ADAS, the parking sensors are by far the most commonly used feature, with 6 participants reporting regular use. Other functionalities such as adaptive cruise control and lane keeping assistance were each used by 4 participants. Blind spot monitoring and automatic emergency braking were each reported by 3 participants, while driver fatigue detection and road sign recognition were used by only 2. One participant indicated the use of a non-adaptive cruise control system. Taken together, these data suggest that exposure to basic ADAS features is widespread among the participants, while there is not a notable variability in the usage of more advanced or specialized systems. This diversity is beneficial for the evaluation, as it allows us to gather insights from users with varying levels of familiarity and experience with in-vehicle displays and ADAS functionalities.

User Experience Evaluation. The UEQ offered a valuable insight into how participants perceived the system across a range of experiential dimensions. It ranges from -3 (extremely negative evaluation) to $+3$ (extremely positive evaluation). Results includes mean values of responses (μ) and variances (σ^2). Overall, the results point to a positive reception of the in-vehicle interface, particularly in terms of usability and clarity. All dimensions are resumed in Fig. 6.

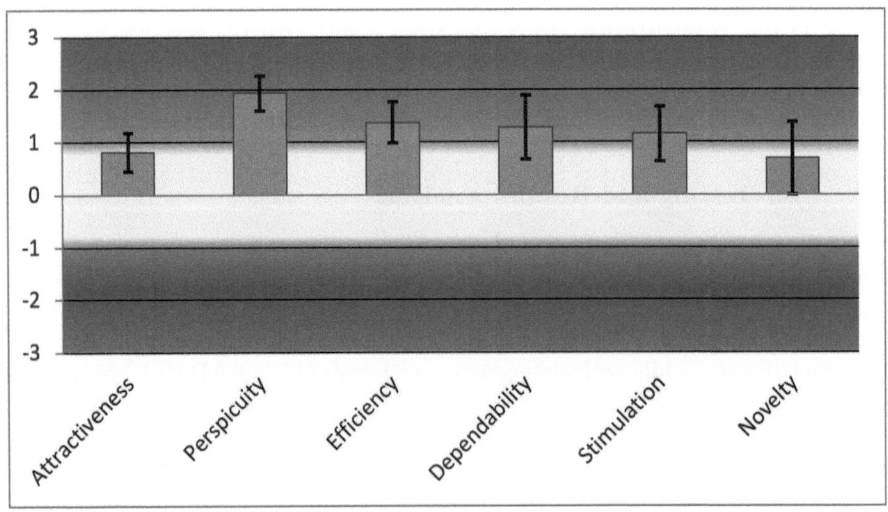

Fig. 6. User Experience Questionnaire results.

The highest-rated dimension was Perspicuity ($\mu = 1.94$, $\sigma^2 = 0.23$), indicating that users found the system intuitive and easy to understand. This result aligns with the emphasis placed during the co-design phase on making alert states and spatial information immediately comprehensible, and suggests that the interface successfully communicates critical information without requiring effortful interpretation.

Efficiency ($\mu = 1.375$, $\sigma^2 = 0.32$), Dependability ($\mu = 1.281$, $\sigma^2 = 0.78$), and Stimulation ($\mu = 1.156$, $\sigma^2 = 0.57$) all received good ratings, indicating that participants experienced the system as functionally supportive, consistent, and engaging. These results suggest that the interface not only aided task performance but also maintained a sufficient level of interest and attentional involvement during use. The slightly higher variance in Dependability and Stimulation may reflect individual differences in how users perceived system reliability and the emotional impact of the visual and interactive elements–possibly linked to the variability of simulated driving conditions and alert scenarios.

Attractiveness ($\mu = 0.813$, $\sigma^2 = 0.28$) and Novelty ($\mu = 0.688$, $\sigma^2 = 1.00$) both scored moderately above neutral, suggesting that while the interface was generally perceived as pleasant and aesthetically acceptable, it was not considered particularly innovative. The relatively high variance in Novelty indicates divergent opinions among participants, likely influenced by the system's intentionally familiar visual language and UI conventions. This design choice, while supportive of usability, may have limited the perceived originality of the interface. Nonetheless, in a safety-critical context such as in-vehicle systems, this trade-off appears justified–favoring clarity and familiarity over visual experimentation to avoid unnecessary cognitive load.

In sum, the results validate the design choices made throughout the iterative process and highlight a user experience that is perceived as intuitive, functional, and engaging. While the overall reception was clearly positive, some variability in perception points to opportunities for refining the interface's visual identity and enhancing its perceived originality. Nonetheless, the current balance between usability and familiarity appears well-suited to the safety-critical context in which the system operates.

6   Conclusions and Future Works

This work presented the design, implementation, and user evaluation of a human-centered in-vehicle visual interface integrated within a Pedestrian Protection ADAS. Leveraging the CARLA simulator and a real-time perception pipeline based on RGB-depth sensor fusion and YOLOv8, the system provides timely and informative alerts to enhance driver awareness and improve pedestrian safety. Through participatory design involving focus groups and usability testing, we validated the interface's effectiveness in conveying critical information without overwhelming users. The UEQ results confirmed the system's strong usability, particularly in perspicuity and efficiency, while highlighting opportunities to improve aesthetic appeal and novelty.

Among the limitations of this work, it is important to note that, for ethical and safety reasons, real on-road simulations could not be conducted. Such simulations would have provided more accurate insights and potentially more valuable results.

We are also aware of a potential usability issue stemming from the fact that the UI conveys critical information–specifically, the level of imminent danger due to a short time-to-collision with a detected pedestrian–exclusively through color. This design choice may pose accessibility challenges, particularly for users with visual impairments such as color blindness. We plan to address this limitation in future work, potentially involving participants with visual impairments in the evaluation process.

Despite the promising results, several directions for future research remain. First, integrating driver state monitoring, particularly arousal and cognitive workload, can provide adaptive feedback based on the driver's Fitness-to-Drive (FtD). Prior studies, such as [1], have shown that biometric indicators such as heart rate, stress levels, and distraction significantly affect driver performance. By incorporating these parameters, the ADAS could personalize alert modalities and intensities according to individual preferences [18], reducing the risk of cognitive overload or under-reaction.

Second, the integration of real-time traffic and environmental context into the ADAS could further improve situational awareness. For example, traffic congestion levels or dynamic pedestrian flow from surveillance cameras can influence the alerting strategy. Techniques using YOLO-based detection on online traffic images [15] or graph-based forecasting models with GNNs [17] provide a promising path to contextualize alerts based on external factors like camera feeds, traffic density, or weather conditions. Integrating this information into the UI can support better decision-making by dynamically adjusting warnings according to traffic scenarios.

Moreover, this work aligns with ongoing efforts to incorporate emerging technologies and sustainability principles into HMI and ADAS design. For instance, virtual reality and haptic technologies have shown promise in early-stage HMI prototyping and usability testing, enabling more efficient and environmentally conscious development processes [23]. Similarly, persuasive and gamified interaction strategies, as explored in sustainable behavior change applications, can be adapted to encourage safer and more attentive driving habits through mobile and in-vehicle interfaces [28]. Finally, integrating intelligent driver monitoring systems into ADAS, as demonstrated in recent research on takeover readiness, can enhance system responsiveness by adjusting alerts based on driver attention and stress levels [22]. These complementary approaches support the broader vision of creating adaptive, intuitive, and sustainable ADAS ecosystems.

In conclusion, this study takes a key step towards designing ADAS that not only detect and warn but also communicate effectively with drivers, taking into account both the environment and human behavior. By coupling technological precision with human-centered interaction, future ADAS can become more intelligent, intuitive, and ultimately life-saving.

Acknowledgment. This work was funded by EU Horizon KDT JU research and innovation programme under grant agreement 101139769 (DistriMuSe).

Disclosure of Interests. The authors have no competing interests to declare that are relevant to the content of this article.

References

1. Andruccioli, M., Mengozzi, M., Presta, R., Mirri, S., Girau, R.: Arousal effects on fitness-to-drive assessment: algorithms and experiments. In: 2023 IEEE 20th Consumer Communications & Networking Conference (CCNC), January 2023, pp. 366–371. IEEE (2023). https://doi.org/10.1109/ccnc51644.2023.10060261
2. Balsamiq: Fast, focused wireframing tools. https://balsamiq.com. Accessed Jun 2025
3. Bosurgi, G., Pellegrino, O., Ruggeri, A., Sollazzo, G.: The role of ADAS while driving in complex road contexts: support or overload for drivers? Sustainability **15**(2), 1334 (2023)
4. Cicchino, J.B.: Effects of automatic emergency braking systems on pedestrian crash risk. Accid. Anal. Prev. **172**, 106686 (2022)
5. Coelingh, E., Eidehall, A., Bengtsson, M.: Collision warning with full auto brake and pedestrian detection - a practical example of automatic emergency braking. In: 13th International IEEE Conference on Intelligent Transportation Systems, September 2010. IEEE (2010). https://doi.org/10.1109/itsc.2010.5625077
6. Damsara, K., de Barros, A.: A systematic review on user acceptance of advanced driver assistance systems (ADAS). Transp. Res. Proc. **82**, 3472–3482 (2025). https://doi.org/10.1016/j.trpro.2024.12.082
7. Dosovitskiy, A., Ros, G., Codevilla, F., Lopez, A., Koltun, V.: CARLA: an open urban driving simulator. In: Proceedings of the 1st Annual Conference on Robot Learning, pp. 1–16 (2017)
8. Gandhi, T., Trivedi, M.M.: Pedestrian protection systems: issues, survey, and challenges. IEEE Trans. Intell. Transp. Syst. **8**(3), 413–430 (2007). https://doi.org/10.1109/TITS.2007.903444
9. Gu, J., Bellone, M., Lind, A.: Camera-LiDAR fusion based object segmentation in adverse weather conditions for autonomous driving. In: 2024 19th Biennial Baltic Electronics Conference (BEC), October 2024, pp. 1–5. IEEE (2024). https://doi.org/10.1109/bec61458.2024.10737955
10. Hasan, R., Hasan, R.: Pedestrian safety using the internet of things and sensors: issues, challenges, and open problems. Fut. Gener. Comput. Syst. **134**, 187–203 (2022)
11. Htike, K.K., Hogg, D.: Adapting pedestrian detectors to new domains: a comprehensive review. Eng. Appl. Artif. Intell. **50**, 142–158 (2016). https://doi.org/10.1016/j.engappai.2016.01.029
12. IIHS: Fatality Facts 2022: Pedestrians (2024). https://www.iihs.org/topics/fatality-statistics/detail/pedestrians. Accessed 03 Apr 2025
13. Inagaki, T., Itoh, M.: Human's overtrust in and overreliance on advanced driver assistance systems: a theoretical framework. Int. J. Veh. Tech. **2013**, 1–8 (2013). https://doi.org/10.1155/2013/951762
14. Kelvin Olaiya, M.A.: unibo-dslab-projects/paper-hcii-pedestrian-protection-adas: User tests (2025). https://doi.org/10.5281/ZENODO.15655734. https://zenodo.org/doi/10.5281/zenodo.15655734

15. Lam, C.T., Ng, B., Chan, C.W.: Real-time traffic status detection from online images using generic object detection system with deep learning. In: 2019 IEEE 19th International Conference on Communication Technology (ICCT), October 2019, pp. 1506–1510. IEEE (2019). https://doi.org/10.1109/icct46805.2019.8947064

16. Laugwitz, B., Held, T., Schrepp, M.: Construction and Evaluation of a User Experience Questionnaire, pp. 63–76. Springer, Heidelberg (2008). https://doi.org/10.1007/978-3-540-89350-9_6

17. Liu, B., Lam, C.T., Ng, B.K., Yuan, X., Im, S.K.: A graph-based framework for traffic forecasting and congestion detection using online images from multiple cameras. IEEE Access **12**, 3756–3767 (2024). https://doi.org/10.1109/access.2023.3349034

18. Mengozzi, M., Andruccioli, M., Mirri, S., Delnevo, G., Girau, R.: Enhancing road safety through fitness-to-drive metrics: the next perception project on driver behavior analysis and gamification. In: 2024 IEEE 21st Consumer Communications & Networking Conference (CCNC), January 2024, pp. 290–295. IEEE (2024). https://doi.org/10.1109/ccnc51664.2024.10454893

19. Nielsen, J., Landauer, T.K.: A mathematical model of the finding of usability problems. In: Proceedings of the SIGCHI Conference on Human Factors in Computing Systems, CHI '93, pp. 206–213. ACM Press (1993). https://doi.org/10.1145/169059.169166

20. Peden, M.: World Report on Road Traffic Injury Prevention. World Health Organization (2004)

21. Pires, F., Lisboa, P., Ribeiro, H., Campos, P., Capdevila, M., Zaina, L.: End-users perspective matters in ADAS: designing a blind-spot alert system from a user-centered approach. J. Braz. Comput. Soc. **31**(1), 50–67 (2025). https://doi.org/10.5753/jbcs.2025.4365

22. Presta, R., Tancredi, C., De Simone, F., Iacono, M., Mancuso, L.: Improving time to take over through HMI strategies nudging a safe driving state. In: International Conference on Human-Computer Interaction, pp. 27–43. Springer, Cham (2024)

23. Presta, R., Tancredi, C., Mancuso, L., Caccavale, D., Riccio, F.M.: Co-designing with experts: exploring scenarios for haptic-enhanced virtual reality in automotive HMI design. In: International Conference on Human-Computer Interaction, pp. 76–95. Springer, Cham (2025)

24. Ranney, T.A.: Models of driving behavior: a review of their evolution. Accid. Anal. Prev. **26**(6), 733–750 (1994)

25. Redmon, J., Divvala, S., Girshick, R., Farhadi, A.: You only look once: unified, real-time object detection. In: 2016 IEEE Conference on Computer Vision and Pattern Recognition (CVPR), June 2016, pp. 779–788. IEEE (2016). https://doi.org/10.1109/cvpr.2016.91

26. Singh, S.K.: Review of urban transportation in India. J. Public Transp. **8**(1), 79–97 (2005)

27. Szilagyi, K., Millar, J., Moon, A., Rismani, S.: Driving into the loop: mapping automation bias and liability issues for advanced driver assistance systems. Digit. Soc. **2**(3), 41 (2023). https://doi.org/10.1007/s44206-023-00066-y

28. Tancredi, C., Presta, R., Di Lorenzo, V.: Promoting sustainable behaviors through mobile apps: SBAM design guidelines. Multimedia Tools Appl. **83**(30), 74021–74052 (2024)

29. for Transport, U.D.: Reported road casualties in Great Britain: pedestrian factsheet, 2023 — gov.uk. https://www.gov.uk/government/statistics/reported-road-casualties-great-britain-pedestrian-factsheet-2023/reported-road-casualties-in-great-britain-pedestrian-factsheet-2023. Accessed 03 Apr 2025
30. Vaezipour, A., Rakotonirainy, A., Haworth, N.: Reviewing in-vehicle systems to improve fuel efficiency and road safety. Procedia Manuf. **3**, 3192–3199 (2015). https://doi.org/10.1016/j.promfg.2015.07.869
31. van Wees, K.A.: Vehicle safety regulations and ADAS: tensions between law and technology. In: 2004 IEEE International Conference on Systems, Man and Cybernetics (IEEE Cat. No. 04CH37583), vol. 4, pp. 4011–4016. IEEE (2004)
32. World Bank: Road safety report (2025). https://openknowledge.worldbank.org/server/api/core/bitstreams/059cbc7d-7b24-5277-baf2-7442af8570b0/content. Accessed 03 Apr 2025

Informing the Design of Mixed Reality Driver Assistance Systems: Opportunities and Risks of Virtual Lane Augmentation

Jan Conrad[(✉)] [iD] and Dieter P. Wallach [iD]

University of Applied Sciences Kaiserslautern, Kaiserslautern, Germany
{jan.conrad,dieter.wallach}@hs-kl.de

Abstract. Mixed Reality (MR) systems using Head-Up Displays (HUDs) offer promising approaches for driver assistance without diverting visual attention from the road. However, unlike aviation applications where pilots receive mandatory HUD training, consumer vehicle drivers lack such preparation. This raises concerns about effective and error-robust HUD design.

In this paper, an exploratory study is presented where two types of virtual lane augmentations in HUDs are empirically evaluated under low visibility driving conditions. Participants completed a within-subject experimental design comparing unsupported baseline driving with two HUD conditions: center-HUD (virtually highlighting the lane center) and right-edge-HUD (highlighting the road edge). A total of six intentional augmentation errors (three for each augmentation type) were introduced to assess participant's error detection capabilities.

Results demonstrate that both HUD augmentation types significantly improved driving precision compared to unsupported baseline drives. However, center-HUD augmentation led to delayed error detection that might have been caused by attentional tunneling: As preliminary eye-tracking data suggests, participants were fixating primarily on the virtual center line, leading to reduced situational awareness. Right-edge-HUD augmentation also improved driving precision significantly while enabling faster error detection.

Participant's subjective evaluations strongly favored right-edge augmentation over center-HUD. The findings reported reveal a critical trade-off in mixed-reality driver assistance design: while center augmentation enhances precision, it might increase vulnerability to system malfunctions. Road edge augmentation, in comparison, seem to better preserve situational awareness. The results suggest important implications for automotive MR system development The findings suggest relevant implications for the design of automotive MR-based HUDs.

.

Keywords: Mixed Reality · Driver Assistant · Head-Up Displays

© The Author(s), under exclusive license to Springer Nature Switzerland AG 2026
P.-L.P. Rau and H. Krömker (Eds.): HCII 2025, LNCS 16336, pp. 342–357, 2026.
https://doi.org/10.1007/978-3-032-12798-3_21

1 Introduction

Favored by recent advances in the development of self-driving vehicles and electric vehicle technology, cars are increasingly becoming computers on wheels. Available sensor technology and, correspondingly, computing power constantly open up new possibilities to entertain, support and unburden a driver during rides. While there are still significant challenges to overcome before successfully achieving SAE J3016 Levels 4–5 [1], Advanced Driver Assistance Systems (ADAS) based on sophisticated sensor technology and innovative interaction approaches are in the starting blocks for commercial release.

An example for an ADAS is the visualization of route information through augmented or mixed reality elements using head-up displays (HUDs). According to ISO/TS 21957:2023 [2] a HUD is a display system that presents information within the driver's forward field of view, allowing drivers to view the information without significantly shifting their gaze away from the road.

In aviation, HUDs are state of the art in military and commercial air flight for many years with a multitude of studies being devoted to investigate their impact on a pilot's performance. Besides numerous positive effects that have been reported [3], the use of HUDs can result in cognitive tunnelling phenomena [4]. Cognitive tunneling is defined as a psychological state of attentional narrowing during deep, concentrated work. In this state people attend to and process only critical, task-relevant information with only very limited processing of secondary information that might also be relevant for successful task completion [5]. The APA Dictionary of Psychology explicitly lists a pilot "focusing on head-up displays without scanning out the windows of the plane" as an example for cognitive tunneling [5]. While selective attention is a critical prerequisite for efficient, goal-directed action in complex environments, it can be a potential hazard when flying an aircraft. A visual focus on a certain area restricts the detection of objects and events in the periphery and impairs situational awareness. Situational awareness refers to a human's perception, comprehension, and projection of the events in the environment [6]. Wickens and Alexander [7] suggest specific HUD-trainings as countermeasures to cognitive tunneling: "It does, however, point to the importance of attentional training for pilots who use this new technology". To efficiently attend to multiple sources of information and to appropriately balance the timing between phases of focused and divided attention, pilots are taught to constantly conduct visual scanning processes, i.e. to briefly attend each source of information in the visual field sequentially and systematically [8].

The usefulness of HUDs, however, depends not only on regular vocational training and the aptitude of a pilot: an appropriate visual presentation of data in the system also plays a decisive role [9].

In the automotive sector—especially when referring to consumer vehicles—there are no restrictive requirements for drivers or (repeated) mandatory trainings as prerequisites for the use of HUDs. When purchasing a vehicle, all a customer needs to do is to tick the respective box in a configurator's equipment list to order an available option. As the enhancement of HUD technologies in cars is emerging, "driving the HUD" without proper instruction and training puts the design of such systems into focus.

One line of HUD development, inspired by computer games like Sony's Gran Turismo [10], makes use of virtual lane augmentations of the road to support, for instance, driving under poor visibility conditions. Such virtual augmentations can be achieved, for example, by virtual visualizations projected as superimpositions on the windshield. This raises questions on how to represent and where to position virtual augmentations in the HUD, as well as how to deal with possible imprecisions or errors in the visualization.

In this paper, two different approaches for driving lane augmentation through mixed reality are investigated. In an exploratory study, participants were supported during drives in a simulator by an augmentation modeled after a HUD in which (1) the *center* of the driver's lane is highlighted and (2) by a system highlighting the *right edge* of the driver's lane. The goal of the exploratory study is to shed light on possible effects of the investigated visualization type (lane center vs. lane edge) on driving precision (

i.e. deviations from the center of the lane). To explore possible effects of augmentation type on situational awareness, errors where intentionally introduced in the lane augmentation (center/right lane) to investigate a potential impact on error detection times. An eye-tracking system was used to monitor the participant's gaze patterns during simulated rides in low-visibility driving scenarios.

2 Related Work

2.1 Mixed Reality and Head up Displays

Mixed reality (MR) is a technology that enhances a user's interaction with the real world by overlaying digital information such as text, images, or videos as superimpositions on the user's view of the real world. Technically, these superimpositions can be realized using a variety of different approaches, including specialized hardware like data glasses or low-cost devices like smartphones and tablets. A specific feature of MR is to provide the user with enhanced context information about the real world, rather than completely replacing direct vision by virtual reality.

The first broader practical use of HUDs stems from the aviation domain. Its origins can be traced back to World War II, where HUDs were explored in military aircrafts. Here, the first experimental HUD was developed by the Royal Air Force in the 1940s [11]. The goal of these early HUD systems was to improve a pilot's situational awareness in order to reduce the risk of crashes. From today's perspective, the first systems were quite simple and consisted of a reflector and a small cathode ray tube (CRT) display. The pilot looked through the reflector, in which an image was superimposed over the real-world view.

In the decades that followed, HUD technology was continuously improved. Further advancements in electronics and display technology enabled the development of more sophisticated systems using larger, higher resolution displays to show a wide range of data. According to the National Aeronautics and Space Administration (NASA), aerospace HUDs typically present critical flight information including navigation data, altitude, airspeed, and attitude information directly in the pilot's line of sight [12]. Eventually, HUDs have found their way also into civil aviation. After successful demonstrations showed that HUDs can replace failing passive automatic landing systems during low visibility operations, airlines began adopting the technology to maintain flight schedules in poor weather conditions. [13]. By the end of the 20th century, HUD-equipped aircrafts had accumulated more than 6,000,000 flight hours and completed more than 30,000 low visibility operations [13].

To use a HUD in an aircraft, it must be certified by an aviation authority, such as the Federal Aviation Association (FAA). The certification requirements for a HUD system depend on the functions performed and are quite complex. This complexity, among other factors, stems from the fact, that, unlike in automatic landing systems, the human pilot is in the active control loop.

The use of HUDs also carries some challenges and risks for design and operation. A significant number of aviation accidents can be traced to breakdowns in task management and prioritization [14]. Nichol [4] associates effects of attention capturing and cognitive tunnelling with the use of HUDs. He describes that new HUD users may notice a tendency to focus attention on one layer of information (e.g., the HUD symbology) at the expense of others (e.g., the outside environment). Nichol argues that the problem of cognitive tunneling may be limited to inexperienced HUD users. However, empirical evidence for this claim is contradictory. Fadden, Wickens and Ververs [15] show that a HUD provides an advantage for most tasks—with two notable exceptions: flight path control during cruise flight and event detection during final approach. However, the cost of using a HUD for event detection during landing only occurs when events are entirely unexpected, reflecting a form of cognitive tunnelling. [15].

2.2 Head-Up Displays in Cars

HUD devices are examples of Advanced Driver Assistance Systems (ADAS), targeted at enhancing driving safety and efficiency by providing the driver with contextual information visualized in her windshield [15]. The visibility, specifications and test procedures for Road vehicles are standardized in the ISO/TS 21957:2023 [2]. According to Liu and Wen [16], Head-up Displays in vehicles offer a significant advantage by reducing driver distraction. Unlike traditional head-down displays, HUDs allow drivers to access essential information while maintaining their visual focus on the roadway, which is crucial for continuously monitoring the ever-changing traffic environment and road conditions.

2.3 K3F Driving Environment

Developing and evaluating automotive user interfaces and (advanced) driver assistance systems is a costly and effortful process. While this is obviously true when using physical vehicles prototypes during development, the effort when using simulators can also be considerable. As an attempt to reduce the expense for defining, conducting and analyzing automotive user studies, we developed the concept simulation framework K3F [17]. K3F is a highly flexible automotive simulation environment that supports a fast configuration and setup of user studies. K3F's hard- and software components—including simulation software, dashboard/infotainment modules, and peripheral systems—can easily be modified, replaced or exchanged. The K3F software simplifies the creation and modification of virtual environments, supports comprehensive data collection and allows for a fast development of real-world street scenarios [18]. Figure 1 shows the K3F driving environment.

Fig. 1. Driving simulation environment K3F.

3   Research Question and Study Design

The aim of the exploratory study presented in this paper is to investigate the impact of augmented lane highlighting on driving performance in a (simulated) mixed-reality ADAS. As virtual augmentation might be particularly useful in low visibility conditions, a dark, rainy and foggy forest road scenario was created. While virtual augmentations in HUDs are typically projected on a car's windscreen, the respective augmentations in our study are superimposed on virtual road scenes on the main screen of the K3F driving simulator. Two different augmentation approaches are explored in the study: One approach is to highlight the *center* of the driver's lane using a virtual green stripe (Fig. 2 left), while an alternative approach is to highlight the *right edge* of the driver's lane (Fig. 2 right).

The augmentation visualizations were intentionally designed to minimize visual obstructions to the actual view of the road scenario. In reality, excessive lane overlap might distract the driver, posing a significant safety risk [19].

Systematic visualization errors were deliberately introduced into both augmentation types, exemplifying technical malfunctions of the HUD. Such errors mean that the visualized augmentation line starts to deviate from its intended position—either from the lane center or the lane edge, respectively. If not discovered, the participant would drive into the oncoming lane or into the forest on the right side of the road when following the augmented line. Drivers were asked to quickly 'reset' the HUD by pressing a button when detecting an error, the system then continues to work properly again. Identification, response times and handling of visualization errors were recorded throughout the study.

Fig. 2. Highlighting the center of the lane (left) the edge of the road (right).

3.1 Participants

A group of 20 participants (N = 20) with a mean age of 23.6 years (SD = 2.62) participated in the study. Seven participants identified as female, 13 as male. Participants were recruited by postings at the local University campus and were paid 10 Euros for their participation in the study. All participants either had healthy or corrected-to-normal eyesight and held valid driving licenses for a mean duration of 76.6 months (SD = 33.8). Participants were driving cars regularly with a mean annual mileage of about 15.000km, 15 out of the 20 participants possessed their own car, 5 participants drove a family car on a regular basis.

3.2 Simulated Driving Conditions

Using the K3F framework (see Fig. 3), real terrain and road data served as a basis to simulate a stretch of an existing rural road with an approximate length of 8.8 km (5.5 miles). To control potentially influencing factors, no oncoming traffic was modelled.

During the study, participants were seated in a simulated, left-hand driven vehicle that was steered on a road with right-hand traffic. The total street width measured 11m, the width of the simulated vehicle was about 1.8m. Steer markings to outline the respective right boundaries of each lane were visualized to be 0.15m of width, the width of each lane measured 3.86m. The two lanes were continuously separated by a center reservation (dashed line: 0.15m). The respective measures correspond to typical measures of German rural roads and are summarized in Fig. 4.

Fig. 3. Selected stretch of a rural forest road.

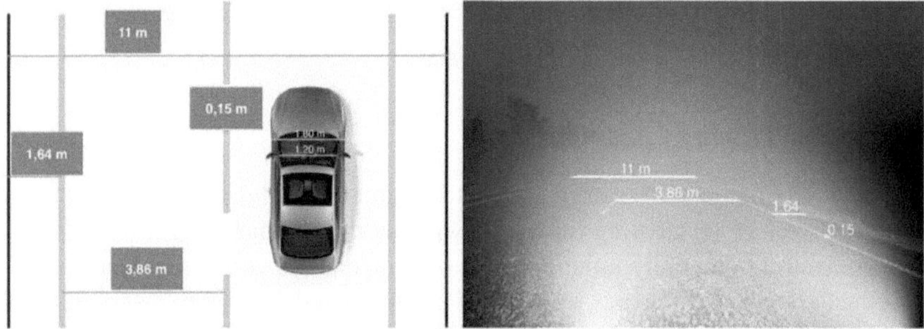

Fig. 4. Road and car measurements.

3.3   Experimental Procedure of the Exploratory Study

The study was set up as a within-subject design where all participants experience three driving phases: *baseline drive, center augmentation* and *right edge augmentation*. During the initial, unsupported *baseline drive* phase, participants were given the opportunity to gain familiarity with the simulated driving situation, i.e. by steering, acceleration, braking reactions on the foggy forest road. The road was illuminated by the headlights of the simulated car. The *baseline drive* phase was followed by either a *center augmentation* drive or a *right edge augmentation* drive, where the respective drive was balanced across the participants to counteract order effects [20]. Figure 5 shows a graphical summary of the study design.

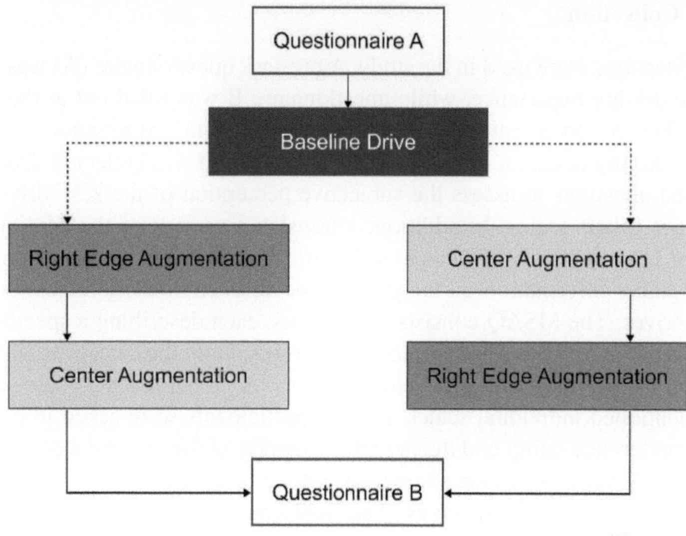

Fig. 5. Summary of the study design.

Participants were instructed to drive as precisely as possible in the center of their own lane throughout all phases. To promote comparable driving speeds, participants were instructed to maintain a speed of about 70 km/h (44 mph) during all drives. A warning tone was emitted when the speed fell below 55 km/h (34 mph). A speed limiter restricted the driving speed to a maximum of 75 km/h (47 mph). A speedometer was available as part of the driving simulator's dashboard. Driving a full course on the rural road took participants approximately 7.5 min to complete. In total, participants drove the course three times (baseline drive, center/right edge augmented drives), resulting in a total driving time of about 22.5 min.

At three defined points in time during both augmented drives, intentional errors in the displayed virtual augmentation were smoothly introduced in the simulated HUD visualization. During the occurrence of an error, the augmented lines were starting to *deviate* from a correct visualization of the center lane/right edge of the road. The first error caused the (center/right) augmentation line to drift to the left of the road, i.e. gravitating towards the lane for the ongoing traffic. The second and third error suggested an incorrect deviation to the right of the driver's lane.

Prior to the driving phases, participants were informed about the "possibility of augmentation errors due to the prototypical development stage of the innovative mixed-reality HUD". Following this cover story, they were asked to indicate their discovery of a "malfunctioning" of the system as fast as possible by pressing a button to "immediately reset the system to normal functioning". The physical button was prominently placed in the driving simulator to support a fast reaction. Participants were neither informed about the number of (intentional) errors, nor when these might occur. When participants failed to detect an error within a time period of 10 s, the system was automatically reset to normal functioning without notifying the participant.

3.4 Data Collection

Two questionnaires were used in the study. A pre-task questionnaire (A) was completed prior to the driving experience, while questionnaire B was filled out at the end of the study (see Fig. 5). In questionnaire A demographic data, information about driving experience, driving licenses, annual mileage and eyesight was collected. Questionnaire B comprised questions to assess the subjective perception of the K3F driving fidelity using 9-point Likert scales. In addition, a translated version of the Motion Sickness Assessment Questionnaire by Gianaros, Muth, Mordkoff, Levine and Stern [22] was applied to gather information on the possible occurrence of motion sickness after the simulated drives. The MSAQ consists of 16 items, each describing a specific potential motion sickness symptom. The symptoms are grouped into the categories *gastrointestinal, central, peripheral* and *sopite-related* factors. A global MSAQ-score summarizes the aforementioned individual scales. Finally, participants were asked to express their subjective preference rating and the perceived support of the experienced augmentation type (center lane/right edge lane augmentation).

During each of the three drives (baseline/center lane/right edge augmentation), speed, distance travelled, deviation from the center line and error detection data were continuously recorded.

A Tobii Pro Glasses 2 eye tracker was used to record gaze patterns of the participants for later analysis. During all sessions of the study, in addition to the participant, a test supervisor and a technician to operate the simulation system were present in the room (see Fig. 6).

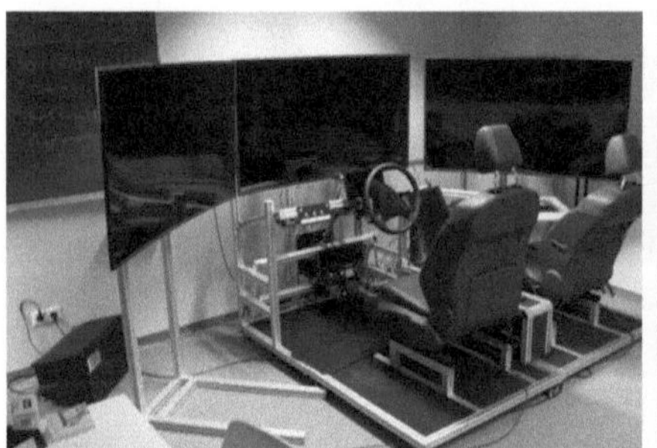

Fig. 6. Experimental setup without participant (left) and with participant (right).

4 Results

The goal of our exploratory study is to investigate potential effects of using virtual lane augmentations in a simulated mixed-reality HUD. Due to the exploratory character of the study, no hypotheses were formulated.

In this section, we provide an overview of the results of the empirical study. While a detailed analysis of the eye-tracking data will be the subject of a forthcoming paper [24], the focus of this section is on reporting our findings regarding the influence of virtual lane augmentation on driving precision (i.e. deviation from the center of the driver's own lane) and the detection of errors in the visualization of the lane augmentation. As reported in Sect. 3.3, three augmentation errors were intentionally introduced in each of the center/right lane edge driving phases.

In the pre-task questionnaire, information regarding the participant's demographic data and the respective driving experience was collected (see Sect. 3.4 of this paper). In the post-task questionnaire, which was applied after completion of the three driving phases, impressions of the perceived fidelity of the participant's driving experience with the K3F simulation was obtained. Two questions were used to assess the subjective perception of the simulation fidelity based on a 9-point Likert-scale. In the first question participants were asked to give their assessment of the following statement: *"The quality of the simulation allows the driving task to be carried out realistically"* ("not at all"… "absolutely", 1–9). The intention of the second question was to understand to what extend participants needed to adjust their driving behavior when driving the simulator: *"I had to change my driving behavior in the simulator compared to my driving behavior in reality in order to carry out the driving task"*. As with the first question, a 9-point Likert-scale was used to collect the participant's answer. The mean value of the obtained results for question 1 *(simulation fidelity)* was $\emptyset = 6.7$ out of 9 (SD $= 1.03$), the mean value for question 2 *(need to adjust driving behavior)* was $\emptyset = 5.2$ out of 9 (SD $= 2.5$). Although we lack benchmark data from prior studies with K3F that would allow for a comparative interpretation, a mean perceived fidelity of 6.7/9 can at least be regarded as encouraging (min $= 4$, max $= 9$). There are obvious differences between a real drive in a car and a drive in the simulation system as an approximation of reality (G-Forces, vibration, driving physics, steering behavior, etc.). It should thus not come as a surprise that participants reported the need to adjust their driving behavior when driving in the K3F simulation system. The mean value of the responses to question 2 *(need to adjust driving behavior)* of $\emptyset = 5.2$ out of 9, i.e. slightly higher than the mean of the scale, suggests that participants had to adapt their driving behavior at least moderately. As with question 1, benchmark data from prior studies that would allow for a comparative interpretation is missing. Upon completion of the final questionnaire, short qualitative interviews were conducted with the participants. While the realism of the simulation was explicitly mentioned on the positive side, some participants report that they had to get used to the steering behavior of the simulated car in the initial moments of the ride.

To assess potential indicators of motion sickness after driving in the K3F simulator, the MSAQ [22] was applied. The MSAQ (Motion sickness assessment questionnaire) is a validated, multidimensional questionnaire for the assessment of motion sickness, consisting of the dimensions *gastrointestinal, central, peripheral,* and *sopite-related.* Each dimension is measured by four items, resulting in a total of 16 (9-Point Likert-scale) questions for the MSAQ. Figure 7 shows a graphical representation of the values of the four subscales of the MSAQ (gastrointestinal, $\emptyset = 16.9$, SD $= 9.45$; central, $\emptyset = 22.8$, SD $= 13.9$; peripheral, $\emptyset = 14.8$, SD $= 7.97$; and sopite-related, $\emptyset = 26.4$, SD $= 12.7$) as well as the mean MSAQ total score (% from max.; $\emptyset = 20.7$, SD $= 9.14$). Czeisler, Pruski, P. Wang, J. Wang, Xiao, M.H. Polymeropoulos and V.M. Polymeropoulos [21] provide reference data to categorize mean MSAQ scores. According to their classification, the observed scores (%) can be interpreted as indicating *none to mild* symptoms of motion sickness, which also corresponds to verbal comments of the participants.

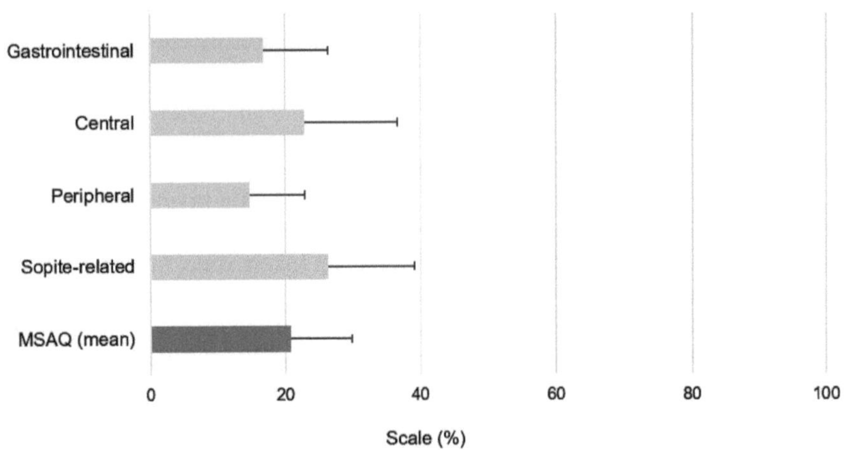

Fig. 7. MSAQ results.

Participants were asked to drive in the center of their own lane during all phases, whether unassisted (base line drive) or assisted by virtual augmentations (center/right edge). As reported in Sect. 3.3, due to a buzzing tone (55 km/h) and a speed limiter that automatically intervenes at a speed of 75 km/h, the mean speed of the participants was about equal in phases of the study. Potential differences in driving precision (i.e. deviation from the center of a participant's lane) are thus unlikely to be caused by speed differences. It should be noted that participants familiarized themselves with the K3F simulator in the (unsupported) benchmark phase. Inspection of the course of mean deviations from the lane center over the driving distance in the benchmark phase gave, however, no indication of a training effect (i.e. a larger deviations in the initial driving sections of rural road course).

Figure 8 shows the deviation from the lane center for all driving phases of the study. Absolute root mean square (RMS) values (in cm) were used to calculate deviations for the respective phases. To compute deviations from the lane center, test drive data was segmented into 1000 equal sections. The use of absolute values ensures that deviations to the left/right of the lane center do not mutually compensate. RMS values were utilized to emphasize higher deviations since these might lead the car onto the lane of oncoming traffic (strong left deviation) or into the forest (right deviation). Right/left deviations were not penalized differently.

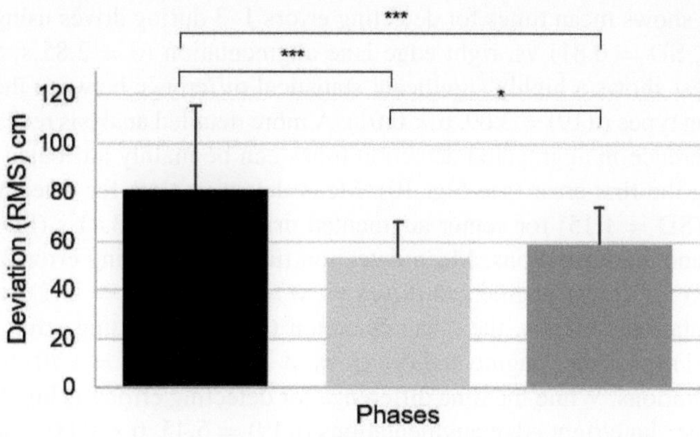

Fig. 8. Mean deviation (RMS).

The mean deviation (RMS) from the lane center in the benchmark phase (without augmentation support) was 84.1 cm (SD = 34.2). During center augmented drives the mean deviation (RMS) was 53.5 cm (SD = 14.4) and drives with an augmentation of the right edge of the lane resulted in mean deviations of 58.8 cm from the center of the participant's lane (SD = 15.1). Paired t-tests reveal substantial statistical differences in the observed lane deviations between unsupported drives and center lane augmented drives (t(19) = 4.43, p < .001), as well as between unsupported drives and right edge augmentations (t(19) = 3.95, p < .001). Paired t-test comparison of observed lane deviations of center augmented drives and right edge lane augmentation also reached statistical significance (t(19) = 2.09, p = .05).

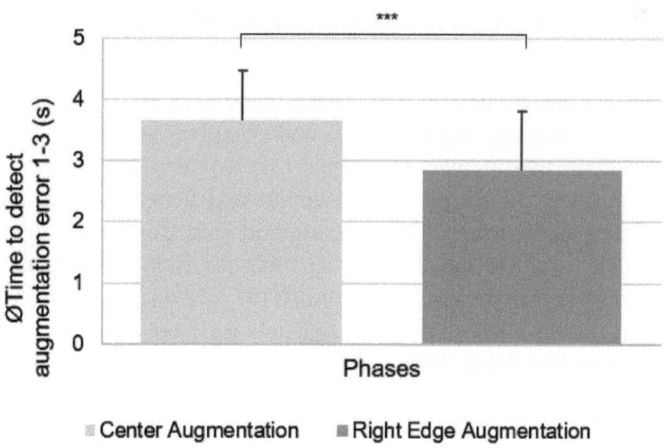

Fig. 9. Overall mean error detection times.

Figure 9 shows mean times for detecting errors 1–3 during drives using center lane (ø = 3.67 s, SD = 0.81) vs. right edge lane augmentation (ø = 2.85 s, SD = 0.96). A paired t-test shows a highly significant statistical difference between the considered augmentation types (t(19) = 3.69, p < 0.01). A more detailed analysis reveals, however, that the difference in aggregated detection times can be mainly attributed to the times for detecting the first error (see Fig. 10). Mean detection time for detecting error 1 is ø = 5.49 s (SD = 1.15) for center augmented drives vs. ø = 3.41 s (SD = 1.56) for right edge lane augmentations. Mean detection time for detecting error 2 is ø = 2.82 s (SD = .95) for center augmented drives vs. ø = 2.89 s (SD = 1.42) for right edge lane augmentations. Finally, the mean detection time for detecting error 3 is ø = 2.7 s (SD = 1.31) for center augmented drives vs. ø = 2.27 s (SD = 1.70) for right edge lane augmentations. While the time difference for detecting error 1 is highly significant between center lane/right edge augmentations (t(19) = 5.45, p < 0.001), no difference was found for error 2 or error 3 (t(19) = 1.23, p = .23). There was no statistical evidence for differences in the number of detected errors nor regarding false alarms.

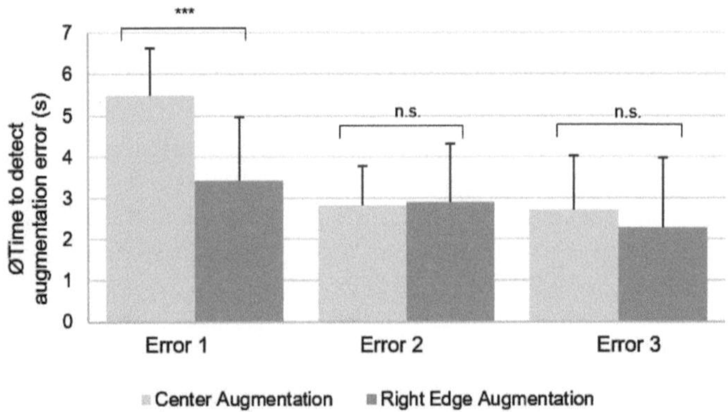

Fig. 10. Error-specific mean detection times.

In the post-task questionnaire, participants were also asked to rate *the perceived support* of the respective lane augmentations and to express how would *rate* the baseline drive in contrast to the two augmentation types. Likert-scales (1–10) were used to collect the subjective impressions for perceived support and general evaluation rating. The results show a consistent picture: The mean support value for center augmentation was 7.5 out of 10 (SD = 2.14) and 8.7 (SD = 1.49) for right edge augmentation. The reported difference is statistically significant (t(19) = 2.45, p = .024). As there was no HUD support during baseline rides, participants were not asked about the perceived support for the baseline drive. While the mean evaluation rating of the unsupported drive is 2.8 out of 10 (SD = 2.55), the mean ratings for center augmentation are 6.55 (SD = 2.01) and 8.95 (SD = 1.23) for right edge augmentation. Paired t-tests show substantial differences between unsupported drive vs. center augmentation (t(19) = 4.66, p < .001) and unsupported drive vs. right edge augmentation (t(19) = 8.34, p

< .001). A comparison of the ratings for center vs. right edge augmentation reveals a substantial difference (t(19) = 8.34, p < .001) in favor of right edge augmentation.

5   Discussion

The goal of the exploratory study presented in this paper is to investigate the impact of virtual augmentations in mixed-reality HUDs on driving precision and aspects of situational awareness like error detection. The findings reported in the previous sections clearly show a positive effect of mixed-reality lane augmentations compared to unsupported driving. The positive effect was present both in behavioral data like observed lane deviations, as well as in subjective data like the perceived support or evaluation rating. While lane deviation was smallest when drivers were supported by center lane augmentation, error detection data points to a potentially critical trade-off. Although the observed effect on mean error detection times was mainly due to the occurrence of the first error, there was a corresponding tendency in the detection times for the third error. Overall, the reported findings point to a differential impact of the augmentation types on situational awareness. Subsequent analysis of collected eye-tracking data from the study will pave the ground for deeper insights into the results presented in this paper [24].

Preliminary inspection of the eye-tracking data suggests that participants' gazes tended to be fixated strongly on the virtual center augmentation line, with comparably fewer saccades targeted towards a broader inspection of the road scenery. An intense visual focus on the (center) augmentation line can be assumed to have a negative effect on situational awareness since it impairs overall visual scanning of the driving environment. In contrast, augmentation of the right edge of the road promotes more distributed gaze patterns. A broader distribution of fixations in the visual field is to be expected when participants, to find the center of their own lane, continuously extrapolate between the center reservation (indicating the middle of the road) and the (augmented) right edge of their own lane. Instead of mainly focusing on a virtual center line, such broader distribution of fixations favors a better situational awareness which in turn supports faster detection of augmentation errors.

6   Conclusion and Future Work

The findings reported in this paper refer to critical considerations when designing mixed reality HUDs: Both augmentation types significantly improved driving precision compared to data from unsupported baseline drives. However, data on error detection time suggests that lane center augmentation might come with potential risks in cases where the system malfunctions. In our exploratory study, road edge augmentation appears to have preserved better situational awareness while still substantially supporting lane following. Our findings are in line with results from aviation HUD research [8] and provide relevant implications for the design and implementation of automotive mixed reality systems.

Participants recruited for participation in the study represent a relatively young sample of drivers. To overcome this limitation, future work should investigate whether the reported findings can be replicated with other age groups. As quite simple augmentations (i.e. lines) were used in the mixed-reality HUD, next steps will include the investigation of different visualization options to understand the impact of MR visualizations on driving precision and error detection. Given that real-world augmentation errors are likely to occur due to environmental conditions, inadequate map data, or connectivity issues, further research is necessary for an informed balance between performance enhancement and error resilience in safety-critical systems.

Acknowledgments. Acknowledgments. "The authors thank Arthur Barz, Aylin Cin, and especially Daniel Kerpen for their valuable contributions and technical assistance throughout this study. We are equally grateful to all colleagues who contributed to the K3F simulation environment.

Disclosure of Interests. The authors have no competing interests to declare that are relevant to the content of this paper.

References

1. SAE International: Taxonomy and Definitions for Terms Related to Driving Automation Systems for On-Road Motor Vehicles. SAE Standard J3016_202104. SAE International, Warrendale (2021)
2. International Organization for Standardization: Road Vehicles — Visibility — Specifications and Test Procedures for Head-up Displays (HUD). ISO/TS 21957:2023. ISO, Geneva (2023)
3. Newman, R.L.: Headup Displays: Designing the Way Ahead. Ashgate Publishing, Aldershot (1995). https://doi.org/10.4324/9781315253596
4. Nichol, R.J.: Airline head-up display systems: human factors considerations. Int. J. Econ. Manag. Sci. **4**(248), 1–6 (2015). https://doi.org/10.2139/ssrn.2384101
5. VandenBos, G.R.: APA Dictionary of Psychology. American Psychological Association, Washington DC (2007)
6. Endsley, M.R.: Toward a theory of situation awareness in dynamic systems. Hum. Factors **37**(1), 32–64 (1995)
7. Wickens, C.D., Alexander, A.L.: Attentional tunneling and task management in synthetic vision displays. Int. J. Aviat. Psychol. **19**(2), 182–199 (2009). https://doi.org/10.1080/105 08410902766549
8. Smallman, H.S., St. John, M.: Chexing the checklist: an overview of display design strategies for improving SA. In: Proceedings of the Human Factors and Ergonomics Society Annual Meeting. HFES, Santa Monica (2005)
9. McDonald, Z.: Augmented Reality HUDs: Warning Signs and Drivers' Situation Awareness. Master's thesis, Rochester Institute of Technology (2016)
10. Sony Interactive Entertainment: Gran Turismo Official Website. https://www.gran-turismo.com/de/. Accessed 28 June 2025
11. White, I.: The History of Air Intercept Radar & the British Nightfighter. Pen & Sword Aviation, Barnsley (2007)
12. NASA: A Review of Some Head-Up Display Formats. NASA Technical Publication TP-1499. NASA Ames Research Center, Moffett Field (1979)
13. Wood, R.B., et al.: Head-up displays. In: Spitzer, C.R. (ed.) The Avionics Handbook, pp. 15-1–15-20. CRC Press, Boca Raton (2001)
14. Chou, C.D., Madhavan, D., Funk, K.: Studies of cockpit task management errors. Int. J. Aviat. Psychol. **6**(4), 307–320 (1996). https://doi.org/10.1207/s15327108ijap0604_1

15. Fadden, S., Wickens, C., Ververs, P.: Costs and benefits of head up displays: an attention perspective and a meta analysis. SAE Technical Paper 2000-01-5542 (2000). https://doi.org/10.4271/2000-01-5542

16. Liu, Y.-C., Wen, M.-H.: Comparison of head-up display (HUD) vs. head-down display (HDD): driving performance of commercial vehicle operators in Taiwan. Int. J. Hum.-Comput. Stud. **61**(5), 679–697 (2004). https://doi.org/10.1016/j.ijhcs.2004.06.002

17. Conrad, J., Wallach, D., Barz, A., Kerpen, D., Puderer, T., Weisenburg, A.: Concept Simulator K3F: a flexible framework for driving simulations. In: Proceedings of the 11th International Conference on Automotive User Interfaces and Interactive Vehicular Applications: Adjunct Proceedings, pp. 498–501. ACM, Utrecht (2019). https://doi.org/10.1145/3349263.3349596

18. Barz, A., Conrad, J., Wallach, D.: Advantages of using runtime procedural generation of virtual environments based on real world data for conducting empirical automotive research. In: Stephanidis, C., et al. (eds.) HCI International 2020 – Late Breaking Papers, LNCS, vol. 12429, pp. 14–23. Springer, Cham (2020). https://doi.org/10.1007/978-3-030-59987-4_2

19. Foyle, D.C., McCann, R.S., Sanford, B.D., Schwirzke, M.F.J.: attentional effects with superimposed symbology: implications for head-up displays (HUD). In: Proceedings of the Human Factors and Ergonomics Society 37th Annual Meeting, pp. 1340–1344. HFES, Santa Monica (1993)

20. Myers, A., Hansen, C.: Experimental Psychology, 7th edn. Thomson Wadsworth, Belmont (2006)

21. Czeisler, M.É., et al.: Validation of the motion sickness severity scale: secondary analysis of a randomized, double-blind, placebo-controlled study of a treatment for motion sickness. PLoS ONE **18**(1), e0280058 (2023). https://doi.org/10.1371/journal.pone.0280058

22. Gianaros, P.J., Muth, E.R., Mordkoff, J.T., Levine, M.E., Stern, R.M.: A questionnaire for the assessment of the multiple dimensions of motion sickness. Aviat. Space Environ. Med. **72**, 115–119 (2001)

23. Draeger, J.: Visuelle Ergonomie im Cockpit. Die Bedeutung der Instrumenteerkennbarkeit für die Flugsicherheit. Ophthalmologe **106**(4), 370–373 (2009). https://doi.org/10.1007/s00347-008-1879-8

24. Wallach, D., Conrad, J. (forthcoming): Augmentations in mixed-reality HUDs: An eyetracking analysis (2026)

A Model of Driver Readiness After Sleep

Jutta Hild$^{(\boxtimes)}$, David J. Lerch , and Frederik Diederichs

Fraunhofer Institute of Optronics, System Technologies and Image Exploitation, Karlsruhe, Germany
`{Jutta.Hild,DavidJ.Lerch,Frederik.Diederichs}@iosb.fraunhofer.de`

Abstract. In this contribution, we propose a model of driver readiness after sleep. It is supposed to cover user states occuring in SAE levels L3 and L4. We propose four states for our model: "Ready to drive", "Relaxing", "Sleeping", and "Affected by Sleep Inertia". We provide first suggestions on transitions between the states and on appropriate transition times. We describe the three states "Relaxing", "Sleeping", and "Affected by Sleep Inertia" in a chapter each as they are new states not occuring in L0, L1, and L2 models.

Keywords: Driver modeling · SAE level 3 · SAE level 4 · Driver states · Driver readiness · Relaxation · Sleep · Sleep inertia

1 Introduction

The field of automated driving has witnessed remarkable progress in recent years, particularly in the development of technologies and human factors solutions [1, 9,10,27], enabling SAE[1] levels 3 and 4 (L3 and L4) automation.

In this contribution, we propose a basic model for the occurring major driver states in driving automations levels 3 and 4. The model describes driver state transitions between driving and sleeping. We think, it could serve three interconnected purposes (1) to provide a structured starting point for empirical research into driver and occupant behavior under L3/L4 conditions, (2) to inform the design of adaptive and context-sensitive human-machine interfaces (HMIs), and (3) to serve as a behavioral reference for Driver and Occupant Monitoring Systems (DMS/OMW), which are critical enablers of safe and user-accepted L3 and L4 driving. Even after thorough review of scientific papers as well as practical guidelines as provided, for example, by Euro NCAP, we did not find a driver model for those levels L3 and L4, hence, starting to carve out one.

1.1 Characteristics of the SAE Levels

Driver modeling is an important means to design and establish safe and comfortable driving. This applies for all SAE levels from L0 to L5. However, the

---

[1] Society of Automotive Engineers

P.-L.P. Rau and H. Krömker (Eds.): HCII 2025, LNCS 16336, pp. 358–371, 2026.
https://doi.org/10.1007/978-3-032-12798-3_22

respective occurring relevant driver states vary for the different SAE levels subject to the drivers' varying roles and responsibilities within those levels [11].

Examining the characteristics of SAE levels, we find kind of a dichotomy between levels L0 to L2 with the driver acting as a driver, and levels L3 to L5 with the driver acting mainly as a passenger. Obviously, this has great impact on their allowed behavior and the resulting behavioral states.

Up to L2, the driver is in charge of controlling the vehicle. Within those levels, the driver is demanded to constantly supervise the applied support features. Hence, besides having the hands on the wheel and the feet on the pedals, supervising requires the eyes on the road and the mind on the driving task. As a result, the large body of available scientific work is focused on driver readiness (perceptual, cognitive, motoric) [14], with a strong focus on driver attention [12,13,24,34,37] and how to support, maintain or restore it.

Relevant driver states are therefore, "Ready to drive" as the wanted state, and "Distracted", "Drowsy" and "Unresponsive" as occurring states that must be treated with countermeasures [32]. As those states are complex human states themselves, research typically addresses only a single aspect, incrementally contributing to a comprehensive understanding of driver behavior in levels 0 to 2.

In SAE levels 3, 4, and 5, the car system is in charge of controlling the vehicle, and the driver is basically a passenger. In our contribution, we do not address L5 as we understand that in a fully automated vehicle with start-to-end service there is almost no limitation for driver as well as occupant behavior. In contrast, in L3 and L4, some driving action by the driver is still required.

By definition, in L3, the driver must take over when requested by the car system. However, during the rest of the time, the driver is allowed to keep themselves busy with non-driving-related tasks including a state of relaxing with eyes closed, hands off the wheel and mind off the driving task. The current limitation is to take back control after announcement within 10 seconds.

In L4, by definition no driver action is required. For the driver, this opens up the option of not only relaxing, but of sleeping. However, the automation time is limited and eventually the operational design domain ends. The vehicle may stop at a safe parking, or the driver prefers to finish the trip by taking over vehicle control.

2   The Proposed Model

In our model, we focus on the situation of relaxing (L3 and L4) and sleeping (L4). With automated driving becoming more common, people might get used to this choice. However, it is necessary to provide safe take over. In order to achieve this goal, typical driver or passenger states in L3 and L4 have to be determined.

As for L0 to L2, the model must include the state "Ready to drive". This state is required in case the vehicle occupant has to take over driving control. As mentioned before, in L3, the occupant must be able to take over in certain situations. In L4, the occupant presumably wants to take over if the car reached its system boundaries and is within a minimal risk state (e.g., stopping at the hard shoulder of a road).

Next, as from L3 the driver is allowed to perform non-driving related tasks (NDRT), like using smart phone or laptop, watching video or gaming, reading, including relaxing with eyes closed, the model should include the state "Relaxing".

Next, as from L4 the driver is allowed to sleep, the model should include the state "Sleeping".

Considering the functional states of the human organism as described by Grandjean [15], we can find the three states "Sleeping", "Relaxing" and "Ready to Drive" as being part of the provided number of stages that occur "(...) between the extremes of sleep and of a state of alarm (...): deep sleep; light sleep, drowsy; weary, hardly awake; relaxed, resting; fresh, alert; very alert, stimulated; in a state of alarm".

Allocating our states to Grandjean's stages, "Sleeping" would cover "deep sleep; light sleep, drowsy". "Relaxing" would cover "relaxed, resting". "Ready to drive" would cover "fresh, alert", "very alert, stimulated" but also "in state of alarm".

However, there is another stage, "weary; hardly awake" which appears to belong neither to "Sleeping" nor to "Relaxing". As a matter of fact, when considering sleeping, we are confronted with the phenomenon of sleep inertia occurring right after waking up from sleep, even after short naps [17,41]. Sleep inertia is defined as a "(...) transitional state of lowered arousal occurring immediately after awakening from sleep and producing a temporary decrement in subsequent performance" [41]. As sleep inertia is known to last for minutes and as take over might not allow for arbitrary duration it appears appropriate considering it as a separate state in our model.

2.1 Model States and Transitions

Hence, our proposed model includes four states: "Ready to drive", "Relaxing", Sleeping" and "Affected by Sleep Inertia" (Fig. 1). Moreover, the model proposes transitions between these states.

Starting with "Relaxing", there is a transition from "Ready to drive". This transition should be completely under control of the occupant's declared intention to relax in case the car drives in L3 or L4 and, hence, should not be subject to any time restrictions.

In contrast, the transition from "Relaxing" to "Ready to drive" might occur surprisingly only after a short time. In a thorough research literature review, we found at least 10 s being required (cf. e.g [29] and below chapter 3).

There is also a transition from "Relaxing" to "Sleeping". When driving in L4, this transition should also not be subject to any time restrictions. When driving in L3, this state must be avoided, requesting a method to safely distinguish between the two states. The reason is that even if the occupant falls only into light sleep where they are relatively easy to wake up again, the take-over would

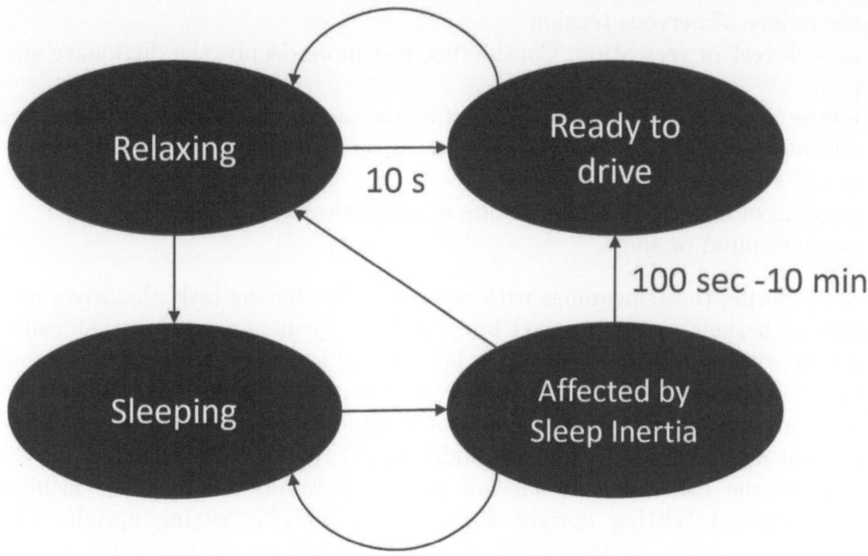

Fig. 1. The proposed model

presumably take longer than 10 s. This is due to the fact that there is no direct transition from "Sleeping" to "Ready to drive".

The reason is that, according to research literature, in between there is always the state "Affected by Sleep Inertia". After thorough review on sleep inertia literature, for now, we propose a time range of 2–30 min for which sleep inertia must be expected [7, 16, 17, 35, 36, 39–44, 46, 47]. As remains unclear which intensity of sleep inertia might be appropriate to call a person ready to drive. Hence, after literature research we came up with a first idea of transition time from "Affected by Sleep Inertia" to "Ready to drive" being within the range of 100 s to 10 minutes (cf. Chap. 5).

Considering the state "Affected by sleep inertia", it might occur that the occupant feels like going right back to "Sleeping" or at least to "Relaxing" in case they feel too uncomfortable. Considering L4 automated driving, these transitions should also not be subject to time restrictions.

We propose that there is no transition between "Ready to drive" and "Sleeping" as before falling asleep, some relaxation occurs (cf. above Grandjean's stages, and below Chap. 4).

3   Relaxing

Merriam-Webster describes *relax* with various nuances or connotations. For us within the driving context maybe of interest

1. the lessening of physical tension/a muscle (fiber) to become inactive and lengthen

2. the relieve of nervous tension
3. to seek rest or recreation. Considering *rest* more deeply, the dictionary suggests
4. repose/sleep, specifically "a bodily state characterized by minimal functional and metabolic activities"; this suggestion builds the bridge between the two model states "relax" and "sleep".
5. freedom of activity of labor/a state of motionlessness or inactivity
6. peace of mind or spirit.

Considering those meanings with respect to the driving task, the driver may relieve both their (1, 5) physical body and (2, 6) mental tension that comes naturally with sustained attention. In L3, this might involve removing the hands from the steering wheel and the feet from the pedals, as well as changing the whole body into a less symmetric and more random pose. Both can contribute to (3) rest and recreation. In L4, in addition, (4) repose is allowed.

Asking the colleagues in our lab how they would relax in this fashion, they mentioned "sitting upright with relaxed limbs", "sitting upright with eyes closed", "sitting in non-upright position", "listening to (favourite) music", "dancing while sitting upright to (favourite) music", and "mind-wandering".

3.1   L3 and Non-driving-Related Tasks

Considering L3 related work, there are plenty of contributions addressing take-over in the situation of NDRT, but only a few explicitly address relaxation as described in the enumeration above.

Jarosch et al. (2019) consider take-over being a time consuming process as there are sensory, motoric, and cognitive state transitions as well as arousal and motivational issues to be accomplished [21]. In other words, the occupant has to (1) perceive the TOR, (2) end the NDRT or relaxation, (3) bring the eyes back on the road, hands back on the wheel and feet back on the pedals, (4) bring back their mind on the manual driving task.

Naujoks et al. (2019) identified NDRTs from existing studies in order to derive their characteristics like the "ability to visually monitor traffic, necessity of sustained attention to NDRT", and they looked into steps of the take-over process that could be impaired by performing the respective NDRT [31].

Kim et al. (2021) provide an overview over 25 studies that investigated the take-over effectiveness of user interfaces for L3 and L4 when drivers are allowed to take their eyes off the road. They report short take-over times (up to 4.32 s) for take-over requests (TOR) "initiated by the auditory modality with high urgency levels". Tactile TOR shows similar reaction times. The longest take-over time (up to 9.46 s) was reported for TOR mediated by visual-only signals [23].

Merat et al. (2014) conducted a driving simulator study reporting that it took the drivers at least 10 s to take-over from a automated vehicle (Level 3 automation) [29].

3.2 Non-driving Postures

Few contributions investigated situations closer to our understanding of relaxation as they consider the issue of changes of the seating position, so-called non-driving postures (NDPs). Yang et al. (2018) report for a L3 scenario longer take-over time when the torso angle of the seat is larger [48]. Muto et al. (2022) investigated six different driver postures, combining upper body and head orientation (forward, sideways) with foot posture (both feet on floor, crossed legs, crossed-legged sitting). They reported that the steering reaction times and the braking reaction times are substantially longer for sideways and crossed legs/crossed legs sitting conditions (steering up to 1.51 s; braking up to 1.69 s) compared to normal posture (steering M = 0.91 s; braking = 0.8 s) [30].

Zhao et al. (2024) considered the impact of NDPs on take-over performance when people are engaged in different NDRTs (L3 driving simulator experiment). The NDPs contained two reference postures and 21 non-driving related postures. NDPs prolonged take-over times, particularly for abnormal right foot positions, trunk deviations, and both hands occupation. Moreover, it appeared that upper body abnormal postures caused slower reaction of the lower body, and vice versa. The authors also report a range of individual reaction capacities [50].

Zhang et al. (2025) address the relevant issue of poor anatomic support considering backrest tilt angles and headrest conditions aiming to provide a reference for future seat design for autonomous driving [49].

3.3 Sound, Music and Active Relaxation Techniques

Choubey et al. (2024) present a study on sound-augmented blankets for relaxation and sleep. Although not a contribution within the context of conditionally automated driving, their contribution might be inspiring as car occupants may utilize a pillow or a blanket to improve relaxation. In an online survey, the authors identified that people prefer an Ocean Waves sound when relaxing [8]. In addition, they provide an overview of the results of sound therapy and on the acoustic characteristics of music and sound for relaxation: natural sounds alleviate everyday stress [38]; fountain sounds and tweeting birds provide quick and pleasant recovery [3]; bird songs and ocean waves reduce arousal and are perceived as especially pleasant [28]. Characteristics of relaxing music are acoustic features (persistent melody lines, basic rhythms, low dynamic levels), aesthetic value, and familiarity [5].

Moreover, Choubey et al. give an overview on relaxation techniques. Examples are Benson's relaxation technique (deep breathing and repetition of chants) [6]; progressive muscular relaxation by Jacobson (systematic tensing and relaxing of muscle groups) [19]; mental imagery relaxation (visualizing calm scenes) [26]; meditation (encourage mindfulness and present-moment awareness) [20]. All are widely used and require active concentration on the body tension and release.

3.4   Deriving Transition Time from "Relaxing" to "Ready to drive"

Based on the above presented contributions, we decided to start with 10 s for the transition between "Relaxing" and "Ready to drive". Even if this duration comes from work on NDRTs, is appears a reasonable starting point. The contributions on NDPs point out that for abnormal postures require longer take-over time. This has to be proved experimentally in the future. Performing active relaxation techniques might also require longer take-over times as not only the body has to be brought back to driving mode but also the mind. In general, Lal and Craig mentioned, that the "relaxed, resting" stage by Grandjean [15] is a condition that is "likely to reduce attention and alertness" [25]. This might also hold for listening to sound or music; however, as this does not demand active involvement it may be an option that allows comparatively short take-over times.

4   Sleeping

In L4, the driver role is that of a passenger. Up to L3, the driver must be awake, quiet wakefulness with eyes closed being allowed as well. In L4, they are also allowed to sleep.

According to Kandel et al. (2021) [22], sleep is a state of "temporary, reversible loss of consciousness". The exact functions of sleep are not yet fully understood. However, it is reasonable that "one function of sleep may be to allow synaptic remodeling and consolidation of memory reflecting the day's experiences" [22]. What appears certain is that sleep "is required for normal brain function, and inadequate sleep, as defined by an increased tendency to fall asleep during the day, is associated with impaired cognitive function" [22].

4.1   Sleep Stages

Typical night sleep is comprised of alternating periods of non-REM sleep and REM sleep. A typical night sleep duration is about 8 hours long and comprises five sleep cycles of non-REM sleep followed by REM sleep, each lasting for about 90 minutes. Non-REM sleep can be distinguished into three stages N1, N2, N3. During all of them, "eye movements are absent, muscle tone is low, breathing is slow and regular, and body temperature falls". The three stages can be distinguished best by measuring brain activity using an electroencephalogram (EEG).

In stage N1, EEG frequencies are slightly slowing (theta waves 4-7 Hz) compared to the fast low-amplitude activity the EEG shows for the awake state. In stage N2, there is some slow activity from theta and delta waves (0.5–4 Hz) as well as two particularly distinctive EEG characteristics, the so-called sleep spindles (bursts of 12- to 14 Hz activity, duration 1–2 s) and the K-complexes (high-voltage single slow waves). In stage N3, the EEG is dominated by very slow delta waves.

Considering consciousness during the non-REM stages, it differs in the following way. During N1, it starts to fade: The "individual becomes drowsy and transitions into light non-REM sleep" [22]. However, they may still be awakened easily. During N2 and N3, "people are generally unconscious of the world around them as the slow cortical activity disrupts information processing" [22].

In contrast, during REM sleep, the EEG shows activity similar to the awake state. Moreover, rapid eye movements are present which differ from the voluntary eye movements present in awake state.

The transition from non-REM fo REM sleep is controlled by a sophisticated system of mutually inhibitory neurons (for detail, please refer to [22]).

4.2   Mechanisms Related to Transitions Between Sleep and Wakefulness

The brain possesses a so-called ascending arousal system that promotes wakefulness. Certain neurons "fire fast during the awake state but much slower during sleep, suggesting that they are wake-promoting" [22]. On the other hand, other neurons cause sleepiness and fire during sleep. Together, a number of mutually inhibitory neurons controls the transition from wake to sleep. They work together like an electrical flip-flop turning each other off.

As a consequence, such a system effects that transitions between wake to sleep, or vice verca, are quick, taking only a few seconds or minutes. This is an advantage, as spending time in a transitional drowsy state makes the individual vulnerable (for detail, please refer to [22].

The regulation of sleep is controlled by two processes, the homeostatic pressure for sleep (established by humoral factors) and the circadian rhythm (enforced by a biological clock in the suprachiasmic nucleus, "clock genes").

The homeostatic sleep pressure accumulates during a longer period of wakefulness. It is mediated by humoral factors that circulate in the brain signaling the pressure for non-REM sleep. Sleep pressure can be measured using the Multiple Sleep Latency Test. A well-rested person "takes at least 15–20 minutes to fall asleep, but a very sleepy person can easily fall asleep within a few minutes in each nap" [22]. The Psychomotor Vigilance Test (press a button as soon as a small lamp is turned on randomly over 5-10 min) can reveal that sleepy people react slowly or not at all, and presumably are in a state of high sleep pressure.

The circadian rhythm "varies on a 24-h cycle, regardless of previous sleep" [22], and counterbalances the homeostatic sleep pressure.

4.3   Deriving No Transition Time from "Sleeping" to "Affected ba Sleep Inertia"

As in L4 the occupant is in the role of a passenger, the transition from "Sleeping" to "Affected by Sleep Inertia" appears to be uncritical in terms of time budget. Hence, our model does not specify any transition time.

5 Affected by Sleep Inertia

Tassi and Muzet [41] characterize sleep inertia (SI) as

- Transitional state of lowered arousal
- Occurring immediately after awakening from sleep
- Producing a temporary decrement in subsequent performance
- Disorientation/decreased performance relative to pre-sleep status

SI occurs always after sleep, both after short naps and after normal 8-h night sleep. SI intensity is influenced by the preceding sleep duration.

SI intensity is also affected by the sleep stage prior to awakening: the deeper the sleep, the higher is SI intensity. SI appears to occur less likely after short naps up to 30 min if they contain only sleep stages N1 and N2 [42]. Brooks and Lack [7] reported that examining nap durations of 5, 10, 20, and 30 min, "10-minute nap was overall the most effective afternoon nap duration". Hilditch et al. considered daily naps of 5, 10, 20 and 30 min, too. They also reported best performance (comparing to pre-nap and no-nap) for an afternoon nap of 10 min duration.

SI intensity is also higher if people wake up close to the trough of the core body temperature compared to the peak core body temperature. SI intensity it is not affected by any other circadian rhythm.

The time course of SI is controversial. SI durations have been reported lasting from 1 min to 4 h. However, without sleep loss, SI duration appears to fade within 30 minutes after waking-up.

Type of task is another variable affecting SI. The reason is that different tasks include different cognitive processes that in turn differ in SI sensitivity.

Hilditch and McHill [17] conclude that "Taken together, (...) studies suggest that circadian timing and prior sleep-wake history influence sleep inertia duration as well as severity".

Sleep inertia is often examined but, so far, not fully understood. Aakersted and Folkart [2] proposed a three-process model of sleep, where sleep inertia is the third process beside sleep pressure and circadian rhythm (cf. Sect. 4.1). It is described as a "short, yet salient, decrease in alertness and performance immediately after waking-up". The exact function remains unclear, however it might be a mechanism protecting sleep at times when sleep pressure is already low (like for example in early mornings hours after night sleep) [33].

The EEG shows more delta activity (associated with N3 deep sleep) and less beta activity (associated with awake) compared to the awake state before falling asleep [45]. Balkin et al. [4] reported that cerebral blood flow velocity is slower for up to 30 minutes after waking-up compared to prior falling asleep. Moreover, fading of SI appears to correlate with reactivation of the brain regions after sleep.

5.1 Sleep Inertia in Autonomous Driving

Several contributions investigated sleep inertia in a driving context. Hirsch et al. [18] reported results from a driving simulator study with 44 subjects. The participants took a nap; in order to avoid N3 sleep, they were woken up after 15–20 min. Three conditions for time budget of take-over were used: 1, 7, and 15 min. The results show that all subjects achieved take-over within 1 min, but were very stressed. On the other hand, 7 min were perceived being too long. Hence, it would be interesting to investigate take-over with a relaxed time budget, for example 1.5, 2 or 3 min.

Wörle et al. reported that in a driving simulator study (L4) performance after short naps was worse than prior to the nap. However, almost all subjects considered 60 s between first TOR and actual take-over being an appropriate time budget [46].

Tomzig et al. investigated in a driving simulator study nap durations of 20, 40 and 60 min. They report longer take-over times for longer nap durations [43].

5.2 Deriving Transition Time from "Affected by Sleep Inertia" to "Ready to drive"

Considering our proposed model, determining the allowed transition time from "Affected by sleep inertia" to "Ready to drive" appears tricky given the results from the research literature. There is no final evidence which SI intensity would be appropriate in order to admit that an occupant is ready to drive. However, we think that SI must not have faded completely in order to be "Ready to drive". Even if 7 min appeared as a too large time budget for take-over [18] we extend the the upper boundary for the transition from "Affected by sleep inertia" to "Ready to drive" to 10 min, simply because in other driving studies yet to come the driving tasks may be more complex and would need a larger time budget.

Concerning the lower boundary, two studies reported 60 s as a manageable take-over time [18,46]. However, as the subjects reported it to be stressful, we suggest a little more time, proposing 100 s in our proposed model.

6 Conclusion and Future Work

We are about to start several driving simulator studies concerning relaxing and sleeping in order to add more information to the transitions between the states of our model.

Future research should further explore the driver's transition between different states. The transition times between the different states are not fully explored. In future work we will further explore the state of sleep inertia and it's effect on the driving performance. Based on this driver state model we will develop AI models that are capable of recognizing the driver state.

Disclosure of Interests. The authors have no competing interests to declare that are relevant to the content of this article.

Acknowledgements. The work has been funded under the funding codes 19A24002K by the Fed-eral Ministry for Economic Affairs and Climate Action of Germany (BMWK) on the basis of a decision by the German Bundestag and by the European Union. The work was performed in the project SALSA (https://projekt-salsa.de/).

References

1. Ahlström, C., Wörle, J., Aust, M.L., Diederichs, F.: Road vehicle automation and its effects on fatigue, sleep, rest, and recuperation. In: The Handbook of Fatigue Management in Transportation, pp. 513–524. CRC Press (2023)
2. Åkerstedt, T., Folkard, S.: The three-process model of alertness and its extension to performance, sleep latency, and sleep length. Chronobiol. Int. **14**(2), 115–123 (1997)
3. Alvarsson, J.J., Wiens, S., Nilsson, M.E.: Stress recovery during exposure to nature sound and environmental noise. Int. J. Environ. Res. Public Health **7**(3), 1036–1046 (2010)
4. Balkin, T.J., Braun, A.R., Wesensten, N.J., Jeffries, K., Varga, M., Baldwin, P., Belenky, G., Herscovitch, P.: The process of awakening: a pet study of regional brain activity patterns mediating the re-establishment of alertness and consciousness. Brain **125**(10), 2308–2319 (2002)
5. Baltazar, M., Västfjäll, D.: Songs perceived as relaxing: Musical features, lyrics, and contributing mechanisms. In: International Conference: Psychology and Music–Interdisciplinary Encounters. Faculty of Music, University of Arts in Belgrade (2020)
6. Benson, H.: Md the relaxation response. New York (1975)
7. Brooks, A., Lack, L.: A brief afternoon nap following nocturnal sleep restriction: which nap duration is most recuperative? Sleep **29**(6), 831–840 (2006)
8. Choubey, A., Cera, A., Pauletto, S.: Sonic blankets: exploring the use of sound-augmented blankets for relaxation and sleep. In: Proceedings of the 19th International Audio Mostly Conference: Explorations in Sonic Cultures, pp. 511–524 (2024)
9. Diederichs, F., Knauss, A., Wilbrink, M., Lilis, Y., Chrysochoou, E., Anund, A., Bekiaris, E., Nikolaou, S., Finér, S., Zanovello, L., et al.: Adaptive transitions for automation in cars, trucks, buses and motorcycles. IET Intel. Transp. Syst. **14**(8), 889–899 (2020)
10. Diederichs, F., Muthumani, A., Feierle, A., Galle, M., Mathis, L.A., Bopp-Bertenbreiter, V., Widlroither, H., Bengler, K.: Improving driver performance and experience in assisted and automated driving with visual cues in the steering wheel. IEEE Trans. Intell. Transp. Syst. **23**(5), 4843–4852 (2022)
11. Diederichs, F., Wannemacher, C., Faller, F., Mikolajewski, M., Martin, M., Voit, M., Widlroither, H., Schmidt, E., Engelhardt, D., Rittger, L., et al.: Artificial intelligence for adaptive, responsive, and level-compliant interaction in the vehicle of the future (karli). In: International Conference on Human-Computer Interaction, pp. 164–171. Springer (2022)

12. Dingus, T.A., Guo, F., Lee, S., Antin, J.F., Perez, M., Buchanan-King, M., Hankey, J.: Driver crash risk factors and prevalence evaluation using naturalistic driving data. Proc. Natl. Acad. Sci. **113**(10), 2636–2641 (2016)
13. Engström, J., Markkula, G., Victor, T., Merat, N.: Effects of cognitive load on driving performance: the cognitive control hypothesis. Hum. Factors **59**(5), 734–764 (2017)
14. Gonçalves, R.C., Goodridge, C.M., Kuo, J., Lenné, M.G., Merat, N.: Using driver monitoring to estimate readiness in automation: a conceptual model based on simulator experimental data. Cogn. Technol. Work 1–16 (2024)
15. Grandjean, E.: Fatigue in industry. Occup. Environ. Med. **36**(3), 175–186 (1979)
16. Hilditch, C.J., Dorrian, J., Banks, S.: A review of short naps and sleep inertia: do naps of 30 min or less really avoid sleep inertia and slow-wave sleep? Sleep Med. **32**, 176–190 (2017)
17. Hilditch, C.J., McHill, A.W.: Sleep inertia: current insights. Nat. Sci. Sleep 155–165 (2019)
18. Hirsch, M., Diederichs, F., Widlroither, H., Graf, R., Bischoff, S.: Sleep and take-over in automated driving. Int. J. Transp. Sci. Technol. **9**(1), 42–51 (2020)
19. Jacobson, E.: Progressive relaxation. University of Chicago (1938)
20. Jain, S., Shapiro, S.L., Swanick, S., Roesch, S.C., Mills, P.J., Bell, I., Schwartz, G.E.: A randomized controlled trial of mindfulness meditation versus relaxation training: effects on distress, positive states of mind, rumination, and distraction. Ann. Behav. Med. **33**, 11–21 (2007)
21. Jarosch, O., Gold, C., Naujoks, F., Wandtner, B., Marberger, C., Weidl, G., Schrauf, M.: The impact of non-driving related tasks on take-over performance in conditionally automated driving—a review of the empirical evidence, vol. 9. Tagung Automatisiertes Fahren (2019)
22. Kandel, E.: Tm; mack sh; siegelbaum sa principles of neural science (2021)
23. Kim, S., van Egmond, R., Happee, R.: Effects of user interfaces on take-over performance: a review of the empirical evidence. Information **12**(4), 162 (2021)
24. Kircher, K., Ahlstrom, C.: Minimum required attention: a human-centered approach to driver inattention. Hum. Factors **59**(3), 471–484 (2017)
25. Lal, S.K., Craig, A.: A critical review of the psychophysiology of driver fatigue. Biol. Psychol. **55**(3), 173–194 (2001)
26. Loft, M.H., Cameron, L.D.: Using mental imagery to deliver self-regulation techniques to improve sleep behaviors. Ann. Behav. Med. **46**(3), 260–272 (2013)
27. Louw, T., Kountouriotis, G., Carsten, O., Merat, N.: Driver inattention during vehicle automation: how does driver engagement affect resumption of control? In: 4th International Conference on Driver Distraction and Inattention (DDI2015), Sydney: proceedings. ARRB Group (2015)
28. Medvedev, O., Shepherd, D., Hautus, M.J.: The restorative potential of soundscapes: a physiological investigation. Appl. Acoust. **96**, 20–26 (2015)
29. Merat, N., Jamson, A.H., Lai, F.C., Daly, M., Carsten, O.M.: Transition to manual: driver behaviour when resuming control from a highly automated vehicle. Transport. Res. F: Traffic Psychol. Behav. **27**, 274–282 (2014)
30. Muto, K., Oikawa, S., Matsui, Y., Hirose, T.: Driving behavior during takeover request of autonomous vehicle: effect of driver postures. Behav. Sci. **12**(11), 417 (2022)

31. Naujoks, F., Befelein, D., Wiedemann, K., Neukum, A.: A review of non-driving-related tasks used in studies on automated driving. In: Advances in Human Aspects of Transportation: Proceedings of the AHFE 2017 International Conference on Human Factors in Transportation, July 17–21, 2017, The Westin Bonaventure Hotel, Los Angeles, California, USA, vol. 8, pp. 525–537. Springer (2018)
32. Palao, A., Fredriksson, R., Lenné, M.: Euro ncap's current and future in-cabin monitoring systems assessment. In: Proceedings of the 27th International Technical Conference on the Enhanced Safety of Vehicles (ESV) National Highway Traffic Safety Administration. No. 23-0286 (2023)
33. Peter-Derex, L., Magnin, M., Bastuji, H.: Heterogeneity of arousals in human sleep: a stereo-electroencephalographic study. Neuroimage **123**, 229–244 (2015)
34. Regan, M.A., Lee, J.D., Young, K.: Driver distraction: theory, effects, and mitigation. CRC Press (2008)
35. Rosekind, M.R., Smith, R.M., Miller, D.L., Co, E.L., Gregory, K.B., Webbon, L.L., Gander, P.H., Lebacqz, J.V.: Alertness management: strategic naps in operational settings. J. Sleep Res. **4**, 62–66 (1995)
36. Schwarze, D., Diederichs, F., Weiser, L., Widlroither, H., Verhoeven, R., Rötting, M.: Are drivers allowed to sleep? sleep inertia effects drivers' performance after different sleep durations in automated driving. Multimod. Technol. Interact. **7**(6), 62 (2023)
37. Singh, H., Kathuria, A.: Analyzing driver behavior under naturalistic driving conditions: a review. Accident Anal. Prev. **150**, 105908 (2021)
38. Song, I., Baek, K., Kim, C., Song, C.: Effects of nature sounds on the attention and physiological and psychological relaxation. Urban For. Urban Green. **86**, 127987 (2023)
39. Stampi, C.: Ultrashort sleep schedule: Sleep architecture and recuperative value of 80, 50-and 20-min naps. Sleep'90 (1990)
40. Tassi, P., Bonnefond, A., Engasser, O., Hoeft, A., Eschenlauer, R., Muzet, A.: EEG spectral power and cognitive performance during sleep inertia: the effect of normal sleep duration and partial sleep deprivation. Physiol. Behav. **87**(1), 177–184 (2006)
41. Tassi, P., Muzet, A.: Sleep inertia. Sleep Med. Rev. **4**(4), 341–353 (2000)
42. Tietzel, A.J., Lack, L.C.: The short-term benefits of brief and long naps following nocturnal sleep restriction. Sleep **24**(3), 293–300 (2001)
43. Tomzig, M., Wörle, J., Gary, S., Baumann, M., Neukum, A.: Strategic naps in automated driving- sleep architecture predicts sleep inertia better than nap duration. Acc. Anal. Prev. **209**, 107811 (2025)
44. Tomzig, M., Wörle, J., Kremer, C., Baumann, M.: Sleep in automated driving-effects of time of day and chronotype on sleepiness and sleep inertia. Transp. Res. F Traffic Psychol. Behav. **102**, 16–31 (2024)
45. Vallat, R., Meunier, D., Nicolas, A., Ruby, P.: Hard to wake up? the cerebral correlates of sleep inertia assessed using combined behavioral, EEG and FMRI measures. Neuroimage **184**, 266–278 (2019)
46. Wörle, J., Metz, B., Othersen, I., Baumann, M.: Sleep in highly automated driving: takeover performance after waking up. Acc. Anal. Prev. **144**, 105617 (2020)
47. Wörle, J., Metz, B., Steinborn, M.B., Huestegge, L., Baumann, M.: Differential effects of driver sleepiness and sleep inertia on driving behavior. Transp. Res. F Traffic Psychol. Behav. **82**, 111–120 (2021)
48. Yang, Y., Gerlicher, M., Bengler, K.: How does relaxing posture influence take-over performance in an automated vehicle? In: Proceedings of the Human Factors and Ergonomics Society Annual Meeting, vol. 62, pp. 696–700. SAGE Publications, Los Angeles, CA (2018)

49. Zhang, J., Jin, X., Huang, Q., Wei, Y., Xu, X., et al.: Human sitting posture changes under different backrest tilt angles and headrest conditions in autonomous vehicle. Int. J. Precis. Eng. Manuf. 1–14 (2025)
50. Zhao, M., Bellet, T., Richard, B., Giralt, A., Beurier, G., Wang, X.: Effects of non-driving related postures on takeover performance during conditionally automated driving. Accident Anal. Prev. **208**, 107793 (2024)

Designing User-Centered Multimodal Output Strategies for Driver-AI Assistant Interaction

Eunju Lee[✉][iD] and Sukjin Chang

Smart Mobility Laboratory, CTO Division, LG Electronics, Seoul, Korea
{lgeunju.lee,sukjin.chang}@lge.com

Abstract. Generative artificial intelligence (AI) in vehicles enables multimodal, context-aware driver interactions, yet practical design strategies remain underexplored. This study derives information prioritization and output modality strategies to minimize driver distraction and enhance user experience, proposing multimodal design guidelines. Using a mixed-methods approach, we analyzed 12 near-futuristic driving scenarios and 44 information types. Surveys with 63 drivers and focus group interviews with 20 early adopters revealed that vehicle warnings and unexpected events are high-priority, while notifications like email alerts are less critical. Pearson correlation analysis identified 23 critical information types in the first quadrant (Q1), confirming that information necessity and preference vary by driving context. Users favored concise, proactive information delivery, minimal voice output, and privacy protection, emphasizing AI intervention timing aligned with driver attention and aversion to information overload. A quadrant-based output strategy was proposed: Q1 information is delivered immediately via voice and haptics, Q2 and Q4 via passive visual displays, and Q3 upon user request. Interaction policies were refined to address output timing, modality prioritization, and user engagement, mitigating overload and excessive intervention. Additionally, a Large Language Model (LLM)-based architecture was proposed to dynamically adjust multimodal outputs using real-time data and user context, supported by user experience (UX) flow examples. This architecture optimizes outputs, enhancing Human-Machine Interface (HMI) processes for Original Equipment Manufacturers (OEMs). This study offers a theoretical framework and practical strategies for generative AI-based in-vehicle multimodal interfaces.

Keywords: Multimodal Interface · Driver Distraction · In-Vehicle Interaction · Information Prioritization · Context-aware Design · Generative AI · LLM Integration

1 Introduction

Advancements in in-vehicle infotainment and voice interface technologies have facilitated intuitive in-vehicle interactions (IVI) [7, 19]. Generative artificial intelligence (AI) has elevated voice assistants to context-aware conversational capabilities [10]. However, single-modality interactions often lead to driver distraction

© The Author(s), under exclusive license to Springer Nature Switzerland AG 2026
P.-L.P. Rau and H. Krömker (Eds.): HCII 2025, LNCS 16336, pp. 372–389, 2026.
https://doi.org/10.1007/978-3-032-12798-3_23

and information omission [29]. Consequently, multimodal interfaces integrating voice, visual, and haptic channels have gained attention [14,24,26], addressing the limitations of single-modality systems [31]. In driving environments, minimizing distraction and providing timely information are critical [20], necessitating the use of diverse channels such as head-up displays (HUDs), AI voice assistants, and gesture recognition [4,25,28,33].

This study investigates multimodal interface design strategies to reduce driver distraction and optimize information delivery. By analyzing the utility of AI assistants, information prioritization, and output channel combinations in driving contexts, it proposes user-centered design guidelines. While prior research has primarily focused on the effectiveness of single modalities or static user preferences [29], this study integrates quantitative quadrant analysis with qualitative insights to develop a context-based information prioritization framework. Furthermore, it proposes a dynamic output strategy leveraging large language models (LLMs) to enhance the efficiency of generative AI interfaces and offers practical design directions for real-world applications. Real-time contextual changes during driving increase the complexity of user needs, underscoring the necessity of qualitative exploration to capture subtle variations in these requirements. This study establishes design strategies that reduce cognitive load based on information importance and deliver complex information intuitively. Thereby, it proposes a multimodal output approach that minimizes distraction and adapts flexibly to contextual variations.

2   Related Works

Multimodal output strategies for in-vehicle AI assistants have garnered increasing attention in the fields of Human-Machine Interfaces (HMI) and Human-AI Interaction (HAII) [7,19]. Efforts to reduce drivers' cognitive load and enhance situational awareness by leveraging modalities such as voice, visual, haptic, and gesture inputs are actively underway. For instance, Smith et al. [15] improved gesture recognition accuracy, while Li et al. [18] enhanced user responsiveness through a visual-auditory tracking system. Kim et al. [17] proposed combining mid-air gestures, haptic feedback, and spearcon audio to minimize physical manipulation and cognitive load. Zhang et al. [35] systematically analyzed voice and visual interface combinations, exploring interaction efficiency. Additionally, Eslami et al. [9] investigated inclusive interfaces for visually and hearing-impaired users, and Chen et al. [5] demonstrated driver state inference using transformer-based behavior recognition. Wang et al. [32] introduced novel possibilities for vehicle UI element recognition using LLMs. These studies have significantly advanced individual multimodal components and demonstrated their applicability in specific interaction contexts.

However, this study adopts a complementary perspective, addressing the following gaps. First, systematic frameworks for dynamically prioritizing information and adjusting output channels based on real-time driving contexts remain underdeveloped. While Kim et al. [17] focused on manipulation methods and

Zhang et al. [35] on review-based analyses, context-driven information adjustment strategies received limited attention. This study employs quadrant-based prioritization analysis to address this gap. Second, balancing user-initiated interactions with autonomous AI interventions requires further exploration. Although Eslami et al. [9] proposed inclusive designs, privacy and information overload issues in driving contexts warrant broader discussion. This study offers context-adaptive guidelines to mitigate these challenges. Third, LLM-driven multimodal HMI integration is in its early stages. Wang et al. [32] proposed UI element recognition, but real-time output strategies integrating sensor inputs and user context data are underexplored. This study extends this through an LLM-based architecture.

In conclusion, this study proposes a quadrant-based information prioritization framework and an LLM-integrated architecture to develop context-adaptive multimodal output strategies, contributing to the safety and acceptability of in-vehicle AI assistants.

3   Research Questions and Exploratory Hypotheses

This study investigates the relationship between driving scenario preferences and information needs, analyzing drivers' perceptual structures to derive practical insights. It focuses on the output of AI assistants, specifically information representation and delivery methods, assuming inputs from drivers' voice queries and in-vehicle/external sensor data. Outputs are designed around core multimodal interface components–voice and visual (display)–and are guided by the following research questions:

- RQ1: In which situations do drivers perceive AI assistants as useful, and why?
- RQ2: What types of information are prioritized in different driving scenarios?
- RQ3: Which multimodal channels (voice, visual, haptic) are effective based on information type (urgent/non-urgent) and driving context?

Based on these research questions, the study proposes the following exploratory hypotheses:

- H1: Drivers are likely to perceive AI assistants as more useful in unfamiliar driving environments or situations requiring real-time, practical driving information.
- H2: Drivers are likely to prefer different information types depending on the driving context.
- H3: Drivers are likely to prefer voice and haptic channels for urgent information and visual channels for non-urgent information.

4   Methodology and Results

To validate the research questions and exploratory hypotheses defined earlier, a user study was conducted. Text-based scenarios and visual materials were developed to facilitate group surveys in a standardized environment, ensuring consistency. A mixed-methods approach, combining quantitative and qualitative data collection, was employed to secure both the volume and depth of responses [8]. Qualitative data were categorized through coding to minimize researcher bias.

4.1 Driving Scenario-Based Design

This study developed driver-AI interaction scenarios to deeply analyze driving experiences [22]. A team of UX researchers, designers, HMI, and AI engineers brainstormed near-futuristic driving contexts, incorporating driver needs identified through a literature review. Initial scenarios were evaluated based on realism, diversity, and technical feasibility, resulting in the selection of 12 final scenarios. These encompass daily driving situations themed around real-time information delivery, personalization, and safety responses. Each scenario includes 2–6 information types (44 in total), as detailed in Appendix A. For instance, the 'Intent-Based Place Suggestions' scenario includes 'Place Details' and 'Why Recommended,' while 'Vehicle Status & Action Guidance' includes 'Vehicle Status Info' and 'Recommended Actions.' Scenario validity was verified through feedback from three external users. Each scenario, composed of context definitions and dialogues, reflects natural interactions. Infotainment screen mockups, created using Figma, served as intuitive visual materials incorporating UI elements and layouts, functioning as standardized cognitive resources to minimize individual differences in driving experiences.

4.2 Quantitative Survey

The quantitative evaluation was conducted through a survey to collect data on scenario preferences, information needs, and multimodal channel preferences. An offline face-to-face survey was administered to 63 participants (aged 20–54, average driving experience 12 years), familiar with HUD and AR navigation, over 90 min under identical conditions. The age distribution included 17 participants in their 20 s, 16 in their 30 s, and 30 aged 40 and above, with a balanced gender ratio (31 males, 32 females). The survey, based on 12 scenarios and 44 information types, comprised (1) scenario preferences (7-point Likert scale), (2) information needs (7-point scale), (3) modality preferences (voice, visual, voice+visual), (4) display location preferences (HUD, cluster, center display), and (5) AI acceptance and intervention preferences. Qualitative responses on scenario preferences were collected to enhance response validity. Survey items were validated for clarity and relevance through review by three experts and pre-testing. Data analysis employed Pearson correlation and frequency analyses (Appendix A). Due to the sample size, the generalizability of findings may be limited.

AI Assistant and Modality Preferences. The willingness to use AI assistants averaged 5.44 on a 7-point scale. Preferred contexts for AI intervention

(Multiple-Answer, MA) included vehicle malfunctions (98.4%), forward accidents or construction (83.7%), and low fuel/battery (79.4%), while intervention was less favored during phone calls (90.5%), parking (65.1%), and reversing (54.0%). This suggests a preference for AI intervention in urgent situations but a desire to minimize distractions during high-concentration tasks. For guidance methods (Single-Answer, SA), multimodal delivery (voice+visual, 81.0%) was predominant, with visual-only (9.5%) and voice-only (9.5%) less common. Preferred display locations (SA) were the center display (58.7%), followed by HUD (15.9%) and cluster (14.3%).

Among the 44 information types, the center display was generally preferred for display location (MA). However, HUD was favored for navigation-related information, such as 'Distance to My Car' (90.5%) and 'Detected Entity Type' (82.5%), while the cluster was preferred for 'Vehicle Warning' (71.4%). Modality preferences (SA) predominantly favored voice+visual combinations, though 13 types, including 'Place Details' and 'Route,' were preferred as visual-only, and 'Detected Entity Type' and 'Dynamic Roadside Elements' as voice-only. These preferences reflect the complexity of information and the challenge of diverting gaze in urgent contexts.

Scenario Preferences and Information Type Needs. Scenario preferences ranged from 4.83 to 6.03 on a 7-point scale. The top-ranked scenarios were 12 (Auto-Edited Dashcam & Incident Response, M = 6.03), 1 (Intent-Based Place Suggestions, M = 5.94), and 3 (Visual Context-Driven Route Guidance, M = 5.90). Key reasons for preference included safety (e.g., incident response), real-time delivery (e.g., intuitive navigation), intuitiveness, and personalization (e.g., place recommendations). Conversely, lower-ranked scenarios (e.g., 8, Driver & Object Behavior-Aware Assistance, M = 4.83) were rated poorly due to feelings of surveillance and unnecessary information. Participants responded positively to functions that reduced psychological burden in incident response and provided practical, user-centered support. Evaluations considered information delivery (volume, presentation), psychological burden, and controllability, with a preference for minimal, intuitive information and user agency. Safety and navigation functions were favored, but excessive information, inaccurate need predictions, and perceived surveillance were identified as barriers to adoption.

Information needs were highest for '11-① Vehicle Warning' and '1-③ Route' (M = 6.89) and lowest for '9-② Received Email Updates' (M = 2.33) and '3-④ Dynamic Roadside Elements' (M = 3.00). These findings suggest prioritizing high-need information types in each scenario. For example, in scenario 3, information needs ranked as follows: '3-② Place Name + Location' (M = 6.44), '3-① Distance to My Car' and '3-③ Static Roadside Elements' (M = 6.33), and '3-④ Dynamic Roadside Elements' (M = 3.00). The need for identical information (e.g., Vehicle Status Info) varied by context (scenario 9: 19%; scenario 12: 85.7%), highlighting the necessity for dynamic output strategies (e.g., voice prioritization in emergencies, visual support when stationary).

Correlation Analysis Between Scenario Preference and Information Need. The relationship between information needs and scenario preferences was examined using Pearson correlation analysis (r>0.3, p<0.01, n = 63). Strong positive correlations were observed for '5-② Detected Entity Location' (r = 0.66) and '7-① Suggested Content' (r = 0.63), while seven information types (e.g., '9-⑤ Weather', r = −0.02) showed negative correlations.

To clarify patterns among variables, information types were classified into four quadrants based on need scores (M = 5.78) and correlation coefficients (r = 0), as illustrated in Fig. 1.

Q1 (23 items, 52%, Strategic Core Information): Items with high need scores and correlation coefficients (e.g., '5-② Detected Entity Location', '10-② External Element Details') are critical for driving safety and should be prioritized in system design. These require immediate delivery, with low expected user resistance to proactive AI intervention [1].

Q2 (14 items, 32%, Potential Value Information): Items with high need scores but low correlation coefficients (e.g., '7-① Suggested Content', '5-③ Suggested Direction') are likely to be perceived as useful if provided contextually. Conditional delivery or user-requested presentation strategies are appropriate.

Q3 (0 items, Non-core Information): No items exhibited both low correlation and low need scores, indicating that low-need information does not actively undermine scenario preferences. Proper management of non-core information is unlikely to negatively impact user experience.

Q4 (7 items, 16%, Low-Impact Information): Items with low need scores and correlation coefficients (e.g., '2-① Place Name + Location', '4-② Route & Alternatives') can be simplified or omitted. These are perceived as expected or lack contextual relevance, contributing minimally to preferences [6,11], suggesting a need for improved information volume, intuitiveness, or timing.

4.3   Qualitative Study

The qualitative evaluation was conducted through Focus Group Discussions (FGD) to explore reasons for scenario preferences and user perceptions in driving contexts [23]. Twenty participants from the quantitative survey, experienced with HUD/AR navigation and electric vehicles (12 males, 8 females; 3 in their 20 s, 8 in their 30 s, 9 aged 40 and above), were divided into four groups of five for 90-min face-to-face discussions. A trained moderator facilitated the sessions using a semi-structured questionnaire. Recorded and transcribed data were processed using thematic analysis [3]. The discussions addressed (1) scenario preferences and modalities, (2) driving behaviors, (3) vehicle function usage, and (4) privacy and AI experiences. During analysis, two researchers independently coded the data, refining 333 initial codes to 89 through consensus, which were organized into 14 sub-themes and 5 main themes (Table 1). Theme significance was assessed based on utterance frequency and mention patterns, with information delivery and interface-related comments being the most prevalent.

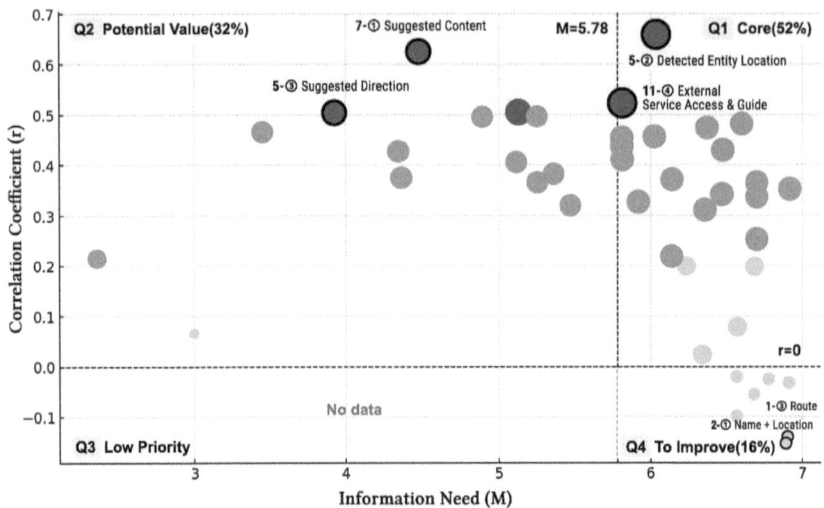

Fig. 1. Quadrant Analysis of Information Types Based on Information Need and Correlation with Scenario Preference. The four quadrants classify 44 types of information based on their strategic implications, considering both the degree of information need (M) and the correlation coefficient with scenario preference (r). Representative items in each quadrant are highlighted with bold-edged markers and labeled accordingly. The intensity (darkness) of each marker represents the strength of the correlation (r), while the marker size reflects the overall importance of the information taking into account both its strategic positioning and correlation strength.

Intuitive Real-Time Information Delivery: Participants preferred proactive driving information (e.g., traffic congestion alerts, P9) and found landmark-based guidance (e.g., "Building-based directions reduce errors", P26) useful. Distance - based guidance required refinement due to age-related perceptual differences (P36), and demand for specific details (e.g., entrance fees, parking) was high. Current navigation systems' unreliable arrival time predictions and lack of lane guidance were identified as limitations.

Personalization and Privacy: Participants anticipated benefits from personalized features (e.g., "I'd subscribe if it planned trips with my kids", P37) but raised concerns about personal data exposure (e.g., "Knowing my card number is excessive", P27) and camera usage (P26). However, they were willing to allow camera use in emergencies (e.g., drowsiness prevention, P17), and the need for a privacy mode with passengers present (P32) was emphasized.

Driving Safety and Emergency Response: Recognizing hazards (e.g., "Scooter detection is needed", P53) and mandatory control during collisions (P37) were deemed critical. Vehicle status notifications (e.g., "Warning light explanations aid troubleshooting", P26) were effective. These findings highlight the importance of context-aware interactions and trust in technology.

Table 1. Summary of Qualitative Research Results: Frequency of Mentions by Theme. The bar chart visualizes the number of times each topic was mentioned by participants during the focus group discussions (FGDs)

Theme	Sub-theme	Utterance
Intuitive and Timely Information	Concrete and Practical Information(10 codes)	134
	Guidance Leveraging Intuitive Elements(9)	116
	Real-Time and Well-Timed Information(6)	103
Personalization and Privacy	Personalization Acceptance & Expectations(8)	106
	Privacy Concerns in Personalized Technologies(5)	85
Safety and Emergency Response	In-Drive Emergency Handling(6)	106
	Awareness of Surrounding Risks(5)	65
	Vehicle Status & Maintenance Support(5)	43
User Interface and Interaction Modalities	Voice Interaction: Efficiency and Limitations(6)	97
	Preferences for Multimodal Guidance(6)	92
	Display Location and Visualization Preferences(7)	76
	Demand for Interaction Simplicity(7)	75
Guidance and Simplification	Contextual Guidance & Intervention(6)	87
	Information Overload & Simplification(3)	38

User Interface and Interaction Methods: Preferences for HUD versus center displays varied (e.g., "HUD simplifies gaze but I prefer the center display", P61), with voice guidance deemed suitable for key information delivery (e.g., "Voice is primary", P30). Multimodal voice-visual combinations enhanced comprehension and error prevention (P1, P18), but voice recognition errors (P1) and excessive dialogue were inconvenient. Haptic feedback (e.g., "Vibration for jaywalking alerts", P61) and routine automation (P30) were also favored.

Context-Based Intervention and Information Simplification: Voice intervention required timing aligned with driver focus (e.g., "Interrupting during focus is fatiguing", P19), and excessive information triggered resistance (e.g., "Too much voice information is overwhelming", P17). Although less frequent, these complaints underscored potential significance. Proactive intervention during traffic congestion was positively received (e.g., "AI conversation in traffic is helpful", P18).

The findings from the mixed-methods study, which integrated both quantitative and qualitative results, are summarized in Table 2.

5   Discussion

This section proposes multimodal interface design strategies and practical approaches by integrating the quadrant classification from Sect. 4.2 and user insights from Sect. 4.3. It further discusses the research questions and hypotheses from Sect. 3 in relation to the collected data.

Table 2. Summary of Mixed-Methods Findings: Qualitative themes from interviews linked to quantitative survey data and integrated interpretations.

Qualitative Theme	Theme-Linked Quantitative Data	Integrated Interpretation
Intuitive and Timely Information	Top 3 Scenario Preferences (1) Auto-Edited Dashcam & Incident Response 6.03/7 (Practical), (2) Intent-Based Place Suggestions 5.94/7 (Real-Time), (3) Visual Context-Driven Route Guidance 5.90/7 (Intuitive)	Preference for practical functions and intuitive, real-time driving information that supports proactive responses
Personalization and Privacy	Discomfort with guidance during passenger presence (50.8%)	Disliked personal data exposure with passengers; Accepted in-cabin cameras only for safety
Safety and Emergency Response	AI assistant activation preferred for front-side incidents or risks (93.7%)	Emphasis on hazard recognition; Support forced vehicle control upon detection
User Interface and Interaction Modalities	Willingness to use AI assistant: 5.44/7; Positive toward multimodal (voice+screen) guidance (81%)	Prefer multimodal over single-modal interaction; Frustrated by repetitive responses from voice errors
Guidance and Simplification	AI assistant preferred for vehicle status issues (98.4%); Disliked during calls (90.5%)	User autonomy is important as users prefer guidance at desired times; Dislike information overload

5.1   Design Guidelines for Multimodal In-Vehicle Interaction

Minimizing Cognitive Load: To reduce distraction, the interface prioritizes information based on quadrant characteristics, hierarchically structuring core (Q1) and secondary (Q2–Q4) information. Voice guidance is designed to be concise, for example, lasting 5–7 s, to prevent cognitive overload (P17: "Too much voice information is overwhelming"), while visual information is presented minimally to reduce cognitive burden.

Cross-Modal Role Optimization: A layered structure separates voice and visual modality roles based on information importance and driving context. The primary strategy assigns appropriate modalities to prioritize information while minimizing user cognitive load. To address voice recognition errors, invocation steps are minimized, using simple phrases like "Please repeat" to facilitate refined requests (P1: "It keeps misunderstanding") (Table 3).

- **Q1 Information (e.g., hazard detection, route changes):** Due to high urgency, active modalities like voice are prioritized, supplemented by haptic feedback (e.g., vibration) when necessary, adhering to NHTSA guidelines [21, 27].
- **Q2 Information (e.g., routine maintenance, content recommendations):** Non-intrusive periodic visual cues or notification sounds are used to avoid excessive distraction, supplemented by voice guidance as needed [30].
- **Q3 Information (e.g., non-driving settings, advertisement alerts):** To mitigate cognitive load, these are hidden by default and displayed only upon user request, using a passive interaction structure [13]. They are placed deep in menus, accessible via navigation-based interactions.

Table 3. Summary of Information and Modality Strategies

Priority		Design + AI Role	Modality	Info Type Example
1st	Q1	Immediate alert, Consider mandatory control in emergencies, Proactive	Voice first (key info), Display (details), Haptics optional	Danger detection (5-①/12-①), Visual route guidance (3-②), Route (2-④)
2nd	Q2	Offer quietly when deemed necessary, User decides to engage, Occasional	Display-preferred to minimize distraction, Voice on request	Content suggestion(7-①), Traffic regulations information (6-②)
	Q4	Better delivery (simplified, menu-driven), On request, Passive	Display-preferred, Brief voice explanations when necessary	Alternative route (4-②), Routine vehicle checks (9-⑥)
3rd	Q3	Omitted, Hidden until user request, Reactive	Display-focused, Concise multimodal response on request	Non-driving related updates (e.g.Advertising alerts)

- **Q4 Information (e.g., vehicle maintenance history):** Given low immediate need, simplified icon displays or request-based menu access are suitable. Exposure intensity and content should be adjusted to prevent perception as unnecessary, with further research needed on delivery timing and frequency.

Context-Aware Design: The interface must adapt flexibly to driving conditions. During driving, information volume is minimized, prioritizing voice interactions (P30: "Voice is primary"), while touch inputs are enabled when stationary [21]. Detailed guidance is provided for unfamiliar routes, with only changes emphasized for familiar ones. When passengers are present, voice guidance is limited for privacy, and sensitive information is output only in emergencies (P32: "A privacy mode is needed") [16]. Proactive AI intervention is restricted to Q1 information (e.g., vehicle malfunctions, 98.4%), with Q2–Q4 provided on request [27]. Appropriate intervention timing and user agency are critical design considerations.

Driver-Adaptive Interface: The interface learns driving habits (e.g., climate control settings, P30) to recommend functions or propose automation based on repetitive patterns [12]. It reflects individual modality preferences, as non-personalized interactions cause fatigue (P58: "Repetitive questions from an AI that doesn't know me are tiring"). The interface must continuously evolve through user feedback.

Figure 2 visualizes an example of the UX flow within a specific driving scenario, reflecting the guidelines described above.

5.2 Design of Generative AI Development Logic for LLM-Integrated Vehicle HMI

To apply the information prioritization and modality strategies from Sect. 5.1 in real-time, a three-stage Sense–Orchestrate–Deliver architecture based on a Large Language Model (LLM) is proposed (Fig. 3). This architecture analyzes driving situations and information contexts in real-time to select and control appropriate output modalities.

Sense Stage: Internal and external vehicle sensors and systems collect data on driving conditions, surrounding vehicles, passenger presence, route history, and

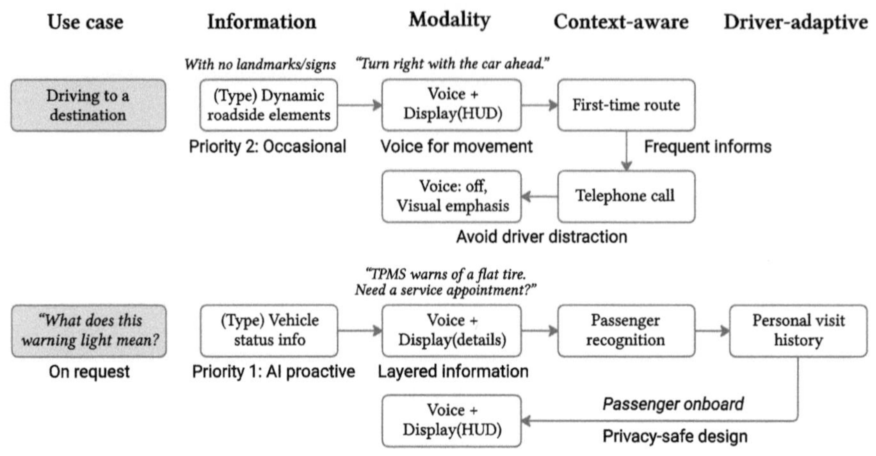

Fig. 2. Example UX Flow for Multimodal Combination

recent user interactions, enabling multilayered situational awareness. This data is analyzed to assess whether the route is unfamiliar, evaluate potential sensitive information exposure, and estimate the driver's cognitive load, facilitating tailored output adjustments for specific driving scenarios.

Orchestrate Stage: Contextual information is structured into a format processable by the LLM. Situational data, system rules, and user requests are transformed into multimodal prompts and fed to the LLM or MLLM (Multimodal Large Language Model), which interprets user requests accordingly. Content is classified by type (e.g., navigation guidance, non-critical updates) and priority (Q1–Q4), and the level of AI intervention (proactive or reactive) is determined to guide subsequent actions.

Deliver Stage: A multimodal output manager translates LLM decisions into modality, sequence, and timing. Outputs are dynamically adjusted by integrating guardrails reflecting safety regulations (e.g., ISO 26262), manufacturer policies, and user preferences. For instance, in emergencies, multimodal warnings combining voice, visual, and haptic cues override user settings to ensure immediate driver attention. Output strategies are refined based on user-preferred modalities, incorporating rules such as 'Q1 information is delivered via voice unless disabled.'

This architecture extends generative AI beyond response generation to decision-making support and adaptive interaction orchestration, enabling human-centered, context-adaptive HMI implementation in complex multimodal environments.

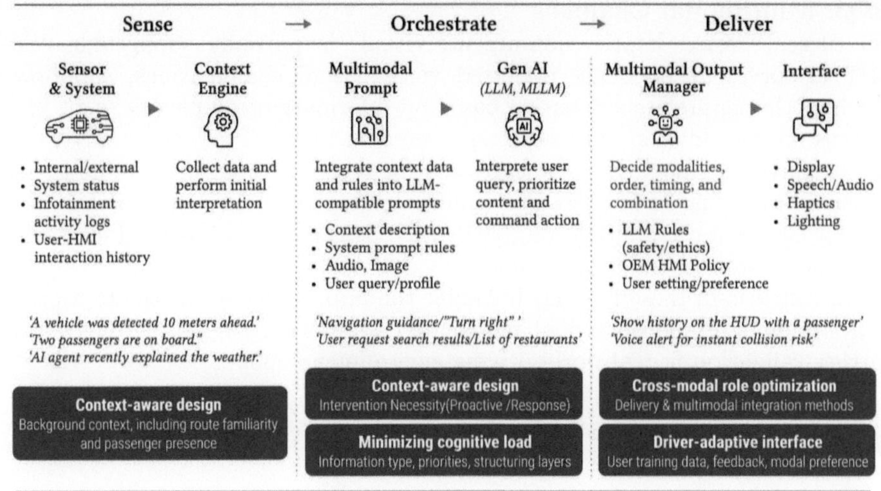

Fig. 3. Multimodal Output Decision Flow Integrated with LLMs (Based on Sect. 5.1)

5.3 Hypothesis Validation Based on Research Findings

This study explored multimodal design elements for driver-AI interactions. By synthesizing quantitative data (scenario preferences, quadrant analysis) and qualitative data (FGD), the results address the research questions (RQ1, RQ2, RQ3) and exploratory hypotheses (H1, H2, H3).

RQ1: Contexts of AI Usefulness

H1 (preference for AI intervention in unfamiliar contexts) is supported. Survey and FGD results indicate that drivers preferred AI intervention for real-time driving information (e.g., "Real-time information is meaningful when provided in advance", P9) and emergency situations (e.g., vehicle malfunctions, 98.4%, Sect. 4.2). This suggests that AI support enhances driver confidence and safety in sudden changes or unfamiliar environments, highlighting the importance of context-aware systems delivering timely and relevant assistance.

RQ2: Information Type Needs

H2 (context-specific information preferences) is supported. Quantitative evaluation (Sect. 4.2) showed that identical information (e.g., Vehicle Status Info) was more needed in scenario 12 (incident risk, 85.7%) than in scenario 9 (pre-departure, 19%). Quadrant analysis (Sect. 4.2) identified Q1 information (e.g., Detected Entity Location, $M = 6.00$, $r = 0.66$) as high-priority due to strong contextual relevance and urgency. Qualitative data (e.g., "Too much voice information is overwhelming", P17) revealed concerns about information overload, suggesting that quadrant-based selective delivery reduces distraction and enhances acceptability. This underscores the need for adaptive systems that dynamically adjust information types and delivery methods based on context [34].

RQ3: Multimodal Channels

H3 (urgent: voice+haptic, non-urgent: visual) is partially supported. While 81% of survey respondents preferred voice+visual combinations, supporting the hypothesis, preferences varied based on information complexity (e.g., Place Details, visual-only) and urgency (e.g., Detected Entity Type, voice-only), leading to partial support. HUD was favored for real-time information due to ease of gaze processing (P61: "HUD simplifies gaze processing"), while the center display suited static information (58.7%) [2]. This indicates the need for flexible multimodal designs balancing immediacy and usability.

In conclusion, these findings highlight the importance of information prioritization, modality optimization, and context adaptation, suggesting the need for further validation in real-world driving environments [30].

6   Limitations and Future Work

This study systematically explored in-vehicle multimodal information output strategies but has several limitations. First, the research relied on scenario-based surveys rather than real-world driving conditions, omitting physical and cognitive data such as real-time distraction, fatigue, or reaction times. Future studies should validate the applicability and effectiveness of findings through simulator or on-road experiments. Second, the study focused on voice and visual modalities, leaving the role of extended multimodal technologies, such as haptics or augmented reality (AR) displays, unevaluated. Qualitative feedback (e.g., "vibration would be useful during pedestrian crossings," P61) suggests the potential value of haptic outputs [48], indicating a need to integrate these in future modality strategies. Third, the sample size for quantitative analysis (63 participants) was suitable for exploratory research but limited in capturing diverse age groups, technology acceptance levels, and driving habits. Notably, older drivers' spatial perception constraints (P36) and privacy concerns (P32) highlight the need for personalized designs addressing individual differences. Fourth, while quadrant-based prioritization was derived from correlations between information needs and preferences, the absence of multivariate regression or causal analysis limits the quantitative understanding of interactions among prioritization factors.

Despite these limitations, this study established user-centered information prioritization quadrants and output strategies through a mixed-methods approach, offering practical guidelines and a system architecture (including an LLM-based multimodal manager) for multimodal HMI design. Quantitative correlation analyses between user-preferred scenarios and information needs, alongside qualitative insights such as fatigue from excessive voice outputs and the need for autonomous control over sensitive information, reveal user-driven requirements not extensively addressed in prior work.

Future research will implement an AI-based multimodal prototype reflecting the design guidelines in Sect. 5.1, measuring driving reaction times (dependent variable) and modality combinations (independent variable) in simulator experiments, with cognitive load assessed using NASA-TLX. Longitudinal studies evaluating personalization adaptability and learning effects with long-term user data, as well as generative AI interface models incorporating real-time conversational feedback (e.g., automatic voice error correction suggestions), are also planned. These efforts will enhance the empirical validity of the guidelines, improving the safety and user experience of in-vehicle AI systems.

7   Conclusion

This study explored user-centered multimodal output strategies for driver-AI interactions. Through an information prioritization framework, it derived design principles based on contextual relevance and cognitive load minimization, proposing modality role separation and context-adaptive Human-Machine Interface (HMI) guidelines. Additionally, a LLM-based architecture was developed to specify a system design responsive to real-time driving contexts. These contributions have the potential to optimize the HMI development processes of Original Equipment Manufacturers (OEMs) and promote the standardization of user-centered In-Vehicle Interaction (IVI) systems. Academically, the quadrant framework extends Wickens' Multiple Resource Theory (MRT) [33] by integrating "contextual relevance" and "information importance" into its resource dimensions, advancing the theoretical framework for driving environments. Modality roles were systematized according to driving contexts, and LLM integration offers new directions for context-aware AI research.

A   Scenarios, Information Types, and Correlation Analysis

Note. M indicates the mean of scenario preference or information need (7-point scale), r the correlation coefficient, and Q the quadrant (Q1: 23 items, Q2: 14 items, Q3: 0 items, Q4: 7 items). Values were calculated with a 95% confidence interval (CI, n = 63).

No.	Scenario Name	M	Information Type	M	r	Q
1	Intent-Based Place Suggestions	5.94	① Place Name + Location	6.56	−0.02	Q4
			② Place Details	6.67	0.37*	Q1
			③ Route	6.89	−0.14	Q4
			④ Vehicle Status Info	4.89	0.50**	Q2
			⑤ Why Recommended	5.33	0.39*	Q2
2	User-Conditioned Route Planning	5.49	① Place Name + Location	6.89	−0.15	Q4
			② Place Details	6.67	0.20	Q1
			③ Itinerary	5.78	0.44*	Q1
			④ Route	6.67	0.26	Q1
			⑤ Why Recommended	5.11	0.40*	Q2
3	Visual Context-Driven Route Guidance	5.90	① Distance to My Car	6.33	0.02	Q1
			② Place Name + Location	6.44	0.35*	Q1
			③ Static Roadside Elements	6.33	0.32	Q1
			④ Dynamic Roadside Elements	3.00	0.07	Q2
4	Real-Time Traffic-Based Routing	5.68	① Traffic Event Type & Location	6.89	−0.03	Q4
			② Route & Alternatives	6.67	−0.05	Q4
			③ Consequences of Ignoring Guide	6.56	0.08	Q1
			④ Lane Load & Suggested Direction	5.22	0.37*	Q2
5	Surrounding Collision Warning	5.06	① Detected Entity Type	6.33	0.48*	Q1
			② Detected Entity Location	6.00	0.66**	Q1
			③ Suggested Direction	3.89	0.51**	Q2
6	Driving Behavior-Based Alerts	5.32	① Past Violation Spots & Distance	5.78	0.47*	Q1
			② Traffic Penalty Info	5.22	0.50**	Q2
7	Driver State-Based Assistance	5.16	① Suggested Content	4.44	0.63**	Q2
			② Suggested Route	5.78	0.45*	Q1
			③ Adjustable Features & Changes	5.44	0.33*	Q2

No.	Scenario Name	M	Information Type	M	r	Q
8	Driver & Object Behavior-Aware Assistance	4.83	① In-Vehicle Object Location	5.11	0.52^b	Q2
			② Adjustable Features & Changes	6.00	0.47^a	Q1
			③ Suggested Content	4.33	0.43^b	Q2
9	Identity-Based Infotainment Home	5.87	① Route	6.22	0.20	Q1
			② Received Email Updates	2.33	0.22	Q2
			③ Personalized News Updates	4.33	0.38^a	Q2
			④ Personalized Content Updates	3.44	0.47^a	Q2
			⑤ Weather	6.78	-0.02	Q4
			⑥ Vehicle Status Info	6.56	-0.10	Q4
10	Environmental Guidance	5.42	① External Elements & Location	6.11	0.38^a	Q1
			② External Element Details	6.56	0.49^b	Q1
11	Vehicle Status & Action Guidance	5.84	① Vehicle Warning	6.89	0.36^a	Q1
			② Vehicle Status Info	6.89	0.36^a	Q1
			③ Recommended Actions	5.89	0.34^a	Q1
			④ External Service Access	5.78	0.54^b	Q1
12	Auto-Edited Dashcam & Incident Response	6.03	① Vehicle Status Info	6.67	0.35^a	Q1
			② Risk Event Type & Penalty Info	6.11	0.23	Q1
			③ External Service Access	6.44	0.44^b	Q1

$^a p < 0.01$, $^b p < 0.001$

References

1. Banerjee, S., Jeihani, M., Khadem, N.K., Kabir, M.M.: Influence of pedestrian collision warning systems on driver behavior: a driving simulator study. arXiv preprint arXiv:2112.09074 (2021). https://arxiv.org/abs/2112.09074
2. Bolton, A., Burnett, G., Large, D.R.: An investigation of augmented reality presentations of landmark-based navigation using a head-up display. In: Proceedings of the 7th International Conference on Automotive User Interfaces and Interactive Vehicular Applications, pp. 56–63 (2015)
3. Braun, V., Clarke, V.: Using thematic analysis in psychology. Qual. Res. Psychol. **3**(2), 77–101 (2006). https://doi.org/10.1191/1478088706qp063oa
4. Charissis, V., et al.: Employing emerging technologies to develop and evaluate in-vehicle intelligent systems for driver support: infotainment AR HUD case study. Appl. Sci. **11**(4), 1397 (2021). https://doi.org/10.3390/app11041397
5. Chen, J., Xu, L., Wang, Z.: Transformer-based multimodal behavior recognition for driver state prediction. arXiv preprint arXiv:2408.12345, August 2024. https://arxiv.org/abs/2408.12345

6. Chen, X., Li, Y., Tang, Y.: Grounded theory-based user needs mining and its impact on app downloads. Front. Psychol. **13**, 875310 (2022). https://doi.org/10.3389/fpsyg.2022.875310
7. Cohen, M.H., Giangola, J.P., Balogh, J.: Voice User Interface Design. Addison-Wesley Professional (2004)
8. Creswell, J.W., Clark, V.L.P.: Designing and Conducting Mixed Methods Research, 3rd edn. Sage Publications, Thousand Oaks (2017)
9. Eslami, M., Rahimi, A., Gupta, S.: Inclusive multimodal interface design for visually and hearing-impaired drivers. In: Proceedings of the 16th International Conference on Automotive User Interfaces and Interactive Vehicular Applications (AutomotiveUI), Ingolstadt, Germany, September 2024, pp. 201–210. ACM (2024). https://doi.org/10.1145/3640792.3640801
10. Gao, J., Galley, M., Li, L.: Neural approaches to conversational AI. In: The 41st International ACM SIGIR Conference on Research & Development in Information Retrieval, pp. 1371–1374 (2018)
11. Hertzum, M.: Understanding preference: a meta-analysis of user studies. Int. J. Hum Comput Stud. **195**, 103408 (2025). https://doi.org/10.1016/j.ijhcs.2024.103408
12. Ho, J., Intille, S.S.: Using context-aware computing to reduce the perceived burden of interruptions from mobile devices. In: Proceedings of the SIGCHI Conference on Human Factors in Computing Systems, pp. 909–918 (2005). https://doi.org/10.1145/1054972.1055100
13. Interaction Design Foundation: Progressive Disclosure (2024). https://www.interaction-design.org/literature/topics/progressive-disclosure
14. Jeon, M.: Emotions and Affect in Human Factors and Human-Computer Interaction. Academic Press (2017)
15. Joo, J., Koh, J., Lee, H.: Hand gesture recognition using ultrasonic array with machine learning. Sensors **24**(20), 6763 (2024). https://doi.org/10.3390/s24206763
16. Kemp, K.: Driving blind: The unexamined privacy risks of connected cars. Univ. New South Wales Law J. **46**(3), 789–823 (2024). https://papers.ssrn.com/sol3/papers.cfm?abstract_id=5025836
17. Kim, S., Park, J., Lee, H.: Multimodal interaction with gesture, haptic feedback, and spearcon audio for automotive HMI. J. Multimodal User Interfaces **18**(1), 45–56 (2024). https://doi.org/10.1007/s12193-023-00412-3. March
18. Li, F., Chen, H., Liu, J.: Integrated visual-auditory tracking system for in-vehicle human-computer interaction. In: 2022 International Conference on Robotics and Automation (ICRA), Philadelphia, PA, USA, May 2022, pp. 2456–2462. IEEE (2022). https://doi.org/10.1109/ICRA46639.2022.9811567
19. Luger, E., Sellen, A.: "like having a really bad pa" the gulf between user expectation and experience of conversational agents. In: Proceedings of the 2016 CHI Conference on Human Factors in Computing Systems, pp. 5286–5297 (2016)
20. McCrickard, D.S., Chewar, C.M., Somervell, J.P., Ndiwalana, A.: A model for notification systems evaluation–assessing user goals for multitasking activity. ACM Trans. Comput. Hum. Interact. (TOCHI) **10**(4), 312–338 (2003)
21. National Highway Traffic Safety Administration: Visual-manual NHTSA driver distraction guidelines for in-vehicle electronic devices. Fed. Reg. **79**(179), 55530–55534 (2014). https://www.federalregister.gov/documents/2014/09/16/2014-21991/visual-manual-nhtsa-driver-distraction-guidelines-for-in-vehicle-electronic-devices
22. Nielsen, L.: Personas - User Focused Design. Human–Computer Interaction Series, 2 edn. Springer, London (2019). https://doi.org/10.1007/978-1-4471-7427-1

23. Nielsen Norman Group: Focus groups 101 (2020). Online. https://www.nngroup.com/articles/focus-groups-definition/. Accessed 15 Jun 2025
24. Oviatt, S.: Multimodal interfaces. In: The Human-Computer Interaction Handbook, pp. 439–458 (2007)
25. Oviatt, S.: Theoretical and empirical foundations of multimodal interface design: advances and challenges. In: The Handbook of Multimodal-Multisensor Interfaces: Foundations, User Modeling, and Common Modality Combinations, vol. 1, pp. 27–61. ACM and Morgan & Claypool (2017). https://doi.org/10.1145/3015783.3015786
26. Oviatt, S., Coulston, R., Lunsford, R.: When do we interact multimodally? Cognitive load and multimodal communication patterns. In: Proceedings of the 6th International Conference on Multimodal Interfaces, pp. 129–136 (2004)
27. Parasuraman, R., Sheridan, T.B., Wickens, C.D.: A model for types and levels of human interaction with automation. IEEE Trans. Syst. Man Cybern. Part A Syst. Hum. **30**(3), 286–297 (2000). https://doi.org/10.1109/3468.844354
28. Politis, I., Brewster, S., Pollick, F.: Language-based multimodal displays for the handover of control in autonomous cars. In: Proceedings of the 7th International Conference on Automotive User Interfaces and Interactive Vehicular Applications, pp. 3–10 (2015). https://doi.org/10.1145/2799250.2799262
29. Salvucci, D.D.: Predicting the effects of in-car interface use on driver performance: an integrated model approach. Int. J. Hum Comput Stud. **55**(1), 85–107 (2001)
30. Shen, X., Eades, P., Hong, S.H., Moere, A.V.: Intrusive and non-intrusive evaluation of ambient displays. In: Proceedings of the 1st International Workshop on Ambient Information Systems, co-located at Pervasive 2007, pp. 3–8 (2007). http://ceur-ws.org/Vol-254/paper07.pdf
31. Spence, C., Ho, C.: Tactile and multisensory spatial warning signals for drivers. IEEE Trans. Haptics **1**(2), 121–129 (2008). https://doi.org/10.1109/TOH.2008.14
32. Wang, Y., Zhang, T., Li, Q.: Vision-language model for in-vehicle UI element recognition using large language models, January 2025. https://arxiv.org/abs/2501.06789
33. Wickens, C.D., Liu, Y.: Codes and modalities in multiple resources: a success and a qualification. Hum. Factors **30**(5), 599–616 (1988). https://doi.org/10.1177/001872088803000505
34. Young, M.S., Stanton, N.A.: Malleable attentional resources theory: a new explanation for the effects of mental underload on performance. Hum. Factors **44**(3), 365–375 (2002). https://doi.org/10.1518/0018720024497709
35. Zhang, C., Yang, W., Zhao, X.: A comprehensive review of speech and visual interface fusion for automotive user interfaces. In: Proceedings of the European Conference on Cognitive Ergonomics (ECCE), Lisbon, Portugal, September 2024, pp. 89–97. ACM (2024). https://doi.org/10.1145/3623489.3623490

Augmenting Driver Situation Awareness Through Distributed Sensing and Driver Adaptive Interfaces: a Research Framework

Roberta Presta[1]([✉])(iD), Chiara Tancredi[1](iD), Flavia De Simone[1](iD), Roberto Girau[2](iD), Alessandro Monteleone[3], and Federica Viero[3]

[1] Università degli Studi Suor Orsola Benincasa, Napoli, Italy
`roberta.presta@unisob.na.it`
[2] Università di Bologna, Bologna, Italy
[3] RE:LAB, Reggio Emilia, Italy

Abstract. Collisions involving vulnerable road users (VRUs) represent a major concern in contemporary mobility, especially in urban contexts where attentional demands, occlusions, and complex interactions can challenge drivers' ability to anticipate risk. Supporting driver situation awareness through adaptive interfaces and intelligent sensing is a promising strategy, particularly when combined with personalized modeling of attentional and behavioral states. This paper presents a human-centered research framework developed to explore the use of distributed sensing and adaptive interaction for enhancing road safety. Starting from a set of high-risk VRU interaction scenarios, such as occluded crossings, unexpected overtaking, and low-visibility intersections, a design rationale is outlined for using real-time data from vehicle sensors, roadside infrastructure, and driver monitoring to generate timely, non-intrusive, and individualized feedback via the HMI. The research focuses on the development of a simulation-based infrastructure for evaluating adaptive safety strategies based on driver-specific patterns of attention and behavior, in alignment with the principles of the Driver Digital Twin (DrDT) paradigm. Methodological insight is provided into the design of this experimental infrastructure, the key performance indicators used, and the experimental hypotheses. This work contributes a theoretically grounded and experimentally structured setup that may inform similar efforts in driving simulations for studying personalized safety interaction strategies.

Keywords: Driving Simulation Environment · Situation Awareness · Vulnerable Road Users · Driver Digital Twin · Driver Monitoring System

1 Introduction

Despite significant progress in automotive safety technologies, collisions involving vulnerable road users (VRUs), such as pedestrians, cyclists, and powered

© The Author(s), under exclusive license to Springer Nature Switzerland AG 2026
P.-L.P. Rau and H. Krömker (Eds.): HCII 2025, LNCS 16336, pp. 390–409, 2026.
https://doi.org/10.1007/978-3-032-12798-3_24

two-wheelers, remain alarmingly frequent and disproportionately severe, particularly in dense urban environments where VRUs are more prevalent and traffic complexity is high [12,25].

Despite their widespread adoption, automated emergency braking (AEB) systems have not resolved the problem. A key limitation is their frequent deactivation by drivers who perceive them as overly intrusive or disruptive. This limits its effectiveness and underscores the need for more nuanced and driver-adaptive solutions.

Furthermore, while the discourse around fully autonomous driving continues to grow, human-driven vehicles are expected to remain dominant for at least the next decade especially in complex and unpredictable urban contexts where autonomous systems still face significant limitations [13].

As such, enhancing safety in manually operated vehicles remains a relevant and urgent area of research.

In this context, maintaining an adequate level of driver situation awareness (SA) is essential for ensuring road safety. SA encompasses the driver's perception of critical elements in the traffic environment, their comprehension of their significance, and the ability to anticipate future developments [10]. A degradation in SA, whether due to environmental complexity, information overload, or limitations in perceptual or cognitive resources, can prevent drivers from correctly identifying and responding to potential hazards. This may result in delayed reactions, inappropriate decisions, or failures to detect road users who are at risk of collision.

Today, several emerging technologies offer promising opportunities to enhance situation awareness in driving contexts, though their integration still poses significant design and engineering challenges. First, intelligent sensing technologies for Driver Monitoring Systems (DMS) are increasingly effective in assessing the driver's psychophysiological state, detecting signs of distraction, fatigue, or emotional stress that may impair driving performance [9,22]. Second, environmental sensing and road monitoring technologies, including external object detection, road infrastructure data, and traffic surveillance, provide real-time information about the vehicle's surroundings. These systems can be leveraged to anticipate critical events such as accidents, hazards, or VRUs who may remain outside the driver's field of view yet are on a potential trajectory intersecting that of the vehicle. Third, communication infrastructures such as Vehicle-to-Vehicle (V2V) and Vehicle-to-Infrastructure (V2I) enable the transmission of this anticipatory information to the vehicle, creating a networked ecosystem that supports predictive awareness [8]. Finally, adaptive human-machine interfaces (HMIs) aim to deliver critical information to the driver in an intuitive and context-sensitive manner, helping to improve situation awareness while striving to limit additional cognitive load [16]. Among these, augmented reality (AR) head-up displays (HUDs) [35,36] stand out for their perceptual continuity with the real environment, which allows them to overlay information directly within the driver's field of view in a spatially meaningful way.

When combined, these components have the potential to deliver timely, context-aware, and cognitively aligned feedback to the driver enhancing perceptual continuity and enabling safer decision-making.

This raises at least two essential questions: (1) how can the integration of intelligent sensing and adaptive interfaces enhance driver performance and safety in complex interactions with vulnerable road users? (2) how can the impact on safety of these integrated solutions on the situation awareness of drivers can be assessed?

To explore these questions effectively and in a human-centered fashion, simulation environments play a key role, as they allow for the safe and controlled testing of high-risk scenarios that would be difficult or unethical to reproduce in real-world conditions without endangering participants.

This paper presents an experimental research framework designed to study how distributed sensing, driver modeling, and adaptive interfaces can be combined to maximize safety in urban driving scenarios involving vulnerable road users. The contribution has been developed within the European project DistriMuSe [1], which aims to support human health and safety by enhancing the sensing of human presence, behavior, and vital signs through multi-sensor systems, distributed processing, and machine learning. The project addresses three main application domains: Health and Wellbeing, Digital Industry, and finally Mobility, within which the proposed work is situated. The framework enables the controlled simulation of critical interactions with VRUs and supports the collection of multimodal data for developing and evaluating driver, environment and vehicle models, as well as adaptive HMI strategies.

The remainder of this paper expands on the conceptual and methodological foundations of the proposed approach. A review of relevant literature in the area of simulation-based research on situation awareness in automotive contexts positions the contribution within the current state of the art (Sect. 2). A narrative scenario is then introduced as a generative tool for requirements elicitation and system specification (Sect. 3), followed by the proposed system architecture (Sect. 4) and a description of the simulation environment (Sect. 5). Section 6 presents the key performance indicators adopted to evaluate safety and interaction quality, while Sect. 7 details the experimental protocol. Finally, Sect. 8 outlines the guiding research hypotheses and discusses the expected contributions, followed by conclusions and future work (Sect. 9).

2   Related Work

To better position our work within the current landscape of systems designed to support situation awareness (SA) in driving contexts, this section presents a structured review of relevant studies. We begin with contributions focused on estimating drivers' SA through experimental setups using Driver Monitoring Systems (DMS). These studies provide insight into how SA is quantified and interpreted via observable behavior and physiological signals. We then consider research on DMS architectures and driver models that integrate internal and external sensing to enrich context interpretation and predictive capability. Finally, we turn to user interface solutions that support the detection and timely response to Vulnerable Road Users (VRUs), translating complex sensor data and driver state information into effective visual or multimodal alerts.

A first set of studies focuses on estimating SA using psychophysiological data and DMS. [19] investigate the link between gaze behavior and hazard awareness using a video-based driving simulation. They find that fixation metrics correlate with SA, though gaze alone does not capture its full variance. Their study supports the use of eye-tracking as a behavioral proxy while validating the ecological relevance of video-based methods. [31] examine how non-driving related activities (NDRAs) impact SA. Their simulator study shows that prior experience with touchscreen interfaces improves task efficiency and driver awareness, suggesting that familiarity can reduce cognitive load in multitasking contexts. [4] propose a fuzzy logicbased DMS that integrates biometric signals, such as heart and respiratory rate, to detect degraded awareness states. The system demonstrates real-time feasibility and highlights the role of physiological monitoring in SA estimation. [2] introduce the Fitness-to-Drive (FtD) index, which combines cognitive, visual, and emotional distraction, modulated by arousal. Simulator results show that FtD scores correlate with driving errors, emphasizing the impact of psycho-emotional states on performance. [23] contribute a large-scale dataset from six simulator studies, capturing synchronized physiological, behavioral, and subjective data under both manual and automated driving. This resource supports research on driver state monitoring and driver modeling.

Building on these foundations, recent work has introduced the concept of the Driver Digital Twin to enable personalized, adaptive support. [17] pioneer a real-time DrDT architecture that combines physiological and behavioral data to monitor driver states such as fatigue, distraction, and stress, enabling responsive vehicle adaptation. [20] develop a DrDT for lane-change prediction based on individual driving preferences, trained with deep learning and inverse reinforcement learning. Tested both in simulation and on-road, the model anticipates maneuvers several seconds in advance. [21] propose a vision-based DrDT for real-time recognition and temporal localization of distracted driving behaviors. Their transformer-based model, enhanced with emotion recognition, achieves strong performance across public datasets. [5] present a dual digital twin architecture linking a DrDT with a Vehicle Digital Twin (VDT). By locally fine-tuning drowsiness detection models using biometric data, they achieve privacy-preserving adaptation and improved accuracy.

Some contributions extend the DrDT paradigm into broader user-centric Internet of Things (IoT) ecosystems. [14] present a modular cloud/edge architecture where Human Digital Twins act as virtual agents managing user profiles and orchestrating personalized services in real time within the Social Internet of Things (SIoT). In the context of vehicle connectivity, [8] explore how cooperative perception between vehicles and infrastructure can improve VRU detection. Their system fuses onboard and roadside sensor data to anticipate risks beyond the driver's line of sight, showing the potential of distributed sensing in critical urban scenarios.

Interfaces also play a central role in enhancing driver awareness, particularly in relation to VRUs and multimodal feedback. [15] study the effects of auditory stimuli–such as music and conversation–on SA during partially automated driving. They find that conversation reduces fatigue but may hinder performance in time-critical situations. [26] compare several augmented reality (AR) cues displayed via head-up displays (HUDs) to support pedestrian detection in low-visibility conditions. Bounding boxes and directional arrows are shown to improve response times and perceived usefulness. [30] investigate the use of AR HUDs combined with thermal night vision for night-time pedestrian detection. Both white-hot and black-hot views improve recognition, with users preferring the black-hot configuration for its visual clarity and comfort.

Taken together, these studies provide a rich foundation for understanding how driver states can be monitored, modeled, and supported through sensing and interface strategies. However, they tend to focus on isolated components– whether sensing, prediction, or feedback–rather than addressing their integration within an adaptive system.

Our approach aims to fill this gap through a unified framework based on the Driver Digital Twin. This architecture models the driver's internal state in real time and dynamically informs interface adaptation strategies. Furthermore, we are among the first to explore how interface design can leverage cooperative strategies based on distributed sensing–both inside and outside the vehicle–to support the recognition of vulnerable road users (VRUs). This integration allows us to reason not only about the driver's cognitive and emotional condition, but also about how external risks evolve in relation to the driver's attention and awareness.

3   Design Rationale

The rationale behind this research effort is grounded in the ambition to improve road safety by enhancing drivers' ability to respond appropriately to complex interactions involving vulnerable road users (VRUs), even in case of low or none VRU visibility and in case of driver distraction. The project adopts a user-centered approach [7] anchored in a narrative scenario [6,11] that guides the design vision and requirement elicitation. This scenario illustrates the types of safety-critical situations the system aims to address and the cognitive and behavioral dynamics it is intended to support.

Scenario

Scene A Occluded pedestrian. Peter is driving in Manual Mode on a busy urban road. It's 6:00 PM, and he is returning home from work. He has just picked up his second daughter, Alice, from nursery school and needs to collect his other daughter, Martha, from the gym after her volleyball practice. Alice is quietly sitting in her car seat in the back. The onboard vehicle system detects a pedestrian moving into the vehicle's path from behind a stopped bus and alerts Peter via the head-up display. Thanks to the alert, Peter is aware of the pedestrian's movement and is able to brake in time when the pedestrian suddenly crosses the street, emerging from behind the obstacle. *Scene B Child distraction and near-miss with cyclist.* Peter realises he is running late and starts driving faster to make up for lost time. Alice begins to cry because she has dropped her dummy. Peter frequently turns around to check on her and tries to calm her down, beginning to drive more nervously and distractedly. As a result, Peter doesn't notice a cyclist passing him on the right, intending to go straight through the intersection where Peter needs to turn right. The onboard vehicle system detects that Peter is distracted and that the cyclist is on a collision course with the vehicle, adding an audible warning to the visual alert on the head-up display. Peter's attention is drawn back to driving, and he becomes aware of the cyclist, allowing him to pass. *Scene C Blind spot motorcyclist.* Peter is almost there. He reaches the last intersection and sees Martha waiting on the pavement in front of the gym, so he hurries to reach her. To pick her up, he needs to turn left. A motorcyclist is approaching from the right, but Peter cannot see him due to the blind spot in the car. The onboard vehicle system detects the approaching motorcyclist and realises that Peter has not noticed him. To prevent a collision, the driver assistance system slows down the vehicle, and Peter is informed via the head-up display about the motorcyclist's imminent passage and the reason for the emergency manoeuvre.

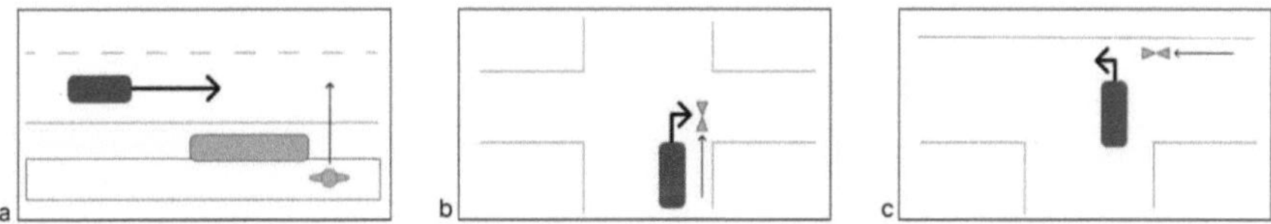

Fig. 1. Graphic representation of the three key moments in Peter's scenario: a) the pedestrian crossing the street from behind an obstacle; b) the cyclist coming alongside him on the right; c) the motorcyclist approaching from the right.

This scenario reflects realistic and everyday occurrences in urban mobility, where driver distraction and occluded VRU visibility can converge to produce high-risk situations. It exemplifies the conditions under which a multisensory and adaptive safety system could significantly enhance the driver's ability to act safely and with minimal stress. The envisioned system is expected to integrate continuous information from in-vehicle driver monitoring and external sensing sources combining these data to assess situational awareness, infer risk, and deliver context-sensitive feedback through a head-up interface. From this scenario, several requirements emerge. These include the need to detect not only

VRUs in the vehicle's environment, but also the driver's level of attention, distraction, or emotional strain; the capacity to communicate alerts in a timely and understandable way that supports quick and correct decision-making; and the importance of balancing support with minimal interference in order to preserve driving comfort and perceived control.

4   High-Level Architecture

The conceptual architecture underlying this research has been designed to address the types of high-risk interactions exemplified in the user scenario presented earlier. Drawing on the insights derived from that scenario where distraction, urgency, and limited visibility converge to challenge driver decision-making, the proposed system aims to integrate multiple data sources to support timely, adaptive, and context-aware interventions.

The architectural concept was developed by the authors as part of a broader co-design effort within the DistriMuSe project. The high-level vision stems from the scenario analysis. The implementation of its various components is distributed among several project partners.

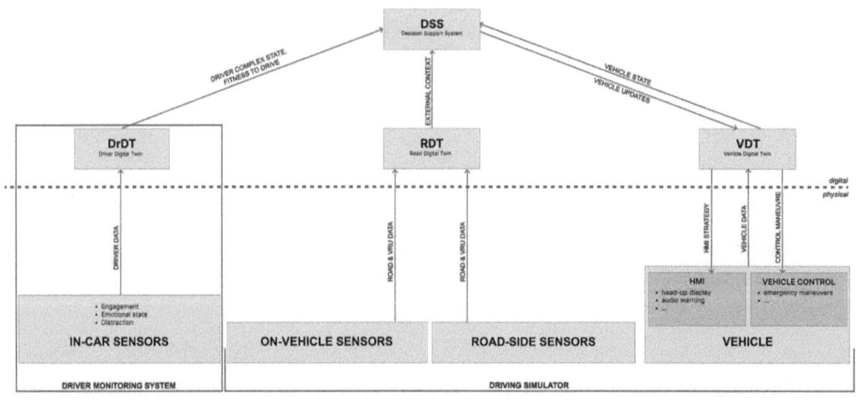

Fig. 2. High-level architecture of the to be developed system.

At a macroscopic level, the architecture revolves around three interconnected digital models: the *Driver Digital Twin* (DrDT), the *Vehicle Digital Twin* (VDT), and the *Road Digital Twin* (RDT). Each digital twin represents a distinct dimension of the driving system and serves as a node in a real-time decision loop.

The **DrDT** models the cognitive and emotional state of the driver (Driver Complex State) based on a Driver Monitoring System leveraging in-vehicle sensor data, capturing facial expression, gaze direction, head pose, and other behavioral cues. Beyond modeling the Driver Complex State, an important objective of the DrDT is to assess the driver's engagement in the driving task and overall fitness to drive, especially under cognitively demanding or emotionally charged conditions.

The **RDT** provides a digital representation of the external driving context, drawing on data from the simulator to model traffic conditions, road geometry, visibility constraints, and the presence and predicted motion of VRUs. It enables reasoning about environmental risks that may not be directly perceived by the driver due to occlusions, blind spots, or lapses in attention. It is fed by external on-vehicle sensors as well as road-side sensors and associated intelligence, enabling a contextualized understanding of traffic conditions and VRU behavior.

The **VDT**, in turn, captures the vehicle's dynamic state, its trajectory, acceleration, braking, and interaction with control systems. It is crucial for estimating how the vehicle is likely to behave in response to the driver's input and external factors, and for simulating corrective or preventive maneuvers when necessary.

These three models are orchestrated by a **Decision Support System** (DSS), which functions as the computational core of the architecture. The DSS integrates data from all digital twins and evaluates the current and predicted state of both the driver and the environment. Based on predefined rules or future learning-based models, it determines whether and how to intervene, whether through a HMI message or a more direct corrective action. Within the proposed framework, both the vehicle and its external sensing components, including on-vehicle sensors directed at the road and road-side sensors, are simulated in the driving environment. In contrast, the driver monitoring system (DMS) is based on real sensor data.

5   Driving Simulator Environment

The RELAB driving simulator provides the experimental environment in which the proposed framework is deployed. In this context, the simulator allows for the controlled simulation of high-risk scenarios involving vulnerable road users (VRUs), such as pedestrians, cyclists, and motorcyclists. These scenarios replicate urban driving conditions where occlusions, blind spots, or lapses in attention may critically impair the driver's ability to perceive and react to VRU behavior.

The simulator supports the integration of simulated on-vehicle and road-side sensors, enabling the generation of synthetic data about VRU position, velocity, direction of movement, crossing intent, and visibility status. Contextual elements such as traffic lights, intersections, signage and lane geometry are also modeled. These features allow for the detailed reproduction of urban complexity in a safe and repeatable setting.

In addition to dynamic traffic modeling, the simulator enables the testing of manual driving behavior (steering, acceleration, braking) and includes support for ADAS components such as collision avoidance and lane keeping. Within the scope of the present research program, ADAS features such as collision avoidance and lane keeping will remain deactivated in order to observe naturalistic driving behavior unaffected by automated interventions, and to better isolate the specific contribution of the adaptive HMI to safety and the overall system on driving performance. Collectable data includes:

- Simulator telemetry (e.g., braking, speed, steering angle);
- Behavioural outcomes, including risky manoeuvres and VRU collisions;
- Recording of the driving scene;

The time at which each VRU becomes visually detectable by the driver (i.e., emerges from occlusion) will be considered a key reference point for computing reaction times, assessing attention allocation, and evaluating the effective window for preventive action. These data are crucial to assess whether drivers respond appropriately once a VRU becomes visible, and to refine the timing and rules of adaptive HMI interventions in the next experimental phase.

Simulated sensors, including cameras, LIDAR, RADAR, and GPS, can be used to reconstruct environmental perception pipelines, and head-up display (HUD) interfaces can be embedded to deliver adaptive feedback to the driver.

Figure 3 shows the equipment of the driving simulator environment for the DistriMuSe research. In-vehicle sensors intended for use in a realistic deployment scenario are represented by a front-facing RGB camera capturing the driver's face and upper body, whose data are used to infer cognitive distraction and emotional state.

In addition to the RGB camera used for real-time driver state monitoring, the simulation environment will also include an additional sensor, a dedicated eye-tracking device, not necessarily intended for real-world deployment, but essential for two complementary purposes. First, it allows for more granular behavioral investigations into visual attention and driverenvironment interaction. Second, it provides reliable ground-truth data to support the development and validation of AI-based inference for visual attention estimation modules under controlled conditions. They will support the definition and detection of VRU miss events, a class of critical occurrences that we aim to model based on the individual driving histories collected during simulation trials. T hese events reflect situations where a vulnerable road user is not registered by the driver in time to allow a safe behavioral adjustment, and represent a key marker of degraded situation awareness. By combining gaze data with contextual information from the Driver Digital Twin (DrDT), the Road Digital Twin (RDT), and the Vehicle Digital Twin (VDT), the system aims to infer whether critical objects or agents in the driving environment are being perceived and acted upon appropriately, thus informing adaptive HMI strategies and just-in-time interventions.

To simulate cognitive load and secondary task interference, a visual-motor dual task is embedded within the simulator environment. This task is a variant of the Surrogate Visual Research Task (SURT) (Fig. 4), commonly used in distraction studies [33] [34] [27]. It is delivered through a web-based application displayed on a secondary touchscreen monitor, positioned to emulate the location of a standard in-vehicle infotainment system. This configuration enables the realistic simulation of driver interaction with central dashboard displays, as typically found in modern vehicles. At configurable time intervals during the driving session, the participant is prompted to identify and touch the quadrant containing a red circle target. The system records response accuracy and reaction time for each prompt, enabling the quantitative assessment of attentional shifts. This setup allows for the structured induction and measurement of driver distraction indicators in synchrony with VRU interaction scenarios.

This simulation environment provides the necessary infrastructure to evaluate the effects of adaptive interaction strategies under conditions that combine real-time driver monitoring with environmental and vehicle-state data. It plays a central role in validating the proposed approach by supporting the reproducible observation of distracted driving behaviors and system interventions in complex VRU scenarios.

Fig. 3. The driving simulator environment.

6   Key Performance Indicators (KPI)

The architecture presented in Sect. 4 is designed to support drivers in enhancing their situational awareness, particularly in relation to vulnerable road users (VRUs). The primary objective is to help drivers anticipate the presence and movement of VRUs, especially those not yet directly visible, so they can modulate their driving behavior accordingly and prevent potential collisions. To achieve this, the envisioned DistriMuSe system relies on a combination of real-time environmental sensing, driver monitoring, and adaptive interface strategies.

The experimental infrastructure described in Sect. 5 plays a dual role: it supports the collection of rich data about the driving behavior and the driver state, and enables the controlled evaluation of the to be designed HMI solution aiming at augmenting the driver VRU awareness.

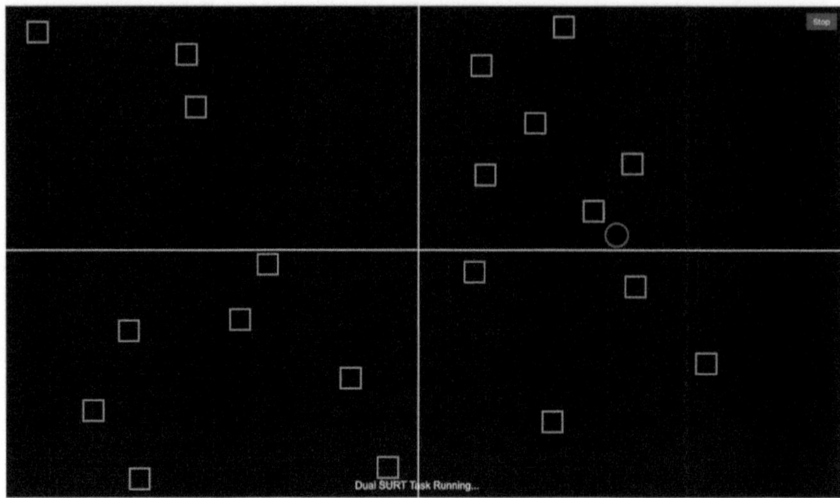

Fig. 4. The SURT distracting task.

In order to systematically assess the impact of the outcomes of the presented research, a set of Key Performance Indicators (KPIs) has been defined [24]. These KPIs reflect both objective safety outcomes and subjective interaction quality, providing a foundation for data-driven analysis and comparison across experimental conditions:

- *Number of accidents with VRUs:* the total number of collisions between the driver's vehicle and VRUs during simulated driving trials conducted under both distracted and non-distracted conditions. This KPI captures instances where the lack of timely driver reaction leads to unavoidable crashes. To assess the system's impact on safety, results will distinguish between total VRU-related accidents, accidents with distraction, and those without. The KPI will be measured in controlled simulator sessions, using system logs of VRU-related collisions and monitoring driver states. Baseline values will be collected in scenarios without HMI support. Comparisons will be made against data from the trial where the to be developed HMI will provide real-time assistance based on driver distraction and VRU detection.
- *Number of risky manoeuvres:* the number of risky manoeuvres drivers perform during simulated driving involving VRUs, both with and without distraction. Risky manoeuvres are defined as abrupt or unsafe actions indicating poor situational awareness or delayed responses. In this phase, five subtypes are tracked: (1) crossing with red light, (2) centre line crossing without indicator, (3) panic braking with stop, (4) panic braking without stop, and (5) sharp turns. Telemetry and behavioural data from the simulator will be used to detect and classify these manoeuvres using thresholds for acceleration, brak-

ing intensity, steering angle, and indicator use. The KPI will be calculated by comparing a baseline (no HMI) condition with a scenario using the HMI.

– *Situational awareness:* the driver's ability to perceive relevant elements, understand their meaning, and anticipate future developments. SA will be measured through the Situational Awareness Rating Technique (SART) [3,32], an ex-post questionnaire to be used both after the baseline driving trials without any DistriMuSe system support and after the driving trials with the HMI support. Since SART has no predefined thresholds, the analysis will focus on comparative increases in SA scores with the HMI. Qualitative feedback will further clarify users' perceptions of how the system supported or hindered their situational awareness by structured interviews after the driving trials with the HMI.

– *Technology acceptance:* refers to how willing users are to adopt a system based on perceived usefulness, ease of use, trustworthiness, and overall value. In systems involving real-time monitoring and feedback, acceptance is critical: a technically effective system may still fail if users perceive it as intrusive or unnecessary. Acceptance will be assessed using the Unified Model of Driver Acceptance (UMDA), based on the theoretical model by Rahman et al. [18, 28]. To explore acceptance further, qualitative data will be gathered via open-ended questions or short interviews. This mixed-method approach will help uncover not only acceptance levels, but also the reasons behind them.

– *User experience:* includes not only usability and task efficiency, but also how the system makes the driver feel, i.e., engaged, confident, or frustrated. UX is particularly critical for systems involving adaptive feedback. UX will be evaluated using the User Experience Questionnaire short version (UEQ-s) [29].

7 Experimental Design

To assess the impact of combining distributed sensing for Vulnerable Road User (VRU) detection with driver monitoring technologies that identify critical driver states, we designed an experimental plan aimed at evaluating the key performance indicators presented in Sect. 6 in simulated high-risk urban driving scenarios.

The plan envisions two data collection cycles involving 40 participants each. The first cycle serves as a baseline, in which neither distraction monitoring nor VRU recognition is active (Cycle 1). The second cycle will assess the effects of enabling an adaptive Human-Machine Interface (HMI) driven by real-time assessments coming from the driver monitoring system (in- vehicle sensors) and the VRU recognition system (simulated external sensors and simulated interaction with roadside infrastructure). In this second data collection, the simulation emulates the presence of infrastructure-based perception units (such as roadside LiDAR, radar, or camera systems) within a limited coverage range of approximately 100 to 200 m from the vehicle. This simulated environment provides localized awareness of VRU presence and trajectories, supporting proactive interface feedback as expected in connected and sensor-augmented road scenarios, such as those envisioned in UC2 of the DistriMuSe project. The data collection campaign for Cycle 1 is structured as a baseline evaluation of driver behaviour and related KPI in the absence of adaptive support. No HMI is presented, then neither distraction detection nor VRU recognition is exploited to help the driver in risky situations. This phase aims to collect behavioural and attention-related data, including reaction times to critical VRU events, performance in the secondary distracting task, and subjective assessments of situational awareness. These measures jointly support the evaluation of attentional dynamics and decision-making under normal and distracted conditions. The same experimental structure will be replicated in Cycle 2, where the HMI will be active and driven by real-time recognition of driver distraction and VRU proximity.

The simulation includes five distinct categories of VRU-related risk scenarios, designed to reflect common urban situations where driver awareness is likely to be challenged (Table 1):

1. *Crossing of a pedestrian from behind a visual obstruction (fig.5):* a pedestrian emerges and crosses the street from behind a stopped vehicle (e.g., school bus, van);
2. *Pulling alongside from the right:* turning right while a bicycle overtakes from the right during the manoeuver;
3. *Blind spot:* turning left with a motorbike approaching from the right in the driver's blind spot;
4. *Unauthorized crossing at intersection with low visibility:* a motorbike or bicycle illegally crosses at a red light, partially hidden from the driver's view at an intersection;
5. *Unauthorized crossing on crosswalk with high visibility:* a bicycle suddenly crosses on a crosswalk, in an otherwise clearly visible situation.

Table 1. Examples of road risk situations and their descriptions.

#	Risk situation	Description
1	Crossing of a pedestrian from behind a visual obstruction	A pedestrian emerges and crosses the street from behind a stopped vehicle (e.g., school bus, van)
2	Pulling alongside from the right	Turning right while a bicycle overtakes from the right during the maneuver
3	Blind spot	Turning left with a motorbike approaching from the right in the driver's blind spot
4	Unauthorized crossing at intersection with low visibility	A motorbike or bicycle illegally crosses at a red light, partially hidden from the driver's view at an intersection
5	Unauthorized crossing on crosswalk with high visibility	A bicycle suddenly crosses on a crosswalk, in an otherwise clearly visible situation

Each category is represented through four variations: two critical events (in which the VRU actively enters the driver's trajectory, creating a potential collision risk), one non-critical event (in which the VRU is visible but does not

Fig. 5. One of the five distinct categories of VRU-related risk scenarios: crossing of a pedestrian from behind a visual obstruction.

interact), and one neutral event (replicating the same driving context but without any VRU presence). This structure results in a total of 20 distinct events (10 that are critical and 10 that are not) per simulated drive. The use of multiple variants per scenario serves to avoid response bias and preserve ecological validity: by introducing ambiguity regarding the presence and behaviour of the VRU, participants are prevented from developing deterministic expectations. This design encourages more naturalistic driving behaviour and allows for a more realistic assessment of situation awareness and decision- making processes. Four different route sequences were designed within the simulator: two for the non-distracted driving condition (ND) and two for the distracted condition (D), where the secondary visual distractin task is introduced. All sequences include the same 20 events, but arranged in different orders to reduce learning or anticipation effects. Each participant completes both sessions (ND and D) in a within experimental design. To control for ordering bias, participants are assigned to one of four experimental groups, varying both the condition order (ND first or D first) and the route. This rotation scheme ensures a balanced distribution of conditions and mitigates potential effects due to familiarity or fatigue. The order of events was also carefully designed to avoid presenting more than two critical events consecutively, preserving attentional balance and limiting overload.

After each session, participants complete the envisioned questionnaires defined for the KPI measurement, followed by a brief interview. An entry questionnaire collects demographic data and driving experience. This baseline dataset serves both as a benchmark for evaluating the effectiveness of the HMI in Cycle 2 and as a foundational reference for behavioural modelling in the development of future Driver Digital Twin (DrDT) solutions. Participants are expected to be healthy adults with a valid driver's license and at least two years of driving experience. In line with open science principles, the dataset collected during the study will be made available to the research community upon completion. It will include simulator telemetry data such as speed, braking, and steering angle; behavioral outcomes such as collisions with VRUs and risky manoeuvres; self-reported measures gathered through questionnaires; eye-tracking data capturing gaze dynamics; recordings of the driving scene; and statistics related to the performance on the secondary task administered during the distracted driving condition. All data collected in this study, including behavioral, physiological, and interactional logs, are anonymized at source and stored in compliance with GDPR regulations and internal ethical guidelines. No biometric or identity-linked data are retained beyond the scope of experimental analysis. The study was designed and approved in alignment with established research ethics standards, and all participants provide informed consent before participating in simulation tasks involving driver monitoring.

8   Discussion

An important component of the proposed framework is the design and evaluation of an adaptive HMI to be represented in a head-up display (HUD) HMI, conceived not simply as an alert mechanism, but as an interface capable of mediating between system-level inference and human-level perception and control. The HUD is intended to provide context-sensitive support in situations where a VRU is on a potential collision course with the vehicle. However, before issuing any alert or adaptive message, the system estimates whether the driver has already perceived the VRU and is modulating their driving behavior accordingly (e.g., by slowing down, maintaining lane discipline, or adjusting trajectory). To this end, we introduce the concept of a *VRU miss*, defined as a situation in which the system determines based on driver attention metrics and vehicle behavior that a vulnerable road user present in the environment has likely not been noticed or cognitively processed by the driver. Identifying VRU misses is critical for calibrating the intervention logic of the HMI: alerts are triggered when such events are detected, ensuring that the system provides support precisely when the driver's situation awareness fails. The estimation of VRU misses draws on multimodal input: eye-tracking and head pose data for visual attention, pedal and steering behavior for motor response, and contextual information from the road and vehicle environment. When a VRU miss is inferred, the HUD delivers a targeted alert, whose intensity and form are dynamically adapted based on both the driver's current state (e.g., level of distraction or cognitive load) and their longer-term behavioral profile. The choice of a head-up display is motivated by its potential to present information in alignment with the driver's forward field of view, supporting perceptual continuity and minimizing attention diversion. In this context, the HUD becomes a key interface for augmenting driver performance without compromising comfort or control.

The experiment has been designed to test the following main hypotheses:

H1: *VRU-related accidents with [A-HMI] < [No-HMI].* Adaptive HMI feedback based on real-time assessments of driver distraction and VRU proximity reduces the number of VRU-related accidents.

H2: *Risky manoeuvres with [A-HMI] < [No-HMI].* The same feedback strategy reduces the number of risky manoeuvres performed during driving.

H3: *Situational Awareness scores with [A-HMI] > [No-HMI].* The presence of the adaptive HMI improves subjective situational awareness, as measured through validated metrics.

H4: *Acceptance and usability of [A-HMI] ≥ acceptable threshold, despite continuous monitoring.* The adaptive HMI is perceived as acceptable and usable by the majority of drivers, despite relying on continuous driver monitoring.

Beyond these immediate hypotheses, the infrastructure also enables exploratory analyses related to driver modeling. One of the mid-term goals of the project is to investigate how individual driver profiles derived from behavioral and attentional indicators may inform the development of personalized interaction strategies. In this perspective, the Driver Digital Twin (DrDT) is not just a real-time inference module, but a representation of the driver's stable patterns of attention, workload resilience, and risk sensitivity. Beyond these, the following exploratory hypotheses are considered:

H5: *Personalized DrDT models predict VRU miss events with higher accuracy than general models*

H6: *Personalized HMI strategies lead to higher Trust and Perceived Usefulness than generic strategies*

This opens new research questions on how the HMI could be adapted not only in real time, but also over time, based on prior knowledge about the user. For example, the system could learn to issue warnings only when a given driver is actually at risk of missing a VRU, reducing alert fatigue and avoiding unnecessary interventions. Such personalization may improve trust and reduce the risk of driver disengagement, a phenomenon sometimes observed when assistance systems are perceived as too frequent or irrelevant, similar to what occurs with users who disable automatic braking or lane-keeping systems.

To explore the benefits of personalizing the Driver Digital Twin (DrDT), we plan to compare different modelling strategies (generalized vs. individualized) by training predictive models of VRU miss events using the data collected from the driving simulator. This analysis will help determine whether personalized DrDTs offer greater predictive accuracy in identifying moments when a driver fails to notice critical road users.

While our setup is highly controlled and designed to simulate complex driving scenarios, it has limitations. Although the simulator allows us to present complex and high-risk traffic interactions with a high degree of realism, ecological validity remains limited. The absence of real consequences and the artificial nature of some stimuli may influence user behavior, attentional dynamics, and emotional engagement. As such, generalizing findings to real driving contexts should be done cautiously, with the understanding that simulation-based responses may differ from those observed on the road.

The participant sample may not reflect the full diversity of real-world drivers in terms of age, experience, driving style, or cognitive traits. This may lead to uniform judgments and averages that do not fully capture the diversity of real-world drivers, that is to be considered especially for subjective evaluations of the system, such as perceived usefulness, trust, or workload. Nonetheless, our research aims to personalize the predictive models of each driver by adopting the Driver Digital Twin (DrDT) approach. This strategy strives to model attentional and behavioral profiles at the individual level and tailor system responses accordingly. In doing so, we hope to improve not only performance and user experience, but also fairness in how the system interprets and supports different types of drivers.

9   Conclusion and Future Work

This paper presented a simulation-based research framework designed to investigate how distributed sensing, driver modeling, and adaptive human-machine interfaces can be effectively integrated to support situation awareness in urban driving scenarios involving vulnerable road users (VRUs). By combining scenario-based design, multimodal sensing, and real-time cognitive workload manipulation within a high-fidelity driving simulator, the setup enables a robust and ecologically plausible evaluation of adaptive HUD strategies informed by both real-time driver state and long-term behavioral patterns.

The system architecture, structured around the coordinated interplay of Driver, Vehicle, and Road Digital Twins and governed by a decision support system, lays the groundwork for exploring novel adaptive support mechanisms grounded in individualized models of human behavior. This approach targets safety-critical phenomena such as attentional failures and missed detections of VRUs. It also opens pathways for designing more transparent, trustable, and user-aligned interaction strategies.

Although the study is still in the data collection phase, the evaluation framework proposed here, particularly the choice of key performance indicators and the structure of the experimental design, offers a useful reference for researchers interested in studying adaptive human-machine interaction in comparable driving scenarios.

In line with open science principles, the dataset collected during the study will be made available to the research community. This includes telemetry from the simulator (e.g., speed, braking, steering), behavioral indicators such as VRU collisions and risky manoeuvres, self-reported questionnaire responses, gaze data from the eye-tracker, recordings of the driving scene, and performance statistics on the secondary task. These data are expected to support future research on multiple fronts. In particular, forthcoming analyses will compare generalized versus personalized Driver Digital Twin (DrDT) models in predicting attentional failures and refining intervention thresholds for adaptive HMIs. They contribute also to assess how personalization affects user trust and acceptance of continuous monitoring systems.

Acknowledgments.. This work was funded by EU Horizon KDT JU Research and Innovation Programme under Grant Agreement 101139769 (DistriMuSe - Distributed Multi-Sensor Systems for Human Safety and Health) [1].

Authors' Contribution. R.P.: Conceptualization, Investigation, Methodology, Writing Original Draft, Writing Review and Editing, Supervision. C.T.: Investigation, Writing Original Draft, Writing Review and Editing. F.D.S.: Methodology, Writing Review and Editing. R.G: Conceptualization, Investigation. A.M.: Software, Resources. F.V.: Methodology, Resources, Supervision.

Disclosure of Interests. The authors have no competing interests to declare that are relevant to the content of this article.

Ethical Approvals. The recruitment and testing procedures have been reviewed and approved by the Ethics Committee of the University of Suor Orsola Benincasa (protocol no. 4403). Informed consent will be obtained explaining the purpose of the study, data protection measures, potential risks and benefits, and the voluntary nature of participation.

References

1. Project DistriMuSe homepage. https://distrimuse.eu/. Accessed 10 Jun 2025
2. Andruccioli, M., Mengozzi, M., Presta, R., Mirri, S., Girau, R.: Arousal effects on fitness-to-drive assessment: algorithms and experiments. In: 2023 IEEE 20th Consumer Communications & Networking Conference (CCNC), pp. 366–371. IEEE (2023)
3. Bolton, M.L., Biltekoff, E., Humphrey, L.: The level of measurement of subjective situation awareness and its dimensions in the situation awareness rating technique (SART). IEEE Trans. Hum.-Mach. Syst. **52**(6), 1147–1154 (2021)
4. Bylykbashi, K., Qafzezi, E., Ikeda, M., Matsuo, K., Barolli, L.: Fuzzy-based driver monitoring system (FDMS): implementation of two intelligent FDMSS and a testbed for safe driving in VANETs. Futur. Gener. Comput. Syst. **105**, 665–674 (2020)
5. Campolo, C., Mammone, N., Molinaro, A., Pizzimenti, B., Singh, G., Zappalà, D.M.: Poster: digital twins for personalized and safer automated driving. In: 2024 IEEE Vehicular Networking Conference (VNC), pp. 277–278. IEEE (2024)
6. Carroll, J.M.: Scenarios and design cognition. In: Proceedings IEEE Joint International Conference on Requirements Engineering, pp. 3–5. IEEE (2002)
7. Chammas, A., Quaresma, M., Mont' Alvão, C.: A closer look on the user centred design. Procedia Manuf. **3**, 5397–5404 (2015)
8. Chen, H., Bandaru, V.K., Wang, Y., Romero, M.A., Tarko, A., Feng, Y.: Cooperative perception system for aiding connected and automated vehicle navigation and improving safety. Transp. Res. Rec. **2678**(12), 1498–1510 (2024)
9. Davoli, L., et al.: On driver behavior recognition for increased safety: a roadmap. Safety **6**(4), 55 (2020)

10. Endsley, M.R., Selcon, S.J., Hardiman, T.D., Croft, D.G.: A comparative analysis of SAGAT and SART for evaluations of situation awareness. In: Proceedings of the human factors and ergonomics society annual meeting, vol. 42, pp. 82–86. Sage Publications Sage CA: Los Angeles, CA (1998)
11. Floyd, I.R., Twidale, M.B., Jones, M.C.: Resolving incommensurable debates: a preliminary identification of persona kinds, attributes, and characteristics. Artifact: J. Design Pract. **2**(1), 12–26 (2008)
12. Forum, I.T.: Safe micromobility. Tech. rep., OECD/ITF, Paris (2020). https://www.itf-oecd.org/sites/default/files/docs/safe-micromobility_1.pdf
13. Gavanas, N.: Autonomous road vehicles: challenges for urban planning in European cities. Urban Sci. **3**(2), 61 (2019)
14. Girau, R., et al.: Definition and implementation of the cloud infrastructure for the integration of the human digital twin in the social internet of things. Comput. Networks **251**, 110632 (2024)
15. Hirano, T., Lee, J., Itoh, M.: Effects of auditory stimuli and verbal communications on drivers' situation awareness in partially automated driving. In: 2018 57th Annual Conference of the Society of Instrument and Control Engineers of Japan (SICE), pp. 690–696. IEEE (2018)
16. Hollander, C., Hartwich, F., Krems, J.: Looking at HMI concepts for highly automated vehicles: permanent vs. context-adaptive information presentation. Open Psychol. **4**, 231–248 (2022). https://doi.org/10.1515/psych-2022-0124
17. Hu, Z., Lou, S., Xing, Y., Wang, X., Cao, D., Lv, C.: Review and perspectives on driver digital twin and its enabling technologies for intelligent vehicles. IEEE Trans. Intell. Veh. **7**(3), 417–440 (2022)
18. Khattak, M.W., Brijs, K., Tran, T.M., Trinh, T.A., Vu, A.T., Brijs, T.: Acceptance towards advanced driver assistance systems (ADAS): a validation of the unified model of driver acceptance (UMDA) using structural equation modelling. Transp. Res. Part F: Traffic Psychol. Behav. **105**, 284–305 (2024)
19. Kim, H., Gabbard, J.L., Martin, S., Tawari, A., Misu, T.: Toward prediction of driver awareness of automotive hazards: driving-video-based simulation approach. In: Proceedings of the human factors and ergonomics society annual meeting, vol. 63, pp. 2099–2103. SAGE Publications Sage CA: Los Angeles, CA (2019)
20. Liao, X., et al.: Driver digital twin for online prediction of personalized lane-change behavior. IEEE Internet Things J. **10**(15), 13235–13246 (2023)
21. Ma, Y., Du, R., Abdelraouf, A., Han, K., Gupta, R., Wang, Z.: Driver digital twin for online recognition of distracted driving behaviors. IEEE Trans. Intell. Veh. **9**(2), 3168–3180 (2024)
22. Manstetten, D., et al.: The evolution of driver monitoring systems: a shortened story on past, current and future approaches how cars acquire knowledge about the driver's state. In: 22nd International Conference on Human-Computer Interaction with Mobile Devices and Services, pp. 1–6 (2020)
23. Meteier, Q., et al.: A dataset on the physiological state and behavior of drivers in conditionally automated driving. Data Brief **47**, 109027 (2023)
24. Orfanou, F.P., Vlahogianni, E.I., Yannis, G., Mitsakis, E.: Humanizing autonomous vehicle driving: understanding, modeling and impact assessment. Transp. Res. Part F: Traffic Psychol. Behav. **87**, 477–504 (2022)
25. Organization, W.H.: Global status report on road safety 2023 (2023). https://www.who.int/publications/b/68866
26. Phan, M.T., Thouvenin, I., Frémont, V.: Enhancing the driver awareness of pedestrian using augmented reality cues. In: 2016 IEEE 19th International Conference on Intelligent Transportation Systems (ITSC), pp. 1298–1304. IEEE (2016)

27. Radlmayr, J., Gold, C., Lorenz, L., Farid, M., Bengler, K.: How traffic situations and non-driving related tasks affect the take-over quality in highly automated driving. In: Proceedings of the Human Factors and Ergonomics Society Annual Meeting, vol. 58, pp. 2063–2067. Sage Publications Sage CA: Los Angeles, CA (2014)
28. Rahman, M.M., Strawderman, L., Lesch, M.F., Horrey, W.J., Babski-Reeves, K., Garrison, T.: Modelling driver acceptance of driver support systems. Accid. Anal. Prev. **121**, 134–147 (2018)
29. Schrepp, M., Hinderks, A., et al.: Design and evaluation of a short version of the user experience questionnaire (UEQ-S) (2017)
30. Singhal, N., Alsaid, A., Talamonti, W., Mayer, K.: Study of night vision configuration with augmented reality in automotive context. In: International Conference on Human-Computer Interaction, pp. 91–98. Springer (2023)
31. Skrypchuk, L., Langdon, P., Mouzakitis, A., Clarkson, P.J.: How does awareness affect performance in an automotive dual task condition? In: Advances in Human Aspects of Transportation: Proceedings of the AHFE 2017 International Conference on Human Factors in Transportation, July 17- 21, 2017, The Westin Bonaventure Hotel, Los Angeles, California, USA 8, pp. 395–406. Springer (2018)
32. Taylor, R.M.: Situational awareness rating technique (SART): the development of a tool for aircrew systems design. In: Situational Awareness, pp. 111–128. Routledge (2017)
33. TS14198, I.: Road vehicles-ergonomic aspects of transport information and control systems-calibration tasks for methods which access driver demand due to the use of invehicle systems. Tech. rep., ISO TC22/SC13/WG8 (2012)
34. Xu, C., Li, P., Li, Y., Merat, N., Lu, Z., Guo, X.: Takeover performance and workload under varying automation levels, time budget and road curvature. In: 2022 IEEE Asia-Pacific Conference on Image Processing, Electronics and Computers (IPEC), pp. 1379–1385. IEEE (2022)
35. Yamin, P.A., Park, J., Kim, H.K.: In-vehicle human–machine interface guidelines for augmented reality head-up displays: a review, guideline formulation, and future research directions. Transp. Res. Part F: Traffic Psychol. Behav. **104**, 266–285 (2024)
36. Zhou, C., Qiao, W., Hua, J., Chen, L.: Automotive augmented reality head-up displays. Micromachines **15**(4), 442 (2024)

The Impact of Encoded Forms of In-Car AR-HUD Warning Information on Drivers' Reaction Time and Subjective Evaluation

Jianyu Shi, Xiang Ben, and Yajing Kan(✉)

School of Mechanical Engineering, Southeast University, Nanjing 211189, China
yajingkan@seu.edu.cn

Abstract. As in-vehicle systems advance, AR-HUDs have become crucial for driver-vehicle interaction, yet unoptimized icon encoding may hinder information processing and increase cognitive load. This study investigates how shape, color and transparency affect driver response times and subjective evaluations by testing 108 icon variants across driving scenarios with diverse participants using a Unity-based simulator. Results demonstrate that color significantly impacts recognition speed, with blue and red icons reducing reaction times compared to yellow due to higher contrast, while line-based icons outperformed area-based designs owing to clearer outlines and reduced visual clutter. Transparency showed minimal effects on reaction time but influenced readability in specific conditions. The optimal combination line-shaped blue icons at 100% transparency yielded the fastest average reaction time (1333.67 ms), with subjective evaluations confirming lower cognitive load for high-contrast, simplified designs. These findings provide actionable AR-HUD design guidelines prioritizing contrast, clarity, and transparency to improve safety and usability, bridging ergonomic theory and empirical data to advance HMI research for future in-vehicle interfaces.

Keywords: Augmented Reality Head-Up Display · Encoding Forms · Unity Experiment · Information Recognizability.

1 Introduction

In the context of the continuous development of intelligent driver assistance systems, Augmented Reality Head-Up Displays (AR-HUD) have gradually become standard equipment in modern vehicles. AR-HUD operates by utilizing optical reflection technology to superimpose virtual information onto real-time road conditions, projecting it directly onto the windshield or at a predetermined distance, thereby improving the driving experience and increasing safety [1]. During driving, a driver's gaze diverted from the target route for 2 s increases the likelihood of a collision by twofold [2]. One reason for this is the inadequacy of interface design, which hinders the driver's cognitive understanding and decision-making, ultimately leading to errors in information reading, analysis, and execution. Compared to traditional HUDs, AR-HUDs not only provide essential information such as speed and direction but also offer enhanced visual

P.-L.P. Rau and H. Krömker (Eds.): HCII 2025, LNCS 16336, pp. 410–422, 2026.
https://doi.org/10.1007/978-3-032-12798-3_25

interaction, intelligent warning functionalities, and realistic road scene reproduction. By experimentally evaluating drivers' gaze behavior, situational awareness, confidence, and workload, AR-HUD systems can assist drivers in responding more quickly [3] (see Fig. 1. Conventional Vehicles and HUD-Equipped Vehicles.). Cheng et al. [4] conducted eye-tracking experiments to assess the impact of AR-HUD systems on driver behavior, with results indicating that AR-HUD can reduce the perception time of hazardous driving scenarios, thereby enabling faster responses to dangerous situations. These features allow drivers to utilize the heads-up display system, thereby avoiding the need to look down at instruments, which reduces the consumption of visual, motivational, and cognitive resources, ultimately enhancing driving safety and interaction experience [5].

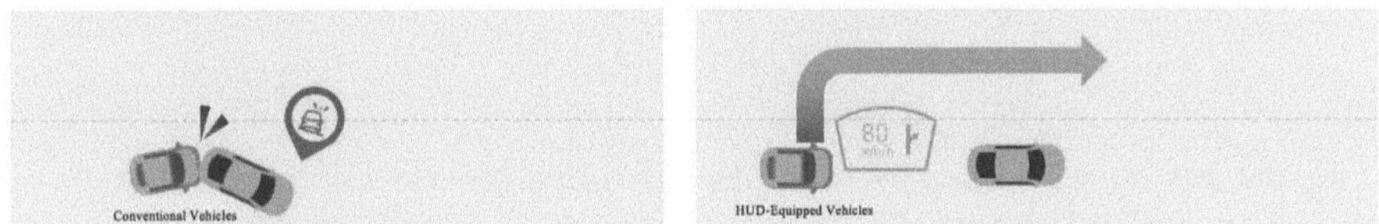

Fig. 1. Conventional Vehicles and HUD-Equipped Vehicles.

However, the abundance of interactive information within the vehicle places a significant cognitive load on drivers, given their limited cognitive resources, which can consequently lead to traffic accidents [6]. According to statistics, approximately 80% of traffic accidents are attributed to driver inattention [7]. If the design of interface information is inadequate, it may increase the cognitive load on drivers, thereby distracting their attention and affecting driving safety. Establishing scientific design standards and guidelines is crucial for enhancing the interaction efficiency of AR-HUD systems and ensuring driving safety [8]. Therefore, throughout the development of HUD technology, research on the content of its display interface has gradually gained widespread attention, in addition to technical advancements. For instance, Li et al. [9] explored the colors and shapes of icons within HUD interfaces; Zhu et al. [10] employed cognitive load theory to analyze the color and layout of HUD icons, proposing optimization design strategies and implementing enhancements. Eye-tracking experiments were conducted to analyze five indicators—visual characteristics, hazard response capability, take-over response capability, speed response capability, and subjective evaluation of the system—of drivers in different scenarios with AR-HUD, aiming to identify the optimal presentation method for interface icon elements [11]. Additionally, Gabbard et al. [12] assessed the colors of AR-HUD interfaces based on user perception, determining stable colors in real-world contexts, thereby providing a foundation for color design in AR-HUD interfaces (Fig. 2).

Tan et al. [13] systematically examined ADAS's current state and future trajectories, elucidating its pivotal role in HMI interactions and how technological advancements optimize human-vehicle communication to boost safety and user experience. Theoretically, in-vehicle Human-Machine Interfaces (HMIs) can provide a wealth of information, including environmental data, vehicle status, and multimedia content [14]. By observing and interpreting this information, drivers can develop a fundamental understanding of the vehicle's operational status and road conditions, enabling them to make informed judgments that are crucial for ensuring safe driving. The driver cognitive system refers

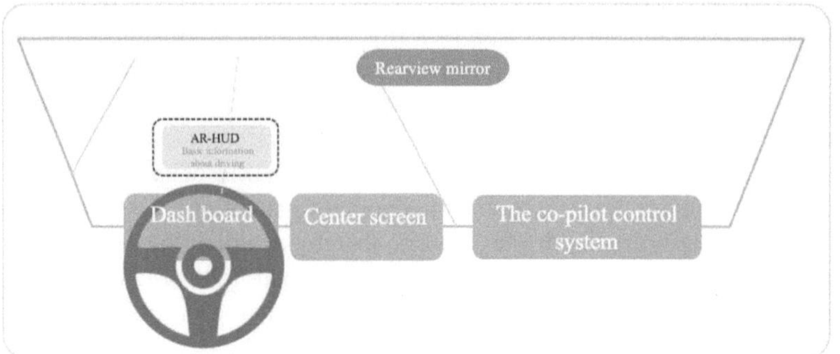

Fig. 2. Spatial Layout of In-Vehicle HMI.

to the process by which drivers make decisions and process information, which can generally be divided into three main stages: perception stage, judgment stage and execution stage (see Fig. 3. Schematic Diagram of the Driver Cognitive Structure System.). Driving behavior is a cyclical process involving these three stages, where perception influences judgment, and judgment dictates action [15]. If the response time of the driver's cognitive system is 3 s, this equates to the driver traveling 50 m blindly during that period, posing significant safety risks. The "3-second interaction principle" is essential for ensuring road safety [16]. Within the first 0–1 s, drivers must complete the acquisition and recognition of information, which is a critical factor influencing driving cognition. By optimizing the interaction design of the Human-Machine Interface, it is possible to reduce the time drivers spend reading information, ensuring that all essential information is acquired within 1 s.

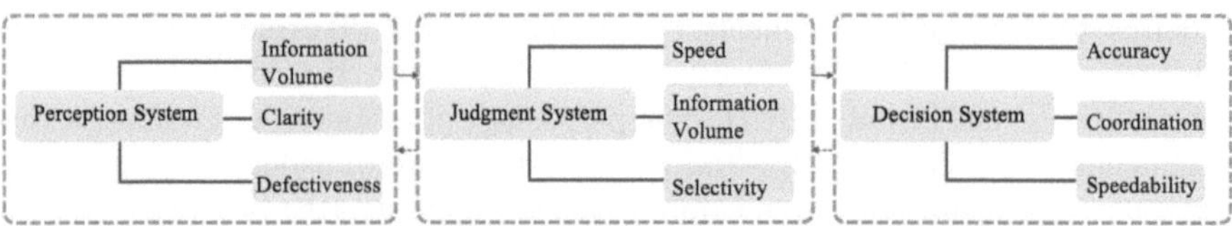

Fig. 3. Schematic Diagram of the Driver Cognitive Structure System.

In summary, HUD technology is evolving to enhance driving safety and user experience, with a particular focus on interactive interfaces [17]. Current research mainly emphasizes aspects like color and shape, while lacking in-depth analysis of data-driven interface encoding forms. Mapping qualitative content to quantitative data is essential for improving human-machine interaction efficiency. Therefore, this paper will utilize Python's Requests and Beautiful Soup technologies to develop a web scraping program for systematically extracting icon information displayed in existing AR-HUD interfaces. Additionally, an experiment is designed to investigate the impact of warning information icons in AR-HUD systems on drivers. This experiment combines objective data (Reaction Time) with subjective scales. By studying the effects of different encoding forms on reaction time, we aim to identify the fastest encoding method and explore visual experiences through subjective measures, ultimately seeking the optimal encoding form for comprehensive effectiveness.

2 Methods

2.1 Evaluation and Optimization Design of Automotive AR-HUD Interfaces

Acquisition and Selection of AR-HUD Interface Icon Samples. This study developed a web scraping tool using Python's Requests and BeautifulSoup libraries. The tool extracted relevant data from websites and saved it to the local file system, effectively creating an interface sample set. After establishing the sample set, a modular analysis was conducted based on the functions of the icons, extracting, and classifying those with similar functionalities. Ultimately, a curated sample set containing 100 interface warning icon elements was compiled.

Existing research has explored the effectiveness of HUD information content. Beck et al. [18] had 51 drivers evaluate 22 items of perceived importance, concluding that six high-priority indicators were identified. These indicators include current speed, speed limit, navigation instructions, maintenance warnings, cruise control status, and low fuel warnings. Park et al. [19] had 21 participants select 11 key items from a list of 24 information items, which included low fuel, engine shutdown, abnormal oil pressure, ABS failure, low tire pressure, door ajar, vehicle speed, seatbelt status, specific doors left open, road speed limits, and navigation information. They indicated that the number of critical information items should be limited to six or fewer.

The collected AR-HUD interface sample set was analyzed for icon element functionality, revealing that the displayed icon information primarily includes six categories: speed indication, navigation prompts, lane change alerts, pedestrian or obstacle notifications, and distance warning indicators. Based on the types of icons, icon extraction was performed on the P1-P100 AR-HUD interfaces, resulting in the following distribution: 5 types of navigation prompts, 10 types of speed indicators, 10 types of straight driving prompts, 10 types of lane change alerts, 4 types of obstacle warning icons, and 5 types of distance warning indicators. This study utilized software such as Photoshop and Figma to organize, synthesize, and standardize the extracted warning icon elements, resulting in a cohesive sample set of interface warning icons (see Table 1. Sample Set of AR-HUD Interface Warning Icon Elements.).

Acquisition of Icon Evaluation Metrics. This study conducted interviews to gather cognitive evaluation information on interface icons from users and experts. A questionnaire was designed for this purpose, and 25 participants (16 males and 9 females, aged 18–30) were invited. Interviews were held in a quiet classroom to minimize distractions. The interviewer facilitated a relaxed atmosphere, recorded the sessions, and each interview lasted 20–30 min. Afterward, recordings were transcribed and key responses on core issues were extracted and organized.

Table 1. Sample Set of AR-HUD Interface Warning Icon Elements.

Event	Icons
Speed	
Driver Information	
Lane Change	
Obstacle	
Distance Remined	
Navigation	

After organizing the interview transcripts, the study will import the extensive textual data into NVivo software for word frequency analysis. By examining the frequency of word occurrences, a frequency table for core issues will be generated (see Table 2. Evaluation Index Keywords.

Table 2. Evaluation Index Keywords.

Order	Index	Frequency
1	Interaction	45
2	Aesthetics	41
3	Simple	38
4	Visualization	36
5	Ergonomics	35
6	Efficiency	31

Initial screening of icon samples. Relevant experts and users are invited to score the normalized interface prompt icons through questionnaires, based on six evaluation indicators: Interaction, Aesthetics, Simple, Visualization, Ergonomics, Efficiency. The entropy-weight method is used to calculate the evaluation results to obtain the comprehensive scores of the prompt icon elements. The icons with the highest comprehensive scores in each group of prompt icons are selected to construct a sample set of advantageous icon elements. The results are shown in the Table 3. Sample of Optimal Icon Elements.

Obtaining the icon color. Yang et al. [20] discuss the important role of color coding in human-computer interaction interface design, emphasizing its ability to enhance information content, improve search efficiency, and reduce cognitive load. Choi et al. [21] conclude that the degree of color recognition is a key factor in enhancing the driving experience. Merenda C et al. [22] indicate that HUD interface elements predominantly use blue as the main color, with red, yellow, and green as auxiliary colors; while the layout of information varies, functionally similar information is presented together. Therefore,

Table 3. Sample of Optimal Icon Elements.

Event	Speed	Driver Information	Lane Change	Obstacle	Distance Remined	Navigation
Icons						

this study selects blue, red, and yellow for the icon coding experiment (see Fig. 4. Color Value of HUD Information.).

BLUE   RED   YELLOW

Blue R: 0 G: 255 B: 255   Red R: 255 G: 0 B: 255   Yellow R: 0 G: 255 B: 0

Fig. 4. Color Value of HUD Information.

2.2 Experimental Test of Takeover Response Time Based on AR-HUD

Obtaining the icon color. The experimental research consists of two parts: reaction time measurement and a post-experiment subjective scale. In the driving simulation system constructed with Unity, we set up six common emergency scenarios encountered during daily driving, including speed indication, navigation prompts, lane change alerts, pedestrian or obstacle notifications, and distance warning indicators. For these six scenarios, we developed a sample set of advantageous icon elements based on the top three icons with comprehensive scores from the prompt. Three encoding forms (shape, color, and transparency) were designed for each scenario. The shape encoding includes line and area; color encoding includes blue, red, and yellow; transparency encoding includes 100%, 75%, 50%, resulting in a total of 108 icons (see Fig. 5. Interface Icons of Three Coding Forms (Shape, Color, Transparency).).

During the experiment, the 108 icons appeared randomly, and participants responded by pressing keys 1–6 on the computer to register their reaction times. The duration of the experiment was between 10 to 15 min. Upon completion of the reaction time testing, participants were immediately asked to fill out a subjective scale combined with memory recall. The scale covered each emergency scenario, requiring participants to select the icon they recognized the fastest, felt most comfortable with, and was most

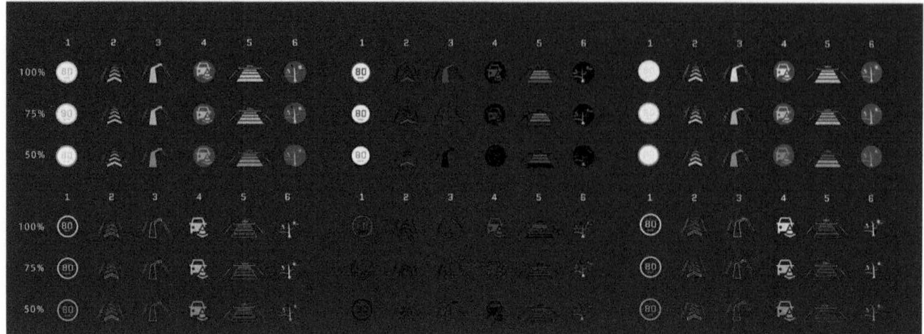

Fig. 5. Interface Icons of Three Coding Forms (Shape, Color, Transparency).

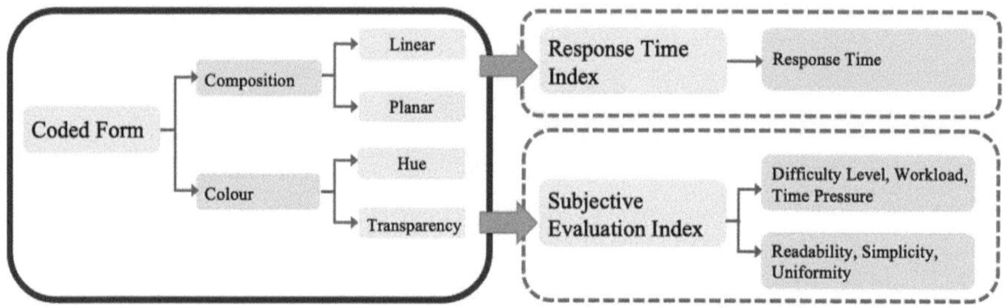

Fig. 6. HUD Experimental Process.

semantically consistent with the scenario. They also rated their eye fatigue before and after the experiment using a 3-point Likert scale (see Fig. 6. HUD Experimental Process.).

Response time data collection. Unity was used as the experimental platform for constructing the driving simulator. During the experiment, one of the six emergency scenarios would randomly appear on the screen, accompanied by the corresponding prompt icon (see Fig. 7. The Corresponding Position of the Six Scenes in the Keyboard.). Participants reacted to the content displayed on the screen (see Fig. 8. Unity Driving Simulation System Experiment Scene.). Reaction time is defined as the interval from the moment the icon appears to the moment the participant presses the corresponding key. This timing data was collected using the timing function built into the Unity driving simulator. After each participant completed a round of the experiment, the reaction time data was exported from the background system.

Questionnaire data collection. The questionnaire is published through the survey platform "Wenjuanxing" and participants can access the questionnaire page by scanning a QR code with their mobile phones. After participants submit the questionnaire, the data will be collected in the backend. Upon completion of the experiment, statistical data will be downloaded from the survey platform and sorted according to the questions (Table 4).

Fig. 7. The Corresponding Position of the Six Scenes in the Keyboard.

Fig. 8. Unity Driving Simulation System Experiment Scene.

3 Results

Shape encoding is divided into line encoding and area encoding, while color encoding offers three options: blue, red, and yellow. Transparency encoding includes three levels: 100%, 75%, and 50%. In total, there are 108 icons (6 shapes * 2 types * 3 colors * 3 transparency).

Table 4. Statistical Table of Information of Drivers Participating.

ID	Gender	Age	Driving time (years)	Colorblindness
1	Male	25 years old	3	NO
2	Male	23 years old	2	NO
3	Male	28 years old	6	NO
4	Male	38 years old	10	NO
5	Male	48 years old	15	NO
6	Male	22 years old	2	NO
7	Female	24 years old	2	NO
8	Female	26 years old	5	NO
9	Female	26 years old	6	NO
10	Female	30 years old	8	NO

3.1 Data Analysis Description

The data is organized as follows: linear encoding is represented by L, area encoding by F; transparency levels are coded as T1, T2, T3; and colors are encoded as B, R, Y (see Table 5. Example Table of Icon Encodings.).

Table 5. Example Table of Icon Encodings.

Shape	Color	Transparency	Icon Example
L (Linear Encoding)	B (Blue)	T1 (100% Transparency)	L - B - T1

3.2 Data Analysis Results

This study analyzed reaction time data from a driving simulation experiment using descriptive statistics and box plots (see Fig. 9. Boxplots of Reaction Time Under Different Coding Forms (Shape, Color, Transparency) in the Driving Simulation System.). Linear shape coding (L, n = 60, M = 1406.83 ms) demonstrated significantly faster responses than planar coding (F, n = 60, M = 1438.5 ms) with comparable variability (SD = 151.71 vs. 155.70). Yellow icons (Y, n = 40, M = 1407.25 ms) showed the fastest median reaction time (1400 ms), outperforming red (R, n = 42, M = 1437.38 ms) and blue (B, n = 38, M = 1422.64 ms) with blue exhibiting highest variability (SD = 162.86). Transparency coding showed minimal effects: 100% (T3, n = 39, M = 1408.97 ms) performed slightly better than 50% (T1, n = 44, M = 1430.68 ms) and 75% (T2, n = 37, M = 1427.57 ms) but without significant differences. These results highlight shape and color coding as critical factors influencing reaction efficiency, while transparency had negligible effects. (M = mean, SD = standard deviation)

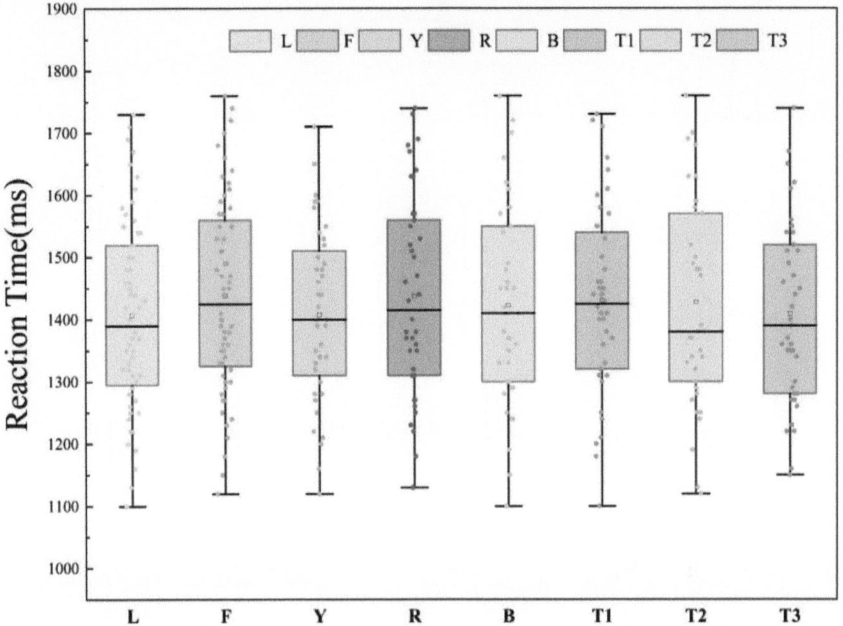

Fig. 9. Boxplots of Reaction Time Under Different Coding Forms (Shape, Color, Transparency) in the Driving Simulation System.

This study utilizes a three-dimensional axis graph with color, type, and transparency as axes to explore the optimal coding combination for the shortest reaction time (see Fig. 10. Three-Dimensional Diagram of Reaction Time under Different Coding Combinations of Shape, Color and Transparency.). In terms of color, the blue area generally shows shorter reaction times, presumably because blue is more attention - grabbing. Regarding the type, the reaction times of linear type combinations are generally shorter than those of planar type combinations, indicating that the linear type is more easily recognizable. As for transparency, the area corresponding to T1 mostly falls within the low reaction time range, suggesting that this transparency level facilitates rapid information transfer. Overall, the combination of blue, linear type, and T1 transparency results in the shortest reaction time and is thus the optimal coding combination.

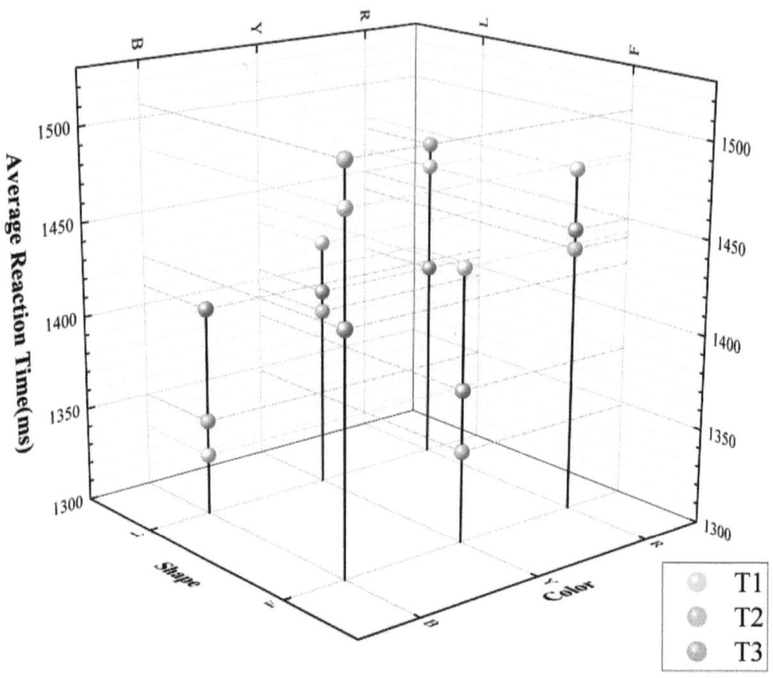

Fig. 10. Three-Dimensional Diagram of Reaction Time under Different Coding Combinations of Shape, Color and Transparency.

4   Conclusion

This study combines objective reaction time data from the AR-HUD (Augmented Reality Head-Up Display) warning information encoding and subjective questionnaire results to explore their impacts on drivers' responses, yielding significant findings.

Data analysis reveals that the optimal encoding combination, consisting of a linear shape (L), blue color (B), and 100% transparency (T1), can remarkably shorten drivers' reaction times and enhance their response speeds to warning messages. In terms of encoding significance, the linear shape is easily recognizable, the blue color grabs attention, and 100% transparency ensures clear information display. Together, these elements improve the efficiency of information transmission. The subjective questionnaire results also confirm that warning messages with this encoding combination are more perceptible and understandable, enhancing drivers' sense of security and trust in the information, thus considering both objective performance and subjective experience.

This research outcome is of great significance in the research field. Theoretically, it provides empirical evidence for the study of the relationship between AR-HUD encoding and drivers' responses, enriches the theoretical framework, and helps understand the mechanism of information perception and response in an augmented reality environment. Practically, it offers clear guidance for the development of human-machine interfaces in ADAS (Advanced Driver Assistance Systems), improving the practicality and safety of the systems.

The current study's limitations include a small sample size and uneven gender distribution, which hinder comprehensive analysis of potential gender-based reaction time differences; moreover, learning effects during the experiment and minor time discrepancies within the simulator may have influenced results. Additionally, findings may be constrained by simulator environments and testing-related learning effects, as real-world conditions—such as varying sunlight, environmental colors, and road lighting—could further impact icon visibility. To address these gaps, future research should expand sample size, balance gender distribution, optimize experimental design to reduce errors, and validate results in actual driving scenarios. Meanwhile, exploring the effects of encoding strategies on drivers' cognitive workload, situational awareness, and overall driving performance can achieve a comprehensive assessment of their practical significance. This exploration will offer strong support for improving driving safety and optimizing the presentation of in-vehicle information.

References

1. Betancur, J.A., Villa-Espinal, J., Osorio-Gómez, G., Cuéllar, S., Suárez, D.: Research topics and implementation trends on automotive head-up display systems. Int. J. Interact. Des. Manuf. (IJIDeM). **12**, 199–214 (2018). https://doi.org/10.1007/s12008-016-0350-3
2. Stojmenova Pečečnik, K., Tomažič, S., Sodnik, J.: Design of head-up display interfaces for automated vehicles. Int. J. Hum.-Comput. Stud. **177**, 103060 (2023). https://doi.org/10.1016/j.ijhcs.2023.103060
3. Kim, H., Gabbard, J.L.: Assessing distraction potential of augmented reality head-up displays for vehicle drivers. Hum. Factors. **64**, 852–865 (2022). https://doi.org/10.1177/0018720819844845
4. Cheng, Y., Zhong, X., Tian, L.: Does the AR-HUD system affect driving behaviour? An eye-tracking experiment study. Transp. Res. Interdiscip. Perspect. **18**, 100767 (2023). https://doi.org/10.1016/j.trip.2023.100767
5. Bellazzi, A., et al.: Virtual reality for assessing visual quality and lighting perception: a systematic review. Build. Environ. **209**, 108674 (2022). https://doi.org/10.1016/j.buildenv.2021.108674
6. Ma, Y., Qi, S., Zhang, Y., Lian, G., Lu, W., Chan, C.-Y.: Drivers' visual attention characteristics under different cognitive workloads: an on-road driving behavior study. Int. J. Environ. Res. Public Health. **17**, 5366 (2020). https://doi.org/10.3390/ijerph17155366
7. Tian, R., Li, L., Chen, M., Chen, Y., Witt, G.J.: Studying the effects of driver distraction and traffic density on the probability of crash and near-crash events in naturalistic driving environment. IEEE Trans. Intell. Transport. Syst. **14**, 1547–1555 (2013). https://doi.org/10.1109/TITS.2013.2261988
8. Park, H.S., Park, M.W., Won, K.H., Kim, K., Jung, S.K.: In-vehicle AR-HUD system to provide driving-safety information. ETRI J. **35**, 1038–1047 (2013). https://doi.org/10.4218/etrij.13.2013.0041
9. Li, Y., Wang, H.: Research on color, luminance and line width of HUD symbols. In: Human Systems Engineering and Design II: Proceedings of the 2nd International Conference on Human Systems Engineering and Design (IHSED2019): Future Trends and Applications, pp. 325–330 (2020)
10. Zhu, Y., Jing, Y., Jiang, M., Zhang, Z., Wang, D., Liu, W.: An experimental study of the cognitive load of in-vehicle multiscreen connected HUD. In: Soares, M.M., Rosenzweig, E., Marcus, A. (eds.) Design, User Experience, and Usability: Design for Contemporary

Technological Environments, pp. 268–285. Springer International Publishing, Cham (2021). https://doi.org/10.1007/978-3-030-78227-6_20

11. Liang, N., et al.: Using eye-tracking to investigate the effects of pre-takeover visual engagement on situation awareness during automated driving. Accid. Anal. Prev. **157**, 106143 (2021). https://doi.org/10.1016/j.aap.2021.106143
12. Gabbard, J.L., Smith, M., Merenda, C., Burnett, G., Large, D.R.: A perceptual color-matching method for examining color blending in augmented reality head-up display graphics. IEEE Trans. Vis. Comput. Graph. **28**, 2834–2851 (2022). https://doi.org/10.1109/TVCG.2020.304 4715
13. Tan, Z., et al.: Human–machine interaction in intelligent and connected vehicles: a review of status quo, issues, and opportunities. IEEE Trans. Intell. Transp. Syst. **23**, 13954–13975 (2022)
14. Murali, P.K., Kaboli, M., Dahiya, R.: Intelligent in-vehicle interaction technologies. Adv. Intell. Syst. **4**, 2100122 (2022)
15. Zhang, X., Chang, R., Wang, M., Sui, X.: The influence of driver's risk perception ability on driving decision-making: an ERP study. Curr. Psychol. **43**, 21995–22005 (2024). https://doi.org/10.1007/s12144-024-05884-y
16. Chen, H.: Predicting driver's takeover time based on individual characteristics, external environment, and situation awareness. Accid. Anal. Prev. **203**, 107601 (2024)
17. Kang, C., Lee, C., Zhao, X., Lee, D., Shin, J., Lee, J.: Safety still matters: unveiling the value propositions of augmented reality head-up displays in autonomous vehicles through conjoint analysis. Travel Behav. Soc. **39**, 100915 (2025). https://doi.org/10.1016/j.tbs.2024.100915
18. Beck, D., Park, W.: Perceived importance of automotive HUD information items: a study with experienced HUD users. IEEE Access. **6**, 21901–21909 (2018). https://doi.org/10.1109/ACCESS.2018.2828615
19. Park, K., Im, Y.: Ergonomic guidelines of head-up display user Interface during semi-automated driving. Electronics. **9**, 611 (2020). https://doi.org/10.3390/electronics9040611
20. Yang, L., Qi, B., Guo, Q.: The effect of icon color combinations in information interfaces on task performance under varying levels of cognitive load. Appl. Sci. **14**(10), 4212 (2024). https://doi.org/10.3390/app14104212
21. Li, Y., Wang, Y., Song, F., Liu, Y.: Assessing gender perception differences in color combinations in digital visual interfaces using eye. Int. J. Hum.-Comput. Interact. **40**(20) (2024)
22. Merenda, C., Smith, M., Gabbard, J.: Effects of real-world backgrounds on user interface color naming and matching in automotive AR HUDs. In: 2016 IEEE VR 2016 Workshop on Perceptual and Cognitive Issues in AR (PERCAR), pp. 1–6 (2016).

Estimation System of Driver Fatigue State Based on Blink Detection

Kisa Takao, Hironori Uchida, Yujie Li, and Yoshihisa Nakatoh[✉]

Kyushu Institute of Technology, Kitakyushu, Fukuoka, Japan
`nakatoh@ecs.kyutech.ac.jp`

Abstract. Accidents involving automobile driving are largely attributed to human error; thus, a system capable of estimating and predicting the driver's condition is essential for preventing such incidents. This paper presents an approach that focuses on Spontaneous Blink Rate (SBR) to detect the driver's fatigue and arousal levels. Experimental results demonstrate a correlation between SBR and the objectively estimated fatigue level when fatigue is present. Furthermore, in the blink classification method, it was confirmed that the EARM (Eye Aspect Ratio Mapping)-based method achieves low-cost yet highly accurate blink detection, outperforming the traditional EAR (Eye Aspect Ratio)-based approach.

Keywords: blink · driver attention · image processing · MediaPipe · EAR · CFF.

1 Introduction

Road accidents are recognized as a global issue, and efforts to reduce the number of fatalities and injuries resulting from such incidents are highly desirable [1]. According to a survey conducted by the National Transportation Safety Board, human factors are responsible for approximately 90% of all traffic accidents [2]. In Japan, a large proportion of traffic accidents are caused by driver error, highlighting the urgent need for technologies that can help prevent accidents resulting from human-related factors [3]. As a countermeasure, numerous studies have explored driver monitoring systems that observe the condition of a driver while operating a vehicle. These systems range from those that evaluate driving behavior [4], such as steering input, acceleration, and braking patterns, to those that extract features from biometric signals [5], including electrocardiograms and electroencephalograms.

In this study, we propose a fatigue detection system based on blink movements using image analysis technology that is non-invasive and does not interfere with the driver's mobility. As a preliminary step, this experiment examines a blink classification method suited for real-world conditions and investigates the relationship between driver fatigue and blink behavior.

P.-L.P. Rau and H. Krömker (Eds.): HCII 2025, LNCS 16336, pp. 423–433, 2026.
https://doi.org/10.1007/978-3-032-12798-3_26

2 Related Works

2.1 Eye Blink

Blinking is typically classified into three types: voluntary blinking, reflexive blinking, and involuntary blinking [6]. Voluntary blinking is controlled by the individual's will, while the latter two occur unconsciously and serve different physiological functions. Blinking has been studied in relation to drowsiness and concentration, as well as in the assessment of attention and cognitive function [7, 8]. In this paper, we focus on spontaneous blinking, which is closely associated with fatigue and arousal, and define it as follows:

Spontaneous blinking refers to the involuntary, temporary, and brief closure of both upper eyelids in a coordinated manner, without any apparent external stimulus. This action is essential for maintaining visual clarity, distributing tear fluid across the ocular surface, and ensuring tear film stability. Spontaneous blinking tends to occur in clusters due to activity changes in the blink control center, which are influenced by the inhibitory effects of the hypothalamic regulatory system and other mechanisms associated with reduced arousal or fatigue [6, 9].

2.2 Relationship Between Fatigue and Visual System Indices

Flicker value is a metric used to measure mental and physical fatigue (stress) by altering the frequency of light flashes. The flicker value (Hz) refers to the number of light flashes perceived per unit time. The critical fusion frequency (CFF) is defined as the threshold frequency at which flickering light is perceived as continuous; a lower CFF indicates a higher level of fatigue. A study by Takahashi et al. [5] confirmed that flicker measuring devices can objectively evaluate ocular fatigue in test subjects.

Many studies have also explored the relationship between fatigue or arousal levels and blink rate. Reports indicate that during the early stages of an experiment, when subjects exhibit high arousal, the blink rate remains unchanged or is suppressed. However, as arousal levels decline, the blink rate tends to increase [10]. The National Highway Traffic Safety Administration (NHTSA) has investigated the relationship between PERCLOS and other alertness metrics, reporting a strong correlation between reduced alertness and higher PERCLOS values [11]. PERCLOS represents the proportion of time the eyes are closed per unit time, and this value increases as arousal decreases.

As demonstrated in previous studies, various findings confirm a clear relationship between arousal/fatigue levels and blink behavior. These insights are highly relevant to driving scenarios, suggesting that indices based on eyelid and eye behavior may provide reliable indicators of a driver's condition.

2.3 Blink Detection Method

Various methods based on different features related to blinking have been proposed in both past and current research. This section discusses several representative studies on blink detection. The Electro-Oculogram (EOG) detects blinking by measuring electrical potentials using electrodes placed above and below the eye [12]. This technique leverages the fact that the cornea exhibits a positive potential relative to the retina. During natural eyelid movements associated with blinking, the potential difference between the two electrodes changes accordingly. Due to the strong correlation between the potential waveform and the blink event, and the fact that head position is not constrained, this method offers high accuracy in blink detection. This approach has been widely used in studies focusing on tracking blink variations in drivers [13, 14].

The Eye Aspect Ratio (EAR) was introduced in research conducted at the Czech Technical University [15, 16]. EAR is a scalar value calculated by first detecting a face in the image, then identifying the coordinates of key eye landmarks, computing their Euclidean distances, and finally applying these values to a predefined formula, as shown in Eq. (1).

$$EAR = \frac{\|p_2 - p_6\| + \|p_3 - p_5\|}{2\|p_1 - p_4\|} \tag{1}$$

Here, p_1 to p_6 represent the 2D landmark coordinates as illustrated in Fig. 1. When the eyes are open, the EAR value remains nearly constant; however, it approaches zero when the eyes are closed. This value is largely independent of head posture and viewing distance and exhibits minimal inter-individual variation under open-eye conditions. Since both eyes blink simultaneously, the average EAR of the left and right eye is usually used. Due to the simplicity of its calculation, EAR provides excellent real-time performance and demonstrates high robustness in practical applications.

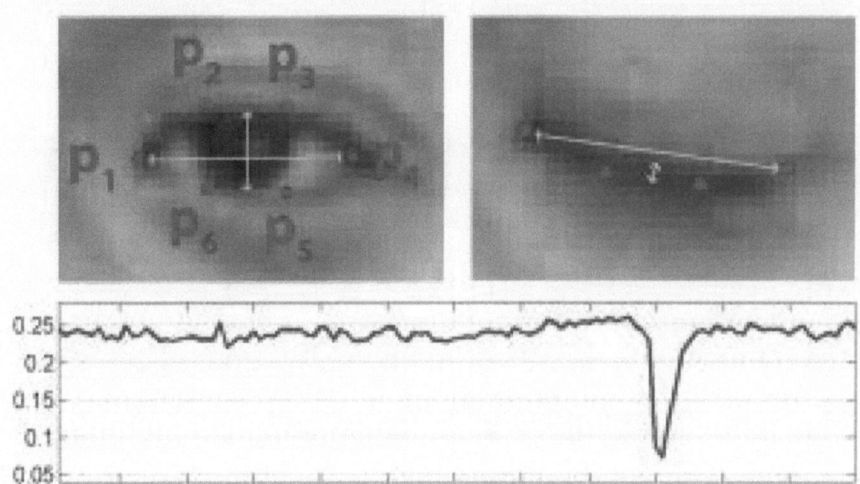

Fig. 1. Eye Aspect Ratio [17].

In addition, Kuwahara et al. [17] proposed a novel blink classification method called Eye Aspect Ratio Mapping (EARM). This method is based on the observation that blinks typically occur within a short time frame (100 to 150 ms), and it defines a blink as occurring once the EARM value exceeds the EAR threshold.

$$EARM(t) = EAR\left(t - \tfrac{X+1}{2}\right) + EAR\left(t - \tfrac{X+1}{2} + 1\right)$$
$$+ EAR\left(t + \tfrac{X+1}{2} - 1\right) + EAR\left(t + \tfrac{X+1}{2}\right) - 4*EAR(t) \tag{2}$$
$$X = Eye\ blink\ time\ flame\ Range(odd\ number)$$

It was confirmed that EARM can reduce a certain number of false positives caused by noise in the EAR signal, such as those resulting from irregular head movements like looking up or down. However, EARM still faces limitations in accuracy when the face moves abruptly or when the distance between the face and the camera increases.

3 Proposed Method

In this section, we describe our proposed blink detection method and the objective fatigue measures utilized in this study.

3.1 Improved Blink Detection Methods

The proposed system for blink detection using full-face images is illustrated in Fig. 2.

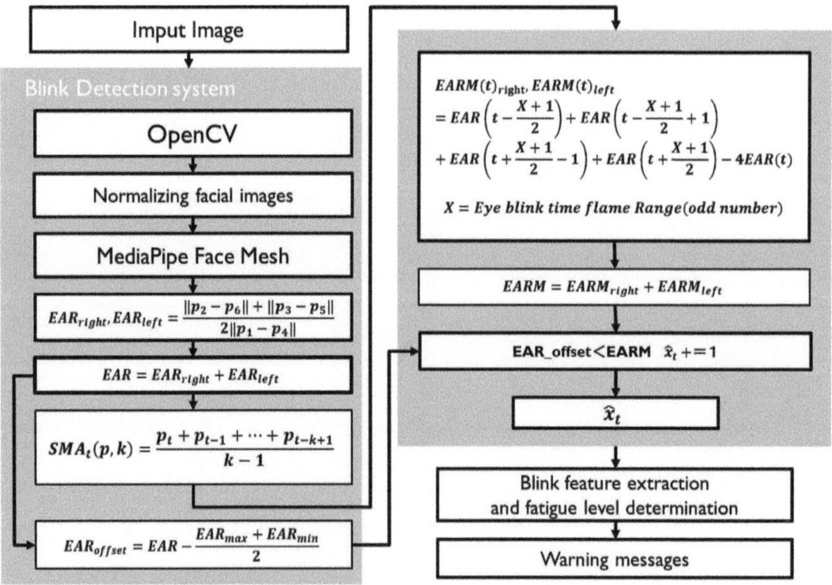

Fig. 2. An overview of the proposed method.

Our method is partially based on the works of Tereza et al. [15, 16] and Kuwahara et al. [17], with several modifications including an updated facial landmark detection technique, a revised EAR computation method, and the integration of noise reduction processing. The system consists of the following steps:

I. Detect and crop the facial region from the input image using OpenCV, and normalize the image size.

II. Use MediaPipe [18] to extract the coordinates of 32 facial landmark points on the upper and lower eyelids from the normalized face image.

III. Calculate the EAR from 12 landmark points around each eye. Apply a simple moving average filter to the time-series EAR data to remove noise. To retain blink features, the moving average window size is set to 5.

IV. Transform the smoothed time-series data into a signal that responds only to spontaneous blinks using the proposed EARM formula.

V. Compare the EARM time-series data with a pre-defined EAR offset threshold to detect blink events.

In previous studies [15, 17], EAR and EARM demonstrated high accuracy and low computational cost. However, preliminary experiments conducted under realistic conditions revealed considerable noise due to unexpected subject movement and limitations in real-time performance.

Therefore, two major improvements were introduced to address the shortcomings of existing methods:

1. Replacement of facial landmark detection library from Dlib to MediaPipe

   The number of eyelid landmark points was increased from 6 to 16 per eye, allowing for more precise tracking of blink movements. In addition, compared to traditional cascade-based approaches, MediaPipe offers superior real-time performance and more accurate facial feature detection.

2. Emphasis on feature points

   Conventionally, the EAR is computed as the average of the left and right eye EAR values. In this study, we instead sum the EAR values of both eyes to enhance the distinctiveness of the EARM signal in subsequent calculations. Blink detection is then performed by comparing the EARM signal with a pre-defined EAR offset threshold derived from the EAR value (Fig. 3).

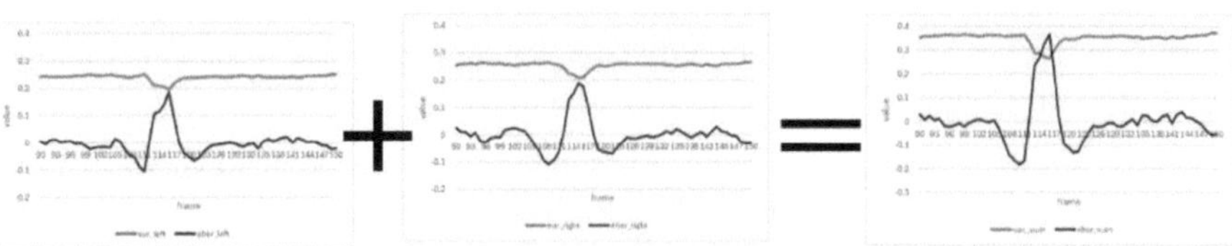

Fig. 3. Emphasis on EAR values.

3.2 Methods of Objective Testing for Fatigue

Fatigue states have traditionally been quantified using various physiological indicators, such as Critical Fusion Frequency (CFF) of flicker and heart rate variability. However, these methods present challenges in terms of simplicity and cost of implementation. For instance, heart rate measurements require resting conditions, and may yield abnormal data due to physical constraints. Moreover, they often require specialized equipment and incur high installation costs, making widespread use difficult. In contrast, measuring flicker CFF is relatively simple and does not require significant training time. It can also be applied across multiple use cases, making it versatile and more cost-effective. However, since CFF values vary across individuals, normalization is necessary.

To address this, the present study introduces a Fatigue Level (FL) metric, based on normalized CFF values, and uses both Spontaneous Blink Rate (SBR) and FL to evaluate the relationship between objective fatigue and blink activity. The SBR is calculated by observing the subject for a set duration and dividing the total number of blinks by the observation time. The result is expressed in units of blinks per second (bl/s).

$$Spontaneous\ Blink\ Rate = \frac{Spontaneous\ Blink\ count\ (bl)}{Time\ (min)} \tag{3}$$

FL is an objective fatigue quantification index introduced in this study and is defined by the following equation:

$$FL = 1 - \frac{CFF_t}{CFF_0} \tag{4}$$

Where CFF_0 represents the CFF value before the experiment, and CFF_t denotes the CFF value measured t seconds after the start of the video viewing task.

Results from preliminary experiments indicated that fatigue began to accumulate when $FL \geq 0.038$. Therefore, the elapsed time at which FL reaches 0.038 is defined as the point when fatigue has objectively accumulated.

4   Experiments

4.1   Dataset

All evaluation videos were captured using a visible-light camera with a resolution of 1080p at 30 fps, resulting in approximately 44,000 frames per subject. The subjects' faces were mostly oriented toward the camera, providing a clear and consistent view during the video-watching session. The ground-truth SBR values were manually verified through visual inspection of all videos. Only fully completed spontaneous blinks were counted; partial or incomplete blinks were excluded from the tally.

Subjects. The subjects included three males in their 20s and one male in his 30s, all of whom possessed a driver's license and drove on a daily basis. To ensure consistent fatigue levels across participants, each subject was given sufficient rest time before beginning the experiment. We obtained informed consent from all participants in this study. The purpose, procedures, voluntary nature of participation, absence of disadvantage from non-participation, and protection of personal information were clearly explained both in writing and orally.

Experimental Environment. The experiment was conducted in a simulated driving setting, with a monitor positioned in front of the windshield of a stationary vehicle located outdoors. The subjects' field of vision was carefully adjusted to approximate that of an actual driving environment.

4.2 Driving Video Viewing Assignments

Currently, no standardized task exists for consistently inducing fatigue. In this experiment, we prepared a driving video viewing task, as shown in Fig. 4. The scenario simulated an urban driving environment, where drivers are required to frequently assess their surroundings at a moderate pace. Each subject watched the driving video four times, with each session lasting 30 min, for a total viewing time of 2 h. To increase the fatigue load, subjects were also asked to perform a Kraepelin calculation task following each 30-min viewing session.

Fig. 4. Driving Video Viewing Assignment.

4.3 Measuring the Critical Fusion Frequency of Flicker

There are several established methods for measuring flicker values. One common approach is the ascending method, in which the flicker frequency is gradually increased and the value is recorded when the subject first perceives the light source as continuous. Another is the descending method, where the frequency is decreased from a fused state, and the value is recorded when the subject begins to perceive flickering. Oikawa et al. reported no statistically significant difference between these two methods [19]. Therefore, in this experiment, both ascending and descending methods were applied, and the average of the two measurements was used as the subject's CFF value. A Flicker Value Analyzer Type II (automatic model) was used for all flicker measurements.

5 Experimental Results and Discussion

5.1 Blink Detection

The Mean Absolute Error (MAE) represents the average absolute difference between the predicted and actual values, and is calculated using Eq. (5). It is commonly used to quantitatively assess the error between predicted and observed values—where values closer to zero indicate higher prediction accuracy. The unit used in this experiment is blinks per minute (bl/min).

$$MAE = \frac{1}{N} \sum_{t=1}^{N} |x_t - \hat{x}_t| \tag{5}$$

The Root Mean Square Error (RMSE) is the square root of the average of the squared differences between predicted and actual values, and is expressed by the following equation. Compared to MAE, RMSE penalizes outliers more heavily and serves as an indicator of the overall accuracy of the prediction model.

$$RMSE = \sqrt{\frac{1}{N} \sum_{t=1}^{N} (x_t - \hat{x}_t)^2} \tag{6}$$

In these equations, x_t represents the actual SBR value, $\hat{x}_t$ is the predicted SBR value, N is the total number of data points, and t is the time index.

Tables 1 and 2 present the MAE and RMSE results for each subject. As shown in Table 1, the improved method proposed in this study outperforms conventional methods in terms of blink detection accuracy. In particular, the average number of false positives per subject decreased from 54.27 bl/min to 7.86 bl/min, demonstrating a significant improvement in detection precision.

Moreover, Table 2 shows that the average RMSE across subjects using the improved method is 9.50 bl/min, the lowest among the evaluated methods. These findings suggest that the proposed approach effectively reduces noise and achieves more accurate blink detection.

However, an RMSE value of 9.50 bl/min still reflects a non-negligible error. False positives in the improved method were observed in cases where the input image featured a slightly overhead angle, resulting in facial landmark detection failure due to rapid blink movement. This limitation is likely due to the sensitivity of the facial landmark detection library to vertical facial tilt. Such issues were particularly noticeable in subjects with narrow eyes, suggesting that enhancements to the landmark detection model are necessary to accommodate individual variations in facial structure and orientation.

Table 1. Performance Evaluation of Blink Detection Method by MAE.

MAE	Blink Detection Methods (bl/min)			
	EAR	EARM	EAR_MediaPipe and Noise Suppression	EARM_MediaPipe and Noise Suppression
Subject A	13.43	1.87	10.14	1.16
Subject B	111.36	5.48	7.97	4.36
Subject C	29.08	38.29	39.98	10.53
Subject D	63.20	15.30	22.11	15.38
Average	54.27	15.23	20.05	7.86

Table 2. Performance Evaluation of Blink Detection Method by RMSE.

RMSE	Blink Detection Methods (bl/min)			
	EAR	EARM	EAR_MediaPipe and Noise Suppression	EARM_MediaPipe and Noise Suppression
Subject A	19.72	2.86	11.72	1.77
Subject B	120.52	6.43	8.99	5.27
Subject C	33.67	40.39	42.30	14.90
Subject D	78.32	17.03	22.45	16.07
Average	63.06	16.68	21.37	9.50

5.2 Association Between Time-Series Changes in SBR and Fatigue Level

The time-series changes in spontaneous blink rate (SBR) are illustrated in Figs. 5 and 6. From both figures, it can be observed that the number of blinks per minute remains relatively stable at the beginning of the video-viewing session, but increases as the session progresses. This trend is particularly pronounced for Subject B. These results are consistent with previous studies, suggesting that blink frequency increases as fatigue accumulates and arousal level decreases.

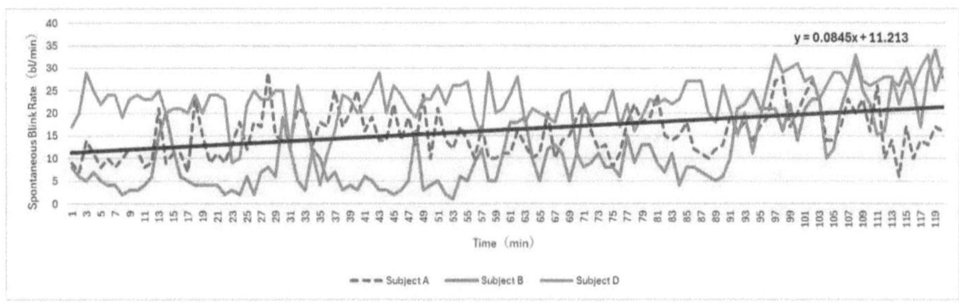

Fig. 5. Time trends of SBR of subject A, subject B, and subject D.

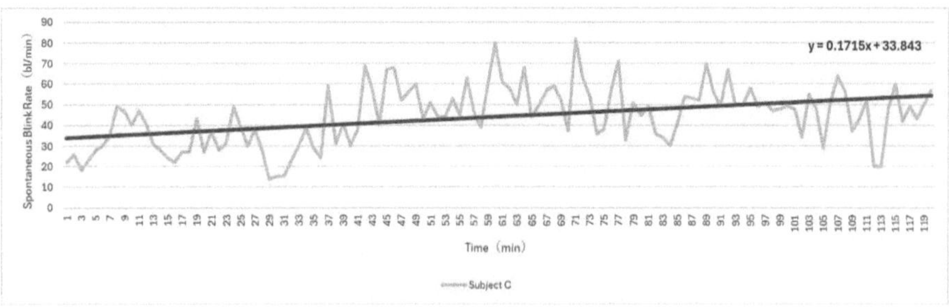

Fig. 6. Time trend of SBR of subject C.

Figure 7 presents a graph of the time-series changes in fatigue level (FL) obtained in this experiment (left), along with the relationship between the time at which fatigue was reached and the rate of change in spontaneous blinking (right).

From these figures, it was confirmed that fatigue levels increased progressively during the video-viewing task. Subjects B, C, and D reached the fatigue threshold between 90 and 100 min. In contrast, Subject A exhibited a sharp rise in fatigue between 40 and 50 min into the experiment. During the post-experiment interview, Subject A reported having performed extended visual display terminal (VDT) work prior to the experiment, which likely contributed to the earlier onset of fatigue.

A comparison of the average 5-min rate of change in SBR (from baseline to the point when the fatigue level was reached) and the corresponding FL value revealed a weak but observable correlation (r = 0.5273). This suggests the potential utility of SBR variations as an indicator for estimating the subject's fatigue level.

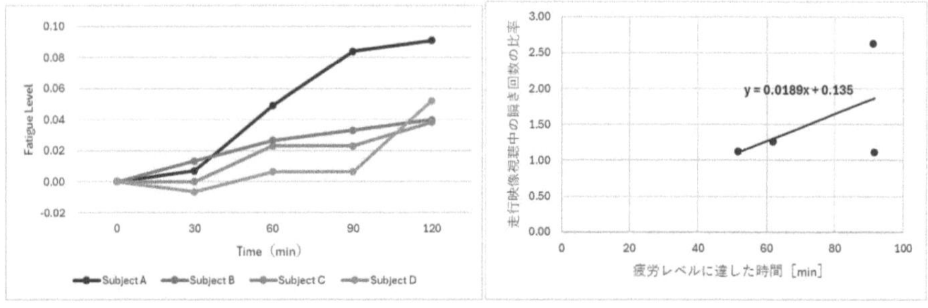

Fig. 7. Time trend of fatigue level (left Fig) / Relationship between rate of change in SBR and time to reach fatigue level (right Fig).

6   Conclusion

In this paper, we proposed an improved method for EARM, a blink detection approach based on facial images, and evaluated its potential application in fatigue estimation. Experimental results demonstrated that the proposed method is simple, low-cost, and achieves high accuracy. Additionally, a moderate correlation (r = 0.5273) was observed between the estimated time at which subjects reached the objective fatigue level and the rate of change in SBR at that point. These findings suggest the feasibility of estimating the onset of driver fatigue by continuously monitoring spontaneous blink behavior. However, the limited dataset used in this study, along with the demographic bias in subject age and gender, indicates the need for further experimentation. Additional studies involving a more diverse and larger sample size are necessary to validate the effectiveness of the improved EARM method and the proposed fatigue estimation system.

References

1. WHO, UN: Global Plan: Decade of Action for Road Safety 2021–2030. World Health Organisation & United Nations (2021). https://cdn.who.int/media/docs/default-source/documents/health-topics/road-traffic-injuries/global-plan-for-road-safety.pdf
2. NHTSA: Critical Reasons for Crashes Investigated in the National Motor Vehicle Crash Causation Survey. NHTSA (2015)
3. Huang, Z.: A comprehensive analysis of US counties' e-Government portals: development status and functionalities. Eur. J. Inf. Syst. **16**(2), 149–164 (2007)
4. Otamani, S.: Effect of driving duration and partial sleep deprivation of subsequent alertness and performance of car drivers. Physiol. Behav. **84**(5), 715–724 (2005)
5. Takahashi: Over-coming drowsiness by inducing cardio-respiratory phase synchronization. IEEE Trans. Intell. Transp. Syst. **15**(3), 982–991 (2014)
6. FukudaKyosuke, Psychology ob blinking -Summary of research on blink behavior-, Kitaohji-shobo, pp 2–7 (1991)
7. Fukuda, K., Stern, J.A., Brown, T.B., Russo, M.B.: Cognition, blinks, eye-movements, and pupillary movements during performance of a running memory task. Aviat. Space Environ. Med. **76**(7), C75–C85 (2005)
8. Stern, J.A., Boyer, D., Schroeder, D.: Blink rate: a possible measure of fatigue. J. Hum. Factors Ergon. Soc. **36**(2), 285–297 (1994)
9. R. w. Ryosuke H.: An approach to the evaluation of arousal level by blinking interval analysis. Jpn. Ergon. Soc. **19**(3), 161–167 (1983).
10. Tanaka, Y.: Arousal level and blink activity. Jpn. J. Psychol. **70**, 1–8 (1999)
11. Kenji SATO, S.Y.: Changes in draivers' levels of wakefulness during automatic driving in an actual driving environment. JARI Res. J. (2018)
12. Asakawa, K., Ishikawa, H.: Clinical application and interpretation of electrooculogram. Rinsho Ganka. **67**(2), 178–182 (2013)
13. I, T., M, K., K, K.: Driver blink measurement by the motion picture processing and its application to drowsiness detection (2003)
14. S, J., L, R.: Eye blink detection for different driver states in conditionally automated driving and manual driving using EOG and a driver camera. Behav. Res. Methods. **50**, (3), 1088–1101 (2018)
15. Soukupova, T.: Eye blink detection using facial landmarks. Res. Rep. Curr. Math. Publ. (5) (2016)
16. Soukupova, T.: Real-Time Eye Blink Detection using Facial Landmarks
17. Kuwahara, A.: Research on Prediction of Ocular Fatigue Using Blink Detection Technology by Image Processing. Kyushu Insutitute of Tecnology (2023)
18. Khabarlak, K., Koriashkina, L.: Fast facial landmark detection and applications: a survey. arXiv preprint arXiv: 2101.10808 (2021).
19. Oikawa, M.: Statistical analysis for critical flicker fusion frequency (CFF). Illum. Eng. Inst. Jpn. **79**(8), 416–419 (1995)

P.-L.P. Rau and H. Krömker (Eds.): HCII 2025, LNCS 16336, pp. 435–436, 2026.
https://doi.org/10.1007/978-3-032-12798-3